Merchants and Empire

Early America
HISTORY, CONTEXT, CULTURE

Jack P. Greene and J. R. Pole
SERIES EDITORS

Merchants & Empire

Trading in Colonial New York

Cathy Matson

The Johns Hopkins University Press

BALTIMORE AND LONDON

This book was published with the generous assistance of the College of
Arts and Sciences at the University of Delaware.

The Johns Hopkins University Press
2715 North Charles Street
Baltimore, Maryland 21218-4319
The Johns Hopkins Press Ltd., London

Library of Congress Cataloging-in-Publication Data will be found at the end of this book.
A catalog record for this book is available from the British Library.

ISBN 0-8018-5602-7

For Sarah

Contents

Acknowledgments

C OLONIAL MERCHANTS were keenly aware that the word *debt* carried many meanings, not the least of them being those of intellectual nurturing, professional assistance, and friendship. My own ledger is long, but it gives me great pleasure to thank publicly some of the people who have helped bring this project to completion. Peter Onuf is my greatest creditor; more than any other scholar and friend, he sustained an interest in my research, provided a model of intellectual rigor, and repeatedly pruned my overwritten sentences. It has been an incomparable privilege to collaborate with Peter early in my career in writing first an article, then a book, and, since then, to have benefited from his sage counsel about almost everything I have written as a historian, including this book.

Stuart Bruchey and Jacob Smit may have long forgotten the criticism and advice they offered me when, as a graduate student at Columbia University, I first began to scour colonial New York sources. Nevertheless, their inspired seminars and close attention to my dissertation provided a foundation for all of my future efforts regarding this project. Over the subsequent years, other scholars and friends lengthened my list of debts. Some of them offered comments on drafts of chapters, some remarked on scholarly papers, some indulged me in discussions about theories of historical understanding or the significance of colonial New York's history. Each has left a mark on the pages that follow. I would like to single out all the people of the New Netherland Project for their conferences, translating, and publishing accomplishments; and members of the Columbia University History Seminar, the New-York Historical Society conferences, and the Delaware Seminar have been patient and critical colleagues. Joyce Appleby, Patricia Bonomi, Paul Clemens, Ed Countryman, Thomas Doerflinger, Paul Gilje, Jack Greene, Margaret Newell, Janet Riesman, Oliver Rink, and Ruth Smith have given generously of their time and expertise to various incarnations of the chapters in this book. Although they are too numerous to name here, students in my undergraduate and graduate courses provide a cherished environment in which to refine my explanations of colonial history, of which New York City merchants were an important part, and to learn from them in turn. They are the invisible underpinnings of this study.

Archivists and librarians at many institutions made countless trips to the recesses of manuscript storage areas to bring me crumbling materials; some of them guided me to information about the linkages among New York City merchants that I might not have found otherwise. Many manuscript curators, special collections librarians, and interlibrary loan staffs tirelessly fetched, copied, phoned, and nagged on my behalf. Especially important were the people at Columbia University Library, the American Antiquarian Society, the New-York Historical Society, the New York Public Library, the Public Records Office in London, and numerous New York City public agencies.

I am also grateful to the many institutions that have provided me with financial assistance, starting with the John Jay fellowships and presidential fellowships from my graduate years at Columbia University, and later including grants from the American Council of Learned Societies, and the National Endowment for the Humanities, each of which made possible a year's leave of absence from my home institution. Summer research grants from the University of Tennessee and the University of Delaware have facilitated travel to archives at crucial junctures and employment of the graduate students Neva Specht, Rob Mancabelli, and Jordie Klienam to help me computerize the collective biography of merchants upon which this study is grounded.

The people at the Johns Hopkins University Press have justly earned their reputation for guiding a manuscript to press with both rigorous standards of scholarship and generous nurturing. Robert J. Brugger is a tolerant and patient history editor, and his many insights, however casually expressed, have left indelible marks on the finished product.

My daughter Sarah has done far more than help me find obscure books in libraries and produce an index. She has been growing up with this book, tolerating the ebbs and flow of my research and writing over the years. I hope she will always know that she brings me the greater joy. To her I lovingly dedicate this book.

Merchants and Empire

Introduction

DURING THE seventeenth and eighteenth centuries, adventurers, sailors, and settlers from western European nation-states engaged in unprecedented rivalries for dominion over the lands, resources, and native residents of North America. Their imperial expansion proceeded alongside an internal transformation of European nations marked by centralized governments, powerful military and financial institutions, rising internal production for growing populations, and new labor and social relations in the countryside. Changes also made it possible for ambitious, rising merchants and manufacturers to accumulate larger amounts of capital, catapulting them to the forefront of many political and economic decisions. All of these activities helped renew the commitment of early-modern people to international commerce and the merchants who conducted it.

At first, England's colonization of distant places proceeded haphazardly and more slowly than the ventures of its European competitors, but by the 1680s, a few towns along the Atlantic seaboard of North America were growing rapidly away from their meager beginnings and acquiring the characteristics of the European cities through which so many colonists had to travel before crossing the ocean. These expanding settlements nurtured the ambitions of international wholesalers who undertook the commercial risks associated with satisfying the material needs and wants of colonists for imported commodities. In a few colonial cities, political authority, flows of goods, and emulation of London's cultural ways combined to give a cluster of eminent merchants disproportionate influence over provincial social relations and policy making. More often than not, historians have assumed a causal relationship between this elite and the gradual, but indisputable, rise in complexity and comfort that maturing urban communities enjoyed.[1]

In colonial New York City's case, there is much to recommend this view. As New Amsterdam had been before 1664, New York was a small outpost of ambitious empire-builders, where successful international commercial competitors could rise quickly to positions of eminent stature. These few men could expect, in turn, to shape immigrants' opportunities for settlement and production in the interior, to spur much of the port city's development, and to inspire provincial policies that responded to economic challenges by colonial neighbors or foreign powers. This economic elite became an indispensable part of the city's rise by cultivating linkages to reputable credit and families in their home countries, undertaking expensive transatlantic voyages in the largest colonial vessels, acquiring great landholdings, making high-interest government loans, and living in a relatively grand style. In most cases, historians—indeed, most contemporaries—identified these individuals as dry-goods importers, wholesale merchants whose most important business was direct trade with English and Dutch merchants for finished household goods, textiles, medicines, and other commodities colonists were unable, unwilling, or forbidden to manufacture. Their ships might carry "all manner of fineries" for wealthy city residents—silks, brandy, or coaches from England and France, and wine or dried fruit from southern Europe. Although their fortunes did not compare with those of renowned English firms, remote ports of call became as familiar to them as the small aggregation of warehouses and homes at the tip of Manhattan. A few of them enjoyed cultural deference and provincial political authority in addition to their comparatively impressive array of capital and goods for elegant living. It has been appropriate, then, for historians to associate these transatlantic traders closely with colonial achievements, and they play an important part in the account that follows.[2]

But we might justifiably ask whether scholars studying New York City's commerce, and, by extension, its social and political development, have not focused too much of their attention on the coterie of individuals at the pinnacle of economic success in the province. Moreover, most studies of merchants in colonial North America have focused on the last decades of imperial rule, a period in which colonial economic maturation is palpable, often measurable, and for which the sources are rich. Perforce, these studies also follow their commercial elites into the excitement of the Revolution and its heightened politicization of economic affairs; and they tend to jump-start portraits of commerce at somewhere around 1750, when merchants entered an exceptional period of intense transformation.[3]

This study takes a longer view of the colony's international commerce, from the time of its founding, through its middle decades, and into the imperial crisis that culminated in the American Revolution, hoping thereby to gain a better understanding of the unfolding of New York City's trade, the development of its merchant community, the fluctuations and intermittent crises of its economy, and the extended time-frame in which many merchants' careers unfolded. Moreover, without disputing that a few eminent merchants made a profound impact on New York City's economic character, we might wonder whether there were not equally significant and enduring influences introduced by other colonists whose lives were shaped by city commerce.

A hasty look at some numbers affirms this. Although dwarfed by London and Amsterdam, New York City was transformed between the 1660s and 1720s into a qualitatively different place. By 1700, it had risen to match the commercial strength of Boston, surpassing it in number of vessel clearances, tonnage, and the value of many exported commodities in subsequent decades. Not until well into the eighteenth century did Philadelphia overtake New York in the volume and value of coastal and West Indian commodities passing through each port, but by then New York City dominated its own satellite regional economy in ways that replicated London's place at the hub of a great commercial wheel. The pace and quality of city maturation required that fully one-quarter of its people be involved directly in commercial activities, from petty officials such as tide waiters to the artisans who helped build and outfit vessels, to the mariners who sailed them, to insurers, inspectors, and other port personnel who processed goods and papers, to captains and supercargoes who bought and sold commodities. Indeed, the commercial elite were just one part of a larger commercial community that has eluded the attention of historians; they represented roughly from 10 to 20 percent of all wholesalers at times during the colonial era and were less than 1 percent of the city's residents in many decades. Moreover, as the number of wholesalers grew from about 80 in 1664 to 135 in the 1690s, over 200 in the 1720s, and nearly 400 in the 1750s, the commercial elite diminished as a proportion of all city merchants.[4]

Who constituted the majority of city traders? What was their role in the larger commercial community? In what ways did their interests coincide with, or depart from, those of the merchant elite? Were their opportunities substantially the same as, or notably different from, those of the men who rose to commercial eminence; were their setbacks the result of poor initial endowments, bad personal judgments about markets and trading relationships, or comparatively worse luck? What economic and intellectual character did they imprint on city life? These are among the many questions that demand answers once the narrative of New York City's commerce is expanded to include the early years of development and we begin to reconstruct its diverse economic community.

In the following pages, I examine an expanding majority of city wholesalers focus whose interests and material accomplishments lay somewhere between those of eminent wholesalers and the myriad petty producers, sailors, and service workers attached to city commerce. Known to many colonists as "lesser," or mid-dling, merchants, they had a significant impact on the city and the region. Although in some respects their commercial activities paralleled those of the great merchants on a reduced scale, they were set apart from the eminent by their modest origins and continuing affiliations with retailers, artisans, millers, and small producers whose livelihoods were not linked directly to international trade. They engaged intensely with local inhabitants to acquire small quantities of goods and watched their prosperity rise to only middling levels; often it fell precipitously. Many of these middling merchants were identified with their energetic trade in coastal and West Indian markets. Although always subject to comparatively volatile fluctuations of prices and buyers, West Indian markets also offered the advantages to rising young men of being closer to New York City; requiring smaller ships and crews, and less start-up capital; and demanding commodities that exporters could acquire within their region. Colonists also connected lesser merchants more with the business of negotiating with the region's aggressive commercial farmers for staples to export.[5]

Reconstructing the densely textured activities of this majority of merchants is only one objective of this study. Beyond that, I hope to explain the relationships lesser merchants enjoyed with other New Yorkers and what economic impact they had on the lives of all ranks of colonists. The view that emerges is one, not of unfolding, relatively uninterrupted opportunity for transatlantic development, but of constant interruptions and all manner of international and internal difficulties. Most city wholesalers did not join a leisured republican patriciate, attain high political office, or achieve great wealth. Those who were tenacious and lucky attained material comfort and social approbation. In other cases, lesser merchants barely earned a living doing what eminent men did. Yet they unwittingly helped to establish myriad nodes of connection between the countryside and the coast. Into the early years of the eighteenth century, struggling city exporters reminded themselves that New York City's commerce was extended—and limited—by the maturation of the surrounding countryside; the port city was never independent of the goods, credit, quarrels, manipulations, and productive potential of the farmers and middlemen in the hinterland, who by negotiating with city merchants enlarged everyone's market opportunities. Similar ever-shifting economic relationships developed between middling merchants and consumers in the urban port, where they collectively welcomed the exchange and consumption of greater quantities of goods. All of which was as consequential for the colony's material refinement as the traffic of the trading elite, if not more so.

Methodological issues go deeper still, for by ignoring the variegated economic experiences of the majority of merchants, historians have also perpetuated too narrow a view of the intellectual and political context in which New York's merchants, and those whose lives were touched by them, functioned. Indeed, we should also be asking whether New Yorkers' commercial opportunities and business choices were related to the explanations of economic life that circulated among them. Did lesser merchants support the commercial goals we have imputed to early-modern development, goals that are closely identified with the commercial elite and political authority? Were middling city traders simply less successful members of an intellectually unified commercial community, or did their distinctive social origins and business affairs set them apart from the commercial elite? Were lesser merchants attracted to elements of a different economic vocabulary? Did they understand imperial economic affairs differently? Did their traffic in different goods, with different places, where the risks and opportunities set them apart from dry-goods importers, have consequences for thinking about consumption in the colony? Did their close connections to the interior sensitize lesser merchant exporters to the colony's productive potential? Were the dissenting behavior and ideas of some merchants harbingers of deeper transformative influences during the Revolution, of changing commerce in the early national era, or of later industrialization?

Colonial American merchants rarely engaged in consistent, systematic, and self-conscious reflection on their political economy, but patterns of economic thought can nonetheless be discerned in traders' personal choices, the extent to which they imagined new commercial possibilities, and the ways in which they framed their disputes with other economic interests. Although I had thought that the daunting exercise of culling through piecemeal writings and fragmentary data would show only that most city merchants' economic ideas could be reduced to the bottom line—profit—I have learned that their calculations with regard to the material comfort and welfare of their people were not "merely economic" and therefore detached from values. Indeed, long before the phrase "political economy" came into vogue during the mid eighteenth century, many merchants affirmed the need for justice in balancing accounts, liberty to negotiate prices, and their right to demand particular legislation. Although terms such as *justice*, *liberty*, and *rights* were used ambiguously at best, and often in a manner baffling to us, they point to a host of interpersonal relations that required merchants' daily attention. In addition, although they had originated in a more traditional time, which was fading rapidly, these concepts could easily be revived in opposition to republican fears about the era's commercial spirit and the mobile wealth it engendered. Indeed, as many colonists joined merchants in celebrating importation of new, and more goods, and export of re-

gional surpluses, the commonwealth tradition seemed inadequate, even antithetical, to these tasks, and the tenets of an emerging economic liberalism
seemed more satisfying.[6]

One species of the genus economic liberalism—what Adam Smith later
called "mercantilism"—has been examined frequently by historians, although
usually from the vantage of the imperial state and its efforts to shape colonization, and less often from the perspective of colonial emulation of that imperial
model. When the Dutch surrendered New Amsterdam to the English in 1664,
Parliament in London was already formulating policies that sought to give
order to unpredictable economic events, to harness centrifugal tendencies in a
world full of hostile nations. The handmaid of political nationalism and international imperial dominion, mercantilism took shape as a series of expedient
responses to perceived threats from foreign competition, illicit trade, and the
relative tardiness of England's own rise. To these ends, legislation shaped lower
export duties, higher import duties on foreign manufactures, lower interest
rates, lower exchange rates for currency, easier credit for private interests, incentives to settle and develop new lands, and deterrents to the flight of specie and
piracy. All of this, and more, required active intervention of governments—in
England and in each colony—to regulate collective economic affairs.[7]

Most scholars are content with the judgment that mercantilism's benefits, in
economic terms, outweighed the formal restrictions it mandated for colonial
activity.[8] But many inquiries have unnecessarily narrowed considerations about
mercantilism to those of statecraft and policy making, ignoring how inspiring
mercantile promoters could be to new commercial interests and activities, how
optimistic their writings sounded to colonists contemplating the compelling
prospects for economic success as members of the English empire. Mercantile
writers continued to insist, as writers for centuries had, that all successful merchants had duties to contribute to the general welfare; but they also distanced
themselves from long-standing ethical injunctions against expansive private
material accumulation through competitive means. No matter how frequently
the authorities reminded colonists of their subordination to the more powerful
imperial center and the interests of English commerce, New York's merchants
could choose to ignore the formal side of the imperial relationship and focus on
its more satisfying aspect: government support for colonial special interests.

Mercantilism guaranteed many material benefits and provided an optimistic
intellectual vision to most of New York City's merchants; it nevertheless had an
ideological counterpoint that coexisted uneasily with a regulation model and
was appealing to a significant minority of city traders. The concept of "economic freedom," or "free trade," became useful, at first, in discussions about

the distinctions between rival empires. Seventeenth-century English observers often explained the success of Dutch trade in terms of the "natural liberty" they perceived Dutch burghers and international wholesalers to enjoy at the open ports of their empire, and their ability to travel without restriction to markets anywhere. The Acts of Trade and Navigation passed in the 1660s were essentially an attempt by British mercantilists to stave off Dutch competition.[9]

Meanwhile, British governors in the West Indies and some inhabitants of recently conquered New York City demanded more freedoms from imperial authorities. In the next generation, some New Yorkers grew accustomed to countering one or another undesirable provincial or imperial measure with kudos for open commerce. By the turn of the eighteenth century, appeals for economic freedom were seldom based on the Dutch example; instead, writers were beginning to extol the natural competition of buyers and sellers in personally responsive exchanges. Lesser North American merchants in the coastal and West Indian trade frequently used this dissenting economic discourse to justify all manner of illicit trade. In addition, as traditional obligations attached to land and inheritance gave way to mobile property and acquisitive social tendencies everywhere in the empire, some writers argued that persons shared universally equal desires and had the potential to become equally endowed with the material benefits of markets, money, and credit. Older notions of political and moral obligation to society and the prescriptive rights of landownership could not, it was boldly averred, unleash self-interest's "sweet" effects—the material elevation of all residents of the empire and eventually an end to costly regulatory legislation and wars.[10]

Of course, political and social relations favored mercantilism's triumph over the opposing intellectual model of economic freedom in the early-modern era. But my examination of New York City's middling merchants points to a series of ironies in this outcome. As New Amsterdam's residents discovered, presumptions of the existence of a "perfectly free" Holland were deeply mistaken; at times, England's arch rival in the early seventeenth century regulated economic activities with a zeal comparable to that of the most ardent English policy makers. Moreover, although the legacy of economic freedom continued to appeal to New Yorkers after the conquest in 1664, and efforts to eliminate commercial restraints surfaced frequently well into the eighteenth century, they proved difficult to sustain. And the reason for these failures is easy to find: most calls for one or another form of economic freedom came from the lesser merchants, who were most vulnerable in trade and least empowered in politics. They achieved only modest amounts of free trade in periods when the provincial government of New York lifted colonial monopolies, embargoes, or discrimination against the New England ports with which lesser merchants traded; and we might add the flourishing smuggling business.

The fact is, too, that hardly any lesser merchant consistently or unequivocally advocated free trade; as most of them understood it, calls for economic freedom in one quarter might be tempered by equally strong calls for regulations in another. Indeed, they regularly behaved as if their goals were both to emulate the imperial model of regulation in order to bring regional, coastal, and West Indian markets into their orbit, just as London had defined New York's place in the larger empire, and to introduce commercial innovations or disencumber aspects of their businesses in the spirit of "economic freedom." Perhaps the most significant examples of this found in this study are, on the one hand, efforts to regulate trade with the interior, and, on the other, the many manufacturing experiments of rising, ambitious city traders who called on their municipal government for aid even as they decried port regulations. As a consequence, it would be remiss of us to impute a vision of unalloyed free-market capitalism to any merchant or early-modern writer discussed in the pages that follow.

This issue merits elaboration. Concepts of regulation and freedom, as they were shaped in the early-modern era, functioned as the poles of a powerful economic discourse, but they were nurtured together in public debates about the delicate equipoise between such other concepts as authority and liberty, scarcity and plenty, and war and peace. Both poles of thought validated the commercial claims of merchants everywhere in the empire against the countervailing interests of the landed aristocracy and customary traditions, promoting a radical shift in thinking about trade, commodities, and international exchange. Mercantilists and free traders alike subscribed to the notion of human perfectibility over time and believed in the universal human desire for refinement. The connection they made between self-interest, property, and national wealth overturned ancient and scholastic conceptions of the common interest by proposing that the promise of material reward lay at the heart of individual inducements to labor and that profits were a justified gain from commercial risk taking. Seeking to avoid the scarcities, insecurities, and widespread unemployment of previous eras, both mercantilists and the advocates of free trade extolled brisk circulation of, and more demand for, all kinds of goods; the resultant wealth, they believed, would make nations and their colonies great.[11]

In the colony's early years, regulation and freedom usually represented irreconcilable poles of belief and policy, not equal possibilities to be chosen or modified as commercial circumstances warranted. But colonists were never simple siphons of hypostatized ideas. In the crucible of their own particular experiences, they innovated and departed from inherited ways; they defied explicit policies, negotiated for favorable ones, or lived in grumbling compliance with other measures. And by the mid eighteenth century, the jumbled legacy of regulation and economic freedom left New Yorkers with a political economy that combined the benefits of living in the empire with another set of benefits that issued from protecting and promoting commerce that lay outside the explicit design of imperial authorities.

Merchants sometimes, but never consistently, grasped the material constraints and commercial opportunities under which they lived, and they usually expressed their understanding in words and concepts that were undergoing rapid change even as they reiterated them. Indeed, whether thought moved along at a snail's pace or by leaps of imagination delivered to the public in treatises fortunate enough to influence a large audience, whether it emanated from legislators or from dissident minorities defining contrapuntal rights and obligations, we cannot claim that the whole merchant community spoke clearly or uniformly. Writers exaggerated, oversimplified, or miscalculated the phenomena they discovered. Publicists created understandings about new economic circumstances and related them to winning over supporters of one or another extreme; they also created fictions about individual motivations, intentions toward others, and the general social consequences of particular policies. Any single thinker might lack consistency, originality, or relevance at times, for underlying their economic choices were all the dotted and disconnected lines of a blueprint for economic success that was imperfectly understood by even the most sophisticated commentator, and variously applied by merchants active in commerce. Mercantilism and free trade were buffeted by shifting circumstances and wrought by imperfect economic knowledge; the boundaries of each cluster of ideas were as permeable as the social groups of eminent and middling merchants.[12]

Colonists tended to find different qualities of either mercantilism or free tradism appealing at different junctures of their commercial experiences. But this should not lead us to the conclusion that city merchants were little more than savvy opportunists. The portrait of city commerce that follows furnishes an important affirmation that economic interests did not all flow into one colonial channel; colonists were not set on an ineluctable course pursuing economic autonomy from imperial authority, and imperial policy makers never attempted to force colonial energies into one great reservoir of homogeneous activities. Colonists' struggles to shape the economic circumstances around them were aided by the existence of intellectual options. Some of them were related to the enlightened and dominant policies that required state intervention, interest-group attachments, and national rivalries; most city merchants agreed that membership in the empire procured economic benefits, and most of them emulated the success of the city's commercial elite, which often seemed to stem from loyalty to mercantile prescriptions.

I make few claims in this book about the connection between long-range economic experience and the potential for politicized visions of economic freedom to sweep colonists along during the imperial crisis. Yet although New York City merchants who aspired to economic freedom failed to prevail ideologically, or to become political majorities, colonists regularly felt their influence. Indeed, by developing habits of criticism and pursuing innovative or forbidden commerce, many city merchants helped other New Yorkers make subtle, sometimes almost imperceptible, forays into new production and consumption, usually based on local or regional considerations. Never was that clearer than during the nonimportation movements that arose after 1764, when dissenting city merchants may have helped alter colonists' views about what Cadwallader Colden, referring to the benefits of membership in the empire, called "freedom in fair trade."[13] New Yorkers came to realize during the imperial crisis that economic freedom could be secured better, not by pure self-interest, but by regulations emanating from sources of authority closer to them. I must, however, leave it to other studies to follow New York's merchants into their American Revolution.

Part I

Engagements with Economic Freedom

Chapter One

Establishing a Port, 1620–1664

I N EARLY NEW AMSTERDAM, only a handful of residents devoted themselves to wholesale commerce, and their material beginnings were noticeably modest compared to the great fortunes of some Dutch burghers. Nevertheless, their expectations of rising economic opportunities ran high, and the colony's merchants took part actively in the persistent dialogue about what kinds of economic policies the Dutch West India Company and its governors-general should promote. Following early-modern thinkers who set down economic ideas systematically, New Amsterdam's merchants were guided in their thinking about commerce by one or another side in the ideological tug-of-war between the proponents of economic freedom and those of economic regulation.

For some time, leaders of the Dutch Republic had proclaimed their commitment to free trade, and the Treaty of Southampton in 1625 stipulated that colonial ports were to "be open and free for the subjects of both parties [in England and the United Provinces] as well as merchants." However, Dutch rulers had set important precedents for mixing freedom and regulation. Chartered by the States General four years earlier, in 1621, the Dutch West India Company functioned less as a free-trade enterprise than as a joint stock company sponsored by the state, with monopoly trading privileges; the right to seize enemy and neutral ships in the Far East, the Gulf of Guinea, and the Caribbean; and authority to pass regulations governing the Dutch Baltic trade. Elaborate Company guidelines channeled resources to Brazil, the Baltic fisheries, and the West African slave trade.[1] The company extended similar regulatory control over its acquisitions in North America, most notably when it reserved exclusive rights to fur trading and exportation for the first of its "servants" sent to New Netherland, and over the next few years, it used its monopoly privileges to penalize noncompany traders with export duties and granted tracts of land in the colony to company loyalists. Almost immediately, these privileges divided settlers bitterly between those who favored company regulation of the economy and those who wanted more autonomy.

As a consequence of clashing interests, inherited economic ideas and policies underwent important changes during New Netherland's fledgling years. Accepted ways of thinking about commerce were altered by local conditions and reshaped by emerging interests in the colony. Differences arose between the inhabitants of the port city and those living in the hinterland, between private traders and company servants, and between eminent and lesser merchants over the fur trade, taxation, colonial prices, and the organization of exporting. Meanwhile, however, settlers' confidence in the promise of their colony was growing. Far from it being an insecure settlement ripe for conquest by the English in 1664, the internal quarrels in which New Netherland's settlers were enmeshed actually betokened steady growth and ripening commercial prospects.

Freedom and Furs

The Dutch West India Company's monopoly privileges placed its factors in New Amsterdam under difficult constraints. They were obliged to pay for peltry at prices set by the company and below what they believed the market would bear; moreover, they also had to pay company taxes and to sell at company prices in Amsterdam. In efforts to create modest returns for themselves, the factors tried to keep down the transport and storage costs of exporting pelts from the interior, while raising the prices of imports as high as colonists would allow. For their part, noncompany merchants in New Amsterdam, most of whom had come from "the General view" of settlers, protested that furs were their basic export, and that their New England neighbors enjoyed better internal gate prices and "open ports" that charged no export duties. Both company servants and rising "interlopers" added that in creating a group of semifeudal landlord-merchants, called *patronen*, company directors had picked men who cared very little about the competitive strength of New Amsterdam's commerce; only one *patroon*, Kiliaen van Rensselaer, and his descendants successfully combined the goals of becoming both a "notable merchant" and a "lord over vast lands."[2]

Back in Amsterdam, company directors, who did not wish to assume the burdens of governing an unruly people, debated ways to reconcile allowing New Netherlanders a degree of autonomy with their own desire for firm company control. In 1629, they revised their earlier expectations of colonists and granted certain "Freedoms and Exemptions" to inhabitants in order to encourage settlement under company auspices. Merchants resident in the fatherland were henceforth allowed to send goods freely out of Amsterdam to the colony, which the directors believed would hold down the cost of colonial imports. They also permitted transatlantic traders to transport intended settlers in company ships and promised that each patroon could expect a generous tract of New Netherland soil. Most important, the company granted both its servants and independent colonial merchants the "staple right" to trade along the North American coastline, exchanging any goods but one for the commodities and currencies they chose, reserving for the company a 5 percent impost on goods they brought back to New Amsterdam. The exception was peltry, which only company factors were permitted to export duty-free. Independent colonial exporters were taxed one guilder per hide after 1629. Private traders were also required to pay a 5 percent import duty on all goods entering New Amsterdam, and to pay at Amsterdam for the entry there of foreign salt, brandy, vinegar, grain, codfish, naval stores, and other major articles of the colonial trade. In order to protect textile manufacturers in Holland, colonists also were forbidden "to make any woolen, linen or cotton cloth" of their own.[3]

Although company directors couched the Freedoms and Exemptions as grants of commercial liberty to colonists, they had, on balance, introduced regulatory legislation that would secure the economic superiority of merchants in the home country and exacerbate the tensions between factors and independent traders in New Netherland. Few vessels paid the new customs duties over the next years. Director-General Pieter Minuit (1626–32) had encouraged open relations between the Dutch and English along the northeast coastline, and the next governor, Wouter van Twiller (1633–37), was helpless to reverse them. Various company servants hired to work tobacco plantations or labor on farms found exporting more profitable than company wages. Joining the colony's independent traders, they abandoned their loyalty to the company in order to trade with New England and the West Indies or exploit the rich fur resources of the interior without hindrance, insisting that the colony's trade would flourish only if the directors in Amsterdam would "sett it free."[4]

The predisposition of early settlers to value commercial ventures more than craft production and farming fueled a tendency for even the lowliest of settlers to enter the fur trade over the 1630s. Among them, Goovert Lookermans and Rutger Jacobsen abandoned craft production for coastal and West Indian commerce, rising to economic comfort and then social prominence between 1635 and 1650. Others stopped producing grain or tobacco in order to export peltry, the source of the quickest profits and the best colonial substitute for always-scarce specie. In the fall of 1626, for example, *The Arms of Amsterdam* carried 7,246 beaver, 853 otter, 81 mink, 36 wildcat, and 24 muskrat skins out of New Amsterdam but only "samples" of grains such as rye, wheat, barley, and caraway. Over the years 1630 to 1635, as many as 15,000 furs were exported annually, according to legal registrations. In 1645, as many as 10,000 may have been transported through the Albany area and then southward to the port. By 1638, the route for marketing fur exports that originated around Albany took traders not only down the Hudson toward New Amsterdam but also into Connecticut River valley towns, Long Island, and Boston, where export duties were lower or nonexistent. When New Netherland traders ran out of skins, neighboring colonies often accepted wampum and imported Dutch manufactured commodities in exchange for the food and household necessities that Dutch settlers neglected to produce. Reports to the company noted how some city importers ordered cargoes of manufactures and handicrafts from Amsterdam to be carried directly to Boston. What did not sell there was transported to New Amsterdam. Such disloyalty to Dutch kinship and imperial goals, the reports continued, reduced revenues in New Amsterdam and impoverished Dutch people everywhere.[5]

Not surprisingly, the States General at home found in 1638 that despite the Freedoms and Exemptions, the company had not encouraged sufficient immigration into New Netherland; while New Amsterdam traders benefited from commercial ambition, they were neglecting the basic requirements of settlement, including agriculture, stable government, and adequate defense of the frontier. The patroonships were pitiful agricultural endeavors. Independent traders secured nothing but furs for export, and in efforts to bypass company duties and shipping fees, they smuggled hides through neighboring ports. Unless the company directors reorganized their management of the colony and brought these disorderly and illicit commercial activities to a halt, they stood to forfeit their entitlement to the benefits of New Netherland's trade.[6]

With their backs to the wall, company directors relinquished the New Netherland trade monopoly they had held from 1621 to 1638. A series of documents, eventuating in a new set of "Freedoms and Exemptions," opened up colonial importing and exporting to both the great firms of the United Provinces and all residents of New Netherland; in order to encourage settlement and end the haphazard coming and going of interlopers, every family of five or more that settled in the interior was guaranteed two hundred acres of free land. The only rights the company retained were those of appointing a governor-general, setting the duty on foreign imports into the colony at 15 percent ad valorem, and retaining a duty of 15 percent on all colonial goods received at Amsterdam. The company continued to send factors to New Amsterdam to buy furs, but by 1642, a flood of new settlers and private traders competed in the colony for resources to export.

Domestic Political Economy

In imperial terms, then, New Netherland was to be developed along the lines of private risk taking rather than joint-stock-company regulation, but within the colony, contention continued over the efficacy of open competition. Rapid development in the 1640s made the resolution of the issue seem all the more urgent.

Although the colony numbered only roughly 300 residents in the early 1630s, its merchants and company factors cleared an estimated thirty to forty ocean-going vessels from the port annually. By the 1640s, these ships, many of them frigates and schooners, not only brought manufactures from the United Provinces but also plied the coastal waters of North America and the Caribbean, returning to New Amsterdam with goods and correspondence that changed the city dramatically during that decade. In 1643, there were some 2,500 settlers in the colony, about 2,000 of whom were concentrated around the fort and port facilities. During the decade, as many as 67 city residents can be identified as merchants, of whom 51 engaged in wholesaling alone, while 16 both exported goods regularly and were retailers as well—generally an option available only to the most successful city traders at that time.[7]

By then, colonial vessels carried to Virginia and the West Indies "the value yearly of several millions" of guilders worth of commodities, "all sorts of domestic manufactures, brewed beer, linen cloth, brandies . . . duffles, coarse cloth . . . in return for which are imported . . . from Virginia, beavers and other eastern furs, considerable tobacco, and from the Caribbean islands a large quantity of sugars, tobacco, indigo, ginger, cotton, and divers sorts of valuable wood."[8] Although many city wholesalers continued to share voyages with the great Dutch traders, a few of them sent captains to Aruba and Curaçao in smaller vessels on their own account, carrying European wares and cloth, along with some foodstuffs, to eager colonists along the Delaware River or at the sugar plantations further south. They then took in peltry at the South River; tobacco, cattle, and slaves at Virginia and Barbados; and cotton wool, horses, and dye-woods at Caribbean ports. On the return trip, they stopped at New Amsterdam to drop off cattle, horses, and slaves for the colony and transferred peltry, specie, conch shells, and tropical luxuries to larger vessels—and wealthier merchants' accounts—for the voyage to Amsterdam.[9]

Important constraints kept this trade smaller than ambitious colonial merchants would have liked. Furs continued to provide the basis for New Netherland's transatlantic commerce, but traders who went to the southern coast-line and the West Indies required more essential provisions. New Amsterdam traders repeatedly lamented their inferiority in this respect to New England shippers, who could meet such demands. Indian wars constantly drained economic resources, and the islands of the West Indies were only just beginning their shift toward sugar and more intensive use of slaves, which would create greater markets for northern colonists after the 1660s. Then, too, the great Dutch merchants had significant advantages in the carrying trade; more and more, New Amsterdam's middling city traders watched their southern imports being transferred into ships suitable for crossing to the home country, where more eminent merchants would realize higher profits from them than middling New Amsterdam merchants could in the coastal trade.[10]

Further threats came with the passage in 1651 of the first major English Navigation Act, which would disrupt the ability of New Netherlanders to carry English tobacco, hides, salt, logwood, cotton wool, indigo, and sugar in their vessels, and to offer liberal twelve-month credit to English firms. Dutch settlers along the coastline had often noted that the English colonies had lower port duties than New Amsterdam; now, the English act, together with a 1651 order from the directors of the Dutch West India Company affirming regulations and duties, seemed to conspire against the Dutch colonists. With passage of England's 1660 Navigation Act—which included tobacco on its list of enumerated items—the route for tobacco transport on Dutch vessels was decisively altered. Fewer of the Virginia and Maryland tobacco shipments touched at New Amsterdam after that year, and although the deputy collector of Newport, Rhode Island, invited free importation of slaves and tobacco through his city, most wealthy Dutch merchants who had the ability to mobilize capital, vessels, and commodities bypassed the northerly ports and made the voyage directly from southern colonies to Amsterdam.[11]

After the West India Company relinquished its monopoly, free competition for pelts within the colony promoted rapid exploitation of the countryside and commensurate prosperity for some exporters. Colonial factors of Dutch firms in the colony were displaced by free agents who sold furs at the market price in far-flung places. But exporters grew anxious when they thought about the delicate balance of distant peoples and markets that this trade required: Indian suppliers, quantities of wampum and trade goods, adequate ocean transport, Dutch and European prices, and the timely and coordinated responses of merchants to all the other conditions. Although Amsterdam's favored position in the international competition for furs kept prices in the home country relatively stable and markets relatively assured until the 1640s, the imperial quests of France and England by then introduced uncertainties about the future of this trade. English and French interlopers to the north of New Netherland offered higher prices to Indians and trappers for furs, and they sometimes paid with silver, gold, or desirable clothing and agricultural implements. Private traders linked to the Van Rensselaer family, as well as a few remaining company factors in New Amsterdam, competed desperately with Albany residents, who in turn traded with French Canadians for northern furs. As that trade grew "worse from year to year," settlers in the Delaware and Connecticut River valleys—especially at New Haven—cornered great shares of territory and furs to the east and west of New Amsterdam's merchants.[12]

Heightened hopes of commercial prosperity, tempered by continual anxiety about the limitations on their trade, sensitized city merchants to even the slightest shifts of commercial policy in the colony. It quickly became clear that the commercial freedoms the company directors had granted were likely to be violated by the States General's appointment of inept or misguided colonial governors-general. Governor Willem Kieft (1637–45), who had been chosen to rule the settlement because of his former experience as a merchant, was openly hostile to the post-1638 commercial freedoms and boldly tightened the reigns of commercial regulation in New Netherland. Known as a primary instigator of a destructive war against the coastal Algonkian peoples, Kieft also, out of loyalty to the company, insisted on passing new port and domestic exchange regulations that flew in the face of the 1629 Freedoms and Exemptions. Kieft complained to company directors that too many nonresidents deprived colonists of their fur trade when they entered the city briefly to collect bundles of New Netherlands furs. In addition, some residents in New Amsterdam had begun to smuggle at English and French ports with impunity. The governor put enforcement agents at the harbor as a first step toward correcting these abuses.[13]

The steeply rising prices of most necessities, which Kieft believed discouraged settlement and encouraged humbler local traders to enter illegal trade with their English neighbors, were his next target. Former company ordinances "against private individuals trading in furs" had never really been enforced, and now autonomous importers were also free to charge excessively high prices for imports. Kieft accordingly formulated new laws requiring all fur traders to have been resident in the colony for three years and to submit all exports to quality inspection. Furthermore, the new legislation required all city laborers and artisans to be in the employ of the company and forbade them to compete for work among the independent fur exporters, a measure intended to curb the smuggling by "diverse, self-interested persons in New Netherland," whose trade had become "publicly apparent to all the world."[14]

Following the model of other early-modern city corporations, additional laws established fairs for regulating the sale of cattle and swine, as well as regular market days and fixed prices of necessary goods sold at the company stores, beginning in 1639. Excise taxes on brewing would provide additional city revenues, while regulation of grain, tobacco, and flour weighing, packaging, and sales would guarantee the city against fraud by rural producers. In 1640, Kieft unilaterally decreed a duty of 10 percent ad valorem on all colonial imports that had not already paid duties to the company in Amsterdam and announced his intention to enforce a 1629 law imposing a 10 percent export duty on peltry, provisions, cattle, and tobacco.[15]

The fact that these measures promoted settlement and protected economic activities in New Netherland was lost on many colonists, who perceived them as hindrances to the opportunities emerging during the 1640s. As a result, the last fifteen years of Dutch rule saw deepened and more complicated quarreling among different economic interests. One fault line of disagreement ran between the "governor's camp" and city traders. Among the former were a small but powerful group of company factors in New Amsterdam, men who enjoyed the privileges of close association with large firms in the United Provinces, including a steady flow of imports from abroad that were sold out of the company store. Also included were the governor's close military and diplomatic associates, who were guaranteed the use of company ships to trade along the coastline and exempted from colonial commercial regulations.

Arrayed against these men were dozens of internal "petty traders" and many of the port's wholesalers, called the "select men" or "best of the commonalty," who in July 1649 united in their demand for "permission to export, sell, and barter grain, timber, and all other wares and merchandise the produce of the Country, every way and every where your High Mightinesses have allies."[16] Their voices were strengthened by the Board of Twelve Men (1641) and a Board of Eight Men (1643–44), originally constituted by the governor from among the freemen of the city to help administer justice during Indian troubles and to provide support for Kieft's port regulations, but soon characterized by their identification with the interests of rising exporters. Under the next governor, Pieter Stuyvesant, a Board of Nine Men (1647–48) would continue to express the concerns of merchants at New Amsterdam who harbored little affection for imperial or provincial duties on trade. Lower export and import duties, allocation of local excise tax money to city-development projects, fair treatment by company inspectors, and deregulation of consumer prices—these became their persistent pleas to both the governor-general in the colony and company directors at home throughout the 1640s.[17]

Pieter Stuyvesant's governorship prompted additional grievances among city wholesalers. Over his term (1647–64), regulation reached new heights. Stuyvesant ordered city laborers to construct a company warehouse on Pearl Street and appointed new port inspectors. An ordinance "obliging merchants to exhibit their books and accounts, when called on so to do," and "providing that all furs be stamp'd" with proof of having paid an export duty of fifteen stuivers for each beaver, otter, and elk hide before being loaded on vessels persuaded many independent merchants to evade the city's laws, which they were able to do with impunity.[18] Stuyvesant further lost the respect of city merchants when he permitted political favorites to trade with company resources and allowed Gerrit Vastrick "to depart [for Fort Nassau] with some thousand skins, without taking a penny [in duties] from him." Moreover, Stuyvesant's port inspectors had violated numerous standards of commercial propriety and justice. The Nine Men and some of their merchant neighbors protested:

Goods must first be sent to, and examined in the Company's store at Amsterdam, before they can be sent on board. Then a man must take a supercargo, also, along, and in New Netherland receive soldiers immediately on board the ship, of which he is no longer master. After which, the merchandize is opened in the Company's store, and what occurs there is an affliction and vexation to behold. For it is all cut open, unpacked, tossed over and counted again, without order or rule; besides that, the Company's servants from time to time destroy and purloin [imported goods].

Stuyvesant also traded openly with Indians and forbade the importation of guns and gunpowder on any vessels but his own. He decreed higher excise taxes on beer brewers and tapsters, expenses that would "probably have to be paid by the poor," in the form of higher consumer prices. The governor and his chosen favorites were even more "brutish" than the internal petty traders, merchants said. They had "fattened here" and "played with their employers [the company directors] and the people as the cat plays with the mouse." The governor's commercial agents in the coastal and West Indian trade were less the guardians of public liberties than they were "a cloak and a catspaw" for his agenda to provide a few loyal wholesalers and landowners with economic privileges, and to tax aspiring traders out of business. By 1652–53, Stuyvesant replaced remonstrants in public office with a new set of councillors and nodded assent to price-fixing.[19]

A second fissure developed between city merchants and nonresident traders who had been forbidden the privileges of importing and exporting at New Amsterdam. "Petty traders" of the interior, as well as foreign merchants' agents, moved freely between the port city and the surrounding hinterland, where they could buy inferior skins at low prices in order to undersell established traders in the colony. The merchant freemen who comprised Kieft's Board of Eight

Men complained to the governor that "the disorders of our commerce" persisted because "private traders had drawn excessive profits from the country" by offering low buying prices to trappers and agricultural producers and insisting upon high selling prices to exporters. Because of such "injurious usury," continued the freemen, country traders "should contribute something to the public service" from those profits in addition to paying the existing export duties.[20]

City merchants also feared peddlers, who took many skins to New Haven, Hartford, Springfield, Long Island, and on to Boston, where they could cut the cost of exporting them by evading duties altogether. Trappers and peddlers were also wandering the city and disrupting regular markets and fairs by the mid 1640s.[21] Boston's "Scotch Merchants and Petty Traders," fussed New Amsterdam's exporters, entered the Dutch port at will without establishing residency and aimed "at nothing else than solely to spoil trade and business by their underselling." They, and not resident merchants selling at markups, were the true "destroyers of trade," "taking as it were the bread out of the mouths of the Burghers and resident Inhabitants."[22]

During the 1650s, complaints continued, centering on the English, who brought "the greatest quantity of tobacco" in competition with city merchants, "admit[ted] of no discount" on bills of exchange drawn on Amsterdam, and demanded payment at English sterling exchange rates. Nor did English merchants allow a discount for the difference between what New Amsterdam authorities charged in fees for weighing and packaging tobacco and the lower fees that English factors charged, which resulted in a "loss on the weight [of peltry] in Holland" and correspondingly lower profits for the colony's Dutch.[23]

That same decade, greater numbers of New Amsterdam traders took advantage of new wagon trails, the expansion of West Indies ports, and the availability of New England goods and credit to enter the channels of "purloined" trade. Small vessels waiting outside Conynen Island evaded export duties and smuggled goods to the South River settlements, Boston, Virginia, and the West Indies. To suppress this "pilfering," the Dutch West India Company engaged in expensive litigation. Company attempts to stifle importation through New Haven—a favored place of entry for Dutch vessels—and the foreign West Indies only exacerbated the situation, since dissenters from Company policy could have "a profitable tobacco trade with the Floridas, the Bahamas," and other areas of the Caribbean as alternatives. Even fines amounting to "5 times the value of the imported smuggled Contraband" failed to curtail the "sorrowful business." Thus, the "daily experience" of contraband trade—into and out of the colony—grew "under the name and cloak of Sailor's freight."[24]

"It is to be remarked," New Amsterdam merchants observed in a petition to the company directors in 1657, "that our Neighbours [in New England] pay no Duties, nor any other charges, not even on the Wares they purchase from us." The result, they continued, was that "a great deal of fraud is committed in this way because several [Dutch] ships go first to New England, and then skulk under our neighbours' wings" as New England vessels. In addition, the "onerous imposts of duties" imposed upon New Netherland's shippers "before we can get our goods home [to Amsterdam]," raised their export and transport costs "28½ per cent," and gave further incentives to smuggle.[25]

Middling traders begged for "some facility in the impost on tobacco" they imported at New Amsterdam and for a reduction of "the weight of the scales" in Amsterdam. "The heavy export and import duties paid here and in the Fatherland, the charges for convoy and direction, the heavy freight bills and premiums for assurance, interest on capital invested in merchandise added to the dangers of leakage and decay make the first cost of goods delivered here more than 70 or 80 p. ct. higher than abroad." As a result, they were compelled to charge markups of at least 70 percent on imports to New Netherland in order to realize any profit at all. Moreover, they insisted, it was crucial to "allow them to sell according to the usages of the Fatherland . . . where commerce has a free course, their goods at such prices, as they think just and reasonable considering the conjunctures of the time, the first cost and expenses." For their part, the independent merchants promised that "it is by no means their intention to overcharge any burgher or inhabitant in the sale of necessary clothing or to demand unfair prices." Should they be allowed to determine their own markups they would behave "like honest traders and good fellow-citizens," keeping goods available and at reasonable market prices. Otherwise, they would withhold goods from city consumers "until the return of better times."[26]

Company directors in Amsterdam were sympathetic to the grievances of their compatriots in New Netherland only to a degree. They agreed that the governors' arbitrary enforcement of colonial legislation and the interference of illegal trade were, "of grave consequence and directly contrary to the course of Free Trade" at New Amsterdam. In 1650, they supported the plea of the merchant Arnoldus van Hardenberg to prohibit Stuyvesant's company servants from raiding his business.[27] In subsequent correspondence, the directors agreed with city merchants that there should be "a universal Trade" with New England and Virginia, "for when . . . the ships of New Netherland ride on every part of the ocean—then numbers, now looking to that coast with eager eyes, will be allured to embark for your island." Private interests, if properly freed from provincial and foreign constraints, would create "an enlarged freedom of foreign trade for the inhabitants" everywhere in the colony, bring new settlers and thus widen the foundations of security for the colony.[28]

Directors also cited the argument of the great Dutch jurist and promoter of commerce Hugo Grotius (1583–1645) that internal trade should not be subjected to the least constraint or limitation, but must be free and unshackled; it should be deregulated, so that "the exceedingly high prices" of imports and exports would, "with the increase of Trade, and the importation of everything in abundance, also cease and disappear in time."[29] In 1658 and 1659, they affirmed earlier statements of New Amsterdam merchants that fixing prices of peltry exports and tobacco reexports also ran against the spirit of economic freedom, for "the merchants there [in New Amsterdam] . . . can make sufficient calculation, without any danger, thereupon; as they doubtless do; for everyone is sufficiently knowing [as] to his own interest and is therefore sufficiently alive and awake thereto." In effect, the directors instructed city merchants to buy furs and tobacco at the lowest possible prices and sell Dutch manufactured wares at higher markups than their customers had borne before. They enjoined city merchants to compete with "the generalitye of inhabitants" and foreigners at the colonial port. "Freedoms," and not "compulsory restriction" would promote private interests—especially those of young starters in commerce—which in turn would be far better for "the advancement of the State."[30]

Up to that point, the merchants of New Amstersdam must have agreed. But the directors also insisted that lifting all duties would be "too excessive a freedom," since it would leave the colony without a source of revenue. Even worse, between 1649 and 1654, the directors granted colonists free trade in French wine and all international grain markets, but they restricted other trade to company servants, as stipulated in the original charter grant of privileges. In addition, certain commodities, especially peltry, were "bound to return [from foreign ports] directly with the freights" to Amsterdam or New Netherland to pay the company's "duties and recognitions." All New England and Virginia imports into New Amsterdam would pay a 16 percent duty, "to the end that a stop may be put to the practice resorted to by some of shipping their Goods to New England, and bringing them to New Netherland under the smaller Duty and that the Merchants sailing direct from here [Amsterdam] to New Netherland be not prejudiced." The company's promise of commercial freedom was, in fact, indistinguishable from the mercantile precepts of England.[31]

Exasperated, some New Amsterdam merchants insisted that the company's directors were subverting the true interests of the colony. Encouraging a modicum of economic freedom within the colony but taxing international trade heavily could never bring the hoped-for benefits to all. In fact, Amsterdam's officials had adopted a policy exactly the opposite of New Amsterdam merchants' hopes. As the latter put it, not higher imposts, but a "free and unobstructed commerce to and fro" with all competitors would reduce costs, encourage honest trade within the Dutch commercial empire, and achieve "peace with the neighboring Republics" in New England. At the same time, judiciously constructed "artificiall" barriers between buyers and sellers, fixing the prices at which merchants bought furs in particular, would guard against greed, excessive consumption, and high prices within the colony. Nevertheless, as New Amsterdam merchants rehearsed these arguments over the coming years, the governor and company factors in New Netherland followed the contrary course of enforcing imposts on many goods as high as 10 percent ad valorem, while the States General in Amsterdam also retained high taxes.[32]

Social Distinctions

For many years, New Amsterdam wholesalers were largely united against the policies of colonial governors, company directors, foreign competitors, and internal interlopers. They were able to frame their commercial interests as a unified, corporate trading community and expressed pleasure when the colonial government enacted discriminatory taxes against foreigners, reaffirmed city merchants' rights to be sole exporters, or censured the governor's untoward interference in city business. The expanding coastal and West Indian trades lent an air of promise to city commerce by the 1650s, and a steady stream of agricultural surpluses from the increasingly settled hinterland added to the opportunities for both exporting and importing.

But economic maturity brought with it the conditions that would both reflect and enhance differences among city merchants—differences of commercial engagement in markets, credit, and social arrangements, and differences of conviction about the appropriate conduct of traders and governments. There was no necessary connection between where a wholesaler traded, what degree of success he might enjoy, and what policies he would advocate to serve his commercial interests. But there was more than a coincidental relationship between the nature of the goods he traded, the commercial relations that prevailed in the markets he chose, and the economic ideas that seemed most satisfying to him.

One distinguishable group of traders in New Amsterdam included men who rose from meager beginnings to places of noted reputation. Jacob Reynsen, for example, was at first no more than a "petty trader" who sold guns and textiles to settlers in the interior for exportable furs but was one of the regular traders to the West Indies by the late 1640s. On the eve of the English conquest, however, Reynsen went under. Johannes de Witt did not have even this degree of success. After making several attempts to sell textiles imported from the United Provinces and to encourage flour exporting, he died in 1668 in debt to most of the merchants with whom he had done business. Francis Boon, a Huguenot who came to New Amsterdam in the early 1650s, survived by trading meager exports of timber and grain to St. Kitts. Jorys Huck fled from the city to Virginia when his debts overwhelmed him. Jacobus Backer, a baker-turned-importer, arrived in about 1658 and immediately rented space in a waterfront warehouse in order to establish his intention to receive goods from Amsterdam. Active, like so many other city traders, in securing peltry for return voyages, Backer nevertheless went bankrupt in 1670, sold his commercial effects to Benjamin de Hart, and returned to Amsterdam without his wife and three children. Pieter Nys, a wine importer for about ten years after 1650, left the trade when his shares in a couple of shipments were lost at sea. Others also enjoyed brief success during longer stretches of uncertainty or a few years of comfort before retiring from commerce.[33]

Augustus Heermans rose higher and more quickly than these fellow city traders. He came to the tiny port in 1633 and immediately established himself as a conduit for furs from the interior and tobacco reexported from the southern English colonies to Amsterdam. In joint ventures with fellow countrymen, Heermans imported goods on the return voyages from Amsterdam. On occasion, the vessels made detours via southern Europe for wine and slaves; sometimes they stopped at ports along the New England coast. By 1650, he was outfitting his own ships and sending them to Curaçao for dyewoods and cotton wool. Shortly thereafter, some colonists thought him the "greatest merchant" of New Amsterdam. By 1670, Heermans had realized the dream of becoming a great merchant and removed to Maryland as a gentleman.[34]

In the last decade of Dutch rule, fifteen to twenty-five New Amsterdammers counted themselves among the "great traders" in a city that had grown to about 2,400. Ten of them imported large quantities of dry goods from Holland and exported most of the furs that left New Amsterdam; seven of them exported fewer hides but handled most of the reexporting of dyewoods, cotton, sugar, and tobacco that arrived from the Caribbean.[35] These established merchants— always a minority—nevertheless enjoyed liaisons with even wealthier Amsterdam and Rotterdam families, from whom they acquired cloth, hardware imports, and long credit. Every year between 1645 and 1664, from seven to eleven vessels cleared Amsterdam for the colony, and as many as thirty others touched at the port on trips to more distant places. Merchants who arrived in the 1650s often survived the vagaries of commerce better than the earliest settlers; some of them also brought capital resources and promises of credit. When the De Hart family's traders—Benjamin, Balthazar, and Matthias—came in about 1654, they already had additional family connections in the West Indies, and they had built a fortune by the early 1670s.[36] Jacques Cousseau, a Huguenot refugee who had established ties in French commerce, arrived in 1658. In shared voyages with Cornelis Steenwyck—the colony's wealthiest wholesaler, who died in 1686 with a fortune estimated at £15,841—Cousseau recovered his former commercial stature; by the time he died in 1683, he was exporting to French and Dutch islands in the West Indies and sending regular cargoes to Amsterdam and Rotterdam.[37] Still other men who arrived during the Dutch period would begin a commercial ascent that endured for generations, including the Loockerman, Philipse, De Peyster, Ver Planck, Van Cortlandt, and Bayard families. In the early years, merchants such as Allert Anthony, Peter Wyncoop, John Winder, Jacobus Backer, Nicholas Jansen Backer, and Paulus Richards had relatively greater initial advantages than most city traders, but they did not advance as high up the economic ladder as the next generation would.[38]

A few New Amsterdam merchants became conspicuously wealthy. The value of the city property alone of Frederick Philipse, the wealthiest merchant in the colony, was assessed in 1695 at £2,610. Gouvert Loockermans died with an estate valued at 520,000 guilders; and Oloff Stevense van Cortlandt added to his initial business as a company brewer with far-flung ventures to all corners of the Dutch commercial empire, expanding family fortunes by helping six of his seven children marry into prominent merchant families by the time of his death in 1683. Each of these men—and as many as seven others—very early in his career combined importation of manufactures with exportation of the colony's furs. Within a few years, each of them had diversified into the coastal and West Indian trade, opened new port facilities for storage, purchased many more shares and entire vessels, begun his family's accumulation of real estate and city stores, and endured the fluctuations in prices and markets by cementing family dynasties. Loockermans, for example, married Maria Jansen, daughter of a successful merchant, and his three daughters married into the Leisler, Keersteede, and Bayard families. Balthazar Bayard, one of the husbands, was Pieter Stuyvesant's stepson; Stuyvesant's sister Anna married Samuel Bayard. In addition, Loockermans counted among his brothers-in-law Oloff Stevense van Cortlandt and Jacob van Couwenhoven, who were wealthy by colonial standards; his father-in-law was connected by marriage to the provincial secretary, Cornelis van Tienhoven, and to another well-to-do merchant, Abraham Ver

Planck. Through marriage, Loockermans linked his interests to nine other colonial business families, many of which extended their own tentacles of influence and reputation to still other "good marriages."

Some city traders rose from modest circumstances to eminence in other ways. Jacob van Couwenhoven, who started as a company servant, and Oloff Stevense van Cortlandt, who was a company soldier, both figured among the wealthiest exporters by 1650. Arnoldus van Hardenberg, Michiel Jansen, Gouvert Loockermans, and Thomas Hall began as sailors and farm laborers; Jan Evertsen Bout and Elbert Elbertsen served first as merchants' clerks; and Adrian van der Donck started as a sheriff on Rensselaerswyck manor. Charles van Brugge and Hendrick Hendricksen began trading in Curaçao and then carried modest mercantile holdings to New Amsterdam in the early 1650s, from where they built prosperous importing businesses; Johannes van Brugge, who may have been Charles' brother, switched from fur exporting to tobacco reexporting as long as ties to Virginia and Barbados were strong. Johannes de Peyster, Mathias and Balthazar de Hart, Robert Vastrick, and Hendrick van der Vin all grew to be wealthy tobacco and sugar merchants after meager beginnings. William Beekman and Pieter W. van Couwenhoven began as city brewers and expanded business to far-flung commercial connections. And among wealthy colonists, there was one—Jan Baptiste van Rensselaer—who successfully produced and exported relatively large amounts of grain during the Dutch period. A few men who immigrated in the 1650s with modest capacities for commerce "married well" and passed on their growing reputations and property to sons, who in turn added material comfort, vessels, and credit linkages. Asser Levy, Isaac de Foreest, Thomas and John Willett, Gerritt Hendricks, Nicholas de Meyer, and Abraham Delanoy fell into this pattern. Together, these few members of a small commercial elite occupied a position between the ambitious, rising merchants of New Amsterdam and the great burghers at home.[39]

By the final years of Dutch rule in New Amsterdam, at least two-thirds of the 112 identifiable wholesale importers and exporters could be characterized as "middling inhabitants." Only a few of them made substantial and lasting fortunes in commerce.[40] Collectively, they were younger, less experienced, and less well endowed with the capital and social connections than their more successful peers. They were often in the early stages of building their careers and depended on family and business partners at nearby ports or relations with small traders and commercial farmers in the interior. Lacking sufficient capital and connections to diversify, the majority of rising traders exchanged goods at regional ports and only occasionally traded with Amsterdam. Coastal and regional trade dominated their commerce. Their small vessels plied along the

Hudson River and to settlements at Fort Nassau—later New Amstel—as well as Virginia, New Haven, and Boston. Although some eminent importers' ships were spotted in the coastal trade—including Stuyvesant's *Prins Willem* visiting the South River settlements and Loockerman's vessels sending goods from Amsterdam to ports along the coastline—small traders needed regional markets not simply to extend their interests but to survive. Sander Liendertsz, Cornelis Coenraetsz, Paulus Leendertsen, Dirck Smit, and Coenradt ten Eyck shipped Indian goods and planks to southerly settlements in exchange for peltry, tobacco, cattle, and slaves; Thomas Wandall and Jan de Kaeper, engaged in voyages to New Haven and Boston.[41]

Reliance on regional and coastal trade qualified the limits to which lesser wholesalers could rise. For each of them, the risks associated with credit and markets were many. Often they straddled possibilities for making autonomous market decisions and disagreeable subordination to established creditors or a father. Jurien Blanck, Pieter Marius, Hendrick Hendricksen, Paulus L. van der Grift, Jacob Steendam, Dirck Dircksz Keyser, Jan de Kuyper, Abraham Staats, Paulus Schrijk, and Johannes Withardt—and many others over the 1650s and 1660s—came from the ranks of small retailers, millers, shopkeepers, or petty traders on the Hudson River. Unlike the more prosperous fur exporters they sent small parcels, shared ventures widely, and doubled as city retailers. Middling merchants depended upon the small producers around them who entered domestic exchange relations with small surpluses of grain, butter, planed timbers, and naval stores. Close contact with familiar local producers and city consumers, combined with the absence of linkages to Amsterdam, affected their views about citizenship, prices, and devaluation of provincial currency and often set them at odds with transatlantic traders. But among the characteristics of greatest consequence for rising traders were the social relations they were compelled to nurture.

Maturing Internal Conflicts

Efforts over the 1650s to secure and extend the position of New Amsterdam reinforced the differing statuses of city merchants, For example, in 1653 a city charter replaced the Twelve Men, authorized the formation of a municipal council, spelled out the obligations and rights of residents, and included a large reserve of authority for two burgomasters and six *schepens* to establish and enforce municipal laws. That same year, an ordinance granted merchants a chance to help fortify the city and develop its port by making loans at relatively high interest; thirty-nine householders, many of them successful transatlantic traders, took advantage of this, becoming municipal creditors. In November, importers were jubilant about the province's grant to the city of control over the wine and beer excise, a privilege that would allay some of the need for high import revenues. Two years later, the city again borrowed money from importers and lowered duties on commodities these merchants of consequence tended to import. Export duties and regional regulations that affected lesser local merchants remained unchanged.[42]

The separation between great and struggling merchants in New Amsterdam was formalized in 1657 when home authorities granted a "burgher right" that established the city's jurisdictional preeminence over the countryside on two levels. Great burghers were defined as loyal residents with exemption from serving on the city guard or performing other civic duties upon payment of 50 guilders; those eligible included all present and past members of the council, ministers, military officers, and native-born residents of the city and their male descendants. Small burghers paid 20 guilders for the right to keep a retail shop or wharf space in the city but were entitled to hold no offices and to share in no city "dignities."[43]

Although Amsterdam officials purportedly sought only to confer familiar structures of authority on the maturing colonial port, the effect of the measure was to establish a code of civic privileges, by which the wealthiest city merchants gained not only symbolic recognition of their interests but also the prerogative of discriminating against lesser merchants when they used their great burgher status to legislate commercial matters affecting the city, a privilege made manifest during quarrels concerning the prices of imports and exports and the value of provincial currency.

As the supplies of peltry began to recede further into the interior, immigrating traders and sons of established families began to seek economic advantages in other markets. Many of them turned with greater determination to the staples traffic with the West Indies, coastal trade in the mid-Atlantic region, and the whaling industry off Long Island. At this early date, few of them could rely on provincial agricultural surpluses to sustain their exchanges. The oft-stated hope of turning New Netherland into a grain-exporting colony still awaited realization, and New Amsterdam's demand for food rapidly outgrew its local supply. Indian raids on the weak northerly settlements curtailed production, and the pitifully small yields barely sufficed to feed the farmers. Entire years passed between shipments of grain from the Esopus area, and the slightly greater exportable agricultural surpluses of Long Island often went to the South River and Virginia settlements rather than to New Amsterdam.[44]

Still, the countryside had acquired a slightly more settled appearance along

the Hudson River by the 1650s, and some markets began to extend beyond familiar locales. As farmers and exporters met more frequently to negotiate exchanges, attachments to custom also underwent change. Anxieties about the
breakdown of customary legislation that had established rural prices and market conditions for centuries had spread across Europe and England by the early
1600s, and experiences in New Netherland pulled colonists into a similar discussion about equity and competition. Although stable, predictable prices might
prove essential for farmers' local trade, many of them regularly raised and lowered the prices of agricultural surpluses intended for New Amsterdam and
beyond. Sometimes, rising city and export demand for rural products fueled
farmers' willingness to raise the prices of the foodstuffs and timber they sold to
supplement family incomes. On other occasions, the impetus for price hikes
was external. Hampstead, Long Island, farmers informed company directors
that stable prices were impossible so long as "traders and factors, who do not
add to the public prosperity . . . come and go solely for their individual profit
and advantage." When outside traders entered towns, farmers were tempted
away from traditional market arrangements and became quite willing to make
their small surpluses as expensive to the intruders—and distant consumers—as
possible.[45]

Middling merchants were doubly opposed to these "free prices" in the countryside. As exporters, they tried to keep the gate prices they paid for grain and
flour low—a direct effort to enhance profits abroad. As consumers in New
Amsterdam, they also decried the rising costs of necessary household commodities, especially grain and flour. One age-old response to these troubles was
to embargo exports of necessary food supplies, but city authorities enacted only
one embargo, in 1649, over many years of shortages. When "manifold complaints" arose in response to rising prices in the city, middling exporters tended
to support price ceilings for vital commodities that were sold at city markets.[46]

But farmers' prices were not the only source of small traders' complaints.
Eminent importers raised the costs of goods, too, in the form of markups on the
"first price" of wholesale commodities to compensate for costs of transport,
storage, and insurance. As consumers, middling merchants found markups on
goods such as imported earthenware, textiles, and agricultural implements especially irksome, since any sudden or steep rise in the coast of these common
"necessaries" was perceived to be "artificiall." Moreover, letting "haggling determine" the value of goods in each transaction produced "excessive and intolerable dearness of all sorts of necessary commodities and household supplies"
and violated community expectations for relatively stable prices. It was not only
merchants who indulged in these evil practices. "Shop-keepers, Tradesmen,

Brewers, Bakers, Tapsters and Grocers [who] make a difference of 30, 40, and 50 per cent when they sell their wares for Wampum or for Beaver" had no choice but to follow importers' lead. The result was that "the poor Commonalty" suffered because "some greedy people do not hesitate to sell the most necessary eatables and drinkables, according to their insatiable avarice, viz. the can of Vinegar at 18 to 20 stivers." Importing merchants also had abused the "weal of the Generalitye"—including lesser merchants in their capacity as needy consumers—by raising markups for imports excessively. Only smugglers' goods did not bear steeply inflated prices, some said.[47]

Importers justified their markups at New Amsterdam by pointing out their own position between colonists who produced little and needed many imports and the agents of Dutch trading companies who exploited this captive market. Amsterdam wholesalers sold goods "at a hundred per cent advance, and higher" because the "common man cannot do without them." New Amsterdam's merchants could no longer sell according to customary notions of the community's needs and ability to pay but were obliged to set prices by the plenty or the scarcity of commodities in competitive markets that engaged merchants of many countries. If they were to make a profit, colonial importers had only one defense against inflation in foreign markets: to pass on the higher prices to the colonists.[48]

Many ambitious merchants appealed for price ceilings in 1652 and 1653 to end the "unfair advantage against the great numbers of persons seeking purchase." In 1653 the city council decreed that merchants could "obtain a living" by charging 120 percent "over and above the first and actual cost." But in order to be fair to city consumers, they were limited to "no more" than that.[49] Three years later, a similar constituency supported city magistrates who created price ceilings on both imports and farmers' goods making their way to New Amsterdam. Lamenting the high prices of "needful commodities and family necessaries," councilmen fixed exchange values lower than prevailing market prices by declaring the value of wampum to be "8 black and 4 white beades for one stiver" and the value of beaver to be the wampum equivalent of 16 guilders. They went on to set "reasonably lower" prices for other commodities, including beaver hides, although in a gesture of compromise toward importers the council added that if the crisis leveled off in the near future, it would reassess fixed commodity prices, "as the general market rate shall require."[50] Shortly thereafter, the council ordered Hudson Valley producers—in particular, Rensselaerswyck manor—to hand over wheat in order to feed residents of the port city; and in 1660 and 1662, the New Amsterdam's court of assizes fixed the prices for flour and bread sold in the city.[51]

But when looking for the greatest commercial advantages, lesser merchants who sought regulation of domestic prices reversed their pleas with respect to international prices and foreign currencies. Locally, New Amsterdam merchants had been able to substitute silver for wampum in order to keep a regular flow of furs coming down the Hudson River. Wampum, Governor Stuyvesant said, "is the source and the mother of the beaver trade." By measuring the value of their goods and services in wampum, tobacco, or beaver skins, not in the recognized international medium of silver, colonists created a relatively efficient local economy. Moreover, the small merchant community did not at first make large profits from international trade, and most profits secured from shipments to Amsterdam were plowed back into outfitting new voyages or used in the form of international paper credit, which was useless in the domestic economy. Hence, the alternative medium of wampum often proved useful all around. But in the minds of most colonists, as everywhere in the early-modern West, the price of goods traded at long distances was linked to quantities of silver or gold in one of its minted denominations. Wampum and other commodity money was useless abroad.[52]

In addition, New Amsterdam merchants were powerless to fix the value of currency and peltry traded internationally; as Albany-area and foreign competitors bid up the prices of peltry, they prompted de facto devaluation of wampum, by as much as 300 percent from the 1640s to the 1660s. In, 1652, Adriaen van der Donck also predicted that the English settling to the south of them would monopolize the production of wampum, saying, "the trade [in furs] will suffer great damage, because the English will retain all the [Indian] wampum manufacturers to themselves and we shall be obliged to eat oats out of English hands." If that came to pass, not only would the absence of local wampum currency bring down the economy of New Netherland; shortages of furs to export to the Netherlands as a medium of exchange would stop importation of manufactured commodities as well.[53]

Given these conditions, exporters protested vehemently when the colonial government devalued "splendid Manhattan wampum" in relation to the "foreign inferior" currencies of neighboring areas. Although their goal was to prevent New Netherland's currency from being "wholly put out of sight" by hoarders, authorities actually created conditions for informal foreign competition to bid up the prices of furs, which pressed down the value of wampum. A few international wholesalers benefited from making foreign sales, but lesser merchants who acquired peltry in the colony and resold it to transatlantic traders suffered from the declared lower value of wampum.[54]

In 1660, when the company's directors in Amsterdam asked the colonial authorities to revalue wampum to a silver standard, even Governor Stuyvesant allowed that such a measure would help a few wholesalers who had great credit with Amsterdam and London, but would harm most internal and regional traders. To adjust wampum to the international standard of silver would present the "considerable risk" of damaging the personal agreements of "man and man, seller and buyer" in the colony, for "the dealer [in New Amsterdam] holds or sells, his goods, according to the abundance of wampum" not of silver. As greater amounts of wampum had come into circulation, said other observers, prices for beaver rose, causing "domestic articles and daily necessaries [to be] rated according to that price, and become dearer." To rate wampum at a higher price would invite local inhabitants to boycott merchants' stores and to invoke customary behavior that could thwart effective enforcement of legislated changes in the currency standard. The larger the circumference of trade stretching beyond the city, the more precarious were the ties of credit and payments in these early years, and the less stable were those based on wampum and other substitute currencies.[55]

By the time Pieter Stuyvesant relinquished his seventeen-year leadership of the colony to the English, city merchants were fractured into various degrees of success and failure. Sometimes the fault lines between eminent and lesser merchants were difficult to discern, for the colony was still gaining a toehold in North America. Even very successful merchants were unable, and possibly unwilling, to turn systematically from commerce to investment in real estate, bonds, or manufacturing. By 1657, the most prevalent "industries" were brewing, milling, distilling, and brick making, all of which investors undertook with traditional forms of technology and traditional social relations. Flour millers were, in all but one case, domestic small producers who did not engage in the city's foreign commerce firsthand; indeed, they were more likely to expand their business to include baking and retailing.[56]

The city supported other "manufactures," which might more properly be conceived of as crafts, since they took place in households and met demand as it was "bespoke": tanning, silversmithing, instrument making, coopering, and house construction. Production of potash and silk was abandoned during the mid 1650s, and between 1661 and 1663, Dirck de Wolff would fail to garner community support for a salt refinery near the city. Meanwhile, some merchants and farmers migrated to New Jersey and New England to join the colony's competitors. In other respects, distinctions between elite and middling merchants were readily apparent in the contrasting lifestyles, neighborhood development, and the sizes of the vessels sitting in New Amsterdam's harbor. Traders had already rehearsed differences between the benefits of regulation in the colony and those of economic freedom in the competitive regions beyond their province.

The English conquest of the colony in 1664 paved the way for greater differences, partly by introducing ethnic conflict and partly by prompting new discussion about where to trade, with whom, and under what conditions. In other ways, the conquest merely changed jurisdiction over economic patterns already established by residents of Dutch heritage. Among themselves, merchants continued to quarrel about the benefits of regulation or freedom in commerce; but together, they sometimes pitted their wholesalers' interests against vocal consumers and farmers. Problems with prices and currency, and thus with the interests of small producers and consumers; rivalries with agriculturalists in the surrounding region; and divisions among merchants with competitive opportunities in international commerce all in their broad contours persisted during the succeeding decades of English rule much as they had during years of Dutch rule, despite the reputed shift from a model of Dutch free trade to one of English strong-state commercial regulation.

Chapter Two

Where Returns Were the Richest

The Transatlantic Trade, 1664–1700

ACQUISITION OF THE fragile colonial outpost that was henceforth called New York represented one more victory for the great commercial and institutional changes of English merchant capitalism between 1600 and 1750. Those changes were marked less by the technological innovations and reorganization of labor processes that would subsequently characterize the Industrial Revolution than by the extension of long-distance trade, new market relationships, and enlarged private profits that derived from owning and moving goods, primarily in commerce. Changing conceptualizations of taxes, warfare, business interests, money, and production challenged previously dominant landed interests and changed the contours of the English political economy, making it more like that with which we are familiar. Although early-modern people seldom fully understood these shifting engagements, they now entered a vital period of public discussion and government policy making, in which particular economic interests steadily expanded commercial dominion abroad and merchant self-interest at home. The dispute between advocates of economic freedom and supporters of economic regulation that had divided merchants in New Amsterdam was part of a much broader debate taking place wherever merchant capitalism took root. It was in this context that England adopted the policies later called "mercantilism."[1]

Although many English immigrants would carry opposing views of freedom and regulation with them to New York City, the continuing presence of Dutch people in the city fostered ethnic identities in which the ideas could thrive. At first, there were concrete benefits of trade to Amsterdam, and Dutch residents of the city continued to play an important role in encouraging compromises between the rival commercial empires of England and the United Provinces. Slowly, however, English immigration and the consolidation of an elite that identified with English imperial goals shifted the ethnic balance and introduced tensions over the appropriate trade policies to follow. Notwith-standing the united pleas of most transatlantic traders for lower port duties, city merchants with English backgrounds or marriage alliances, credit from English firms, and preferences for carrying English goods stood to benefit most from their home country's policies; their association with New York's English officials also helped to consolidate tangible material success for this new immigrant elite by the end of the century.

The maturing city was also home to many new middling merchants seeking trade with Dutch and English ports. But although the city's improving standard of living and the growing number of New York–owned ships in the harbor bol-stered the aspirations of young residents and sons of recent immigrants, Eng-lish lesser merchants had no more reason to expect that they would rise any higher into the ranks of the city's wealthy than most of their Dutch peers had in earlier years. Middling traders—men who relied upon more widespread shar-ing of voyages, smaller quantities of goods, fewer customers, and less frequent opportunities for taking transatlantic risks—became an even larger proportion of the merchant community as a whole over the decades, especially in the local and West Indies markets. As a consequence, a separation of policy interests between great and lesser merchants endured under a succession of English gov-ernors, even as the differences between people of Dutch and English origins diminished.

An Ideological Crucible

After prolonged economic trauma throughout the empire at the opening of the seventeenth century, English manufacturers made significant strides toward expanding cloth exports, and merchants began to build more of their own ves-sels, conduct commerce with their own bills of exchange and credit arrange-ments, and put many skilled immigrants to work. The city of London emerged as an emporium to rival Amsterdam, and policy makers boasted that England's exports doubled between 1600 and 1640, and by about 1660 had doubled again. Producers made myriad new commodities for home consumption and export; investors formed over three hundred joint-stock companies; merchants gath-ered at the exchanges, coffeehouses, brokerage, and insurance firms; the mar-kets for securities and bonds expanded; goldsmiths aided the rise of banking by offering discounts and paying interest to merchants; and Dutch and English financiers formed joint enterprises in London. All of these developments re-flected and furthered great changes in production at local levels, while port cities all around the coastal perimeters of the Atlantic Ocean provided indispensable gates of exit and entry for the goods of four European empires.

Until the 1690s, a number of factors conspired to dampen many English observers' unmitigated enthusiasm for commercial development. The country's general advance was marred, according to some of them, by poverty, underemployment, and a low rate of internal population growth, which hindered productive potential; they pointed to scarcities of vital foodstuffs in the early years of the century, as well as below-subsistence wages for rural and urban labor. For those who were in the woolens trade, which showed significant decline after the 1620s, it was not yet apparent that sugar refining, tobacco reexporting, and the manufacture of glass, metal, and paper goods could replace the "Old Draperies." Moreover, merchants still struggled with credit and currency shortages, dearth and glut, hostile competitors, pirates, and hostile public opinion. Jamaican and Barbadian traders continued to plead with home officials for "the necessitye of a Free Trade" at their islands, and merchants in Virginia and Maryland remained attached to the "holland free trade" in tobacco after the imperial authorities decreed its close regulation. Above all, the contours of a "gentlemanly capitalism" that merged the interests of a resilient aristocracy with those of aggressive emergent merchants were still being negotiated over the early decades of the seventeenth century; agricultural innovation, financial revolution, and the gentrification of the commercial elite only slowly came into alignment. The rising standards of living and great fluidity of goods and people in England over the seventeenth century detected in hindsight by historians were often imperceptible to contemporaries.[2]

Part of the reason for this lay with the long commercial shadow cast by Dutch commercial success, a shadow some English observers attributed to the wide individual autonomy that the States General gave its merchants. Moreover, in the early seventeenth century, Dutch merchants had already secured a hold in the West Indies, the East Indies, and former Portuguese colonies when England had only begun colonizing. The Dutch were the world's greatest carriers: they dominated the northern fisheries and Baltic trade; had a strong presence in the colonial carrying trade; and had developed superior warehousing, credit, and banking systems. English merchants had observed Dutch business acumen firsthand in the cloth-finishing trades. Perhaps, argued some early-modern English writers, emulation of these successes, rather than their destruction, offered the greatest prospects for England's economic unfolding.[3]

They also believed that the unprecedented commercial ascendancy of the United Provinces was due to well-calculated commercial enterprise and to the Dutch state's policy of "free ships, free goods," which until 1713 meant that neutral Dutch goods could be transported on enemy vessels in wartime and neutral vessels could pass unmolested through Dutch lines. In his widely read treatise of 1608, *Mare Liberum*, Hugo Grotius laid down that whether in war or peace, "freedom of trade is based on a primitive right . . . which has a natural and permanent cause."[4]

Another Dutch writer, Pieter de la Court, extended Grotius's arguments in his work. Bellicose English state-makers, he insisted, did not understand the many salutary effects of free trade upon the domestic well-being of a people, one of which was to provide a natural antidote to the early-modern era's periodic "clogs" in the circulation of goods. But more: free trade established the principle of "natural liberty," which permitted more opportunities for international commerce and promoted more domestic production than regulated economies did, thus establishing the means to overcome the endemic and cyclical hardships caused by Europe's economic systems. The great Dutch statesman Johan de Witt (1625–72) pointed out how quick the English were to *politicize* commercial affairs at the opening of the seventeenth century. Factions in English government had unnecessarily conflated their role in collecting and redistributing resources for the public welfare with the role more properly played by commercial interests in coordinating the natural relationships of consumption and circulation. Left free to calculate and take risks, few merchants needed government in the way some English observers thought they did.[5]

Earlier, England's Sir Walter Ralegh (1554–1618) might have agreed. Dutch commercial success, Ralegh insisted, derived from more than efficient transportation; low import duties and a policy of importing great quantities of goods that were warehoused until reexport prices were favorable seemed central to Dutch commercial greatness. As Ralegh put it, "smallness of custom, and liberty of trade . . . draws all nations to traffick with them." For Ralegh and others in the early seventeenth century, open ports meant "liberty of traffick for strangers." They pointed out that Dutch freight, storage, and shipbuilding costs were one-third to one-half lower than peacetime English costs. Dutch ports charged no tariffs on naval stores, Dutch commercial loans could be had at 3 percent interest—as compared to English loans at 5 to 8 percent—and Dutch artisans knew how to build the *fluitschip* (fly boat), a large transport with a narrow, rounded stern and a broad bottom, which the Dutch put to efficient use transporting heavy commodities in overseas trading.[6]

Arguments for imitation of Dutch success were never ideologically dominant, but they were nevertheless of consequence. During the seventeenth century, as Holland and England collided in warfare, much of it commercially motivated, statesmen and publicists attributed the origins of the conflicts to the different cultures, material developments, and intellectual traditions of the two countries. Indeed, for fully two centuries after 1550, many writers clung to a belief in competing national characters, which in turn grounded their reasoning about the political economy of each nation and its colonies. By 1600, writers had polarized perceptions of the two competing nations into commercial models, pitting Dutch economic freedom against English economic regulation.

Their voices grew loudest after England suffered a downturn in agriculture and textile production. When West Country woolen manufacturers began to replace regulated companies in cloth exportation by the 1620s, they chimed in on free-trade arguments. Devonshire clothiers argued loudly for free trade in woolen manufacture. A few prominent policy makers in England noted that the Dutch reaped huge profits in the Newfoundland fisheries because they forbade monopolies there. Moreover, a few prominent writers emigrated from the Low Countries to England, where they gained a hearing for Grotius's belief in the "natural and permanent" rights of nations to observe a "freedom of trade" on the expansive, uninhabited, and unconquerable open seas. Sir William Petty (1623–87), an ambitious English official, who was educated partly at Leyden; Gerald Malynes, a former Dutch merchant; and, later, Matthew Decker, a Dutch immigrant in England, expressed belief in the rights of individual commercial activists to "find vent" without constraint. "Only freedom in trade can make the trade great," as John Pollexfen put it.[7]

The tenets of open commerce were not completely unknown in England. During periodic legislative debates about securing new trade routes without the state's restraining regulations and monopolied company privileges, various interests had promoted "open trade" for all competitors and no need for specific charters. At the end of Elizabeth's reign, writers associated it with the separation between dominion and colonial settlement; whereas the former was premised on mere conquest and force, the latter would be promoted best if autonomous commercial interests outfitted voyages and determined the most beneficial conditions of commerce for themselves. Negotiations with Spain for peace in 1599 included the demand for English free trade wherever Spanish conquest had not resulted in permanent settlements, and James I's Treaty of London in 1604 carried on this dialogue.

Historians have concentrated on the rise of joint-stock enterprises and the foundations of mercantilism in the seventeenth century; but private ventures to found plantations in the Western Hemisphere occupied more capital and people than corporations did, and private planters explained their need for free ports to compete against pirates, smugglers, and foreign competitors who sold at low prices and thereby cornered markets. The Englishmen John Cary and

Josiah Child maintained that merchants and their foreign agents were the best judges of commercial opportunity. Economic freedom, they held, solidified legitimate enterprise and won colonists' loyalty to the crown's overall objectives. Their most sophisticated arguments proposed that there ought to be a perfectly direct relationship between the international trader and the colonial consumer, and that colonies were most useful to the home country if its commercial interests were left free to find their own markets. And, as we shall see, these more radical economic spokesmen also celebrated the ability of unfettered merchants to do things that other discourses hedged—to meet growing colonial demand, create new economic desires, and broaden consumption.[8]

In the first half of the seventeenth century, this reasoning was strongest among traders and governors in the British West Indies. Some calls for free ports represented desperate responses to high levels of competition and the need to manipulate the prices of staples on the islands and in England. For example, production of tobacco and sugar began to stabilize, then rise, by the 1640s. The price of Jamaican sugar also began to rise, in part because of under-cultivating, thus reducing supply of the commodity to England and enabling merchants to force up prices. This, they claimed, was no state-sanctioned monopoly; it was a private combination on the island to "give us a free trade" in periodically glutted markets. More typically, however, assertions about "the necessity of free trade" between the 1630s and 1670s included a straightforward recognition of the rights of merchants to seek the best markets among all foreign islands, whether or not the commodities being traded proved suitable for sustaining the nation as the English government defined it.[9]

Dutch commercial successes also challenged certain long-standing beliefs about the English domestic economy. Most economic policy makers in England affirmed long-standing beliefs in low wages, low prices, and relatively high interest rates, which would encourage merchants to become government creditors. But John Cary joined a few innovative writers who reasoned that merchants and manufacturers were more likely to benefit from low interest rates, which also reduced usury and encouraged commercial exchange, as the Dutch had demonstrated. Dudley North, John Pollexfen, and Joseph Massie were sure that unregulated Dutch interest rates had enriched Holland and made it populous. Gerald Malynes, Henry Martyn, and William Goffe agreed with Cary about another issue: that wages need not be low in order to encourage diligent labor, for chronic poverty and underemployment could be remedied by open admission to trades at competitive wages. Nor did the prices of many imports need to be low in order to ensure their consumption.[10]

Of course, Dutch greatness in the seventeenth century was built upon a degree of commercial regulation and protection that these observers over-looked, and that the New Amsterdam example had made manifest. Neverthe-less, by the second half of the seventeenth century, Dudley North, Nicholas Bar-bon, and Jacob Vanderlint extended praise for "Dutch freedoms," and argued that uninhibited circulation of both goods and coin was the most "natural" posture. As Dutch policies had shown, a small amount of inflation—repre-sented by rising prices—was a minor evil compared to economic stagnation and widespread personal bankruptcies; likewise, the periodic export of specie was preferable to deep-going "clogs" of commercial exchange. Although peri-odic government restraints on the flow of goods and coin might be necessary in the worst periods of shortfall harvests, commercial gluts, or injustice in price movements, the goal of policies ought to be individual latitude in markets. Indeed, unregulated prices would invite, not the chaos that English statesmen feared, but the social consensus and order resulting from myriad market en-counters and continual negotiation.[11]

Advocates of "natural prices" and open trade waxed optimistic about the role colonies could play as partners in the empire. Dalby Thomas and John Old-mixon witnessed the great accretion of things through the empire and noted the colonies' rise alongside England's.[12] Charles Davenant reminded readers that colonists were subject to the same universal human appetites as the inhabitants of England, and that they ought to be seen, not only as subjects of military out-posts and sources of naval stores, but as coequals in free exchange within the empire, capable of adding to the total "stock" of material things; founding more colonies implied the piling up of total wealth, which in turn made the empire great.[13] Others pointed to the free Dutch ports of St. Eustatius and Curaçao as sources of far more specie and goods, and a more favorable exchange rate, than the English possessions. Even as late as the 1750s, Matthew Decker noted how these "free ports must carry trade to its utmost height." No wonder, he contin-ued, that northern colonists centered their illegal traffic there.[14]

This vocal minority was overshadowed—but never totally defeated—by a chorus of publicists and statesmen in England who were committed to a vision of transforming distant lands and peoples into the satellites of a rising empire by means of a stronger state. Intellectual ponderings and rival economic inter-ests seemed to demand the imposition of imperial coherence on the great changes at home and abroad. By the early seventeenth century, they were coun-tering the "free ships, free goods" practices of the United Provinces with argu-ments for the web of regulations, bureaucracy, and special-interest policies that Adam Smith later called "mercantilism." Much of this legislation stemmed from anxieties about foreign competition. Cloth weavers spoke out in 1605 with scorn for "Dutch strangers" who encroached on the West Country trade. London brewers and silversmiths moaned about the "hollander invasion" from "new upstarte townes in Holland," which purportedly brought in habits of transience, luxury, greed, and usury. From 1617 to the 1630s, the Merchant Adventurers of England, a monopolied company in the cloth trades, harangued against the importation of Dutch cloth—although they also accepted Dutch capital to renew their monopoly charter with the English government. Animosities against Dutch successes in the fisheries had also emerged in England by 1620, and they grew when the Dutch competed aggressively for the East Indies trade for years thereafter.[15]

Some English writers noted that the absence of large landholdings among the Dutch exacerbated their tendency to engross commerce. Long-standing ethical and social concerns in England had privileged the position of landed interests, who regarded rising merchants' claims skeptically. Despite the guarded approval of private gain in commerce by ecclesiastical authorities such as St. Thomas Aquinas, as well as the self-promotional efforts of trading companies, merchants' corruption of the polity with luxuries remained a source of anxiety. In time, landed interests would use such reasoning to shift taxation onto certain imported commodities; but before 1650, the general tendency was less to tax merchants than to scorn them. Theorists such as Thomas Mun, Sir William Petty, Charles Davenant, and Josiah Child dwelt upon the differences of character in nations and persons that arose from the various inherited, educational, social, and even accidental circumstances. "Gain is their God," Sir William Temple (1628–99) declared, referring to the merchants of the United Provinces in 1673; Dutch lace and skilled tradesmen were undermining the strength of England. Doubts about England's balance of trade were fueled by the growing quantities of East India and French luxury goods imported by monopolied trading companies, goods that were thought to be far too expensive for even the wealthiest consumers of the realm.

These anxieties spilled over into observations about England's feeble efforts to colonize abroad. Dutch preeminence in the carrying trades made permanent and profitable settlement of overseas colonies seem only a remote possibility; Spanish and French footholds in the Caribbean and the North Atlantic from the 1620s to the 1670s fueled additional fears. And compared to the rising importance of their rivals' sugar production, Englishmen's meager output of tobacco was not the stuff of which viable competition was made. By midcentury, even this beginning was threatened by falling tobacco prices at Barbados and Antigua—a problem Virginia had already experienced—as well as soil depletion. Moreover, piracy remained a persistent threat. Formerly an advance guard for both private venturers and imperial designers, pirates had become a menace to orderly colonial dominion by the early seventeenth century.[16]

Perceptions of the need to reverse Dutch successes and English domestic weaknesses came together in an edifice of legislation premised upon economic order, political power, and patriotism. The Navigation Act of 1651, one of England's most encompassing commercial statutes, was directly connected to imperial aims against Dutch interests in the Caribbean and the northern fisheries, and in the first of three wars with the United Provinces, from 1652 to 1654, enforcement of the act was the goal of English policy. England's greatest prize in the second war against the "Cabal of Holland" (1664–67) was New Amsterdam, and by the end of the third war, in 1674, the Dutch were willing to concede the lion's share of the West African slave trade and the Caribbean staples trade to England. By then, four important Navigation Acts had been passed, setting the parameters of England's official commercial policies for decades to come.[17]

The Navigation Acts were piecemeal, ever-changing in their particulars, and easily evaded by colonists, but they made at least four contributions of consequence to many generations of New Yorkers. First, they protected the home country's shipbuilding industry and merchant marine by requiring that British commerce be carried in English-owned and crewed vessels, or colonial vessels employing crews that were at least three-quarters English. Second, they sought to serve the interests of English merchants and manufacturers by channeling all imperial commerce through English ports, imposing tariffs and customs inspections on goods clearing all British ports, and setting up a machinery of enforcement. Third, "enumerated" commodities were designated to be traded only with England, or to be reexported through English ports, where merchants paid import duties and gained drawbacks of duties. Enumeration not only guided goods to markets and secured state revenues; it also privileged particular shipping services and special-interest groups in England and addressed complaints about colonial smuggling with foreign enemies. Regulations must be set for ports and commodities prices, special interests insisted; piracy and illicit trade must be stamped out. Finally, the state prohibited manufactures in the colonies that interfered with English producers' efforts, and it approved of protective laws to govern conditions of manufacture, pricing, and sale of finished goods from England. Henceforth, Sir William Petty declared, a new "political arithmetick" would guide the forward steps of England's expanding empire.[18]

Historians may never agree about whether these measures were largely promotional or substantially restrictive of imperial development.[19] Certainly, by the Glorious Revolution in 1688, new men of property required special legislation to further their emergent interests—at the expense of both foreign and

British colonial ones—and gained a more favorable hearing from shifting coalitions of parliamentary representatives. Moreover, the principle of keeping colonies underdeveloped and staples-producing was a clear objective of seventeenth-century legislation, as when the Woolen Act of 1699 prohibited the transport of finished cloth and clothing from one colony to another, and manufacturing interests in England pressed for fuller prohibitions on colonial production that affected the ambitions of New Yorkers.[20]

However, the authority of mercantilism—faith in its ability to create the appropriate conditions for England's rise—was not at first assured. Doubts arose early about whether Britons should eschew customary wisdoms about specie, prices, and economic exchanges in order to prop up the "mushroom" merchants rising from below in this new commercial order. Some regretted the fluctuations of credit and financial paper. Others worried that the first major mercantile legislation had been passed by the Rump Parliament without the consent of the House of Lords, which Parliament had abolished, or of the king, whom it had executed. In fact, Charles II held the legislation to be null and void when his line was restored in 1660. Parliament's subsequent ratification of the Navigation Acts of 1660, 1663, and 1673 began the era of regulation in earnest, however, and by the end of the seventeenth century, mercantile policy operating through the Board of Trade and a bureaucracy of customs collectors served myriad emerging interests; an early sociology of public welfare based upon of counting and distributing goods had also emerged. Changes in the management of credit, banking, and stocks accompanied these developments, and the English government began to borrow more systematically from individuals and monopolied companies, especially during the century's many wars. In the wake of the Glorious Revolution, Parliament exercised growing control over taxation, as well as the right to earmark a "sinking fund" out of tax revenues to pay competitive interest rates of first 8 percent, then 6 percent, and finally 4 percent to the government's creditors. Exchequer bills issued in return for loans not only bore interest but were highly liquid and only a short-term risk. Annuities offered the alternative of a safe long-term investment, although they tended to depreciate over time. The Bank of England, founded in 1694, provided a capstone to these changes, but it was preceded by the establishment of many private "country banks," which held large funds for the landed gentry and somewhat smaller amounts of money for merchants, who borrowed from the banks in order to speculate in government securities.[21]

Institutional and social changes accompanied a new intellectual orthodoxy by the end of the seventeenth century. Notions about the just price, usury, local scarcity, and religious justifications for regulating individual market behavior gave way to certainty that merchant capitalism would rise and, in time, to confidence in England's ability to excel in calculated and aggressive expansion. "True political knowledge," Petty wrote, was grounded on a keen sense of "the public accounts of a nation," in the same way that the risks a merchant took were based on "careful calculation." As the Duke of Albemarle put it in 1664, with reference to the appropriateness of taking New Amsterdam: "What we want is more of the trade the Dutch now have."[22]

Mercantilists began to shift economic discussion from the issues of local equilibrium and relative stasis to the dynamic expansion of national economies. Commerce, said many writers between the 1640s and the 1680s, would help solve rampant price inflation, underemployment, and periodic scarcities in agriculture. Writers who accepted the desirability, or just the fact, of commercial development called for a "national monopoly," a united, energetic coalition of national interests against the idleness and waste of an outmoded aristocracy and all foreign competition, in order to acquire more of the world's constant wealth. The manufacture of hosiery, ironware, and refined goods, some observed, laid the basis for national self-sufficiency in a hostile world of rival nations.[23]

At the center of mercantilists' attempts to create orderly development was the "balance of trade." Before the seventeenth century, the term *balance* often referred to the unwritten English constitution's mixture of political powers based on stasis or organic harmony among classes of people in hierarchical order. Imbalance resulted when domestic factional or warring international interests abused power for selfish ends. In its more economic meaning, however, *balance* referred to the movement of goods or their aggregate values. A favorable balance of trade did not imply mutuality or equality in exchange, any more than political balance implied political equality; rather, it meant that England exported goods of higher total value than it imported, and that the "overplus" would be returned to England in the form of specie and bills of exchange. Such an overplus was more than personal gain, however; it was, wrote Charles Davenant, "the *Profit a Nation Makes by Trade*." Already by the 1620s, the idea of a balance of trade was premised upon the ideal of enhancing national greatness by exporting more to external markets than the nation imported, thereby enlarging the nation's "stock" of money and goods and, by extension, its social well-being. It emphasized the constancy of the world's wealth and a domestic economy operating on the basis of simple exchanges that satisfied individual needs. England's power was presumed to increase, not merely by the rising productivity of its own people, but at the expense of other nations as well. As Sir

Francis Bacon observed, "The increase of any estate must be upon the foreigner (for whatsoever is somewhere gotten is somewhere lost)."[24]

A favorable balance of trade, according to mercantile wisdom, required an elaborate system of import restrictions, export incentives, revenue schedules and collection officials, drawbacks on reexports, rebates on raw materials used in manufactures, bounties to encourage new enterprise, inducements to import specie and keep it at home, and temporary special monopolies in cases of new commercial risk taking. Thomas Mun, Charles Davenant, and others also shifted emphasis from acquiring national treasure—specie that could be viewed as the measure of commodity values—to the circulation of goods that embodied value. Joining these writers, Sir William Temple, William Wood, Richard Gouldsmith, and John Houghton insisted upon the useful role of merchants, for if "the natural matter of Commerce is Merchandize," it was the commercial risk takers who circulated goods for their profit and the stability of the nation who must be accommodated with legislation. In 1673, Temple proposed exporting the best of particular commodities that had high values, while keeping inferior goods for the home market; other writers insisted that a well-balanced trade would, more generally, result in greater values of exports than imports, fewer luxury imports, and the rising capacity of the domestic economy to produce finished goods that formerly were purchased abroad. Within a few decades, hopes ran high that a favorable balance of trade would not only yield personal profits to merchants, but that chronic poverty and underemployment would be remedied. Not importation, but, as Davenant put it, "the Exportation of our own Product . . . must make England rich; to be Gainers in the Balance of Trade, we must carry out [the surplus] of our own Product." Goods produced cheaply, wrote Gouldsmith somewhat later, by the "natural Frugality of the People that Export, or as from the low Price of Labour," were the best kinds of exports. Luxuries, many earlier writers argued, were the worst sort of imports.[25]

"Balance" was the leitmotif of colonization as well. Until the 1660s, "violence abroad"—the competition among nations for dominion—was a foregone conclusion. "It is true, That hee that commaunds the sea, commaunds the trade, and hee that is Lord of the Trade of the world is lord of the wealth of the worlde," Sir Walter Ralegh wrote. The poet John Dryden, among others, conflated the economic and military interests of England in popular formulas, especially because commercial interests convinced them that England would have to capture markets from foreign rivals in order to expand—to rebalance the net profits and power of the world in England's favor. But once North American colonization began in earnest, some commentators lamented this view. Wars, they said, were "a transient Hell" that disrupted the normal channels of commerce, siphoned off taxes to pay for unprosperous activities, and raised factional quarrels that led to internecine strife. John Locke added to this kind of reasoning in his *Second Treatise* when he invoked the hypothetical vision that when "all the world was America," there had been no need for government. Others proposed that the colonies would provide "useful employments" at home by supplying English laborers with continuous supplies of raw materials—a balance between the natural bounty of North America and underemployment at home.[26]

By the end of the seventeenth century, the rough symbiosis envisioned by writers like Henry Pollexfen, Charles Davenant, and Josiah Child had been elaborated to provide that colonial plantations would exchange their primary resources and specie for England's finished goods. By 1721, writers often stated, "We have, within ourselves and in our colonies in America an inexhaustible fund to supply ourselves, and perhaps Europe, with what we are now beholden to foreigners for." Colonies would take England's incorrigibles, provide markets for its finished goods, and answer the demand in England for commodities it was forced to buy from its European competitors.[27]

This relationship between the emporium and its satellites was seldom formulated creatively enough to take into account the expanding needs of and opportunities in the colonies. The myriad pieces of legislation, and mountains of transatlantic correspondence were sometimes restrictive, sometimes promotional; still, mercantile policies were not so much whimsical as designed to enhance the national wealth and power of England and deny the colonies an equivalent level of prosperity. Colonists were expected to "serve the favorable balance at home, being London." "Manufactures in the Plantations," said an anonymous pamphleteer, "is that very Means by which the Kingdom is drained of its People." Thus a colony ought not to diversify so as to drain England of labor; its prices and wages ought never to compete favorably against England's; and its rival domestic manufactures ought never to be exported if an English equivalent would suffice.[28]

In truth, the legislation prohibiting particular colonial exportation or manufactures did not touch some of New York City's most important commerce, including bread and flour, fish, livestock, processed meats, staves and boards, salt, and—until the eighteenth century—wine. Of the items enumerated, dyewoods and sugar filled New Yorkers' vessels frequently, peltry was one of their major provincial exports, and naval stores rose as a proportion of all exports from the colony. Sometimes enumerated commodities were not of major concern to colonists, as in the case of whale oil, iron, potash, pearl ash, hats, sugar, tobacco, indigo, ginger, and cotton wool—all of which were enumerated but shipped in significant quantities only during the eighteenth century.[29]

Nevertheless, the very existence and conceptual intentions of these English laws provoked many New York merchants into declaring dissent from England's imperial goals. And their dissent was shaped by the ideas associated with economic freedom, ideas that provided merchants with powerful means to articulate interests antithetical to mercantilism. Of course, the adherents of both regulation and freedom shared many perceptions about commerce, including antipathy to landed aristocracies and tradition. Both mercantilists and free traders advocated a radical shift in the notion of property, from rights *in* something—an office, an entitlement to political authority—to property in *things* themselves. The sheer scale of international trade by 1600—the aggregates of people, commodities, and exchange across many uncharted miles—invited both regulators and free traders to agree that the most fundamental individual actions stemmed from accumulation of property. Both persuasions also accepted scientific rationality, the perfectibility of peoples over time, and the universal human desire for refinement; they both proposed that people labored for material reward and not for an abstract common good. And both kinds of writers welcomed commerce and merchants, new goods, and greater human comfort. Neither regulators nor free traders provided a crystalline explanation of economic conditions, for both groupings emerged in circumstances of shifting and tentative economic knowledge, and each had permeable boundaries of understanding about the social relations of commerce.

Continuing Dutch Trade

As New York City welcomed greater numbers of English migrants after 1664, policy makers at home contrived additional Navigation Acts, on the supposition that the delicate international balance of trade had tipped against England and that stronger remedial measures had become necessary. But the crown gave Governor Richard Nicolls (1664–67) and his few followers no explicit plan by which to develop the colony. Already colonists had experienced a pattern of clashing interests involving the States General, provincial governors-general, West India Company directors, and a divided merchant community. The same pattern would give shape and meaning to developments in the first decades after the conquest, when city residents witnessed the alternating rhythms of peace and war, salutary neglect and restrictive imperial policy, and coexistence and conflict with other colonists in the region. Although English mercantile policies undergirded the conquest and many migrating English merchants remained loyal to them, New Yorkers also enjoyed commercial opportunities that lay outside the designs of policy makers. Piracy and smuggling were regular aspects of colonial development throughout the seventeenth century, as they had been under the Dutch, and contests for economic privileges developed among city merchants and their provincial rivals on Long Island and along the Hudson River, as they had under the Dutch. Then, too, new developments challenged the city's hoped-for domination over the region: the creation of a colonial assembly in 1684 gave voice to landholders, who often prevailed against the interests of city merchants; the separate functions of New York City merchants and rural small producers became clearer; and the uncertainties of elongating market structures grew, with all their train of debt, interdependence, and anonymity. But until the end of the century, many conflicts over the appropriateness of one or another policy were expressed as preferences for either economic freedom or economic regulation, along lines that had been familiar during the Dutch period.

The port did not grow rapidly at first; a quickened pace of settlement and commerce was effectively delayed until the 1680s. At the time power was transferred to the English crown, the colony's small population of no more than 9,000 was a notable advance over the earliest Dutch period, but weak compared to neighboring New England, whose inhabitants numbered about 50,000. Few of New York City's 2,400 inhabitants lived beyond the wall yet, and portions of the city were given over to pasturing livestock, a sight that must have amazed immigrants who had embarked from London, which had reached a population of over 460,000 by the 1660s. Colonists hardly could have foretold that their number would more than double by 1698, to a calculated 18,067 inhabitants, 4,937 of whom resided in New York City.[30]

Nor could they have predicted the growth of the city's fleet. In 1678, Governor Edmund Andros (1674–77, 1678–81) reported a few "smale shipps and a ketch"; by 1684, Governor Thomas Dongan (1682–88) noted six oceangoing ships, 26 sloops, and 46 riverboats, owned fairly widely among international and domestic traders. In 1687, Dongan reported that the fleet comprised 31 to 33 vessels of 46 tons on average, of which nine or ten were "sturdy ocean going ships" of 80 to 100 tons registered by eight of the colony's most eminent merchants. In 1694, a new estimate indicated there were 40 ships, 62 sloops, and 62 riverboats registered to New Yorkers, and that the large ships were concentrated in the hands a few traders. By 1700, Governor Richard Coote, Lord Bellomont (1698–97, 1700–1701), estimated that although most of the fleet continued to consist of vessels of 40 to 60 tons, it had reached 124 vessels altogether. He wrote what any city merchant knew: that small colonial vessels were important for

Fig. 1. New York City around the Time of the British Conquest. A 1673 engraving of
"New Amsterdam, a small City on Manhattan Island, new Holland, North America,
now called New York . . . about 1667," published in 1702. An original in the possession
of the New-York Historical Society is described by I. N. Stokes in *The Iconography of
Manhattan Island, 1498–1909* (New York, 1915–32), 1: 220–21.

transporting goods along the coast, but the city still relied upon larger Dutch
and English ships for transatlantic voyages.[31]

The colony was, in other important ways, a classical satellite of the mother
country during the seventeenth century: its main activities were the acquisition
and export of furs; its hinterlands were sparsely settled; a single port city dominated the political, economic, and cultural life of the colony; and the majority
of inhabitants were dependent on an imperial center for manufactured goods.
No wonder so many city wholesalers hoped to continue trading in the proven
channels to Amsterdam and Rotterdam after the transition in government to
English rule. The colony's first two English governors, Richard Nicolls and
Francis Lovelace (1667–73) could hardly overlook the benefits that would come
from cementing friendly relations with both the local Dutch population and
firms in the Low Countries. New York's direct trade with Amsterdam continued
legally for a brief period in 1664, until Governor Nicolls received orders from

London to freeze the remaining assets of the Dutch West India Company and to bring Dutch traders under mercantile regulations. Still, trade to Amsterdam was not entirely forbidden.[32]

Pieter Stuyvesant, the former director-general of New Netherland, spoke out in favor of continued trade with the United Provinces. In 1664, he asked Nicolls for permission to send four to six ships a year to the Low Countries until London could absorb the peltry and tobacco New Yorkers exported. Three years later, Stuyvesant pointed out to crown officials at London that "a free Trade was esteemed to bee of most considerable importance" when the Dutch surrendered to English rule; unless the duke of York's colony traded with Amsterdam, French interlopers would redirect New York's fur trade through Canada, and Spain would capture the budding West Indian connections of the northern colonies. Besides, he insisted, Dutch residents of the colony had rights to a free trade with *their* mother country that antedated the conquest; their original national attachments superseded the changing political rights of different states over their inhabitants.[33]

Early English immigrants did not cleave closely, on the whole, to the tenets of mercantilism. For one thing, Nicolls admitted to being under pressure to permit more open commerce because of the example of New Jersey's "free ports" and their attraction for New York's merchants during recurring commercial difficulties in the first years after the conquest. Moreover, reports reached New York that about seventy Dutch merchants stood ready in 1667 to continue trading with colonists despite the English takeover; some Netherlanders announced intentions to send their sons and agents to New York to cement business liaisons. Resident merchants of Dutch descent also sensitized Nicolls to the economic and social importance of continued trade with Amsterdam. Since the population of the city was, by Nicolls' reckoning, three-quarters Dutch, he hoped Parliament would grant them the rights of citizens. Even more, he hoped that immigrating English merchants would not be "blowne up with large designes" in the future, but instead try "to become wiser" about settled practices in the city. Otherwise, "not knowing the knacke of trading here to differ from most other places, they [would] meet with discouragements" and quickly leave the colony. It was far better for all parties, Nicolls argued, to grant exceptions to the Acts of Trade and Navigation for ships headed to Amsterdam.[34]

Lovelace was also favorably disposed toward open Dutch commerce in the first years of his administration and approved lowering import duties from 10 to 7 percent, as well as specific duties on wine, dry goods, cocoa, and reexports up the Hudson River for the fur trade with Native Americans, measures that city burghers had pressed for under Dutch rule.[35] Rumors also circulated that he favored the established importers over new and struggling traders when he appointed Cornelius van Huyven as the customs collector, a man who proved his loyalty to his Dutch compatriots by overlooking port regulations that affected arriving foreign vessels. Moveover, the Dutch West Indies Company appointed two agents—Pieter Stuyvesant and Cornelis Steenwyck—to forward goods and commercial information from New York to Amsterdam, appointments Lovelace applauded. In the face of rumors in 1668 that English laws would be enforced soon, Stuyvesant continued to argue for the trading privileges of Dutch merchants in New York, who had sustained the fur trade by importing "Indian goods" during a time when English ships did not arrive in sufficient numbers. Samuel Maverick, a Long Island merchant, added that New York's Dutch and English inhabitants shared a need to send ships to Amsterdam because of a more serious threat: "Boston invaders" had "found the way hither againe from Virginia," bringing tobacco and carrying away New York's grain. For the short term, English officials agreed to renew permission in 1668 to license three ships per year from New York to the Low Countries; this was reduced in 1669 to one per year.[36]

Between 1664 and 1668, an average of three or four vessels per year (eight in 1667) cleared New York for Amsterdam; from late 1667 to late 1668, a royal allowance permitted three ships per year to clear from Amsterdam and Rotterdam; reports indicated that the quota was filled, but the privilege was revoked at the end of 1668. Governor Lovelace continued to support the Dutch trade, but not out of disinterested concern for the future of the colony. He and his brother Thomas owned shares in the *Hopewill* (with Steenwyck), the *Good Fame*, and the *Duke of York* and traded through Dutch agents resident in New York, Eagiduis Luyck, Francis Hooghlandt, Nicholas Gouverneur, and Isaac Bedloe.[37]

In these first years of English rule, eminent Dutch merchants dominated transatlantic commerce, but they did not actively exclude English newcomers or reject the new political arrangements in the colony. Indeed, they welcomed the greater number of settlers, which boosted the demand for imports and shipping services in the city. Nicolls and Lovelace officially released farmers and fur traders outside the city from the regulations of the Dutch West India Company and its agents, only to place them under similar economic constraints that bore the imprimatur of the English crown. Unfazed, many Dutch merchants in the city allied with immigrating English merchants to enlarge the urban community's privileges in opposition to the outlying areas during the 1660s and 1670s. Dutch and English served together on the Governor's Council, groping for policies that would serve their mutual interests.[38]

During a brief interlude of renewed Dutch rule from July 1673 to November 1674, the government ordered a "loan by the most affluent inhabitants of this city" to build much-needed fortifications. At the very top of the assessors' list of some sixty-three households were five Dutch merchants: Frederick Philipse, Cornelis Steenwyck, Nicholas de Meyer, Oloff Stevense van Cortlandt, and Jeronimas Ebbingh. Philipse was already the wealthiest man in New York and would continue to outstrip all other merchants until his death in 1702. Savvy investments, vast estates and numerous house lots in the city, and many children who would marry into established fortunes—all of these cemented Philipse's wealth. His deathbed bequests to family members reveal a commercial empire beyond most colonists' imaginations: houses and warehouses in New York, Yonkers, Bergen, and elsewhere; scores of slaves and tenements; thousands of acres of land; mills, cattle, and sloops for the inland trade; and at least four solely owned ships for the external trade were scattered among his children and surviving wife. Cornelis Steenwyck, also known as an "affluent" city merchant in the 1670s, left an estate valued at £15,841, a very great amount for any northern colonial trader but nowhere near the achievement of Philipse.[39]

Thirteen merchants whose wealth was rated at 10,000 florins or more followed the top five men; they, too, enjoyed diversified markets, owned many vessels, and often engaged in the slave trade. Over subsequent years, they proved more capable of weathering the competition of English immigrant merchants, as well as the more stringent regulatory policies of English governors, than their peers of middling stature. Of the remaining ninety-two "affluent" inhabitants in 1674, most of whom were wholesalers or wholesaler-retailers, another twenty or so would rise into the top ranks of commercial standing along with new English merchants in the next ten years, while thirty-seven would remain comfortable for five to ten years; many of the remaining forty-three probably attained no more than middling stature at the peaks of their careers. In 1692, William Blathwayte listed the nine wealthiest and most respected merchants in the city: seven were of Netherlands origin; six traded higher values of goods to Amsterdam than to London before 1689. Later in the 1690s, some immigrants with commercial ties to prominent firms in London happily joined the Dutch in sustaining trade with Amsterdam, and at least three prominent English-born merchants were then counted among the city's wealthiest.[40]

Anglicizing City Commerce

Affiliation with the firms, credit, and goods of the Low Countries would influence the commercial character of New York City for years to come, but it was vain to hope to sustain Dutch hegemony over the city's trade. In the first place, new immigration into New York City was overwhelmingly English in origin by 1685; moreover, the immigrant stream was steady, and the merchant community grew from about 115 in 1664 to over 180 at the end of the century. At least fifty new traders entered the colony from England—a few of them French Huguenots—during the prosperous years of 1675 to 1685; although few merchants migrated into the city during the recession years of 1685 to 1692, and some of them out-migrated to neighboring colonies or the provincial interior, approximately forty more merchants assumed residence in the port from 1692 to 1699.[41]

Moreover, the four or five ships clearing New York for Amsterdam annually from 1674 to 1680 were often not full. And although fifty or so city merchants traded with Amsterdam between 1670 and 1690, only a few survived and prospered into the years that followed, and fewer still filled the places of former Dutch connections. Francis Hooghlandt, Nicholas Gouverneur, Isaac Bedloe, Gabriel Minvielle, Johannes de Peyster, and others transported goods in smaller vessels and less frequently, often along the North American coastline, and supplemented their Dutch trade with new ventures to the British West Indies to find goods that were in demand and undutied. By the 1690s, the remaining Amsterdam trade was concentrated in the hands of twelve New York merchants, ten of them of English origin, who made regular shipments of hides and southern tobacco to Amsterdam and ordered return cargoes of cloth, weaponry, and gunpowder. At least seventeen English firms—some of them world-renowned—traded regularly with the colony's merchants irrespective of ethnic background.[42]

Seventeenth-century warfare had also taken its toll on the Dutch carrying trades and reduced the States General's diplomatic standing. By the opening of Queen Anne's War in 1702 many city merchants of Netherlands origin could no longer secure goods and credit enough to trade "on their own accounts." One of their options was to act as factors in New York for London firms for a 2½ to 5 percent commission; another was to relocate to England to serve as factors for New York merchants. Levinus van Schaick, having lived in both New York and Amsterdam, availed himself of his connections in London when he returned there and factored for the Livingstons, Schuylers, Ten Broecks, Wandelaers, and Rosebooms until at least 1710. Other Dutch New Yorkers married into English families to consolidate commercial capital and reputation or, envious of the "free ports" of New Jersey and Rhode Island, moved to those places. Still others routed their trade to both Amsterdam and London via customs officials who permitted smuggling.

Eminent transatlantic traders of both Dutch and English heritage commingled in the merchant community, sharing vessels and goods, intermarrying, and vouching for one another's good reputations. As close associates at the top of the social ladder, they drew together around two important issues: their shared view that they could, and should, create a metropolis dominating an extensive economic region; and their conviction that port duties often rose too high for them to be able to secure favorable markets. Both Dutch and English traders also benefited from provisions of the Navigation Acts, especially from imperial attempts to seal English trade off hermetically from the intrusions of foreigners and pirates by using convoys escorted by navy ships, and from drawbacks on some duties paid at English ports. In addition, England offered colonists a ready market for timber masts, naval stores, and completed vessels. Because the return trip to New York normally brought goods of little weight in proportion to their value, New Yorkers were glad to sell their vessels in England, apply earnings from the sale to outstanding debts there, and pack their purchases into one ship for the voyage home.[43]

Merchants carefully balanced the benefits with regulations channeling all New York's legal overseas trade to England. It was difficult, however, to apply this mercantilist model within North America, and the city's best-placed English immigrants reported that "all of New England" and New Jersey had been trading with New Amsterdam since the Dutch West India Company settled on the Hudson River. They predicted that this trade would continue, and thereby thwart attempts to strengthen New York City, unless all officials reduced their own provincial import duties and stringently discriminated against "disorderly" neighboring provinces.[44]

To the end of his two terms as governor, however, Andros attempted to raise port duties and refused most requests by New York's importers for measures disadvantaging New Englanders. At most, colonial merchants may have applauded efforts by royal officials to strengthen the corporate character of the city during the 1680s and to treat outlying settlements in their economic region as subordinate satellites. Already the "burgher right" under Dutch rule and the Duke's Laws of 1665 excluded both foreigners and hinterland peddlers from doing business in the city. Now, in 1686, a new city charter reaffirmed city privileges: "our frontier province of New York does in a greater measure depend upon the welfare and property of our said City wherein the Trade and Navigation thereof are chiefly and principally carried on." Like the Duke's Laws, the charter recognized that the "natural distinctions" between city and country gave rise to urban claims to dominate producers and consumers throughout the colony. The charter bolstered merchants' confidence, even as they argued for lower import duties, in the ability of economic regulation to create a superior trading entrepôt, with a supportive, subordinate region surrounding it and city traders at the helm.[45]

Lesser merchants supported efforts to reduce import duties, especially since as consumers, they hoped that the prices of necessities would remain low. But their stronger interconnectedness as traders with New York's hinterland and the New England coastline pitted their commercial interests against those of the city's elite when issues related to regional discrimination arose, as we shall see. Moreover, middling traders were more likely than their eminent peers to blame any faltering of opportunities on an elite that supposedly retained strong Dutch ethnic qualities. Andros, allegedly an ally of this elite, was said to have used tax revenues to repair the wharves and warehouses of his wealthy "Dutch tribe," and parallels were drawn between favors to the "dutch harpies" in New York and the city elite's inability to regard those who traded with Amsterdam as little more than "foreigners" who could never have the best interests of the city or the empire at heart. Reports by lesser merchants to the duke of York centered on the supposed "obstruccions and hindrances" put in their way by importers of Dutch descent. By 1680, ethnicity had become a greater target than class; objectors charged that Andros was "favoring Dutchmen before English in trade" and "admitting Dutch ships" into the port for his own private benefit. John Lewen, appointed by the duke of York to investigate city commerce, found that the governor's customs collector, William Dyre, "lett pass such Contraband Goods as ffrederick Philipps had come from Holland." "Some few Dutch Merchants" had made "such rigid usage to others that hath caused a great Obstruccon to Trade by those discouragements given indeed to all England," and had tempted "true Englishmen" of reputable commercial and political backgrounds to engage in this trade, thereby undermining the security of English settlement.[46]

As a consequence, elite and middling city merchants had different reasons to withdraw their support from Andros and to regard subsequent governors cautiously. For example, in the mid 1670s, a few lesser traders blustered that Andros supported "a free trade" with "our Dutch enemy" in direct violation of his duties to the English crown. Although these charges no doubt contributed to the inquiry that led to his recall in 1682, they were unfounded. Andros in fact raised specific import duties and reinstated an export duty on hides, to the chagrin of eminent and lesser merchants alike. When Andros further demanded that all city residents take oaths to the English crown, eminent merchants with transatlantic interests joined with protests of their own against import duties and held a few "tumultuous meetings" to declare their "ripening system of interests" under attack by an overzealous governor. The same protesters refused to pay colonial port duties in 1680–81 to demonstrate withdrawal of support for the governor. Lesser merchants' ethnic fears about wealthy Dutch in their city briefly joined cause with all merchants' desire to hold down import duties.[47]

Complaints continued under Governor Dongan, who focused his administrative efforts on appeasing the emergent landed interests that assumed prominence in the provincial New York Assembly created in 1684. Although he had been instructed to encourage all trade except that which interfered with the Royal African Company's monopoly of the slave trade, and to "suppress the ingrossing of Commoditys tending to the prejudice of the Freedom which Commerce and Trade ought to have," he chose to support steeper taxes on imports of foreign origin and from neighboring colonies, more rigorous regulation of the city's trade with New England and Philadelphia after 1685, and suppression of smuggling to Amsterdam. The rationales given by legislators in the Assembly for New York City's high imposts did not differ from those of their Dutch predecessors: increasing competition from Long Island, New England, and budding Philadelphia-area traders required discrimination against their "foreign" goods in the interest of developing the province of New York overall. The proceeds from these duties were essential, too, legislators argued, to fortify the city against Indian attacks and during the almost continuous imperial warfare between 1682 and 1694. But eminent English importers in New York, who were just as anxious as their Dutch predecessors to eliminate onerous imposts, disagreed with this reasoning. In any event, they ignored the decrees and simply smuggled in dutied goods by "greasing the palm" of Dongan's appointed port inspector with "ready money." Faced with diminishing opportunities, many lesser traders left international commerce and shifted their focus to coastal and overland trade.[48]

Most English merchant immigrants who arrived after 1680 did not become prominent in city commerce. But a few who traded in textiles, clothing, seed and agricultural implements, glassware, earthenware, and any number of household items from great London firms could boast of being prominent dry-goods importers in time. The merchants John Robinson, William Pinhorn, and Edward Anthill were among these earliest English merchants in the city, and at least thirteen others—ten of them young and ambitious men who departed London with the assurance of credit and ample commodities—also began creating a web of debts for imported finished goods that were of significant value overall in the city's trade. These were the prominent merchants that Andros had in mind when he reported to the Privy Council in 1681 that commercial ambition had "increased [the city's trade] att least tenn tymes to what it was" under Dutch rule, and that customs duties accounted for over £14,000 a year.[49]

Colonists' need for textiles and manufactured goods drove much of their importation from England, but return cargoes and payments were not always easy to secure. Although many New Yorkers sent back bills of exchange or a few commodities in ships owned by other colonial merchants, a few could ship on their own accounts. Their goal, reasonably enough, was to make up large cargoes of unenumerated goods that would "land free" in England, or to send goods that were enumerated but also entitled to drawbacks of a portion of the duty when they were reexported to foreign ports. Of course, the choice was not entirely their own; until the end of the seventeenth century, New York merchants were more likely to reexport Caribbean logwood and sugar, South Carolina rice, and southern furs than to export their own naval stores or grain. The latter commodities awaited noticeable extraction and production by a more populous provincial countryside after the 1690s.

The relatively high amount of starting capital that was necessary in transatlantic trading, and the reported difficulties of outfitting vessels and maintaining good credit relations with England, gave these merchants an air of privilege. In truth, however, the effects of alternating periods of economic well-being and crisis fell differently upon individual wholesalers at New York, in part because they judged markets differently, but largely because of the natural divisions of initial capital, market fluctuations, shifting conditions of warfare, or sheer luck that separated merchants. As a consequence, successful importers could expect their profits to be higher than those of local and coastal traders if English credit relations were good, if colonial demand remained stable, and if sources of supply did not become costly or scarce. New York's most eminent merchants were typically sole owners of local trading vessels by the 1680s–1690s, but few of them solely owned large transatlantic ships until at least the 1720s. They could, however, augment their profits by adding higher markups to the price of English imports than merchants added to commodities originating in their region, so that despite freight, insurance, and storage charges, dry-goods importers typically gained 25 percent over first cost, a profit higher than wholesalers in other arenas of trade could expect. Indeed, if dry-goods importing had not required substantially more starting capital and long credit, it would have been a far more competitive sector of the colony's trade, despite its uncertainties.

Instead, effective monopolies in particular markets and goods often followed periods of intense competition and concentration of commerce in the hands of a few well-situated traders. The fur trade provides one important example of this.[50] Importation of southern European wine, brandy, and "fancy stuffs" was another of the city's concentrated trades before 1700. Rip van Dam and Abraham de Peyster imported most of these commodities in the 1680s and even in 1701–2, they ranked among the top four in this trade.[51]

Yet even as they consolidated markets in particular commodities, New York's great traders also hoped to extend networks of their correspondents and discover additional ports of call. Indeed, such diversification was an important means of extending city commerce. English ships might originate in London, touch at a port in the Low Countries, and proceed to New York before going south, or originate in New York and reexport commodities from the southern colonies to Amsterdam, with or without a stop at an English port to pay duties, depending on the attitude of the ship's owners to smuggling, and sometimes with an illegal entry at New Haven. From the start, English merchants sought business relations with Boston, New England, and far-flung markets throughout the Caribbean and southern Europe, often in complicated forms of multilateral trade between two empires.[52]

Robert R. Livingston, one of the most successful of the new immigrants, began by trading with Amsterdam. In partnership with Stephanus van Cortlandt in 1678–81, Livingston sponsored voyages that included stops at the British colony of Barbados. He shipped goods to London on a relatively regular basis after 1692, and he subsequently diversified even further.[53] Adolphe Philipse began with both Dutch loans and Dutch commission business in the fur, lumber, and slave trades; but by 1700 he had branched into British West Indies logwood, Virginia tobacco, southern cotton, and southern European wines, which were reexported to both Dutch and English buyers. Gerard Beekman sent pearl ash and potash to Ireland, in return for which he received hosiery and linen to sell to New York, Rhode Island, and Connecticut colonists. From those regions, he received flaxseed, iron bars, flour, rum, hams, and horses. Large portions of the foodstuffs he centralized went on to Barbados, South Carolina, or Curaçao, from which places he accepted indigo, cotton wool, rum, raw leather, and sugar. Beekman also occasionally traded in southern European wine, Honduras logwood, and African slaves. This diversity of goods and markets doubtless made Beekman the envy of his rivals, for it decreased the risk of major losses as a result of gluts, dramatic price shifts, and many other potential mishaps.[54]

By the 1690s, most of the city's great merchants enjoyed a relatively unimpeded—and unprotected—commerce with southern European, Irish, and African ports. Although trade to southern European ports grew slowly because markets were distant and New York's supply of agricultural surpluses was unstable, a few prominent transatlantic traders had enough capital to outfit one or two successful voyages a year that returned a profit of from 25 to 40 percent. According to Governor Andros, Jacob Leisler had established connections with Iberian wine merchants by the mid 1670s, and other New York City merchants were exporting up to 60,000 bushels of grain to Lisbon and Madeira some years during the 1680s. Even in the crisis-ridden 1690s, one or two New York vessels a year entered southern European ports. And after the 1690s, there were routes to Lisbon, Cape Finisterre, Madeira, the Canaries, and the Azores. Lisbon was the preferred port, however, because it collected no reexport duties and had no official pass requirements. Moreover, waters near Lisbon were relatively free of pirates, and numerous London brokers facilitated bills-of-exchange transactions there for New Yorkers. By 1710, Adolphe Philipse exported fewer bundles of furs to London than casks of flour and grain to southern Europe, returning with Madeira wine.[55]

Rip van Dam, who was born in Albany in 1661, rose quickly in the ranks of provincial fur exporters during the 1680s, adding the West Indies and Carolina trade, as well as shipbuilding and dealing in real estate, to his activities over the 1690s. By 1695, however, his estate of £330 was only a portent of his continued rise in the southern European wine trade and African slave importation. Allied in this transatlantic commerce with the Bayards, Beekmans, and Livingstons, van Dam was one of the very wealthiest traders in New York City by 1701. Caleb Heathcote arrived in New York City in 1691 at the age of twenty-six and quickly established himself as a diversified trader with interests not only in English dry goods importing but in the Antilles, Madagascar, and Madeira trade as well. From his profits in wine and other luxury imports, Heathcote purchased extensive city lots and an estate at Scarsdale; but he continued to spend most of his time in New York City and his assessment of £640 in 1695 was based upon his owning several warehouses and shops, which he rented to other city merchants.[56]

A few advantaged city merchants integrated voyages to West Africa—where they acquired slaves for North American settlements—with their stops at Amsterdam and the Canary Islands; a few others engaged in slave-trading ventures that touched at Newfoundland on the way back to New York. By the 1690s, merchants who could afford ventures to acquire slaves from Madagascar or West Africa often ordered their captains to return direct. Upon the vessel's return, the slaves would be shared out among the original investors and either enter these merchants' homes or be sold along with other merchandise. Only occasionally did New Yorkers acquire African slaves for southern destinations such as Virginia or Barbados. After the *Prophet Daniel* was captured by pirates along the coast of Africa in 1698, fifty slaves intended for auction in New York were even-

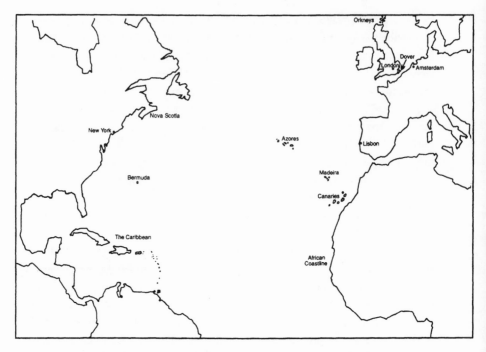

Map 1. New York City Merchant's Major Transatlantic Ports of Call by the 1690s

tually taken on board a slaver from London and sold in Barbados. Members of the crew who returned to New York after the ordeal noted not only the serious property loss to the ship's owners but also how irregular it was for the city's ships to detour in a southerly direction on their return voyages from Africa.[57]

Many of these well-placed city residents broke imperial law by trading with pirates. New Amsterdam's Council had lamented the crimes of the former merchant Thomas Baxter in the 1650s but could not put a stop to his and other pirates' marauding in the Caribbean.[58] In 1664–65, English policy makers admitted their own lack of success in suppressing piracy, and with renewed warfare against the Dutch, they instructed the governors of British colonies to grant letters of marque—formal permission to seize enemy vessels—against the Dutch and to enlist pirates for the purpose. Aboard eminent merchants' vessels, and guaranteed a portion of the merchants' booty from every capture, hired pirates proved equal to the task: they captured, lost, and recaptured most Dutch and Spanish possessions and a few French ones as well. In addition to serving British war aims, they brought windfall profits to a few city merchants and much public esteem.[59] But within the Caribbean theaters of war, British officials were not as quick to praise these arrangements. Lord Willoughby, governor of Barbados, scorned their disregard for military or civil order, as well as their immoral subculture. "They are all masters, and reckon what they take to be their own, and themselves free princes to dispose of [it] as they please," he said. "This cursed trade has . . . so many of it, that like weeds or Hidras they spring up fast as we can cut them down," Governor Lynch of Jamaica wrote eight years later.[60]

By the 1680s, New Yorkers had learned that the South Seas and the African coastline offered good markets for their grain and flour exports, and that pirates could supply them cheaply with luxury commodities and specie from many nations. From 1674 to at least 1681, the customs collector of New York's port, William Dyer, selectively admitted pirates and their vessels into the harbor, and with Governor Benjamin Fletcher's arrival in 1692, Dyer found a high-placed ally. In the otherwise difficult trading conditions of the 1690s, Fletcher became notorious for favoring pirates with asylum in New York and lining his own purse with their loot; the governor also licensed merchants to outfit "privateers (a soft name given to Pirates)," permitted merchants to loan pirates money at steep interest rates, and blinked their random seizures of goods off the coast of Africa. Among the merchants widely known to have benefited from piracy in the 1680s were the councillors William Nicholl and Nicholas Bayard; during the 1690s, the merchants Caleb Heathcote, Barent Rynderston, Thomas Lewis and Josiah Rayner threw in with the famous Red Sea pirates, and John Barberie, John Cruger, Ouzeel van Swieten, Richard Lawrence, Stephanus van Cortlandt, Stephen De Lancey, Philip French, William Pinhorne, and Frederick Philipse used profits from piracy to buy shares of city and Westchester County real estate, wharf space, and newly constructed ships. Philipse and Thomas Marston supplied Madagascar pirates with essentials such as clothing, liquor, guns, and ammunition; their captains returned with cash, slaves, and East Indies goods, and were "permitted to egress and regress without control, spending such coin there in the usual lavish manner of such persons." Robert R. Livingston traded with French buccaneers at Hispaniola regularly over the same years.[61]

Governor Bellomont faced stern resistance to suppressing piracy at New York City, complaining in 1699 that eminent traders hated him because "they say I have ruined the town by hindering the privateers (for so they call pirates) from bringing in £100,000 since my coming." Even enlisting the support of the pirate Captain Kidd and the prominent merchant Robert Livingston failed to stop the "constant Intercourse of Trade and Commerce from New-York, and the other northern colonies to Madagascar, and other parts of India, from whence are brought Muslins, and other Indian Goods, which are privately run into the

Colonies." Merchants at New York helped "one [Giles] Shelly, a New-York man[, bring] about sixty Pyrates . . . with great quantities of Goods from those Parts" into New York, and then "into Pennsylvania, the Jerseys and other neighboring Colonies." Shelley "went into New-York afterwards and was never questn'd about it." Despite concerted attempts by the Admiralty Court to try cases during Queen Anne's War, merchants continued to evade the ten armed ships placed in the harbor; only when peace returned in 1713 after Queen Anne's War did city merchants divert their attention to other forms of trade.[62]

During wars, other opportunities to consolidate commercial advantages arose. Robert R. Livingston, Stephanus van Cortlandt, and William Bayard purchased the privilege of supplying the resident British troops, the Four Independent Companies, with grain and provisions, in return for which they received much-coveted specie or London bills of exchange. From 1683 through 1697, their business yielded profits, they said, of up to 100 percent when they sold the bills to other merchants, especially when they "pinch'd out of the poor soldiers bellies" a portion of the agreed-upon rations. Another kind of contract—the flag of truce issued to privateers during imperial wars—also offered the chance to engage British ships in profitable ventures. Since at least the 1620s, colonial governors or provincial supreme court justices had issued these contracts to visit enemy colonies for the purpose of exchanging prisoners of war; but they had always implied the chance to return with valuable plunder to sell as well. Privateering, or legal plunder cloaked in patriotic purposes and national sanction, enjoyed favorable public opinion, since what was gained in personal advantages by the seizure of enemy vessels was unquestionably a service to the war effort, and the "condemned" commodities would find their way into the shops of the city to some extent. From the merchant's point of view, privateering also offered the advantages of lower wartime interest rates on marine insurance, and it was of great advantage for newly immigrating English merchants to secure these plums.[63]

Initial advantages, diversification, ethnic intermarriage, and repeated good luck contributed toward shifting the wealth of New York from Dutch to English families by 1695. In 1678, Governor Andros reported that "A mercht. worth £1000 or £500 is accompted a good substantiall merchant & a planter worthe halfe that in moveables accompted [rich]." If that generalization stood up over the next two decades, then only a few city merchants could have been counted among the "substantiall" when New York City's government made its first full tax assessment of households and estates in 1695. Of the 761 resident heads of households assessed, 134 assumed the title "merchant"; of the latter, 49 were assessed for at least £150 of real and personal wealth, the median amount of all assessments. Five merchants—all of Dutch heritage—were very wealthy: Gabriel Minvielle at £710; Nicholas Bayard at £766; Stephanus van Cortlandt at £885; Abraham de Peyster at £1,050; and Frederick Philipse at £2,610. Below these men were another 24 merchants, 15 of whom were assessed at from £300 to almost £600, and nine more were assessed between £250 and £300. These 24 were only slightly more Dutch than English in origin, only slightly older than the city merchants of lower assessments, and would rise or fall in fortunes in roughly equal numbers over the coming years. Only one Dutch family, the De Peysters, had as many as three descendants appear on the list of very wealthy residents. In short, new—primarily English—merchants were establishing themselves in city commerce by the 1690s.[64]

Credit, Interest, and Personal Reputation

During the seventeenth century, the prices of primary imports fluctuated according to the terms of transatlantic peace or war, and slow population growth kept consumer demands low. Warehousing, insurance, wharfage, freight, turnaround time, and losses owing to delays and to piracy could amount to 24 percent or more of merchants' costs, and this proportion fell only after 1713. Although ship repairs and mariners' wages did not rise until well into the eighteenth century, the costs of building a ship remained high relative to most merchants' starting capital.[65]

Importers tended to compensate for these risks and inconveniences with higher markups, reasoning that after subtracting ordinary commercial costs and insurance, the resulting customary prices of imports allowed but a small cushion against damaged goods, slow markets, or adversity. In the 1670s, 50 percent was "looked upon as an indifferent advance"; there was generally a markup of 100 percent on imports from England—"yea sometimes 400" percent in the 1690s. Governor Bellomont reported in 1699 that 90 percent was a typical markup on the wholesale price of necessary household goods, and other writers believed that markups had become tolerable to "the generalitye" of colonists. Only as the prices of imports declined by the beginning of the eighteenth century did markups begin to stabilize at lower levels.[66]

Markups became a source of periodic tension between importers and provincial consumers, but a more persistent form of anxiety developed around merchants' need for getting and giving commercial credit. On the one hand, city wholesalers regularly sought credit from their correspondents abroad. England's great firms were more likely to grant credit to established colonial traders than to risk placing their money with new investors, since the personal characters of the former had already been tested. As London correspondents reasoned, only the most reputable could be trusted on a regular basis with nine- or twelve-month promises to remit payments, and only they should, in turn, be permitted the risks of personal security, personal recommendations, and personal guarantees associated with extensive trade. At the same time, conventional wisdom held that inexperienced traders were more likely to default on debt repayments. If commercial conditions were favorable, merchants met their commitments to English creditors from the profits of carrying cargoes and offering shipping services. But when markets were overstocked or sales delayed, even the most substantial traders found it difficult to make timely payments; problems were magnified if a portion of their capital was tied up in government loans and local small debtors were falling behind in payments to merchants. To cut imports would only prolong the cycle of indebtedness; to demand government repayment of loans was fraught with political difficulties. Yet until the end of the colonial period, New Yorkers tended to blame, not economic instability generally or political quarrels particularly, but the "avarice of the home merchants" in London, who seemed to call in debts precisely at times when payments were most difficult.[67]

On the other hand, the web of trading relationships became ever more complicated, and many city wholesalers became eager creditors to myriad local consumers and producers. Colonists also had long been warned about the fantastical nature of credit, how it "hangs on opinion, depends upon our passions of hope and fear; it comes many times unsought for, and often goes away without reason." "Too much credit" also was believed to underlie many gluts of commodities or sluggish sales; personal miscalculations and, especially, the overly long periods of repayment to London correspondents seemed responsible for many economic downturns, not more general dislocations of the business cycle. A complaint often heard during recessions was that "overgenerous extensions" of credit encouraged "imprudence" in the "transient trader." But the lure of expanded credit was universally irresistible.[68]

Closely related to colonists' changing conceptions of credit were those of "usury" and "interest." Usury had been feared most among people who exchanged goods and money in a defined community of interests where personal reputation and the expectation of equal treatment dictated that all parties strive to maximize the benefits of exchange so that no single person need fear usury or the ill will of another. In the early seventeenth century, some writers still believed usury to be the bane of an orderly state and a sign of immoral individual behavior. Usurers, said Sir William Petty, were "like rats in a ceiling" that "live upon prey" and gnaw at the sinews of society. But since Aquinas, at least, ideas about usury had been undergoing significant alterations, until by the sixteenth century most commentators accepted the legitimacy of taking interest. As the principles of corporatist reciprocity and familiar personal relations gave way to long-distance markets, many communities ceased to define productivity and ownership in terms of imagined limits, beyond which virtue gave way to selfishness. In the emerging acceptance of continual expansion, money could justifiably earn interest without the stigma of "usury."[69]

Even in New York's earliest years, usury was being stripped of its associations with excessive extraction of fees from a borrower who had need of another's money, or the immoral augmentation of one's fortune without honest labor. As more capital became necessary to start up new enterprises, or to extend oneself in new risk taking, public and official attitudes shifted from protecting the reputation of a borrower against usurious charges of interest by the lender to guarding the right of the lender to make his money work as if it were capital. After all, the new view held, the lender was forgoing the use of his own money for a period of time and could not be expected to tolerate that it remain idle. At the same time, however, there were concerns about the form of investment on which interest was being charged: Western capitalist economies commercialized rapidly after the 1660s, and borrowers were increasingly risking their money in trade, rather than buying land.

With the new respectability of interest, some writers called for limits on the rates borrowers could be expected to pay. For as long as most early-modern observers could remember, loans for developmental improvements had earned only about 3 percent a year in Amsterdam and London. When the Bank of England began operations in 1694, and the British government became a public borrower of funds from individual investors, the low interest rates paid, from 3 to 4 percent, were in accord with traditional morality and landholding custom. It seemed fitting that the costs of new commercial growth ought also to be low, which entailed low rates of interest for merchants' needs. Indeed, the legal rate of interest allowable between private parties declined in England from 10 percent in 1622, to 8 percent in 1664, to 6 percent in the 1670s, and to 4 percent by the end of the seventeenth century, probably because there was so much money in circulation, but ideologically in conformity to arguments favoring low interest rates.[70]

While borrowing merchants might have been satisfied with the falling legal rates of interest, those who were occasional creditors preferred the interest rate to rise. Among the latter were some of New York's eminent city traders, and at times when the provincial government justified loans at higher-than-usual interest as a means of securing revenue for the "general welfare," prominent merchants in New York became eager for contracts, privateering privileges, and issues of stocks and securities. For example, the profits from wartime ship-building and exports of naval stores provided funds to invest in provincial government loans. Dry-goods importers also benefited from diverting capital from purchases of commodities in England to in their government's wartime needs. Jonathan Swift's sentiment about English merchants during Queen Anne's War applied as well to many New York merchants: "The Bait of large Interest would draw in a great Number of those whose Money by the Dangers and Difficulties of Trade lay dead upon their hands."[71]

Beginning with Robert R. Livingston's loans in 1674, at least some merchants chose to seek the profits of about 4 percent interest associated with government public projects and wars. During the years Livingston risked his funds to victual the Four Independent Companies, he received sterling bills of exchange on London in payment, thus collecting negotiable instruments, which he mused about reselling at 100 percent profit. Between 1683 and 1687, William Bayard and Livingston separately loaned Governor Dongan £3,500 and nearly £1,200 at 5 percent interest—together more than ten times New York City's annual revenue—with the additional stipulation that they receive the privilege of victualing the colonial troops, from which they earned commissions. In 1690, the rebellious Leisler government borrowed heavily from merchants to support a new garrison and then levied a tax on assessed city property in order to repay merchants at 4 percent interest. In addition to abetting piracy, Governor Fletcher also made generous land grants to favored transatlantic traders and secured loans from them at generous rates of interest.[72]

Following Fletcher, Governor Bellomont borrowed frequently from men he called "london traders" to support military campaigns, and he discovered the power merchants had to withhold such funds to gain political leverage. Moreover, Bellomont complained bitterly to the crown that suppliers had received sterling bills of exchange for supplying the garrisoned troops, but paid wages and acquired food rations at lower New York currency valuations, thereby making as much as 30 percent additional profit. "The deduction [between sterling and colonial currency] is an intolerable oppression upon the officers and soldiers, and unless it be taken off, we shall never be able to keep full companies," he wrote. When Bellomont also grew suspicious that contractors were providing inferior supplies and falsifying the record about the quantities they delivered in order to enlarge their commissions, he interceded, selling the bills of exchange on London merchants for local currency, which he then paid out direct to soldiers and local suppliers. Although a few city inhabitants must have profited from Bellomont's sales, he undercut the plans of Livingston and some other "most influential merchants," at least until he found himself in the compromising position of begging city merchants for more and more local currency for military purposes. As he lamented in 1700, "were it not for one Dutch merchant and 2 or 3 Jews that have let me have money, I should have been undone." The labyrinthine nature of drawing credits and making payments in order to feed the troops continued with the subsequent governors Nanfan and Cornbury.[73]

Consistent with early-modern wisdom about commerce, New Yorkers tended to explain economic trauma as a shortage in their circulating medium and resorted quickly to innovations that would provide alternative forms of currency. Unlike small producers and exporting merchants in the colony, who could turn to local remedies such as commodity payments, wampum, and, after 1708, paper currency, international wholesalers had to pay external creditors in bills of exchange or specie. The tug of war between coin, bills of exchange, and seasonal trade imbalances—circumstances experienced in all parts of the empire—was most acute in zones where consumer demand for imports rose precipitously, or where imports exceeded exports over a period of time. Then, specie flew "like bolts from the skye," prices fell, and insolvencies occurred. Some merchants reacted by hoarding specie, counterfeiting notes, or clipping coins. Andros suggested that colonists might import English copper farthings or melt and recoin Spanish pieces of eight to correct the "dearth of trade."[74] But two other practices proved to be more enduring in New York.

One of these, a tested practice since the eleventh century, was the use of bills of exchange, or assigned credit instruments, which were elastic among agreeing correspondents. There was, said Robert R. Livingston, "no better way of making returns" in international commerce when specie was scarce. English merchants who had earned specie by selling goods overseas and wished to ship it home could avoid the risks of piracy and inconveniences of transporting heavy metal by purchasing a bill of exchange from a second merchant at the foreign place. These bills could then be exchanged for specie by submitting them for payment to a third party in the merchant's home port, who might also be actively buying English sterling bills of exchange and forwarding them to other locations, where they were sold for specie available there. Thus, bills of exchange—normally payable within thirty to sixty days, until the New York City Council extended the official period to ninety days in 1747—required communication among at least three, and often four, parties; when need rose, they circulated faster and among more hands. Moreover, as these bills became more valued as circulating credit, merchants rediscounted them by assigning, or effectively selling, a bill to a third party for less than the original obligation or cost of the bill, so that the party holding the bill could acquire currency with which to transact business.[75]

Bills of exchange might have had a "likeness to coin," but they were never an equivalent. Their successful use required that the drawee—the person asked to pay the value of the bill—had debtors somewhere who were honorable, as well as a favorable balance of accounts with other merchants. In addition, colonial laws required witnesses and notaries to rediscount bills, making the procedure cumbersome, and the private nature of bills was confusing and often frustrating. When debtors failed, a New Yorker could write pleas for compliance with the stated terms of the bill, and if that did not produce payment, he could ask friends resident in the delinquent merchant's city to confront him. In a final step, protesting a bill of exchange, or seeking legal redress for nonpayment of a bill, a merchant might choose to undertake time-consuming and costly proceedings. The holder of the bill protested first to the notary public, who sent a formal notice to the drawer of the bill that the merchant's debtor had refused payment and thus dishonored the transactions between the original drawer and both of his correspondents in the distant place. The drawer was then responsible for contacting the original drawee and seeking compliance; if he failed, formal legal proceedings could be initiated by the holder of the bill of exchange against the responsible drawee. Of course, any of the negotiating parties might have reason to doubt another merchant's claims upon him and to insist upon his own financial reputability. English and New York law addressed abuses in the use of bills of exchange by assigning penalties and potential jail sentences for nonpayment; however, since a merchant's reputation could be tarnished seriously by failing to honor the terms of a bill of exchange, abuses tended to arise among smaller traders in the domestic economy rather than among the established international wholesalers, who had so much more to lose, as well as more extensive credit relations upon which to rely for help.

Still other uncertainties might arise. The price of a bill of exchange was determined by the quantity of specie in the city and its valuations, the quantities of paper currency and paper credit circulating, the velocity at which foreign demand kept currencies in motion, and the imperial government's stipulated rate of interest. Whatever the prices of bills of exchange were in New York from season to season, the international rate of exchange—or price cited at New York for a sterling bill of exchange that would be accepted in England—provided an index of how faithfully colonial merchants could satisfy English creditors. Dry-goods importers applauded low international rates of exchange, since they indicated favorable credit relations with English firms and rapidly circulating commodities; conversely, rising exchange rates indicated tightening credit, possibly gluts of imports and their falling prices, or smaller surpluses of agricultural staples and sluggish markets in the West Indies. If the price of foreign exchange rose high enough, it was more desirable to export specie to foreign creditors than bills of exchange until city traders could curtail imports, sell off surplus goods at reasonable prices, and await the return of specie and bills of exchange from the Caribbean and southern European trades.

But merchants' second remedy for presumed specie shortages circumvented some of these risks. Overvaluation of coin, which the Dutch colonists knew much about, could attract more foreign coins to the colony by setting its value higher than the money of account—English pounds, shillings, and pence. This overvaluation grew out of a long historical debate and the twists and turns of English policy since the 1540s, when Parliament had begun the practice of reducing the amount of silver or gold in coins, while retaining their face value— the economic equivalent of overvaluation—thereby attracting coin to England and helping debtors repay merchants. In the 1670s, Governor Andros "Encouraged Severall [merchants] . . . to Trade to fforeign parts, By Means of which Trade, Gold and Silver Moneys were first Imported" into New York City; he further promised to overvalue this foreign coin from 6s. to 6s. 8d. per ounce of silver. But the Duke of York's secretary, Sir John Werden, issued a stern reminder of an older wisdom: "The rayseing of any money in a country far above its intrinsicke value, is a certaine way of debaseing the Comodityes of that Country; and therefore a kind of impoverishing it." In 1692, the crown gave Governor Fletcher explicit instructions: "You shall not, on any pretense whatever, permit any alteration to be made in the value of the current coins." Early the next year, Fletcher and his council fixed the weight and value of currency as a remedy for its unreliable fluctuations, the first of several attempts to do so in the colony. But over the years, overvaluation gave way to devaluation informally among colonists; most of the pieces of eight, reales, pistoles, and bitts were reduced from, not raised over, their English valuations, "being very much Diminished in [their] Intrinsick Value by Clipping The light & heavy Money then passing Indifferently in Common Payments. The Merchts . . . began to give an Advanced price for heavy pieces of Eight in Order to Export them to Other parts where they Disposed of them at a higher rate." Thus, while domestic exchanges suffered from poor circulating currency and disputes over prices, merchants found ways to pay debts by enhancing the value of bills of exchange when their purchase was made in colonial currency for sterling debt payments. Over time, merchants who favored this means of increasing their commercial assets from domestic transactions habitually demanded that their government set the price of specie higher than money of account, thereby striking at the heart of received wisdom about the intrinsic value of specie.[76]

Although moderate overvaluation potentially provided easier exchanges among far more colonists than bills of exchange, it, too, could backfire. For one thing, sterling exchange rates might rise precipitously and thus create an unacceptable gap between the price of bills of exchange and New York's devalued currency. Or, when creditors received depreciated local currencies from their debtors—usually paper money—they could in turn increase prices for consumer goods. As a consequence, overvaluation could increase latent tensions between debtors and creditors, small producers and merchants. Small producers might favor overvaluation in the domestic economy when they were in the position of repaying debts with specie; but in their position as consumers, they rarely favored monetary manipulations that tended to raise the prices of necessary commodities.

Even at the end of the seventeenth century, the Dutch were a numerical majority among city merchants and small traders; but they owned less, collectively, of the wealth of all merchant householders than the newer English part of the community, many of whom took advantage of connections with over a dozen renowned London merchant firms trading in New York City. The principle of a favorable balance of trade with England offered transatlantic traders a rubric within which to make calculations about cargoes, pay careful attention to accounts, control the flow of regional goods with timely legislation, and create cautious trust all around. Of course, not all international dry-goods wholesalers accepted the tenets of economic regulation uncritically, and day to day, they sought the opportunities of smuggling, argued for diminished import duties, and looked for the means to enhance their provincial control over credit and financial matters. Overall, the city's comparatively successful wholesalers promoted the regulatory model taking shape in the empire and directed their commerce into transatlantic channels. Middling traders, as we shall see, adjusted mercantilism to suit the promise of commercial negotiation in regional and coastal trade to a greater degree than their eminent peers.

Chapter Three

"Where There is the Least Hindrance"

The West Indian and
Coastal Trade, 1664–1700

TO LONDON POLICY MAKERS and great merchants, New York City's emergence as an important port was represented by a few prominent transatlantic traders. Governors and provincial officials were quick to reinforce this impression in their reports on the city's rise, as when Governor Andros observed in 1674 that he "found the place poore, unsettled & without Trade, except a few coasters," yet by late 1681 boasted that the city had "greatly increased in people, trade, buildings, & other Improvements . . . the Navicacon increased att least tenn tymes . . . and plenty of money . . . and all sorts of goods at reasonable rates." Exaggerations aside, Andros and his seventeenth-century successors, Governors Anthony Brockholls, Thomas Dongan, and Benjamin Fletcher, attributed the city's emergence to its commercial elite.[1]

From the perspective of more disinterested travelers, however, the city seemed to struggle against commercial mediocrity. Although both successful and lesser wholesalers must have mingled on the docks and shared prices and gossip regularly, outside commentators readily separated traders by status, lifestyle, and the areas of their commerce. Charles Lodwick, an ardent royalist and opponent of Leisler's Rebellion, hardly hid his dismay that most English merchants in the city were of middling stature in 1692: "the Dutch [are] generally the most frugall and laborious and consequently the richest; whereas most of the English are the contrary, especially the trading part." In 1695, the Reverend John Miller also noted about New Yorkers that "as to their wealth and disposition thereto, the Dutch are rich and sparing; the English neither very rich, nor too great husbands; the French are poor." But it was the middling, of both English and Dutch ethnicity, that drew his frustration: "As to their way of trade and dealing, they are all generally cunning and crafty, but many of them not so just to their words as they should be."[2] Jasper Danckaerts insisted that seeing the title *merchant* appended to correspondence should not mislead outsiders; they were, in fact, no more than petty traders—almost all of them "gain[ed] their living by trade, namely, in tobacco and liquors, thread and pins and other knick-knacks."[3]

A few great importers boasted brick mansions near the water's edge by 1680, most of them homes and businesses combined. But most city ordinances for construction addressed the problems of a crumbling fort, hogs running wild in the streets, garbage flung from shops and houses, and great crowding of wagons, dogs, and citizens conducting petty business in the open. Harlem was still a half-day's walk from New York City, and would be joined to the original settlement by a road only after 1670. Country traders walked freely about, selling their small parcels of timber and containers of foodstuffs to city residents, who offered pickled oysters, wooden containers, or small crafts they had imported from New England or abroad, in a fashion not unlike the way business was conducted in rural areas. The wealthy few stood out conspicuously against a background of slow material rise.

It was of great consequence that the provincial authorities imposed only minor port duties on merchants' traffic during these early decades, and that most duties could be negotiated by commercially inclined members of the city and provincial governments. Moreover, the Navigation Acts did not significantly channel New York's trade with the West Indies and along the North American coastline, and it was in these arenas that the majority of city merchants started and sustained their trade. Indeed, no more than 5 to 10 percent of the value of New York's agricultural, extractive, processing, and transport activities associated with external commerce came under the provisions of mercantile policy before 1699. In years when the colony's supply of grain, flour, timber products, and naval stores outstripped English demand for them, merchants switched their flow toward the West Indies and neighboring ports, where demand grew rapidly. There, colonists collected specie, bills of exchange, sugar, and tobacco, which were of incalculable importance to the city's late-seventeenth-century rise along the Atlantic rim.

The West Indian and coastal markets also attracted some of the city's eminent merchants who wished to branch out from the transatlantic trade, but they became the primary ports of call for rising and new city traders. The pressing needs of colonists all along the Atlantic seaboard and the relative proximity of foreign possessions also encouraged middling New York merchants to argue for a political economy based on free exchange with neighboring and Caribbean colonies, lower export duties, and currencies that could be exchanged at comparable values across colonial boundaries. Lesser merchants were less directly connected to English credit and English laws through their trade, and they had little to cushion them against adversity; consequently, they argued for commercial freedoms that would enhance their opportunities closer to New York, and were likely to pursue those freedoms illegally when government policies worked against them.

The West Indies

Beginning in the 1640s, Dutch vessels began to carry West Indian sugar to the duty-free ports of Rotterdam and Amsterdam. Given Dutch superiority in the carrying trades at this time, and their preference for transporting staples rather than refining sugar and distilling rum—both of which they taught early English settlers at Barbados—Dutch captains were able to convey sugar from English and French possessions almost unhindered for about three decades. Then, with England's efforts after 1660 to channel Caribbean sugar to its own ports in the holds of its own vessels, Barbadians reluctantly gave up their "free trade" with the Dutch. In numerous statements to Parliament, planters explained that their "trading liberty" was being crushed by "the great inconvenience of the Act of Navigation and Trade," "which by constraining them to bring all they produce to one market, so beats down the price of sugars and advances freight [charges], that in a short time it must bring ruin on his Majesty's plantations." Governor Windsor of Jamaica urged planters to seek "free commerce with the plantations . . . of Spain" despite international rivalries, and also to try "to admit them to a free trade" at English ports. Merchants everywhere, he insisted, must go "Where There is the Least Hindrance." Following the second Anglo-Dutch war in 1674, British West Indies governors and merchants pleaded with home officials to recognize "the necessity of free trade" and "free credit" in young colonies. "Free Trade is the life of all Colonies," Lord Willoughby, the governor of Barbados, declared in 1666 in words reminiscent of Grotius. The Navigation Acts, he said, would bring only disaster to the island. The higher costs of English shipping and falling sugar prices in Europe brought on a serious recession in the West Indies, and in 1667, thirty-four Barbados residents left to settle in New York City.[4]

When prices of West Indian commodities fell in Holland and England during the 1680s to one fourth of what they had been in the 1620s, New York's rising traders made it abundantly clear to the provincial authorities that their grievances derived neither from enumeration, which did not affect the colony's grain, flour, and timber exports anyway, nor from colonial duties, which were occasional and low, but from the prohibition on trade at the ports of other European powers. In some cases, protesters had become enthusiastic about trading with Surinam and Curaçao. As early as 1626, a few West Indian slaves were sold to New Amsterdam residents; by the 1650s, many of the upwardly mobile merchants of the city were acquiring slaves for frontier agriculture and urban craft shops. Geurt Tyssen, for example, sold eight seasoned slaves to a Miss Verlett for 2,600 guilders in 1652, only one of his many sales of Caribbean slaves over the few next years. After 1654, West India Company directors permitted city merchants to trade in slaves as chattels, fixing a duty of 10 percent on black persons exported from New Amsterdam to Virginia or Maryland. The number of West Indian and West African slaves imported continued to rise in the last years of Dutch rule; for example, in 1664, Symon Gilde transported some 300 slaves from Curaçao to New Amsterdam.[5]

Although few vessels carried large numbers of slaves over the 1660s and 1670s, even an occasional delivery of 20 to 45 slaves to Virginia could be exchanged for large cargoes of rice for reexport to southern Europe, bills of exchange and specie for London creditors, or tobacco for transshipment to Rotterdam and Amsterdam—with or without a stop at a British port to pay duties, depending on the vessel owner's attitude toward smuggling.[6] By and large, however, this lucrative trade was confined to merchants with good connections, as when the Philipse family borrowed Dutch capital to make early fortunes in the fur, pirate, and slave trades, and in turn invested in ships commissioned to the Caribbean. Over the 1680s, the ships of Adolphe Philipse, often in partnership with Stephen De Lancey, regularly carried Virginia tobacco, Honduras dyewoods, and West Indian muscovado (raw sugar) and cotton to both London and Amsterdam, as well as a few slaves per voyage to New York City.[7]

The Cortlandt, Schuyler, and De Vries families had traded furs to Amsterdam before the 1660s, and they expanded their connections to include direct voyages to the Dutch islands of Surinam, St. Eustatius, and Curaçao, as well as the English possessions of Barbados and Jamaica.[8] Nicholas Bayard, who had imported Dutch and English dry goods in the 1660s and expanded during King William's War by exporting regional commodities to Curaçao, ranked among the wealthiest five men in the city in 1695. He passed on a fortune to his son Samuel when he died in 1711. Gabriel Minvielle, who migrated to New York City in 1669 and married into the wealthy Laurence family in the 1670s, was another West Indies trader of outstanding wealth by 1695. Lewis Morris, although by birth a gentleman, and associated with New York's landed elite, traded with the British and Dutch West Indies from 1675 to 1691, often in his own vessels. Stephen De Lancey, who married Anne van Cortlandt in 1686, pooled his small starting capital with established Dutch traders, and by the mid 1690s, he was reselling West Indian cocoa in Amsterdam.[9]

Unlike these men, who viewed the Caribbean as an arena of supplemental opportunities, lesser merchants treated it as indispensable to their modest returns. Start-up costs in this trade were relatively lower, since turnaround times were shorter and smaller vessels could be commissioned or purchased for the southerly voyages; it took about thirty to forty days to reach Jamaica, and a captain could expect to spend about twenty-four to thirty days in port at Barbados. Moreover, the complementarity of supply and demand between New York and the islands proved far more alluring to them than the long haul and debt payments to English firms involved in the transatlantic dry-goods trade. Insurance rates also were lower during peacetime: 4 or 5 percent of the value of goods carried in each direction.[10]

The rising traders Gabriel Ludlow Sr., Gerritt van Tright, and George Heathcote sent provisions or timber products to St. Eustatius two or three times a year. Ludlow, one of the more recent entrants into commerce, found the West Indies more compatible with his means than English trade; his estate was assessed at no more than £25 in 1695, and contemporaries judged his family home outside the city to be modest. Van Tright, who was in New York by 1665, was assessed at a low £70 for a dwelling and small warehouse in 1695. Heathcote, who arrived in 1678, had at least three small sloops engaged in West Indian commerce by the 1680s; he was assessed at £150 in 1695, and until his death in 1710, he made roughly two voyages to the Caribbean annually, although he never reaped great benefits from them.[11] By the 1680s, many new city traders added one to ten slaves to their return cargoes on occasion, and by 1699 it was a received wisdom that New Yorkers "supply themselves with a great many goods from Suranam and Curassow . . . and in return for these goods, they send to those Dutch Colonys, several of their Productions, for which they find no Market any where else." Indeed, they marketed a "multitude of Dutch wares" from the islands throughout the northern colonies until at least the end of the century.[12]

A few lesser merchants would rise from modest beginnings in the 1680s to positions of relative success after 1700. Joseph Bueno, for example, who traded local surpluses and slaves to the Dutch West Indies over the 1670s to 1690s, owned at least two mid-sized sloops before 1690. He was assessed at £240 in 1695 and by the early 1700s was a primary sugar importer. Richard Willett and Robert Watts Sr. started out trading with the Dutch West Indies upon their arrival at New York in the 1690s, but they soon included British possessions in the West Indies among their southern stops. Willett imported dry goods occasionally but concentrated on importing rum from Curaçao and Barbados and wine—which originated in the Canary Islands—from Bermuda. By the early 1700s, he was among the top nineteen city wholesalers, and in 1708 he was among the top thirty-seven in a rapidly expanding merchant community. Watts began his career modestly by exporting grain and flour to islands in the West Indies, primarily Barbados; by 1700, he owned four vessels and expanded business to Curaçao, Jamaica, and the Leeward Islands. When his son took over the family's commercial operations around 1710, Watts was no longer at the bottom of the middling layer of merchants, but neither was he among the eminent; Robert Jr. would see to that.

Regional Political Economy

Early Dutch merchants had enjoyed a thriving trade with colonists of both Dutch and English descent along the Chesapeake and New England coastline, and the first English immigrant merchants looked forward to building fortunes in the same manner. Together, merchants of English and Dutch origin shared the benefits of exchanging goods of many regions; many of them also provided services to English insurance brokers, bullion brokers, underwriters, packers, supercargoes, and shipbuilders across the Atlantic Ocean. As the years passed, however, New Yorkers came to recognize an unevenness of result in the coastal trades. In the first place, the Navigation Acts threatened to harm coastal traffic more than West Indies trade, especially the cargoes of middling traders, and it was not long before they were blaming both English governors and the original Dutch elite for their difficulties. Some frustrations were expressed as scorn for Governor Francis Lovelace's "shortsightedness" and closeness to wealthy "Dutch usurers" in the colony. Middling merchants hurled the blunter epithet *hogs*, long a term of abuse in England for the Dutch, at the successful transatlantic traders Cornelis Steenwyck, Cornelis van Ruyven, and Thomas Delaval. When Dutch privateers took ships belonging to some of the city's best-placed merchants—the *Good Fame*, Steenwyck's *James*, Thomas Delaval's *Margaret*, and Frederick Philipse's *Frederick*—in 1673–74, ethnic fears were exacerbated. Captain John Manning wondered who was the greater "enemy in our Bowells," Dutch enemy ships or residents of the port who continued to trade with Amsterdam. After peace returned, declarations by diplomats and provincial governors that "free trade" would no longer be tolerated reinforced regional traders' biases, as did the appointment of the wealthy Dutch merchants Stephanus van Cortlandt and Cornelis Steenwyck to positions of power in the new city government.[13]

But ethnic hostilities began to wane in subsequent years when most eminent merchants, of whatever national origins, closed ranks against the interests of rising traders over issues of imperial and provincial policy. Discriminatory policies against regional ports, for example, divided merchants along lines of status, relative success, and chosen areas of commerce. The city's great merchants tended to favor more elaborate regulations to protect New York City against the competition of its neighbors, but lesser merchants, who collaborated closely with their peers in other colonies, disputed the wisdom of such legislation. Throughout the 1670s, trade with New England, Maryland, and Delaware was vital to the interests of middling New Yorkers. Along with Cornelis Steenwyck, men such as Johannes Verbrugge, Nicolas Varlett, Johannes de Witt, and Henry Coutary sent regular shipments of grain from Esopus and Long Island producers to Maryland, where they acquired tobacco for reexport from New York, along with wine, vinegar, and other items, to London and Amsterdam.[14] After the warfare of 1673–74, Jacob Leisler, Francis Rombouts, Gillis Verplanck, Nicholas Cullen, and Edward Lloyd joined this circle of traders more regularly, and established closer connections with Dover and London; Henry Coutary moved to London to aid these ventures, while Jacob Milbourne and Anthony Brockholls extended their Chesapeake trade to include stops at Barbados and Hartford.[15]

Governor Andros's determination after 1674 to tighten royal control of the city's commerce implied less encouragement for small traders, especially when his government levied steeper duties on imports. Men with secure international relations simply passed on higher costs of trade to colonists, as they had in the past. By 1680–81, however, Andros and his port officials faced not only angry urban consumers and Long Island middlemen, but also failing small merchants, who openly defied the port regulations. When Andros's customs officers attempted to impound the goods of small vessels trading with New England, he was confronted by an enraged group of citizens, who forced his departure from the colony by 1681. Middling traders who charged the government with creating monopolies favorable to wealthy Dutch residents and imposing arbitrary duties were the backbone of the rebellion.[16]

Following Andros, Thomas Dongan made concessions to landed interests that hurt all merchants, especially lesser traders. Not only did Dongan raise import duties; he also approved new legislation to force New England merchants into a subordinate place, measures that struck hard at the middling merchants who relied on neighboring producers and small traders for exports. Unable to enter the southern European trade or coveted English markets with their slender capital and small vessels, these men both depended on duties at New York City being low enough to attract the goods of neighboring colonies and required easy communication among the ports of the economic region. At times they joined with "vocal free traders" such as Samuel Winder of Staten Island to protest the rough treatment they received from port collectors who expected bribes. When Dongan closed Long Island ports in order to steer trade through New York City, he drove modest traders throughout the region into the opposition.[17]

Dongan also exacerbated the divisions among city merchants by granting large tracts of land to a few of the greatest wholesalers. Philipse, Kip, Rombouts, van Cortlandt, and Livingston, among others, settled members of their families on rural estates and began to attract agricultural laborers and millers. By the mid 1680s, they had developed transportation and marketing strategies that brought those families great material benefits and placed them in a position to set the terms for internal commercial relations. Additional grants from 1685 to 1687 on Long Island and Staten Island strained relations between would-be gentry and small producers linked to lesser merchants.[18]

The Leislerian Experiment

In its initial phase, Jacob Leisler's Rebellion and government (1689–91) gave concrete political focus to lesser merchants' anxieties. Although the rebellion was inspired by the Glorious Revolution in England and its rhetoric arguably was grounded in ethnic tensions between rising English and displaced Dutch and French inhabitants, it also developed at an especially poignant moment of economic distress, which accentuated the fault lines between the great importers and ambitious lesser merchants in New York City. Leisler himself was associated by marriage and notable commercial success with city merchants who had risen quickly to prominence after 1680, but he drew together the threads of discontent that had unraveled over previous English administrations: resentment over higher duties, discrimination against neighboring ports, and increasing privileges for residents of the port city at the expense of those of the hinterland (a subject to which the next chapter turns). His bitterest enemies were not immigrant English merchants, among whom were some of the most sorely aggrieved city traders, but anglicized Dutch merchants, whose wealth had grown over the preceding years, and the Dutch population of Albany, who resented his close attention to the needs of New York City.[19]

Given that the Amsterdam trade diminished yearly and that the London trade was open to only a minority of traders with good connections, while governors perennially favored merchants whose fortunes were already secure, whether Dutch or English, it is not surprising that Leisler's Rebellion united many middling inhabitants against wealthy and privileged merchants in general, Dutch and English alike. Moreover, some of the dissent ripening in New

York originated with rising business and farming families along the Hudson River, constituencies that were both Dutch and English in origin. For a while, many middling city exporters, commercial farmers, bolters, and millers perceived the rebellion as an opportunity to realign economic privileges. As a consequence, the Dutch merchants David and Jonathan Provoost, Johannes and Abraham de Peyster, Cornelius Cuyler, Johannes van Brugh, Peter Delanoy, and Samuel Staats were among Leisler's initial middling supporters. But so were rising immigrant English and French merchants such as Robert Walters, Thomas Weaver, John Coe, Abraham Gouverneur, and Cornelius Pluvier. Established wholesalers in the Teller, Cuyler, and Loockerman families were conspicuous for their wealth in this group of otherwise middling city residents.

Once in control of government, the Leislerians began to abolish city privileges that had been irksome to lesser merchants. For example, discriminatory duties against merchants in neighboring colonies quickly fell away. But in August 1690, when Leislerians established "equal freedom to boult and bake and to transport any thing" from the various settlements of the province through New York City, the new government risked losing its supporters among lesser merchants involved in grain and flour exporting. Although they supported the principle of more liberal commerce outside the colony, free exchange in the interior ran against their interests. Leisler's introduction of free bolting and transport of grain clearly favored country over commercial interests, some of them argued. Later that year, he alienated even more of the merchant community when he asked the New York Council to approve new port duties. He also favored the great city wholesalers with more privateering contracts against the French in 1690 and 1691.[20]

Before Leisler was removed from power, most middling merchant supporters had abandoned hopes of tax relief and promotional economic policies. Nevertheless, long after the rebellion was crushed, colonists conflated two interests in the Leislerian constituency: merchants of middling stature and merchants of Dutch origins. Among the primary charges against Leisler at his trial was one that he had "ruined merchants" of the city who had worked hard to establish their status under English rule, and that he intended to "raise up" new commercial interests. Nicholas Bayard, a wealthy dry-goods importer, believed even in 1701 that Leisler had attempted to put "the meanest and those of Dutch extractions" "in all the offices and places of trust and power," while "the principle and peaceable inhabitants and especially those of the English nation have been oppressed."[21] Others spoke merely of rank, as when, in 1692, William Blathwayte divided city merchants into three groups: the well-to-do and loyal elite; the reputable but economically insubstantial majority; and "insipid wretches" who had few commercial successes and seemed to have gathered around Leisler's cause.[22]

Bayard and Blathwayte exaggerated, and anti-Leislerians persisted in the belief that eminent wholesalers could not be served by the illegitimate political claims of dissenters who had risen from middling station. Indeed, as governors, Thomas Sloughter (1691), Richard Ingoldesby (1691), and Benjamin Fletcher (1691–97) retained import duties that transatlantic traders protested but extended the privileges of land grants, blinked piracy and port briberies, and granted government appointments and military contracts to the advantaged commercial families of the city down to 1697. Middling traders, however, weathered commercial recession in the 1690s poorly. King William's War, competition from Boston shipping and shipbuilding, neglect of the regional trade, and comparatively high duties drove much trade to neighboring ports, seeming to confirm the complaints of struggling traders.[23]

Struggling exporters also felt the sting of the provincial currency devaluation that eminent wholesalers favored. When provincial officials raised the value of coin by "artificial means" in relation to mediums of exchange, lesser traders protested that they would be forced to accept depreciated local currencies from small producers and colonial consumers trying to repay their debts. Eminent importers could raise the prices of their goods in order to receive enough compensation to pay debts to England, but "lesser men" of trade would have to watch as export prices lagged behind import prices for a period and the initial advantages of devaluation for the small producer and agriculturalist vanished. Farmers, of course, would in turn raise gate prices. Stuck between rising consumer prices of imports, and rising gate prices for exports, middling traders feared that the spiral of upward-moving prices would know no end once the value of specie was altered. Competing domestic economic interests would vie for their respective advantages, Adriaen van der Donck said, but no side could remain satisfied for long. To the extent that they were middling consumers themselves, lesser merchants decried devaluation, because they would need more and more of the declining currency to pay for necessities.[24]

As a consequence, lesser merchants fought hard to defeat measures that depressed the value of domestic currency, and they often succeeded. Governors Dongan and Bellomont, in 1684 and 1700, entertained the notion of a mint in New York, but the proposal was widely rejected by colonists, who feared that more circulating coin would devalue the colony's currency and reputation together. Denunciations of piracy, despite its ability to bring in as much as £100,000 a year during the 1690s, represented awareness by these same constituencies of the potential for the de facto price inflation that resulted. Stiff popular resistance met schemes to import devalued coins from England, until, beginning in the 1720s, colonists campaigned to prohibit the circulation of small-denomination coppers minted in England, centering their argument on the fact that the coins did not contain copper commensurate with their declared values. In the following decade, William Wood, whose earlier *Survey of Trade* had bolstered the mercantile cause, gained sanction from George I to send at least three shipments of coppers to New York, but as each ship arrived, lesser merchants and their neighbors organized public protests to prevent their circulation in the city.[25]

Smuggling: The Opportunity and the Rationale

Smuggling had long been a common feature of English trade. Dutch and French woolens, tea, sugar, and spices made their way from Sussex to London, Yorkshire, and Edinburgh. Even periodic show trials in London staged at the behest of mercantile interests failed to deter the customs officials, hawkers, and affluent metropolitan merchants involved in the trade. Later, widespread knowledge of the large supply of French wines in the cellars of Sir Robert Walpole (1676–1745), King George II's chief minister, as well as popular acclaim for the daring exploits of smugglers, bolstered what was expressed as a "right according to tradition" to evade customs duties. Historians have estimated that at least 8 percent of London's imported goods were smuggled, and there may have been a far higher percentage at other ports. Up to one half of some shopkeepers' tea and sugar may have been smuggled between 1650 and 1750.[26]

The Dutch colonists of New Netherland had often resorted to smuggling in defiance of mercantile regulations, and under English rule the illicit traders of New York drew justification from the popular belief that merchants would benefit more from open than from regulated trade. Their prosperity, they insisted, would in turn benefit all inhabitants. Undoubtedly, some merchants were keen to avoid the high costs of delays between unloading and reloading at ports, including wharfage and crew wages. Others expressed the belief that smuggling, like piracy, provided a means to sidestep persistent currency shortages. Still others argued that smuggling was justified on the basis of a simpler maxim: reducing costs and maximizing individual profits. Given that colonists were the pupils of traders who defied mercantilism at its point of origin, few were surprised to hear their governors report that colonial merchants conducted a "common" and "practicable" trade with Amsterdam, via Portugal or Boston, on illegal terms.[27]

Despite the laws to stop smuggling that New York legislators layered upon imperial legislation, merchants landed cargoes of contraband goods from ports in the French, Spanish, and Dutch West Indies at the coves and inlets of New Jersey, Connecticut, and Long Island on a regular basis. As Governor Dongan noted, "Last year two or three ships came in there with goods and I am sure that the Country cannot . . . consume [them] . . . in two years soe that the rest of their goods must have been run into this Government without paying his ma[jes]ty['s] customs." The *Blossom* and *Rebecca* were reported to have been engaged in this trade since at least 1677. And enumerated items bound for Amsterdam could be rendered "legal" by stopping at Dover or Falmouth and bribing port officials to allow the vessel to continue without making formal bonds and payments.[28]

Adolphe Philipse, John Barbarie, Stephen De Lancey, Robert R. Livingston, Henry van Rensselaer, Cornelis Jacobs, and Stephanus van Cortlandt, all among the great traders of the city, increased their illicit trade after 1675.[29] But so did some of the city's middling merchants. Novice traders were tempted by smuggling, because it did not require great capital or risky long-distance voyages to smuggle goods via Long Island Sound or the New Jersey coastline. For example, while he was still a rising middling merchant, Abraham de Peyster promoted Leisler's cause in 1689–90 because the rebels promised greater commercial opportunity. In the meantime, he stationed members of his growing family network throughout the empire to receive "Holland pots," West Indian logwood, peltry, Madeira goods, and enumerated commodities; at New York City, he cultivated the friendship of port collector and receiver-general De Reymer, who was willing to blink "unlawful ships and goods." In part by smuggling West Indian goods, De Peyster became one of the next decade's wealthiest merchants.[30]

De Reymer was appointed directly by the governor and was responsible for using part of his annual salary of £200 to create the offices of haven masters, who searched ships' entry papers, comptrollers, who kept customs accounts, surveyors, searchers to list all entering goods, and pilots and waiters to bring vessels safely to dock. All of these "servants" depended on the collector's commands, which often included instructions for smuggling, fraud, bribes, and destruction of documents. In 1680, Collector John Lewin, formerly a special "Agent and Servant" of the Duke of York, reported that orders for illegal entries came directly from Governor Andros, who had allowed a "Connivance practiced to some few Dutch merchants, vizt. ffredrick Phillipps and Stephanus Van Cortlandt" "to bring in goods contrary to the Acts of Trade." Van Cortlandt and Philipse continued smuggling under the eye of the colony's third collector,

William Dyer. Already infamous among middling merchants for stopping their small vessels for needless searches, Dyer earned their further anger when he passed the blame for smuggling on to his paid servants, Peter Delanoy, the provincial bookkeeper, and Henry Filken, the port searcher. When the latter two, rising city merchants, could not produce sufficient receipts to prove their honesty, they were dismissed for permitting illegal entries into the port. Predictably, other small exporters registered their anger.[31]

Undeterred, Collector Lucas Santen openly defrauded the government of at least £3,000 in customs revenues from 1682 to 1686 and encouraged "free" entrances and clearances for those able to pay him "private sums." When sued, Santen and his port servants were tried by a commission that included the renowned illicit trader Stephanus van Cortlandt. Santen was cleared of the charges, but when he tried to redeem his image as a good public servant the following year by drawing attention to Governor Dongan's collusion in smuggling French and Spanish goods, the Assembly replaced him with Matthew Plowman.[32] Under Leisler, similar abuses continued. Nicholas Bayard lasted as port collector for only a few days in 1689, and although hopes ran high among middling merchants that Leisler would appoint a collector more open to their need for unimpeded trade, they were once again disappointed when the Assembly appointed Peter Delanoy, one-time servant of Dyer, and George Brewster; as was their inheritance, these two discriminated in favor of the great importers.[33]

No doubt, men of more modest means found ways to smuggle as regularly in regional trade as great importers did on a transatlantic scale. Indeed, lesser merchants' opportunities for illegal transport of small quantities of West Indian goods were many times greater than for very long voyages, and their use of small vessels permitted entry at coves or inlets where great ships could not dock. Although imperial officials attempted to make enforcement of customs legislation more alluring in the 1690s by allowing the collector to keep 5 percent of port revenues, this was insufficient to match the funds that Governor Fletcher's appointee, Chidley Brooke, could otherwise collect in fraudulent vessel entries. By 1698, when Bellomont took office as governor, reports noted the growing number of small vessels "entering by cover of night" and how New York City "grew rich" with Spanish silver. Good Whig that he was, Bellomont was confident that right principles and parliamentary sanctions would bring an end to smuggling. But opposition in New York proved formidable, and he complained to the Lords of Trade that the "Merchants of this town" had "raised such a Clamour" that his efforts to suppress illegal trade were ineffectual. "I have made all the court that a man could do that [had] the soule of a gentleman, to those angry merchants," including "[Fletcher's] sycophant Councillors Nicholl, Bayard, Brooke and the rest of the bloodhounds."[34]

Brooke repeatedly delayed the seizure of illegal cargoes and, with the help of about twenty city merchants, cajoled the tide waiters into ignoring Bellomont's orders to measure and weigh cargoes and to check ladings carefully. Brooke and Sheriff Samuel Wilson invested in smuggling ventures themselves in 1698, concealing East India goods in eminent merchants' homes, while lesser merchants unloaded countless containers of commodities acquired along the coast. One of the searchers of customs, a Mr. Monsey, received bribes to ignore the entrance of small parcels from the West Indies, while Bellomont continued to lament that city residents applauded the "reproachful and scandalous" behavior of its merchants.[35]

Bellomont further alienated the interests of city merchants from his rule by requesting in 1699 that the Lords of Trade appoint tide waiters, searchers, and port collectors from London to replace the corrupt officials his council appointed earlier. "I covet to have gentlemen from England to be in [these] employments," to serve on "the Council of New York to balance those of the country, who have interests to manage that do not always square with the interests of England," and to displace city merchant interests at the same time, Bellomont wrote to London. It was to little avail; he faced formidable opposition from men like Samuel Bayard, Thomas Willett, Gabriel Minvielle, Philip French, Stephen De Lancey, Rip van Dam, Lewis Morris, and Myndert Schuyler, who had combined their commercial interests with ownership of great tracts of real estate. These "merchant-gentlemen" regularly tampered with port registration forms, taunting fellow importers who tried to comply with the Acts of Trade. They joined with about two dozen rising lesser merchants in early 1700 to petition the king for a new governor, inasmuch as Bellomont had caused "the decay of Trade" by his attempts to suppress smuggling.[36]

London firms with whom New York City's eminent dry-goods importers did business grew concerned that Bellomont's excessive zeal would strike hardest at existing lines of transatlantic trade, especially the colonial city's most successful liaisons with London. If they fell prey to a governor's crusade, interlopers might try to supplant them. The London wholesalers Thomas Byfold, Micajah Perry, Thomas Starkey, Simon Lodwick, and Jonathan Blackall also wrote to the crown noting that New York's trade was "in danger of being ruined" by middling traders, some of them no more than ship captains, or hired transporters, who had "encouragement given them by the Governor." Bellomont, they said, had mistakenly identified the aggressive "middling Leislerians," rather than the established great wholesalers, with crown interests and the future of the colony. In any event, suppression of smuggling failed to become a priority among imperial aims in New York over the coming years, and merchants of all degrees there continued to engage in illicit traffic.[37]

Middling Traders

The maturing West Indies and coastal trade gave ambitious young immigrants and sons of resident traders their greatest prospects. But their rise was in no way certain during the seventeenth century, and a great deal of untested terrain lay to New York's south. In some ways, new optimism about the role of merchants in the empire's rise encouraged city merchants to take risks in the Caribbean. After generations of doubt about the value of merchants to a stable or rising people, observers on both sides of the Atlantic were beginning to link economic maturation with these "servants of trade." In England, Charles Davenant noted that while labor and its "Natural, or Artificial Product[s]" were the "Spring and Measure" of all commerce, merchants should be guaranteed "some Overplus," a "clear and certain Profit" for themselves. Their fortunes, said optimists, were their reward for taking commercial risks and their incentive to continue improving the lives of all inhabitants of the empire.[38]

Of course, this intellectual shift did not provide New Yorkers with concrete business opportunities; not even the Acts of Trade much affected their exports to the coastline to the south and the West Indies in the seventeenth century. But a more favorable view of merchants, attached to the public welfare, garnered respect for new ventures, albeit for small profit. For example, the "much respected merchant" John Sprat, who imported wholesale earthenware and other household necessities until his death in the late 1690s, possessed only a modest fortune. The inventory of Sprat's estate in 1697 gives a total of £1,797, £120 of which he held in specie, £240 in unimproved real estate, £145 sunk in a warehouse and house lot near the docks, and £3.10.0 in books. Two other "esteemed merchants," Andrew Teller Jr. and Jacob Teunis de Kay, were no richer. Teller's inventory reveals a similar decision to acquire real estate near the end of the century—his dwelling on Pearl Street, two small rented houses down the same street, and two additional houses and lots nearby—but his cash reserves were depleted and his debts remained high at the end of his life. De Kay died in 1706, leaving his oldest son a city lot, his next son a country lot, his grandson another country lot, and his creditors a house lot on Whitehall Street across from Bowling Green.[39]

Even at the ends of their careers, most middling merchants owned little—

typically, only minor household goods, modestly assessed dwellings, and few trade commodities in the sections of warehouses they rented. Peter de Groot and Matthew Ling died at the turn of the seventeenth century with little to leave family members, after many years trading out of New York City. Anthony Lispenard Sr. died in 1696 leaving £50 to his oldest son and "all my wearing apparell, house, arms and tackle." John Coesant died four years later with 9,196 guilders on hand, but a list of debts for his family to repay that would more than absorb all his capital and savings; John Haines passed on in 1691 with £100 available for the many creditors who claimed that his commercial debts amounted to far more. When Henry Mayle died in 1692, he left only £10 to a friend's son, and four gold rings valued at 20s. each to four associates in trade; his brother Jacob, also a merchant, fared little better.[40]

Peter Marius, active in city politics during the last years of the seventeenth century, rose somewhat above the stature of many city merchants. Two merchant friends took an inventory that revealed about £150 "cash in chests," "91 Dutch books, valued at £6 by the appraisers," and household goods—auctioned later by Robert Lurting—valued at £446. In addition, Marius left a great amount of improved property on the lower end of Manhattan Island, including a large dwelling with a shop in front, a living room behind, a "great kitchen" attached, great and small storehouses, a "thatched chamber," a "writing closet," a "coach loft," cellar, and sleeping chambers. The sale of the effects of the estate realized nearly £5,291, and hundreds of small debtors owed Marius another £4,679.[41]

De Kay was more typical than Marius, however, of New York's middling merchants, whose numbers continued to swell with new immigration. Most focused on exporting, but it was not unrealistic for some of them to combine their retailing or rural peddling with modest importation. A few were not so much part of the ambitious cluster of city craftsmen and retailers aspiring to upward mobility as they were representative of falling fortunes. Depressed conditions in the fur trade or failed international ventures accounted for consolidation of trade into fewer hands and elimination of recent entrants during the 1660s. Warfare also brought about continuous change in the city's composition throughout the 1680s; while some already-advantaged traders benefited from demand for war supplies or government interest rates on loans, many others did not.

By 1695, one-third of the city's merchant community—49 of the 129 property-holding merchant residents—paid assessments between £100 and £250, figures that straddled the mean for all inhabitants. Fully two-thirds of the total were assessed for no more than £150; a few owned such small dwellings and so few household items that their assessments stood at only £20 to £40. As in earlier years, the level of assessment often reflected the stage of a merchant's career. On the one hand, new or young entrants to trade often had little city property to report, and the assessors did not include shares of vessels or outstanding commercial debts. As a consequence, some city merchants with low assessments would undoubtedly improve their condition over subsequent years. On the other hand, of the 129 assessed city merchants in 1695, as many as 80 had been trading in the city for five years or longer; 51 of these were assessed below £250. Another 21, who had earlier advanced into wholesaling from being captains, flour bolters, or small retailers, were assessed below £100, claiming property worth no more than many of the city's cordwainers and tailors. Not surprisingly, many were recent arrivals of modest means; it often took years to build a colonial fortune in the seventeenth century, especially during periods of warfare and doubtful supplies of exports. Indeed, the five years on either side of the assessment were fraught with major international tensions that would test the ability of even great traders to prosper and ruin many aspiring traders.[42]

Other problems beset this majority of city traders. For one thing, English and European demand remained centered on bulky unprocessed goods from the Caribbean and southern colonies; English consumer demand for colonial agricultural products or urban manufactures was low. The eminent transatlantic traders were best able to transship the dyewoods, logwood, tobacco, and sugar that found ready markets in England. Lesser merchants owned smaller vessels, had more locally established connections, consolidated their small quantities of commodities with a number of other city merchants, and often aided the great traders by centralizing goods from the region in New York City for re-export. Or, pooling their small quantities of goods to fill the hold of a sloop, they often proceeded to southern ports or went on to Boston, where the New York commodities would be transferred to a larger transatlantic vessel. They also generally spread risks by sharing the costs of outfitting vessels and taking dozens of orders for small quantities of West Indian or southern colonial commodities. Returned vessels at New York might bring large quantities of sugar, molasses, or rice, which were then broken up into myriad small parcels for city shopkeepers and inhabitants who had placed orders for the items.

Lesser merchants were less likely to be linked by marriage and credit to far-off suppliers and customers. Not only did they have less credit to extend to others; they also had more to prove in asking for it on their own behalf, and late payments, faulty judgments, imprudence, and uncertainties about debt repayments plagued most of them from time to time. Even when overseas firms granted credit as long as twelve months, and New York merchants extended domestic credit for six to nine months, transactions might take two years or longer to complete; sometimes trade seemed to drag on at nearly imperceptible levels. Despite their best efforts, middling merchants also had trouble entering markets in bills of exchange or availing themselves of opportunities for making private loans: either of these would have required sufficient prior success and a reserve of investment capital. So would any attempts to make loans to the colonial government or bids for military supply contracts.

As a consequence, middling merchants—who were no less ambitious than the great traders—actively sought trade in other channels, primarily along the New England coastline, in the West Indies, and in the shuttle traffic to and from Long Island, avoiding the more costly ventures to England and southern Europe. Thomas Willett Jr. and Gerritt van Tright, for example, struggled to find supplies of provisions for West Indian buyers and sent small parcels on many different vessels during the late 1680s. In the cases of Peter Delanoy and Gabriel Ludlow, long-standing dealings in Amsterdam gave way to securing supplies of peltry or local produce for export to regional markets; like many other lesser merchants in the 1690s, they gave up shipping goods on large vessels in partnership with big merchants and undertook ventures with smaller parcels of goods in ketches and sloops.[43]

As a group, merchants in the coastal and West Indies trades typically accepted whatever commodities were available for transport; individually, few of them consistently secured more than two or three types of commodities. When demand at new markets or for new commodities was incalculable, diversifying would exhibit foolish daring. Few of them imported cloth, ribbons, nails, small implements, buttons, and earthenware from England on a regular basis. Most of the city's aspiring, ambitious merchants sent New York's wheat, flour, staves, barreled pork, and other agricultural surpluses to the Carolinas or the West Indies, returning with sugar, cash, bills of exchange, and slaves. Coastal traders distributed wares at the ports of New England, Philadelphia, and in the Carolinas, or picked up agricultural commodities that were centralized in New York City before shipment on larger vessels to the West Indies or southern Europe. Some of them held goods for a while, waiting for room on a clearing vessel; others disposed of the goods to port-city consumers when debts pressed them or the goods stood too long. Rhode Island cheese and barreled pork, Long Island whale oil and fruit, and parcels of woolen cloth from all over the surrounding area made their way on small vessels to New York City.

By the end of the colony's first century, aspiring merchants' lifestyles and property assessments reflected modest commercial achievement, which could be identified with the opportunities of the coastal and West Indies trade to a greater degree than importation of dry goods from England and Europe. Their imports of tobacco, molasses, cocoa beans, and sugar, some of which was reexported by the better-placed city wholesalers and some of which was consumed in the region around them, were rising rapidly by the 1690s. These commodities were "of a less necessitous nature" to most colonists than the agricultural implements, textiles, and earthenware imported from England in the last half of the seventeenth century, but they provided the means to pay for imports and expand the arena of city commerce.

The development of noticeable "ranks" within the commercial community, made more apparent with each tax assessment, each new commercial law to raise duties or discriminate against different portions of the community, and each petition to the crown for redress of commercial grievances, also kept alive lesser merchants' sensitivity to economic freedoms. In some ways, those freedoms were still attached to the persistence of Dutch ideological influences and culture. In other ways, the unprotected markets of the Caribbean and the potential benefits of illegal trade created new appetites for unimpeded commerce. Indeed, while it was clear to many colonists that a few eminent dry-goods importers prospered under imperial regulations and with favors from officials, they also began to identify rising lesser merchants, not only with the West Indies and coastal trades, but with smuggling and dissent. Although these popular perceptions were erroneous and exaggerated with respect to many city merchants, they nevertheless deepened over the years, reinforced both by the self-conscious distinctions merchants drew among themselves and by their interactions with another vocal economic interest, the commercial farmers and traders of New York's hinterland, to whom we now turn.

Chapter Four

Creating a Regional Economy, 1664–1700

NEW YORK CITY'S DEEP HARBOR, open all year long, adjoined the Hudson River, along which rural sellers of flour, butter, staves, shingles, and peltry found transportation to be faster and cheaper than overland traffic to or from neighboring colonies. At first, the cargoes moving toward, and then down, the Hudson consisted largely of furs and naval stores. By the end of the century, however, agricultural goods filled small boats headed for both city consumers and merchant exporters.[1] Throughout most of the seventeenth century, the gathering momentum of rural production and exchange drew less attention and policy controversy than city commerce did. Only a few owners of the country estates granted from the 1670s to 1690s improved their lands before 1700; instead, city lots and warehouse space provided merchants with mortgages that could be converted into valuable credit instruments for raising commercial capital or form an inheritance of rising value. But before the late 1720s, most merchants held only two significant city properties, a warehouse and a residence. Instead of developing tenantable properties in New York City, or creating a fluid market of buyers and sellers of land, most wholesalers invested in ships, goods, and commercial credit.[2]

City commerce could only thrive, of course, if wholesalers secured sufficient exports to offset, at least partially, the cost of imports. The fur trade filled this need in the early years of colonial development and provided a basis for the commercial fortunes of a few exporters who were graced with fortuitous combinations of good prices, plentiful supplies, and beneficial credit and marriage connections. Lesser merchants found it more and more difficult to enter the fur trade by the 1680s, but they were attentive to other opportunities in their region, the most important of which was trade with the maturing settlements that produced small quantities of exportable commodities, the clusters of farmers and petty craftsmen along rivers. By the end of the seventeenth century, the agricultural hinterlands provided sufficient quantities of exportable grain, timber products, and partially processed farm goods to support the entry of dozens more merchants into commerce. The demand for foodstuffs, shingles, and dairy goods, which grew very rapidly in the West Indies and coastal trades, proved alluring to men with modest capital and reputations to build. As a result, a number of New York City's middling—and some few of its great—merchants set about the task of developing and subordinating the surrounding agricultural region.

Lesser merchants were already familiar with the contrapuntal discussion about economic freedom and regulation; they had pursued port freedoms with neighboring merchants, they had supported dry-goods importers' desires for lower duties, and they had opposed unlimited markups for some time. But in their capacity as exporters of agricultural surpluses, the same rising merchants often reversed their ideological commitment from freedom to regulation. Ambitious commercial farmers, millers, and country tenants provided consistent and consequential opposition to exporters' goals for prices and terms of sale. Years of informal negotiation with residents of the hinterlands gave rise to concerted efforts by merchants to create new provincial policies for quality control, regulated exchange relations, and gate-price ceilings on regional commodities. And for their part, small producers in the hinterland proved quite willing to compete with merchant exporters for the terms most suited to their interests.

The Declining Fur Trade and Export Monopolies

During their first years under English rule, New Yorkers experienced a temporary lull in regulation of the Indian trade in the colony and fur exports. As we have seen already, Governor Richard Nicolls and his council were eager to keep the trade with Amsterdam open. With similar reasoning, Nicolls argued in 1666 for "a Generall Liberty" of exportation from New York; free competition, he insisted, would encourage immigration and keep prices in the colony down. Cheaper local commodities and imports would in turn help exclude expensive New England goods and encourage more local production. "Our neighbors of Boston have made good use of our Necessityes" by "raysing the price of their Goods" shipped into New York. "Freedom of the Trade," "without molestation," would bring down prices and discourage New York's merchants and bakers from raising their own prices. Ideally, said Nicolls, "Shipps of any Nation may Import or Export into or from hence all sorts of Merchandize whither they please." Like many others of his times, Nicolls was sure that higher prices arose solely from the avarice of monopoly interests, rather than the scarcity of goods. In the interests of "encouraging this Place," consumers required predictable, low prices for daily necessities.[3] Two years later, Nicolls decreed the Indian trade to be open to all merchants of the province irrespective of ethnic background, city of residence, or prior advantages. There should be, he wrote, "the privilege of a free Trade" throughout the interior, of the same kind that merchants enjoyed with respect to external commerce.[4]

Arguments for an open fur trade were kept alive by small trappers who plied the woodlands north of New York City, sloop captains and middlemen who wanted access to the port city's consumers, and some members of the Livingston and Morris families—early recipients of large land grants—who wanted to buy peltry from trappers and market it independently to city residents or exporters. As many of them noted, a city export monopoly would only worsen the odds in their competition for good prices and markets, especially with interlopers to their west and Philadelphia exporters, who were said to enjoy "great freedom" of trade. Robert R. Livingston, who served as agent for Hudson River valley towns and Albany, agreed about the harmful effects of trade into Canada when provincial laws failed to regulate it, but argued that an open trade throughout the interior was essential for maximum competition among all peltry exporters. But merchants in the de Meyer, van Cortlandt, and Philipse families disagreed; they retained purchasing and transport agents—often relatives—in Albany, in order to corner supplies of peltry, which they later exported from New York. Without personal "monopoly" privileges over the Albany fur trade, they reasoned, settlers in that northern area would raise the prices of furs sold to merchants' agents inordinately high. City exporters concurred about the benefits of monopoly privileges, using familiar customary language about preserving the public weal to support their cause; a temporary provincial monopoly, they insisted, would help minimize the risks of economic ventures in an era of persistent insecurities and guard England's interests against French encroachment. Unlike great trading monopolies created by the crown, local ones had a favorable effect on the lives of a majority of colonists, for they gave order and stability to competition. Shortly thereafter, exporters would use similar arguments deriving from customary considerations to promote more corporate city control over other hinterland interests.[5]

Governors and councillors at first supported such reasoning, as when Governor Francis Lovelace granted city merchants a monopoly of the Hudson River carrying trade in 1670, thereby easing exchanges of imported Indian goods as well as exportation of furs. But in 1674 Governor Edmund Andros imposed a higher duty of 1s. 3d. per beaver skin passing through the city of New York; and although in 1678 he granted city merchants the sole right to export furs, he also imposed stronger inspection and export controls and enforced assiduous collection of duties.[6]

Merchants unleashed their anger when Andros's legislation expired in 1680 and the customs collector William Dyer attempted to secure duties for which there was not yet a new law. In mock dismay over Dyer's conduct, the merchants William Nicolls, John Laurence, Henry Beekman, and Jacob and Stephanus van Cortlandt asked how a public servant could enforce an act that was no longer in force; besides, Dyer had blinked the entry of dutiable Dutch and French goods, and the great city wholesalers easily bribed him into overlooking their obligations to pay import duties on English goods. When Dyer seized a vessel in 1681 for nonpayment of export duties, the merchant owner promptly sued him for illegally confiscating private property, an act of "high treason" against "his majesty's commerce." Although an English inquiry cleared Dyer of the charges, exporters had succeeded in blocking new export duties for two years.[7]

Even when Andros lowered export duties in 1683, exporters seethed with discontent. By then, middling traders were joined by wealthy merchants such as Philipse and van Cortlandt, who petitioned the authorities to the effect that there was a fundamental distinction between grants of trading privileges and grants of revenue: acts channeling the fur trade toward New York City, they insisted, gave order and stability to internal exchanges, while duties of any kind would cause merchants to pass on the higher costs to city consumers and Indian traders, thus diverting trade to French Canada. City merchants enlisted the support of twenty-one London merchants who concurred that if this eventuated, "the whole Bever trade will be lost." But while the next governor, Thomas Dongan, assented to greater corporate privileges for the city, including a 1686 decree that made New York City the sole port of entry for the colony, he failed to satisfy hopes for city control of the fur trade. That same year, Dongan granted Albany the coveted monopoly rights over collection and marketing of peltry within the northern area, prompting exporters such as William Beekman and Nicholas Bayard to establish residences there, leaving family members in New York City to receive their furs for export.[8]

From this vantage, the Van Cortlandt, Philipse, Livingston, and Bayard networks continued to build family fortunes by capturing most of the fur trade. Once they had consolidated the greatest share of it into their hands, they then ventured into other areas of commerce, while newcomers to New York and rising sons of local retailers shared smaller and temporary portions of the fur-export markets. Consolidation of the fur trade into already-advantaged hands was made easier by irrevocable changes on the frontier and in Europe. For one thing, fur supplies were rapidly receding away from settled areas by the 1690s, and the level of exports fell from about 40,000 pelts per year in 1664 to about 10–15,000 annually, and often many hundreds fewer, by 1700. Governor Dongan estimated in 1689 that the typical "35 or 40000 Beavers besides Peltry" exported each year in the early 1680s had fallen to 12,000 in 1687, and "9000 and some hundreds Peltry in all" by the end of the decade. In addition, between 1664 and 1700, the price of beaver fell from 14s. to 5s. a pound in London. Some of the Albany area's dealers made continuous efforts to steer peltry through French Canada, where Indian trade goods were of higher quality and relations with local middlemen often more amicable. In addition, fashion preferences in England and Europe shifted away from beaver hats and collars during King William's War, producing artificial gluts in England and making it very difficult for even eminent city merchants to earn credits to buy a return cargo. Even well-connected English arrivals to the city—men such as John Lewis, Charles Lodwick, James Graham, Edward Griffith, Caleb Heathcote, and Samuel Winder—consistently exported fewer furs by the 1680s than the "monopolists," and eventually they staked their futures on different kinds of ventures.[9]

New York's rising merchants, who had less starting capital, shunned voyages that became prohibitively expensive during the war. A few of them began to factor for Dutch or English merchants and traded only regional goods on their own accounts. Those who could still count on small supplies of furs took up smuggling through neighboring ports in order to avoid fees and duties. Still others fell outside of the tight-knit network of fur-trading relationships by 1690. Collectively, however, small traders had begun to learn a valuable lesson about economic freedom: that absence of regulations during good times could spur city commerce forward, but benefiting from port freedoms during hard times depended on the extent of one's initial position on the ladder of commercial success. Middling status was fraught with the danger of downward slippage or failure during periods of fierce competition.[10]

The Rise of Grain and Flour Exporting

Even from afar, observers recognized that New York's future depended on the agricultural production of myriad small proprietors on the vast lands that spread out beyond the port city's wall. The Dutch had not been complete strangers to farming; since the 1650s and 1660s, they had exported small quantities of rye along with peltry, and during the brief interlude in 1674 when the Dutch retook the colony, they hoped its settlers would provide Holland, Curaçao, and Surinam with "a granary." But periodic scarcities, sparse settlement, a dearth of agricultural skills, and absorption by city consumers of most available food products ensured a slow start for grain and flour exporting.[11] Since the 1630s and 1640s, New Amsterdam's traders had "contended with New-

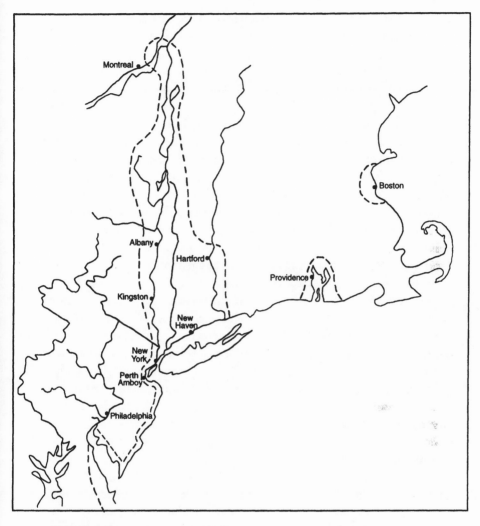

Map 2. New York City's Trading Region before the End of the Seventeenth Century

Plymouth . . . for the first possession of the river Connecticut," and also carried on a lively competition with New England for transshipping Delaware Valley tobacco to England. But when West Indian demand for foodstuffs rose noticeably in the late 1660s, New Yorkers lamented that grain and flour constituted little more than an additional small portion of the commerce they enjoyed with England, Holland, and southern Europe.[12]

Ambitious exporters expressed frustration with these conditions, especially because the fur trade did not provide enough opportunity for the growing merchant community. Would-be flour wholesalers noted that internal settlement proceeded slowly. The population of the colony rose from probably little more than 9,000 in 1664 to about 11,500 by 1680 and 18,000 in 1698. New York City had been growing comparatively faster—from 1,500 in 1664 to 3,200 in 1680 and 4,937 in 1698—and provided a ready market for grain, horses, timber, and small farm surpluses from the New York hinterland, Long Island, New Jersey, and Connecticut. In comparison with the dangers of frontier life and the difficulty of acquiring desirable freeholdings close to roads and rivers, the city's safety, opportunities for employment, and community were attractive; but the result, complained merchants, was a dearth of goods to export.[13]

Moreover, a handful of commercial fortunes had been amassed in New York City by the 1670s, to the astonishment of foreign visitors, who also remarked on the contrast between the city and the great stretches of unsettled frontier. To some extent, they were correct. The prescriptive rights attending ownership of a country estate in England, and bequeathed as a family inheritance to subsequent generations, appeared comparatively rarely in New York's seventeenth-century political economy. Rensselaerswyck had been the only viable estate during the Dutch period, and although at least eight large tracts were granted through political favoritism in the first twenty years of English rule, they went unimproved for the most part. Governors Dongan and Fletcher granted at least twelve more vast tracts of real estate in efforts to consolidate loyalties to the crown, but few of the new landlords leased smallholdings or settled freeholders or tenants on their estates for some time. As a consequence, a colonial landed interest, which defended its interests against the seventeenth century's rising commercial ones, appeared only slowly, and some country estates produced noteworthy exportable surpluses only after 1700.[14]

The primacy of commercial interests is exemplified, for example, by William Pinhorne, a merchant of note by 1679, who owned one of the best garden houses at the foot of Broadway and traded from his warehouse nearby. In the 1690s, for a rent of one beaver skin a year, Pinhorne secured a land grant fifty miles long and two miles back on both sides of the Mohawk River, but he did not develop this estate. Similarly, the Beekman family, which owned thousands of acres along the Hudson River by its second and third generations, only partially tenanted its lands with farmers. William Beekman owned mills in and around New York City but chose to invest chiefly in shipbuilding, exporting commodities from a wide region, and the bills-of-exchange market. Asser Levy died in 1682, after twenty-eight years of entirely commercial enterprise in New York City, worth the great sum of 57,000 guilders; yet little of his property was real estate. Even at the end of the century, most city merchants continued to occupy old housing near wharves in the southeasternmost part of the city, along the East River.[15]

Of course, some merchants did aspire to become landed gentlemen. One such was Philip Schuyler, who was descended from Dutch traders doing business in the colony since the 1650s and had intermarried and traded with the Van Cortlandts, De Lanceys, Livingstons, and Van Rensselaers. The Schuylers acquired their first real estate outside of New York City in 1665, and they still "confounded" their commercial interests with extensive landholdings around Albany and along the Hudson in the late 1740s. In the 1750s, Schuyler was what his biographer calls a "frontier aristocrat," seeking "fortune and distinction" in both commerce and a country estate.[16]

Two of the Hudson Valley's great estate holders enlarged their commercial fortunes and landed stature together, turning partly to grain and flour trading to do so. One, Robert R. Livingston, combined farming, gristing, sawing, and fur trading in a grand commercial farming enterprise by the 1690s. The other, Frederick Philipse, father-in-law of John van Cortlandt, had an extended commercial network, which included sole ownership of many oceangoing vessels familiar at Antigua, Madeira, Jamaica, Virginia, South Carolina, and London. By the end of the century, a visitor, Charles Wolley, heaped praise on Philipse as "the richest *Mein Heer* in that place," noting his thirteen houses, several city lots, bolting house, and three warehouses in New York City. But the great merchant also owned extensive land, slaves, and mills in Ulster County and in Bergen, New Jersey. From the two Philipsburg manor wharves, sloops carried grain produced by well over one hundred tenants to New York City for bolting and export as flour. His son Adolphe and brother-in-law Philip French expanded the family lands, mills, blacksmith shops, coopering works, and tenant settlements even more in the next generation.[17]

The unevenness of internal agricultural development and the growing demand in the West Indies for food and timber created a tension that New York City's exporters tried assiduously to resolve. Helpless to quicken the pace of settlement or motivate large landholders to turn over more of their soil, exporters tried to shape port policies that would both encourage more production for export and discriminate against conflicting economic interests. Governor Nicoll's policy of economic freedom was replaced after 1668 by regulations that discriminated against weaker neighboring ports. In 1668, too, great and lesser merchants together hailed the granting of commercial privileges to city residents. When Long Islanders petitioned for fewer port fees and "free trade" for their cattle, and then threatened to sell valuable supplies of grain and flour "to Strangers neare and farre" "in a free manner," New York City exporters assented to a provincial embargo on exporting foodstuffs from all New York ports until the local population had sufficient provisions to meet its needs. While singing the praises of serving "the Public Good" by curtailing their trade, exporters nevertheless admitted that an embargo would also stifle their Long Island rivals and privilege their own commerce.[18]

For the city's lesser merchants, then, economic regulations were neither a universal good nor a universal privilege; in the face of an embargo that stymied their own traffic as well as Long Islanders', they demanded more economic freedoms. By mid 1670, despite the continuing embargo, city exporters had resumed shipments of grain to coastal and Caribbean ports, incurring the anger of millers and consumers, who worried about the double threat of rising import prices and food shortages. When the embargo expired, millers and consumers appealed publicly to Governor Lovelace to prohibit export of foodstuffs, and renewed embargo legislation in 1671 once again challenged grain exporters to choose between their interests either as city consumers and millers or as merchants who required goods for foreign trade. Not surprisingly, many were reported to have "encrease[d] their private Welfare" by demanding free "transportation of fflower made of Wheate[,] bread[,] or Biskett for the use of Merchants . . . who are or may be engaged to make payment therein." They insisted upon the right to export at will in order to compete with Boston for West Indian markets; otherwise, they felt justified in defying custom by hoarding and forestalling outside the city wall to force provisions prices upward and compel the opening of external markets.[19]

The pendulum of appeals from city merchants swung once again toward economic regulation in the case of East New Jersey traders in 1676. Having suffered the effects of New York's discriminatory duties and grown jealous of New York's external trade, New Jersey officials declared Perth Amboy a free port. Merchants there declared that they had awakened to their "true interest," which was to defend the lower price at which they could acquire grain and export it, when there were no city monopolies, and lower costs of importing, when there were no duties. "Free ports" were the only way to attract commerce, they believed, given New York City's "Commercial prejudice."[20]

For a few years it appeared that New York City and Perth Amboy would go their divergent ways. But events in New York conspired against New Jersey's dissidence. In the first place, New York merchants were exporting at least 60,000 bushels of grain a year by 1680 and gristing an equal amount of flour for the Newfoundland fisheries and West Indian plantations. Predictably, they were keen to buy grain from New Jersey and Connecticut and to monopolize regional exportation if possible.[21] Then, too, New York's Governor Andros was intent upon bringing all the northern colonies under close commercial regulation. He reminded New Jersey traders that despite their proclaimed political independence, they fell under New York's commercial laws by order of the crown and were obliged to collect import duties at New Jersey ports and forward them to the treasurer at New York City. To these ends, Andros placed the troublesome William Dyer at Perth Amboy to collect import and export duties ranging from 5 to 10 percent ad valorem. Eminent New Yorkers who wished to create stronger ties between themselves and London merchants pledged Dyer their support and praised these efforts to "bring order to city commerce," but they reminded the governor that Long Islanders had already taught the metropolis how easily the outlying areas could violate official dictums. Some vocal lesser merchants in New York expressed quite a different sentiment. All regulation between neighboring colonies was a hindrance to building regional markets, they argued; should New York become "excessively regulated" it might not draw grain and flour from the countryside to the extent of New Jersey's free ports, thereby undercutting their livelihoods.[22]

Some of their fears were ill founded, for New Jersey's sparse internal settlements were well connected by rivers to New York City. Perth Amboy was not as convenient as the larger port to the north, especially for colonists who used the Passaic River to transport commodities, and New York City's exporters promised shorter turnaround time for perishable commodities. In any event, praise for the "natural channels" of intercolonial commerce was muted when prominent city merchants used their influence over Governor Dongan's provincial council in April 1685 to secure measures forbidding all New York vessels to trade at neighboring New Jersey and Connecticut ports. The council also appointed the merchants Stephanus van Cortlandt, William Creed, and Nicholas Bayard to arbitrate the act as port officials. Predictably, rising traders who were linked directly to the regional countryside for supplies of exports questioned the wisdom of these measures; however, the provincial authorities preferred not to emphasize the prospects for interregional cooperation but rather to create a mercantile "monopoly of the export" in their own city with provincial regulations. New York City's mayor and city council agreed with the trend: "this Citty [of New York] & Albany . . . are the only pillars on which Your Majesty's revenue is erected," and it was an "absolute necessity" to draw "Connecticut[,] East and West Jersey, [and] Pennsylvania . . . as extends from the Falls of Susquehanna" into New York's commercial region with firm guidelines for the exchange of commodities.[23]

But the enforcement of such mercantilelike commercial order remained elusive; Governor Dongan was sure that small traders in New Jersey and New York were evading the latter's legislation with impunity. Everyone, he lamented, knew that smuggling was rife between New York and the "free colony." In a further effort to orient the lion's share of this commerce toward New York, Dongan and the New York Council extended the 10 percent ad valorem duty on foreign imports to all goods arriving at New York, including imports that landed at another colonial port before transshipment to New York City. In this way, city merchants and the commercial farmers of Long Island, New Jersey, and Connecticut no longer enjoyed the benefits of shipping via Boston, Perth Amboy, or New Haven before touching at New York City. Foreign goods routed through intermediate ports would prove more costly than those imported direct to New York City. Considering such costs, small producers would also be more likely to take their grain and flour to New York and exchange them there for cheaper imports. When these measures proved less successful than Dongan and his merchant supporters hoped they would be, the governor closed the Long Island ports altogether. Meanwhile, Dongan and his successor, Governor Thomas Sloughter, urged the home authorities to annex New Jersey, Connecticut, and Rhode Island to New York as a means to resolve the persistent regional contention.[24]

Exporters continued loudly to negotiate their interests in trading with the merchants of neighboring colonies, but their skirmishes with commercial farmers proved even more consequential by the end of the century. Fraud, ignorance, and agricultural failure had damaged New York's reputation, many exporters averred, and there was nothing worse than the practice of allowing farmers to bolt (i.e., sift and grade) flour anywhere in the colony, creating a "libertism of trade and confusion of market," with "every man doing what seemeth good in his own eyes." New flour mills were springing up "in all parts" of the colony, attesting to rising prosperity in the hinterlands, but also threatening a kind of anarchy. "Greedy farmers" got rich by raising prices, and country millers overcharged for gristing and transport too; New York City grew poor, while "every homestead [became] a market." Country millers—especially those north of the city wall and on Long Island—ignored Council orders to bring flour into New York and evaded sheriff's instructions to seize all flour bolted and packed in the countryside. This struck at the general welfare. Poor-quality, irregularly packaged grain and flour from New York's hinterland could not compete with Boston and Hartford shipments to the West Indies, and if their own commercial reputations faltered, exporters warned, the prices they offered farmers would have to fall as well.[25]

The weight of these arguments proved strong enough to influence provincial policy once again. Following upon merchants' victories in winning an exclusive monopoly of the Hudson River carrying trade in 1670, a monopoly of peltry exporting in 1678, and legislation discriminating against neighboring ports, they were granted a monopoly by the provincial Council in 1680 providing that "noe flower be Bolted or Packed nor Breade made for Transportation in Any Place whatsoever within this Government Except in the City of New Yorke."[26] The act was justified, merchants exulted, as a measure to build New York's "Credit and Reputation Abroad"; an additional unstated aim must have been to purchase grain from farmers at lower prices and control the markups added by country millers. In November 1683, New York City's mayor and common council—all prominent merchants—petitioned the home authorities to allow the act, citing the charter privileges granted to New York City in 1665 and insisting that grain and flour were "in greater request in the West Indies and the only support and maintenance of the Inhabitants of this Citty." Governor Dongan nodded assent to the legislation, and sent it to England for approval.[27]

Members of the provincial Council defended the bolting monopoly to mercantile powers in England over the coming months by pointing out the colony's dependence on exporting staples: "the manufacture of flour and bread . . . hath been and is the chief support of the trade and traffic to and from this city and maintenance of its inhabitants in all degrees." Unlike England's more diverse economy, or the "other parts of this province [that] have some particular advantage and way of living as Long Island by husbandry and whaling; Esopus being the fat of the land by tillage; Albany by Indian trade and husbandry; this city [has] no other advantage or way of living but by traffic and dependence one on another chiefly upheld by the manufacture of flour and bread."[28]

Middling exporters added their voices of support to those of Common Council and provincial Council members. The monopoly, they insisted, would improve the quality of exports, regularize their prices, and add predictability to merchants' trade abroad. For merchants who doubled as bolters, the city monopoly provided direct personal benefits. For example, Johannes Clopper owned a female slave who could work the mill when he was out scouring the region for grain or collecting some of the thousands of guilders owed to him by small producers. Peter Sympkam went into the coastal trade with his brother, a carpenter; together they operated a bolting mill that produced flour for city consumption and export. Unlike these and other examples, however, Robert Story was an exceptionally successful New York City bolter, who branched out into dry-goods importing, the slave trade, and internal exchange of all kinds. He kept a mill house at Esopus as well, which supplied exportable grain to New York City ships, while his sloops returned up the Hudson River with imported goods for storekeepers in the hinterland.[29]

An official English communication in late 1684 ratified the bolting legislation and noted that colonists were correct to "always care [for] the interest and
advantages of your City of New Yorke, that being the staple of your trade and
indeed the key of your Country." But the colony's Assembly, sitting for the first
time in 1684, disagreed. In the name of "the generalitye" of inhabitants—most
certainly including some of the great country landholders—assemblymen distinguished between making the city the sole port of entry to the colony, which
did not discriminate against anyone, because the object was to keep prices stable for everyone, and city control over bolting, baking, and packing of grain and
flour, which disrupted livelihoods within the colony by granting privileges to
some inhabitants. They countenanced only setting the assize of bread as a city
privilege over the country.[30]

Continuing disagreement among economic interests in New York underscored the insecurity of the exporters' 1680 victory. But for its brief few years of
existence, the bolting monopoly probably aided the city's overall development:
from 1678 to 1692, the number of houses within the city limits grew from 343 to
983, grain exports rose steadily, and revenues from import duties tripled because of rising urban demand. Connected to this, the surrounding countryside
was yielding greater amounts of grain and flour by that decade, some of which
fed growing city neighborhoods and some of which was exported to markets
along the coast and in the West Indies. Indeed, the bolting monopoly fortu-
itously coincided with rising agricultural productivity.[31]

Although the bolting monopoly was not directly responsible for promoting
the immigration of more merchants, the rising importance of grain and flour
exports provided opportunities for young and rising men to enter regional
commerce when other avenues of international trade proved formidable. By
the end of the 1680s, over fifty city wholesalers exported grain regularly. Ten to
twelve of them already had established their commercial eminence in foreign
importation and the fur trade and to some extent had shifted their export preference toward grain by then. Another ten can be counted among a younger generation of traders who rose quickly to prominence as grain exporters, wine and
dry-goods importers, and estate holders. Well below them in stature—roughly
adduced from their shares in vessels, numbers of voyages, landholdings, quantities of goods, and distances of voyages—were seven to nine middling former
fur traders who enlarged their connections with a few regional grain producers
in order to export to new West Indian markets. The larger group of middling
merchants, however, included many ambitious newcomers to New York who
had started out in business by collecting surpluses from regional growers, which
were then marketed along the coast and in the West Indies, and who often did

not go on to build significant connections with dry-goods merchants in Europe. By 1700, such men constituted the majority—between seventeen and twenty-two—of city grain exporters, and over the following years, their number as a proportion of all city exporters grew by leaps and bounds.

Still, merchants' successes were mingled with failures and frustrations during these early years, which in turn fueled animosities between city and country. The grant of a city charter of incorporation in 1686 enlarged the formal powers of the city over the hinterlands; but these were mitigated by rising landed interest in the Assembly, rivalries with New Jersey and New England ports, and the grant to Albany of extensive privileges in the fur trade. Governor Dongan began to despair of creating a powerful port city that mirrored the role of London as an entrepôt; despite his best efforts, he lamented, "wee are like to be deserted by a great many of our Merchants," who found New Jersey's free ports alluring. The ensuing turmoil of war and political factionalism exacerbated divisions among New Yorkers.

The 1690s

When Leisler's government introduced numerous commercial changes during April 1690, the Bolting Act was one of the first city privileges to fall. John van Cortlandt, a city merchant who had favored the monopoly, relayed to ex-Governor Andros the elation of commercial farmers when the law was repealed, adding that he felt certain economic chaos would result. "All towns and places," he complained, would "have equal freedom to boult and bake and to transport where they please directly to what place or country they think fit, anything their places afford, and that the one place shall have no more privileges than the other."[32]

Although wealthy traders had diversified their commercial interests, ensuring that grain exporting was not their sole risk, lesser merchants were dazed by Leisler's repeal of the Bolting Act, and they drew together their anger into formal appeals. Most important, thirty-six city merchants petitioned the crown to restore their bolting and export privileges. Most of them were rising men who traded throughout the region and had supported the bolting monopoly since 1680. Some noted that Leisler himself owned a major bolting mill in the city and had traded grain and flour from Esopus to Maryland and Rotterdam for over twenty years. In power, Leisler seemed to be alienated from regional commercial interests, since free gristing in the interior reintroduced all the pricing, quality, and exchange difficulties with which any exporter was familiar. Subsequent governors treated grain and flour exporters no differently; under Fletcher, for example, rumors of graft and political favoritism grew to the charge that "four hundred pounds was contracted ... by the Country of [Es]opus" to pay the governor and a councillor for their affirmation of free bolting.[33]

Complaints crescendoed during the 1690s, for coinciding with the repeal of the bolting monopoly, a transatlantic commercial crisis was gathering momentum; the fur trade continued to decline; and there were poor harvests at many Hudson River settlements, with regular reports of wet and adulterated perishables being sent to hungry city consumers. Consumers must at first have enjoyed the benefits of trading directly with farmers and negotiating down the price of wheat—from 4 shillings per bushel in 1684 to 3s. 6d. per bushel by 1691—but bad harvests in the latter year so reduced supplies that provincial councillors lamented the "penury and want of bread" affecting the city. Ironically, despite the free bolting policy, Abraham and Jean Hasbrouck were two of a very few millers in the interior who sent flour to New York City for export after the repeal; given the reduced quantities of grain, most bolting was more efficiently done in the port city. Then, too, warfare from 1689 to 1697 created a high demand in the West Indies for foodstuffs that New Yorkers were eager to supply, but high costs of shipments and low external prices for New York's products reduced profits regularly after 1692. At Barbados, "the price and value of New York Flower fell five shillings in the hundred below the price of Pennsylvania," resulting in gluts, failure of merchants to return to New York with specie in enough quantity for remittance to England, and idle ships.[34]

Numerous exporters accounted for the city's trauma by noting two well-rehearsed conditions: excessive private competition in New York's hinterland, and continuing rivalry with neighboring colonies. In the first case, exporters regretted the "talk of liberal trade" throughout the countryside, a situation that had destroyed New York's reputation abroad and made city residents' grain expensive. The landed "country merchant" Robert R. Livingston was a primary target of their attacks, given his loud protests in the General Assembly against the bolting monopoly. Exporters predicted that he and others on large estates would create a formidable alliance with independent small farmers, country millers, and transportation middlemen around Schenectady and New Paltz who would use the Assembly against city interests, on the grounds that freedom to make marketing choices without the encumbrances of legislation that taxed and channeled exports was vital to their rising wealth.[35]

Before 1700, collusion between the great landlords and myriad small farmers in defense of the commercial interests of the interior would have been problematic at best, although their separate voices offered similar rationales for "country freedoms." Middling exporters, however, who identified closely with millers and bakers in the city, reminded colonists that their own collective well-being also hinged on exports of grain and flour to the West Indies being of reputable quality. New York could never become the granary of the colonies, they maintained, so long as the inhabitants of the hinterland persistently avoided inspection and careful packaging; country bolters mixed Indian corn and other objectionable products with wheat, giving rise to "country forestalling," shortages in city granaries, and a general "anarchy in the Province," which both "destroyed the reputation of New York flower" abroad and hurt consumers at home. In this, exporters echoed city complaints against the Dutch West India Company almost fifty years earlier: although a high degree of economic freedom was desirable in external trade, the greater welfare and basic peopling of the colony required judicious internal quality and market controls.[36]

But middling exporters, who had already experienced favoritism by provincial governors and legislators with respect to import duties, piracy, land grants, and currency devaluation, watched in dismay as officials resorted, not to improving the quality and quantity of exports, but to embargoes on exports of many agricultural goods in 1693, 1696, and in 1697, and to measures to license bakers more stringently in June 1696. New Yorkers' daily bread deserved to be safeguarded, exporters agreed, but they implored city and provincial authorities to consider their own plight too. Because they depended both upon small wagonloads of grain and flour from farmers in New England and New Jersey and on markets in the West Indies, embargoes of more than seasonal duration would doubly disadvantage their trade: they would prevent exportation of provincial goods, thereby giving the advantages of meeting external demand to rival colonies, and they would encourage producers in the hinterland to do business with merchants at other ports who could offer faster turnaround times.[37]

These disadvantages would, said middling exporters, grow worse if the colony persisted in its discriminatory policies against the inhabitants of Boston, East New Jersey, and Connecticut. Aggressive attempts by neighboring governments to attract trade by creating free ports had not abated. As New Yorkers said, "our trade [is] clogged when our neighbors goe free . . . their trade flourisheth, ours decays, they draw away both our riches and people." With rhetorical flourish, merchants on the city's Common Council asked the crown in August 1691, "what merchant will come to New York and trade and pay . . . the excise . . . if they can at two or three miles distance . . . be free from any duty or imposition whatever[?]" Already having lost their bolting monopoly, New York's exporters could only compare their regulated conditions unfavorably to the free ports around them.[38]

In 1693, Customs Collector Charles Lodwick had to agree that New York's

comparatively high import duties, periodic embargoes, and absence of a bolting monopoly were a flawed combination: "our neighbour governments are
wholly exempted from any impositions or customes as are paid att New York;
which greatly discourages the trade of this Province and apparently lessens the
revenue for the support of their Maj'ties interest here." The result: "our merchants and traders [are] removeing thither."[39]

Just how many merchants were relocating to other ports is unclear, but middling inhabitants insisted that bolters, coopers, and small transporters were
leaving the colony regularly.[40] Lesser merchants suspected rural producers who
stayed behind of brash attempts to take control of prices and quality of grain.
"Every Planters hutt throughout the Province is now become a Markett for
wheat Flower and Biskett," cried some. Yet "the Cry in the Streets is the want of
Bread." Why? Because "liberal farmers" attempted to free precious agricultural
commodities from regulations in order to market them at prices, and on conditions, that suited their country interests alone. City exporters also found fault
with merchants who developed large landholdings, men like William Beekman,
whose fortunes continued to rise over the decade. Beekman, argued a few exporters, exacerbated their problems when he set up bolting and gristing operations in the countryside. Together, landed merchants and country millers had
made urban consumption exorbitantly expensive, the former by allowing the
price of grain sold from their estates to rise, and the latter by raising their fees to
farmers. Artificial hoarding, they charged, was only one pernicious by-product
of these practices. Moreover, grain exporters on the Common Council insisted
that free bolting had "taken away the livlihood of two thirds of the Inhabitants
of this Citty." After experiencing the plentiful supplies of grain coming through
New York City in the 1680s, attributed (only partly correctly) to the effects of the
bolting monopoly and regional discrimination, colonists now faced city stocks
reduced from "fourty or fifty thousand Bushells of wheat" in 1692, and to almost none at all by 1698. Merchants could not "procure Corne Enough in Store
to Supply [city] Inhabitants with their dayly Necessities of bread." With appeals
to the "ancient privileges" of the city over its hinterlands, some city merchants
insisted that if colonists put flour bolting under merchants' "Providential Care
and Industry," New Yorkers could "have a Certain Benefit by the Encrease of
[their] Revenue, the husband man A Certain Profitt by having A Mercate for
his Corne and the Province in General A great Advantage by Encourageing the
Citty whereby itt may Grow in Strength and Navigation." At the same time, the
wisest policy would be to drop all discriminatory duties against those who lived
in the interiors of other colonies, who were potentially valuable allies.[41]

James Graham, a flour exporter and temporarily the port collector, noted in

1698 that "the humour now running amongst the most eminent of our people," was divided between wanting "freedoms" and wanting "proteccions." Speaking for the latter group, Graham insisted that without a bolting monopoly, "the market [would be] placed at every Planter's doore through out the Province," and then "every Creek and Bay in the Province is a port, and by that means [colonists] manage their unlawfull trade without controule." Although King William's War exacerbated export conditions, said Graham, provincial harvests had begun to recover their former levels, and the time had come to wrest control from Boston decisively. Otherwise, foreigners would dictate prices and selling conditions to New Yorkers, and other colonies would corner exports from the northern settlements.[42]

When Governor Bellomont assumed office, discussions about the economy took on a heightened factional character that would last for years to come. On the one hand, assemblymen threatened to withhold tax revenues allocated for defense of the port if its merchants pursued the bolting monopoly any further. There had been legislative turmoil over smuggling, piracy, and Leisler, and since Bellomont's salary depended on the Assembly's largesse, he could support no legislation that would renew the city bolting monopoly or impose taxes on flour bolted outside the city. In fact, in 1699 he assented to an Assembly proposal for import duties of 2 percent on all goods entering the city port, 7 percent on all "indian goods," and high taxes on imported rum and wine; in addition, he allowed peltry export duties of 9d. per hide and free exchange of furs in the interior. But he also implored the Assembly to recognize the centrality of New York's international commerce, and sought the support of New York City importers by instituting severe penalties for piracy and removing "Fletcher's traders" from public offices. Equally important, Bellomont pledged to support importers' requests for port discrimination against New England competitors. Persuaded that higher import duties on flour and bread imported from surrounding areas would add revenues to New York City's coffers and preempt landings along the New Jersey coast, where duties could be avoided, Bellomont assented to a new Common Council ordinance to those ends. In short order, he also approved higher duties on "foreign"—that is, neighboring—barrels, woolens, beer, malt, and small boats.[43]

Lesser merchants were consistent losers in all of these activities. A few big wholesalers had diverse enough interests to weather the adversities of the 1690s, but many middling traders relied more and more on grain and flour, which were no longer protected by a city bolting monopoly or quality controls. Some of them complained bitterly that the new port duties were the last straw, and that they would be forced to leave the colony. Into the early eighteenth century,

Governor Cornbury, among others, insisted that flour was "vitiated" by farmers' addition of foreign matter and "ingross'd" by country merchants. City bolters and coopers left the city to be closer to rural supplies of grain and obtain lower prices, which fueled the recurring notion that "the City will in some years be unpeopled." Anxieties were tied inextricably to continuing smuggling along the East Jersey shore, to uncertain supplies of grain and flour for export, and to West Indian markets, where the pendulum kept swinging between high and low prices as merchants of various colonies competed with their irregular supplies of grain and flour. As before, in any given bad season, some lesser merchants faded out of commerce altogether.[44]

Custom and Negotiation in the Interior

Harvests of grain in the Hudson River Valley grew over the years. Until the end of the century, however, few producers had agricultural surpluses to spare for long-distance trade on a regular basis from one season to the next. They oriented most of their producing efforts toward meeting family and local needs first, using traditional farming methods. Moreover, some commodities produced in the interior were less suited to long-distance travel than to trade from community to community, including livestock on the hoof; animal by-products used in making candles, soap, and wax; eggs and cheese, which would spoil on all but short trips to neighboring colonies; and salted butter, fruit, seeds, and saplings. By the 1690s, settlers in almost any locale could acquire a range of necessary commodities from neighbors; they did not need to obtain feathers, herbs, wagons and wagon parts, barrels, cider, or malted beverages from merchants. Flocks and herds in and around New York provided clothing for local markets, but until the eighteenth century, they yielded little extra for other colonies and the West Indies.

Some surpluses exported from the interior may have been an unanticipated means of overcoming the winter scarcities that families and their laborers regularly experienced during the seventeenth century. Few farmers had sufficient capital and labor to plant only one staple crop for long-distance marketing; diversification was a hedge against adversity and the best way to better oneself over time. Moreover, colonial importation was only beginning to rise enough to sustain rural demand for the textiles, agricultural implements, and other goods that farmers would stop making if they turned too quickly, and too thoroughly, toward commercial agriculture. Although a couple of large estate holders directed their laborers to concentrate on one or two exportable commodities, which they traded for finished commodities, the more typical rural producer before 1680 oriented sales of his small surpluses toward New York City only infrequently, rather selling his surpluses at local villages.

For some, suspicions about new market relations continued to shape decisions about trading to faraway places; for others, optimism about controlling prices and conditions of sale grew, because agriculturalists provided vital necessities to colonists and foreigners. Then, too, country producers did not universally accept the commercial instruments of merchants; many colonists persisted in the belief that a locally accountable magistrate should govern economic relations, and they grew fearful of the emergent commercial elite, with all of its aggressive, self-interested characteristics. How was the small producer far from New York City to distinguish trustworthy from untrustworthy exporters? To compound the problem, agricultural producers often sold their surpluses to agents traveling through the countryside, who then ferried the goods of whole villages to New York City; these middlemen were all too often careless with shipments or untrustworthy in remitting the profits of sales back to the countryside. In any event, nonlocal traders might force agriculturalists into dependency on them by means of fees, credit advances, or commercial services.

Questions about the wisdom of more extensive internal trade also preoccupied exporters, for they faced competition not only from neighboring merchants but also from overland wagon masters and peddlers looking for goods to market in the port city—some of which they might resell to exporters or retailers. Expensive transportation also prevented some merchants from integrating markets into more efficient or monopolized systems of distribution. Bad harvests could raise prices exorbitantly without warning. Labor shortages and high wages could make gristing and sawmilling prohibitively expensive as a secondary investment; poor workmanship on barrels and improperly packaged grain diverted many merchants from exploiting disreputable local markets. Exporters lamented that the woolens, leather goods, and salted meat marketed at New York City were readily consumed by the families of craftsmen, small retailers, and sailors there, so that after feeding and clothing New Yorkers, there was little left to export. Likewise, there was only a trickle of imported manufactured goods into the countryside, because local craftsmen in small towns and Albany supplied many necessities.[45]

By the 1680s, merchants were noting clear signs of a change in rural attitudes and trade patterns. Slowly, many settlers in the interior had begun to test the soundness, and profitability, of selling their small agricultural surpluses to country merchants and city exporters. Soon, they began to send small amounts of grain and flour regularly on sloops to New York City, and the boldest of them began to extract, process, mill, and transport goods to the city themselves when they perceived the conditions of sale there to be beneficial. Without introducing new technology or significantly altering rural social relations, the quantities of exportable grain and flour issuing from New York's hinterlands rose noticeably. Having settled into rural patterns of cultivation, harvest, and the internal development of local villages, myriad rural families had passed the earliest stages of intensely converting the frontier and overcoming scarcities.

In time, this trade drew farmers into more sophisticated business relations, which evoked more complicated compromises among the various economic interests throughout the province, even when rural producers' techniques remained the same and local social expectations about trade harked back to a distant past. Indeed, country producers entering markets away from their familiar surroundings, whether by plan or because of unanticipated bounty, did not uniformly or unquestioningly adopt the attitudes to money, credit, and prices to which exporting merchants had become accustomed. They learned that shortages of specie in their economy became consequential as soon as anyone exchanged goods away from his immediate rural locale, thereby promoting all buyers and sellers to seek credit and accept debt networks. But it did not necessarily follow that farmers should develop all of the credit and debt arrangements that merchants did. Early on, for example, country producers found merchants' bills of exchange or notes for long credit from London to be useless when they returned to rural settings. Instead, they preferred the benefits of barter, commodity money, and book credit in daily affairs.

Barter was useful primarily in local exchanges and endured in the seventeenth century as a means to compensate for scarce money. Jasper Danckaerts noted, with only some exaggeration, that "no money circulated among themselves, and they pay each other in wares." During the Dutch period, colonists had been permitted to pay some provincial taxes with beaver pelts, which presumably could be exported on the Dutch West India Company's account against commercial credits in Amsterdam. Beaver continued to be a useful exchange commodity into the 1680s, when merchants sometimes paid export duties with peltry; by then, however, English officials forbade transmitting peltry abroad to meet payments, and most hides were offered for sale to local furriers in order to get cash or bills of exchange for commercial transactions.

By then, too, wampum supplies had diminished so that it was no longer reliably available as a medium of exchange. Instead, farm goods—butter, feathers, wood products, cheese—often served as commodity money. Wholesalers doubtless found payment in kind and commodity exchange to be cumbersome, especially when it involved perishable goods; many of them gave commodities a money valuation if they were intended to be exchanged for merchants' imports and offered discounts for purchasing goods with specie. Rural traders seem to have accepted merchants' practice of raising the prices of imports that they sold to the interior in order to compensate for the inconveniences of commodity money. After all, the merchant would subsequently have to enter into another negotiation with city retailers or the owners of market stalls to dispose of farm goods he could not use or obtain convertible bills of exchange.[46]

Book credit was also available and probably widespread by the end of the century. By entering credits in money amounts without exchanging goods and services reciprocally, farmers and storekeepers created an intangible purchasing power that could be called upon or transferred to another person as debt payment without needing cash in hand. Storekeepers' advances and loans to rural consumers or merchants' agents might take the form of book credit, which was entered in the money of account, usually wampum or sterling until the end of the century. However, balancing accounts often entailed further exchange of goods—merchants' imports, for example—which domestic producers did not necessarily want, and could not transport conveniently. Moreover, producers in the Albany and Esopus areas sometimes found it inconvenient to accept payment in kind or notes good for purchases in New York City. Under these circumstances, cash was preferable to goods, and rural people increasingly asked for payments in a more transportable and convertible medium accepted at any place and at any time in the colony.

Rural producers were able to enter both local and long-distance markets most effectively by variously using commodity money, book credit, and cash, thereby permitting new kinds of economic exchange to bind them to exporting merchants when desirable. They also learned that flexibility in negotiating the prices of their goods was more effective than appeals to customary prices. Traditionally, prices were thought to represent a true measure of the worth of a good or service to a purchaser, or a true measure of the labor added to natural resources by the seller. And in familiar local conditions, country sellers continued to conceptualize prices as a calculation based upon economic justice and the mutual best advantage of the exchanging parties. But long-distance commerce and its train of credit, goods, middlemen, and degree of anonymity just as easily introduced reconsideration of prices. Early in the province's history, traditional views coexisted alongside emergent ones. For example, early in the colony's history the manor lord Kiliaen van Rensselaer drew a line between familiar, nearby associates and those who were resident in New York City. In writing to his agent in the port city, Van Rensselaer noted that a 50 percent markup on imports was his break-even point, the wholesale price plus all charges he had incurred during importation. "Therefore," he instructed the agent, "[you] must sell all such goods as can bear it, somewhat higher than 50%. But I do not wish my own people [on his estate] to be charged more than 60% since they must gain it by hard labor. But from other people, for whom I need not care, you may take as much as is the market rate you can get."[47]

Van Rensselaer's distinction between custom and competition occurred at a time when many early-modern observers were reevaluating the origins and meaning of money. Some English writers—including Gerard de Malynes, Sir William Petty, and John Locke—urged readers to connect the money supply to everyday transactions and the general welfare. Money, they argued, had more than an intrinsic value; it was also the measure of value of commodities and a means by which to circulate the goods of a nation. Greater amounts of money in circulation would reduce the values of all commodities in the same markets, bring down prices, stimulate consumption, and increase domestic production.[48] Other writers went further by the end of the seventeenth century: prices would derive from the level of productivity and the speed of circulation; in the marketplace, myriad private transactions, completed by individual reckoning and demand, created "natural prices" that were far more equitable than government declarations. The market, not price fixing, was "the best Judge of Value," said Nicholas Barbon.[49]

Seventeenth-century New Yorkers lived with many ambiguities about domestic money, credit, and markets. Already, exporters had argued for a mixture of freedoms and restraints: lower duties, open external ports, repeal of export embargoes, quality controls, and city monopolies. The regulations they supported drew upon both traditional and mercantile wisdoms about the corporatist character of economies. And the economic freedom they envisioned never entailed unlimited universal competition. Similarly, rural producers were becoming sensitized to a range of ways to manipulate prices to serve one or another conflicting interest. Van Rensselaer's reasoning about different economic interests proved infectious in the hinterland. Before the end of the seventeenth century, many rural producers did not hesitate to enter the confusing whirlpool of fluctuating demand and negotiable prices. Farmers and shopkeepers who otherwise adhered to local regulation of economic activities adapted to regional or international prices that followed the imperatives of supply and demand. Indeed, their success in wresting agreeable prices for grain and flour they sold to New York exporters drove them into opposition to the bolting monopoly. Bolting at New York City introduced the risks and costs of transport to the port, loss of timely information about millers' prices, and nagging middlemen's fees. After 1690, they were free to find a miller who gave the best prices for gristing, or to wait until millers' seasonal prices rose. With respect to lumber and small agricultural surpluses, they actively sought long credit from nearby retailers or argued with merchants over prices. More often than not, they could demand higher gate prices on the assumption that they had what city and foreign consumers needed.[50]

Rising agricultural prices were the bane of international traders. Nevertheless, country producers pushed up the prices of grain, flour, flaxseed, and timber products about 20 percent in some years of the 1690s. Then, after fluctuations at the end of the 1690s, prices rose between 60 and 70 percent at the opening of the eighteenth century.[51] By then, some of the great landlords of the valley had reached a level of improvement that permitted them to exercise even more authority over rural gate prices than independent farmers had. The Philipse, Robinson, and Kip families, for example, regularly "set the market for their wheat" sent to the port city. Not surprisingly, Robert R. Livingston, whose many rural enterprises included gristing and bolting, criticized commercial policies enacted by "city interests" and insisted that internal development depended on free bolting. Frederick Philipse, whose estates were already producing great quantities of exportable grain and flour, welcomed the bolting monopoly's defeat because it coincided with his vigorous building of mills, blacksmith shops, and cooperage works at his main manor after 1693. Freedom to make marketing choices without the encumbrances of legislation that taxed and channeled his exports was a vital component to enhancing his wealth. Along with others of the "landed interest," Philipse argued that fixed prices were "a grievance and a violation of the people's property."[52]

Merchant exporters continued to argue for relatively fixed conditions of purchase from commercial farmers, and for quality controls over agricultural exports. At the same time, they lived by competitive prices in international trade. They regularly cited fluctuating market evaluations, or "prices current," in their correspondence, calculated balances of credit obligations in specie, paid or earned interest in changing percentages, and offered varying discounts to other merchants in order to speed the circulation of bills of exchange. Until the 1720s, there were no newspapers in New York to cite the prices current, but long before that colonists had inched toward a new conceptualization of prices.[53] Most farmers and merchants accepted the notion that prices were open regularly to renegotiation, and they were equally likely to reject attempts to fix prices at "perpetual" ceilings; in most years they entered "liberal trade" in the region for linens, woolens, sugar, and small finished goods.[54]

When merchant exporters attempted to impose some expected price, or condition of sale, on rural producers, they were liable to meet with utter frustration. Gerard Beekman, for example, told Henry Lloyd of Boston exactly how

much he would allow for casking, cartage, storage, and commissions in exporting flaxseed to Ireland; if the price of flaxseed should rise too high locally, he
would lose foreign markets and, he told Lloyd, "it will not be worth your While
either." Small producers would have to take the price exporters offered for their
flaxseed or see the commodity pile up in their barns; for their part, he predicted,
merchants would collude with one another to standardize the "best price." But
Beekman and his kind delivered more threats than cheap flaxseed, however, for
in contrast to the myriad municipal regulations of market days in New York
City, designated terms of sale at city stalls, and city retailing laws, they won
comparatively little regulation of exchange throughout the interior.[55]

Lesser merchants, who depended far more upon trade within the region for
goods to fill their vessels than upon transatlantic communication, could justify
paying farmers higher prices for grain only when Caribbean orders were certain. Barely able to afford the initial investment of foreign commerce, they were
the first to retrench in times of high internal gate prices and low prices for their
grain and flour in the West Indies. Furthermore, lesser merchants were, by definition, also middling consumers, who could ill afford to pay higher prices for
food in New York City. Eminent traders, who had connections with the great
firms in England that supplied colonists with imports, and who had more diversified exporting activities, could endure seasonal fluctuations of prices because they had larger reserves of capital and goods, which enabled them to avoid
exporting any particular commodity when farmers' prices rose steeply.

After three decades of rule by English governors and settlement by predom-
inantly English immigrants, the colony had shifted the focus of its exporting
decisively from furs to agricultural surpluses. To be sure, few servants or wage
laborers resided on the small farms dotting the area beyond the port city's immediate trading orbit; and few farmers specialized their production for market
exchange yet. Still, market prices and money relations became more important
in settlers' overall networks of buying and selling, and the port city's fate was
tied ever more to the development of its hinterlands. In this process, merchants
who had argued strenuously against port duties and mercantile regulations,
repeatedly appealed to this same regulatory model when acquiring exports of
grain, dairy products, timber products, salted meat, and other goods sent from
farms surrounding the port. These commodities were relatively unaffected by
English mercantile legislation, but New York merchants argued that they should
be brought under their own regulatory aegis because the region's internal agricultural surpluses were the source of their greatest economic expansion.

By 1700, New York's grain exporters—most of them lesser merchants—had
thoroughly rehearsed their demands for economic regulation, and they saw

little contradiction between those demands and their hopes for economic freedom in external commerce. Nevertheless, the most consequential regulation—the bolting monopoly—had been defeated by the economic interests of many landed magnates, commercial farmers, millers, and small transporters, and, in a temporary political guise, Leislerians. However much rural producers adhered to customary concerns in their local and household economies, those who chose to enter commercial relations gained a significant degree of competitive, private control over provincial markets and prices.

Over the next century, these conflicts recurred, albeit less urgently and less frequently. Grain and flour production rose dramatically, the countryside acquired a more settled appearance, and partners to exchanges began to regularize their expectations. Occasionally, great demand for grain and flour in the West Indies or southern Europe permitted New York's exporters to offset farmers' high gate prices by passing on the increase to foreign buyers. Farmers' prices and productivity rose comparatively faster, too, than prices of many imported manufactures, which in turn fueled their expectations of material advancement.[56] Eventually, however, the prosperity farmers and exporters enjoyed gave rise to new conundrums for New York's political economy: whether, and what, to manufacture for themselves and others; and the effect of new kinds of consumption on the people of the province.

Part II

Encounters with Imperial Maturity

Chapter Five

The Spur of Success

Ideology and Experience in
Transatlantic Trade, 1700–1760

NEW YORK CITY'S INTERNATIONAL COMMERCE grew in both planned and unanticipated ways during the eighteenth century. New routes, more immigrants ambitious about trading abroad, more credit and debt dependencies, new goods that changed importers' and consumers' perspectives on their material condition, and innovative approaches to extending trade opportunities—in each way, city residents witnessed their own commercial maturation. Ethnic quarrels between Dutch and English families were not quashed in the first half of the eighteenth century, but their most visible public manifestations subsided. Piracy almost disappeared in Atlantic waters, but privateering and smuggling rose to unprecedented highs.

To the casual eye, many things about the merchant community did not change in the eighteenth century. Aside from their larger numbers, the city's elite continued to seek their profits in transatlantic trade with Britain, southern Europe, and the Low Countries, while the middling merchants found more opportunities in the coastal and West Indian trade. Many day-to-day concerns—about quality of goods, the level of import duties, and the city's competition abroad—united merchants in opposition to other interests. But material changes also created deeper economic and social rifts in the trading community. Between 1700 and 1760, the gap between elite and middling merchants grew wider, whether colonists evaluated the degrees of social and cultural refinement, counted the ships at the New York docks, or took note of family tax assessments and inheritances. Then, too, shifting groups of city merchants disagreed about the appropriate strategies for protecting and extending trade, and diverged in their perceptions about new consumption, manufacturing, and the place of merchants in the political economy. By the eve of the imperial crisis, city exporters and importers were at once a "community" with certain shared concerns and a stratified, shifting collective of interests, nurtured in the rhythms of business cycles, interimperial warfare, and the different arenas in which merchants conducted their commerce. Over the century, imperial authorities also learned to think of New York City merchants in dual terms: on the one hand, English authorities greeted New York's maturing commerce as an important contribution to the strength of the empire; on the other, they grew to fear the colony's potential for prospering beyond the allowable parameters mercantilism had established.

Shifting Rationales for Freedom and Regulation

New York's eighteenth-century commercial development continued to be linked to England's maturing economy and its changing definitions of empire abroad. Between the Dutch defeat in 1674 and 1702, England's registered exports to northern colonies tripled; after more than a century of contention, the Dutch had become England's subordinate in western commerce. English observers began to connect urbanization and nonagricultural growth to the home country's ability to produce more food and clothing in the countryside, develop new transportation linkages and more sophisticated distribution networks, and specialize in the production of cheaper necessities that reached great numbers of consumers throughout the empire. Praise for "trade" had begun to encompass not only the ventures of ships to exotic lands but the home crafts and web of activities in the domestic economy that bound country and city inextricably together and linked them both to a world of goods.[1]

The quickening pace and thoroughness of material changes in the empire inspired greater confidence in merchants' activities. "Trade and commerce are the pillars of prosperity and safety to England," said William de Britaine. Carew Reynel seconded this view: "Riches are the convenience of the nation, people are the strength, pleasure and glory of the nation, but trade preserves both." And, wrote James Whiston, commerce was so important that "its neglect will be England's ruin and confusion." Few, however, matched the passion of Daniel Defoe for the trade that was, he said, "the life of the nation, the soul of its felicity, the spring of its wealth, the support of its greatness, and the staff on which both king and parliament must lean, and which (if it should sink) the whole fabric must fall, the body politic would sicken and languish, its power decline, and the figure it makes in the world grow by degrees contemptibly mean."[2]

Merchants' reputations grew along with their opportunities, while England's landed interest entered an era of insecurity and anxiety about domestic social and economic changes. Through self-promotion and greater public visibility, merchants gained a reputation for business acumen that they employed against many odds—pirates on the high seas, deceitful debtors and foreign agents, the vicissitudes of war, and the difficulties of getting agricultural goods to the coast. For centuries merchants had been open to the charge of committing "fraud upon strangers," but by 1700, myriad Englishmen deemed them vital to exchange of provisions and necessities. "Universal merchants," wrote Defoe, "men who carried on foreign correspondences, importing the goods and growth of other countries and exporting the growth and manufactures of [his nation] to other countries," moved goods, united locales, and created linkages between anonymous producers and consumers. They performed an array of activities that included wholesale importing and exporting, shipbuilding, and money lending.[3] As Richard Campbell explained, "Wherever he comes, wherever he lives, Wealth and Plenty follow him; the Poor is set to work, Manufactures flourish, Poverty is Banished, and Public Credit increases." Joseph Addison, who was in many respects ambivalent about the effects of commerce, nevertheless declared: "There are not more useful members in the commonwealth than merchants. They knit mankind together in a mutual course of good offices, distribute the gifts of nature, find work for the poor and wealth for the rich, and [grant] magnificence to the great."[4]

Although commerce introduced higher levels of material comfort, it did not render England a peaceful nation. Over the eighteenth century, the English state engaged in four, increasingly broader, wars, which riveted attention on the enmity of France and Spain. Following Queen Anne's War (1702–13), the Treaty of Utrecht marked the beginning of British preeminence over those countries; by then, England had acquired Nova Scotia, Newfoundland, Gibraltar, Minorca, and Hudson's Bay, as well as the coveted *asiento*—the right to supply African slaves to plantations in the Caribbean and South American colonies—that England won from Spain, and that Parliament bequeathed to the newly chartered South Sea Company. The treaty also established boundaries of colonial expansion that remained relatively unaltered for decades to come, and it gave international traders confidence that England's hegemony could be challenged by other nations only at great risk to themselves. Aggressive expansion into the North American interior and over the Caribbean, argued mercantilists, complemented English manufactures, shipping, and dominion. "Our interest is our Trade," said Daniel Defoe in 1728; "to invade our commerce is to invade our property, and we may and must defend it." France and Spain nonetheless challenged the English balance of power repeatedly in a series of confrontations over settlement and trade, and more warfare, between 1713 and 1763.[5]

For English policy makers, the promise of commerce and the reality of imperial wars heightened the need to shape their national and colonial economies with a more elaborate edifice of regulations. At home, they argued, revenues should be raised from exportation and excises on luxury goods. By 1705, British export duties on manufactured goods had reached about 15 percent; by 1745, they stood at 20 percent; and by 1759, they topped 25 percent, more than colonists in British North America would ever be asked to endure. Equally important, many mercantilist writers presumed that England's power would increase at the expense of other nations; over a century after Sir Francis Bacon's famous phrase "Beggar thy neighbor" became public property, Joseph Harris insisted that there should be "a limit to the vent and consumption of all sorts of commodities" in the nation, and Matthew Decker believed that "if the Exports of Britain exceed its Imports, Foreigners must pay the balance in Treasure and the Nation grow Rich." Even as commentators heralded the salutary effects of the financial revolution, new credit relations, and flexible instruments of exchange, they continued to subscribe to the influential, if mechanistic, balance-of-trade theory.[6]

England's colonies had become close, although subordinate, partners in this plan. "Colonies are the strength of the kingdom, while they are under good discipline, while they are made to observe the fundamental laws of this original country, and while they are kept dependent upon it," Charles Davenant wrote. Half a century later, Malachy Postlethwayt restated Davenant's sentiments: "Colonies ought never to forget what they owe to their mother country in return for the prosperity and riches they enjoy. Their gratitude . . . and the duty they owe, indispensably oblige them to be immediately dependant on their original parent." Over the eighteenth century, writers elaborated on this view of obedience with the complementary one of colonists' "unrefined" economic efforts and consumption of England's finished goods. The appetites and ambitions of colonists had the potential to grow without limit, as they would in any collective of successful human beings; but "the very nature of colonies" demanded "that they ought to have no culture or arts, wherein to rival the arts and culture of their parent country," for "colonies cannot in justice consume foreign commodities, with an equivalent for which their mother country consents to supply them; nor sell to foreigners, such of their own commodities as their mother country consents to receive." As state makers worried about the importation of French luxuries and the excesses of the English aristocracy, they expressed corresponding concerns in the new century about whether colonists knew how to reasonably restrain their new consuming habits.[7]

Just where the boundaries of this restraint lay, and how colonists might recognize them, remained unclear. Even while professing their dependent circumstances, colonial merchants pursued commercial opportunities that radiated outward from colonial and English ports into unplanned channels. For example, few English observers denied that the rise of the northern "bread colonies" depended on rising demand in the West Indies. Even governors knew that "there is no island the British possess in the West Indies, that is capable of subsisting without the assistance of the Continent," for England could not supply the islands with commodities in large enough quantities or at cheap enough prices, and West Indian planters provided New Yorkers with valuable specie and bills of exchange to pay debts elsewhere in the empire. By 1720, West Indian sugar planters imported nearly as many shiploads of necessary foodstuffs, other provisions, and work animals from New England and New York as of finished goods from England. Within another decade, New Yorkers were shipping more goods to British islands in the West Indies than they could absorb, with the result that colonists were tempted into the ports of foreign islands on a regular basis.[8]

Non-British transatlantic trade drew worried comments from policy makers in London. Joshua Gee, for example, argued in 1721 that although English subjects paid taxes on textiles and clothing manufactured in the home country, colonists obtained these commodities at wholesale cost plus "minimal" merchants' markups because of generous drawbacks for exporting these goods to the colonies. But colonists failed to appreciate this "free traffick" and chose instead to do business in "several ships, the major part of whose owners live in Holland," which were loaded "with linnens, threads, and other Dutch effects" that colonists needed and English manufacturers could not supply as cheaply. Unless a duty were laid on these goods in the colonies, said Gee, "foreigners [would] run away with our Trade."[9]

As New York's merchants became increasingly capable and willing to satisfy the material needs and wants of a growing population by reaching out to new markets, mercantilists in England resolved to regulate more colonial trade. Some laws bolstered staples production in the West Indies, some prohibited trade with the enemy and smuggling, and some curtailed colonial manufacturing. Their object was to protect, tax, and channel trade in all segments of the empire in the interests of England's national stability. Never thorough, never systematic, these policies built upon the procedures and bureaucracies that had been created in the seventeenth century.

After 1699, new legislation, some of which directly affected New York's wholesalers, enumerated specific commodities: the waning fur trade was still taxed; new regulations were imposed on naval stores, masts, dyewoods, and whale oil; new laws covered the voyages of vessels, the size and origins of crews, and the ownership and conduct of ventures; fees and drawbacks circumscribed many activities. By then, enumeration also covered staples that New Yorkers reexported in significant quantities or consumed in the colony: sugar, indigo, ginger, and cotton wool. Between 1705 and 1727, Parliament added more goods of consequence for New Yorkers' carrying trade, including hemp, rice, molasses, fur hats, wine, and flaxseed. Direct trade to French Canada, Amsterdam, southern Europe, and Ireland became more difficult when Parliament put enforcement machinery into place. By the late 1720s, unparalleled lobbying efforts by English planters in the West Indies, whose estates and capital investments in sugar, molasses, and slaves had eroded slowly because of lower prices at foreign islands, pressured Parliament to legislate on their behalf. Their arguments made clear that New York merchants benefited doubly from lower buying prices for sugar at Dutch and French islands and higher selling prices for colonial provisions. Passage of the Molasses Act in 1733 was a triumph for the view that government regulations ought to force colonial trade back into English ports, so that planters could better dispose of their goods and eliminate their need to "sell excessively low" in order to get northern colonial business.[10]

Lengthening lists of enumerated goods affected transatlantic wholesalers differently than their lesser peers in the coastwise and West Indian trades. Overall, the new regulations proved less detrimental for merchants who were distinguished by their successful English connections than they were for the merchant majority; anyway, dry-goods importers accepted a degree of restraint because it was offset by the security of membership in the empire. Moreover, when exchange rates for specie payments rose too fast some seasons—usually a function of trade conditions in the West Indies—city merchants could look forward to getting British bounties and drawbacks, and to orders for New York vessels. Then, too, transatlantic importers enjoyed rapidly growing opportunities to import, not only English manufactures, but "European goods" as well. And they were the major beneficiaries of a burgeoning reexport trade in West Indian goods acquired, most often, by lesser merchants. Proof of their commercial gain was visible in the accoutrements of commerce, city real estate, slaves, and household refinements they touted.[11]

It was otherwise with coastal and West Indies merchants. In the first place, grain, flour, salted meats, livestock, fish, and staves and boards, their most important commodities of trade, left the colony freely. The quantities of these goods exported from the colony rose precipitously after 1700, enriching many new young city traders. Secondly, these merchants had long since discovered easy ways selectively to violate the mercantile code. Indeed, as the principles of regulation and subordination gained more legal coherence, thereby providing some merchants with the order and protection they needed, others with greater frequency rehearsed the benefits of open ports and smuggling. Most significant of all, lesser merchants had become accustomed to marketing their goods at many West Indian ports, including foreign ones. The new enforcement machinery accompanying Parliament's stepped-up enumeration threatened to become the most onerous burden of all the changes introduced.

The combined impact of rising colonial productivity and exportation, and merchants' habits of smuggling and foreign trade, reinforced the appeal of free-trade ideas after Queen Anne's War. Free-trade thinking owed much to policy reformulations during the eighteenth century. Until 1713, the official definition of "free trade" held that the rights of merchants to transport goods in wartime were defined by the neutrality of commodities rather than the destination port or registration of the ship. Thereafter, the ability to transport goods freely depended upon the status of the vessel's owners and port of origin; goods transported on enemy vessels were no longer neutral, but "infected," which enabled privateers to plunder foreign competitors on the high seas when other risks were low.

The new definition also invited merchants to distinguish between unethical trade with foreign nations, and the benefits of more open commerce within the empire. Already New Yorkers were familiar with such arguments, as when they debated discrimination against New England and New Jersey. In England, Joshua Gee promoted more thorough exclusion of foreigners from colonial trade over the 1720s, but he also believed that so long as colonists purchased manufactured goods from England, there should be a "free trade in provisions and staples" between the northern colonies and the West Indies. For Gee, and other writers, the empire was to be a closed system of mutually dependent Britons, in which lawgivers need not be overly concerned about restraint if colonists were obedient about how, and with whom, they traded.[12]

The new conceptualizations of commercial freedom in the empire also evoked criticisms of the nation-as-war-machine, consuming endless taxes and goods. Universal human appetite, free-trade advocates wrote, would drive the industry, exchange, and development of British subjects. The most radical critics of regulatory measures claimed that international peace would follow from allowing the natural behavior of prices and appetite for new goods to unfold.[13]

In New York City, a vocal minority of merchants found that the tenets of colonial subordination sat ill with this promise of mutuality throughout the empire. This was especially true of lesser merchants in the West Indies and coastal trades. The mercantile model worked relatively well when these ambitious, rising traders aimed to bring the economic region under urban control, but these same merchants wished to pursue unimpeded opportunities for commerce throughout the Atlantic. Thus, while formulations about economic freedom were muted by the salutary effects of the visible hand of government, they provided inspiration for myriad autonomous activities away from the colony. Ironically, the city's lesser wholesalers experienced fewer imperial constraints of a direct sort, but their comparatively more fragile positions in commerce fueled greater sensitivity about economic regulations and more volatile reactions to the few imperial impositions that were passed over the century. Cornelius Cuyler was one New Yorker who believed that the city's rise had been slowed over the early eighteenth century "for want of a Free Trade."[14]

The Ladder of Success

New York City's population growth in the eighteenth century was a baseline for commercial growth. A 1703 city census revealed a population of 4,500 white residents and 750 slaves; of the former, 110 were listed as "merchants." Of course, New Yorkers did not need to be reminded that their city was small compared to London, with 550,000 inhabitants in 1700, or Amsterdam, with 250,000. Still, New York County had grown to 6,622 white and black inhabitants by 1731, of whom 2,250 were white males over 10 years of age. By then the top 10 percent of the city's taxpayers owned 46 percent of the assessed wealth, and the entire colony had grown to over 50,000. By 1737, the city population had climbed to 8,800, and in the next thirty years, it grew to about 17,000, while the colony as a whole increased to over 120,000. By 1771, estimates of the city's population climbed to 19,000, of whom at least 299 were merchants.[15]

As imperial and colonial officials puzzled over the permissible limits of merchants' activities, the bewildering gyrations of boom and recession focused many colonists' attention on very immediate concerns. They could not agree about the causes of the periodic recessions they faced. Hard times, said some, stemmed from Philadelphia merchants' ability by the 1720s to deliver better quality and cheaper commodities to West Indies markets. Others found fault with provincial export duties or the provincial Assembly's decision to allow a tonnage duty on "foreign" ships from Bermuda, Boston, Newport, and other places, enacted in 1715, to lapse after 1721. Still others blamed the reduced shipping on more successful merchants said to have conspired with foreign traders to corner markets. And some critics charged that instead of investing in shipbuilding or new processing industries in New York, a few wealthy traders indulged in "a kind of usurye" by loaning money to the government or English

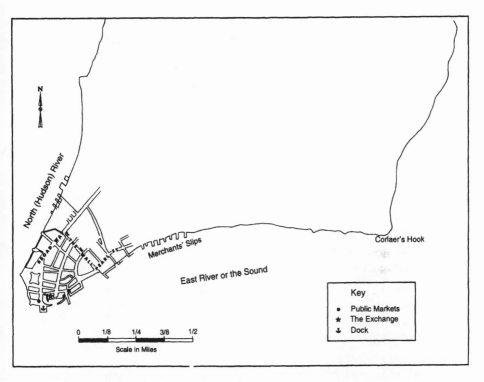

Map 3. The Extent of New York City in about 1695. The placement of streets and commercial activities is based on I. N. Stokes, *The Iconography of Manhattan Island, 1498–1909* (New York, 1915–32), vols. 1–2.

factors at a steep 8 percent interest. "Usury," like the drainage of specie to pay English creditors, tied up specie that might otherwise have "oyled commercial wheels," and "salve[d] wounded interests."[16]

Try as they might to provide satisfactory explanations for recurring recessions, colonists were helpless to prevent them. Warfare from 1689 to 1697 had produced acute economic stagnation, and the renewed hostilities of Queen Anne's War after 1702 caused yet another slump and the loss of many vessels. In both cases, exporters were unable to get goods out of New York safely to destined ports; during the second war, exports filled an average of only four ships per quarter from 1701 to 1704 because of the dangers of transatlantic commerce, tight English credit, and Boston's ability to attract more of the region's trade with lower port duties. Although 74 vessels entered and cleared the port of New York from June 1701 to May 1702, most of them were English-owned. Aspire as they might to look and act like the great merchants of London, with their town houses and coaches, New Yorkers who were not already opulent in 1700 rarely rose to such heights during the early years of the eighteenth century.[17]

After a brief flurry of recovery following the war—in 1715 there were an astounding 391 entrances and clearances at New York—hard times came again in the early 1720s. Isaac Bobin wrote George Clarke in England in 1721 that there was "a Consumption of Trade," "a Languishing Commerce," in the city. Even in 1734, Governor William Cosby wrote that immigration had all but halted and tradesmen had only "expiring hopes" that shipbuilding would revive. "John Trusty" lamented the multiple scourge of New York's "Deadness of Trade" in the early 1730s: "Our shipping are sunk. And our Ship-building almost entirely lost. Navigation is in a Manner gone; and Foreigners are become our Carriers, who have been continually draining us of that Money, which formerly was paid to our Seamen." A much-reduced fleet since Queen Anne's War also stymied the capacity of merchants to export agricultural surpluses from 1716 to about 1734; from a fleet of 125 vessels in 1700—fourteen of them oceangoing—it shrank to 67 in 1715, and to 50 in 1734. When demand for exports failed to recover quickly, merchants had little available capital or incentive to build more vessels; imports also fell 14 to 24 percent below 1722 levels during 1726 to 1736. Although the population of the city rose 22 percent over the 1720s, shipbuilding and new registrations languished.[18]

New York lagged behind both Boston before 1730 and Philadelphia after 1750 in the construction of new vessels and the number of clearances, but between those dates a few prominent city importers flourished. For those who had already established important ties of credit, reputation, and marriage with London firms, inbound vessels brought more dry goods in 1738 and 1739 than colonists had seen for many years, and "invisible earnings" from new vessel registrations and shipping fees rose; indeed, these were signs that colonists were winning away from English merchants more of their own ability to carry commodities. But not all city merchants recovered in that decade. Robert Livingston Jr. and Peter Livingston, for example, failed to sell even modest imports of cloth from 1735 to 1737, and many middling merchants competed for sales to neighboring colonists along the coastline, sending out vessels averaging only forty tons and dreaming of voyages across the Atlantic. For them, commerce did not confer significant opportunity and profits in the third decade of the century; there were more rungs on the ladder of assessment that separated the middling from the eminent international wholesalers over the 1730s and 1740s.[19]

Between the 1730s and the time Parliament began to reorganize the empire in 1763, transatlantic traders carried larger weights and values of goods to England and brought more goods home to colonists, but because of the tremendous development of other areas of trade, the proportion of all New York trade to England did not grow. Then a postwar recession, beginning in 1764, marked by gluts of goods and severe specie shortages, undermined their very best calculations and disrupted long-distance trust. Colonists' first nonimportation movement, organized to effect repeal of loathsome imperial legislation and spur trade, rekindled some optimism, as did the confidence of a few great dry-goods importers that they would soon return to commerce as usual. But over subsequent years the proportion of trade merchants conducted with England, Holland, Ireland, and southern Europe on their own accounts did not grow. The level of total transatlantic exports and imports changed little in its overall character during these final colonial years—even as it sustained the economic foundations of New York.[20]

Still, in their methods of doing business, the social roles ascribed to traders, and a host of accidental circumstances, the great dry-goods importers were quite distinguishable from others who made a living buying and selling goods. A peddler, or "gypsy merchant," for example, often borrowed cash to purchase from the docks or warehouses, or from retail shopkeepers, the goods that did not sell quickly, slightly damaged, moldy, or out-of-fashion wares that went for "a fair price under" the "first price" of commodities, and sold them outside the city. In an unstable economy such as New York's was at times, a peddler's ability to transmit information about prices or become the conduit for interpersonal deals was valuable indeed. But few peddlers rose as high as Haym Solomon, who prospered enough to buy a small shop, from which he sold textiles and sewing notions, and then to venture into coastal ports as part-owner of two or three vessels. Solomon became a sutler in the Revolutionary War, and after 1777, he spied for the patriots, escaped British capture, and fled to Philadelphia, where he became Robert Morris's chief broker of currencies; he ended his career as a creditor to James Madison.[21]

More typical among peddlers, however, were the individuals who learned a craft or provided services as tradesmen or shopkeepers. Colonists associated peddlers with smuggling, trafficking in illicit goods, and secreting stolen items —although this was true of some of the wealthiest traders of New York City as well—and talking fast to cheat customers. Peddlers were known to take advantage of their face-to-face encounters with women who were at home unattended by adult males, as when the petty trader Jacob Lucena was arrested in 1670 for liaisons throughout New York and Connecticut. A New York court charged him with being "notorious in his lascivious daliance and wanton carriage and profers to severall women." Other peddlers attracted notoriety as members of an imagined underworld of rabble and criminals and were derided as hucksters, "Lying and Cheating grimy Strangers" who undersold sedentary entrepreneurs or closed off potential markets by going directly to the customer. City suppliers increasingly criticized itinerant salesmen who slipped through the nets of indebtedness, and a 1738 law that required them to obtain licenses and limit their hours of selling in the city. In 1752, city merchants promoted additional legislation to exclude peddlers from city markets and auctions, and in 1766, attesting to their continued presence, a provincial law prohibited them from selling anywhere in the colony.[22]

The separation between retailers and international wholesalers was never complete in the colonial era, for some wholesalers often marketed imports in their own stores, and a few retailers ventured abroad with established merchants. The two groups were more distinct by the 1720s, however, both in the public mind and in practice. Some storekeepers started with only a small amount of capital earned as skilled craftsmen or brought to New York from Europe or the West Indies as investment capital. Sidelines of repair work, bookkeeping, notary or minor legal services boosted the incomes of others. The retailers Richard Sause, John Milligan, Samuel Deall, and Henry William Stiegel supplemented their specialized sales of wine, sugar, and candy by lending small sums to local inhabitants, for example, and their account books show that they were sometimes owed debts large enough to threaten them with economic misery.[23]

Larger stores in Dock Ward, close to the waterfront, tended to be owned by former wholesalers who had been "men of substantiall means," for prosperous shopkeepers who had succeeded earlier as wholesalers sometimes decided to go into the retail business at the end of their careers. Based on his access to the colony's internal markets, including estate holders in the Hudson River Valley, John Wetherhead made standing commitments to a few importers to sell whatever they acquired. Elias Desbrosses' widow converted her husband's Canary-wine-importing business to a retail trade, and eventually added sundry English dry goods to her stocks. William Bradford sold coffee, tea, oatmeal, and a variety of textiles in his printer's shop; John Miller started out importing seeds and agricultural tools but expanded to include cosmetics, drugs, cutlery, and groceries in the mid 1730s. Gerard Duyckinck's "Universal Store" supplied hundreds of different items to customers in the New York area, including country estate holders and urban wholesalers. Giles Sylvester, John Merrett, George Talbott, Samuel Bourdet, John Miller, a Mr. van der Spiegel, and Jane Blundel advertised a variety of both essential and exotic goods in the *New-York Gazette* in the late 1720s.[24]

Shopkeepers were often the first to go under when credit tightened or supply and demand reached serious disequilibrium, usually because they owed wholesalers more than they could collect from numerous petty debtors. The example of Moses Michael Hays is instructive. After rising steadily in his retail watch and clock business, Hays formed a partnership with Myer Polock in the 1750s to import "mechanical goods." Soon their business expanded along two other lines: legitimate trade along the coast, involving all manner of local goods, and a lucrative smuggling business in West Indian rum, brought in through Newport. In the postwar slump of the early 1760s, however, Hays and Polock could not collect even the smallest of payments from their regional debtors, and they were driven to bankruptcy by wholesalers in New York City and London, who dunned them for payment.[25]

Artisan-entrepreneurs like Hays and Polock generally enjoyed a reputable place among the city's middling citizens, but they were vulnerable to public criticism during economic downturns or personal failure. As "inferior burghers" who lacked the credentials to correspond with the great firms in England, they were perceived as squandering their small profits on "exorbitant luxuries" when their personal fortunes faltered. In 1769, for example, the retailer Arnoldus de la Grange was ridiculed by his neighbors because he "dressed up like a great fop," even though he made his living "busily employed in his shop, packing and marking . . . a parcel of ribbons which he was going to send to Barbados." La Grange, scoffed his critics, traded in no more than "tobacco and liquors, thread and pins and other Knick-Knacks." Because of these public perceptions of a man living beyond his means, it was easy to accuse him of "constantly cheating and defrauding" his customers.[26]

Colonists dwelled on the visible distinctions between wholesalers and other kinds of traders, and within the community of wholesalers as well. Homes, carriages, and dress all became symbols of a merchant's place in the world. People watched closely as neighbors and their relations acquired or lost ships, wharf space, credit, slaves, and real estate. Although estimates of the amount of capital required to go into business varied, Edmund Andros believed in 1678 that the £500 to £1,000 necessary for outfitting a venture was available to only the "good substantiall merchant[s]" of the city. Charles Wolley seconded this estimate in 1701, when there were as many as 180 city wholesalers, about 30 of whom had acquired significant family wealth.[27]

Many within this successful minority developed important liaisons with English firms and diversified their trade to include southern European, African, and West Indian ports of call; some of them continued to rise in stature after 1710 by turning from the waning fur trade to provisions and lumber exporting. Samuel Vetch's decision in about 1700 to buy Captain Kidd's house on Pearl Street for £1,000 is indirect evidence of his "substantiall" fortune. Ledgers enumerating imports and exports from 1701 to 1708 show that the twelve most active merchants in the city ordered nearly 60 percent of imported commodities and regularly shared the same ships. One of them, Rip van Dam, had been born in Albany in 1660 of old Dutch stock; he moved to New York City as a young man but stayed firmly linked to the northern fur traders over his adult lifetime, even as he also allied with the landed Livingstons, Beekmans, and Bayards, who helped secure him exportable surpluses of furs and agricultural goods. Van Dam also built an extensive network of correspondents in the West Indies, and ran his own shipyard with the investor James Mills. Van Dam, Abraham de Peyster, and Richard Willet imported well over half of the city's wine in 1703, and from 1713 to 1715, van Dam figured among the city's greatest wine and rum importers and ranked high among dry-goods importers as well. His large family of nine white members and six slaves resided in a "great mansion" on Sloat Land. He served as the city's mayor and then temporarily as provincial governor, from which positions he supported looser provincial regulations and lower export duties. Van Dam's worth was assessed at £330 in 1695, a modest sum for a merchant rising so rapidly; by 1703, he was near the top of the city's assessment list.[28]

More than any other city wholesaler at the beginning of the century, Benjamin Faneuil extended his inherited position to a huge network of family, diversified markets, and foreign liaisons. The son of Peter Faneuil, of the prominent Boston merchant family, and related to the famous Andrew and Peter Jr. of Boston commerce, Benjamin became a freeman of New York City in 1699. Dozens of entries in customs records from 1701 to 1719 show his vessels clearing direct for West Indian ports or entering direct from Antigua, Martinique, Barbados, or St. Thomas with rum, sugar, slaves, and European goods. Just as often, however, his vessels cleared to Boston before proceeding to England or the Caribbean. Boston merchants may have been pleased with Benjamin's efforts to link the two ports, but he was pragmatic about accepting bundles of furs from New Yorkers and sending them wherever demand arose. After carrying peltry to London, his captains often proceeded with a half-cargo of dry goods from London to pick up wine in Madeira and then returned to either New York or Boston. Between 1713 and 1716, Faneuil owned a prize vessel, the *Hope*, which plied between the West Indies and New York thirty times; he also diverted some of his trade from exporting hundreds, even thousands, of skins per year to London to exporting provisions to Barbados, Jamaica, St. Thomas, Hispaniola, and the Bay of Honduras. In 1703, assessors listed Faneuil among the minimal property holders in New York—indeed, as a tenant—but by 1715, he was among the ten most highly assessed merchants in the city, and his jointly owned *Swallow, Royal Prince, Revenge,* and *New York* brought goods regularly from Cowes, Holland, Grenada, and Rhode Island.

Wills and estate inventories, which record end-of-life fortunes, also point to a few outstanding fortunes in the colony's commercial elite. Although Moses Levy's bequest of £8,000 in New York currency when he died in 1728 came nowhere near the £300,000 in sterling that his primary correspondent in London, Isaac Franks, left in 1737, it was among the most notable fortunes of the decade in New York. A few other city merchants died between 1700 and 1745 with estate valuations rated between £2,000 and £4,000; about forty merchants died during those years rated between £550 and £2,000. By their third generations, the Van Cortlandt, Livingston, De Lancey, Beekman, and Philipse families left fortunes that rivaled those of the lesser London merchants with which they did business.[29]

Steven De Lancey, a city resident since 1686, who married Anne van Cortlandt in 1700, combined the two family fortunes to establish a commercial empire that touched at almost every port frequented by New Yorkers. By 1713, he had taken his place alongside the great traders such as Faneuil, De Lucena, Cruger, Gomez, Fresneau, Levy, Pacheco, and Van Dam, and by 1720, he was the sole owner of the *Pearle,* the *St. Stephen,* the *Albany,* and the *Sea Nymph,* and part-owner of many other vessels. Like many other great merchants, he sent a cargo to London only two or three times a year, but the quantities entered or cleared in his name surpassed the trade of his peers during the 1720s. Moreover, De Lancey also ventured logwood, sassafras roots, copper ore, leather goods, and peas to Ireland, St. Thomas, St. Kitts, Bristol, Havana, St. Lucia, and South Carolina. The cargoes he sent to London included such diverse goods as wine, oil, whale fins, snuff, indigo, logwood, coconuts, foreign produce, turpentine, copper ore, ginger, and various household manufactures. Then followed a period of more specialized importation, during which De Lancey's exports tapered off; by late 1729, he was almost solely an importer of dry goods from Dover, Perth Amboy, and London, although his captain made two voyages to Lisbon and Amsterdam that year. In his final years, De Lancey resisted the temptation to retire to the country and continued to import bricks, hemp, wrought iron, and silks. He left his heirs over £100,000 when he died in 1741.[30]

Abraham van Horne and his three sons entered city commerce after Queen Anne's War by outfitting voyages to Madeira with grain and flour, which returned through Boston or Perth Amboy with wine, rum, and English dry goods. In the next few years, they ventured to Campeche for logwood on occasion and shipped horses and lumber goods to Surinam and Curaçao as well. Cornelius van Horne also began to join ventures to Guyana, while continuing to make frequent trips to Madeira, Dover, Cowes, Perth Amboy, and Virginia through the mid 1720s. His brothers, John and Garitt, stopped at South Carolina and Virginia on their way to St. Eustatius, St. Kitts, and the "salt islands." John, who began as a flour bolter and had an assessment of £140 in 1695, rose to join the top thirty merchants in 1703 and 1708. Indeed, the Van Hornes endured the hard times of the 1720s and became one of the first important partnerships to trade with Philadelphia regularly, where Abraham sent frequent cargoes of leather, hides, sassafras roots, and logwood; they also shipped barrels to Amsterdam, along with barrel staves, beeswax, horses, and the family's famed good-quality flour. The Van Hornes together owned at least six vessels—the *Three Brothers*, the *Endeavor*, the *Dragon*, the *Catherine and Mary*, the *Margaret and Mary*, and the *Hope*—and each of them also owned additional shares with three or four other merchants. Cornelius van Horne Jr. figured among the top forty shipowners in 1730 and would carry on the family reputation for at least twenty years to come.[31]

Compared to these individuals, most city merchants aspired to a level of comfort that remained just out of reach, their lives intersecting as closely with those of artisans, shopkeepers, and commercial farmers as with the great traders. Flour exporting brought a merchant close to bakers and millers if he could not hire agents; textile importing required him to associate with tailors and retailers if he did not have hirelings to "break cargo" and distribute it; sugar importing might put him in touch with great reexporters when he transferred the cargo to a larger, oceangoing ship, but it could just as easily bring him into contact with female consumers. A few of the 232 (85% of the total identified) middling merchants who wholesaled for shorter or longer periods of time during the century's first decade rose quickly after Queen Anne's War, when immigrants created demand for imports and agriculturalists produced more exports. But most of them rose and fell in a swirl of shifting opportunities that left them with few household goods and little land even at the ends of their lives.[32]

Tax assessments and customs ledgers at different points during the eighteenth century corroborate this. In 1701, the city assessed 95 merchants taxes; about 20 of them were in the top 10 percent of all wealth holders that year, while at least 59 fell into the next 10 percent; 7 merchants fell into the bottom 50 percent of assessed citizens. That same year, 12 to 15 wholesalers imported a very great share of the dry goods dutied at the port, and over 50 others imported small quantities of dry goods, sugar, Carolina rice, or regional agricultural goods, or exported small parcels of peltry. In the assessment of 1703, 110 of the roughly 1,200 adult male residents whose real estate was taxed styled themselves merchants. Of these, 28 were in the top 15 percent of assessed value and jointly imported about 60 percent of the goods that entered the city legally; they also owned most oceangoing vessels, made the most frequent voyages, and provided most city loans and funds for improvements. Some of this top group had dropped out of sight by the 1708 city assessment, and at least 18 of them imported less by then, despite their having reached generational maturity.[33]

In that same year, 1703, there were over 80 middling wholesalers of fluctuating stature within the trading community. Many had been peltry exporters for decades but secured only modest quantities of skins in any given year; others changed from peltry to grain and flour but gathered only modest quantities of regional exports. Some had only just risen from a modest economic position as regional traders, while others had already reached a point of maturity in their careers, and a few had known better years before entering a period of personal economic decline. Jacob de Kay, for example, owned a house in which five white family members and six slaves lived in 1703, but he often failed to secure supplies from farmers for the West Indies trade or encountered "dead markets" for New York's grain and flour in other colonies. Adrian Hoghlandt, who became a freeman of the city in 1695, was assessed for only £20 of personal and real property that year; by 1703, assessors noted marriage, five children, four slaves, and a house, but his exportation was infrequent and slight, and his widow imported European goods only three times from 1713 to 1715. Adrian's cousin, Johannes Hoghlandt, was rated in 1695 on two homes valued at £115 and other property amounting to £190, and in 1703, his household of four white inhabitants and two slaves indicated only slight advancement toward the top of the bottom third of city taxpayers.[34]

Some of the De Peyster family enjoyed outstanding commercial success early in their careers, but not all members of the family were so fortunate. Johannes de Peyster Sr. died in 1684, leaving his widow to carry on trade; she was assessed for £270 in 1695, one of the top city fortunes that year. Their son "Colonel" Abraham de Peyster may have inherited some of his father's commercial capital by then, but he was widely acknowledged as a premier wine importer and his tax assessment of £1,060 in 1695 included a household containing nine slaves and seven indentured servants. In contrast, the colonel's three brothers never rose into such fortunate circumstances, although their inheritances were roughly equal. Johannes de Peyster Jr., who served as both mayor and alderman in the 1690s, was at the peak of his career when he was assessed below the top forty merchants in 1703 and 1708. Cornelius de Peyster's West Indies trade brought him a £380 assessment in 1695, and a rise into the ranks of the top twenty city merchants by 1703, but he experienced a precipitous decline during Queen Anne's War, when his grain and flour did not reach good markets. Isaac de

Peyster, the third brother, ranked lower in 1695 than his brothers and mother—at £170, or roughly the city average—and although his household had grown by 1703 to include three natural family members, five indentures, and three black slaves, his trade to the West Indies and Perth Amboy was irregular thereafter.

Even without a great inheritance, some sons of these struggling merchants might expect to do better than their fathers by building a sounder commercial reputation and marrying an associate's daughter. A few sons of middling merchants even "married up" the economic ladder after 1720 or pledged their undivided affiliation with eminent merchants. However, these cases represented a small proportion of middling merchants; on the whole, only wealthy men were able to join their own substantial fortunes in marriage to women of roughly parallel social stature. Far more typical were men like John Cholwell, whose trade in European and West Indian goods brought him a low assessment of £90 in 1695 and a ranking close to the bottom third of property holders in 1703; his patterns of trade remained the same over the next few years and could not have raised him much higher in the city's tax ranks. Similarly, Lewis Gomez, born in 1666 and a freeman of New York City by 1706, exported grain and flour to both the West Indies and Madeira, returning with rum and southern European wine through the years of Queen Anne's War. But he never built a "great house" or owned ships outright. Only in the next generation, when Gomez's six sons were inducted into family credit and trading patterns abroad, did the family gain noticeable stature among city merchants.[35]

Expanding one's connections to the interior for supplies of grain and flour was not necessarily a blueprint for rising stature. Cornelius Low, who was born in Kingston on the Hudson in 1670, used his connections there to collect grain surpluses for export to the West Indies; in coming years, his son Cornelius Jr. added numerous small producers from Connecticut and New Jersey to the list of family liaisons, but debts proved difficult to collect and markets hard to meet. Isaac Gabay and Abraham Juneau sent out six to eight small cargoes of grain in 1702, and even in the boom years after Queen Anne's War, they continued to export modest quantities. Gabriel Ludlow developed connections in the United Provinces in the 1680s and continued to send skins and grain there into the 1710s; but his assessment stood at only £25 in 1695, and his inventories remained small. None of these traders owned a vessel, made loans to the government, or borrowed in London; they and many others left their heirs less than a seasonal craftsman's annual income. In fact, 57 of the city's roughly 110 merchants in 1708 had been trading since at least 1701, but only 16 of them rose measurably, while 18 fell from a prominent or a middling assessment level into the lowest third of city taxpayers.[36]

A 1730 city assessment and the 1729–30 shipping returns reveal a "middling" core of traders growing faster than the elite, and failing to close the gap in the scale of their enterprises: 24 merchants in the top 10 percent of city's assessed wealth controlled 54 percent of the entering and clearing tonnage that year, but the remaining city traders—at least 69, and maybe as many as 93 resident merchants—moved few goods and paid only modest taxes. Indeed, bankruptcy and poverty had been inescapable for a significant number of them, even at the ends of their lives. Some, like Isaac Levy, Moses Hart, and Michael Jacobs had promising careers as West Indies traders in their early years, but then lost their edge by 1730, perhaps because of the transatlantic recession of the 1720s. Aaron Machado and Myers Cohen died poor because many colonists owed them back debts, and Peter Marius died in 1702 with dry goods that sold at auction for £446, cash on hand of £148, and debts on his books due from other colonists in the amount of £4,679. Joshua Isaacs left a debt of £9.14.3 in 1744. David "Ready Money" Provoost was one of the few New York merchants who borrowed extensively from London and New York connections to invest in promising ventures, but one after another of his calculated risks turned sour, and he died at about midcentury with £500 less than what he owed.[37]

Transatlantic Patterns of Trade

Dutch trade did not vanish in the decades following the city's conquest, but merchants' attention shifted decidedly toward English firms that could supply New Yorkers' needs and luxuries. For example, the *Blossom*, a New York–owned ship that arrived from London on December 28, 1703, brought a variety of goods that had been ordered by a host of wholesalers and retailers:

David Low	1 box, 1 barrel medicines
Robert Dawkins	1 box women's apparel, sundry rugs, blanketts, chairs, cheese
Cornelius Lodge	1 sm. cask merchandise
Joseph Nunes	3 barrels, 1 box merchandise
Augustus Crossett	55 bars iron, 200 ells brown ozenbrigs
William Smith	1 bale, 2 cases merchandise
David Provoost Jr.	2 bales, 1 box merchandise
Thomas Wenham	23 to 30 casks of ironware, one chest stuffs, 33 to 35 cases sm. armes, 1 to 19 casks of bulletts, 20 to 22 cask lead bars, 47 one box hatts, 41 to 43 bails sail

	cloth, [quantities of] cordage, cables, brimstones, iron shott, reams carbon paper, laces, copper ladles, bills, prime pig iron, wormes, powder, lennengo, cotton, linneing, cloth, strouds
John Barbarie	cotton ruggs, pennistones, gingerlius, kersies
John Hardenburgh	nails
Gabriel Minvielle	iron, broad cloth, strouds, blanketts, cloth, shifts, ozenbrigs, haberdashery, aggott, pins, pennistons shatto; combs, canary seeds
Abraham Wendell	1 case of merchandise
John Tiebold	powder, shott, gloves, silk, calicoes, checked hollands, marling, cordage, haberdashery
Thomas Burrough	2 casks pewter
Robert Lurting & Co.	grinding stones, stuffs, haberdashery, tobacco pipes, blanketts
Hannah Wool	lead, shott, glass goods
Elias Noan	bales of goods, miscellaneous "stuffs"
Stephen De Lancey	duffles and cloth
Gerard Schuyler	iron, pewter, blanketts, "goods"
William Whiting	box of goods
Richard Harris	box and bundle of goods
Arnold Crook	barrels and box of goods
Joshua Solefire	small amount of "goods"
Lewis Richard	iron ware
Solomon Jesreau	household goods
Anthony Brockholst	duffles, blanketts, strouds, lead, powder, sundry goods
Nicholas Bayard	strouds, blanketts, goods, lead, shott, powder
Arendt Schuyler	iron goods, nails, powder
Gabriel Ludlow	seeds, tools, pewter, anvils
Dan Armigoa	small chest of goods
John Burroughs	bales of cloth
Jacob Ballargue	one box medicines

In these early years, traders of all distinctions shared the holds of transatlantic vessels, importing large and small quantities according to their ability. Still, although importation of dry goods involved 133 city merchants in 1701, only a few well-placed importers ventured to bring in wine from southern Europe. As the century progressed, other transatlantic importation was concentrated in the accounts and ships of New York's most advantaged wholesalers. Still, even in 1725, most ships still brought necessities; that year, merchants paid duties on 806 bales of woolens, 854 cases and boxes of linen, 282 trunks of silks, 797 packs of calicoes, hundreds of crates of earthenware, glassware, bottles, tiles, and bricks, and fully 819 grindstones from English firms.[38]

By the early 1730s, New York consumers' tastes for, and English manufacturers' ability to sell, new kinds of commodities became noticeable. What had been deemed luxuries, including coaches, silks, snuff, perfume, and great quantities of tea, entered the colony, along with ever-greater quantities of typical necessities. Textiles and clothing made up about 25 percent of the legal volume of imports from England over the three decades following 1735. Linens and silks continued to arrive regularly, but as the orders of David Clarkson and James Beekman illustrate, manufactured Yorkshire cloth from Bristol, as well as worsteds, cotton checks, tin buttons, diaper, and calico from London, found ready buyers in the colony.[39]

It is not hard to pinpoint reasons for colonists' continuing dependence on London firms for such fundamental household goods. It was "but natural," according to many contemporaries, to exchange necessities throughout all parts of the empire. Textiles were both essential and nondurable. New Yorkers were still unable in the 1730s to provide sufficient quantities of cloth and clothing for themselves. Traditionally, most family members played some role in the continual production of cloth when they were not otherwise engaged in trade, agriculture, or crafts, but New York's families could not keep up with the demands of growing towns and new country settlers who devoted most of their energies to clearing land. Moreover, some items could be imported more cheaply than they could be produced in New York, including certain kinds of textiles. And many craftsmen learned early that they could earn a better living producing household goods that families could not make themselves—barrels and firkins, wagons, axes, wheels, pewterware, rope, shoes—and in turn buy what they might otherwise have tried to produce in their own homes. As colonists specialized more, the prices of some English textiles fell slowly over the eighteenth century, and most dry-goods importers understood them to be a readily saleable commodity.[40]

The 1730s brought other realizations, too. Although the transatlantic trade offered New York merchants greater profits per voyage than most other kinds of commerce, it likewise continued to be a more difficult arena of trade to enter. As a consequence, fewer middling city traders outfitted vessels for England as the century wore on. In mid-career many middling merchants opted for the security of the regional and West Indies trade, and many newcomers chose to avoid British markets. But paralleling this development, goods associated with lavish lifestyles—usually of English and European origin—were both imported by, and enjoyed by, the families of eminent importers. Having assiduously cultivated their taste for new goods, the city's elite began to wrest some transatlantic shipping from London merchants and invest in shipbuilding and shipping services. In the first two decades of the eighteenth century, only some 4 to 10 vessels had been built annually in New York dockyards and registered by provincial owners; nearly half of the colony's entrances and clearances were in English vessels. Around 1730, English merchants still owned about 40 percent of vessels bound for London, but New Yorkers owned 67 percent of those going to the West Indies, 60 percent going to coastal ports, and 25 percent going to southern Europe. In 1738, 53 vessels were registered at New York City, and in 1747, 99 vessels; in 1749, Governor Clinton reported to the Lords of Trade and Plantations that the city's fleet comprised 157 vessels, of 6,406 registered tons. By 1764, city merchants' share of vessels clearing for England had risen to 49 percent, of those bound for the West Indies to 68 percent, and of those going to southern Europe to 42 percent. And New York built vessels carried fully 89 percent of the city's rapidly growing coastal trade.[41]

The importance of New York's shipbuilding was not lost on English merchant firms, as when Kilby, Baker & Co. found that colonists were "able to supply us with ships thirty per cent cheaper than they could be built in Great Britain." New Yorkers were happy to oblige English buyers, for they could ship bulky cargoes from New York to England, sell the goods and ships there, and import lighter finished goods back to New York in someone else's partly full vessel. Exporters to southern Europe often sailed in ballast from the Canaries or Portugal to London, where they sold the colonial vessel and loaded orders for New York into the hold of an English ship. When New Yorkers not only sold a vessel to a London buyer but saved turnaround time by adding orders to another merchant's return cargo, they called it a "double advantage."[42]

One consequence of sinking more capital into shipbuilding was that the city's best-placed merchants also began to concentrate vessel ownership in two or three partners by the 1730s, and some specialized in fewer goods, but larger quantities, from English firms, abandoning the many retailing functions their fathers had performed for decades. Only a few merchants imported the tea that so many colonists had grown accustomed to having by then, but those men rarely imported other commodities by the 1750s, when legal imports probably rivaled the great quantities smuggled directly from foreign ports. Newspaper advertisements of city retailers and contemporary opinion testified that by 1750 tea had become only one—albeit an increasingly important—item in the extensive collection of "superfluities" offered to whet the public's appetite. In 1765, importers brought in legally entered tea valued at £75,410, representing three-fourths of the foreign goods reexported from London to New York. It is hardly surprising, then, to read Levi Coit's encomium to colonial trade in 1759; colonists, he insisted did not take what was "left over" after their English counterparts organized the lion's share transatlantic business; they were equal partners in the great network of imperial trade, like "a torn half of a correspondence fit to its mate half."[43]

Another small coterie of city merchants specialized in reexporting Caribbean goods from New York to England after the 1720s. Typically, they purchased a few containers of sugar or salt, or a full load of logwood, from lesser merchants who were unable to transship to London. Others formed valuable linkages to agents of English firms and performed just part of the voyage. John Theobold, the three Van Horne brothers, Andrew Fresneau, Gilbert Livingston, and Robert Lurting, among others, carried logwood into New York City, where it was loaded onto the English-owned ships *Drake, Hopewell,* or *Benjamin.* Unlike middling city traders, these men did not resell their West Indian goods in New York, thus ending a bilateral voyage. Instead, they reloaded onto English vessels and proceeded to sell the goods on their own accounts in London. Only three city merchants imported southern European wine regularly before 1720— all of them previously successful in other forms of commerce—but into the next decade they created a consignment system in which at least a dozen aspiring merchants at Boston or Rhode Island received foreign wine for them and then forwarded at least some of the bottles and casks to New York, having paid the lower duties in New England.[44]

City merchants shipped wheat, flour, and whale oil to southern European and Newfoundland ports infrequently before the 1720s because of great distances and uncertain demand there, not to mention New York's still-meager exports of those goods. At the beginning of the century, only Samuel Vetch and John Livingston sent the struggling residents of Newfoundland small quantities of flour and barreled meats once or twice a year from New York; their vessels returned with peltry, wine, linens, textiles, and other goods that had been taken from the northern interior or left by English ships. Those few who overcame southern European risks, however, reported prompt payments in cash and bills of exchange, drawn on London creditors who kept agents in those places, and selling prices that brought returns of 25 to 40 percent per voyage. The Treaty of Methuen in 1703 prohibited British subjects from trading at French ports, thereby making Portuguese and Spanish ones more attractive to New Yorkers; then with Queen Anne's War, which created shortages in France of exportable foodstuffs for Portugal, a few New Yorkers discovered "a very profitable Trade with Lisbon for wheat, by which several have made estates." But "the Distance [to Lisbon] made the carriage so chargeable, being the Ships were obliged to return empty" that only Abraham de Lucena could continue this trade for more than a few seasons at first. By 1716, however, at least six city importers had resolved to return with their holds full of wine from Portuguese-held Madeira and the Azores. Repeated entries in William Bolton's letter book covering 1695 to 1714 note how his vessels went directly to Lisbon with cargoes of wheat, staves, and whale oil, and cleared directly for New York or Amsterdam with undutied wine and brandy from the islands. Abraham de Peyster, Charles Nicoll, Rip van Dam, Anthony Rutgers, and Anthony Lynch followed in his footsteps.[45]

Into the next decade, wine's popularity with the elite and middling population kept wholesalers anxious to secure it in exchange for grain. Yet the recession of the 1720s prevented many fall and spring voyages to Madeira. The trade was, as Cadwallader Colden put it, "to our loss, this Province consuming more wine from thence, than can be purchased with our commodities which obliges the Merchant either to send money or to pay the Ballance in Bills of Exchange for London." In addition to insufficient grain surpluses, New Yorkers confronted provincial embargoes during wartime and a tax on wine imports; soon plentiful harvests of grain in eastern Europe undermined their markets in southern Europe as well. Moreover, wartime insurance on exports from Madeira cost four times what it did from London, and during troubled times, Colden complained, "the intelligence of a demand [from southern Europe] reaches us so late, that the markets are supplyed before our vessels come there . . . and by the length of the passage [grain] often grows musty."[46]

Even during years of peace, English carriers arrived at the southern European islands of Madeira and the Canaries with late summer harvests sooner than most ships sailing from New York. In order to compete effectively, a few New Yorkers experimented with new commercial linkages from the 1730s to the 1760s. Anthony Duane and Paul Richards exchanged West Indies products at New England ports for the fish Catholic countries of southern Europe needed. Others brought back limes, lemons, and spices for New Yorkers to try, or salt, an undutied commodity from the Caribbean and southern Europe, which they reexported to Newfoundland or coastal fishing regions. Compared to New York

City's average of eleven clearances per year between 1715 and 1718 (5% of all clearances), about 31 ships cleared for southern Europe per year during the 1730s, and most of them returned with large amounts of silver and gold.[47]

Thomas Newton continued prospering in the wine trade into the 1760s, but his unusually well cultivated business connections were exceptional. By then, city merchants had grown accustomed to gyrating demand for wine, the high costs of freight and insurance, and consumers who might reject the product if markups were too high. At the close of the Seven Years' War, an imperial tax of £7 a tun on wine imported directly from southern Europe into the colonies also dampened importers' enthusiasm for that trade. In their capacity as exporters, they also experienced difficulties: southern European demand for New York's grain fell precipitously when there were high winds to drive Mediterranean windmills and a moderate rainfall, and during the last two major wars of the colonial period, England embargoed Spanish and Portuguese trade. Then New Yorkers' own government embargoed exports of foodstuffs during the late 1750s, just as news reached city merchants that exporters in the Levant and Sicily could not supply Mediterranean demands for wheat. Colonists registered vociferous protests in their newspapers against such "obstruktiv legislashun." But only after 1762 did some conditions change for the better. A demographic explosion in England and a series of inadequate harvests forced English traders to turn from exporting to importing grain, thereby encouraging New Yorkers to redirect grain exports to the mother country and southern Europe. By 1770, New York's cargo tonnage to southern Europe reached 3,124, or about 12 percent of the value of its exports.[48]

England still treated Ireland like a colony in the eighteenth century and permitted the island to import from North America only provisions, horses, servants, linens, and—after 1731—flaxseed. Only in the 1750s, however, did New York's production of the latter, and Irish linen manufacturers' demand for it, rise high enough for Gerard Beekman and Samuel Horner to concentrate their energies on that trade. Indeed, they were known throughout Rhode Island, Connecticut, western Massachusetts, and the Hudson Valley as the "monopolied men" in flaxseed exporting. Once in Belfast, Beekman collected payment in bills of exchange drawn on London, where he acquired orders for New York customers. William Snell acted as Beekman's agent in London in case of protested Belfast bills or to procure advance cargoes, insurance, and price lists. Samuel Horner, a lesser dry-goods merchant, usually arranged to have his flaxseed shipped by two Boston merchants. In 1765, he commissioned a Rhode Island captain to collect flaxseed from the countryside, accumulate it at Boston, carry it to Belfast, and return via Liverpool to pick up salt for Boston buyers.[49]

By then, Bristol rivaled the Irish demand for flaxseed, and Henry Cruger became the city's primary—nearly sole—exporter of flaxseed and oil to that port. Returning from Bristol, his ships brought linen, candles, small manufactures, and bills of exchange, which Cruger could either sell in New York or remit to London creditors in the future.[50]

Although England had risen to commercial preeminence over Holland by the eighteenth century, Amsterdam firms continued to offer New Yorkers strouds (coarse woolen cloths), guns, gunpowder, tea and fine cloth at consistently lower wholesale prices than English firms. Indeed, dry-goods merchants often cited both English and Dutch prices for the same commodities in their letters. Many Dutch merchants also offered a full year of credit, usually without interest, and their warehousing and bulk-storage techniques allowed them to purchase ahead of demand when supplies were available. Dutch ability to market logwood, dyewoods, tobacco, fish, and slaves broadly also permitted merchants in Holland to take commodities of inferior quality along with the better ones, a policy their English peers rarely dared to try. In 1750, Lewis Morris, then a judge of the provincial vice admiralty court, asserted that the Dutch still "are known to be the cheapest carriers in the world."[51]

These benefits proved irresistible to the few New Yorkers who could secure large ships and the trust of Dutch creditors. In 1714, Governor Robert Hunter feared that copper from "Mr. Schuyler's mines" in New Jersey would be "carried into the channel of our Trade to Holland" (notwithstanding that it was a perfectly legal transaction), and the customs searcher Francis Harrison confirmed in 1721 that this was happening. Other observers commented that New Yorkers were shipping wine from the Azores, Madeira, and the Canary Islands to Amsterdam after 1715 in order to pay for cargoes of dry goods going to New York. John van Cortlandt imported large amounts of West Indian sugar for New York refiners; but he also reexported almost half of the unrefined sugar to London, Amsterdam, and South Carolina. Through the 1730s and 1740s, the merchants John Sanders, John Cruger, Cornelius Cuyler, William Johnson, and Johannes Bleecker exported ginseng and potash to the firms of William Snell and Storke & Champion, who acted as intermediaries with Dutch firms. From 1748 to 1750, during a postwar boom, Gerard G. Beekman placed orders with Amsterdam merchants and insured New York vessels bound for the Low Countries, while Waddell Cunningham speculated in the purchase of prize goods, which he sent in bulk to Amsterdam.[52]

In the 1720s, Robert R. Livingston Jr., Henry Cuyler, and Rip van Dam exported peltry to Samuel Storke in London, where it was sold and the net proceeds forwarded to Dutch firms; cargoes were then made up at Amsterdam for shipment to New York via Dover or the Orkneys.[53] That same decade, four merchants of English descent—John Lewis, Charles Lodwick, James Graham, and Edward Griffith—each shipped a few hundred furs directly to Amsterdam, but the Wendell and Ten Eyck families, as well as other Dutch descendants, shipped larger quantities. Cornelius Cuyler, an established exporter of Dutch heritage, averaged 5,500 furs annually in the period 1730–34, a large proportion of the entire trade by that date.[54]

New Yorkers maintained close liaisons with four prominent partnerships in Amsterdam. A few colonists knew the bankers John de Neufville & Son from London introductions, and John Hodshon had moved to Amsterdam after years of doing business in England. Daniel Crommelin & Son had been founded about 1735, after the firm's major partner, a Huguenot refugee from France, had lived in both the West Indies and New York. Crommelin had facilitated and backed shipments between Amsterdam and New York since about 1720, doing business as the Holland Trading Company with bankers like Willincks, Ten Broeck, and Schemmelpennick. In about 1733, he moved to Amsterdam, and after 1755, the Dutch firm became a banking house, Crommelin & Zoon, which lasted until Crommelin's death in 1768. His son Robert kept commercial liaisons with New Yorkers over these years, and his daughters married the New York merchants Gabriel Ludlow and Gulian Verplanck. John Ludlow, Gabriel's brother, bought over 25 percent of his imports from agents of the Crommelin family; in 1757, he exported over five times more to Crommelin than to any English merchant.[55]

Levinus Clarkson, the fourth Dutch liaison, had the double good fortune to have been raised the son of a well-to-do New York City merchant, Matthew Clarkson, and to be related to Charles Lodwick, a successful New York trader, who returned to London after 1710. Levinus visited the Lodwick household and met many of the metropolis's commercial elite; by 1736, he was prepared to join his uncle in Amsterdam, where they launched a vigorous export trade to New York that also involved an elaborate service in converting bills of exchange and extending credit. Occasionally, Clarkson imported New York goods and bills in Daniel Crommelin's name. Through his connection with Lodwick in London, Clarkson also secured goods and credit for Francis Goelet, Anthony Rutgers, and the Roosevelt brothers in New York; until the end of his career, he also held on to his portion of a 5,000-acre colonial estate that had been granted to his relatives the Van Cortlandts.[56]

Continuing ties to Amsterdam's good and credit afforded some city merchants another opportunity to argue for commercial freedom. Philip van Cortlandt and Cornelius Cuyler wrote of their frustration with New York's and Parliament's regulation of colonial exports over the period 1713 to 1727. In 1728,

Cuyler notified his London correspondent, Richard Janeway: "I can assure you that all the goods which I have Received from you in June last are all unsold for Want of a free trade." High import duties at New York, he explained, forced importers to raise the prices of English goods higher than undutied Dutch ones. Cuyler urged Janeway to help "get those unnatural acts [of Parliament] Repealed," or else the "self-Interest" of London and New York City merchants would be destroyed by flourishing Dutch connections and even more smuggling than usual.[57] Cuyler was one of a few New York merchants who pleaded for the reduction of import duties and complete suspension of export duties, especially those on furs. Their plaints, directed at English creditors, were aimed at reducing future prices. But the feasibility of turning their trade elsewhere, and an alternative commercial model of more open trade, emboldened them to shape their trade as they chose and to imagine a larger sphere of mutual interests than the English empire could offer. The merchants Groesbeck, Philip Livingston, Cornelius ten Broeck, Johannes de Peyster, Hans Nansen, Rutger Bleeker, Evert Wendell, and Ryer Gerritse all pointed to the "freer trade at Amsterdam" as an appropriate example to emulate.[58]

The intermittent presence of Dutch factors in New York underscored all of these beliefs and actions. Although city legislation denied Dutch agents the licenses required to insure departing cargoes or to become auction masters, Dutch factors did both. One of them collected grain and lumber from dozens of New York exporters for Albert Hodshon over the years 1706 to 1714; for a commission of 4 or 5 percent on most voyages, the factor also received Dutch goods to sell in New York or reexport to Moses Lopez in Curaçao, from whom he received cocoa, molasses, and slaves. Other Dutch factors broke up cargoes of cocoa and molasses into small parcels for numerous city retailers or reexported one great load of goods to Amsterdam; some fulfilled instructions to purchase vessels, discount bills of exchange, forward cargoes of West Indies goods, or make money transfers.[59] Imperial enumeration of furs in 1722 did not have the intended effect of concentrating the trade at London. Demand fell in England, peltry supplies dwindled, and Parliament soon halted the drawback of duties for goods reexported from England to Amsterdam. As a result, furs, which made up 40 percent of New York's exports to Holland before 1720, and about 20 to 25 percent after enumeration in 1722, fell to negligible amounts by 1730. Yet even without sure exports for Amsterdam, Robert and Richard Ray smuggled Dutch goods into New York City, while William Alexander and Cornelius Ludlow imported Dutch goods directly to the port in subsequent decades. By the time Parliament passed more strenuous revenue legislation to pay debts incurred during the Seven Years' War, New Yorkers were well practiced in skirting what Cuyler called "those unnatural acts."[60]

Innovating, Adapting, and Staying Afloat

Only a handful of New York's wholesalers enjoyed a level of wealth that turned colonists' heads, but they set the tone for many other men's aspirations and for much of our scholarship about colonial commerce. Their successes were linked firmly to owning large ships; concentrating certain goods and London credit in few hands; selling at city auctions; and the privileges of personal banking, marine insurance, markets for bills of exchange, and government loans. Initial advantages were further secured by intermarriage and tight-knit commercial networks, which in turn permitted established merchants to stay in trade longer than New York's newer ones. Until the 1720s, colonists also associated commercial greatness with a coterie of dry-goods importers, as when, in January 1701, the public awaited the arrival of the *Endeavor,* owned by eighteen prominent dry-goods importers in New York, which brought large quantities of cloth and clothing, implements and medicines, seeds and pewter wares. Some of this group loaded up the vessel with peltry for the return trip to London, while others put their peltry and timber masts on the *Betty,* the *Antiqua,* or the *Helena.* Within four months all four vessels were bound to London again, and the following January, sixteen of the original group announced the impending arrival of the *Endeavor* with dry goods once again. In 1710, ten of them still traded together.[61]

Success and persistence over time eluded most city traders, however, and before midcentury, names rose and fell with regularity on the city ledgers of registered vessels and dutied goods. Having started out in the Hudson River transport of peltry and Indian trade goods in the 1690s, for example, Peter van Brugh, Clauss Wyngart, John Wandler, John Rosebau, Abraham Wendell, Adrian Hooglandt, Paul Droilette, John van Allen, and others acquired enough credit by 1701 to venture into transatlantic trading. By the end of Queen Anne's War, another set of names filled customs ledgers, and still other immigrating merchants or young sons in the colony temporarily occupied the ranks of middling traders following the recession of the 1720s. Some lesser merchants traded a few goods over many years, but most failed within five to seven years.[62]

Distinctions between elite and middling business arrangements widened in other ways over the century. From 1701 to 1709, ten to twenty-two city merchants shared vessels entering from London; when Isaac de Peyster and Rip van

Dam traded as sole owners of a vessel in 1701, it was unusual. In 1715, there were at least 122 merchants with shares in city vessels, although only twenty-four of them owned shares in three or more vessels or fully owned one of their own. By 1729, merchants still tended to own ships jointly, but by 1764, roughly 10 percent of New York ships sailing to Britain or southern Europe were solely owned, and by then the typical number of shares per vessel was five to eight.[63]

Partnerships—usually a short-term agreement between two or three merchants for the duration of one or two voyages—were indispensable arrangements for all merchants, since they defrayed the high costs of transport, dispersed the risks of "dead" markets, and pooled any single merchant's slim exports with others. Most merchants must have availed themselves of these benefits at some time during their careers, for at least five-sixths of the trading ventures from 1701 to 1709, and three-fifths of those between 1768 and 1772, were conducted as partnerships. But by the 1720s, the great sugar and logwood reexporters tended to form more lasting partnerships, from two to seven years, and to unite all their goods in a single long-distance cargo, while middling merchants had too much at stake in any particular voyage—and comparatively little capital to invest—to agree about such terms. Their captains competed fiercely for sales upon arrival at the ship's destination, and they tended to carry the cargoes of many traders who kept separate accounts, branded separate containers, and personalized their bills of lading.[64]

The city's elite also tended, when possible, to specialize their services and transport a particular commodity exclusively. Jacobus van Zant became known as a "cloth merchant." Walter Livingston earned the appellation "earthenware importer," while John Abeel was identified as a "flour merchant" and John Watts as a "wine and molasses merchant." Correspondents almost always wrote to John van Cortlandt with reference to his "sugar business," and John Ludlow occasionally entered the slave trade but preferred the regular "Holland trade," with its reduced costs of insurance and sailor's wages, short turnaround time, and ready supplies of Amsterdam wares. This kind of specialization was also more likely among merchants who did not market goods into the interior or across the city, but sold directly from the docks.[65] Lesser merchants specialized, not in order to extend risks and create economies of scale, but to retrench when capital grew short, supplies of exports grew slim, and their reputations faltered. For them, specialization might be compulsory in their early careers and preferable during prolonged recessions or shifting strategies of extraction or production in the countryside.[66]

Specialization was but one way for members of the commercial elite to enhance their trade; diversification was more typical among aspiring traders and marked the careers of many merchants at the peak of success. Caleb Heath-cote, for example, was an outstanding success by 1710 because he supplemented well-known international markets with uncharted ones and invested in new provincial experiments related to wholesaling. Having expanded his commercial activities rapidly and then built grist mills, a leather-tanning shop, a fulling mill, a linseed-oil mill, and a saw mill, Heathcote then promoted the colony's only significant flaxseed and hemp production before midcentury. Earlier, Peter Jay remarked that he survived transatlantic competition by investing in shares with many of "our major merchants"; but even at the peak of his career, Jay did not retreat to the security of just a few tested correspondents. Philip Livingston diversified his exporting when peltry for London fell to a trickle of Hudson River traffic in the 1730s, turning to flour shipments to Amsterdam and wheat sales at Barcelona; salt purchasing at Gibraltar; sugar and rum acquisition at Jamaica; and trade for specie at any foreign West Indies port his captain could enter. Livingston even supplemented his dwindling fur supplies to London with local turtles, oysters, native seedlings, and other "exotic" commodities. But he was only one of many reputable merchants whose agents scoured the region for new commodities to export and new customers to buy imports.[67] By 1736, Cornelius Cuyler, formerly almost exclusively a fur trader, corresponded with David van Brugh in the West Indies to buy up all the silver they could mutually afford. By the early 1750s, Cuyler had established additional connections with London firms that agreed to receive all the "curing plants" and "dye plants" he could send, and Amsterdam and Curaçao became regular stops for his vessels. Cuyler "planted" his son Henry in Antigua and assigned his son Philip to over-see the exportation of ginseng grown around Albany, from where he also distributed English tools, apparel, and cooking wares to internal shopkeepers.[68]

Many other eminent wholesalers diversified during the 1750s, including John Ludlow, Robert Murray, John Watts, John and Stephen van Cortlandt, and David Provoost.[69] John and Henry Cruger traded all manner of commodities on four continents, where collateral relatives often extended credit and shipping ser-vices. Henry Beekman's general provisions stores in New York were one part of an extensive network of agents in eight other colonies. Gerard G. Beekman, his brother, imported glass and sea coal from England for Rhode Island retail-ers; reexported rice from South Carolina to Boston in his vessels; and shipped Dutch cloth and tea to ports in the West Indies, where he then picked up rum for northern ports. Beekman also sent coffee and cocoa from wholesalers in Hol-land to southern colonial correspondents; he paid European correspondents with the local produce of Rhode Island and Connecticut, and bought gun shot, china, and lumber for those colonies. Oddly enough, Beekman did not import many English finished goods; his flaxseed exports went to Ireland, his provisions exports to the West Indies and southern colonies, and his trade in small finished crafts linked buyers and sellers in New York, New Jersey, and Connecticut. James Beekman, another brother, distributed imported cloth through his chapmen along the Hudson River to Kingston, Schenectady, Fishkill, New Rochelle, Rye, and Albany.[70] Like the Beekmans, Daniel Gomez built his far-flung reputation with an amazing array of goods and correspondents. From 1739 to 1765, Gomez imported every conceivable kind of dry goods, including stockings, metal wares, earthenware, pottery, linen, silks, and farm implements; and he exported a long list of local produce, including preserves, salted meats, tanned hides, grain and flour, whale fins and oil, cheese, and straw wares, which made their way to markets in the West Indies, Amsterdam, London, southern Europe, Madeira, Charles Town, and throughout New England.[71]

An integral part of early modern commerce involved relationships of trust—with other merchants, with local consumers and distributors, and with suppliers and insurers. But all merchants did not trust in the same ways. Traders of meager means might find it easy to establish ties of credit and debt in local surroundings, but these were often also the most fragile or burdensome connections; and when they made contacts abroad, modest traders had little choice but to accept the judgment of captains who assessed conditions on the spot or were handicapped by distance and anonymity. Trust, then, was indispensable but not a guarantee of success.

Distinguished wholesalers also relied on face-to-face trust, but their relationships tended to be founded on a more elaborate set of negotiations or compromises, often involving consolidated families or broad networks of correspondents. They might send their goods, captains, and ships to the limits of the empire, and thus have to place their trust in commissions agents at foreign ports in order to gain the most timely information and first customers. As markets became more competitive, it was imperative to act "with dispatch" to arrive "in season," but city merchants did not want to risk sending goods "to find an open market" or to sell exports "without the assistance of the request," for demand and prices were too changeable and the degree of anonymity among strangers required caution in "infant markets." That is why John van Cortlandt kept "sugar agents" in Philadelphia and North Carolina who received West Indies goods and prepared vessels full of naval stores for direct voyages to southern Europe or Bristol, thereby helping to reduce the vessel's turnaround time and ensuring Van Cortlandt that a close associate would tend to his affairs. John Watts and John van Cortlandt consigned small quantities of myriad commodities from New England, Long Island, and New Jersey to agents in Jamaica,

London, and Newfoundland who would "value themselves upon" small buyers in those places, transmit bills of exchange, dun debtors, and procure insurance. John and Henry Cruger frequently instructed agents in the West Indies to send sugar to New England or logwood to Amsterdam, "upon your commission of 2½%," during years of peace. In time, New York's diversified great merchants began to rely on consignment sales to expand business, too. In the 1750s, when William Alexander's New Jersey iron works began to yield small quantities of bar iron, kettles, chain links, and plowheads, he felt it was hazardous to undertake all productions and sales operations in his own name. Instead, he consigned goods to Newport, Boston, Salem, and other New York City wholesalers, who in turn linked up with Philadelphia and West Indies agents.[72]

Well-appointed city merchants also consigned exports of foodstuffs to London firms after Queen Anne's War in hopes of decreasing the risk of losses and spoilage and reducing storage fees with quicker turnover of goods.[73] In the following decades, other firms sold West Indian dyewoods and sugar or naval stores from South Carolina on commission for Walter Livingston and Philip Cuyler. In the 1730s, Peter Livingston, Henry Cuyler, John Cruger, and Rip van Dam all consigned merchandise to Samuel Stork, whose son took over these commissions sales after 1740. Henry Beekman's flaxseed buyers in Ireland often sent the proceeds of sales to agents in London, where they were applied to Beekman's credit, or his London connections subscribed insurance premiums or collected orders from smaller traders to make up cargoes for New York. John Ludlow's dry goods came from at least twelve different suppliers, any one of whom might be asked to outfit vessels for return trips to New York on commission.[74]

Some of New York's wholesalers welcomed the opportunity to provide these services in return, at a commission of 2½ to 5 percent for outfitting vessels for departure and filling printed orders. Nicholas Bayard, Frederick Philipse, and Isaac Adolphus began the practice in the first years of the century, and John van Cortlandt, Philip Cuyler, and Anthony Bleeker were active in the 1750s. By the 1760s, John Watts and Gerard Beekman agreed with Bleeker that providing "all manner of goods on [5%] commission for persons at home or abroad" would attract new correspondence from New England, Quebec, and Virginia.[75]

Some of these men found it easier to secure commissions if they put up an advance to cover the debts of a foreign merchant with third parties, or covered the cost of goods sent to a third port. In the parlance of international traders, worthy consignment merchants would treat their correspondents "as I would treat myself," faithfully sending lists of prices current and estimates of local demand for commodities. In some cases, they could warn against a venture, as when Gerard Beekman groaned to Irish correspondents about the competition from "Scotch Merchants here [who] sell [textiles and clothing] at 12 month Credit and Comes cheaper then yours." Beekman was sure that neither "Our Poor Nor Negroes," nor "New England people" would buy Irish wool and linen. "Really, it would be giving Your Property Away to urge the Sale of your goods at Present."[76]

Middling traders rarely earned commissions in New York, and they were less likely to enjoy the connections of "good marriage" or extended family linkages in distant ports that grounded many commission arrangements there. John Barbarie, who was well known in New York as a fur exporter until his supplies declined in the 1690s, was not able to corner sufficient grain supplies to redirect his commerce; instead, he sent sons to Barbados and Jamaica to clerk for other families and secure cargoes of sugar for reexport out of New York to England, for which he made advance payments. His returns to the islands consisted of English and European goods that had gone unsold in the city. Even very late in the colonial period, young men just getting started in the West Indies traded directly as Barbarie had. Some of them fared well; others fell into great debt and fraud. Alexander Hamilton, a West Indies agent in the 1760s for the wealthy Cruger family's far-flung network of trade, expressed frank annoyance with the reputations and credit of his neighbors. Although the intimacy of commercial connections secured a degree of fairness, timeliness, and standardization where firmer regulation lacked force, Hamilton's apprenticeship opened his eyes to the uneven effects of these networks and the disregard many traders had for both personal trust and the law.[77]

Exchanges of goods and money, partnerships, and sharing voyages could not have flourished without the confidence traders placed in each other. In an era of currency shortages, uneven flows of commodities, and few ways to invest profits outside of land and commerce, some wealthy traders sought to make their money grow by another kind of trust: a kind of "private banking," by which city merchants loaned "ready money" or "prompt cash" to local acquaintances who wished to purchase cargo, insurance, sailors' wages, and ship repairs. A personal bond drawn up between two merchants for six months to five years, at 5 to 7 percent interest, represented one merchant's promise to provide security to another for future payments of commercial debts. Like bills of exchange, bonds were transferable by the second quarter of the eighteenth century; the intimate nature of the agreement and nonspeculative character of the contract also proved very desirable, especially among dry-goods importers who had larger sums of currency on hand.[78] But great merchants like Oliver De Lancey, Peter Warren, and Gerard Beekman also lent small sums as advances against goods and fees for particular voyages, not to other prominent merchants but to lesser peers in their own neighborhood, sometimes at high rates of interest. Although the New York Assembly fixed the rate at 6 percent in 1717, personal loans rarely could be secured for less than 8 percent, and in the absence of imperial enforcement machinery, the Assembly raised the legal rate to that level from 1720 to 1738.[79]

Early in the eighteenth century, merchants also loaned cash from commercial profits to urban and rural retailers. One anonymous factor for Amsterdam and Curaçao merchants, for example, put out portions of the foreign merchants' credits from commerce to city shopkeepers and artisans. "Whereas many Persons in this Province have often Occasion to borrow Money at Interest, and others have Sums of Money lying by, which they want to put out," merchants would lend and borrow "on good Personal Security" at various locations in the city, newspaper advertisements announced in 1728.[80] Gerard Beekman, who tried to keep his money "working," wrote to Thomas Freebody of Rhode Island, "It is now upwards of 12 months your money Layn by me without Any Advantage Either to you or myself." Beekman advised that this was wasting an opportunity to put out the money at interest: "If you think You Shall want it in 12 months and its Agreeable to you I will make use of the same and allow you 3 per[cent] per annum for it which is much better then to Let so much money Lay dead."[81]

Of course, Freebody, among many others, risked *not* having his money repaid at interest in twelve months. John Watts was one of many frustrated merchants who loaned money extensively and then lacked cash for further negotiations when debts to him became overdue. He wrote to Gedney Clarke of his failed attempts to retrieve money from Thomas Astin somewhere in New England: "I cannot for my Life account for his extraordinary Conduct. We are perfect Strangers and without any recommendation in the World . . . He now stands indebted to me about a thousand pounds and I have God knows how many Bills and other Expences to pay." Although most merchants would not have loaned money to "perfect Strangers," Watts hoped that strangers would be utterly diligent about obligations and not "plague my hart out."[82]

Loaning money to the crown was only slightly more secure than loaning privately. Before 1739, public loans carried the promise of greater interest and quicker returns. But once the crown halted the practice of giving direct victualing contracts to appointed colonial merchants during imperial wars, replacing them with a system of subcontracting with New Yorkers via London appointees, that promise was buried under numerous complaints of favoritism, late payments, and impossible assignments.[83] Frederick Lentz, David Clarkson, and others found it was more convenient to contract with their own provincial Assembly in 1747 to furnish it with £5,500 sterling (£9,075 in New York currency), at higher interest rates than private lending. Christopher Bancker's four loans to the city between 1748 and 1750 were rewarded with municipal bonds for twice the value of his investment and 6 percent interest on the initial loans, which the city renewed at 7 percent in subsequent years. Oliver De Lancey and John Watts loaned the provincial government sums between £700 and £1,000 at 5 and 6 percent interest during the Seven Years' War. By 1771, John Bogert, Henry Cruger, Pierre de Peyster, and the subscribers to the New York Hospital and New York Marine Insurance Society—almost all of them prominent dry-goods importers—held many city bonds. When British troops arrived there in 1776, New York City owed merchants over £13,000 on bonds, which was more than it collected in taxes each year.[84]

English correspondents invited city traders to invest in stocks and the Bank of England, but John Watts, among others, scorned the 3 percent interest rate on Bank of England offerings as "too slender for an Annual Crop," and feared the "Devilish" swings of stock values in England. For years, many New Yorkers harbored deep fears of England's financial revolution in general, preferring to keep their money under closer watch in New York. The spectacular failure of the South Sea Company between 1711 and 1721 reinforced their worst anxieties. During those years, untold numbers of newly rich "projectors" had pooled their capital under a government charter of incorporation to finance England's imperial ventures against foreign West Indies trade. Company brokers promised wealthy merchants, landlords, and members of the royal family enormous profits on the sale of South Sea stock to people in all walks of life, and company directors negotiated with the government to underwrite large portions of the national debt in exchange for a monopoly of trade with newly acquired foreign possessions in the West Indies. Capital for the underwriting would derive, they said, from public loans at relatively high interest rates. As the project drew cash out of circulation quickly, the supply of circulating stocks expanded and myriad small investors committed future income to the South Sea Company by selling stocks on an "installment plan."[85]

But the company failed to pay out regular dividends, and its directors never expanded trade in the Caribbean. When the bubble burst in September 1720, internal credit was frozen, the luxury trades collapsed, bankruptcies rose, and the government itself was discredited. Amid the ruins, Sir Robert Walpole's government initiated a conservative posture toward government finance, but too late to appease middling English investors, who had to be content with a pittance of the value of their "flimsy chimerical paper." Sir Isaac Newton invested hugely during 1719–20 and sold his shares on April 20, 1720, at 100 percent profit, which cleared him £7,000, but he later reinvested £20,000 and lost it all when the South Sea stocks collapsed. As he commented to a fellow investor, "I can calculate the motions of the heavenly bodies, but not the madness of people." Like so many others, Newton worried about the ethics of building fortunes without direct labor, and he was perplexed that the "science" of financial speculation had failed to control the behavior of stocks. Daniel Defoe, probably one of the architects of the South Sea Company, was dismayed that what should have "further[ed] the interest" and the "property of all England" had dissolved into mere "fantasies."[86]

The New York City merchants John Catherwood and George Clinton had first-hand experience of the South Sea Company's unreliability. When they loaned Parliament and the province substantial sums during Queen Anne's War, they received repayments "in South Sea stock, which they [were] obliged to [accept] at par when [its value stood] at a very large discount, and had no interest allowed them for being out of their money so long a time." They still had not been repaid when the company went under, and as the decade's trade recession deepened, many city merchants (wrongly) blamed the South Sea debacle for glutted West Indies markets and failing regional debtors. Only two New York merchants are known to have invested in Bank of England stock thereafter: John Watts and William Alexander held stocks in the funded debt at 4 percent interest in the 1750s. Merchants who watched the annual interest rates on British exchequer bills and annuities fall from 10 percent in the 1690s to about 5 percent after 1720 pronounced them a "slim inducement" to invest abroad.[87]

Marine insurance premiums were uncommon until the 1690s, and from 1700 to about 1730, London agents underwrote most New Yorkers' insurance risks. But a few eminent traders in the colony began to offer the service thereafter. Lawrence Reade's New York Insurance Office advertised that any exporter with a cargo might declare to it the details of his intended voyage, apply to Reade for a policy, and settle upon the level of coverage and the premium, which the exporter paid in advance. Reade kept the policy, and solicited five to ten other merchants to subscribe amounts of the coverage up to the entire risk, at which point the vessel left port. If it arrived safely, the premium, plus interest, was divided among the broker and subscribers; if it suffered losses at sea, the broker collected the subscription sums from the merchants and forwarded them— minus his own commission and any fees he had paid—to the insured merchant.[88]

During the Seven Years' War, the speculative character of these contracts became abundantly clear. Hugh Wallace had over £10,000 out at interest from 1757 to 1759, much of it in shipping insurance, and Jacob Walton raised his percentage for insuring New York vessels returning from the West Indies from the usual 4 to 4½ percent to an average of 20 percent, and for the round trip, he sometimes charged 50 percent of the value of goods entered at customs. London brokers decried the "usurious am[oun]ts" of interest New Yorkers charged, but Corbyn Morris, writing from London, saw these investments "as a source most fruitful of *private Speculation* and *public Benefit*; And is so far from being justly reproachable as a Plan of Gaming that it removes the Business of the Merchant from that of the State and greatly reduces the Risk upon the whole, dissipating it in such a manner as to leave even the Insurer himself liable to little Hazard." Gerard Beekman, who incurred a debt in one month of "near £500 to pay for Losses of other merchants whom [he and others] had insured" would have agreed about the wisdom of "dissipating" insurance risks, but he was undeterred from insuring the same merchants' commerce in years to come.[89]

As a few city dynasties wrested some control of their commerce from London firms, they grew sensitive about the presence of "foreigners" in the city— especially auctioneers who sold "overstocks" of goods at reduced prices. The practice originated when returning privateers tried to dispose of goods seized from enemy ships, or when a bankrupt or deceased inhabitant's creditors wished to turn warehouse stock into ready cash. By the early 1700s, however, nonresident factors sold large quantities of imports without having to "break packages" and distribute small amounts to local retailers, thus underselling city wholesalers. As Madam Sarah Kemble Knight recorded in her 1704 journal, damaged or out-of-season goods could be auctioned, and if the onlookers were "treat[ed] with good Liquor Liberally," they would "Bidd up Briskly . . . after the sack [of spirits] had gone plentifully about." That year, city authorities required outsiders to acquire a license to make these "cheap sales" in an effort to discourage them, stabilize prices, and "prevent the flight of our currency."[90]

But consumers who celebrated cheaper prices for goods such as stockings, gloves, and various uncut cloths were at odds with importers, and helped to make auctions popular in the 1720s and 1730s. By 1750, the licensing system lay in complete disarray, and city merchants protested shrilly against unsolicited Irish and Scottish imports being "dumped" on their docks. The "flood" of British commodities, most of them sold at a "Multiplicity of public Sales" for reduced prices between 1750 and 1755, and again between 1763 and 1766, was, they insisted, "injurious to the regular Trader."[91] John Ludlow concluded that the "Grate plenty of goods we have here" rendered his "Trade Over Don[e]"; the problem, he was convinced, was not changes in wartime consumption but auctioneers who offered great quantities of goods in cities to be "sold vastly Cheap." Gerard Beekman shied from the dry-goods importing business altogether when he realized that the costs of importation could not be passed on to city consumers, so that merchants could not make a living; instead, "Our Vendue House[s] are Crowded with Goods that must be sold if they fetch no more than [New York] Currency for [English] Sterling [value]." Under such conditions, it was "Intirely Out of [his] Way to Sell dry goods."[92]

Other "honest Traders" and "Humble men of Commerce" also despaired. A Philadelphia woman visiting New York City remarked that "the city is overstocked with goods that . . . you may buy cheaper than in London, and the needy Trader is constantly obliged for the sake of ready cash to sell his goods (often with the bales unopened) to vendue." City wholesalers could not "get in Money [from debtors], as 'tis a great temptation to the Country to lay out the Money due [to merchants] at these Auctions." Although importers were hopeful that a 1766 law to tax auctioned goods at 5 percent of their value might "stop a pernicious practice" of selling dry goods, rum, sugar, wine, "and so forth" in that manner, they were disappointed. By 1770, insurance brokers—themselves members of the city merchant community—were using the "fair price" at the city's six active auction houses to determine the level of compensation they would offer, thereby leaving some of the city's "best merchants" with the impression of being underinsured.[93]

The most eminent dry-goods importers experienced the uncertainties of demand and supply from time to time. Scarcities, whether of necessary commodities in short supply from English craftsmen or of luxury goods for which fashions had changed abruptly in England daunted the most experienced city traders. During the 1730s, for example, Rodrigo Pacheco of London and James Alexander of New York were hopeful about rising from middling stature to a notable dry-goods partnership. They regularly corresponded about the meals and clothing of their potential customers. "Rice last year did very well at London," but prices had been declining, and it would sell better at Lisbon, Pacheco predicted in 1732. In order to get the rice—not a commodity that New Yorkers grew—to its destination, Alexander outfitted the *Albany* to sail with "flour, bread, pork, pease, tarr, staves," and other goods to Jamaica, buy "Sugar, Rum, Limejuice, Negroes, and Cash to the value of about £800" there upon selling the New York goods, and then proceed to South Carolina to acquire a full load of rice for Lisbon. In another letter, Pacheco wrote from London to Alexander in New York that because of Queen Caroline's recent death, most traders "at the Merchants Exchange and at the City [are] in Black, Greens and Blues." Predicting that New Yorkers would honor the queen likewise, he did not wait for them to order the mourning cloth, but simply sent it to Alexander, along with a lengthy description of how the English cut and wore "bombazeen, silk, and cambreck" to show respect for a queen in high fashion.[94]

Gerard Beekman also studied public fashion and cultivated his correspondence carefully, using mutual friends and close family connections to seal every transaction in his rising multilateral trade. When he was "a young beginner in trade," he wooed London and Rhode Island firms with the promise that "though I am a Stranger to you I take the Liberty [to] Tender you and your friends my best services" and if any commodity should be "sent to my Care I will ... on Receipt of the same per first Conveyance advance One half The Value and remit it in Such Effects ordered." Like so many others, Beekman assured new correspondents of his financial stability, as well as his capacity for "safe dealing and Speedy remittances."[95]

However, one bad judgment, one bad year of debts, one seasonal miscalculation of prices, or one venture with a deceitful liaison could send a merchant reeling. Frederick Jay wrote from the West Indies to his brother John that he was "much surprised" that Henry White and Abraham van Horne had not sent flour from New York, although the two merchants had been unable to fill their vessels. "They have missed it this time, flour being very dear and Scarce here." Strikingly, it was more important to Jay that his recurring difficulties flowed not from generalized gluts, bad harvests, or warfare that he could not control, but from young men of poor individual judgment. Others, too, often blamed the shippers and producers upon whom they depended. Gerard Beekman thought small traders outside New York City "shuffled" in an "ungrateful" manner when it came time to repay loans, and that he "had suffered much here tofore by Putting too much Confidence in Men," especially the commercial farmers and shopkeepers, who were little more than "Damned scoundrels." He was sure that the whole "damn'd Cuntry" of Connecticut was full of "lost money." As for Rhode Island, he would place no orders there, "for I have been Long Enough Tryfled with about it." Over two hundred debtors owed Christopher Bancker small sums, while at least three hundred in five colonies owed money to William Alexander by the 1760s. Walter Livingston and John van Cortlandt drew up periodic lists of from two to four hundred debtors. To a Boston merchant, Beekman once lamented that although John Clarkson was a major city merchant, he was deep in debt; "being young and frolicksome" he could not have been expected to guard his fortune well, but many people took advantage of his "untested temperament" to withhold payment of debts.[96]

Of course, debts—even large ones for a short time—were not in themselves an evil. But regular indebtedness, coupled with bad judgment, imperfect skills, and "weak character" brought frowning scrutiny from one's fellow merchants. The worst judgments fell upon those merchants who did not see, or would not admit to, their failings. Honest men, it was held, would confront their dilemmas and make arrangements for settling accounts, often by appointing peers to accompany them about town to "lend their reputation" and vouch for the best intentions of the erring merchant. Indeed, although the mayor's court of New York City and the provincial Assembly heard formalized cases of bankruptcy, absconding, or unpaid debts by the eighteenth century, most merchants arranged for debt settlement through kin and peers. James de Peyster's prolonged time in jail for bad debts was exceptional.[97]

Bad goods caused as much consternation as bad debts. Willful deception by trusted correspondents was not as frequent as importers claimed it was, but the record of unintentional disappointments is massive. Eminent and middling alike shared dismay on opening a crate that contained goods of inferior quality marked at appallingly high prices. At times, city traders, even smugglers, returned orders, as when Rhode Islanders received a return shipment of illicit sugar from dissatisfied New Yorkers, carrying the message, "Extremely bad, not fit for shop use." Gerard Beekman at times found clothing from England "a wretched Parcell of Refuse Shop goods," which he speculated had gone unsold in England; woolens, he lamented, always arrived "out of season." More than once, he rejected munitions from his London agent, Thomas Davis, saying they were "the worst Trash I Ever saw." To Luke Babcock of Rhode Island, Beekman wrote that the hogsheads of flaxseed transshipped to New York City for export were, in one case, "a barrel of dirt," and, in the other, "may doe for your horses mixed with Oats," but were unfit for sale abroad. Walter Livingston pleaded with his Jamaica correspondents to sell the goods he sent, rather than leaving them to rot on the wharf. John Watts wrote in exasperation to merchants in Virginia, "Your oats are confoundly gritty; we are forced to pass it all through a sieve; when your folks are richer and can construct barns, I suppose that evil will be removed." To his Irish correspondents, Watts complained about careless ship captains: "The shoes and linen have arrived, but by the negligence of the vile Master they have come . . . among the coal and suffered by downright carelessness to get wet." Watts complained to shippers in Salem, Massachusetts, of shoddy workmanship: "From some defect in Cooperage, or want of Coopers, your Rum frequently arrives in a very dangerous state." While Watts agonized that his exports never seemed to bring the high prices he sought abroad, William Alexander complained that his imports were "charged against my account too high." Peter R. Livingston heard a rumor that one of his vessels lay wrecked on the coast of Hispaniola after some foul play, but it took him a year to discover the extent of the damage.[98] There was no easy way to allay anxieties. Even when a venture had been concluded, ledgers tallied, and arguments about the final reckoning of accounts in a uniform currency settled, the results, from all points of view, might be paltry.

Despite material growth in New York City, complaints about the "want of cash" arose with regularity. "Money begets money," wrote Daniel Defoe, "trade circulates and the tide of money flows with it; one hand washes the other and both hands wash the face."[99] Although merchants had begun to comment on structural conditions such as the effects of bad harvests, epidemics, and prolonged underemployment, their thoughts more often turned to the policy and personal conditions of currency devaluations, tariffs, the nature of credit and debt, and individual manipulation of prices. "Silver and Gold will never tarry among us, till by retrenching our Expenses and improving our Trade, we bring the balance in our favor," Cadwallader Colden reflected in the early 1720s. "The money imported from the West Indies seldom remains six months in the Province before it is exported to England, current cash here being wholly in current bills of the province and a few Lyons Dollars." Another colonial writer reflected a few years later that when money was short, he was "at a Loss who to Trust."[100]

In compensation for scarce specie, more and more New Yorkers set aside their anxieties about credit between buyer and seller. As Isaac Gervaise put it in a widely read English publication: "Man, generally speaking being eager and greedy of Gain, is impatient in Trade; so that when he cannot have the Value of things, as soon as he would, he chuses rather to allow unto the Buyer more or less time, at once to force the Vent, and to prevent any other's supplanting him." Credit, he continued, "proceeds from Fear and Desire," the first originating from the lack of trust between two parties to an exchange or two sellers who competed for first sale to the buyer. Desire, on the other hand, prompted the buyer to pay interest on the credit he received in order to gratify himself immediately, and it provided the merchant with a constant means to help his goods circulate. Forty years later, John Hope wrote with even more confidence that credit "quickened commerce" and represented "the trust that one man gives another." It showed "confidence . . . in the honesty or solidity of the borrower" to use money wisely for trade opportunities, thereby keeping "the general opulence of the Kingdom" growing and preventing merchants' capital from laying "useless in an iron chest." Although a debt was "founded on the opinion of mankind," it was "as much a real possession as any property" bought and sold.[101]

Likewise, a few city wholesalers suffered periods in which bills of exchange grew scarce, as when the level of export trade from New York declined, when

Fig. 2. New York City in the Early Eighteenth Century. A portion of a 1747 line engraving on copper of a drawing done by William Burgin of Boston between 1716 and 1718 and known as "The Bakewell View" (after the engraver, Thomas Bakewell of London). Burgin's original drawing is in the possession of the Museum of the City of New York, and the view is described by I. N. Stokes in *The Iconography of Manhattan Island, 1498–1909* (New York, 1915–32), 1: 272–74.

West Indies demand fell and thereby curtailed the primary supply of bills, or when colonists' debts to England rose so high that bills became, as Robert Sanders put it in 1753, "so rare that I know not when I shall [remit payments]." But at other times they were so plentiful that a few city traders could corner sufficient quantities of them to establish a business sideline marketing them. Stephen Bayard advertised in 1728 that he would "take, receive, or Exchange all Pistoles" for bills on English creditors. Gerard Beekman wrote to a firm in Philadelphia in 1752 that he "could readily sell 6 or 8 hundred pounds in Bills at 30 or 40 days sight but must have them soon for there will be plenty here in three weeks time." William Bayard, John Watts, and Daniel Crommelin wrote to their London connections to buy bills that could be resold in New York at an advance, "for all [merchants] here will accept them," and at its founding meeting in 1768, the city's Chamber of Commerce established limits for damages to be paid on protested bills, thereby reducing the risk of speculating in bills of exchange.[102]

Already merchants had learned about the potential of currency devaluation to attract money to the colony, and of the dangers it posed for consumer prices. For example, Bostonians reduced their pieces of eight between 1693 and 1704, thereby impoverishing New Yorkers who depended on specie for international trade but could not get it because silver "flew" to their neighbors in New England. In 1704, too, Queen Anne's government ordered the devaluation of the pound sterling in relation to Spanish silver, in order to draw the metal into England. Not in itself a burden to colonial commerce when all regions complied with it, the law became unbearable when Bostonians began clipping coins (which had the same effect as devaluation, but carried moral and legal stigmas as well), and emitted great sums of paper money. New Yorkers decried how "several persons here . . . sent away as much money by the Post [to Boston] as [the postman] could carry, and for four or five days all manner of Trade was stopped; there was no Market, nor one could buy anything with ready money [at New York]."[103] Within a few months an angry correspondent to a newspaper declared that "one hundred Pounds current in New York here will scarce pay or purchase Fifty Pounds worth of goods when the same money at Boston will goe currant for £100 and purchase to that value." Rancor shifted from neighboring colonists to the crown when, in 1705, the clamors of merchants for a New York devaluation—finally approved by the Assembly and Governor Edward Hyde, Viscount Cornbury—was condemned by the Board of Trade. The colonists, said the king's ministers, deserved sound reprimanding "for their assuming a right to settle the value of coin." However dire their circumstances, they must not interfere with the political judgment of the crown.[104]

Subsequently, an act of Parliament in 1708 not only affirmed the 1704 devaluation but also fixed the value of English sterling at 6s. to the milled Spanish dollar in the colonies and 4s. 6d. in England, a measure that New Yorkers were sure would pull all silver out of the colony and to England. They disregarded the crown edict regularly and openly over the next few years, continuing the colony's own plan of devaluation, which the courts upheld in debt cases and the Assembly honored in its tax levies. As Governor Hunter put it in 1715, "'Tis not in the power of men or angels to beat the people of this continent out of the silly notion of their being gainers by the augmentation of the value of plate [silver]." Indeed, devaluation struck a popular chord and inspired confidence to try other ways to increase the colonial money supply, the most important of which would be New York's paper currency emissions, starting in 1709.[105]

The Bane of Taxes

Few issues meliorated the differences between great and rising traders, and set them against the shifting coalition of landed interests, as much as provincial and imperial taxes did. Despite the fact that New Yorkers paid lower duties than their compatriots in England, they rehearsed antipathy to provincial taxation over and over, especially when the 1720s recession added poignancy to all efforts at raising revenues. Already during Robert Hunter's administration (1710–19), the merchants John van Cortlandt, Stephen De Lancey, William Nicoll, and Samuel Mulford used their positions in the Assembly to note that importation burdens had been rising during Queen Anne's War and, with the return of peace, should fall. But Hunter and members of the provincial Council retorted that higher duties on imports secured vital revenues to the province and, anyway, importers could pass on some of their rising costs to consumers. Besides, noted councillors, the traffic being discussed involved primarily luxury goods, which only the wealthiest colonists purchased, while the "sober, industrious, prudent or needy part" of the province could forgo them and satisfy its needs with homespun, domestic cider, beer, and spirits. "The burden will only lie on those best able to bear it—gentlemen of estates in towns and cities and rich farmers in the country."[106] Importers withdrew from protests after that, and when Parliament raised duties on wines, European goods, and additional English dry goods, they accepted the imposition without significant protests— probably because the goods, as Hunter wrote, often arrived in London-owned ships and did not amount to "one per cent as the goods are sold here." Only when London merchants vigorously lobbied Parliament in 1724 were the increases discontinued.[107]

Protests against port duties crescendoed again during the traumatic 1720s for a host of reasons. The international recession signaled sluggish markets, falling prices, and depressed shipbuilding in New York. Governor William Burnet (1719–27) promised a coterie of landed magnates that he would expand the fur trade westward—a project that drew approving nods from exporting merchants—but the plan proved chimerical. During the same decade, larger paper currency emissions assuaged certain needs throughout the regional economy but could not pay transatlantic bills. But merchants who desperately sought new markets when old ones foundered began to object loudly to the duties on wine and rum from southern Europe, commodities whose import values rose more than six times over early years of the century. Malt, hops, molasses, and sugar importers decried their burdens as well, especially when distillers who paid rising excise taxes on liquors sold in the colony, and brewers who paid a tax covering the production of beer, threatened to buy their raw materials from New England importers. In 1725, city merchants narrowly fended off proposed Assembly legislation to tax imported southern European salt, a commodity not enumerated by the Acts of Trade, and a tax on molasses imported from the West Indies, which had as yet not been duby Parliament.[108]

The recession of the 1720s had compounded the burden of import duties for New York's wholesalers. Perhaps for this reason, they played a more active role in provincial policy making that decade and participated in a lively public debate about commercial difficulties and the best kind of taxes to support the common weal. Subtle concerns had arisen about the merits of land, as opposed to commercial, taxes, and about the very character of merchants. Earlier, vocal opposition to merchants was couched in arguments against the luxury, usury, and opulent lifestyles of elite traders. These arguments attacked the personal character of merchants and proposed that many imports were either unnecessary or, in any case, sold to them at unjust prices. Misgivings subsided when colonists began to associate merchants more closely with the beneficial nature of trade and to look favorably on the consumer goods, migration, and general communication merchants made possible. By the 1720s, there was less doubt about the role of merchants in the city economy, with the result that some writers supported the elite's material gains as a degree of privilege earned in the course of rendering a vital public service. By then, colonists had less fear about the effects of expanding consumption on their lives, and merchants reasoned that colonists' overall development enabled payment of rising duties without sacrificing public necessity.[109]

It was in this context that Cadwallader Colden's pamphlet *The Interest of the City and Country in Laying Duties* circulated widely in 1726. Like Hunter's speeches, Colden argued that international trade deserved to bear taxes because it was associated with luxuries and the doubtful character of merchants; the city's rich would either curb their conspicuous consumption or support the colony's defense and development by paying higher duties. In any event, "superfluities," gambling, drinking, and ornate consumption were unbecoming displays by colonists and deserved to be taxed. The tax on imported southern European wine was especially wise, because that commodity continually drained the colony of specie and bills of exchange that would have been better used in the trade with England for necessary textiles and small hardware. Colden also shifted the ground of the tax debate when he proposed that duties had the indirect incentive of promoting not just virtuous living but active production of new things. Duties on West Indies rum and molasses could have the effect of turning tastes toward local cider and honey. Duties on foreign tonnage might not only deter unwanted entries of other merchants' goods but encourage New York's own shipbuilding industry as well. In more modern terms, Colden argued not only for revenue-producing luxury taxes but for a protective barrier that might spur New York's self-sufficiency.[110]

City traders regarded this argument, and others like it, as veiled proposals to keep the burden of taxation on commerce in order to avoid taxing land—especially the great estates of the hinterlands. Their voice appeared in *The Interest of the City and Country to Lay No Duties*, a pamphlet possibly written by Colden himself. Duties, it argued, were not only a direct tax on merchants' pocketbooks, but were paid in turn by all "country" people, along with city residents, in higher prices. Most imports, the essay insisted, were not luxuries but necessities. Tonnage duties might discourage foreign shippers who brought the "luxuries" that the first pamphleteer censured, but the same ships also carried away the surpluses of the colony to meet demand in other parts of the world. Did not merchants best exemplify frugality and industry, the twin engines of national prosperity? Did they not create markets at their own risk?[111]

These writings coincided with efforts, spearheaded by the merchants Adolphe Philipse and John van Cortlandt in the provincial government, to reduce import duties. When the costs of "fair traders" fell, they insisted, consumer prices would fall too, and smuggling would dwindle in significance.[112] An editorial in the *Weekly Post-Boy* in 1751 sounded like an early clarion for Adam Smith when it pleaded for readers to understand that customs duties had climbed so high that the costs merchants could pass along to consumers had almost been met, since selling prices were "fixed by their scarcity and plenty" and not subject to the whim of importers' responses to legislators. It behooved colonists to examine landed interests who paid no taxes on their unimproved estates, and who were prone to "violent Distempers of Luxury and Extravagance."[113]

Colden himself offered a rejoinder to both views, a declaration of shared interests among landed and commercial men together to avoid taxes that were, in any event, passed on to consumers and small producers: "I would ask . . . in what country . . . the whole Burthen [of government support] was taken off the poor, and laid on the Rich: Is it not generally the Rich that lay Taxes, and do they not constantly take care not to Overburthen themselves?" Both landed and commercial interests were prey to the same base passions: "Can they expect to be proof against the deep Designs of men . . . whose Interest is so highly concerned to avoid a heavy Load themselves, and to shuffle if off upon others?"[114]

Cynical as Colden proved to be in print, his pragmatic political posture was to support western land developers and Hudson River planters, and to seek import duties. More than once from 1726 through 1732, Colden squared off against Philipse and Van Cortlandt in the Assembly; although the merchants' representatives lost then, over the years 1732 to 1736, Philipse, Franks, De Lancey, Van Dam, Beekman, and Clarke used their positions in provincial government more successfully to reduce commercial duties. But renewed imperial warfare after that quieted all attempts to reduce taxes, and from 1736 to 1738, men like Robert R. Livingston, William Johnson, James De Lancey, William Smith Sr., and the three Van Horne brothers abandoned their political support for commercial interests—where they had made their fortunes—and associated with frontier expansionists to defeat new land taxes, gathering support for their view from numerous colonists with small parcels of land to nurture. Arrayed against them, the merchants John de Noyelles, Christopher Bancker, Gabriel Ludlow, John Alsop, and John McEvers—all of them prominent dry-goods importers— stood firmly against higher commercial duties, but from 1743 to 1753, Governor George Clinton abandoned efforts to relieve New York City merchants. The Duty Act of 1753 reinstated long-standing import duties, and added brandy, shrub, and "European and East India dry goods from the British Islands" to the list, forcing disappointment upon importers once again. Legislators renewed the act each year until 1774.[115]

And so it went, with merchants associated with dry-goods importing renegotiating their commercial interests regularly over the eighteenth century. From the vantage point of policy making, most provincial duties were not as burdensome as contemporary rhetoric might lead us to conclude; neither were imperial restrictions a serious curtailment of merchants' traffic. Still, city wholesalers frequently wrote to their correspondents that it seemed as if the imperial model of balance and protection was falling short of these goals. From the vantage point of personal commercial choices, there were noticeable improvement in colonists' material lives, more sophisticated networks of exchange and important innovations in business practices, and a few dry-goods importers rising dramatically to new pinnacles of fortune. But here, too, difficulties qualified the material success of all transatlantic traders, and almost no city merchant was consistently successful in taming the economic conditions confronting him or avoiding personal hardship, suspicious behavior, and bad weather. Yet out of these persistent ambiguities, we might fairly conclude that the tendency of New York merchants anxiously to scrutinize their government and their competitors, rather than complacently to acclaim their accomplishments, stemmed from their holding the imperial model in high regard. They had helped establish a thriving port city at the hub of a region of expansive commercial enterprise and had subordinated a significant number of regional markets to New York City in emulation of London's place at the center of a powerful empire, but their accomplishments were still but a miniature reflection of their collective aspirations. The final irony is that energetic emulation of the imperial model had, unwittingly, created habits both of commercial innovation and of dissent from the very subordination to imperial interests that all colonists were expected to uphold. Intellectual and professed political commitments to imperial goals had opened up opportunities for well-situated city traders to press at the allowable limits of arrangements in the empire, as the Seven Years' War would make abundantly clear.

Chapter Six

The Prospects for Satisfying Appetite

The Transforming Qualities of West Indian and Coastal Trade, 1700–1760

B Y T H E E N D of the seventeenth century, a few "mushroom gentlemen" enjoyed "considerable fortunes" in New York City, and attracted the favorable attention of visitors. Some policy makers and treatise writers in England, too, pointed favorably to New York's combination of rising commercial prosperity, favoring it over the staple-producing colonies of the south or testy New England. "The City of New York" had "long been held at home, the first in America," Peter Delanoy said, once the tumult of the Glorious Revolution and Leisler's Rebellion had subsided and the conspicuous consumption of the city's wealthiest merchants became secure. In the next century, Peter Kalm noted of New York City that "with regard to its fine buildings, its opulence, and extensive commerce, it disputes the preference" with neighboring Boston and Philadelphia. "New York," he continued, "probably carries on a more extensive commerce than any town in the North American provinces." Even at the end of the colonial era, Lord Adam Gordon wrote that New York City's links to the surrounding hinterlands gave it "preference over the other ports of America."[1] What constituted first place in the minds of many optimistic commentators was the degree to which a few New Yorkers emulated the lifestyles and decorous social relations of the commercial elite in London, and the extent to which many others improved their material lives, thereby supposedly creating a "harmony of interests" among the parts of the empire.

In truth, however, the commercial elite was not alone in extending the material comfort of New Yorkers, and merchants' ledgers reveal many difficulties in achieving each stage of advancement. Ever greater numbers of middling merchants entered commerce, and in their aggregate, they contributed to colonists' refinement to a very great degree. Most important, the coastal and West Indies trade was both a source of many exotic commodities and the means to "raise up" newcomers to trade with opportunities they could not obtain in transatlantic markets, and for those reasons seemed to open up more possibilities for innovation and growth all around. Indeed, in the century's opening decades, the number of lesser merchants grew from nearly one hundred to well over two hundred, most of them gaining commercial security from the coastal and West Indies trade. By 1760, there were nearly three hundred middling merchants, about three times more than the city's eminent traders.

Moreover, although merchants' personal successes were still mixed with periodic setbacks, their aggregate growing presence in all important ports created qualitative changes in the city's merchant community. This, in turn, shifted the balance of consequential policies and intellectual considerations toward growing areas along the Atlantic rim. More middling traders contemplated the benefits of commerce beyond the boundaries set by the imperial authorities, becoming vocal advocates of policies that they understood to uphold economic freedom. At times they secured more open trade through legitimate reforms of provincial or imperial laws; when policy makers failed them, some middling men, and a handful of eminent ones, reaffirmed and extended smuggling—the open violation of commercial laws. Growing public affirmation of material comfort aided city wholesalers' efforts, too, and bold reformulations of ideas about interest, wealth, and appetite accompanied their pursuit of buyers and sellers.

Thinking about Trade and Consumption

Until far into the eighteenth century, received wisdom held that certain people bore the social responsibilities arising from material improvement better than others, and perpetuated fears that most people would be corrupted by new articles of importation. How, asked some New Yorkers, could they support the "prodigious increase of American luxury" when so many colonists were spending less on "necessitous" finished clothing from England and more on exotic goods? Others were less certain that luxury consumption would preempt necessary goods, but they were certain that unnecessary items were difficult to sell. English factors, they lamented, used New York City as little more than a dumping ground for goods colonists could not afford. Items imported from the Far East by trading monopolies had flooded shops and invaded unwary homes in England, too, draining English silver reserves and creating both a large foreign debt and growing consumer indebtedness. In New York City, the factors of international firms tricked an unwitting public in similar ways. The threat was not dangerous to merchants of great stature or officials of the royal government; rather, it was that the unrestrained acquisition of "superfluities" by middling folk, in emulation of an elite to which they did not belong, would result in their coming to expect a share in the social and political power to which they were not entitled. Consumption beyond one's means could be attached by this reasoning to dire social consequences.[2]

Such fears were based on long-standing views about the nature of goods and their exchange. Few early-modern people treated commercial goods as instruments for capital investment or a source of funds for provincial development. Most of them thought of the commodities exchanged in long-distance trade as belonging to an imperial "stock" of goods, which provided a measure of a nation's wealth, and as the tangible rewards for the risks that merchants took privately. Up to some unstipulated—indeed, unknowable—quantity of amassed wealth, merchants received public approbation for reaping the benefits of their commercial ventures. But early-modern writers also tended to introduce a heavy dose of ambivalence about which merchants were entitled to such approval, which goods they might enjoy without fear of their corrupting influences, and in what quantity. Concerned observers of England's imperial rise focused their attention on the dangerous consequences to middling and poor inhabitants arising from unchecked desire for goods, the rising prices they paid, and the proportions of their private incomes diverted into unnecessary spending. Sir William Petty, for example, believed that costly goods tended to be "used up" quickly in private pleasure or social frivolity and waste; for nonelite members of the empire, incomes might be depleted very rapidly. Hence only policies that suppressed the level of wages and prices would curtail vanity, pride, and idleness. Low interest rates would stifle urges to invest beyond one's means, said Petty, and prevent merchants from lending money at high—usurious—interest.[3]

Certain critics of luxury attributed its rise in England to the quickening pace of commerce and the astounding numbers of new traders, which were not matched by rising purchasing power. When Parliament broke the power of the English trading monopolies, it freed up competitive merchants, who quickly sought any and all markets for trade. Rising London firms transported goods freely and sold them in vast quantities to people who could not possibly pay for them, critics noted in alarm. By the end of Queen Anne's War, Joshua Gee, Henry Martin, Erasmus Philips, John Egleton, Daniel Defoe and others had expended much ink condemning the importation of French lace, wine, silks, brandy, and an "infinite number of other curiosities" too extravagant for England's budding national economy.[4]

Received wisdom held that only the "better sort" had qualities of character suited to enjoying the material finery and comforts pouring in from abroad. Distinctions of social class might break down if merchants fulfilled their promise to expand the tastes and refinement of all citizens. In New York, governors reported home, valuable colonial naval stores and agricultural staples were being exchanged for unnecessary French salt, sugar, wine, spices, and brandy—a perversion of imperial relationships established in trade agreements between England and France in 1713. By the early 1720s, some English mercantilists expressed concern about the extensive exportation of grains, timber, and work animals from colonial North America to French possessions in the West Indies, where New Yorkers received payment in "the least necessitous of life's goods," which not only robbed British West Indies possessions of an outlet for their sugar and molasses but perverted the moral fiber of the colonies as well.[5] The elder William Pitt attributed the domestic and imperial turmoil of the 1760s at least in part to the new and excessive "influx of wealth into this country"; wealth, he added, that had not been produced by "the regular, natural produce of labor and industry," but constituted a kind of "Asiatic luxury" that should in no way be conflated with the wealth that issued from the collective industry of a nation.[6] Even toward the end of the eighteenth century, Adam Smith warned of the social dangers of luxury consumption, for "people that are least able to go to the expense, must have their tea tho' their families want bread."[7]

Slowly, beginning late in the seventeenth century, another view began to erode the influence of these warnings by advocating a natural economy—one that celebrated the role of expanding commerce and ambitious merchants. In 1691, Sir Dudley North praised the inherently acquisitive character of every Briton: "the main spur to Trade, or rather to Industry and Ingenuity, is the exorbitant Appetites of Men . . . when nothing else will incline them to [work]." Nicholas Barbon argued that "desire" drove much trade; "it is not Necessity that causeth the Consumption. Nature may be Satisfied with little; but it is the wants of the Mind, Fashion and the desire of Novelties and Things Scarce, that causeth Trade."[8] "Prodigality," Barbon went on, "is a Vice that is prejudicial to the Man, but not to Trade." Excessive spending might ruin individual consumers, but faster and greater circulation of goods would more likely benefit society's majority of modest inhabitants. Thus, he also recommended that imports be admitted free, but that high excise taxes be placed on luxury articles circulating within the nation, so that the "merchant has his traffick," while prices for some unnecessary commodities "will remain sufficiently high" to discourage average consumers.[9]

After the 1720s, a chorus of New Yorkers echoed explanations of riches as a reward for commercial efforts and the sign of a natural desire to prosper and refine one's circumstances. Strong voices began to detach customary economic notions from their classical agrarian and prescriptive natural-rights origins and to approve of the mobile commercial wealth accumulating in the hands of international traders. Throughout the empire, the traditional moral system that sought to restrain self-interest began to give way to expansive, multivariant, and inclusive interests, talents, and tastes, which in turn created possibilities for competitive encounters between buyers and sellers of all social strata. Optimists proposed that when self-interest became persistent and calculating enough, it could not only lead to great material acquisition but also help to build the public good. In 1729, an essayist in the *New-York Gazette* reflected on the "common view" that "Men are always powerfully influenced in their Opinions and Practices by . . . their particular Interest." As William Livingston's *Independent Reflector* put it in 1753: "'Tis true, every Man ought to promote the Prosperity of his Country, from a sublimer Motive than his private Advantage: But it is extremely difficult, for the best of Men, to divest themselves of Self-Interest."[10]

The central concern, of course, was to control the far-reaching effects of self-interest without stifling the benefits of expanded consumption. But this was so very hard to do, for as an early visitor to the colony put it, "Interest that governs all the world, tyrannizes at New York." William Alexander, a merchant of long standing, wrote to a business partner in 1756: "Interest often Connects People, who were intire Strangers, and it sometimes separates those who had the strongest natural Connections." Some writers proposed that the rise of individual interest emanated from the volatility of politics and the unreliability of trading relations; but many others believed that unfortunate political factions and commercial misfortunes did not cause, but rather resulted from, self-interest run amok. Commitment to collective ideals was waning, Philip Livingston noted of his fellow merchants: "we Change Sides [in politics] as Serves our Interest best." In commerce Livingston self-consciously chose relations that enhanced profits, even when they required that he break trusted business liaisons. For example, he let a relatively newly acquired Jamaica correspondent refer his business to other locations in the West Indies, rather than rely upon the recommendations of long-standing correspondents in that part of the world, for they would act out of the same self-interest; as he explained, his older West Indies correspondents "have Relations at N. York [and] may Deceive me and Serve themselves" by giving better terms of trade to Livingston's competitors.[11]

Livingston and others had, in a small way, adapted to the changing tides of self-interest in the early eighteenth century. As with any merchant in the city, his commerce alternated between success and failure. Traditional thinking posited that when rising traders enjoyed too much success, they would evoke public suspicions of an indulgent self-interest. The emergent view of merchants held, however, that they were not only the agents for accumulating treasure or specie for the national coffers but the servants of a public interest who circulated goods at competitive prices and improved people's lives. New writings defined markets not only as arenas of conquest and adjuncts of political power, but also as locations to receive ships and export goods to satisfy expanding demand. Collective self-interest unleashed desires and creative energies and was thus a beneficial force. Josiah Child went so far as to judge that "the laws of England . . . were a heap of nonsense, compiled by a few ignorant country gentlemen, who hardly knew how to make laws for the good government of their own private families, much less for the regulating of companies and foreign commerce."[12]

It would be far better, Child reasoned, to put control of commercial legislation into the hands of the rising merchant and manufacturing firms. A few decades later some writers added consumers and small producers to the portrait of worthy subjects. Not goods in the abstract, wrote Isaac Gervaise, but all "the Labour of each Nation . . . opposed by all the Labour of the rest of the World," created England's ability to compete against rival empires. Peace was a vital alternative to costly wars; and freedom from internal and external regulations would promote rising individual accumulation in all corners of the empire. As Gervaise continued, "if Trade was not curbed by Laws, or disturbed by . . . Wars . . . Time would bring all trading Nations of the World into that Equilibrium, which is proportioned, and belongs to the number of their Inhabitants." Trade laws diverted naturally harmonious economic activities "by Force, and against [the trader's] Will," thwarting spiraling desires. Indeed, given conditions of peace and economic freedom, the "middling sort" might raise themselves by their own labors and frugality to stations of comfort that were as worthy as those of "the luxurious sort."[13]

Matthew Decker concurred. Policy makers had too often presumed that merchants overshot the ability of consumers to absorb the great shiploads of goods entering the empire, and that merchants themselves were to blame for the rise of unpaid debts and warehouses full of unsold goods. Taking exception to the mercantilist Joshua Gee's 1731 statement that high port duties might "check the vanity of a people" for "excessive consumption . . . of foreign superfluities," Decker insisted that it was, instead, the state's creation of "artificial" markets that harmed merchants' business and consumers' preferences. Citing Locke's belief that fashion and vanity drove up the prices of foreign commodities, Decker nevertheless shrugged off Locke's misgivings about the effects of consuming these high-priced goods and welcomed the quickened circulation and employment they brought. Besides, he added, "Extreme fondness [for unnecessary commodities] checked, naturally breaks out into madness." Consumers must retain their right to buy, or pass by, any imports; passions for "Japan goods" and "french fopperies" would not go away simply by discouraging their importation with higher duties.[14]

Others contemplated the differences between perishable or rare "luxuries," and the "wealth" in money, real estate, ships, and household refinements within the grasp of many citizens by mid eighteenth century. One's wealth—the totality of tangible goods accumulated—was far from corrupting; in the new argot, wealth was ennobling and civilizing.[15] Wholesalers applauded legislation that restricted importation of foreign luxuries, which siphoned off great amounts of specie, and prohibition of imports that competed with domestic production. But they scorned a blanket policy of disallowing the entry of gewgaws and non-nutritive commodities, since the widespread desire for them could become a spur to employment, consumption, or useful exchanges of agricultural surpluses. Luxury consumption, they noted, resulted only when two other conditions prevailed: when too many competing interests or goods vied for limited markets, thereby stifling the flow of commerce and interrupting the delicate system of credit and debt; and when modestly endowed inhabitants staggered under the weight of debt. Until that point, colonists could accumulate and consume without limitation, since it was all positive wealth.[16] The desire for refinement beyond necessity, David Hume affirmed, was both universal and innate, and its effects were to spur production and exchange. To accept and release this passion was a first step toward achieving more lasting natural balances in the economy than governments ever could create.[17]

Of course, by the time these voices joined peace, material comfort, and freer importation, there were visible signs of rising consumption everywhere. "The present increase of wealth in the city of London spreads itself into the country, and plants families and fortunes" of such influence that the true gentry would soon be "bought out," Daniel Defoe observed. Goods, Horace Walpole remarked in 1768, had changed people's characters more than politics: "The immense wealth that flowed into the country . . . bore down all barriers of economy, and introduced a luxury . . . unknown to empires of vaster extent."[18]

But how did writers confront the relationship of the imperial center to colonial outposts? Thomas Dalby and John Oldmixon suggested straightforwardly that colonists shared the universal human appetites of all Britons, and that the colonies ought to be seen, not only as military outposts and sources of naval stores, but as partners in free exchange within the empire. They welcomed exploration and settlement, placed the acquisition and circulation of private property at the center of human endeavor, and associated new spending with a growing layer of ambitious, rising colonists. By the end of the seventeenth century, London importers supplemented their cargoes of wheat, flour, and naval stores from New York City with ginseng, flaxseed, whalebone products, oysters, preserved turtles, and colonial reexports of cocoa, coffee, and exotic fruits. The importation of such "rarities" or newly discovered "scarcities" from the colony invited merchants to reverse the standard mercantile balance-of-payments argument: perhaps it was not the finished manufactures they sent to New York that drove commercial relations, but English demand for New York's goods that aided their own search for distant liaisons.[19]

Likewise, they admitted, colonists had begun to shape their own clear preferences for goods, and all merchants "must suit [their] cargo to the taste of [their] customers; and not to old-fashioned notions of parsimony of former days." Others stressed the mutuality of interlocking interests among North American colonists, Caribbean planters, and English traders and producers. In the crucial discussion of foreign West Indies sugar trading after 1728, for example, some writers insisted that the "universal bent" to produce, transport, and consume that commodity had transformed it from a luxury to a necessity. An anonymous work dating from about midcentury assured readers that colonists could effect the same transformation with any commodity that they chose to ship to English consumers in great quantities; "then those things that are now luxuries would cease to be so, and become our common Commodities." By 1763, John Campbell noted that "the increase of our consumption is an indubitable proof of the increase of our riches," not luxuries. As we shall see, this mutuality of interests among English, northern colonial, and Caribbean peoples would also buoy New York merchants' arguments for more open trade.[20]

In New York, even skeptical supporters of new consumption admitted that the tide of diversifying importation in New York City refined the lives of many inhabitants, aided employment, and called forth a manufacturing interest that allied itself with commercial interests. Markets, writers began to notice, were significant public spaces, in which colonists made a mind-boggling array of new consumer choices; they were also powerful arenas for interpersonal negotiation of prices, credit, and reputation. Indeed, colonists began to articulate linkages between goods and politics, linkages that distinguished the worthy from the unworthy, the corrupt from the virtuous, and struggling producers from idle placeholders in ways that politicized their conception of markets and goods. The linkages, by the time of the imperial crisis, suggested a critical question to some observers: if universal desire led to universally rising consumption, how would New Yorkers respond to specific economic policies directed against them as inferior, dependent colonists by specific political agents in the empire? Answers varied in New York, but they tended to be inspired most by commercial experiences in the burgeoning West Indies and coastal trade, the channels of illegal commerce, and efforts to transform the provincial interior.[21]

The Range of Material Refinement

Toward the end of the colonial period, Cadwallader Colden, whose own many political and economic interests defied classification, nevertheless placed his fellow colonists in "Ranks"; there were (a) landowners with 100,000 acres or more; (b) lawyers and judges; (c) merchants, "many . . . suddenly rose from the lowest Rank . . . to considerable fortunes"; and (d) "Farmers and Mechanics" who "comprehend[ed] the bulk of the People."[22] Men he identified as having "considerable fortunes" tended to draw public attention. As Governor Fletcher escorted a visitor through the city in 1697, he showed off "the multitudes of great & Costly buildings erected since his arrivall about 4 years since . . . Amongst wch none appeared more Considerable than that of Coll. Abr. Depeisters a noble building of the newest English fashion, and richly furnished with hangings under pictures." But the city also boasted "abundance of Lofty brick & stone buildings on the same range, th[eir] back doores & wharfes, warehouses & gardens Lookeing into the Sound, & Harbour." Residents knew De Peyster as a man "whose entertainment is generous & like a Nobleman though a merchant by his profession." Like Fletcher himself, "back'd with the grandeur of a Coach and six horses," and "more plate . . . than all our former Governors ever received," De Peyster abetted piracy and illicit commerce; unlike Fletcher, the great majority of his commercial ventures knitted together relationships with firms and their goods in many countries and colonies.[23] The commercial elite in New York had joined royal officials in consuming nonessential stimulants such as tea, coffee, sugar, and tobacco since the first decades of English rule. Tea, at first used as a medicinal cure-all, became the preferred drink of "polite" society by 1700, a breakfast custom that replaced the heavy repast of beef, and a symbol of quiet, private company that contrasted with tavern life. Tea also became a symbol of the colonial elite's refusal to be siphons for England's "common manufactures."[24]

A host of new commodities adorned the persons, dining tables, and homes of successful wholesalers. Like his counterpart in London, the well-to-do New York gentleman spent lavishly to display the returns on the economic risks he had taken. Whether they acquired new vessels, warehouses, and waterfront property or invested in town houses, real estate, and sumptuous banquets, colonists often measured merchants' success by the visible signs of wealth. John Watts and John Low vied with fellow merchants to give the most splendid turtle barbecues, to serve the most exotic banquets, to wear fashionable, well-coiffed wigs and to shave with fish-skin razors. By the later years of the century, there were sixty-six coaches and chaises in New York City, most of them owned by merchants. Skilled slaves worked as coachmen, valets, cooks, and smiths to maintain the wealthy merchant's lifestyle. A few households had as many as three to five white bond servants and three to five black slaves. Two- and three-story brick mansions became the pride of the De Lancey, Stevens, and Livingston families, as well as the city's great sugar merchants, the Rhinelanders, Bayards, and Alexanders; the distillers and brewers George Harrison, the Lispenards, and the Beekmans; and the shipping magnates William Walton and John Watts. Isaac Roosevelt and Rip van Dam indulged themselves in fountains, roof gardens, and brightly wallpapered townhouses that imitated the lifestyles of British East India merchants, although most of their fellow wholesalers preferred to live near their counting houses in the city. Some spent lavishly on unnecessary "superfluities" because their means to reinvest profits were limited by the extent of markets or their ability to put money out on loan. Others believed that their coaches, mansions, and wigs elevated their business connections to the public.[25]

As extant commercial correspondence indicates, city traders took time to import reading materials from England. Although books often were decorative accoutrements in merchants' households, or additional validation of leisured habits, merchants reported reading many of their titles too. Their libraries included not only the popular moral and classical republican texts but also the works of dissenting political economists and critics of imperial arrangements. Some traders in New York listed the free-trade writings of Hugo Grotius among their collections, and by the final colonial decades, merchants' import ledgers and private letters mention histories and early English novels, as well as economic titles by Malachy Postlethwayte and John Locke. The printer and bookseller James Rivington wrote to William Johnson of titles he had recently imported for New York merchants, including Robertson's *History of Scotland,* Lord Littleton's *History of Henry II,* editions of popular plays, the *Annual Register,* Captain John Knox's *Historical Journal . . . for 1757, 1758, 1759, and 1760,* as well as "many literary works" that, he believed, circulated from household to household. William Johnson often shared the *Gentleman's Magazine,* Homer and other classical writers, and London newspapers with his New York City whole-sale merchant liaisons. The merchant Samuel Judah's personal library, from which a few prominent city traders borrowed, included the following list:

Postlethwaite's *Dictionary*, 2 vols.

Watson's *History of Philip the 2d*, 2 vols.

Hutchinson's *History of Massachusetts Bay*, 2 vols.

Abbe Reynall's *History of the East and West Indies*, 5 vols.

Gibbon's *History of the Roman Empire*, 1 vol.

Saxby's *Brittish Customs*, 1 vol.

Baldwin's————ditto, 1 vol.

Spectator, 8 vols.

Tour through Britain, 4 vols.

Life of John Bundo, Esq., 4 vols.

Remembrancer, 13 vols. in 8 books

The Profest Cook, 1 vol.

Malcolm's *Arithmetick*, 1 vol.

2 vols. of *Shakespear*, 3rd and 4th

The Universal Gazetteer, 1 vol.

Salmon's *Geographical Grammar*, 1 vol.

Two of Bayle's Dictionaries

Bailey's *English Dictionary*

Town and Country Magazine

Annual Register, 2 vols.

Parliamentary Register, 2 vols., No. 1 and 3

Swift's *Works*, 2 vols.

Gentleman's Magazine, 1 vol.

Commodore Walker's Voyages, 1 vol.

The Grecian Courtezan, 1 vol.

Nature Displayed, 1 vol.

Tryal of Doctor Sachaverell, 1 vol.

Pope's *Works*, 1 vol.

Peregrine Pickle, 1 vol.

Don Quixote, 1 vol. in French

The Young Man's Book of Knowledge, 1 vol.

Lady Chudleigh's *Poems*, 1 vol.

Court Calendar, 3 vols.

Adventures of a Jesuit, 1 vol.

History of Canada, 1 vol.

Earl of Warwick, a Tragedy

Peerage of England, 3 vols.

German Grammar, 1 vol.

Acts of Parliament, 1 vol.

Trials for Adultery, 5 vols.

Death of Abel, 1 vol.[26]

There is no necessary connection between what merchants read and the economic choices they made; we shall never know what texts influenced their commercial behavior, or how elements of texts may have entered their thoughts about market relations. Although more readers chose works on "political economy" by the 1750s, they may have found written support for commercial innovations *after* they had already initiated forms of economic behavior consonant with the views they encountered in printed texts. For example, it is doubtful whether Locke's analysis of the origins of money and English coinage actually prompted merchants to rethink their trading patterns and business practices; merchants' experiments and risks with devaluation and new forms of credit may, in fact, have been the model for what tractarians would only later record on the printed page. However, by midcentury, certain printed texts articulated and ratified their commercial aspirations. Books helped put into words and systematically conceptualize things that practical businessmen did regularly. More than merely symbols of pretension, books were shared around and valued highly in personal wills. They also provided affirmation not so much of a merchant's advancement out of his commercial station into one of gentility as of his valued place in city life as a merchant.[27]

It seemed natural at first for resident New Yorkers and visitors to link the city's changing economic welfare to the rise of this eminent group of wholesalers. But when, following the recession of the 1720s, more colonists began to eat and wear a greater variety of commodities, and to replace certain household wares as fashion instructed, some of them noticed that their well-being depended on a variety of conditions outside of elite influence. Expanding internal production and demographic growth had created demand and purchasing power, as well as exports. The province had developed more roads and ferries, and wagons traversed the regional byways for the commodities needed—or simply desired—by villagers and semirural settlers. A greater division of functions between country and city evolved; middlemen began to market certain agricultural surpluses, and storekeepers held larger varieties of finished goods or gave credit in the form of advances on future crops or retail trade business in small towns. Local exchange relations, never totally dominant in New York anyway, began to break down almost visibly. By the opening of the eighteenth century, the metropolis integrated its expanding international trade with the production of grain in New York, New Jersey, and Connecticut; exports of furs declined, but merchants sought them even into Canada. Domestic small traders transported timber and small quantities of metal ores, ginseng, flaxseed, and myriad farm surpluses of dairy and preserved meat products into merchants' warehouses for consumption in the city or export. As city commerce ranged to the farthest corners of the world, markets for bills of exchange grew, thereby easing payments to England for its manufactures. An active shipbuilding industry increased earnings on freight, ships, and insurance. Commercialization of the frontier prompted the rise of new towns around the city, which created demand for even more importation. As merchants' economic opportunities expanded, so too did the "revolution in desires" for new commodities. All of these changes, colonists admitted, played a role in their rise.[28]

In their "perpetual restless ambition . . . to raise themselves," middling New Yorkers adopted some commodities formerly found only in elite households. In 1731, at least one observer believed that "habitual Tea-Drinking" "so universally prevail[ed]" among New Yorkers that reforming their preferences seemed impossible. Women and men alike consumed it "as often as . . . Salt at Meals . . . or to fill up little Intervals of Discourse." William Smith had been "credibly informed that tea and china ware cost the province, yearly, near the sum of £10,000." By 1750, others affirmed that new economic preferences, especially the "fashion for luxuries," which "we now deem necessary," had "uncontrolled sway" on both sides of the Atlantic Ocean. "Commerce engrossed the attention of the principle [sic] families" and also "attracted shopkeepers, and tradesmen, who sustain the reputation of honest, punctual, and fair dealers. With respect to riches, there is not so great an inequality amongst us as is common in Boston and some other places. Every man of industry and integrity has it in his power to live well, and many are the instances of persons who came here distressed by their poverty, who now enjoy easy and plentiful fortunes."[29] Tastes did not change over night. Dry-goods importers continued to bring in many essential goods; agricultural tools, glassware, anchors, anvils, bells, hammers, grindstones, panes, cutlery, copperware, cast-iron wares, earthenware, pewterware, saws, scythes, shovels, and vises represented about 40 percent of New York's annual average of legal imports from England even at midcentury. But importers' ledgers and retailers' inventories show that about one-quarter of the city's imports from London and Bristol firms from 1722 to 1765 were "oriental goods" such as spices, teas, pepper, and chinaware.[30]

Above all, however, the expanding West Indies and coastal markets offered great varieties of goods colonists had never before experienced. In addition to the great quantities of sugar and molasses flowing into New York City by the 1720s, there were ginger, salt, rum, lime juice, pimento, oils, ginseng, and "cocoa nuts" from the West Indies, goods that created new impressions of the world of trade and introduced new habits of consumption. Southern colonies sold rice, tobacco, cotton wool, and lignum vitae. More New Yorkers processed chocolate, snuff, and distilled spirits in New York, or reexported various dyewoods (referred to as fustic, Jamaica, or Honduras), ebony, whale fins, deer skins, mahogany, dried fruits, indigo, coconuts, coffee, sugar and candy; and importation of these goods prompted larger exports of grain, flour, ship's biscuit, lumber products, beeswax, and flaxseed by the 1730s, and of potash and pearl ash by the 1750s, while city chocolate and candy manufacturers purchased cocoa beans in large quantities.[31] Local shopkeepers or small entrepreneurs pickled, candied, sliced, and packaged West Indies pimento, lemon, and ginger. For a growing number of New Yorkers, "superfluities" never before imagined from places they would never visit adorned city shop windows:

To be sold, wholesale and retail . . . on Rotten Row: Fine Heyson, Green, Congoe and Bohea Tea; Coffee and Chocolate; single and double Refined Sugar; Powder and Muscovado do.; Sugar Candy; Sugar Plumbs and Carraway; Confects; Jarr Raisins and Cask ditto; Currants, Figgs, and Prunes; Almonds in the Shell; Cloves, Mace, Cinnamon, and Nutmeg; Ginger, Black Pepper and Allspice; Dry Citron by the Box or smaller quantity; West India Sweetmeats of all Sorts; Preserves of all Sorts, such as Currants, Jellys, Quinces, Grapes, Strawberries, Raspberries, Damsons, Peaches, Plums, and sundry other sorts. Pickles of all sorts in small quantities, very fit for the Army, such as Walnuts, Cucumbers, Mangoes, Pepers, Capers, Anchovies, etc. Pickled Oysters and Lobsters.[32]

However accessible these goods became to people with middling incomes, their acquisition depended on an intricate web of commercial relationships developed by an ever-shifting, always creative, community of merchants trading to the West Indies and ports along the North American coastline.

The Caribbean Linchpin

Distinctions between eminent and rising merchants became most palpable when colonists contemplated their West Indies commerce, in no small part because that arena of trade continued to provide much of the opportunity for new merchants and optimism for new consumption. By 1700, merchants had established solid trade routes to the Caribbean, and by 1730, traders along the Hudson River and on Long Island had settled into exporting patterns that persisted until textile factories appeared in the nineteenth century. More and more, colonists shaped their tastes and spending patterns around West Indies goods; the trade in turn provided the specie and bills of exchange for their expanding imports from transatlantic sources. As a petition of sixty-seven merchants put it in 1704, "the principall staple of the trade of this Province is the manufactory of wheat expended chiefly in the West Indies." From this trade, they noted, colonists expanded their consumption and "returns [are] made for England . . . [with] heavy pieces of 8. and other produce of the West Indies." In 1748, Peter Kalm recorded a common wisdom that "the goods which are shipped to the West Indies, are sometimes paid for with ready money and sometimes with West India goods, which are either first brought to New York, or immediately sent to England or Holland." He might have added that many West Indies merchants paid New Yorkers with bills of exchange drawn on London firms, a vital means of redressing the colony's trade imbalances with England. Only when wars disrupted this set of happy arrangements did wheat become "of small value in the West Indies, to our great impoverishment." Consumer demand for sugar, muscovado, molasses, coffee, and rum coming from the Caribbean seemed to keep pace—and sometimes outrun—merchants' ability to import them in larger quantities after 1730. Rum that colonists did not consume could be reexported toward Albany for the Indian trade, or to the Newfoundland fisheries, while sugar and molasses became universal sweeteners and ingredients in over 300 medicines. By midcentury, a few city sugar merchants turned to refining and candy making. Distilling, brewing, and refining were industries capitalized and owned by merchants who traded primarily with West Indian islands.[33]

From 1715 to 1765, half of New York City's entering and clearing vessels plied the West Indies, and almost half of its cargo tonnage left the city for West Indian destinations. Those markets also permitted more sole or dual ownership of mid-sized vessels than the transatlantic trade. Between 1700 and 1709, partnerships of three to twelve merchants owned fully 78 percent of the city's vessels clearing for the West Indies, while sole ownership or dual partnership accounted for only 9 percent of city clearances to that region. By 1729, those figures had become 60 percent and 35 percent, and in 1764, three to five traders jointly owned 58 percent of clearing vessels, while one or two men owned 37 percent of them. Although the city's well-established merchants ignored the West Indies trade at their peril, the Caribbean attracted mostly lesser merchants. Once piracy and warfare abated after roughly 1700, new traders found it cheaper to outfit a voyage to the West Indies than a transatlantic one, and thus more feasible when one lacked much capital. The shorter and less perilous voyage to the Caribbean increased the likelihood of quicker disposal of cargo and an earlier return than dry-goods importing from England or the wine trade with southern Europe. Since the merchant capitalist of the eighteenth century had few means for coping with high labor and transport costs, the proximity of numerous trading towns in the West Indies also reduced docking time and kept goods circulating. Moreover, voyages to the West Indies cost less to insure during times of peace.[34]

Changing demographic, ethnic, and political influences in New York City by the second generation of English rule did not at first shift interest significantly away from Dutch Caribbean coffee and sugar.[35] Routes from St. Eustatius, Surinam, Curaçao, and Guinea to Amsterdam were well established, of course, but fewer New Yorkers ventured from the Caribbean across the Atlantic Ocean by the start of the century. Instead, they shuttled between New York City and the islands and relied upon Dutch factors to transship goods to their home country or to market West Indian returns throughout Europe. A factor in New York for the Amsterdam merchant Albert Hodshon received dry goods over the years 1706 to 1714 at 5 percent commission, which he then dispersed in two different ways. Merchants sold some of each shipment to retailers in the city in exchange for grain and flour, which they loaded on vessels bound for Curaçao. Middling merchants marketed some dry goods in the West Indies for Hodshon, and occasionally the factor sent goods up the Hudson River to Jacob Nutsen in Esopus. Vessels returning from Curaçao to New York City brought cocoa, slaves, molasses, and plenty of bills of exchange and cash to be credited against the accounts of city traders who had shipped the Dutch goods (as well as local products on their own accounts). Finally, after subtracting his commission, the factor forwarded a large portion of the bills of exchange and cash from the West Indies to Hodshon.[36]

At least ten city exporters who had started out sending furs to Amsterdam and London shifted to Dutch West Indies trade by 1715, and "Robert and Peter Livingston and Company" followed this pattern during the 1720s and 1730s, as did Cornelius and Philip Cuyler. The Cuylers also realized the value of free, or open, trade at the Dutch islands and the Low Countries, and they increased their trade with the West Indies "of necessity" because of "those unnatural acts" of Parliament. By 1723, Surveyor-General Cadwallader Colden reported that "a Considerable Trade with Curacoa" in time might rival the British West Indies traffic; indeed, over the decade, most of New York's flour went to Curaçao and the British possession of Jamaica.[37]

Spanish possessions figured more prominently in New Yorkers' trade once piracy had been reduced and peace returned in 1713. Before the 1720s, British West Indies merchants depended on foreign money, rum, sugar, and molasses

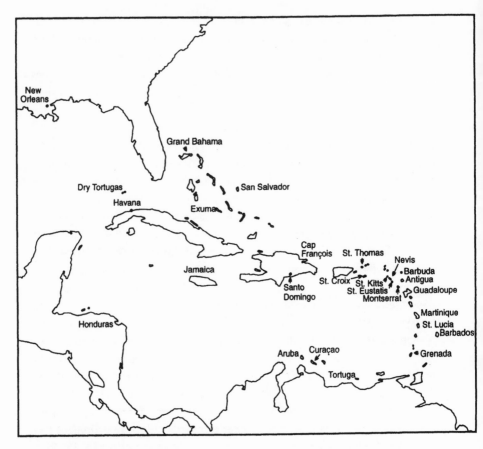

Map 4. New York City Merchants' Major West Indies Ports of Call by the *1690s*

from *asiento* factors at Havana and Monte Cristi to supplement their own smaller exports from Barbados and Jamaica. By the late 1720s, a few New York merchants sought direct connections with Spanish factors at Havana and the Bay of Campeche, and by the mid 1730s, some of New York's grain and lumber exporters had established a regular trade with the Spanish Caribbean. Philip Livingston, for example, diverted some of his wheat shipments intended for Antigua to Spanish ports during the war year of 1735, and despite official decrees cutting off the Spanish trade in 1739, London writers were convinced that northern colonists conducted a regular trade with their enemy merchants in the Caribbean.[38]

Between 1688 and 1717, the French West India Company held monopoly rights to trade with French Caribbean possessions. However, its home government forbade the company either to import West Indies rum into France—as a means of protecting brandy distillers—or to reexport muscovado from France—on the assumption that France ought not to provision rival nations. With their home market thus circumscribed, French merchants in the Caribbean had a major rationale for expanding their illicit trade with colonists in British North America, to whom they sold sugar and molasses cheaply, and from whom they bought the fish, salted meat, grain, lumber and horses that the French colonies required. Even when the French government opened this illicit trade to legitimate competition, prices of French molasses and rum remained comparatively low; over the years before 1729, merchants reported French prices 25 percent below those in English possessions such as Barbados, Antigua, and St. Kitts. French commodities also did not carry the 4½ percent export duty at British islands during this period. One report estimated that England's northern colonies "took as much or more from the French and Dutch" in molasses and rum as they did from British islands.[39]

English possessions—Barbados, Jamaica, Antigua, Nevis, and St. Kitts—became an important source of demand for colonial goods that England could not absorb, and for reexports to the mother country. Colonists had little use for dyewoods such as logwood and fustic from Honduras and the Leeward Islands, and only erratic demand for lime juice, lignum vitae, cotton wool, indigo, and coffee from the islands; until the 1740s, West Indies merchants often commissioned more sugar and cocoa beans than their own regional markets could consume, with the intention of transshipping those commodities—along with their own regional products—to London. Although some of the sugar traffic went directly from the West Indies to England, most transatlantic traders preferred to reexport sugar brought back from the West Indies in smaller vessels, in part because New Yorkers owned few oceangoing vessels until the 1730s, and reexporting permitted consolidation of cargoes. From 1750 to 1755, the value of sugar from New York reexported to British ports was about £2,500 to £4,500 a year; from 1757 to 1763, it rose to from £25,000 to £50,000 a year, because privateersmen captured great quantities from enemy vessels, and because New Yorkers could by then refine the less desirable muscovado into finer grades of sugar for English buyers.[40]

Middling West Indies merchants and great traders to London benefited together from these opportunities. For one thing, middling merchants' steadily rising imports helped fill the holds of ships clearing for England faster than otherwise, thereby reducing port costs and turnaround times. West Indian reexports were surety against large financial losses or even bankruptcy, because New Yorkers frequently sent cargoes to England of less value and volume than those they imported, or when bills of exchange were in short supply. Then, too, the colony's agricultural goods rarely found sufficient demand in the mother country. For the newcomer to transatlantic commerce, reexports of dyewoods and coffee, mixed with cargoes of grain, refined sugar, and bar iron, were a low-risk entrance into the British trade.[41] By some accounts, New Yorkers' "independence" in reexporting and monopolizing local exports additionally discouraged some London traders from factoring and auctioning goods in the city. For example, some members of the Cruger family in the West Indies procured sugar, while John Cruger "monop'liz'd" the export of flaxseed and flaxseed oil from New York to Bristol by purchasing numerous small cargoes from regional merchants; together, the Crugers undermined the attempts of Bristol merchants to place their own agents in New York City.[42]

Patterns in the shipping career of Moses Levy illuminate the interdependent relations of modest traders, New York consumers, and London firms. It is unclear when Levy immigrated into New York, but it could not have been much sooner than mid 1695 when, at the age of thirty, he became a freeman of the city. That same year, assessors valued his real estate at a mere £5, one of the lowest assessments for a merchant in the city; other untaxed wealth probably included shares in two or three vessels, a small quantity of West Indian goods in the warehouse of a friend, and household belongings. By January 1700, Levy shared the risk of importing on London-owned vessels with seventeen to twenty-two other city merchants; from 1700 to 1709, he sent parcels on the New York ships *Endeavor, Palmtree, Dove, Hope, Anne, Unity,* and *New York Merchant* about once a year to London, and with four to eleven merchants, two or three times a year to Barbados and Jamaica on the *Supply, Isaac, Joseph, Mary, Dolphin, Eagle,* and *Fortune.* Like transatlantic voyages, those to West Indian ports involved long layovers in the early years of the century; merchants sometimes waited six months to make up a return cargo. Also, voyages to both London and the West Indies involved more diverse cargoes and risks more widely spread among many city traders than they would by the 1720s and 1730s; Levy, like others, imported what he thought might sell—fustic, strouds, brandy, or iron, but also sugar, coffee, molasses, and "trunks of merchandize" filled with notions, cloths, and seeds, or large orders for sugar or "English hats." Levy's trade extended to Rhode Island, where he sent parcels of dry goods, and to Madeira, where he acquired portions of wine shipments.[43]

Just after Queen Anne's War, Levy joined many city traders in efforts to extend their routes and add new ports of call. Some of them had built their own vessels in New York by 1715 and formed partnerships with one or two other merchants rather than three or more, thereby assuming greater risks in each voyage, but hoping to make greater gains. From November 1715 to November 1716, Levy engaged shares in the *Abigail* to export provisions, wine, onions, vinegar, and grain to St. Thomas; import potatoes, straw ware and bills of exchange from Bermuda in March; set out a month later with provisions and boards for Barbados; return four months later with rice and pitch from South Carolina and bills of exchange from Barbados; set out again in a month with provisions, grain, and coconuts for Lisbon, return with wine, and reload at New York City with provisions for Jamaica.[44]

By early 1717, Levy had become part owner of the *Charlotte* with Jacob Franks, Samuel Levy, and Henry Cuyler, and of the *Curaçao* with Samuel Levy; both ships set out from New York City about four times a year with provisions and lumber—and less frequently with candles, copper ore, and grain—for the West Indies. Both ships also arrived at New York City from West Indian ports about once a quarter, laden with rum, sugar, molasses, European goods, pimento, lime juice, and coconuts. Occasionally, the captain returned with a whole cargo of salt from the Salt Islands or a few slaves from Barbados. Before 1720, Levy joined only once with a London merchant, for a trip to Madeira with 4,100 bushels of grain, and only once with other city merchants—Stephen van Cortlandt and Adolph Philipse, along with his close associate Jacob Franks—in a venture of the *Abigail* to acquire a shipload of annatto (a yellowish red dyestuff) and indigo, which they reexported to England. In September 1720, Levy sent the *Charlotte* to Amsterdam loaded with furs, dyewood, and sugar, but he made no other known trip to that port over his career.

Following this basic pattern of dependence on West Indian demand, Levy branched out to include Nathan Simpson as a partner on a few voyages in 1720 and traded with correspondents at Jamaica, Nevis, and St. Thomas, where he acquired snuff, cotton wool, old iron, and fish. Roughly once a year, from mid 1720 to mid 1729, Levy also sent the *Rachel*—of which he was sole owner—to Jamaica full of provisions and lumber, and the *Prince Frederick* to London with a variety of West Indies commodities. These two vessels also involved new partners, David and Matthew Clarkson, Robert Livingston, and Paul Richards, while the older vessels continued to sail under the original partnerships. In 1728 and 1729, the last two years of Levy's commerce, the troubled recession markets forced him, and many others, to diversify even more. City export ledgers show him venturing grain and flour to Madeira, and more regional commodities to Surinam, Jamaica, Newfoundland, and South Carolina; import ledgers show that small amounts of mohair, silk, berries, coffee beans, Indian goods, wine, cordage, pitch, tar, fish, and old bottles came to New York on his ships, but he purchased far less sugar and molasses. By late 1729, failing health and a continuing recession influenced Levy's decision to halt transatlantic commerce and concentrate his voyages on bilateral West Indies–New York routes.

Although transatlantic dry-goods merchants often diversified when they had built up large stocks of capital and goods, as well as far-flung reputations for carrying a great array of goods, for Levy and many of his middling peers, diverse cargoes provided hedges against adversity. By the time of his death in 1729, Levy had sustained an above-average, but never superior, position among city traders for years. Two of his sons, Isaac and Michael, carried on the family's trade with Jamaica and Barbados and developed trading connections in Boston and Philadelphia in the 1730s. Their cousin Hayman Levy and two of his sons also carried a variety of West Indies commodities, as well as slaves and logwood, over the 1740s and 1750s. All were recognized as reputable regional wholesalers, albeit of modest stature.[45]

Moses Levy was one of many New Yorkers who gradually extended their markets and increased the number of their correspondents, but never profited exceedingly. Gabriel Minvielle, who had arrived in 1669, had little more than a house in New York in 1692, but he bought two commercial buildings in the next nine years, boasted many household adornments, and owned two household slaves. Minvielle later served as mayor, ardently opposed Jacob Leisler, and married into the well-to-do Lawrence family. But his commerce, as Minvielle was the first to admit, never grew to the level he had hoped to achieve. When he died in 1702, he had few debts to settle, but neither did he leave his family much in the way of goods or investments.[46]

Matthew Ling, who arrived in the 1680s, did not rise as high as Minvielle, possibly because his trade included only the islands of Barbados, Nevis, St. Kitts, and Jamaica and he did not enter the fur trade. Ling's flour and grain business linked him to city bolters, and his provisions exports found ready markets in the Caribbean. His captains returned with rum, which he sold to tavern-keepers and Boston factors who came to New York City looking for business, and small quantities of sugar, cocoa beans, nails, and dry goods, which he sold to city retailers from the dock. In 1695, Ling's personal and real property was assessed at £50, a small sum for an ambitious merchant; but by 1703, he was a widower living in a fine brick city residence and owned wharf space, a warehouse, and three female slaves. Having attained modest comfort, Ling retired in 1704.[47]

As the staples-producing economies of the Caribbean plantations grew, New York merchant families transplanted some of their sons and cousins to the islands to act as factors or buyers for them. William Lloyd, for example, went to Kingston, Jamaica, in 1752 to enter a partnership with the importer Charles

Seymour. The firm of Perry & Ludlow and the businesses of John Harris Cruger and Henry Livingston also served New York merchants almost exclusively because of their family connections. The Curaçao merchants Telemon Cruger, Philip Livingston, John Cuyler, Myndert Lansing, Nicholas and Isaac Gouverneur, and members of the De Peyster, Duyckinck, Bowen, Lefferts, and Remsen families all did a brisk trade with New Yorkers. Cornelius Kortright and Nicholas Cruger set up counting houses in St. Croix, and David Beekman, whose older brother Gerard lived in New York, became a sugar planter. William Livingston and Peter van Brugh Livingston went to the West Indies as young men to learn the business before they started out "on their own account" in New York, and Alexander Hamilton clerked for the West Indian firm of David Beekman and John Harris Cruger, whose wide network of kin covered Curaçao, St. Croix, St. Thomas, New York, and Bristol.[48]

The profound dependence New Yorkers created upon West Indian commerce was not an unmitigated blessing. By the 1720s, merchants' letters dwelled on periodic commercial difficulties. Caribbean growers often enjoyed a favorable balance of trade with England, which allowed them to spend more for lumber, livestock, and grain in British North America. The greater flow of cash and bills of exchange into New York in turn fueled merchants' ability to place large orders with English creditors. But those orders hinged on the illusion that New York's exports grew at a pace commensurate with staples production in the West Indies and New Yorkers' own demand for imports. This, however, was not consistently the case; New Yorkers consistently exported goods of lower value than those they imported from England and southern Europe, sometimes four to six times lower.[49]

The West Indies trade was "hazardous" or "torturous" in other ways, too. After the 1690s, Jamaican planters expanded sugar production and boosted the island into the most favored position in the British West Indies. Not only was Jamaica the only English possession in the West Indies not to levy export duties before 1756, which kept the cost of exporting sugar and molasses lower than it was at competing islands. Planters also aggressively expanded sugar production by concentrating their resources on it and avoiding other food and crafts production, with the result that demand for imports of foodstuffs, horses, and clothing in Jamaica rose rapidly. Upward swings of sugar prices in England— 1689 to 1713 and 1734 to 1758—pleased many New York merchants too, as did rising prices for New York's wheat in the West Indies from 1698 to about 1725, 1739 to 1744, and 1747 to 1748.[50]

But if successful voyages might bring profits of 25 to 30 percent, in the context of overall European competition and the transatlantic recession of the 1720s, traders in the West Indies expressed fears about sustaining such earnings. Proximity to West Indian markets offered merchants an alluring prospect of rapid turnover and frequent trips, but it also attracted competitors in large numbers. Wars, slave revolts, high mortality among slaves, the speed at which land was converted to sugar production, and the reliability of captains and the resident agents who received and sold New York cargoes in the West Indies also affected the prices of British North American exports. Then, too, when the prices of colonial exports to Havana or Port-au-Prince rose, the news traveled quickly to hundreds of northern correspondents by eighteenth-century standards, resulting in glutted markets and downward-spiraling prices within months.

By the late 1720s, New Yorkers were pressing London for policy changes to compensate for the uncertainties of commerce at Jamaica. But conditions worsened until about 1735, low export prices and soil depletion forced Jamaican merchants to limit their production of sugar, molasses, and rum and indirectly to reduce importation from New Yorkers, who in turn reoriented some of their trade to Barbados and the Leeward Islands. At those islands, too, New Yorkers despaired of selling their goods at "reasonable prices"; through the War of Jenkin's Ear, some wholesalers looked in vain for places to market the colony's grain and flour. The years 1740–46, 1748–52, 1757–62, 1765, and late 1766 through 1769 evoked additional complaints of very low prices in the West Indies; and the years 1753–56 and 1762–64 witnessed wide fluctuations in prices within months. Unless a captain or factor chose to wait in port for prices to climb again—a costly decision—he was forced to take losses on the early sale of his commodities or to accept pledges against the following year's sugar crop. Abraham Keteltas simply despaired of sales to familiar correspondents in Jamaica and left one hundred barrels of flour at Kingston "unsold there." Others brought flour back to New York.

Challenges to imperial goals and private interests spurred a debate by the late 1720s that reassessed colonial commerce in the West Indies. Not only the conditions of island production, warfare, and competition with other ports, but the imperial political economy itself seemed flawed from the vantage point of British planters. They complained about competition in Holland and France, where sugar imports remained cheaper, and return goods to the islands were consistently of inferior quality, but more easily disposed of to islanders. Rankled by their loss of profits in the West Indies, British planters also noted the loss of English customs revenues when North American colonists imported foreign sugar direct from the West Indies. Over the 1720s, some Londoners singled out northern colonial wholesalers for their violations of imperial trade laws; their reexports of French sugar to England, tracts argued, cost the Exchequer at least £1,000 per year in duties colonial merchants would have paid if English ships had carried English sugar. London merchants linked closely to New York exporters believed that the best way to reduce the wholesale and retail price of sugar and molasses carried to England and restore more legal trade was to deregulate those commodities, thereby making them competitive with the French ones. But hardened mercantile observers refused to lower export duties at British Caribbean islands or—turning their backs on some New York pleas—to create free ports there. Represented by a West Indian planters' lobby, favored since the late seventeenth century by the fawning solicitude of mercantilists in Parliament, they persuaded the House of Commons to discuss a bill to disallow North American colonists to carry sugar, molasses, and rum into their ports and subsequently reexport large portions of it; instead the bill proposed to enforce an earlier law requiring direct transport of those goods from the British West Indies to the home country. When New York merchants, reinforced by their own Governor Cosby's letters to Parliament, confronted the powerful "sugar interests" of Barbados, Jamaica, and the Leeward Islands, however, and argued strenuously about the value of northern colonial carriers for the entire system of West Indian relations, things took a different turn; within weeks, legislators shelved the bill.[51]

Not all merchants in England wanted a direct trade with the British West Indies that would exclude northern colonial carriers. A London importer, Micajah Perry, wrote to Cadwallader Colden in late 1731 of his opposition to the notion "that the Islands were the only usefull Colonies we had & that the Continent was rather a nusance." His counter argument was to show, by invoking the proof of customs returns, that he and other London merchants had exported "more of the Manufactures of this Country [England] to the [American] Continent than the Island of Barbados Ever took off in one year." Further, since the French could not consume anywhere near the full quantity of molasses and sugar from their possessions in the Caribbean, those commodities "must in probability be thrown away, if your [New York] people did not take it." Or, Perry continued, an even worse possibility loomed; if British colonial merchants did not transport the molasses of foreign islands, "it seems very naturall to me that they [the French] will fall to distilling it themselves & supply the whole fishery at Newfoundland," which remained vital to imperial interests. Finally, Perry agreed with colonists' argument that if the laws forced them to buy British molasses at higher prices, they would "grow Barley & provide [them]selves with spirits within [them]selves"; and if they could not sell their lumber to foreign islands, northern colonists would divert their commerce through "Quebeck, Cape Briton & the Mississippi which however difficult it may appear necessity will make Easy."[52]

In 1732, a writer in the *New-York Gazette* extended arguments against the intended parliamentary legislation by claiming that none of the northern colonies imported much rum from the West Indies because they made their own. Deprived of markets for sugar and molasses to distill into rum, the Indian trade and northern fisheries would languish; French remittances of silver and cocoa, which traders sent to England to pay for finished goods, would cease; and shipbuilding and marine employment would decline. New York merchant petitioners and publicists readily acknowledged their carrying trade with foreign islands, but insisted upon its probity, since the British West Indies could not provide colonists with large enough markets for their grain, flour, and lumber. No nation could wish to stagnate economically in order to honor the misguided notion of increasing the "Luxury and Extravagance" of a few planters. In fact, they quarreled, if policies cut off New York's means to buy manufactures, it "must be reduced to Nakedness or to make our own Clothing." New Yorkers must have "the open way of Trade."[53]

In addition, New York merchants reminded Parliament that the Caribbean plantations had been too large to attend properly to soil fertilization, slave discipline, and harvesting, so that returns from Barbados and the Leeward Islands had fallen. While corrupt clerks ran their plantations, absentee planters lived in idleness and luxury far from the miseries of tropical life. They matched each particular of their attack on British planters with a favorable view of French and Dutch methods: foreign planters' holdings were newer and smaller, owners often resident, slavery more socially stable, and French settlements along the Gulf coast and in the Caribbean populous and mature. An act to deny British North America the right to trade with the foreign West Indies would not only destroy British interests but aid England's enemies as well; New York merchants "must have the Sugar business" of France and Spain "because they have no manufactures of their own by which to remit to [England's] creditors." The Danish possessions, according to a captain's letter to New York merchants, lowered import duties at St. Croix, because "without America they cannot live." Others noted that the French and Spanish planters put most of their capital resources into sugar production and slaves, and reserved little of it for sustaining agriculture, with the resulting high demand for provisions, construction materials, and shoes from British North America. Merchants at the French possessions did not depend entirely on home markets, and their imperial center allowed sales directly to neutral Dutch and northern colonial merchants. Citing

Lord Coke's treatises, one New Yorker insisted that trade "is the livelihood of the merchant, the life of the commonwealth." Why, then, should "trade, commerce, arts, sciences and manufactures . . . not be as free for an American as for an European?"[54]

From 1729 to 1732, sugar planters deluged the English press and Parliament with tracts to refute these arguments. What, asked many of them, had the concerns of subordinate colonies to do with the burgeoning demand for sugar throughout Europe and the potential for making it a foundation of English prosperity? Sugar, they continued, called forth an array of manufacturing and distributing services, including carriers, refiners, distillers, commission agents, and bank funding. Rum was a vital link in the slave trade and in Indian diplomacy throughout the empire. They estimated that while £10 million of English capital was sunk in mainland North America, over £66 million—much of it spent on the slave trade—depended upon the continued prosperity of the British Caribbean. Moreover, the northern colonies consumed less of England's manufactures than the West Indies did, and the duties on the direct trade boosted England's welfare. Foreign competition brought on an unquestionable decline in sugar prices from 1729 to 1733, aided and abetted by the debilitating rise of smuggling among the islands, and between the islands and northern colonies. In reflecting back upon the 1720s, William Smith conceded that England had almost always had a favorable balance of trade with all of its colonies, and that it would be an even larger balance "if a stop was put to all clandestine trade." But, he insisted, "our importation of dry goods, from England, is so vastly great that we are obliged to betake ourselves to all possible arts to make remittances to the British merchants. It is for this purpose we import cotton from St. Thomas and Surinam, lime juice and Nicaragua wood from Curacoa, and logwood from the [Honduras] bay, etc." Still, this foreign trade was not enough and "it drains us of all the gold and silver we can collect."[55]

The Molasses Act of 1733 gave the victory to the West Indies sugar planters. It put duties on all foreign rum (6d. per gallon), molasses (6d. per gallon), and sugar (5s. per cwt.) imported into the colonies, stipulating that these duties be paid in cash before landing, and also permitted drawbacks of duties paid at British ports when merchants carried the commodities direct from the West Indies. However, the act had minimal effects from 1733 to 1759. Although its imports of sugar and molasses never reached Boston's levels in that period, New York imported more each year; when city traders had trouble acquiring West Indies commodities, regional or world economic tendencies were the cause, rather than the Molasses Act's prohibitions. Moreover, many merchants persistently invested their personal fortunes in illegal voyages, and all exporters sought to manipulate regional markets in their own interests, quite aside from imperial designs. Moreover, there were three distilleries in New York in 1730, but twelve by 1748.

Despite these advances, New York merchants gave it as their impression very early that the new legislation was harmful, and that open trade with all Caribbean markets would prevent the annoying gyrations of prices there. The balance of trade was not so favorable as New Yorkers thought it ought to have been, and it did not keep pace with debts due to London firms. Indeed, the Molasses Act drew greater fire from city exporters and importers than other trade acts. Merchants' letters expressed fears that the act might undermine trade with coastal and southern European ports, and some of them turned toward contemplating the remedy of making New York a "free port," or simply evading the act.[56]

Worsening conditions fueled fears and organized opposition over the next few years. England's declining demand for sugar from New York carriers and insufficient processing industries in New York to absorb large amounts of sugar and molasses were but two of merchants' complaints. City imports and re-exports slowed by midcentury, which in turn curtailed the ability of New Yorkers to dispose of surplus grain at West Indian ports and to import English goods, and a series of successful grain harvests in the 1730s and 1740s in Europe lowered the price of the middle colonies' grain exports to southern Europe and Amsterdam. Although some New York exporters diverted portions of their grain trade to coastal markets, these shipments could not entirely relieve the effects of shifting trade patterns. In the late 1740s, New Yorkers petitioned Parliament to open the Dutch trade in the West Indies for "profitably exchanging with our enemy the luxuries of life for sugar, a commodity of great and general demand throughout Europe." French molasses continued to have little home market, because monopoly legislation protected brandy distillers there, so that northern colonial merchants believed they provided a justifiable service to exporters at Cayenne, the Mole, and other French possessions when they purchased their molasses. During a post-1760 recession in West Indian markets, Cadwallader Colden remarked that New York merchants had been demanding "freer sugar" and "freer trade" for years since passage of the 1733 Molasses Act.[57]

The Intricacies of the Coastal Trade

Many of the young and modest traders who achieved a degree of success in coastal shuttling are enigmas in the historical record. Colonists, however, never understated the trade's significance. It was a preferred beginning for men who had not yet built their credit and reputations with more distant correspondents, or for third and fourth sons of wholesalers who could not afford to outfit their many children in transatlantic commerce but might hope that a more modest investment in the coastal trade would add to family prosperity. Before 1700, New York's coastal trade to New England allowed merchants to use book credits, promote diverse reciprocal exchanges of commodities, obtain quick turnaround times, and transport and resell small shipments. By 1700, these voyages rose faster in number than any other part of the city's commerce; from 1717 to 1742, the number of New York vessels returning from New England doubled, and the number of clearances to northerly colonies increased by one-third. Ports to the south, excluding Philadelphia, received over twice as many vessels over the same period. Although earlier acts of Parliament attempted to tax goods shipped from colony to colony at the same rates as international exports and imports, enforcers never held close to the law. Hats, woolens, and small iron implements from New York continued to meet the needs of its New England, Chesapeake, and southern colonial neighbors.[58]

Enjoying the relative predictability and regularity of demand from a steadily rising regional population, a host of New Yorkers carried goods valued at £100 or less in their sloops, averaging three or four voyages annually to Boston, Rhode Island, or New Jersey, with occasional trips to the Carolina or Virginia shores. While merchants commonly stashed staples such as wheat, flour, rum and molasses in the holds of coastal sloops, they also redistributed small crafts, household manufactures, cheese, butter, shingles, feathers, and foreign imports that New Yorkers had not purchased. In addition to "natural productions" of the land, they received in return "Fish, Oil, Blubber, Whale Fins, Turpentine Oil, Seal Skins, Hops, Cyder, Flax, Bricks, Cole, Lamp Black, certain Wrought Iron, Tin, Brasiery, Joinery, various carriages and Chairs," and many other commodities from their neighbors. John Theobold, Francis van Dyke, John Williams, Job Carr, Edward Burling, and John Hallock brought raisins, currants, pails, iron goods, Indian strouds, and small amounts of wine for the shops of New York City retailers during the earliest years of the century. Into the 1720s, William Ellison, John Deane, David Townsend, Thomas Barnet, and David Carmer still transported goods of the same kind, but on more frequent voyages. Between 1699 and 1709, the *Mary and Sarah* entered New York twice a year from Boston, sometimes with hundreds of gallons of local rum, sometimes with European goods and English textiles, on order by a dozen or more minor city merchants; and many small wholesalers traded in the reverse direction to Boston on small vessels laden with local goods. Gerard Beekman and Philip Cuyler, both of whom rose quickly to positions of some importance in city

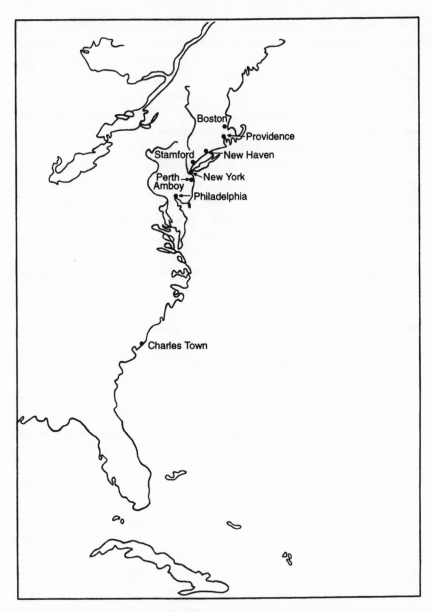

Map 5. New York City Merchants' Major Coastal Ports of Call by the 1690s

commerce, imported goods from afar and kept accounts with dozens of minor wholesalers who reexported portions of the cargoes "on their own accounts."[59]

Boston, which was periodically unable to depend upon its surrounding countryside for exportable foodstuffs, welcomed supplies of wheat, flour, refined sugar, and dairy products from New Yorkers such as Samuel Horner and David van Horne. A significant increase in this trade engaged New Yorkers over the 1730s and early 1740s, and as much as 20 percent of New York's 40,000 bushels of exported wheat and flour went to Boston each year in the 1760s, where it was either consumed or reexported abroad. Moreover, the Boston merchants Peter Faneuil, Charles Apthorp, John Rowe, and Thomas Avery had access both to British credit and dry goods and to imports from the West Indies and South Carolina, which could be transferred in small quantities to New Yorkers' vessels for consumption in their colony.[60]

New York's physical proximity to New Jersey made feasible the creation of a network of family ties uniting lesser merchants to great traders. John Stevens, who got his start as a New Jersey port collector shortly after 1699, married John Campbell's daughter, Anne, and moved to New York by 1700. The Stevens and Campbell families held only modest quantities of trade goods, sloops, and household belongings at this time, but soon Stevens invested in the West Indies and Madeira trade, joining return voyages to New York City to stops at his wharf near Perth Amboy. As both families deepened their connections to farmers and merchants in New Jersey, their stature—and their wealth—rose steadily until Stevens' death in 1737.

Other New Jerseyites pinned their futures on connections with New York. During the 1730s, Andrew Johnston and his brother-in-law John Parker, both of New Jersey, owned shares of at least four vessels that sailed regularly from New York or New Jersey to the West Indies. Johnston's son married a Van Cortlandt, and two of Parker's sons married into the Alexander family, matches that boosted the traders into the social ranks of the most successful shippers in New York, enabling them to do business with the Philipse and De Lancey families as well. Cornelius Low of New York and his son-in-law Joseph Reed of New Jersey jointly sent three vessels to Lisbon in the 1720s. Anthony van Dam did business with the merchants Thomas Chapman and William Bethell of Perth Amboy, and John Watts exported timber and staves for James Neilson of New Jersey. During the 1730s, Philip Livingston worked with correspondents in Perth Amboy to corner wheat and flaxseed for export to Leghorn, where Stork & Gainsborough credited Livingston's accounts. Over the same decade, a large number of New York and New Jersey partners owned shares together in the *Catherine*, *Sally*, and *Little David*, all of which sailed to Africa for slaves or Madeira for wine, and by the 1740s, many New Jersey wholesalers were entrusting goods to Waddell Cunningham of New York City, who owned thirteen vessels engaged in the dry-goods trade with England and Ireland. Fewer of Connecticut's commercial farmers and middling wholesalers linked up with New York City merchants until the 1720s, but thereafter agricultural exports provided men like Philip Livingston with many cargoes of wheat and flaxseed from New London and Matthew Clarkson with great quantities of "country commodities" for transshipment from New London to New York City or Amsterdam.[61]

Newport and Providence traders often relied upon New Yorkers, whose residence in a larger metropolis permitted access to credit, to underwrite their insurance and share the expenses of outfitting West Indies or privateering ventures. Many regional shippers who lived in Rhode Island kept warehouses and stores in New York. It was worth paying commission fees to New York brokers, they wrote, because bar iron, hats, leather and hides, shingles, beer, refined sugar, bricks, candles, English finished goods, artisan implements, and Boston rum sold more quickly there. Until New York's own population began to grow rapidly after the 1720s, some of its own homespun and other home manufactures had found ready buyers in Newport, Providence, and Hartford, where New York's wholesalers collected grain and flour for export. Subsequently, New York wholesalers imported, not only foodstuffs, but cattle, horses, and linen and homespun made from surpluses of flax and wool from New Jersey, Rhode Island, and Connecticut.[62]

The city's coastal trade with the southern colonies emerged more slowly than its nearby regional commerce. The Delaware and Maryland trade, which had looked promising under Dutch rule, subsided and all but disappeared when Philadelphia began to grow, and the imperial duty on tobacco was high enough to deter New Yorkers from carrying much from that region until the 1720s. Thereafter, when customs officials relaxed enforcement of these duties, John Scott and others imported sufficient quantities to manufacture snuff in New York.[63] At about the same time, connections at Charles Town, a convenient stop on the way to the West Indies, attracted a new generation of shippers, including John van Cortlandt and Isaac Roosevelt, who traded New York's leather, bar iron, refined sugar and provisions and New England's small manufactures at the southern port. Their vessels returned quickly with cash, bills of exchange on London firms, or rice and naval stores to be reexported to England.[64] Van Cortlandt's rice trade with South Carolina reached £2,000 to £3,000 value in a typical year, and as New York City's largest "Carolina merchant," he tended to fill three or four vessels a year with nonenumerated commodities.[65] By 1750, Peter van Brugh Livingston and William Alexander made regular trips to North Carolina for furs and naval stores, and once Virginians converted portions of their agricultural production to wheat, exports of their flour proved alluring to many rising New Yorkers, as well as to the more eminent John Watts and John van Cortlandt.[66] By the eve of the Seven Years' War, Philip Cuyler joined in more intricate voyages to the southern colonies that involved pooling goods from New York and Boston in joint ventures, dropping off goods at Charles Town, proceeding with cash or credit to Virginia and Maryland, where captains purchased wheat, and returning to Boston or New York City before reexporting the grain to southern Europe or milling it into "inferior" flour for New York's local use.[67]

By the early 1730s, many New York wholesalers tended to attribute these accomplishments to the city's having become the metropolis at the epicenter of a trading region—the cosmopolitan source, not only of necessities, but of refined new articles of consumption. While they not only imported goods from foreign nations and England for their own and the adjacent colonies, they also distributed the products of the entire region among its people, in an area encompassing Long Island, the Jersey shoreline, points north into New England, and all of New York's Hudson Valley. "Several of our Neighbors upon the continent can not well subsist without our assistance as to Provisions for we yearly send Wheat and Flower to Boston and Road Island," Cadwallader Colden remarked in 1723. "Connecticut to the East, and New Jersey on the West, are fertile and well cultivated Colonies, and thro' natural Necessity, must always contribute their Aids in rendering this City a plentiful Mart, because their Exports cannot with equal Ease be conveyed to any other Port of considerable Traffick," William Livingston wrote confidently in the *Independent Reflector* in 1753. Of course, disgruntled local suppliers, unable to carry their own trade or set prices and conditions of sale, saw things differently. Convinced that he had been undersold, one Connecticut trader expressed the hope "that the plumes of that domineering city may yet feather the nests of those whom they have long plucked." Many of his New England neighbors would surely have concurred.[68]

Views emphasizing domination represented the rising confidence of city wholesalers in their material accomplishments, but they obscured merchants' mutual dependence upon regional traders, especially those in Boston and Philadelphia. For example, New Yorkers shared shipbuilding and marine insurance risks extensively with traders in neighboring cities by the 1730s. John van Cortlandt sent his refined sugar to Philadelphia, and Gerard Beekman sold vessels and bills of exchange there. John Ludlow and John Waddell bought foreign goods at lower prices in both Boston and Philadelphia than they could obtain abroad themselves, and carried them to New York for resale. Exporters shipped goods to Philadelphia when they moved sluggishly in New York.[69] These mutually beneficial arrangements tied together wholesalers of many locations and reinforced the increasing productivity of thousands of rural inhabitants, who together contributed to the city's continued rise at the center of its economic region.

Slavery

New York City's slave trade from the Caribbean rose noticeably after Queen Anne's War, when England made significant territorial gains and wrested control of the right to transport and sell slaves to acquired Spanish and French islands. Ventures to Africa had long been held to be more profitable, but maturing West Indies connections proved to be more integrated with regular lines of commerce into the eighteenth century. In addition, concerted government efforts to reduce piracy in British waters, and the refocused attention on the West Indian and southern European markets, raised middling merchants prospects of entering the slave trade from roughly 1713 to the 1740s. Once New Yorkers established linkages to correspondents who could offer slaves in return for northern grain and provisions, they acquired a steady, if small, stream of seasoned island labor as partial payment for cargoes. Indeed, in those years, one-third of New York City's vessels returned home with slaves from the West Indies.[70]

Early in the century, city traders showed little enthusiasm for the slave trade, preferring instead to obtain specie and bills of exchange from West Indies merchants; besides, some of them observed, the merchant's responsibility to exchange or sell imported slaves at New York City added to commercial burdens. Even between 1714 and 1721, although well-established venturers seized the occasional Spanish vessel in encounters near the Leeward Islands, which netted both slaves and silver, rising beginners in West Indies commerce rarely returned with slaves for auction.[71] William Walton, Rip van Dam, Garrit van Horne, and Philip Livingston engaged consistently in a large, diverse exchange of goods at Caribbean islands; as the importers of more slaves in the early century than all other West Indies merchants combined, however, it is significant that they instructed captains to take slaves only on occasion in lieu of specie and bills of exchange.[72]

After the 1720s, the free and slave black population of New York City grew rapidly, mostly through direct imports of slaves from Curaçao, Bermuda, and Barbados. With the exception of 1702, when merchants imported 165 slaves legally, and 1763, when they returned with 205, the heaviest years of slave importing involved an average of over 150 slaves a year from 1725 to 1735, with a high of 309 in 1731. Merchants reexported a few slaves to Perth Amboy and Philadelphia, or to the small towns on Long Island, but the great majority stayed in New York City and its environs.[73]

Lesser merchants in the West Indies trade carried slaves to New York City only on an occasional basis as part of their mixed cargoes. By the third decade of the century, William Vernon, Robert Stevens, Thomas and William Taylor, and Thomas Rogers conveyed more slaves than many merchants, although normally they brought only five to nine on a given voyage, and usually as partial payments to their captains for grain and provisions delivered to British or Dutch ports in the Caribbean. Many other city merchants, however, purchased an occasional black slave for a local customer or for their own households, and Captains Jasper Farmer and Thomas Miller, to name but two, began their careers carrying slaves and goods for city merchants. But even these opportunities diminished after 1740, as the slave trade pivoted once again toward the African coastline, as transatlantic voyages grew safer, and the prices of unseasoned slaves from Africa fell relative to the rising prices of seasoned slaves from the West Indies. By 1747, almost all of the city's slaves entered from Africa on the vessels of a few very successful transatlantic importers.[74]

Some city merchants had made the voyage to the east side of Africa all along. From 1716 to 1721, New York City's *Postillion* and *Crown Galley* returned directly from the west coast of Africa at least six times with cargoes of more than one hundred slaves each trip, although smuggling through neighboring ports and underreporting of entrances at New York City make it impossible to establish how many slaves actually entered the city. At least twenty-one entrances introduced dozens of Africans for sale at auction between 1715 and 1740; at least 130 voyages to various parts of West Africa took place between 1748 and 1772, returning to New York City with greater numbers of slaves than previously. By the eve of the Revolution, city merchants could make the dubious claim of having imported or smuggled at least 3,000 slaves.[75]

Consumption and the Illicit Trades

Expanding West Indies and coastal trade underscored important opportunities to expand outside the parameters of mercantile restrictions. After all, most goods that West Indians bought were not enumerated, and England controlled only a few of the many Caribbean islands that needed supplying. Attempts to stifle open commerce to all Caribbean markets seemed especially narrow-minded. As Cornelius Cuyler remarked in 1728, "Several Principal Inhabitants and merchants" of the city believed that "unnatural acts" "exceedingly chan-nelled" their commerce, stymieing independent commercial initiatives. A third-generation descendant of New York settlers, Cuyler was intent upon establish-ing his commercial reputation in a city that had overcome its meager origins by then and was rapidly becoming a premier port in the northern colonies. He, like so many others, believed that the best way to do this was to identify with aggressive expansion into West Indian markets. His letters to London, Antigua, St. Eustatius, Boston, Perth Amboy, Albany, and elsewhere betray impatience with imperial designs to keep New York a subordinate satellite in the empire.[76]

The Acts of Trade permitted colonists to convey nonenumerated goods to England or foreign ports provided they transported them in English or colonial vessels and with British crews. But authorities forbade New Yorkers to buy enu-merated goods at foreign ports, or to allow any foreign vessel carrying them to enter or clear the port of New York. The city's most important exports—flour, grain, and lumber products—were not enumerated, of course, but English law carried the further stipulation that New Yorkers post bonds verifying ports of destination, which imposed extra responsibilities on colonists whose vessels did not go directly to England. Caribbean traders who followed intricate routes through the islands, hoping to change their captain's instructions as opportu-nities arose, expressed their dismay with imperial legislation, connecting the regulations to their many commercial obstacles, incomprehensible changes in prices, fluctuating supply and demand, vagaries of competition, and recurring shortages of circulating currency. The remedy they proposed over and over was greater economic freedom; in the case of the West Indies, not just lower duties, but a wider range of free transport and open commercial relations filled their appeals.[77]

Captain Fayrer Hall, a retired West Indies trader, gave elaborate testimony in 1732 to the House of Commons—then debating the future Molasses Act—about the conditions merchants and planters experienced in the islands. Hall had become convinced that officials should not tamper with the competitive prices merchants enjoyed for West Indies molasses, rum, and sugar, for "All Things that have an intrinsick Value"—raw materials, as well as silver and gold—and "though you hinder it in one Instance, it will find its Way in an-other." Impending parliamentary legislation to force West Indies goods into legal channels, where high duties would prevail, could only fail, Hall insisted. Colonists would seek French trade, for without it the northern colonies would languish. Furthermore, suppressing the molasses trade might force colonists to buy French rum and sugar; in that event, North American merchants would lose both the benefits of manufacturing their own products and ready sales of lumber, casks, horses, grain, and other provisions. Merchants would naturally seek the highest price for New York's provisions and foodstuffs and the lowest price for sugar and molasses; it was "but natural and of practical Sense" to "follow to these markets of Martineco . . . and Coracoa" where they might "follow their own Interest." Like Cuyler, Hall believed in the benefits of uninhibited commerce with foreign islands, and that the "natural values" of goods ought to be "left free of artificial value" created by "monopolies." Goods in competition, they wrote, eventually cost less and spurred consumption everywhere.[78]

In order to obtain the bills of exchange, cash, and deferred payments for shipping services that reduced colonial debts to London, New York's wholesalers looked to the West Indies to sustain the colony's development. Since England's demand for the items New York was capable of exporting was limited, merchants' payments to London creditors depended on West Indies cash and bills of exchange on London merchants. But anxieties did not end there; traders complained that their own provincial government had passed duties and periodic embargoes, but "our Neighbors are Free." The conclusion seemed "clear to all" West Indies traders: so long as Dutch, Spanish, and French foreigners agreed to pay higher prices than British merchants did, and to offer cheaper staples in return, that trade must help subsidize the colony's expanded importation from England. And if the memorialist William Smith was correct, shippers found that British merchants paid "little cash" and sold their produce "at a higher rate than either the Dutch or French islands," while the Spanish merchants paid "wholly in cash." Before the Molasses Act, English molasses and sugar was exported from Jamaica duty-free and from Barbados for 4½ percent ad valorem. But there was never enough of it to satisfy growing colonial demand, so the French islands became frequent stops, where, because of comparatively steep duties, merchants smuggled liberally. After 1733, the Molasses Act imposed greater risks on this trade, but incentives to smuggle also grew, because New Yorkers obtained higher prices for colonial commodities at the forbidden islands.[79] As a consequence, the West Indies became the most important testing ground, not only for legitimate trade, but also for the evasion of mercantile laws altogether by a few bold New Yorkers.

Parliament intended the "Act for preventing Frauds and regulating Abuses in the Plantation Trade," a pillar of the mercantile system passed in 1696, to curb smuggling; and in subsequent years it was reinforced with many bureaucratic appointments, some public chastisement, a few financial penalties, and, as a report in 1734 reminded colonists, even a hanging. But at no time during the entire colonial period did such measures put smuggling under effective legal restraint. Governor Cornbury was certain that smuggling through New England and Long Island was a kind of "liberty of trade" that knew no moral restraint, and future authorities reiterated his refrain.[80]

Strictly speaking, merchants who evaded port duties, whether by under-reporting the value or quantity of cargo, or by hiding goods from port officials, were smugglers. The practice also involved either reporting foreign goods as English ones or, what was riskier, bringing in foreign goods surreptitiously. During times of war or imperial prohibition, this trade was indisputably illegal, but many merchants saw warfare as an opportunity to organize business rela-tions with the small producers and merchants of neighboring provinces, where they could rely upon secret orders or illegal face-to-face transactions by their captains.[81] For example, John Cannon and John Pintard of Norwalk received "most of the fictitious clearances from the Customhouse at Newhaven, [on behalf of] the Merchants here [at New York]." At Newport, the firms of Henry Collins, John and William Tweedy, Richards and Coddington, and Joseph Wan-ton all sold fictitious "flags of truce" to the New Yorkers Philip Cuyler, Isaac Roosevelt, Lawrence Kortright, Leonard Lispenard, and David Jamison "by way of Stealth." Others cleared port without entering the required description of goods to be transported, instead filling out only a general bond with customs officials. The boldest smugglers, and those who forged reputations as the pop-ular heroes who delivered desirable goods at cheaper prices, simply weighed anchor under cover of night.[82]

Evidence for smuggling is neither systematic over time, nor direct, for by definition smugglers would not appear in customs records; private correspon-dence divulges evidence of illegal transactions, but often fails to draw a com-plete picture of trading networks. In addition, many critics of smuggling exag-gerated to the point of our disbelief, as when Governor Bellomont proclaimed, "Here at New York the merchants run [smuggle] all the goods they can."[83] Somewhere between the silences and exaggerations, there is a body of indirect evidence suggesting the extent of smuggling, although never its precise magni-tude. It includes accounts of governors and watchful officials who remitted reports to England, as well as the newspaper advertisements for commodities in city retail stores and at auctions, and the comments of many colonists about the variety and quantities of goods in their city.

Imports that originated in Barbados or St. Kitts became legal entries, but merchants took on much of the tea, lime juice, dried fruits and numerous other items New Yorkers consumed at other ports. Related to this, the number of clearances for Holland, southern Europe, and the West Indies was rising, but equal numbers of entrances are seldom recorded in any given year; since cus-toms officials recorded even empty vessels that entered legally, and most unreported entering vessels left port within a few months, the uneven balance between incoming and outgoing ships suggests illegal entries. Moreover, travel accounts and private letters indicate a rise in the illegal trade. Voyages to Amsterdam early in the century often went via West Indian possessions, the Orkney Islands of Scotland, or southern Europe, where safe conduct passes could be procured. Although port records show entering vessels from the Low Countries or Dutch vessels stopping at English ports only rarely, New York's retailers regularly announced "holland goods" for sale by the 1720s.[84]

By then, New York wholesalers favored commodities of two kinds when they smuggled: items such as molasses, sugar, coffee, dyewoods, and brandy, which agents acquired more cheaply than their British equivalents by evading the prohibitions on trading with enemy nations or forbidden ports; and goods such as gunpowder, tea, and linen, for which neither steep duties at New York nor drawbacks at British ports existed, and that cost less to import if merchants traded with foreign nations directly. But in return for New York's "Flower, pork, peas, and other provisions," bound by the 1720s not for New England but for Surinam and Curaçao, "the vessels that carry them to those places *pretend* always to return in ballast." In fact, captains complied with some very specialized orders. Philip Livingston asked his agents Storke & Gainsborough to forward "Dutch powder" to be landed "at Block Island," even though he expressed "fear of being discover'd" and having it seized by customs officials. Francis Harrison, the customs collector in 1722, reported that "toy looking glasses," "felt hats, and razors" came in regularly from the Continent without paying duties as European goods. By then, William Smith was sure that "we ought not to presume upon [the] fidelity" of customs officials or dismiss the public's approval of contraband traffic.[85] Earlier, Governor Cornbury had written to the Lords of Trade that Customs Collector Byerley regularly "gave Bills of Store" to New York merchants who paid no duties "for Enumerated Comodities to be Carried to foreigne plantations." Among the smugglers, "one Capt. Chelwell (who is a Mercht. of this City)" received free entrance at the Sound "for two hundred weight of Cocoa" carried in the sloop of Charles Evertsen, a Surinam merchant. Byerley reportedly helped smuggle cocoa to the Rhode Island firm of Joseph Bueno and Son as well, and he complied with New Yorkers who landed contraband goods at Connecticut and eastern Long Island ports or evaded the customs vessels watching the harbors.[86]

Colonists' new taste for tea, silks, fashionable pottery, citrus fruits, and other exotic imports helped smuggling become "well nigh respectable." Merchants could, in fact, lose their commercial reputations if they suddenly refused to supply goods. "Scarce a week passes," observed one resident, "without an illicit

Trader's going out or coming into this Port." There was little reason to fear the condemnation of seized cargoes in 1739, since they were commonly released without forfeiture of goods, the customs officials being open friends of the smugglers. Around that time, the assembly refused to seat Benjamin Pratt on the supreme court because of his known opposition to illicit traffic. The oft-cited traveler Andrew Burnaby, who passed through New York in 1748, was sure that although only a few merchants "grew rich" in this trade, most colonists applauded it.[87] Favored places of entry included Providence, Perth Amboy, Stamford, Norwalk, and Long Island Sound. In 1700, Governor Bellomont lamented that a "Major Selleck" of Stamford "has a warehouse close to the Sound" where "he receives abundance of goods from our vessels, and the merchants afterwards take their opportunity of running them into this town." In subsequent years, Perth Amboy and Newport became havens as well; the latter, reported the surveyor-general, had a "greater plenty of European goods than in any place on the Main, tho' they have not so much as a vessel that goes thence for home [England]" to register cargoes.[88] Captains might carry small quantities of many different regional goods up and down the New England coastline and be tempted at times "to sing of the independency tunes" rather than abide by laws that dutied "Provisions, Chocolate, Lumber, European and Indian Goods," or goods intended for reexport to England. John van Cortlandt, for example, became New York's greatest "Carolina merchant" by trading all manner of northern commodities and smuggling rice from the southern ports to foreign ones after that commodity's enumeration in 1704.[89]

Unsurprisingly, Amsterdam and the Dutch West Indies proved to be valuable nodes of New York's illicit trade. In 1684, New York vessels had carried Virginia tobacco to Holland and then "return[ed] neither to this Kingdom [England] nor the said plantations." By the end of the century, Governor Bellomont reported that many vessels "lurked" at Nassau Island, then stopped at Oyster Bay, before setting out for Amsterdam, and Robert R. Livingston and others jointly ventured illegal cargoes to Daniel Crommelin of Amsterdam in 1701. Jeffrey Jeffreys watched officials seize two of his ships in New York's harbor in 1704 for smuggling "holland goods" from the Dutch West Indies, and Rutger Bleecker sent out at least one illicit voyage a year from New York to Curaçao, and thence to Holland, from 1701 through 1710. An anonymous merchant cleared New York City in 1710 to take illicit goods directly to Amsterdam himself. Some colonists thought it was "common" and "practical" to sail for Amsterdam, then carry fish to southern Europe or salt and wine to the Newfoundland fisheries, and make a return voyage through Amsterdam without paying duties at London on enumerated commodities. In still other cases, New York vessels carried enumerated Carolina rice directly to Holland or Lisbon, or held the commodity at Newport without paying duties until it could be transshipped to southern Europe. In 1739, Governor George Clarke reported that the seizure of the *Mary and Margaret*, loaded with gunpowder and molasses from St. Eustatius, was the uncommon interruption of a very common business. In 1743, officials in Antigua seized the *Charming Molly* of New York for carrying a load of Dutch cocoa from St. Eustatius for which the captain had not taken out a bond.[90]

Although the fur trade waned steadily in the eighteenth century, a few established exporters sustained their long-term linkages to Amsterdam with illicit communication. From 1713 to about 1720, Evert Wendell's trade was unexceptionably legal; he exported furs to his correspondent William van Nuys in Amsterdam and imported dry goods and tea at Newport's free docks or through family members at Boston. But after 1722, when Parliament enumerated furs, Wendell shipped his commodities through Stephen De Lancey in New York City, who in turn sent mixtures of enumerated and nonenumerated goods to Amsterdam, sometimes by way of Boston, without posting bond at New York.[91] Indeed, long after Parliament enumerated furs, Isaac Low, William Glencross, Olaf van Sweeten, John Barbarie, Benjamin Faneuil, Rip van Dam, Henry Cuyler, and John Cruger shipped peltry direct to Amsterdam for Albany merchants, while others, including Stephen De Lancey, Philip Livingston, Robert R. Livingston Jr., and Hyman Levy, sent skins straight from New York to Amsterdam. Merchants at Amsterdam then made up cargoes for the New Yorkers, which touched at Dover or the Orkneys, a port where customs officials could be corrupted easily, before crossing the Atlantic. When furs could not be obtained for export, the Bleekers borrowed capital from Charles Lodwick of London and transmitted it to the Bleekers of Amsterdam, who in turn supplied the colony with goods that were slipped into Long Island Sound by night. When the fur trade gave way to ginseng and potash exporting during the 1730s and 1740s, Robert Sanders, John Cruger, Cornelius Cuyler, and Johannes Bleecker kept the trade with Amsterdam open.[92]

Comparatively few New Yorkers smuggled tea, but because it was of high value for its weight, even three or four ships a year represented a significant contribution to some merchants' incomes and many colonists' consumption habits. Some tea entered New York on Dutch ships cleared from Holland for a Dutch West Indies port, with an unscheduled stop at New York. More frequently, Philip Cuyler, John Ludlow, John Waddell, and Cornelius Ray brought Dutch tea to New York through a New England port, where, with various ruses, captains paid a fraction of the duties on their cargo and obtained falsified documents that would permit entry at New York City without additional cost. Ludlow ordered his captain to secure tea in Amsterdam, pay cash for it, and return through New London, where the merchant Nathaniel Shaw would unload and disperse the cargo. On other occasions, Ludlow ordered his captain to the Bay of Honduras to get enumerated logwood and take it direct to Amsterdam; subsequently, with a return cargo of tea, the captain landed "near Connecticut" where "Mr. Lloyd sends his sloop" to unload the ship before customs officials created a record of entry. Elias Desbrosses, later the third president of the Chamber of Commerce, used "Holland Clinkers" to purchase Dutch West Indies goods, which he then smuggled through Rhode Island into New York City. David "Ready Money" Provoost, a prominent tea smuggler who married the widow of James Alexander, chief justice of New York City in the 1720s, had customers throughout New England. Dutch tea, gunpowder, heavy clothing, and linens were consistently cheaper than their English equivalents before at least the 1740s; smuggling made them cheaper still, so "as to totally discourage the Importation of these commodities from Great Britain."93

Although many crown observers admitted "impolitick and unreasonable" trade in Dutch commodities, there was little to be done. Philip Livingston was one of many city wholesalers who eluded officials with complicated indirect and multilateral return voyages and a confusing variety of goods. From 1735 to 1736, he sent New York wheat to Barcelona, from where his captain sent part of the proceeds to London creditors and carried the balance to Amsterdam, where he purchased "Dutch powder," paper, glass, cloth, and tea. The returning ship proceeded to Block Island to unload at night. With credit from the Dutch merchant Levinus Clarkson, Livingston imported large quantities of "that Article"—presumably tea—"which we discover'd of great Demand here."94

Cornelius Cuyler, another inveterate smuggler, seemed to delight in the risks of seizure. In 1754, he instructed his son Philip to proceed from London to Amsterdam with cash from peltry sales, where he was to purchase Bohea tea and other "Holland goods," followed by a return "direct to New York." The father noted that this was "a trip not without Danger," but "Capt. Keteltas understands these affairs" and would guide the novice son's adventure. That same year the elder Cuyler smuggled tea through Rhode Island and Connecticut; but he stopped short of smuggling through Oswego, "that Great Carrying Place," because of the extreme danger of being caught. In the fall of 1756, the father learned that port officials seized a large parcel of his imported "Dutch checks" at New York City, whether because his son Philip bungled the job of secretly entering the goods into New York or because the Dutch correspondent, Daniel Crommelin, had failed to be deceitful enough in his paperwork. Cuyler nevertheless agreed to pay all the fees in connection with the seizure. Only two weeks later, Cuyler learned that customs officials had taken another of his illegal cargoes at Stamford.[95]

In the 1740s, fur traders in the Wendell and Livingston families supplemented return cargoes of sugar and molasses from the West Indies with rice from the Carolinas and logwood from Honduras, or consigned their captains to carry the goods direct to Amsterdam without posting a bond for their destination. Philip Livingston periodically added New York and New England flaxseed and lumber to his grain shipments to the West Indies; these he had transferred into Dutch ships at St. Eustatius and routed to Amsterdam. Livingston, along with Robert and Barent Sanders, Hendricke ten Eyck, and John Cuyler, also arranged with their captains occasionally to trace a forbidden triangle: after selling cargoes bound from New York to a West Indian port, the captain purchased a second load and headed for Amsterdam without a bond or stopping to pay British customs. Robert Sanders preferred to ship French sugar from St. Eustatius to New York for Robert and Richard Ray, city sugar refiners, for two decades after passage of the Molasses Act, or to the Van der Grifts of Amsterdam.[96]

French ports also attracted illicit trade. In 1700, officials seized Abraham de Lucena's *Hester* for nonpayment of duties on Madeira wine transshipped from an unnamed French island, and then auctioned its cargo in New York City. The next year, a sloop owned in New York returned from the French Caribbean bound for French Quebec with smuggled flour, tobacco, and earthenware; when it was wrecked off Martha's Vineyard on its return to New York, tide waiters pulled the soggy contents out of the vessel and sought out the owner, one "S.V." Investigation by Lieutenant Governor John Nanfan (1701) revealed the owner to be the merchant Samuel Vetch, a prominent friend of the crown in New York, who had married Margaret Livingston of Albany, and had ventured capital for this voyage with her brother Robert Livingston Jr. Although authorities publicly chastised Vetch and fined him £200 in 1705, New Yorkers were neither surprised nor outraged by the offense; close associates predicted that this would not be his last smuggling expedition to French Canada.[97]

Until the 1740s, France's Caribbean possessions supplied more staples to colonists—especially sugar—on more favorable terms than English planters could. Some city observers believed that the Molasses Act hardly affected the regular flow of sugar out of Martinique, where many ships "lost their identity" as New York vessels by obtaining French registers and thus becoming foreign bottoms. With "a little greasing" of foreign customs officials, smugglers also got safe conduct passes to the French islands from neutral Caribbean ports, and from there they proceeded to southern Europe.[98] Jamaica proved the best

British port at which to sell provisions and, with the cash proceeds and a false cocket (customhouse permit), clear for a French port. From January 1735 to October 1752, 2,503 vessels cleared Jamaica for the northern colonies; 763 of these left empty, and about 900 left with one to five hogsheads of sugar or molasses. Yet most New York–registered vessels in this trade reported large cargoes of sugar entered at their home port just months later.[99] Then, too, the French islands permitted other creative adaptations, as when Philip Livingston's captain stopped at the Carolinas to pick up rice, for which he failed to pay duties, and proceeded to French West Indies ports to acquire "Dutch Curacoa's" valuable logwood and sugar.[100] Christopher Bancker on occasion sent shipments of Madeira from French possessions directly to his business associate, Daniel Crommelin, in Amsterdam; Cornelius and Philip Cuyler, and John Ludlow ordered their captains to make similar voyages.[101] During King George's War, a few city merchants made regular trips to French Caribbean possessions via Louisbourg and Nova Scotia with rum, sugar, and flour; after the capture of Quebec, they also sent dry goods along the same routes, lured by the high prices they could charge to replace spoiled, damaged, and scarce goods in Canadian stores. Others turned their wartime attention to the illegal trade with the French West Indies as a "recourse to . . . cutting losses in beseiged [sic] portions of Canada."[102]

The Spanish Caribbean also drew New Yorkers' attention. Although Parliament forbade trade to the Spanish West Indies during Queen Anne's War, Governor Richard Ingoldesby noted that without taking their flour there, city traders would be "much impoverished." Under Governor Cornbury, concerns grew about the salt and logwood trades, both of which Parliament prohibited intermittently until the 1740s; yet New Yorkers continued to trade between the Spanish factors at the Gulf of Campeche in Mexico and the great firms in Holland.[103] Even in years of peace, the authorities made stern reminders, such as Governor Clarke's in 1736, that the Spanish trade was disloyal, although evidence from newspapers and governors' correspondence indicates that New Yorkers were reluctant patriots. By the 1730s, customs officials took the mere presence of logwood on a northern vessel as "evidence" of smuggling with the Spanish, although many of them blinked the traffic and collected a few coveted Spanish pieces of eight for their own pockets. Renewed warfare between 1742 and 1748 again evoked official sanctions against the Spanish trade, but New Yorkers continued to run goods to those islands. When Spain made Monte Christi and Havana free ports in 1752, New Yorkers were already well known and welcome there.[104]

No laws altered the definition of smuggling or the punishments for engaging in it over the eighteenth century, and many New York City merchants still scorned the illegal traders in their midst. But smuggling grew, and officials were helpless to quash the "liberality concerning the traders of northern ports." In 1747, Malachy Postlethwayt waxed indignant that colonists evaded the Molasses Act assiduously, and that New York vessels carried on a direct trade to Marseilles, Toulon, and Holland from the Caribbean. He cited "New York's freedom" as particularly odious to the tenets of mercantile order. Ten years later, he reiterated that smuggling into the northern colonies was a "manifest subversion of the fundamental maxims of the British policy, for . . . [illicit traffic with French colonies] strengthens their power at the expense of our own . . . to our eternal ignominy." Governor Clinton agreed with English policy makers that New York was controlled "by Merchants who find their private advantage is the breach of these Laws." Customs collectors had to "suffer by a performance" of their duties, while evasions reached "enormous height."[105]

In the early 1740s, the House of Commons sought the means to encourage more legal trade and enforce the Molasses Act. Members listened to arguments from former smugglers and ship captains who shared the "common wisdom" that high duties drove many traders to seek the lower prices of smuggled West Indies and Amsterdam goods, and great public approval facilitated their decisions. They pointed to the decline in English smuggling during the decade, which they attributed to lower import duties for certain commodities, and related the rise of illicit traffic through northern colonial ports to the Molasses Act. Written reports from colonists also insisted on the influence of ideas about the moral justice and economic benefits of free trade. A few years later, during the Seven Years' War, colonial merchants again pointed out the degree of economic freedom in the foreign West Indies, and demanded access to Spanish and French ports as a matter of survival. Although imperial officials pointed out the ease with which North American merchants could obtain privateering and supply contracts during the war, replies made it clear that those were avenues open only to the already-advantaged merchants. Middling merchants, they insisted, needed more long-term assurances of open commerce in the Caribbean and drawbacks of duties at English ports equal to those English merchants enjoyed. Failing this, however, a number of New York City merchants simply continued to serve the growing "taste for refinements" such as sugar, tea, and coffee in the manner to which they had become accustomed. By the mid 1750s, New Yorkers probably imported more sugar through Rhode Island and Connecticut, or under the noses of customs collectors at New York City with false cockets, than legal sugar purchased in the West Indies or from captured enemy ships' cargoes. Before the close of the Seven Years' War, 11,500 hogsheads of molasses reached

New York via Rhode Island, having originated in French and Spanish islands, while only 2,500 hogsheads came from British possessions. At neutral St. Eustatius New York crews loaded thousands of hogsheads a year for the return trip to Hartford, Long Island, or Newport. Under auspicious conditions—ineffective enforcement of legislation, favorable prices for foreign staples, and widespread public support—more, rather than fewer, New York merchants joined the ranks of smugglers in the 1750s and 1760s.[106]

Chapter Seven

The Promise of the Domestic Economy

Expanding Internal Trade and
City Manufacturing, 1700–1760

B Y 1 7 0 0 , New Yorkers' production, exchange, and consumption relations took in not only the Hudson River Valley but much of Long Island, New Jersey, Connecticut, and Rhode Island. Wealth still came to merchants, retailers, or commercial farmers in old ways; risks and failures were still frequent; diversification occurred according to established patterns of commerce; markets connecting villages and households were not yet an integrated system of cash and commodities exchange. Still, as more sons and new immigrants sought entry into commerce, and as the province's population grew and created demand for agricultural goods, colonists crossed each other's economic pathways more extensively and more intricately. People of all social strata moved goods or provided services, merchants' sons relocated to other colonies' ports, and many farmers' sons situated themselves in New York City. Middlemen began to market agricultural surpluses for rural producers, and storekeepers held larger varieties of finished goods or gave small credit advances on future crops, while merchants ventured into the countryside or sent their chapmen to collect small surpluses of agricultural goods for export. By the 1720s, some city merchants took an active part in promoting domestic manufactures. And by then, country and city shared overlapping, interdependent destinies.

But interdependence did not always produce agreement among different economic constituencies in New York. Already, middling merchants who were identified most with the West Indies or coastal trade knew that they would sometimes collude with, and sometimes oppose, the interests of the great dry-goods importers. So, too, did lesser merchants learn that their interests could be at odds with those of ambitious commercial farmers, or city residents, or internal developers. The grain and flour trades flourished in the eighteenth century, but there would be no new Bolting Act, because farming and landed interests combined more formidably than lesser merchants could. Demand steadily rose in the port city and abroad for New Yorkers' provisions, but lesser merchants' efforts to make "the best price" were often thwarted by farmers who haggled effectively over prices and quality of exports. Moreover, despite having social origins close to those of the thousands of middling consumers and retailers in New York, lesser merchants sometimes made economic choices about exporting goods or freeing their commerce from municipal regulations that put them at odds with those consumers and retailers. The large numbers of colonists entering the West Indies and coastal trade testified to the overall maturation of the province, and the significant number of opportunities that trade still offered. But close daily contact with countless producers and consumers in the domestic economy made merchants' domination over economic affairs a subject of continuous and contentious negotiation. And their ideas about and efforts at provincial manufacturing kept alive their differences with the great importing wholesalers as well.

The City and Province

A variety of imports trickled into the remotest parts of the countryside after 1700, introducing new habits of consumption and encouraging rural inhabitants to produce for export. Although luxuries such as imported wine, oriental rugs, spices, teas, pepper, and chinaware appeared in only the wealthiest homes, other commodities sold quickly, albeit in small quantities, at country stores, where more modest exchanges occurred: cheap cloth from England and Holland; salt from northern Europe; linen and canvas from Ireland; sugar, molasses, ginger, snuff, rum, lime juice, pimento, oils, ginseng, cocoa, and many other items from the West Indies; and rice, tobacco, and cotton wool from the southern colonies. Farm families welcomed the opportunity to put windows in their homes, buttons on their clothing, or dishes on their tables. Imported commodities represented no more than 25 percent of the goods provincial New Yorkers consumed during the eighteenth century, but their purchase required careful planning and much time; commercial farmers probably spent as much time collecting small surpluses of locally grown produce—theirs and their neighbors'—and forwarding it to buyers more than a day's journey from home as they did providing the minimum requirements of clothing and food for their families.[1]

New York City was much more than a siphon for country goods on their way to foreign ports or for exotic imports to be loaded onto bateaux bound for rural homesteads. The city itself was the locus of resources and employment in the shipping trades and the greatest single body of consumers to whom provincial goods were sold. Its growing population depended on the food and household necessities supplied by rural producers to supplement imports from abroad, with the consequence that before the 1720s, grain, flour, and lumber products made up most outgoing cargoes, while other farm goods reaching the mouth of the Hudson River were consumed in the port. Many rural traders knew New York City best as the place to meet urban consumers face-to-face in the five urban markets situated along accessible waterways and the East River, a meeting ground for the expanding population of artisans, household servants, rural producers, and small shopkeepers, where long-standing laws regulated tightly the times of sales, quality of goods, and sometimes the prices of certain necessities.[2]

As the century progressed, the great wholesalers became less visible to the majority of rural producers and city consumers in daily marketing, even though they became more visible in their conspicuous display of commercial success. Dry-goods importers spent more time along private docks that accommodated entering vessels in deeper water or waited for retailers and distributors to approach their warehouses to receive pre-ordered parcels. And the eminent were far more likely than middling merchants to hire city laborers and craftsmen to build ships and transfer Caribbean fustic, Honduras wood, mahogany, ebony, cocoa beans, coffee, or sugar to large transatlantic vessels. A few great merchants were also the only employers of city residents in chocolate, sugar, candy, snuff, and distilling "manufactories."

But lesser traders mingled freely with their buyers and sellers in familiar pubic places. Minor exporters bridged international markets and local trading spheres frequently as they strove to hold down farmers' and millers' selling prices, collected supplies, bribed customs officials in order to keep their costs down, or haggled for the best terms of sale. Some exporters sent chapmen and agents into the countryside to gather goods for their ships in efforts to prevent rural surpluses from reaching city retailers or open-air markets. Others sent their sons into the small towns of Rhode Island and Connecticut to learn about local affairs and provide points of commercial contact, in the same way that London merchants sent their sons to the West Indies. Israel Abraham lived with his family in New York until about 1741 and then moved to Newport to market grain, horses, and cheese; Nathan Nathans joined him a few years later, and together they built a significant commercial firm. On the advice of his father, Moses Lopez moved in 1752 from New York to Rhode Island, where he manufactured potash. In 1765, Samuel de Lucena moved to Norwalk, Connecticut, for the same reason, and was joined by his father shortly thereafter. Andrew van

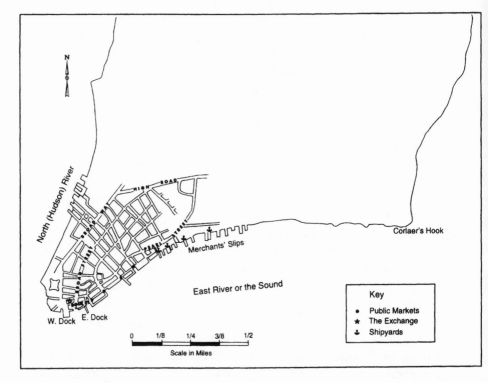

Map 6. The Extent of New York City in about 1730. Positions of residences and businesses are based on documentary evidence used in this study and a survey of the city made by James Lyne in 1728 entitled "A Plan of the City of New York from an Actual Survey," reproduced in *The Memorial History of the City of New York*, ed. James G. Wilson (New York, 1893), 1: 185.

Horne established gristing, bolting, and flour marketing in New Jersey in connection with his brothers' far-flung commercial activities. In each case, middling wholesalers valued links to local producers in the countryside as much as their distant kin and associates abroad.[3]

Lesser traders were as familiar with city markets as they were with the great docks, and they identified their interests as readily with the households of city consumers as with international ports of call. City council and provincial Assembly members reported that rising traders had actively promoted regulations to protect the city's economy from encroachments by commercial farmers. Although they failed to win legislation fixing the prices of farmers' produce, and it would have been foolhardy to forbid country farmers from entering city markets, they helped enact many city ordinances requiring farmers to meet merchants and household consumers on regular market days in fixed public places. Merchants also helped ensure that "country inhabitants" asked for no more than a "fair exchange" of the goods they could not sell at regular markets when they approached general-store retailers—of which there were at least sixty-four by 1760—to take surpluses. Lesser exporters not only benefited as city consumers from the guiding hand of quality controls and marketing regularities, their commerce as flour and grain exporters also improved with the greater predictability of city trade.[4]

Exporters joined with city consumers to prevent forestalling or engrossing of agricultural commodities intended to reach the city, and they applauded legislation to set assizes; fix weights and measures; establish the dimensions and styles of containers made of lumber; set the proportions of brine to packed meat and the grades of lumber; and prohibit mixing lime and sea salt with potash, wood chips with tar, and sugar, honey, or pepper in beer. Acts of the city's Common Council regulated exports of packed meats and fish, naval stores, and sole leather in order to correct the "Discredit of the Said Staple Commodities of this Colony at foreign markets" and to set limits on the degree to which city exporters could compete among themselves in a system of "free prices" in New York City and abroad. As they insisted, controlling inhabitants in the swath of trading activities twenty to one hundred miles around them boosted the reputation of the city abroad. Of course, exporters also hoped legislators would raise necessary city revenues from noncommercial activities. They were, in fact, pleased with the city's corporate charter, granted in 1730, which gave aldermen the authority to collect urban revenues from liquor excises, tapster licenses, ferry franchises, and sale of dock, market, and water lots; permission given by the provincial Assembly for public works funded by special tax assessments also diverted attention away from taxes on commerce.[5]

In other respects, middling city merchants identified less with city interests, and more with the requirements of profitable external trade. Periodic embargoes, for example, benefited city consumers during times of food scarcity, but they frustrated exporters' hopes for shipping goods. During imperial wars the Common Council often forbade exporters to take grain from the city, in order to conserve labor and vessels, and provide necessary food for the local population.[6] Governor Cornbury and the Assembly were not entirely deaf to merchants' interests when they levied an embargo in 1706; in order to alleviate the "Clog or Hindrance on Traffic or Commerce," legislation after 1708 permitted the free export of grain and flour and exempted New York vessels from tonnage duties.[7] In 1711 and 1713, the Common Council again issued embargoes on grain exports, in response to urban protests about the rising costs of bread and the need for military provisions, to the consternation of exporters. Abraham de Lucena and Justus Bosch appealed for special permission to get wheat and flour to Jamaica, but the need for foodstuffs, vessel transports, and seaport labor for the military cause overrode their pleas.[8] With the return of war, city government embargoed provisions exports again—in 1740, 1741, 1746—and merchants' vessels stood in the port half full.[9] By the latter year, exporters had framed familiar arguments against embargoes; not war, they insisted, but farmers who sent poor-quality grain and flour for sale, and small producers who manipulated the quantities of goods available for trade, were at the root of shortages and rising prices. Petitioners, who identified themselves as provincial consumers, retorted that merchants' unregulated, ceaseless exportation of grain, flour, and butter was at fault. The "Great and Unusual Exportation of the produce of our Country to foreign Markets in the West Indies has Occasioned so great a scarcity of provisions . . . [that] they are become most Excessive Dear[,] to the Very great Oppression and Loss of all Degrees of people."[10]

No doubt, constituencies of farmers, consumers, and exporters each told part of the truth, and greater levels of production would have resolved many quarrels. But they continued. In 1748 the ire of consumers and city bakers made itself felt more strongly than usual when city merchants won their appeal to Lieutenant Governor James De Lancey and the provincial Council to refrain from putting an embargo on provisions exported to the West Indies. Such, said one of them in the New-York Post-Boy in 1748, was "the Force of Money" that even in the midst of King George's War, exporters refused "to divest themselves of Self-Interest," preferring to export grain and flour to external markets, some of them foreign, during a war fought for the "public welfare."[11]

City exporters continued their earlier disagreements with retailers and consumers about the wisdom of discriminatory regulations passed by the Assembly against sister colonies, primarily in the form of higher import and tonnage duties on their "foreign" trade with New York. City and provincial legislators echoed the popular perception that the city ought to become the mercantile center for an expanding region of exchange; discrimination against neighboring colonies promoted more importing by New Yorkers, fuller employment, and cheaper commodities. But lesser merchants could not agree with their isolationist fellow New Yorkers that discouraging coastal shippers from entering their port would ensure more employment for city inhabitants; legislation intended to defeat neighboring colonial competition with stiff duties or port prohibitions, they insisted, would only force that trade into illicit channels where they could find multilateral trade connections. As for hoping that regional discrimination would prevent the importation of socially polluting luxuries on foreign ships from foreign places, lesser merchants assured colonists that their fellow dry-goods importers were the main purveyors of such goods.[12]

Following Queen Anne's War, governor after governor pursued regulatory and taxing policies that, merchants railed, would do little to make New York City a dominant entrepôt in a region of subordinate economic satellites. Commercial legislation periodically taxed at higher rates those foreign goods coming into New York that had first landed at Boston, Providence, or Hartford. In 1715, the Assembly, responding to demands of a rising landed interest and urban consumers, approved a flat 5 percent duty on all goods entering from Boston; wine and cocoa were to pay a double duty if they first stopped at Boston.[13] Discriminatory duties of two shillings per ton on vessels registered outside of New York City added to lesser merchants' burdens, since they often combined voyages with neighboring merchants or accumulated surpluses for their long voyages from many small boats in the region. But port fees drew their greatest anger: "The excessive sums of money screwed from masters of [neighboring] vessels trading here under the notion of port charges, visiting the said vessels by supernumerary officers, and taking extraordinary fees" only produced a "great discouragement of trade . . . beyond the precedent of any other port, and without colour of law."[14]

By 1734, the voices of rural landholders and city consumers who wanted discrimination were joined by yet another interest: the great transatlantic dry-goods merchants. When the Assembly stiffened the tonnage duty to three shillings per ton on foreign-built and foreign-registered vessels, exempting only whaling vessels engaged in coastal commerce, a few eminent wholesalers spoke out: "Vessels built or owned here are of far greater Benefit" to the city, because they would pay duties and fees that would stay in the city, unlike "Strangers coming hither for Freights, . . . [since] Money Earned by them is carryed out of the Colony." In addition, before there were tonnage duties on foreign vessels, "the Number of our own Shipping . . . Decreased to Such a Degree that at Present the Vessels of other Ports . . . become almost our only Carriers." "Strangers" earned New York money on foreign manufactures and drew it out of the colony, while New York's produce "Remains and Circulates Amongst us" at no increase to the colony's balance of treasure.[15] Exporters who shared cargoes and vessels with the now-taxed neighboring merchants did not give up. David Provoost, John Jansen, Jacob Kipp, and Garret van Horne, who had not yet built the fortunes they would later enjoy from the West Indies trade, had already been defeated in pleas to eliminate peltry export duties and fix prices of grain and flour drawn from the surrounding hinterlands.[16] Although tonnage duties never brought in a significant amount of revenue, writers admitted, they nevertheless "drove trade to [the] Jerseys," where ships entered virtually duty-free from 1723 to 1758. But by the 1740s, multiple interests demanding embargoes and discriminatory port legislation seemed to have conspired against rising exporters' hopes.[17]

The Final Years of the Fur Trade

When Surveyor General Cadwallader Colden asserted in 1723 that "this Province has a more considerable share in [the fur trade] than any other in His Matys. Dominions," colonists involved in the trade knew that his statement was only relatively accurate. By then Pennsylvania's fur trade was still growing, while New York's had stagnated and then declined; peltry was being eclipsed by other exportable commodities; from 1700 into the 1720s, furs represented roughly 25 percent of the volume of New York City's exports, and by 1750 this figure sank to 16 percent; by 1774 it was a mere 2 percent.[18] Since the 1690s, exporters had faced glutted English and Dutch demand, declining prices of beaver in London, and rising export duties at New York City. By the end of Queen Anne's War, the city exporters Cornelius Lodge, Thomas Davenport, Cornelius de Peyster, Stephen De Lancey, Frederick Philipse, Gabriel Minvielle, and John Barbarie also lamented the intrusion of interlopers who traded on their own accounts—especially the great valley men like Robert R. Livingston—and the smuggling between Albany and Canada.[19]

De Lancey and Philipse diversified into the West Indian markets that absorbed the flow of agricultural surpluses from Long Island and New England, and they were joined by newcomers like Benjamin Aske, Onzeel van Sweeten, Ebenezer Wilson, Brandt Schuyler and Walter Thong from 1700 through at least 1710, and Jacob Wendell and Henry Beekman after 1720. Philip Livingston, Cornelius Cuyler, Abraham Wendell, Gerard Beekman, Cornelius ten Eyck, David van der Heyden, Robert Sanders, and others began to buy up flour, wheat, ginseng, and dried peas from the interior and instructed their agents in New York City to send the commodities to West Indian ports.[20]

Only established fur exporters were positioned well for consolidating the internal trade and monopolizing foreign correspondence; John Lewis, Charles Lodwick, James Graham, Edward Griffith, Caleb Heathcote, Samuel Winder, and others, all of them recent arrivals to the city, consistently exported fewer of New York's furs than the original traders.[21] Lewis, for example, shipped 400 to 550 hides per year between 1702 and 1709, while the veteran Cornelius Cuyler often shipped that many hides from Albany to his New York agents in one month between 1725 and 1740. In order to continue prospering from 1732 through 1735,

Cuyler shifted most of his peltry export business with London from Samuel Baker to the firms of Storke & Gainsborough, and then Joseph Mico, because they had cornered great portions of the trade in fur imports in England and offered higher prices to colonists than Baker could.[22] In New York, he faced fierce competition with other successful exporters, including Stephen De Lancey, Cornelius ten Eyck, and Philip and Robert Livingston, but by shrewd collaboration he was able to acquire more furs in the interior for city manufacturers and transatlantic shippers than his competitors. In 1732, he continued to "sell yearly here to our hatters above 3000 lbs. of Beaver." Cuyler's exports averaged from a high of over 5,500 pounds of beaver in 1731 to a low of about 950 pounds in 1734, with wide differences over the entire period. From 1752 to 1755, he exported roughly the same quantities per year, despite the trade's declined prices, but Cuyler also diversified enough to market dozens of hogsheads of ginseng and hundreds of barrels of flour. Middling fur exporters, including Olaf van Sweeten, Rip van Dam, William Glencross, John Barbarie, and Benjamin Faneuil had to content themselves with small quantities of peltry from local suppliers.[23]

Although in their private letters city exporters admitted that the decline in supplies of furs was a major source of their difficulties, they insisted publicly that unwise policies were ruining them. The Treaty of Neutrality with Canada and the Iroquois from 1701 to 1722 had aided Albany merchants' in keeping an "open trade" with their northern suppliers. But such freedom of exchange and transport, argued city wholesalers, was a seriously flawed grant of privilege. "Tyrannises" remarked in 1709 that direct traders to Canada conducted illicit activities and kept prices for peltry exceedingly high.[24] Philipse and De Lancey sent letters to Parliament explaining the diversion of beaver supplies to the French, and the consequent inability of importers to pay for goods from England from 1700 to 1715. Remonstrances to the provincial Council over 1725 and 1726 noted that peltry exports had fallen by half since 1690, and the prices charged by Indians and middlemen had risen 25 percent. Although Governor Burnet urged exporters to pursue "the far western trade" as a means of avoiding animosities with the French while they found new supplies of peltry, city merchants were reluctant to try it. Instead, they argued, the government ought to pass more stringent legislation to channel furs to New York City and set their prices.[25]

Meanwhile, the exporter Philip Livingston joined with some of the rising "country interest"—led by Cadwallader Colden, Lewis Morris, and James Alexander—in trying to corner peltry for the London market over the early 1720s. They soon discovered, however, that "free trading independents" from New York were able to get closer to the sources of furs, and that they favored trade with the French. Livingston reasoned desperately with his London buyers that because of this, only the inferior furs were shipped through New Yorkers' hands, while the best hides trickled northward to the French, because there was no effective provincial legislation. He complained in 1734 that the French got seven-eighths of the colony's furs, and by 1736–38 his letters to Storke, Gainsborough & Mico in London insisted that the French had cut off the trails to Oswego. By then the interloping New York traders, "a parcell of wild brutes" who were "govern'd only by an unruly Passion of getting money by fair or foul means," were beyond influence. And as it turned out, these "wild brutes" were the men to whom Mico turned, bypassing Livingston and other city merchants by the late 1730s.[26]

For their part, members of the "country interest" supported Livingston's urgent appeals for regulation because they were convinced that free traders would not only destroy colonial Indian relations, but would also move to Montreal to sell cheap English strouds and trinkets to the French illicitly. Equally harmful, argued this country interest, were the efforts of a "monopoly" in city fur exporting whose "selfish" intentions led its members to smuggle and bribe at ports, and to promote the principle "that trade cannot be interrupted." Governor William Burnet agreed: "[I]f to get any thing by trade it was necessary to pass through hell, [they] would venture to burn [their] sails"; the comparatively greater prosperity of smugglers to Dutch ports, and the failures of three city merchants who traded to London, proved the point.[27]

Parliamentary enumeration of furs in 1722 was not exactly what Cuyler, Livingston, and others had hoped to achieve, for the sanctions provided against the Canadian trade were enforceable, and the law also "restrain[ed] them from a free commerce" to Amsterdam in Dutch or New York vessels. Henceforth, exporting directly to non-English ports proved risky, and trade through England and then to another port proved prohibitively expensive.[28] Cuyler, Thomas Bayeaux, Stephen De Lancey, Dirk Schuyler, Jacob and John Wendell, and Telemon and John Cruger all laced their correspondence with arguments for leaving the international trade "equally free in all parts to all your majesty's subjects in America." Firm regard for internal regulations was wise; imposition of restraints on exportation was "unnatural."[29] But the colonial Assembly failed to oblige them. In 1726, it renewed internal duties on Indian goods shipped up the Hudson, thus increasing city merchants' expenses; simultaneously, it refused to regulate the export traffic, thus defeating merchants' hopes "to give free peltry the spirit of regulation" necessary for channeling it to New York City.[30] Legislation the next year and in almost all subsequent years down to 1754, curtailed open trade with Canada and the western frontier, but exporters reflected bitterly that the measures were intended to guard New York's northern boundaries and expand its settlement westward, and not to address their commercial needs.[31]

Not all New Yorkers saw the issues in such unambiguous terms. Archibald Kennedy, appointed customs collector in 1731, believed that there was merit in regulating the fur trade according to imperial interests, especially in light of provincial efforts to recover it from French Canada. But he also realized that export duties and taxes on the goods used in Indian diplomacy harmed the trade of Albany and New York merchants. Perhaps, wrote Kennedy, the principles behind the original Acts of Trade were not durable under changing conditions in the colonies; perhaps they raised divisive jealousies that weakened the colony's ability to prosper. Years later, in 1750, Kennedy returned to these issues, and changed his mind. In building northern defenses and paying for the goods used in Indian diplomacy, land taxes were a better revenue source than export duties. Kennedy proposed that the government free the fur trade of monopoly privileges and encourage open trade in the northern reaches beyond Albany. But fixed prices for Indian goods were essential, too, to tame "a Tribe of Harpies" within the community of New York City fur merchants. Ultimately, he envisioned, there might be a zone of friendship between English and French dominions, and the application of mercantile policies in a spirit of compromising diverse interests and evoking imperial peace.[32]

But in any case receding supplies of peltry muted the quarrel between exporters and their rivals and shifted activities to the scattered interlopers who pressed into the frontier and smuggled goods into Canada. In the 1740s, few city merchants could collect enough furs for export. Cornelius Cuyler was able to send a few hundred furs to the merchants Samuel Storke, Richard Champion, and William Baker in London, but most of them were illicitly gotten from Canada. After the Seven Years' War, Cuyler and new men such as John Wetherhead, Alexander McComb, Daniel Campbell, Hayman Levy, James Sterling, and two merchants named McTavish and Duncan cultivated connections with far western trappers, and shipped their exports to Benjamin Booth and John Blackburn, merchants who rose to prominence in London during the war. Indeed, their far-flung connections survived well into the 1760s, when the imperial crisis made them problematic.[33] By then the frontier diplomat William Johnson had noted to crown officials how local inhabitants of Albany and Schenechtedy had joined nonresident smugglers to pursue "what [the independent traders] call their rights" and to demand that "every Trader be at Liberty to go where, & do as he pleases." Not only did such activities violate obligations to mercantile authorities; they also disturbed Indian land usage and culture. Johnson de-

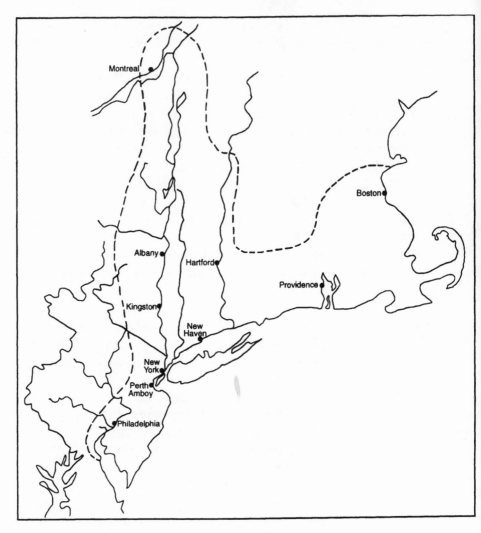

Map 7. New York City's Trading Region by the 1740s

spaired of arriving at justice for all parties: "as extravagant Gain will often tempt people to overlook [Consequ]ences, & run all hazards I have long thought it best to [Wave every] part [of the regulations] which co[ul]d possibly be dispensed with" when trading to the north.[34] Although they were otherwise distinct from Johnson in their economic interests, city exporters might have concurred with his judgment of interlopers. Ironically, interimperial wars and provincial expansion westward kept alive the conflicting claims of regulating interests and ambitious independent colonists, even when furs were themselves of little consequence for their economy and there were few fur traders in the province.

The Preeminence of Grain and Flour

Exporters who prevailed over the recession of the 1720s, as well as many newcomers to commerce, welcomed the shift toward grain and flour exporting to coastal and Caribbean ports in the next decades. External demand for the colony's provisions fueled their confidence, as did the prospects of shipping clothing, foodstuffs, work animals, implements, staves, beeswax, pork, beef, butter, candles, and tanned hides in exchange for coin and staples. Greater emphasis on West Indian markets would not only benefit city merchants, they argued; it was undoubtedly a part of "Her Majesties interest" as well.[35] Already by the late 1690s, Stephen De Lancey, Samuel Vetch, and Philip Schuyler were among many rising wholesalers who concentrated their attention on obtaining wheat, rye, and "our own Indian corn" for export to the war-ravaged Caribbean.[36] By the 1720s, "the Staple Commodity of the Province [was] Flower and Bread which [was] sent to all Parts of the West Indies."[37] Supplies of these exports came from docks at Albany, Esopus, and throughout the Hudson Valley, Connecticut, Long Island, and New Jersey. Millers of other colonies were reputed to choose New York City over their own provincial ports, so that by the 1750s, William Smith wrote in his *History* that New York City "command[ed] almost the whole trade of Connecticut and New Jersey."[38]

Agricultural producers mixed their lingering reliance upon customary relations with their ambitions to cultivate larger portions of their fields in exportable commodities. Given good soil and weather, seven to eight acres might yield eighty to ninety bushels of wheat per year, forty-five of which were necessary to help feed a family of five. Some of the remainder might be used in the web of local labor and commodities exchanges over the winter season, while perhaps ten to twenty bushels might be available for export. Indeed, hundreds of families in New York produced thousands of bushels of wheat by the 1720s. It is uncertain how much country produce from regional farms was consumed in New York City; a conservative extrapolation that accounts for a maximum possible quantity of exportable grain and the probable quantities exported over the years leaves the impression of a port city highly dependent on the commercial farmers around them.[39]

Although ideas about justice between buyer and seller continued to exist in the countryside, there is little evidence in New York that farmers had deep attachments to customary social relations when they sought the best prices and markets for goods sent out of their communities. Storekeepers, producers, and merchants reckoned most country services and goods in a money value, not time or skill; the money value might be recorded in customary terms referring to barter or labor exchanges, or in "prices current," and debts might be settled at year end or not. Trust must have been some part of the equation between commercial farmers and city exporters at all times, but negotiations over the precise terms of sales created habits of calculation as well. Indeed, difficulties arose between country and city traders precisely because both sides traded on common ground, regularly and intensely confronting each other over the quality and prices of goods brought to market.[40]

When rural producers had the advantage of knowing about the conditions and productivity of their neighbors, and of having what exporters keenly wanted, they could insist that goods moving toward the port city "be left free" of regulations that set the terms of sale, regulations favored by New York City's exporters.[41] Or they could try to control the conditions of sale in order to get favorable gate prices. Long Islanders were among the first to complain bitterly about the combination of low prices merchants offered for farm goods and the burdensome regulations the government imposed on them. The bolting monopoly in the 1680s had already convinced them that city merchants and millers intended to monopolize exports behind a thin guise of promoting the colony's commercial reputation. Thirty years later, Long Islanders still protested city discrimination and proposed the creation of new ports of entry closer to their "country grain." For their part, exporting merchants wished to divert trade out of Oyster Bay into New York City and to prevent the rise of overland shipment to Boston, where merchants paid higher prices for grain. But rural sellers were not above withholding produce in order to get better prices: when wholesalers complained that having to go to Long Island to pick up commodities would be prohibitively costly, small producers there chose to let "wheat and grain lay by them till the Vermin [ate] and Spoiled it."[42]

New Jersey's many "country merchants" and their "wood boats that bring firewood and pipe staves" to New Brunswick or Perth Amboy developed a very different relationship with New York City exporters. Because Jerseyites' ports were free of duties, and their port officials granted quick clearances for Madeira, the Canary Islands, or Caribbean ports, New York's exporters were content to collect great quantities of grain near New Jersey ports. Country traders were in turn grateful to see New Yorkers visit New Jersey ports with large vessels and agreed to accept lower gate prices from New Yorkers than they had hoped to receive. Even when Perth Amboy recaptured part of this trade in the 1740s, its merchants continued to be middlemen and port waiters for New York's exporters.[43] Connecticut and Rhode Island traders—many of them also commercial farmers and sloop owners—noted that their preference for New York's exporting arrangements over Boston's stemmed not from New Yorkers' prices, which were less favorable than Bostonians', but from the efficiency of their shipping and marketing abroad.[44]

The tension between merchants and producers in New York's own hinterlands is evinced by dissatisfaction about prices for necessary imports, which country buyers insisted rose exorbitantly outside the city. A growing colonial population created regular demand for many commercial imports by the 1720s, and most savvy traders knew that this should have kept prices relatively low and predictable. In fact, some goods from England were cheaper than those produced in the colony: durable dishware, agricultural implements, and, by the 1740s, some cotton textiles. Furthermore, rural producers had some knowledge that wholesale prices were falling on the other side of the Atlantic Ocean, and they were by no means ignorant of merchants' markups; indeed, people in the hinterland frequently blamed colonial importers for charging an "excess[ive] price."[45]

Over the 1720s and 1730s, for example, Samuel Storke imported commodities intended for the average consumer and often added a 50 percent markup, which he calculated as barely enough to cover his costs of storage, transport, and insurance, but a level beyond which he dared not go. When it came to finer cloth, New Yorkers were acutely sensitive to any rise in textiles prices that might be due to markups or "artificial" impositions. As a merchant told his British correspondents more than once, "purchasers here pay No Regard to the [prices you ask] but are Govern'd by their own Judgement." They "are Not Ignorant of the Quality and Prices" of textiles, and commercial farmers even expected prices for imported clothing and agricultural implements to remain stable or decline in relation to the commodities they sold to merchant exporters. Later, John Wetherhead was sure that the principle of adding markups worked in reverse for country buyers of common cloths; some of them, he lamented, expected to negotiate prices downwards: "I always understood there was a Certain price fixed for the different Packages from which there was no Deviation—I shall however know better for the future."[46]

Of course, there were good reasons to resist price hikes, especially when rural families accumulated steep debts for merchants' imported goods. Some countryfolk provoked angry correspondence when they did not, or could not, repay traders, as when Philip Cuyler prodded William Seeber to pay a debt that "was upwards of two Years" overdue. Seeber was one of many who were in his debt, and Cuyler regretted his experiment in "country dealing." Gerard Beekman aimed to corner Boston's trade with Newport, Hartford, and New London storekeepers between 1747 and 1764, although he also felt it might have been a waste of time: seven-eighths of the people of New England, he charged, were given to such "d————d ungrateful cheating, that I am almost afraid to trust any Connecticut man."[47]

Many New York City consumers were also in debt to merchants who had sold them both marked-up imports and expensive grain. By the 1720s, taverns, newspapers, and shopwindows posted price information, providing a basis for "cost-comparison" shopping and demystifying the cluster of merchants associated with changing prices. Retailers felt compelled to standardize the prices of common imports; deviations from them could erupt into consumer protests, "popular boycotts" of goods, or price-fixing demands. And grain merchants—usually rising, modest traders—assented to be "reasonable" about their food prices to homemakers. For their part, merchant importers were less sympathetic to consumers' demands, and they defeated every proposal sent to the Common Council for fixing ceilings on markups. In 1763, they won—although only narrowly—their case for "liberal trade" in linens, woolens, sugar, and small finished goods by defeating a law to limit profits.[48]

What continued to cause exporters the greatest consternation, however, was rural producers' ability to negotiate rising gate prices in the countryside.[49] For example, William Beekman, the colony's largest flaxseed exporter after mid-century, was not sanguine about being able to buy farm goods at prices he considered low enough. Over the fall and early winter months, he accumulated thousands of bushels of seed in New York City and exported it as soon as farmers agreed on a price to charge exporters; but "the Seller will not make a Price Untill the Bulk of the Seed comes to market, so that there is but Little Chance of one [shipment] being Cheaper then Others." Compounding Beekman's problems, some middlemen who transported seed to New York City for upriver farmers wanted "to Engroce the Whole" and set artificially high prices for the commodity. Beekman was not alone in decrying the timidity of the colonial Assembly when it refused to "limit the price of provisions at market" because farmers protested; along with his merchant neighbors the Crugers, Beekman "monop'liz'" supplies of flaxseed and flaxseed oil, declared an acceptable price, and sent shipments to Bristol.[50]

Frustrations were compounded before 1740 because a medley of circumstances prevented uniform prosperity, including uneven grain harvests, fluctuating prices and markets abroad, and periods of citywide distress throughout the eighteenth century. At the heart of many merchants' troubles lay the irregular maturation of regional agriculture, especially widely varying quantities of exports, which made it difficult to judge markets in the West Indies, Amsterdam, or southern Europe; and despite larger surpluses, the pace of settlement along the Hudson River seemed glacial, vast tracts of land being only partially improved or tenanted early in the century. Prospective settlers who entered New York City from abroad often migrated to Boston or Philadelphia because received wisdom held that these rival cities offered more competitive advantages for artisans and retailers, easier acquisition of the much-coveted "yeoman tract," and busier city docks, where rising merchants could earn greater returns.[51]

Even when merchants' country agents inspired rural producers to orient more production toward exportable commodities, to hire nonfamily labor, and to accept cash payments and the bookkeeping methods of country storekeepers, they remained dismayed at the thinness of settlement. West Indian demand soared in certain years, but social conflicts over the prices and quality of marketable surpluses, as well as quarrels about rural withholding of surpluses or bad harvests, made it hard for merchants to "get enough for shipload" in the century's early years.[52]

Given the missed opportunities of long-distance trade and the vagaries of regional exchange, some lesser merchants believed that raising the prices of goods they marketed to the interior was their only means of economic survival. Some of them echoed Cadwallader Colden's argument that colonists everywhere raised the prices of goods "over their intrinsic value" because producers needed a profit and buyers would assess their needs along with the justice of a sale. As "the great Locke" had insisted, value proceeds initially from the "natural necessity" of a thing, whether it be air, water, specie, trade, or any item of trade. But it also proceeds from the "voluntary choice of mankind" to measure the labor put into producing an item, to judge its plenty or scarcity, and make a calculation between buyers and sellers. Prices changed "naturally" if exports were plentiful or scarce, depending upon the "industry" of inhabitants who brought products to depots along the seacoast, and upon the bargain struck with exporters. The final price of a commodity might not be known to producers and exporters simultaneously, said Colden, although all parties made predictions about the prices they anticipated upon the arrival of commodities in a distant market. Indeed, it was disastrous to establish the price of commodities before they had arrived at the point where they would satisfy demand, for all buyers sought the lowest prices from sellers, and the latter wished to charge the highest markups.[53]

Such wisdom was, of course, perfectly acceptable to farmers who wanted "free prices" and the best possible terms of sale to exporters. But the latter disagreed, and added that their price increases, or markups, were not only an immediate market decision but a means to cover losses on shipments of commodities for which there was not advance demand and markets were limited. It was just, they insisted, to counter small producer's freely shifting prices with markups of 200 to 300 percent on goods sent up the Hudson River, although few of them would take the chance of losing sales altogether by charging the 500 to 600 percent that the great wholesalers added to luxury furniture and fine textiles. In the 1750s, a "150 per cent advance" on imported clothing or housewares was still typical, and in 1774, Governor William Tryon was under the impression that markups on dry goods finding their way into the countryside began, not at New York City, but at London, where exporters entered them on cockets for "two and often five times their original cost."[54]

Wholesale prices of textiles, agricultural implements, and earthenware declined slowly but surely over the century. The costs of sugar, molasses, tobacco, rice, and dyewoods fluctuated more, but they too were cheaper in some years. In addition, storage and transportation of the commodities, insurance, freightage, losses due to piracy, turnaround time, and wharfage fees all declined starting in the 1690s. Although 15 percent of New York's imports originated in Europe and had to be dutied and reexported through English customs—thereby increasing merchants' costs—their original prices fell slowly, as did the English ad valorem duties on them. Some shipbuilding costs may have fallen over the century, but merchants' ledgers indicate that the costs of outfitting or repairing a ship held steady, as did mariners' wages.[55]

Why, then, did city merchants seek higher markups? Importers argued that charges for freight, storage, commissions, and crew's wages still whittled down their margin of profit by as much as one quarter of total returns, and wars pressed up insurance rates manyfold. Then, too, West Indian goods were subject to fluctuating demand by rural colonists; in efforts to dispose of them, great importers could afford to dispatch small quantities of sugar, tobacco, molasses, or cotton wool into the countryside and wait for payments from country storekeepers, or "put [them] in storage in hope of getting Something More for them" at a later time. These were the traders whose many credits with country buyers often went uncollected. Lesser merchants, however, could neither afford excessive insurance rates nor wait for goods to sell more slowly at higher prices; they did not have the credit, reputation, or cash reserves to keep up international trade while they waited for expensive goods to sell. Indeed, there were times when middling merchants faced formidable efforts by country buyers to press down prices of goods sold in the interior, and most evidence points to rural victories.[56] Worst of all, middling city merchants feared that the rising production of finished goods in the countryside would lead to diminished purchases of imports, and that farmers might in turn demand more cash for their agricultural surpluses, or decrease their reliance on staples exporting altogether.[57]

The fluctuating quality of goods offered to merchants' country chapmen also thwarted exporters' expectations. Since the defeat of the bolting monopoly in 1690, they had decried the "anarchy in the Province" resulting from the fact that the prices and quality of goods brought to market were controlled by "rapacious farmers" and colluding country millers. Moreover, new kinds of middlemen interfered with relations of exchange. Rural retailers who had themselves been local farmers became indispensable purveyors of goods to village homes, centralizers of small farm surpluses that were subsequently sent to New York City for sale or export, and often the rural community's bankers. Wholesalers often benefited from their services, but during times of scarcity or high prices, village retailers were prone to cause friction between commercial farmers and middling exporters. The storekeepers, charged merchants, tricked unsuspecting customers into buying "artificialities" and unnecessary goods of inferior quality, at costs beyond their means, and then deliberately arranged for "unnatural shortages" of exportable surpluses in order to "oversell" merchants' wares and cheat exporters. They dunned people for payment of overdue debts and plagued merchants with the malign practice of hoarding. Competitive advertising, which first appeared among shopkeepers of the province, not among the importing merchants of New York City, further aroused merchants' hostility.[58]

Merchants also looked with disdain and alarm upon the prosperous stone mills erected far into the New Jersey and Hudson River countryside. Enterprising millers who did very little farming themselves had built structures here and there along streams that were three stories high, complete with hoisting pulleys, washing and sorting equipment, and overshot waterwheels. Most commercial farmers took their July and August harvests to these "country mills," where they paid 10 to 20 percent of their grain for use of the mill and then consigned portions of the flour to middlemen and storekeepers at their own designated prices. It was this dispersed milling and individually set prices that "destroyed the reputation of New York flower," city merchants charged. Many grain exporters blamed trouble in the West Indies on farmers who "charge[d] overly dear," middlemen (who had begun to market surpluses by the 1720s), and storekeepers who stocked too many finished goods at exorbitant prices and allowed farmers too little—and unreasonably short—credit.[59]

These concerns usually did not apply to the "merchant mills" emerging near New York City, where farmers sold their grain to mill owners at set prices, expecting the miller to market the flour as his own commodity, often by collaborating with city exporters to keep up the quality of barreled flour and to regularize the flow of exports into the port.[60] In fact, some city merchants were connected to merchant millers by birth or marriage, and established a well-integrated business for securing supplies of grain, controlling the gristing and barreling of flour, and arranging for its transport and sale in distant places. William Beekman and Caleb Heathcote built gristing mills and hired all kinds of laborers and craftsmen to collect grain, run the mills, package and transport flour for export out of New York. Andrew van Horne, one of the city's rising exporters, kept a farm on the Raritan River near New Brunswick from the 1720s to 1745, at which he had an orchard, livestock, a gristmill, a bolting house with two mills in it, and a bakery. The operation was, he noted, "convenient both for a foreign and inland Trade." Indeed, his three brothers were among the most eminent West Indies traders in New York City, and regularly carried Andrew's grain and flour to Barbados, Jamaica, and Antigua. Adolph Philipse, son of the manor lord, Frederick, took over operations of the complex of mills and craft shops some time after 1700, and from his nearly one thousand tenants collected enough grain to produce about two tons of flour a day during peak seasons of the 1740s.[61]

These were exceptional operations, however, and most exporters prevailed upon commercial farmers and local millers to send modest amounts of grain to New York, and upon their Assembly to support a city bolting monopoly. Importers of West Indian goods also lent their support to reinstating the bolting monopoly, and innumerable city millers, coopers, bakers, and middlemen involved in the grain trade did likewise. Everyone, merchant petitioners declared in 1698, knew that "there was never a greater Act of Improvidence," than to permit free purchase and sale of vital grains. Regrating (buying in bulk with a view to immediate resale) and forestalling inevitably resulted from deregulating markets. Merchants paid more for farmers' surpluses under such deregulation, they insisted, and were helpless to raise prices in foreign markets. Moreover, since the city's population was "chiefly dependent upon flour," the higher prices would hurt countless inhabitants.[62]

These objections were to no avail. When prices in the West Indies dipped low once again in 1700, "city merchants [who] were . . . obstinate for maintaining their ordinance" to bolt only in New York City persuaded a few Assembly members to refuse to provide revenues for the support of government without a city monopoly on grain and flour exporting. Although Governor Bellomont assented to the measure, the Assembly majority voted against the act, and free bolting continued.[63] A few years later, in 1708, Governor Cornbury again condemned free bolting, and associated it with falling prices abroad. "The Country," he said, "don't care what becomes of the city provided they have goods cheap. They think the more goods are brought in the cheaper they will be no matter whence they come nor how much the trade of the province is destroyed." He agreed that only bolting regulations could ensure merchants quality exports, at competitive prices, and thereby secure their international reputations; companion legislation to regulate the quantities and prices of imports would prevent the gluts that merchants dreaded; land taxes would distribute the burden for raising revenues to residents of the interior. And elimination of export duties would be essential to this program, for they were "found by experience to be the expulsion of many, and the impoverishing of the rest of the planters, freeholders and inhabitants of this colony; of the most pernicious consequence, which, if continued, will unavoidably prove the ruin of the colony."[64]

But Cornbury's attempt to appease all economic interests in fact disgruntled most colonists. Indeed, his intemperate requests for higher taxation all around, prevailed upon both constituencies to sharpen their respective justifications for opposing legislation. The Assembly, by then dominated by the landed interest, sternly rejected Cornbury's reasoning. Only imports, they said, were just objects of taxation; these, their reasoning held, were imposed on goods made elsewhere and marketed to colonists by strangers, and the taxes could justifiably weigh heaviest on luxuries. Revenues raised from export taxes would, however, be paid either by the great Hudson River magnates (some assemblymen among them) who brought their grain and flour to New York City for export or by middlemen for the merchant exporters, who would pass on their greater costs to farmers by offering lower gate prices. As for land taxes, to raise these without the consent of the province's proprietors was, everyone knew, "a grievance and a violation of the people's property." And the Assembly had a duty to protect the interests of the majority of inhabitants, for "it is and always has been the unquestionable right of every freeman in this colony that he hath a perfect and entire property in his goods and estate."[65]

Grain and flour exporters, called the "regulating interest," must have been pleased to share one demand with the landed interest: antipathy to export duties. Yet they also upheld their proposals to shift the burden of taxation from city to country, regulate exportation more strictly, and create an excise on country milling. In 1715, when specie was needed to cover a large issue of paper currency, the Assembly assented to most of this formula and added modest import duties as well. At first, exporters sighed with relief and enjoyed the rising postwar foreign demand for provisions. But soon the currency emission's effects waned, and port officials refused to abide by the new flour inspection laws. And although import revenue laws were renewed over the coming years, land taxes did not materialize, and excises on milling lasted only from 1715 to 1722. Farmers, too, continued their informal practices of adjusting prices and resisting merchants' buying conditions.[66]

Conditions accounting for divisions between city and country, and between great merchants and lesser ones, endured. Dry-goods importers continued to fret about import duties, estate holders continued to oppose increased land taxes, and their interests tended to meld when the great wholesalers invested capital in land and established ties of marriage with landed families. Export-oriented lesser merchants were not overly concerned about import duties on luxury or fine goods, but they were not indifferent when the duties affected trade from neighboring colonies and the commodities they sold to storekeepers and farmers in the hinterland. Furthermore, until the end of the colonial period, most great importers did not deal directly with rural producers in getting grain and flour, so they did not join in persistent efforts by exporters to win regulatory legislation over the countryside; importers' justifications for higher prices in New York City stores also implicitly set them apart from middling merchants, who were themselves among the consumers who could not easily afford the higher prices.

Possibly because they wished to distance themselves from their humble wholesaling peers, prominent dry-goods merchants periodically charged rising exporters with complicity in the "decay of reputation." Unbranded cargoes, they noted, often concealed the deceits of two or three men in the blended mediocrity of an entire shipload, and the mixed cargoes of many regional farmers elevated the possibilities for deceit. Since the defeat of the Bolting Act, established merchants believed that increased forestalling and shortages were due as much to lesser merchants who illegally cornered supplies for export as to calculating farmers. On one side, lamented the great importers, they were besieged by the despised commission auctioneers who came from England to sell large unbroken containers of goods at reduced prices; on the other, the joint ventures of middling merchants in the city threatened to ruin them. For example, in December 1715, the successful importers Dugdale and Searle brought a suit against a newcomer to exporting, Thomas Kearney, charging that he had brought merchants "into great Discredit" at Bridgetown, Barbados, where 57 of 100 half-barrels of flour were "bad and mixt" with foreign matter. Although Kearney was only one of many New Yorkers who had put together the cargo, he alone paid over £20 for the collective deceit.[67]

In this and other cases, rising exporters responded firmly that they were helpless to make up good cargoes because they had so little control over the quality of colonial goods. The merchants Paul Richard, Robert Livingston Jr., Philip French, and Mordecai Gomez brought familiar pleas to the Common Council in 1733: "The Credit of the Trade of this City . . . is very much Lessened, and . . . will in a Short time be wholly Ruin'd unless some Speedy Method be fallen upon to prevent . . . Frauds and Abuses for the Future." The blame lay with farmers, great and small, and Hudson Valley millers who "suffered Fair Traders to receive" poor-quality grain at exorbitant prices.[68]

Shortly thereafter, Governor Cosby, already unpopular among merchants because of tonnage and slave-importation duties that had been passed early in his administration, redeemed his image in part by favoring flour inspection and export regulations. "The main bent of our farmers," wrote Cosby, "is to raise wheat," but they tended to overproduce and sell poor-quality commodities to merchants' agents. A loose coalition of influential leaders, including the landed Lewis Morris, the publicist John Peter Zenger, and "the populace" of the country, persuaded the Assembly to defeat Cosby's legislation in April 1734 on the grounds that the city should not have greater privileges than "the generalytie" of inhabitants through the province.[69] Under Governor Clark, from 1736 to 1743, the same clash surfaced again when Hudson Valley magnates declared themselves in favor of free exporting from their estates, pointing to the combined benefits of developing the interior, expanding provincial power to the west, and taming neighboring colonies. Lesser exporters reminded the Assembly once again that such aggressive instincts would undermine their and farmers' abilities to prosper.[70]

Into the 1750s and 1760s, middling exporters accommodated country interests without the help of wished-for quality and price regulations. Abraham ten Eyck, for example, periodically revived use of commodity payments in order to increase the circulation of flour in his warehouse, or to purchase more for sale to Jamaica markets, especially during times of scarce specie. One of his advertisements announced a long list of "country Produce" he would give "in Payment for [flour]," which he hoped would "make considerable easement to the Purchasers thereof," especially because the flour would "answer their Ends as well as Cash, as they must pay Cash for such articles." Late in the century, other merchants believed they could speed up sales of imports if they "Truck[ed] them away" for exportable commodities.[71]

Economic maturation in the region, the libertarian impulses of scattered regional farmers, and the measures of their provincial legislature with respect to exporting, defined many parameters of opportunity and restraint for dozens of lesser merchants. But these traders also depended on the all-important, if unreliable, West Indian markets to absorb colonial staples and provisions. Although they sent more grain and flour each year from 1710 to 1747 to English Caribbean ports, there were periods of rather sudden and sometimes dramatic fluctuations in prices, especially when West Indian and continental European economies faltered between gluts and subsistence crises.[72]

Anxieties also rose each year as the autumn months approached, for that was the time when markets in southern Europe tended to become saturated with Polish grain and warehouses in the West Indies overfull. Over the 1730s, British demand for sugar and molasses from the West Indies also declined, which—quite aside from the Molasses Act—depressed prices for those commodities, reversed the terms of trade for West Indians, and made their payment of debts to New Yorkers difficult. Then in the late 1730s, New York City's merchants experienced good fortune: West Indies sugar and molasses prices fell, because the commodities were readily available, and North American grain and flour prices fell in many seasons because of bountiful harvests. Trade out of New York had never seemed better.[73]

A similar cycle of events recurred when high international demand from 1747 to 1749 gave way to gluts and low prices in 1750. Confronted with poor international markets, New York's exporters turned against the farmers and millers of their own interior. Merchants, William Livingston wrote in *The Independent Reflector,* reported "great Frauds carried on in the Manufacturing Wheat into Flour," and "in the Article of Bread, Beef, Pork, Bacon, [they] are so notorious abroad" that merchants buy only what is ordered by foreign correspondents.[74] William Alexander, a merchant, made the point quite clearly in 1750: "What makes the most noise here at present is the inspection of flower, our Staple Commodity . . . the Great frauds Committed in the manufacturing thereof and the great necessity there is of some remedy being applied." At a time when high quality was of utmost importance, "about seventy of the merchants of this City petitioned the Assembly . . . and the next day attended the house with above thirty Evidences of the discredit our flower is in through all the Islands in the West Indies and . . . letters by which it clearly appeared that neither the English, French, Dutch, Spaniards or even the Negroes would buy a barrel of New York flower while philadelphia flour is to be had."[75]

At first, the 1751 Inspection Act "to prevent the Exportation of unmerchantable flour" seemed to address these difficulties; in addition to the usual controls on quality and weights of exported flour, the act provided stern penalties for recycling condemned flour and made unbranded flour forfeit. Close observers were convinced that "we have a good law, appointing officers to inspect and brand every cask before its exportation," and that it accounted for relatively good markets at the West Indies between 1749 and 1764. Moreover, with each renewal of the act until 1768, colonists noted how their own exports of good-quality grain kept rising. But deeper economic trends were at work, undermining exporters' optimism, for colonial importation had risen steeply by the late 1750s, and even the best years of West Indian trade came nowhere near to offsetting the debts of colonists to English firms. Then, colonial embargoes during the Seven Years' War reduced what producers could sell to exporters. New York's bakers, millers, and shopkeepers raised their prices to compensate for greater wartime cost of living or to profit from consumer need, demanding from the Common Council that they be "allowed the freedom of the market," just as rural producers had enjoyed it for decades.[76] Farmers responded with a rising spiral of gate prices; in contrast to the 10 percent price increases city exporters enjoyed in the West Indies, exportable flour and grain flowing from the countryside to New York rose about 30 percent in price from 1750 to about 1762. As a consequence, during the few years in which their trade was not under embargoes, city exporters faced seriously declining returns for those commodities.[77]

Postwar adjustments were painful. With each renewal of the Inspection Act, exporters and producers took opposing sides, as if the issues were being argued for the first time; farmers and landed Hudson Valley "flour merchants" clamored for a "free price" when taking grain and flour to New York City for export, while exporting city merchants such as John Watts and John DeVoe united with city consumers and bakers against rural people who, Watts said, acted "most avaricious."[78] Even when provincial agricultural prices dropped slightly, London credit became more available, and foreign demand revived by 1766, exporters reiterated appeals for city privileges. In 1768, leaders in the newly formed Chamber of Commerce petitioned the Assembly to pass legislation to inspect, set a standard of fineness, and brand all barrels of exportable flour intended for export with millers' initials and county of residence. In the round of public discussion accompanying passage of yet another flour regulation, exporters reiterated their hope that the statute would "retrieve the general disrepute [of New York flour] in all parts of the world." Until it was passed, however, they would have to suffer selling "foul trash."[79]

In the following year, Isaac Low, a prominent city grain and flour exporter, took time out from the rising tide of agitation against imperial rule to call attention to the rising costs of sugar and falling prices for grain at French and English possessions in the West Indies. He recommended that the colony upgrade its flour with new agricultural techniques, including the use of French buhrstones in grinding, the transport of grains in covered wagons and containers, the use of German mill screens to filter flour, and weighing flour casks only upon loading them into export vessels. The proposals proved more costly and

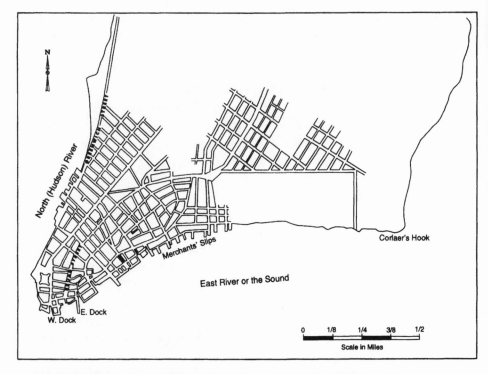

Map 8. The Extent of New York City in about 1766. From "Plan of the City of New York, 1766–1767, Surveyed by Lieut. B. Ratzer," reproduced in *The Memorial History of the City of New York*, ed. James G. Wilson (New York, 1893), 1: 344.

innovative than farmers could, and government officials would, undertake at this time. Until the eve of the Revolution, then, correspondents in the British West Indies reminded New York's merchants that their wheat was "of very ordinary Quality."[80]

Can a Merchant Favor Paper Money?

Quarrels about devaluation, bills of exchange, or customary accommodations to money shortages in the interior contributed to divergent economic interests in New York, as did the revisions of financial orthodoxy that were taking place throughout the empire about banking, credit, auctioning, and thinking about the "stock" of circulating currency. Early in the eighteenth century, under pressure to increase war spending, New Yorkers created a modest supply of paper currency—bills of credit issued by the government that were redeemable in tax payments—for provincial usage, and devised plans for its quick retirement. In the process, colonists also entered a widespread discussion that accompanied policy experiments, about the quantity theory of money and the source of economic value.

For some time already, discussions about changing the value of New York's silver in relation to the money of other colonies and other metal currencies had evoked the long-standing adage that overvaluing silver in New York was unnatural. Silver was the surest money, of intrinsic value, and of constant value against all other monies of account. According to the same wisdom, when other colonies overvalued their silver in order to attract more of it to their dominions, the reliability of silver as a bedrock of exchange was corrupted. When Queen Anne established one standard valuation of silver in 1704, colonists hoped that international exchange rates would stabilize; but silver rates in foreign ports began to rise in relation to England's valuation, and merchants were left with little recourse but to raise their prices to compensate for the de facto devaluation of silver. Still, attachment to the intrinsic value of silver, and opposition to issuance of a paper medium of exchange occupied the attention of many influential thinkers, including William Pollexfen, Thomas Mun, William Petty, John Locke, and Josiah Child.[81]

If silver, the most fundamental of all exchange values, was unstable, early modern writers argued, how could mere pieces of paper of no intrinsic worth salve and extend the colonial economy? Some of them felt certain that the majority of people would never accept so flimsy a means of exchange without the grounding of both personal reputation—which bills of exchange and government loans had—and a redeemable "fund" of some true value. Some observers in New York were sure that colonists would not accept paper money at face value, but instead depreciate its value a little bit in each transaction until it was worthless. Still others insisted that paper money would lower prices and speed circulation of goods—both beneficial effects—but that at some point, it would prompt an unchecked "thirst for money," increase desire and spending by myriad colonists, and so bring ruin.[82]

Beyond these general social considerations, dry-goods merchants had particular concerns of their own. Those who required cash and bills of exchange to pay London creditors, and who adhered to the orthodoxies of mercantilism, opposed the losses they would incur upon conversion of debts from paper into sterling valuations. Furthermore, great merchants in the city had made loans in specie to the government for the 1709 expedition to French Canada, and in some cases were under contract to supply troops with goods for which they were obliged to pay cash; the issuance of paper money would undercut the ability of specie to pass at near par, and would "give public preference" to the "artificiall currency," to the detriment of sound war finance and their own self-interest.[83] Besides, the Assembly would have to pass higher taxes—some of which would no doubt fall on imported goods—in order to retire circulating currency. Tied to this concern, expressed in remonstrances to the governor and Assembly in 1709 protesting the first emission of paper currency, was importers' worry that middling West Indies traders who drew their exports directly from the small producers of the hinterlands would honor the new currency, even if it depreciated moderately, because their "insignificant debtors" had need of it. Meanwhile, among the "old porshun of our trading city" an inevitable gap would grow between the values at which paper currency passed locally and the price of bills of exchange on London. However, two more emissions followed in 1714 and 1717.[84]

The benefits of having an "artificial," as opposed to an "intrinsic," medium of exchange had been acknowledged since at least 1650, when William Potter's *The Key of Wealth* proposed that more rapid circulation of trade goods might be facilitated by paper money. Nicholas Barbon, John Law, William Lowndes, Bishop Berkeley, David Hume, and Sir James Steuart, to name a few, refined an argument that favored moderate emissions of paper money in England. Most of them adhered to long-standing beliefs that any addition to the money supply would raise prices of commodities and services, because the quantity of money established a fund against which all commodities were supposedly priced. As the debate was joined on both sides of the Atlantic, a vocal constituency in New York reiterated that whether the increase in money came from more silver in circulation or from paper issued by government, the price of commodities would rise. In an ideal economic pie of equilibriums and symmetry, the quantity of goods would rise commensurate with the value of silver. So, advocates of artificial currencies had to permit the new, disconcerting view that emissions of paper money would inflate the total value of money, and depreciate the total value of goods. As one colonist put it, "issuing new bills of credit had altered the value of silver" and tempted many citizens into buying frenzies; plentiful money, high demand, and high prices went together, or, put another way, the "value of monies fell as the plenty of them rose."[85]

A responsible government, others insisted, could not eschew the benefits of issuing paper currency; moreover, it would legislate the appropriate policies for withdrawing paper money in a timely fashion. The original device by which New York's advocates of paper money tried to make their plans palatable was the "sinking fund"—taxes or specie set aside for government expenditures—by which paper currency could be drawn out of circulation after it served as a temporary substitute for scarce specie. The fund would mitigate the inflationary effects of paper money. Lesser merchants had to agree that more domestic currency might facilitate exchange and payments without harming the market for bills of exchange that sustained remittances of debts to English firms. Indeed, they applauded the Assembly's declaration in 1714 providing that if creditors refused colonial bills of credit, or overpriced goods for which they accepted paper money—a common practice among merchants who wished to protect themselves from depreciated values of the paper—debts owed to them would not be upheld in civil courts. With this second currency emission, paper currency became legal tender for private debts. In addition, the legislature issued the bills for longer periods of time and increased taxes on imported wine, rum, and brandy because retirement of colonial paper money would be delayed—to the consternation of dry-goods importers who had predicted just such an outcome.[86]

By the end of Queen Anne's War, paper money's lines of support and opposition had been drawn. Lesser merchants and inland traders attributed their ability to prosper with the return of peace to the issuance of a flexible medium of exchange, while transatlantic importers decried the Assembly's continued recourse to paper money. But as William Smith reflected years later, the war loans of great importers lay at the root of even more currency emissions: "Incredible were the numbers of the public creditors; new demands were everyday made. Petitions came in from all quarters, and even for debts contracted before the [Glorious] revolution. Their amount was nearly 28 thousand pounds. To pay this prodigious sum, recourse was had to the circulation of bills of credit to that value."[87]

Nevertheless, when the Assembly emitted another £16,607 in bills of credit in 1717, dry-goods importers joined provincial Council members to demand royal disallowance of the law, with the backing of the London merchants Charles Lodwick, Samuel Baker, and Samuel Stork. An unlikely alliance of commercial farmers, landed magnates in the Assembly, a frustrated and long-unpaid governor (Robert Hunter), and a group of middling exporters invoked rhetoric against colonial "monopolies" in trade—a barb against the great importers— and pressed for the emission. The most vocal advocates of the provincial currency were merchants who had intricate business connections with grain and lumber producers of the hinterlands and reasoned that the new means of exchange was essential for securing exports and facilitating farmers' debt payments. A few of them pointed to other personal benefits as well: offering depreciating paper money for wheat transported down the Hudson River toward the entrepôt would help offset the losses incurred for falling sugar prices in the West Indies trade. Moreover, they reasoned that no international trader wanted to pay drafts in sterling for debts contracted in depreciating paper money, but the alternatives of collecting debts in commodities or extending debtors' periods of repayment were even less desirable. A few renowned West Indies traders— Lawrence Reade, Robert Walters, David Provoost, John Cruger, Johannes Jansen, John de Peyster, and Jacob Kip—added their names to the lesser merchants who favored the bill, possibly because their country agents required a ready means of exchange.[88]

Loud protests by transatlantic traders ensued in 1718. Merchants and captains complained that cargoes of English goods had declined at least 35 percent in value because they had to take freight earnings in paper currency. As they waited at New York City to unload goods and negotiate for bills of exchange, potential profits were diverted to paying wharf fees and sailors' wages; in the end, they also had to sell their goods at New York prices for New York currency, knowing "it is of no value elsewhere." The same London captains had to sell the paper money "back again [to New Yorkers] at their own rates" in order to receive the necessary bills of exchange.[89] Despite a parliamentary investigation, Governor Hunter affirmed that the Assembly's bills of credit would circulate with his approval because they were good for commerce and encouraged "the many to venture their Stocks in trade to the prejudice of the few who had so long monopoliz'd it." The great wholesalers, said Hunter, were men of "private views piques and interests," which worked against the "general view" of the colony. Hunter also approved legislation to fund new emissions with higher taxes on the wine, dry goods, and ships built in New York, taxes that would fall heaviest on opponents of paper money. A 1718 printing of paper currency circulated for two years without crown intervention, until the Board of Trade learned that provincial duties used as a backing for the currency discriminated not only against some colonial wholesalers but against English shippers as well.[90]

Divisions among New York's economic interests over the appropriateness of issues of paper currency continued into the next decades. On the one hand, opposition during the 1720s centered on the provincial Council's core, Adolph Philipse, Peter Schuyler, and Stephen De Lancey, who complained that "Humble inhabitants" and regional traders allowed Massachusetts and Rhode Island currency to pass at large discounts, while transatlantic merchants strove to pass the same currency at face value in order to give their bills of exchange "good reputation." Into the 1730s, John Reade, William Walton, and Robert Watts concurred that when the value of currency fell—as it did when greater sums circulated—bills of exchange became more expensive and New Yorkers' reputation declined abroad. On the other hand, landed gentlemen and western expansionists such as Cadwallader Colden, James Alexander, and Robert R. Livingston tended to agree with lesser merchants that paper money paid the governor's salary, attracted new settlers, and promoted better trade relations between exporters and internal people. Even Governor Burnet noted in 1724 that bills of credit were "compulsive" in young economies and during wars of defense against France; moreover, "the bills of New York keep up their credit," not because "common opinion" regarded them favorably but because the New York Assembly retired them efficiently. "It is not the names things get for the present," insisted Burnet, "but the real nature of them, that will be found to hold against all events," as well as the "just laws" that regulated otherwise fickle public opinions.[91] Outside observers such as John Wise of Massachusetts noted that New York's currency had a salutary effect because, unlike some neighboring colonies, the Assembly emitted it in moderation. The governor of Maryland wrote that New York was "vastly improved in foreign trade as well as home manufactures by a paper currency."[92]

Between 1724 and 1734, the Assembly ordered no new money to be printed, and over the next three years, it authorized only a small amount. But as the colony was once again fell short of funds to sink its outstanding currency, the Assembly levied tonnage and slave duties, which added to transatlantic importers' grievances, and tied emissions of paper currency to appropriation bills for provincial defense in 1738. Importers grew alarmed about the "popular cry for paper," pointing out in a memorial to the Board of Trade that colonial currency did not bear the required suspension clause—a guarantee to Parliament of its right to disallow any colonial act deemed harmful to imperial goals. Although a House of Commons inquiry in 1739, and a Board of Trade report issued in March 1740 reprimanded the Assembly's insubordination to imperial authority, renewed warfare after 1738 drove Governor Clinton to approve new emissions under the usual colonial provisions. By the end of King George's War in 1748, New Yorkers were circulating enormous sums of paper money, much of which was still outstanding in 1755.[93]

During the 1730s, the New York Assembly supplemented its paper currency with a second kind of money, one subscribed through a colonial Loan Office by the private collateral of land and improved real estate, a commodity of unquestioned reputation. When government expenses increased to over £9,000 in arrears in 1739, the first Loan Office Act authorized the printing of bills to the value of £40,000, earning 5 percent interest annually, payable from the colonial treasury, and secured by the collateral of colonists' real estate. Unlike earlier experiments in Europe and New England where a consortium of individual sponsors established private land banks,[94] New York's Assembly kept close watch over its public Loan Office. Support for it grew quickly, especially with the publication of soothing views about its salutary effects on the economy. As one observer put it, the best way to help "Revive the Commerce Trade and Navigation... of the Colony" was to keep commercial interest rates low and the amount of circulating medium plentiful, for "plentiful Currency will occasion Interest to be low." Only "usurers" who loaned over the legal rate of interest, he said, would oppose the plan. The bills, in denominations of £25 to £100, circulated for up to twelve years, provided the real estate mortgages of subscribers remained two times the value of the loan.[95]

For commercial farmers throughout the countryside, Loan Office bills of small denominations were a significant convenience. Even when West Indies traders objected that military suppliers and a "landed interest" outside the city participated heavily in the Loan Office, they also conceded their pleasure at having a greater medium of exchange.[96] But by 1751, London officials grew alarmed about the rapid expansion of paper currency throughout North America. Parliament's Currency Act that year was aimed against New England, but many New Yorkers grew defensive about the benefits of their own provincial money. Along with farmers and West Indies merchants, Assembly representatives stated clearly that paper currency—whether funded by taxes or land—had become one of the instruments by which they remained autonomous from the will of governors and allied with the will of colonists.[97] When the prospects of yet another war loomed, and the crown ordered the colonies to raise a permanent revenue in 1753, Lieutenant Governor James De Lancey wrote to the Board of Trade that "as the assembly are averse to Taxes at this time," the only means to build necessary fortification was to emit more paper currency. Furthermore, although the Board of Trade agreed to the emission, so long as bills of credit were not "declared to be a legal tender," the Assembly countered that "to emit Bills of Credit without making them a lawful Tender, we are confident, will be absolutely useless and without Effect, for we are fully persuaded that no man in the province will be willing to accept that for money which he knows that another may refuse to receive as money from him." War preparations began in earnest over the next months; assemblymen raised import duties and instituted a provincial stamp act, but in 1755 they also ordered a printing of £525,000 in bills of credit—over twice the amount printed between 1709 and 1754—which were to pass at legal tender. The Board of Trade could only blink these violations of imperial laws in order to secure defense of colonial territory.[98]

Over the years, New York's paper currency and cautious Land Office loans depreciated very little, and many colonists became willing to tip their opposition toward support. John Watts and Gerard and Henry Beekman, for example, reassessed their former scorn and admitted that "unless a large sum of money is struck in this and the neighboring governments we shall never get in our debts."[99] So connected in the minds of many New Yorkers were paper currency and government finance by the Seven Years' War that even perfunctory protests against emissions disappeared from the press. By 1757, most merchant military suppliers readily accepted colonial bills of credit, and English contractors were pleased to exchange Parliament's interest bearing treasury bills for New York currency in order to facilitate supply movement. The interest earned on treasury bills provided New York City merchants with an incentive to profit from public service without concern for currency depreciation. And after the war ended, Cadwallader Colden reminded Lord Hillsborough that "Whatever other effect the granting of a paper currency may have, it will certainly increase the consumption of British manufactures in this province."[100]

A few transatlantic wholesalers accepted paper money's indirect capacity to facilitate war and a better balance of trade with England, but most dry-goods importers continued to blame the amount of circulating paper currency for poor foreign rates of exchange, although often erroneously. When exchange rates and agricultural gate prices rose dizzyingly high during times of crop failures in New York, foreign market gluts, or postwar slumps, transatlantic wholesalers demanded less paper money, on the assumption that depreciating paper currency undermined the value of foreign bills of exchange. When agricultural production ran apace with foreign demand or wartime need arose, they accepted paper currency and Loan Office money as valuable support to the economy. But to the end of the colonial period, they linked a supposed overabundance of paper currency closely to the periodic trade crises or lurching international prices they experienced in the wider international economy, and tended to overlook the more structural causes of commercial difficulty. Direct manipulation of specie by overvaluation and their personal reliance on bills of exchange constituted their preferred means of redressing trade difficulties.[101]

Many middling traders linked paper money more directly to competitive regional exchanges. Firsthand experience in the West Indies and coastal trade prompted thinking about the fluctuations—and thus the manipulability—of economic conditions that varied from transatlantic ones, and changing relationships in the countryside invited comparable new thinking about the benefits of detaching paper currency from notions of intrinsic value and desire for specie. By the mid eighteenth century, a few writers on both sides of the Atlantic argued that additional amounts of paper currency in circulation did not affect the value of silver, which would rise and fall in value irrespective of the quantity of paper currency. Indeed, said some, silver should not be conceptualized as a unit of intrinsic value against which all exchange commodities were measured; it was a commodity like other commodities, and its value derived from its plenty or scarcity. Paper money and specie both changed values according to levels of trade.[102]

The Appeal of Manufactures

In 1670, Daniel Denton observed how the demands of early settlement had constrained most colonists from experimenting with "manufactories": "this country is not yet ripe for manufactures. Labor is too high—too much land to be settled." Into the next century, other writers echoed the difficulties of starting up enterprises that required innovative technologies or uses of labor; population was too low to support manufactures, said some, and people "find it more their interest to cultivate their lands and attend the fisheries than to manufacture." Indeed, the investor Peter Hasenclever wrote late in the century, artisans and manufacturers of England "imagine that the inhabitants of the colonies . . . make many things and export several manufactures to the exclusion of British manufactures of the same kind," but start-up costs were too dear in New York.[103]

Officials reporting to the Board of Trade understated the range of manufacturing activities, largely because it was their job to ensure that colonists did not rival English producers. In 1732, Governor Cosby felt certain that "the Inhabitants here are more lazy and inactive than the world generally supposes, and their manufactures extend no further than what is consumed in their own Family's." Cadwallader Colden was less convinced that colonists were lazy. "The reasons which have hindered the inhabitants from going upon any . . . manufactures are the difficulty with which people can be persuaded to leave the common means by which they have supported their familys to adventure upon any new methods," he argued instead. Farmers and merchants together would "not readily adventure [their] Stock in raising Hemp or making Tar," for "the charge of labor" was too steep to warrant such investment, and even "the benefit of [bounties] . . . does not so immediately reach the Planters." Indeed, wrote Colden, "There is a considerable difference betwixt encouraging the exportation and sale of a commodity which is already the manufacture of the country and the engaging people to go upon a new commodity."[104]

Other colonists concurred that it would be difficult at best to reorient rural producers toward new types of production until costs declined. "No manufactures of note have as yet been established here; at present they get all manufactured goods, such as woolen and linen cloth, etc. from England, especially from

London," Peter Kalm recorded in his travel journal in 1748. Negative assessments appeared in Andrew Burnaby's travel accounts as well; he was so unimpressed with New York's "inconsiderable" manufacturing that he would "not take notice of them," and William Smith wrote in 1757, with significant exaggeration by then, that New Yorkers had "no manufactures of their own."[105]

Many views underscored how difficult it was to sustain an "industrious character," the energy directed to improve private and public welfare in a socially appropriate manner. Virtuous industry might easily lapse into cheating, deception, or a quest for luxuries. An excess of industry without adequate attention to social obligation led to the evils of dissipation, "ambition," and "artful wiles," qualities that were most likely to appear with the rise of manufacturing, since it, unlike commerce, could be conducted by men of lesser means, such as rising shopkeepers and people whose business acumen was not grounded on adequate personal reputations. Furthermore, manufacturing separated people from their "natural" agricultural surroundings and local attachments, thereby endangering the security of country labor and community relations.[106] For their part, some merchants argued that a shift in rural production toward "country manufactures" would prove too costly with respect to both the capital required for new improvements and the reduction in agricultural exports from the province when farmers diverted their energies. Indeed, colonists "are not hindered from making any commodity they might have thought for their own use," but the "better prices for their labor" involved exportation of agricultural goods.[107]

Worries were allayed somewhat by definitions of "manufactories" as nontechnical procedures or the management and distribution of familiar commodities made with familiar tools. Gristmills, sawmills, and small spinning shops minimized both the relocation of individuals from home and changes in the structures of work authority. Mild mercantile protection of certain colonial enterprises, said some writers, could help draw metal crafts, cloth, and processed foodstuffs out of the countryside without luring farmers entirely away from agricultural production. Bold as it seemed, this view did not foresee expanding consumption patterns, universal markets for cheaper commodities, or a rising standard of living. Its proponents tended to imagine manufactures of small scale, small capital, low levels of accumulation, familiar social relations, and the mercantile balance of trade.[108]

Of course, mercantile notions about the proper role of colonies reinforced the opponents of manufacturing. Even the Dutch, who had been exemplars of economic freedom, forbade New Netherland colonists from making cloth in order to protect the weavers, dyers, and manufacturers of Holland, and after 1664, England's state builders protected new manufacturing interests rising alongside powerful commercial ones, thereby refuting the old privileges of landed aristocrats and trading monopolies.[109] Arguments promoting English manufactures included dictums about northern colonial exportation of agricultural and primary goods, and manufactures limited to homespun and family farm subsistence foods. In 1701, "An American" contested Charles Davenant's call for unregulated manufacturing because too many farmers would rush into new enterprises, leading to unbalanced production and too little necessary food.[110] "Manufactures in the Plantations," said an anonymous pamphleteer, "is that very Means by which the Kingdom is drained of its People," its skills, and its proper authority. Thus, a colony ought not to grow so as to drain England of its laborers; its prices and wages ought never to compete favorably against England's; and its domestic manufactures ought never to be exported if an English equivalent could suffice.[111]

In 1726, the Board of Trade affirmed earlier manufacturing prohibitions and laid down the sweeping dictum that "all the products of the colonies for which the manufactures and trade of Britain has a constant demand be enumerated," and that "every valuable merchandize to be found in the English colonies and but rarely anywhere else and for which there is a constant demand in Europe shall also be enumerated in order to assist Great Britain in the balance of trade with other countries." New York City's transatlantic merchants reinforced such policies by restating the belief that manufacturing was a useful alternative when "our commerce be clogged" but it was at best a secondary grounding for the rise of empires.[112]

Others in New York were not so sure. By the 1720s, some observers expressed a heightened awareness of colonists' role as consumers with expanding material demands, which spilled over into discussions about manufacturing to meet this demand. Few of them had "discovered," theoretically speaking, an understanding of how consumers saved for their purchases, what role there might be for labor and wages in developmental scenarios, or what effect internal improvements would have upon enhancing the value of land. But they noticed rising standards of living, maturing agricultural production, more sophisticated business relations, and accumulation of significant wealth in the hands of a few colonists. Maybe, a few hazarded, refinement stemmed not only from circulation of goods across oceans, but from new production, credit, and debt relations in the countryside as well. Although there was no early and complete adaptation in New York to the production, wage, or exchange relations that we identify with a system of manufacturing, regional commercial farmers entered the "cash nexus" and anonymous long-distance exchange willingly, some of them by marketing as much surplus as possible by the 1720s. Middling merchant wholesalers hardly ignored that they played a vital role in the general economic maturity of the region as facilitators of the "universal industry" so many early modern writers praised, and as the initiators of new "country manufactures."[113] Some went so far as to imagine the mutually reinforcing network of new and more goods, rising population, new technology, and inducements to "industry."[114]

Periodic gluts in the West Indies inspired some support for manufactures. "The Markets for your Flour," Governor Clarke warned colonists, "are already so much over-done, by the great Importations that are made [in the West Indies], that unless some Manufactures be set on foot that are wanted in Great Britain, or do not interfere with theirs," credit would tighten, shipyards close, and commercial exchanges eventually fail. Clarke, and Governors Hunter and Colden before him, also lamented that giving exclusive emphasis to grain and flour exporting had encouraged trade with the enemy. By 1737, New Yorkers, in the midst of a trade recession, reached a level of "universal Discontent." "Extream poverty have overspread the Country and threatened its utter ruin" because, said commentators, they had so thoroughly concentrated production upon subsistence for home consumption and staples for export. Small producers and merchants alike, wrote Clarke, "intirely neglected" to experiment with new agricultural commodities; their reliance upon staples exporting "Cramps the minds of the People from thinking to Launch out into [new] trade which has given other Colonies the opportunity to become almost our Sole Carriers." New York's commerce had not come to such disastrous ends as these, but it is significant that some of its inhabitants—among them governors appointed by the crown—struggled to overcome perennial commercial problems by means of manufactures.[115]

Already by the turn of the century, almost every town in the colony boasted a central gristmill to which local farmers brought grain, which might find its way to New York City for urban consumption or export. Farmers also used millstones to sharpen tools, shred rags for the colony's paper mills, press flaxseed for its oil, or grate bones for pastes and medicines of various kinds. The upper stores of larger mills were rented for storage; the horses were rented for farm labor; the miller himself often functioned as a local handyman and received cash in payment.[116] By the 1740s, communities all along the Hudson marketed dairy products, beeswax, ginseng, barreled meats, planed timber, beaver hats, lampblack, linseed oil, shoe leather, flaxseed, and small quantities of leather goods, which in their aggregate provided a rapidly growing export trade to New England, South Carolina, and the West Indies. While grain remained its most important single export commodity, the portion that it represented in the widening array of exports fell from 33 percent in 1720 to 21 percent in 1770.[117]

Domestic "manufactures" accounted for many of the new goods available for export, and were possible in the first place because they derived from familiar materials and skills in rural production, and the aggressive marketing strategies of middling merchants. In the case of hemp, a few investing merchants attempted to persuade the "selfish farmer"—who was at first reluctant to divert part of his resources away from subsistence toward an "industrial" crop—that he would benefit from expanding its production. Caleb Heathcote, still gaining a toehold in colonial commerce, proposed in 1705 that hemp and flax production would be a spur to country settlement and prosperity because many farmers knew how to process those commodities; and they would be alluring to merchant exporters because they were of high value for their weight.[118] Like the sheep raised in many northern areas for their wool, flaxseed and hemp could be grown as one of a commercial farmer's annual crops alongside the grain and orchards that were vital to his family's existence. They could be planted on less desirable soil, harvested later than ripened food and grains, and processed into marketable manufactures during the winter months. Moreover, hemp had become essential in making linen, bags, plow traces, halters, and rope. Indeed, if it is true that settled farmsteads could produce more grain than external markets demanded until the 1760s, commodities like hemp may have been an important export substitute for ambitious farmers.[119]

Lesser merchants welcomed the relief that hemp exportation brought when West Indian sugar became expensive to reexport, and joined in the hemp enthusiasm early. As they actively encouraged commercial farmers to produce hemp, they reiterated the arguments of Cadwallader Colden and George Clarke in the 1720s that more exports would provide more credit for imports, and there was hardly a more "useful commoditie" because hemp undercut England's need for Scandinavian supplies and kept colonists focused upon agricultural production.[120] To these ends, colonial policy makers assured the Board of Trade that Hudson Valley inhabitants would start production in earnest if they had bounties—cash incentives to extract, produce, or transport specific items—of 6d. per pound of hemp delivered for export.[121] Although middling merchants stood to benefit more from these arrangements than the great transatlantic wholesalers, a few of the latter contemplated how they might employ laborers at iron works and establish wineries in New York and New Jersey with government bounties paid to small producers.[122]

Although it only cost about £3 to £7 to start manufacturing potash, and it could be marketed cheaply, being a lightweight commodity, few colonists undertook this enterprise before 1700. Colonists produced potash and pearl ash—useful in making soap and candles, and in washing raw woolens—in their homes for generations before colonial bounties promoted their export. So universally did colonists use potash in regular household activities that it could be offered frequently as a barter commodity at country stores. After 1757, bounties encouraged its production for export to the glass-making, soap-making, and tanning industries of England, from which there was an astounding result: before the bounties, New Yorkers exported a meager 10 to 40 pounds of ashes a year, but by 1765 they sent England 89,927 pounds, and in 1771, they sent just over two million pounds. New business relations developed too: during the 1740s to 1760s, a few middling merchants' sons went off to Connecticut or Rhode Island to manufacture potash for export from their fathers' docks in New York. Israel Abraham and Nathan Nathans went to Newport in about 1741 for this purpose; Moses Lopez went to Rhode Island in 1752; and Samuel de Lucena went to Norwalk in 1765. Hugh Wallace, a wholesaler rising quickly in New York, advertised that he wished to "purchase a Small Quantity of [potash,] about 100 wt. at any price and send it [to] Ireland, where I could have a certain ac[coun]t of its goodness and the value of it." By 1764, Peter Remsen, Francis Ruppert, and Peter Hasenclever also had joined the ranks of potash exporters.[123]

Textiles, made in myriad homes throughout the region, were the most ubiquitous and elusive of New York's manufactures. Parliament's 1699 prohibition of colonial woolen exports coincided more with the rise of cloth manufacturing in England than with noticeable colonial production. Moreover, the law at first affected New Yorkers minimally, because it did not prohibit local or intercolonial exchanges, or country sales to coastal towns. Daniel Denton, who was skeptical about the rise of new "industries" in New York, thus also thought that textiles production was a special case, since "every one [was] making their own Linnen, and a great part of their woolen cloth for their ordinary wearing." The real constraint on producing even more, including textiles made for export, was the unarticulated marketing structures of the interior; "had they more Tradesmen amongst them, they would in a little time live without the help of any other Countrey for the Cloathing." Rural producers had no desire to remain self-sufficient, argued Denton, but wished to extend markets from the countryside to as far away as demand arose; chapmen, peddlers, and itinerant weavers helped them meet these goals to a modest degree before 1700.[124]

Beginning in 1702, formal reports of governors and private communications of merchants pointed to the potential for greater textiles production in the province, although commentators held two different views about its desirability. Governors tended to fear its subversive effect on imperial relations. Noting that colonists already made "very good serges" for themselves, Governor Cornbury surmised that they would in time also make "coarse cloth, and then fine" to substitute for imports. A few years later, he warned the imperial authorities that colonial home manufacture

sets men's witts to work, and has put them on a trade which I am sure will hurt England, in a little time, viz., the woollen manufacture on Long Island and Connecticut. These colonies, which are but twigs to the main tree, ought to be kept entirely dependent upon and subservient to England, and that can never be if they are suffered to go on in the notions they have, that, as they are Englishmen, so they may set up the same manufactures here as people may do in England.[125]

Caleb Heathcote, one of the dry-goods importers who voiced opposition to colonial textile manufacturing, observed that whereas hemp and flaxseed bounties promoted exportable surpluses that would enhance the colony's purchasing power abroad, textile production would interfere with wholesale importing from London. Heathcote remarked—with some exaggeration—that "3/4 of the linen and Woollen they use [in New York], is made amongst 'em." Long Islanders were beginning to export their own textiles to coastal ports in the region, cloth as fine as any from England.[126] Governor Hunter was one of many observers who grew dismayed at how many "country folk" wore cloth of their own manufacture, but he blamed importers' 100 percent markups. Later, in 1737, a merchant's comments in the *London Daily Post* scorned the quantity and quality of "woollen . . . which they . . . are now creeping into," and its adverse effects on London sales to New Yorkers, but had to concur that it was very popular among colonists. In response to these reports finding the unmistakable signs of colonial market ambition, the Board of Trade condemned the "pernicious practice" of making "advanced manufactures" and "fine stuffs" that competed with England's goods and renewed prohibitions on cloth manufacture for external sale, adding new ones on colonial sailcloth.[127]

Defenders of country textiles manufactures included ambitious middling merchants whose ledgers show increasing competition to buy and sell them, as well as more leisured strategists of empire-building. Archibald Kennedy, the imperialist who had advocated compromise to reconcile quarrels in the fur and grain trades, lamented the narrow-mindedness of English policies on manufacturing. The Wool Act compelled colonists to buy too much of their cloth from England, he wrote. The Molasses Act barred them from a source of cash that they needed to pay for imported textiles. The Hat Act deprived them of an industry that had never competed with England's milliners and tailors. Such acts, which colonists had "no hand in . . . contriving or making," were mere "Solecism in Trade, and the Bane of Industry."[128]

For their part, colonists had failed to formulate viable "industrial" policies of their own. There were limits, Kennedy said, to world demand for New York's agricultural produce. New Yorkers needed to exploit new resources, people the colony, and "usefully employ" colonists in the "arts and manufactures." Logging, shipbuilding, potash manufacture, and pitch and tar extraction would benefit from provincial and parliamentary bounties, but investment of risk capital by individuals was also needed. Combined "Liberty and Encouragement" would cement all parts of the empire, for "it is infallibly true, that . . . Industry and Labour of the Plantations . . . never fails to increase the Wealth and Power of Great-Britain."[129]

A few inhabitants advanced the notion that regulations against colonial manufactures did not create neatly interlocking pieces of one prosperous empire; rather, they stymied New York's natural propensity to expand the sphere of its commerce, dissuaded immigrants from settling in the colony, and retarded investments in the colony's economy. Such regulations were not simply unwise; they were impossible to enforce, for the "universal tendency" among New York's hinterlands producers was to find their way into new markets with new commodities, especially textiles. Even more, manufacturing restrictions would affect New York's patterns of spending and consumption. Throwing over the older belief in fixed wealth, these observers proposed that if the colony did not advance economically, it must regress, for movement in some direction was certain. Nothing less than liberating colonists from restraints on manufacturing would ensure the continued prosperity of the empire in the face of the designs of foreign powers.[130]

As arguments unfolded, production of "rough stuffs" rose in the countryside, even as cotton, cambrics, oznabrigs (a coarse linen that took its name from Osnabrück in Germany), "common cloths" and "fine stuffs" continued to arrive from abroad. Colonists exchanged small quantities of their own "natural manufactures," sometimes to villages at significant distances from their farms, sometimes to merchants who resold them in New York City to obtain remittances to England for finished goods that colonists could not produce. Contemporaries often noted how omnipresent home manufacturing of cloth and clothing provided barter or commodity money in local exchanges. New York City ledgers give us glimpses into the rising quantity of cloth and clothing brought from the countryside over the entire century. For example, New York City merchants imported over £1,200 worth of linen from East Jersey in 1754 alone, and in 1756, Albany retailers imported about 200 "woolen Boston jackets" through port city traders. Although peddlers and auctioneers periodically undersold importers with "rough stuffs" from rural producers, urban demand for English textiles grew, too.[131] In 1767, Governor Moore explained that even with rising imports, farm families were able to produce "a sufficient quantity [of cloth] . . . for the use of the Family" and New York City consumers. Moreover, there was ample work for itinerant weavers and "every house swarms with children, who are set to work as soon as they are able to Spin and Card."[132]

Relatively cheap river transport of commodities to New York City, steadily declining export freight rates, and falling prices in the West Indies all made processing the interior's timber lucrative and easy "to go upon." Indeed, planed and finished lumber products became the province's most important export commodity after grain and flour; naval stores, although enumerated in detail at an early date, were in much demand in England and the West Indies. More efficient sawmills motivated farmers and millers to fell trees and cut them to the specifications desired by English naval contractors in New York City or sell them to colonists constructing new residences and wharves. Farmers-turned-sawmill owners enhanced their incomes by producing resin, pitch, and tar for export. Governor Clinton's report to the Board of Trade in 1749 noted that colonists favored shipping lampblack out of the country; and they had been producing and distributing linseed oil around the province for thirty-four years. Both of these commodities were easy to produce as by-products of rural and frontier living; whereas most planed timber and barrel staves went to the West Indies, lampblack and linseed oil were shipped to transatlantic markets.[133]

In order to compete with Philadelphia in sales of staves, shingles, barrels, planed timber, masts, and other wood products, New York's rising exporters turned early and frequently to their provincial authorities for mercantilelike regulations, including bounties granted for timber products regularly in New York after 1705. Seen as an encouragement to productive activities that complemented the home country's manufacturing and did not promote large concentrations of industrial capital and wage labor, bounties suited policy makers' goals of keeping the colony economically subordinate and also securing necessary supplies of wood products. For their part, colonial lesser merchants hired laborers to cut trees or construct sawmills, transport the timber down the Hudson, or make pitch and tar for export.[134]

An array of internal economic interests consistently thwarted attempts to control the prices of lumber goods, but quality controls, especially those imposed under Governor Andros, established a long-term habit of regulating the size and quality of staves, shingles, boards, and other lumber exports. Usually, city exporters, country mill owners, and farmers all applauded these laws, for they ensured the competitiveness of New York's products abroad. However, when a law in 1719 not only extended these provisions to uphold the quality of lumber exports and the reputation of the colony abroad but went on to tax the importation of staves, barrels, and casks from neighboring colonies at a higher rate, the provincial "lumber interest" divided. Agrarian producers and millers seeking additional forms of income from selling small quantities of cleared timber praised the responsiveness of their Assembly to provincial interests, while lesser merchants who relied on a wider region of buyers and sellers in order to fill the holds of their vessels decried the government's discrimination against sister colonies.[135]

In years to come, Assembly laws "to restore the credit of our Lumber and enable us to share that Branch of Trade with Pennsylvania and other provinces . . . at the West Indian markets" kept most interests satisfied, while acts to prevent "Stave-Getters from New Jersey and other Parts . . . to work our good Timbers" divided small producers from merchants to the end of the 1760s.[136] Lumber exporters continued to blame rural interests for their difficulties in securing supplies of staves and barrels that could be sold competitively in West Indian markets. Some merchants believed that individual farmers marketed cords of firewood, homemade casks, and other wooden containers directly to city residents, from whom they got higher prices than wholesalers would give. Others believed that sawmill operators and their country agents cornered local supplies and withheld various lumber products and boards until exporters were willing to pay exorbitant prices. Caleb Heathcote, who had been encouraged by the Board of Trade to promote extraction and export of "the Masts and Timber in the Woods, that are fit for the use of her Majesty's Royal Navy," argued that he could get valuable wood products cheaper outside of New York. But the cost of cutting and transporting timber from the hinterlands proved exorbitant, and so Heathcote, like others, contracted to carry Honduras dyewoods from the Caribbean to England or Amsterdam.[137] Transatlantic wholesalers joined lesser merchants' protests against "country prices" when the rising costs of timber affected the building of ships they hoped to sell abroad.[138]

Other efforts to regulate production or promote greater exportation from the countryside drew out middling merchants' skepticism about provincial policies. For example, leading colonists made plans early in the eighteenth century to attract settlers into New York's hinterlands and "put them upon country productions" of "industrial crops." Governor Hunter, one of the colony's most avid developers, was determined to tap the interior for exportable tar, pitch, turpentine, and pine masts, and in 1709, he led a venture to secure English financial backing to transport thousands of Palatines, refugees from religious oppression and wartime hardships in the Rhineland, into the colony to produce those commodities. Although mercantilists frowned upon the emigration of skilled labor from their mother country, they approved of this scheme to produce naval stores, a most valued "simple manufacture," and to settle the unpeopled countryside as well. Hunter enlisted skilled superintendents and well-connected merchant exporters, including Robert R. Livingston, to train each Palatine immigrant to extract timber in return for a 40-acre land grant free of quit-rents for seven years. As productivity increased, promoters believed the Germans would pay off their debts to their English backers, help stock the empire's war chest with naval stores, and build New York's commerce by helping to fill the holds of exporters' ships with commodities for which there were considerable drawbacks on customs duties at London.[139]

Parliament granted £10,000 that same year for minimum necessary supplies and housing costs for the Palatine laborers. But unreliable supply arrangements, and troubled land and labor relations between Livingston and the immigrants, quashed hopes of extracting great quantities of naval stores. By mid 1712, many Palatines had hired out as farm laborers; when London and New York City merchants refused to rescue the project, other refugees scattered into New Jersey and Pennsylvania. Complaints spread quickly that instead of producing good-quality tar and pitch for export, the Palatines had fallen "upon Woollen and other Manufactories to the prejudice of the manufactures of [the] Kingdom." In truth, the project overreached itself; short of capital, and failing to coerce the Palatines to work for them, its organizers abandoned the plan, and middling city exporters gloated that their "natural conneccions" to the countryside produced modest, but sure, exports.[140]

In another case, lesser merchants welcomed Hunter's and the Assembly's aid in regulating the "whaling interest" of Long Island by legislating that all marketable supplies be loaded at, and cleared from, New York City. In 1708, outlying traders on the island retorted that these merchants' hindrances, "if continued, will undoubtedly prove the Ruin of the Colony," but by 1714, the provincial authorities reaffirmed that all fish, whales, and whale by-products had to be entered at New York City. The Long Island whaler Samuel Mulford insisted, in arguments reminiscent of Hudson Valley flour millers and inland timber producers, that such discrimination violated the spirit of the economic freedom due to all Englishmen. Regulation of external commerce was right and good, said Mulford, but justice required that the "undoubted right and property by the law of God and Nature, settled upon the subject by Act of Parliament," could not "be taken from them by the supreme power without due course of the law." The Assembly swiftly and thoroughly subordinated Mulford's argument for the property rights of individuals to New York City exporters' collective commercial interest and passed regulations that enhanced New York City's domination over the region. Governor Hunter ridiculed the whalers' case in his 1714 drama *Androboros*, in which a central character named

"Mulligrub" is chastised for presuming to promote the "free traders" involved in Long Island whaling at the expense of New York City exporters, who are presumed to serve far broader regional interests.[141]

Conflicts continued among farmers, middlemen, and exporting merchants, who adapted creatively to new manufactures. But one imperial measure united their voices because it suited none of them: the Iron Act of 1750. Andrew Burnaby noted that New Yorkers were "exceedingly dissatisfied" with this act; although it permitted colonists to export their larger quantities of pig and bar iron, it also prohibited them from manufacturing nails, tools, and pots. They had been extracting iron ore from their "inexhaustible quantity in the Highlands" and shipping it for manufacture into pig and bar iron in New Amsterdam as early as the 1630s, and by 1730, a smelting furnace at Center and Reade Streets produced a regular supply of "reputable pigs."[142] These were permissible activities even after 1750. But by midcentury, small "company towns" around wooded areas with plentiful supplies of water power, where barracks and forges were constructed for itinerant laborers also engaged in "country mining and manufacture." Robert Livingston's Ancram works, the Sterling works in New Jersey, and the Ringwood forges supplied the city with ready exports to London of rough iron, which was in demand by the metal trades of England. Word was out, too, that colonial production had reached "high levels" and that manufacturing had begun. Ancram, for example, produced 3,318 tons of iron from 1750 to 1756, and operations at other works grew sophisticated enough to manufacture finished kettles, nails, and farm implements.[143]

With such success, it was tempting to defy parliamentary legislation. Despite the Iron Act, William Alexander continued manufacturing iron goods at his Hibernia works and consigned them to New York City for sale; investors in New Jersey's Vesuvius Furnace sold cooking and farm appliances through their warehouses on the city wharfs. The New York City merchant Myer Myers, in partnership with Michael Gratz of Philadelphia, owned and operated a lead mine outside of New York City during the 1760s. By 1768, Nicholas Gouverneur, three Abeel brothers, Peter Keteltas, Jacobus van Zandt, Edward Laight, Garret Rapalje, William Hauxhurst, and Peter Hasenclever held shares or sole ownership of new mines and forges around the city, and added a variety of locally produced iron goods to their West Indies and coastal cargoes. Peter Curtenius, Gilbert Forbes, Richard Sharpe, and Thomas Randall formed a partnership in 1767 to construct a furnace to cast iron. Peter Hasenclever started his operations with European capital, and by 1768 owned twelve forges and four blast furnaces around the city. When he went bankrupt in 1773, Curtenius lost little time competing for Hasenclever's clientele and the generally rising colonial demand.

Along with Richard Sharpe, he also proposed a project to bring fresh water into New York City and began to manufacture cylinders for a city aqueduct. Although the approaching Revolution thwarted efforts to complete the project, Governor Tryon's report to the Board of Trade in 1774 recognized it as one of many efforts to defy the Iron Act.[144] Before 1760, the highest value of bar-iron exports for New York was £284. Then, with the discovery of new iron deposits and the willingness of some colonists to invest profits from the Seven Years' War in smelting and forging, production rose. By 1775, the colonies together were exporting £50,000 sterling value in bar iron, and New York's share of the trade was over £15,000; reports also indicate that New Yorkers marketed pails and nails throughout the region by that time.[145]

Although copper mining developed without particular incentives or prohibitions in the early years of the century, English policy makers decried colonial efforts to extract and ship the ore. In 1714, Governor Hunter noted that New Yorkers were mining copper ore destined for Bristol. Francis Harrison, a surveyor and customs searcher at New York City, concurred, saying that unless copper ore, "very rich and in great plenty in a newly discovered mine of one Mr. Schuyler in New Jersey," were regulated, it would be "carried into the channel of our Trade to Holland." In 1721, Harrison wrote that merchants were indeed "loading casks of Copper Oare for Holland," and this time the Lords of Trade responded by enumerating the commodity. Yet despite legislation against the Dutch connection, observers in the early 1730s saw persistent "clandestine running of [copper] oares" to Amsterdam.[146]

Rural manufacturing rarely introduced new kinds of processing or new technologies, although some writers began to imagine their usefulness. In the port city, however, the greater availability of labor, and its integration with commercial services, encouraged some enterprises of distinctive character. Silver- and goldsmithing, glassmaking, and candy making were centered almost entirely in the city. Rope walks, which occupied a lot of public space, and slaughterhouses and tanneries, which produced "noysome smells," relocated north of Wall Street in order to relieve some neighborhood congestion. Although smaller craft shops were exempted from the Common Council's orders for banishment to the periphery of the city, tanneries, shipyards, ropewalks, earthenware ovens, slaughterhouses, and at least five distilleries were located on its outskirts by 1760. In fact, distilling was an important investment for a few of New York's formerly middling merchants, who prospered over many years of bringing sugar and molasses to the colony. Isaac de Foreest and Jacob Wolfertsen van Couwenhoven had distilled rum for local consumption, the Indian trade, and reexport to the northern fisheries during the Dutch period, and by the 1670s,

Nicholas Bayard, Oloff van Cortlandt, and Jacob Kip imported molasses for their distilleries. In 1730, Nathaniel Hazard owned a ninety-gallon still in the city, and before the close of the decade, six merchant firms produced rum and a little brandy. By 1768, at least seventeen importers distilled in the city, all of them eager to purchase greater quantities of sugar and molasses from West Indies traders.[147]

Brewing beer, on the other hand, was a ubiquitous household undertaking and could be expanded to export production with readily available local commodities. Females throughout the countryside were probably taught at an early age how to brew for household consumption, but New York's demand for publicly sold beer grew steadily as well. The earliest brewing houses were owned by the distillers De Foreest and Van Couwenhoven. Soon, merchant familes such as the Beekmans and Gansevoorts also brewed beer for public sale. But by the 1730s, families that ran taverns or inns owned most breweries, as in the case of Nicholas Matteysen and John Hold. Moreover, since beer was cheaper than distilled spirits, and increasingly identified with the tastes of the "lesser orders," its production dispersed over time into the various neighborhoods, where brewer-tavernkeepers also dealt directly with rural producers for hops, barley, and containers.[148]

New York City manufactures were not only more diverse than any given village's operations; a few of them surpassed even the largest country mills in scale of operations and level of capital investment. Sugar refining was second only to distilling among wealthy merchants' preferences for capital investment; although discouraged at various times during the eighteenth century because of its potential to compete with English production, refining was never disallowed by law, and even when enumeration forbade export of refined sugar from New York, its manufacturers found ready demand within the colony and along the coastline. Robert Hooper built the first sugar refinery in 1720. Hooper, a West Indies merchant who obtained a city monopoly to refine for local consumption, lost this privilege in 1727 when he failed to abide by the terms of the monopoly. Thereafter, other merchants took up the enterprise without monopoly grants. Among them was Nicholas Bayard, who built the city's most successful "sugar manufactory" in 1729 near City Hall and the main market house, and Henry Cuyler and Peter Livingston, who expanded their West Indies trade enough to start refineries on Crown (now Liberty) Street in the 1730s. In 1763, Cuyler sold his lot and buildings to the Rhinelanders; by that time, Nicholas Roosevelt was operating a refinery on Queen Street and John van Cortlandt was refining at the northwest corner of Trinity churchyard; the partners William Alexander and Peter van Brugh Livingston operated sugar refineries nearby. On the eve of the

Revolution, James Baker began manufacturing chocolate, a luxury commodity for which demand would grow rapidly. His mill was a relatively sophisticated combination of water wheel, a two-story building, millstones, kettles, and wage labor, and Baker established many liaisons among West Indies merchants who brought imports of the necessary sugar and cocoa beans.[149]

Snuff, produced easily from a common agricultural commodity, tobacco, also attracted merchant investors by the 1720s. Mordecai Gomez and his son Luis produced snuff for a while that decade, and William Bayard processed payments in tobacco from Virginia merchants in a New York City mill attached to his sugar refinery. In the 1740s, he announced that snuff was "most sought among the ladies now." The smugglers Peter Lorillard and John van Cortlandt expanded into the manufacture of this increasingly popular item in about 1760, when it became difficult for them to market South Carolina's tobacco elsewhere. From 1763 to 1765, Van Cortlandt was in partnership with Frederick Lentz and Nicholas Bayard, who together ran a "small snuff manufactory." Van Cortlandt apparently provided capital and imported some Virginia tobacco, Bayard rented space and also imported tobacco for the partnership, while Lentz supplied the operation with labor (both black and white), iron goods, rum for rations, firewood, and various tools.[150]

The candle maker Solomon Simpson depended upon many Connecticut and Long Island tallow suppliers over the 1750s and 1760s. At first, small producers around the city made candles in typical "out work" circumstances. By the mid 1760s, his company of "Sampson and Solomon Simpson" was widely known, and much of the household production of candles for New York City was located in a more centralized establishment. But even in 1761, it had become clear to the Simpsons and other candle manufacturers that in order to protect the infant industry from rising prices for raw materials and labor, business combinations would be wise. In 1761, eight New York candle makers formed two different partnerships in efforts to obtain raw materials from rural inhabitants and coordinate distribution of candles to consumers. By 1773, these merchant-manufacturers had combined into the United Company of Spermaceti Candlers. Solomon Simpson, Isaac Stoutenburg, William Jarvis, and their partners united with Connecticut and Massachusetts candle manufacturers against whalers and shopkeepers in attempts to set prices and dominate the collection and processing of tallow.[151]

New York City exporters and inhabitants of the interior engaged in continuing conflicts over prices, quality, and conditions of exchange, as well as methods of exchange and transport. But then, too, long years of negotiation had also prepared exporters and small producers to creatively transform their economy in mutually advantageous ways. Both constituencies shared support for the three most significant internal changes in New York's hinterlands during the century: intensive efforts to convert newly occupied tracts of land, not merely into family sufficiency, but into exportable surpluses; experiments to extend their means to buy and sell with paper currency and innovative forms of credit; and willingness to extend home and village manufacturing into more complicated arrangements to refine, process, and market goods that would be sold at some distance from them.

A great number of inhabitants in the niches of New York's countryside aggressively engaged in long-distance market relations, watched prices closely, produced ahead of demand, and experimented in new agricultural manufactures. Crops of flaxseed and hemp, linseed-oil mills, and gristmill operations adjacent to general stores all betokened efforts of rural producers to improve their condition beyond family or local sufficiency. Along with the harvesting and partial processing of agricultural surpluses, large quantities of which would find their way to New York City for consumption or export, these internal efforts also collectively abetted the efforts of merchants to extend commerce. Indeed, many enterprising lesser merchant-exporters pinned their hopes and expectations for commerce on internal developments, as they sank their capital into the labor, transport, and fees associated with New York's maturing countryside. Of course, grain and flour were preferred exports, largely because farmers and exporters alike could count on them to be in demand. Home manufacture of textiles was also a familiar activity and required no new technology or labor arrangements in order to produce small amounts for needy immigrants or the West Indies.

Few of these colonists feared disrupting the imperial status quo. By 1750, many of them believed that it was in accord with the "laws of nature and nations" to "push the manufacture of iron beyond the making of a horseshoe or hob nail." Indeed, some reasoned, if manufacturing was a natural and inevitable stage in the development of nations—a belief that had become popular among English historians and theorists—perhaps New York must turn modestly to manufactures or stagnate. The exigencies of the Seven Years' War heightened these perceptions among colonists of their own productive capacity, even as many fellows warned against entering the province's historical manufacturing stage too quickly. A few vocal city merchants contemplated a future of "free manufactures" in New York, in which they would have the opportunity to take up new enterprises without meddlesome regulations, in the same way that some of them had advocated open regional trade and innovative currency schemes. Perhaps, they argued, prohibitions on colonial production served home interests more than colonial ones. Ironically, many of these same city wholesalers continued to advocate quality and price controls contrary to the interests of rural inhabitants and to regulatory measures that promoted certain manufactures. In truth, the clusters of ideas known for so long as economic regulation and economic freedom continued to influence the practical choices that colonial merchants made, separately and together, and never unambiguously.[152]

Chapter Eight

The Vagaries of War and Depression, 1754–1770

B Y   T H E   S T A R T of the French and Indian War in 1754, all the routes of trade, innovations of business organization, patterns of regional economic relations, and policy alignments that would shape New York merchants' responses to the imperial crisis were in place. The British government's need to mobilize economic energies in the intercontinental struggle gave North American traders unprecedented new opportunities to advance their interests. By then, they had learned a great deal about wartime opportunities or setbacks; the scope and intensity of the conflict would create unparalleled scope for privateering, military contracting, government loans, and smuggling.

Some, however, experienced setbacks, especially lesser merchants who could not afford the rising costs of exports and commercial insurance, the near halt to Canadian trade, and wartime embargoes that interfered with exporting and the West Indies trade. Middling traders seldom benefited from government or military favors to the degree that well-placed merchants did, and they were adversely affected by altered economic circumstances. Many of their earlier concerns about regulation of exports, securing external markets, and developing the hinterlands resurfaced when British troops were sent from the mainland to the Caribbean region in 1760, and new concerns emerged when prolonged debate began in England about colonial credit, currency, revenue duties, smuggling, and manufacturing. For all merchants, the intercontinental discussion after 1763 about the future of the empire took on special poignancy when set against the dramatic postwar fluctuations in international commerce. And in the context of political choices being made everywhere in the colonies during the imperial crisis, the distinctions between lesser and great merchants proved consequential once again.

The Benefits of War

Already, King George's War (1739–48) had worked a remarkable change of attitude among New York merchants. Above all, it had taught many young traders that imperial conflicts did not necessarily lead to universal dislocation and hardship. Indeed, city merchants felt quite unexpected relief with the outbreak of war. Governor George Clarke, among others, noted that military spending put many shipbuilders back to work after a long lull; ship registrations in the city had totaled only 53 before the war, but they had climbed to 157 by 1749. Imports from England rose precipitously over the same years, and more than sixty privateers returned with vessels and goods worth thousands of pounds sterling each. Merchants traded vessel shares at the city coffeehouses and docks at a rapid clip, while war contractors like John Watts, Peter Livingston, and James Alexander became wealthy beneficiaries of the privateering and troop-supply businesses. A few exporters took New York's and the region's flour—some 80,000 barrels a year by 1740—to West Indian ports when embargoes did not prohibit it; flour that brought the New York miller 18 shillings a barrel sold in Jamaica for 25 to 30 shillings per barrel at the end of the 1740s, and in Barbados for 32 to 34 shillings a barrel.[1]

Although a few city merchants had made fortunes by 1748, peace revived well-rehearsed commercial difficulties. Minor traders grew disappointed when gluts of foodstuffs and lumber in the West Indies drove down prices; their meager returns of specie and bills of exchange were much less than what the dry-goods merchants needed to offset English debts, with the consequence of steeply rising markups on necessary imports. By mid 1752, "every branch of trade was stagnated," there was a "leadness of times and . . . scarcity of money" once again. Although the causes were multiple, city merchants were divided as to who to blame. The prosperous dry-goods traders of the 1740s turned against smugglers, decrying their competition, while less-advantaged exporters, who were hamstrung by falling demand in the West Indies, claimed that their woes could be rectified by more careful rural regulation and open trade in grain to northern and southern Europe.[2]

There was a degree of truth in both charges. Continued attempts to cut off illicit trade with the Cape Breton "interlopers" who were the "most notoriously guilty of supplying the French with Provisions" in Canada failed utterly, and proposals to turn the "free trade to the northern places" into a regulated trade that awarded formal privileges to a select few merchants who could be trusted to abide by legislated regulations fell on deaf ears. Meanwhile, others resumed smuggling with more lucrative markets. Gabriel Ludlow, Robert Livingston,

James Jauncey, John Watts, William Bayard, Henry Cuyler, David Provoost, Evart Byvanck, Gerard Beekman, and John Tiebout kept accounts with Spanish logwood dealers in the Caribbean and often transported the commodity to Amsterdam without paying duties. The Cuylers joined their capital with that of Edmund and Josiah Quincy of Boston in order to smuggle mixed cargoes to the Hopes of Amsterdam. Christopher Bancker carried on a similar business from Perth Amboy and Newport with Daniel Crommelin of Amsterdam.[3]

Philip and Cornelius Cuyler, Gabriel and John Ludlow, Elias Desbrosses, William and John Waddell, and Richard Ray all sold grain to French and Dutch agents in St. Eustatius and Curaçao and smuggled molasses and sugar into New York, where it supplied distillers.[4] Indeed, New York dry-goods merchants' frequent comments to English firms about the extent of West Indies smuggling were predictable and believable. In truth, without the foreign Caribbean trade, it is doubtful whether New York would have enjoyed even the modest development that it did, since England's demand for its exports was limited even in the best of times.[5]

Furthermore, the postwar optimism of farmers and West Indies grain and lumber exporters vanished when the Stephen De Lancey faction in the Assembly, whose majority identified with London connections in dry-goods importation, rejected new issues of paper money in 1752. When they assented two years later to an emission of £40,000, they insisted that the money circulate in the colony without legal-tender provisions, ensuring that it would not affect the prices of foreign bills of exchange or the value of debts due, ultimately, to London firms. About then, they also approved higher export duties, a direct infringement on the internal and regional trade of lesser merchants. Unable to secure exportable provisions because of wartime shortages, or to sell commodities in the West Indies at even very low prices, because of gluts there, some middling traders moved to Connecticut or New Jersey to become country millers or storekeepers. Of course, dry-goods importers eventually suffered, too, when they failed to get bills of exchange in sufficient quantities to pay London manufacturers and merchants, and when city consumers began to curtail purchases at poorly stocked stores.[6]

In this context, Gerard Beekman reflected on the extension of the French and Indian War into the Seven Years' War (1756–63) with the comment, "War is declared in England—Universal Joy among the merchants."[7] Joy may not have been universal, but until 1759, troop supplying, privateering, and smuggling increased to levels never before experienced in New York. The greatest benefits accrued more often than not to merchants who could lend money to the government and survive occasional losses as they scrambled for timely windfall profits from imports—which increased by a factor of four between 1756 and 1759—to support troops. The twelve merchants active on the provincial Council—three-fourths of its membership—were also poised to create policies favoring commercial interests.[8] And some city merchants found it rewarding to become insurance brokers when the costs of transatlantic commerce rose steeply after 1754. Some temporary partnerships of two to five merchants withdrew from trade altogether and sold marine insurance rather than face such steep rates themselves.[9]

Supplying troops for the provincial government attracted a few of the colony's best-placed men of commerce. In principle, fixed scales of payments for delivery of particular provisions, or construction of particular bridges, wagons, or barracks might yield significant profits if merchants could keep down the prices they paid for colonists' supplies and services. Well-positioned traders who could pay country producers with cash reported some successes. But the high prices set by city bakers for flour and bread, and years of struggle with country producers and farmers, did not prepare exporters for the "exhorbitant" (sic) prices of grain, flour, and lumber products that they had to acquire by traditional means from the region.[10] Nor could wealthy Oliver De Lancey and John Watts secure provisions at desirable prices under their more formal contracts from 1750 to 1753, and again from 1760 to 1764; they regularly complained about the high cost of English blankets and clothing since the start of the war and "excessive" charges for provincial flour, pork, and beef.[11]

Subcontracting with English firms to supply troops proved no less frustrating, as when Watts extended his provisioning operations to affiliate with Colebrooke & Nesbitt in England, from whom he contracted to earn between 5 and 6½ percent commission. Watts could not obtain payments, however. After 1756, William Alexander and Peter van Brugh Livingston took over as agents for the distant firms, with similar results after the first few months. Another group of provisioners—the merchants William Kelly, Hugh Wallace, George Folliott, Wadell Cunningham, and Judah Hays—serviced northern New York in 1755 and 1756 under the same trying conditions, while William Bayard and Cornelius Cuyler reported that local farmers and merchants plagued them with pretended shortages, sabotage, incompetence, and spoilage, which only disappointed their collection of commissions further.[12] Only the syndicate built up around Jacob Franks of London, who served as a crown agent in the last half of the war, provided smoothly flowing goods and currency through local secondary suppliers such as Judah and Moses Hays, Elias Desbrosses, Gerard Beekman, and Peter de Peyster.[13]

Lending money to the provincial government at relatively high interest proved to be a better risk than provisioning troops, but it required "substantial ready money." De Lancey and Watts, as well as Frederick Lentz and David Clarkson, had enough in August 1755 to bargain for 5 and 6 percent interest, which the Assembly paid promptly. William Axtell, Beverly Robinson, Nicholas Bayard, John Wetherhead, and other city merchants also invested in city real estate and government projects down to 1760, and John Bogert, Henry Cruger, and Peter de Peyster held large amounts of city bonds by the close of the war.[14]

Privateering—the capture of enemy vessels and goods by privately owned ships commissioned to do so by colonial governors—often became legalized piracy, but was attractive to wholesalers of all stations. In previous wars, it had become received wisdom that Spanish and French vessels anchored in large numbers near Guadaloupe, Curaçao, Rio de la Hache, and St. Kitts; in addition to their becoming British prizes, the crews of those vessels became captive customers for New York's grain and livestock, paying prices even the most prosperous wholesale merchants had not imagined. Since 1708, an imperial law had allowed the governor to take a share of the booty from sales of prize ships and goods, while the sailors and captains of the expeditions earned regular commissions. Not all colonists were sanguine about privateering's benefits, for "money so easily got was as lightly spent," but over time the 1708 law regularized the condemnation of seized vessels and provided the province with coveted specie. Although eminent traders such as Frederick Philipse, Nicholas Bayard, David Provoost, Abraham Keteltas, Leonard Lewis, Johannes Tiebout, Adrian Claver, and Martin d'Frels took the lion's share of foreign vessels in Queen Anne's War (1702–13), many lesser merchants pooled their resources to privateer as well. As many as thirty of the latter prospered as privateers during King George's War; Samuel Bayard, Abeel Kiersted, Abraham Brasher, and George Cunningham each brought in more than one Spanish ship a year during the war and earned the approbation of Governor Clinton in 1744 for providing the public with a valuable service while in the pursuit of profit. Lesser merchants did not succeed to the extent that the owners of great ships did—as when the *Dolphin* netted about £51,000 from twenty prizes from 1744 to 1747—but a few of them earned from £400 to £8,000 in foreign goods and specie before King George's War ended.[15]

At the opening of the Seven Years' War, then, New Yorkers quickly took up such "an Opp'y of Laying our Cash to Advantage." A few prominent dry-goods importers and logwood reexporters whose connections to London were seriously disrupted in the early months of warfare became the first to apply for letters of marque against the French. They were joined by a few lesser merchants who purchased shares in smaller vessels, many of them rum importers who found that they could combine military demand for their rum imports with the search for French ships in the West Indies.[16]

By the second year of warfare, nearly three hundred city merchants owned shares of vessels and traded goods outside the colony, and almost half of them engaged in privateering. In June 1757, twenty-three privateering vessels crowded the docks at New York, and in the fall of 1758, customs officials counted even more. Lieutenant Governor Cadwallader Colden reputedly made a fortune from his commissions of one-third of the value of each prize condemned in the admiralty court, but only a few wealthy investors out of some eighty-six identifiable eminent men privateering in 1756 can be identified as having derived much profit from it. Of the sixty-four lesser merchants who can be identified among city privateers early in the war, most invested only occasionally when they obtained high prices from sales of rural commodities. Lewis Gomez and Charles McEvers, for example, made noteworthy gains from successful forays into the Caribbean for French prizes, but those who went into privateering in the later stages of the war achieved little profit.[17]

As it happened, smuggling was more regular than privateering. Rhode Island's governor, Stephen Hopkins, never tired of noting how dependent New York exporters were on his colony's grain and provisions markets, and how vital the New York merchant carriers were for Rhode Island's prosperity. But this trade had limits, and "after all the English inhabitants, as well of the continent as of the islands, are fully supplied, with as much as they can consume with the year, there remains a surplusage of at least one hundred thousand barrels [of flour]," and great amounts of beef, pork, fish, and lumber. These, Hopkins noted in 1758, could only be fully disposed of "to the Spaniards, French, and Dutch in America," enabling merchants in England's North American colonies "to make their remittances to the mother country for the British manufactures consumed in them." The delicate balance of production and consumption in New York, New England, and the West Indies would be entirely disrupted if home officials suppressed the illicit trade with foreigners.[18]

Governors George Clinton, Charles Hardy, and Stephen De Lancey, along with the provincial Council, failed, in fact, to halt smuggling through Sandy Hook and at Connecticut, Rhode Island, and New Jersey ports during the war. Much of this trade grew out of long-standing connections of city traders with neutral St. Eustatius and Amsterdam, but it spilled over to French Montserrat, Nouvelle-Orléans, and Cap François (the Mole), as well as Spanish Monte Cristi. John Ludlow, for example, sent French coffee and French indigo to English firms in 1757, and a number of city traders sent goods cleared for Jamaica and Antigua to St. Eustatius, where they traded with French agents or got false papers to proceed to the islands of St. Kitts and Nevis. Alternatively, they sailed to Spanish Monte Cristi or Hispaniola. Too many traders, wrote New York officials, indulged in the machinations of this trade to calculate who was responsible; too many colonists proffered ruses rather than help in stopping the trade; and too many customs officials in London collaborated with the New York merchants in giving false cockets for half a cargo, which could be altered to suit collectors and tide waiters in other ports after the vessel had left Britain.[19] In an effort to stem the greatest flows of smuggled goods—French commodities carried in Dutch vessels or loaded at Dutch ports for the mainland—the British Parliament passed the Rule of 1756, designating any neutral Dutch carriers involved in trade with French ports as enemy vessels. However, the law equally affected the importation of gunpowder from St. Eustatius, a lifeline of support for the English troops, who were supplied by at least four New York merchants.[20]

The Rule of 1756 did not go unremarked in New York; indeed, some city traders felt certain that it represented yet another curtailment of their long-standing "free access" at neutral ports and a serious impairment of necessary wartime commerce. Still, they learned quickly of imperial intentions to enforce the Rule. Alexander Colden noted that port officials had seized the merchant Nathaniel Marston's goods, and others grew "vastly uneasy as they find bribing will not do." Colden predicted that most of New York's traders to the Low Countries would be cautious in the future, and, he told Dutch liaisons, "I believe few goods will be ordered from your place this season." Philip Cuyler wrote that the "officers here have lately made great Seizures of Illegal goods Imported from Holland and are determined to put a stop to the counterband trade." Between 1755 and 1758, Cuyler left many shipments at Stamford, Providence, and Norwalk until enforcement abated; his correspondent John Lloyd sent small parcels slowly overland to New York City. As his father, Cornelius, warned him, merchants "must Consider the advice with [their] friends," for "sending them Direct to New York is not without Danger unless the Captain is acquainted with those affairs." Crown officials found some of the family's tea and gunpowder that had been "shipped that way" and forwarded it to city auctioneers for public sale. When Cuyler bid for his own goods, he was careful to "bribe the Custom House officers that they should not bid, for which Reason they went so low." Cornelius declined the Amsterdam trade thereafter, although his son continued smuggling on his own account.[21]

Governor Hardy had to admit that the Rule of 1756 hardly stemmed the rise in smuggling of Dutch tea, canvas, and gunpowder through Rhode Island and New Jersey, where customs officials were notoriously corrupt and associated in the smuggling business; Jonathan Freebody Jr., for example, paid rather large sums to them for the privilege of avoiding payments into royal coffers. "If some effectual means are not used, the greatest part of the commerce of the American colonies will be withdrawn from the Mother Country and carried to Holland," Hardy wrote the Board of Trade in mid 1757. When he ordered seizure of vessels that unloaded Dutch goods at Sandy Hook under cover of nightfall, merchants simply took future shipments to Connecticut first and transferred them through Long Island Sound inlets. James Beekman, William Leroy, Robert Rutgers, and Leonard Lispenard picked up Dutch tea at St. Eustatius or Curaçao and entered it through the Sound.[22]

Other outbound captains rounded St. Eustatius to drop off embargoed grain for French buyers and to pick up cocoa and sugar intended for Amsterdam without paying duties.[23] Waddell Cunningham bought up prize goods and shipped them to Amsterdam during the war, relying on the Londoners William Snell, Richard Champion, Joseph Mico, and Samuel Storke to transfer funds or underwrite insurance for the voyages. Some of these trips complied with mercantile obligations, but Cunningham also brought undeclared cargoes of dry goods through New England ports for New Yorkers.[24] John Ludlow often ordered his agents in the West Indies to purchase logwood and load it onto a Dutch vessel bound directly for Amsterdam; alternatively, he instructed the captain to obtain a return cargo of linen and tea for shipment into New York by illicit means. Merchants who reportedly sent some 1,000 to 2,000 tons of logwood to Holland each year in the 1750s showed no balance of payments in goods or money sent to New York, or bills of exchange remitted to London creditors on Ludlow's orders, so that Ludlow, Leonard Lispenard, Peter Keteltas, David van Horn, Philip Cuyler, and Henry Bogert almost certainly unloaded return cargoes from Amsterdam at New England coastal towns, where they avoided paying duties.[25]

Although smuggling with Holland was persistent, contemporary assessments of that clandestine trade exaggerated the number of merchants, ships, and cargoes of goods involved. In 1752, Governor Clinton clung to the earlier perception that Holland received "more benefit from the Trade of the Northern Colonies, than Great Britain does." Other colonists referred to any commerce that competed with their interests as a generic "hollander trade" or "dutchified interests." Still, although there is no conclusive evidence that *more* tea or Dutch textiles made their way into New York over the years, colonists readily and willingly obtained them at cheaper prices than their English equivalents. Moreover, whether availability of these goods created demand or demand motivated the continued liaisons with Holland does not affect another generalization: that *awareness* of the trade's tenacity, its competition with the English dry-goods trade, and the economic advantages Dutch trade brought drove late colonial governors to distraction by the opening of the imperial crisis, while a few prominent city merchants argued for recognition of the "Dutch free trade."[26]

As the interimperial war progressed, conflicts also arose between English authorities and colonists. Planters in the British West Indies noted how ineffectual the Rule of 1756 was and pressed London legislators for a monopoly on transporting sugar. Meanwhile, manufacturers in England became alarmed at the number of new distilleries in British North America—at least eight were added at New York City alone during the war. Lord Loudoun wrote in 1757 that self-interest had surpassed itself by then; blatant evasion of the Acts of Trade made many merchants "extremely successful . . . all make Fortunes." Clearly, all city traders did not make fortunes; but large numbers of them grew indignant over crown recommendations to supplement the Rule of 1756 with provincial embargoes on all provisions exports, whether to enemy or neutral ports. In July 1756, Governor Hardy ordered an embargo on all provisions that were not intended for British forces, a measure to which the Council and Assembly assented, while a "great outcry" arose from city exporters, who had quite different orders to fill. As before, imperial trade proved permeable. "It is thought an Embargo will be laid tomorrow but it's too late[,] for most of the Trading people here and in Philada. have for a Considerable time been a-crowding provisions to 'Statia [St. Eustatius] from whence it goes Imediately (some in the same Bottom's that carry it from hence) among our Enemies," William Kelley wrote from New York City to William Johnson. Hardy gained small consolation from an act passed the same year stipulating that all shipmasters clearing the port of New York not only specify their port of destination—a customary regulation—but also post bond on their cargoes. For vessels of 100 tons or less, merchants posted £1,1000, and for vessels over 100 tons, they posted £2,000, enormous sums for average city traders. A year later, in July 1757, Parliament's secretary, Thomas Pownall, enjoined New Yorkers to halt all exportation of provisions except for those commissioned by English and Irish firms. A "Flour Act" passed that year restricted exporters' choice of markets even further, and the colonial Assembly extended the provisions embargo to all outward-bound vessels in August, a hardship not lifted until May 1758.[27]

The provincial elections in 1759 seated more representatives of the "Livingston," or "country," faction than previously, and when Cadwallader Colden gained the governorship in 1760, merchants feared the loss of many commercial privileges, a fear borne out when Colden wooed Thomas Pownall, a prominent mercantilist bent on suppressing colonial smuggling and paper currency. Moreover, just as the Assembly lifted its provincial embargo in 1758, Parliament imposed a full-scale embargo of its own on the export of provisions to enemy islands. The act forced New Yorkers to shift their routes but not to change their aims. After that date, Philip Livingston and others began to buy molasses from the British West Indies with specie acquired from troops stationed in British North America. The New Yorkers then sold the molasses to French merchants and used the proceeds to buy provisions from neutral ports such as Curaçao and St. Eustatius. Or New York vessels took advantage of Monte Cristi's status as a free port after 1761 to seek Dutch and French goods or falsified clearances and safer points of entry than the French islands afforded. Until 1759, Monte Cristi had "exist[ed] no where but in the airy Regions of Imagination," but in the last months of the war, the firm of Greg & Cunningham was one of at least forty-six partnerships that brought sugar from that Spanish port to New York.[28]

War's Limitations

The Seven Years' War produced uneven material success in New York City, and not all of its merchants shared the "universal Joy" that John Watts noted. Lesser merchants tended to rise more modestly and fall harder during the war than their eminent peers. High prices charged by regional farmers, millers, and river transporters defeated attempts by many provisions exporters to profit during the war years; and when city bakers, shopkeepers, and small retailers failed to obtain "freedom of the market" in New York City, they raised their prices to compensate for higher costs of living.[29]

Embargoes proved especially onerous to middling traders, who had difficulty diverting their commerce to New Yorkers, the moving armies, or southern European markets.[30] By 1758, their voices joined those of consumers and small producers who linked acute currency shortages to commercial difficulties and called for more emissions of paper money. Already, farmers had raised grain and flour prices, mostly because of embargoes, shortages, and rising import costs, but also because of glimpses they had of English silver being infused into the economy. But by 1758, the upward spiral of prices brought a halt to many colonists' ability to do business at all, and so they turned once again to the remedy of paper money.[31]

Outside the province, prices for New York wheat and flour declined—some said "alarmingly"—in the French West Indies, and by 1757, sugar was costly once again, while privateering stimulated a rise in insurance rates. Despite William Smith's belief that "British and American merchants had grown opulent by [French sugar] commerce in spite of all the calamities of the war," only merchants who were well established at the onset of war invested regularly in privateering and endured lower prices for sugar, because the sheer quantity they carried enabled them to make some profit. The multiple difficulties of exporting expensive flour and wheat, selling the same goods at declining prices at the islands, and importing sugar or tea that did not sell quickly in New York drove many lesser merchants out of trade altogether, however. By fall 1758, New York City wharves held so much French molasses and sugar that their prices declined "enormously." By 1760, the flow of specie and bills of exchange reversed, so that many lesser merchants could not pay their growing debts to correspondents in the West Indies. New York recovered its favorable balance of trade with the sugar islands only in 1764, and by then a different kind of trouble was brewing between them. Not surprisingly, then, although a significant number of middling merchant privateers, captains, and rising regional traders became reputable wholesalers during the war, many a lesser merchant who had been at the beginning or midpoint of his career in 1750 was no longer commercially active in 1760.[32]

Even the great sugar importers were sorely tested by postwar difficulties. The correspondents in Jamaica who had helped Gerard Beekman falsify clearance records so that he could trade with enemy islands in the Caribbean without detection in New York preferred to keep trade in the islands after in 1760 when British reinforcements reached their area. "I say dam [sic] them all!" Beekman exclaimed when he learned how his long-term liaisons at Jamaica had forcibly unloaded his ships to acquire provisions for the arriving troops. Other New York sugar and molasses merchants struggled to reexport those commodities to London, where demand for nonessential goods fell quickly. Failing in that trade, they tried to sell cargoes in New York, but distillers and refiners were already feeling the pinch of the decaying export business and did not have the means to sustain their usual network of relations. Compared to Gerard Beekman, Philip Cuyler, and Evert Wendell, who could find English and neutral markets for wheat over the war years, most of their peers had poor success in getting orders to ship grain, flour, and sugar once they had lost their valuable connections. For a while after 1760, the only New Yorker who was able to keep a sugar house open full time was John van Cortlandt, who had the advantage of possessing his own ships, managed to corner portions of West Indies markets, and refined a popular finely granulated sugar. Other traders waited for the return of better conditions.[33]

Dutch and English prices for logwood, fustic, and other dyewoods from Spanish possessions declined dramatically, too, so that all but the best-placed city merchants retreated from that trade. Although John Ludlow was able to sustain his own investments in logwood, he noted that "most merchants here don't care to trust to the chance of it." Those who could afford to take the risk in this illicit business often set fine examples of financial success; but logwood trading was not a lucrative venture for lesser merchants during the war.[34]

Postwar Optimism and Recession

Divisions within the trading community reflected the greater ambiguities of prosperity and the setbacks experienced in the city as a whole. By the end of the war, the population of New York City had grown to nearly 18,000, and over 300 merchants clustered their commercial establishments along the East River, on Queen and Dock streets, and along a few of the crowded smaller side avenues nearby.[35] Within the neighborhood, the wealthiest importers preferred both Hanover Square and the area around the Fort and the governor's mansion. "The Force of Money" ensured that the elite community enjoyed most of the benefits of economic regulations and public works over the decades; homes in Dock Ward displayed imported fineries, and new mansions rose alongside the warehouses or were set off at a distance from them, while more coaches filled the streets. At Burns' City Arms, a local tavern that was a meeting place for the trading elite, merchants spoke of investments in British bonds, stocks, and annuities. One observer, reflecting on the signs of opulence gracing the city, predicted that New York might soon supplant London, as Byzantium had once done Rome.[36]

Travelers to postwar New York City adduced the city's prosperity and gentility from the examples of eminent wholesalers. James De Lancey, John Watts, Nicholas Bayard, and John Cruger, for example, were all valued at £50,000 to £100,000 by 1760—fortunes to rival those of many London wholesalers.[37] James Beekman made profits during the war that astounded his fellow colonists, and both Henry White and Hugh Wallace had risen from middling stature to prominence by 1763.[38] "Never," wrote William Smith, "was the trade of this Province in so flourishing a condition, as at the latter end of the late French war."[39] A few of the great city merchants reopened former lines of foreign trade: Leonard Lispenard, Thomas Buchanan, Samuel and Walter Franklin, John and Henry Cruger, and John Watts sent vessels to Guyana (British Guiana) for logwood and fustic after 1763, and Thomas White and Walter and Samuel Franklin sent to the Isle of Man, "that citidel of smugglers," for wine and soap.[40]

A few eminent wholesalers continued to rise after the war through their illicit connections, including Peter R. Livingston, Abraham de Peyster, Theophylact Bache, and Lawrence Kortright, who were reportedly "too generally concerned in this illegal trade" with enemy ports. During 1762, Thomas Lynch sent out large amounts of flour, beef, fish, and butter "to the [French] enemy" in spite of renewed provincial embargoes, while John Watts sent "an odd kind of mungrell Commerce" to Spanish and French buyers, who sold their sugar and molasses at "give-away prices." Watts, like others, was not above complaining about the risks of this trade, especially when French and Spanish men-of-war seized British North American vessels in their waters: "the Evil is suffered to go on with determination. The Subject is torn to pieces by Robbers, Lawyers and all sorts of Vermin."[41]

Despite such somewhat disingenuous indignation, New York's smugglers developed a well-trodden course after 1760. After taking "large quantities of provisions to New England governments for which the merchants give Bond as the Act [of Trade] directs," giving the illusion of trading within their own region, their ships proceeded to the West Indies. In time, they brought back "French Sugars to New Jersey and the New England Collonies which are from thence imported into this place with proper [i.e., falsified] cocketts of their having been legally imported." A network of city merchants kept one another informed about the "numbers of fictitious clearances for Different Persons . . . also their method and Price for doing it," information that they obtained from their friends and partners in New England and the West Indies. Many clearing vessels took goods to New London, North Carolina, Pennsylvania, and Jamaica that could never be sold there, but probably went on to Hispaniola instead. "So many people I suspect have been interested in this illicit Trade from this place that it is very difficult to find Persons to execute any orders [from crown or provincial authorities] who have not connections with them." Customs officials proved all too willing to help conduct "the sugar traffic" by falsifying documents, even to a ludicrous extent. As the report of one watchdog put it:

Inclosed is a list of Vessels Cleared out of this Port with Provisions which are suspected to be on illicit trade. Among them it is observable that the sending of Onions, Boards, Hoop-poles, Apples and Oyl to New London, the sending of Tar to South Carolina, Beef and Butter and the sending of Provisions, Bricks and hoops to Pennsylvania are all of them like sending Coals to New Castle.

Other merchants took advantage of falling transatlantic insurance rates and a calmer ocean after 1760 to start up the slave trade again; they usually landed in New Jersey, where there were no import duties on human cargoes. The logwood trade with Spanish ports also increased once again, and undutied Dutch tea entered New York each season in the early 1760s.[42]

Lesser merchants were poised, in some cases, to share the benefits of postwar

optimism with their peers, but for different reasons. Living in the neighborhoods of small retailers, shopkeepers, and artisans in the East and North Wards,
they resided close to many of the open-air markets and some of the new "manufactures"—distilleries, breweries, sugar refineries, tanneries, and snuff refineries—that developed north of Wall Street.[43] Many of them quite self-consciously promoted new habits of consumption in the city by the end of the war.
New Yorkers of all ranks had "run too much into habits of luxury . . . War had
allmost turned their Heads," John Watts thought. Farmers often shared in the
general confidence in commercial expansion and were willing to bring grain
and flour to New York exporters. Milling, blacksmithing, peddling, and weav-
ing had also increased in the hinterland as a result of the Seven Years' War, creating new networks of internal trade along rivers and alluring prospects for
importers who would supply many of the initial wants of frontier inhabitants.[44]

Far-sighted city merchants explained that the mutual prosperity of countryside and port city provided capital and labor for new mining, smelting, refining, candy-making, and food-processing enterprises in and around New York
City. Urban small producers' efforts made some imports superfluous after the
war, and the enterprise and natural bounty of their interior assured colonists
that they would be well fed. Indeed, Sir Henry Moore noted, many rural colonists could not help but produce more than their own needs.[45] In time, as country farm yields increased and the rural population stabilized, the city's small
manufacturers would enlarge the domestic net product and strengthen the
empire against foreign commercial competition and political power. Already
David Hume had begun to formulate his thoughts on "refinement," and other
writers began to imagine manufacturing as the companion of agriculture and
commerce.[46]

Shipbuilding, cordage and sailmaking, iron smelting, tanning, rum distilling, and potash, soap, candle, and chocolate manufacturing were enthusiasti-
cally begun by merchants who realized that greater quantities of exportable
country goods complemented rising production in the city. Some new under-
takings compensated for losses in the Caribbean trade, while others were attempts to find useful ways to invest commercial capital. A number of lesser merchants also discovered opportunities in transporting and marketing rurally
manufactured textiles. Although cotton and linen fabric from England, Holland, and Germany, along with silks, lace, and fine haberdashery, imported as
"European goods," accounted for perhaps half of New Yorkers' annual need for
clothing and household textiles, production in the city's economic hinterland
now contributed substantially to satisfying a portion of the other 50 percent.[47]

Despite growing optimism about the domestic economy, city merchants seldom lost their primary attachment to overseas commerce. In 1760, the New York Assembly drew up four resolutions that both summarized merchants' experience of many years and linked their expectation of postwar commercial prosperity to the destiny of the empire. In time, crown officials also would understand the resolutions as a statement of the dissenting commercial arguments colonists had long put forward.

The first of the resolutions embodied importers' plea to sustain the trade with Spanish and Portuguese possessions that supplied the wine that colonists in British North America had consumed in ever-greater quantities since the 1720s. The second, speaking for a broader group of commercial interests, pointed out that English firms had traded actively with neutral Danish and Dutch islands in the West Indies during the war and argued that it was only fitting that American colonists, as "true Englishmen," should be permitted open trade with those places too, and that any charges brought against them for smuggling there violated the principle of commercial equity applicable to all citizens of the empire. The third resolution pointed out what merchants had said informally in their correspondence for years: that trade with French and Spanish merchants for sugar, rum, and molasses served the public weal; consumer demand was growing throughout the empire, and these commodities provided valuable staples to refiners and distillers. The fourth resolution sounded a familiar refrain. As the Assembly put it, the reputation of New York merchants had grown substantially at Montserrat, Monte Cristi, and other foreign ports, with the consequence that they could import more English manufactures. But Parliament had ignored this mutual relationship, and "the Sugar Islands" had "gained a preference" over the northern colonies, although this was "inconsistent with the true interest of their mother country." To suppress the "free trade" to foreign islands would "cramp and impoverish the poorer Northern colonies; when yet this Conduct brings no real Advantage to themselves [in England]," and could call forth "a thorough Alteration in [the colony's] whole domestic Oeconomy."[48]

Crown officials reminded colonists of their subordination to the laws of Parliament in London. Cadwallader Colden, then lieutenant governor of New York, forwarded the Assembly document to Prime Minister William Pitt, who in turn brought it before anxious policy makers and West Indian lobbyists. At about the same time, Pitt sponsored a bill to enforce the 1733 Molasses Act and empower courts in the West Indies to try cases of smuggling, which dashed merchants' hopes that Pitt might secure them "the Liberty for a free Trade."[49] He spoke angrily to Parliament about the "illegal and most pernicious trade . . . by which the enemy is . . . supplied with provisions and other necessaries, whereby they are principally, if not alone, enabled to sustain and protract this long and expensive war."[50] Shortly thereafter, Lord Shelburne added to the arsenal of incriminating evidence against the "too free" New Yorkers a charge that smuggling not only destroyed orderly collection of the king's revenues; it also "expose[d] every fair Trader to . . . Danger of Ruin by his not being able to carry his Commodities to market on an equal footing with those who fraudulently evade the Payment of the just dues and Customs."[51]

Colden had to agree with British authorities like General Jeffrey Amherst that if colonists were to gain any leverage for the West Indies trade, they must put a stop to "so open and Barefaced a contempt and Infringement of the Laws." In August 1761, Amherst secured written evidence that a Mrs. Willett of New York City had smuggled provisions to the French on the Mississippi.[52] Later that month, Colden used information from two captured sailors to disclose that many other merchants in the city used Norwalk, Connecticut, as a port of entry and quickly wrote to that colony's governor to punish port officials who abetted illicit trade.[53] By April 1762, Amherst had collated "Several Papers, relative to the Illicit Trade Carried on from [New York] Port" to French Guiana and Cayenne. A calendar of those papers named Peter Robert Livingston, Theophylact Bache, Philip Livingston, James de Peyster, a Mr. van Solen, a Mr. Rieux, a Mr. Tetard, and the De Peyster, Livingston and Fragier company, and many vessels whose owners had not been ascertained.[54] In May, additional evidence showed that Jacob van Zandt, Jacob Townshend, Thomas Lynch, Thomas Witter, Abraham Lott, Bogardus van Solingen, Wadell Cunningham, and Thomas White shipped goods illegally from Norwalk. These "free trade spirits" regularly offered bribes to authorities who had pledged to suppress the trade, and easily sent goods on to Spanish and French islands. In 1764, three vessels sailed from New York to Newfoundland, then on to Amsterdam, and returned to Rhode Island with untaxed linen, sailcloth, gunpowder, tea, and bricks for New Yorkers.[55]

Once it became general knowledge that Colden intended to prosecute as many of these merchants as possible, based on the written evidence and testimony of detained sailors, at least fifty "fair traders" signed a pledge in 1762 to stop smuggling if he would release the known offenders.[56] Amherst, for one, did not believe them, for they "consider nothing but their private profit." His assessment was not far off the mark. Over the coming years, West Indies traders continued to ignore imperial laws and crown officers, reiterating that "a free Trade with the foreign West-India Islands, is of far more consequence to North America than any other Considerations." Moreover, if the legislation passed after the Seven Years' War to halt the foreign trade had been enforced, the wheels of empire would have screeched to a halt. As the authors of *An Essay on the Trade of the Northern Colonies* and a *New-York Mercury* article put it, the revival of the

French and Dutch trade made it easy in practice to discount the intentions of policy makers.[57]

Optimism about both the domestic economy and West Indies trading was offset by another postwar economic downturn that deepened after 1762. John Watts, an importer of rum and dry goods, noticed the first signs of difficulty even earlier: "The Tipling Soldiery that use to help us out at a dead lift are gone to drink it in a warm Region, the place of its production." And, of course, they took their silver and demand for colonial goods and services with them. Although the London merchants Colebroke, Thomlinson, and Nesbitt retained Oliver De Lancey, John Erving, and David Franks in New York as suppliers even to the end of the 1760s, the removal of British troops to the West Indies brought an abrupt halt to the extensive system of provisioning and transport contracts.[58]

City merchants also found that privateering in the Caribbean had become more costly and riskier.[59] And after a brief flurry of importation to relieve pent-up wartime denial, the city entered a period of steadily rising debt to English firms, due in part to diminished demand for agricultural goods in England until the mid 1760s, and in part to lower returns from the West Indies trade.[60] English manufacturers' prices rose during these years, and so did prices for agricultural goods purchased in the countryside.[61] Merchants who reexported logwood or extracted furs watched their fortunes reverse, too; from an annual average business in logwood of £30,000 in 1753, the trade fell quickly to £2,000 in 1755 and to a mere £115 in 1761; furs had fallen to one-tenth of their prewar export values by 1760.[62]

By June 1761, debts had risen in all quarters of the trading empire to the worst in memory. "Thus the consumers break the shopkeepers, they break the merchants, and the shock must be felt as far as London," one writer observed.[63] "The Times are Very Uncertain," said another. "The weak must go to the Wall," yet a third observer declared. Philip Cuyler was one who did. Failing to complete transactions on his Seven Years' War contracts because of currency shortages, he was bankrupt by late 1760.[64] Even the very successful John van Cortlandt came near bankruptcy when his refineries stood still for the first time, and Charles Thomson wrote to London firms that he and other New York City distillers were "wholly strangulated."[65] Anne Grant commented that some merchants had lost all hope of financial gain after 1760, as "trade languished . . . their British creditors grew clamorous; the primitive inhabitants looked cold upon them; and nothing remained for them but that self-banishment, which . . . was the usual consequence of extravagance and folly."[66]

Some city traders had predicted the downturn, having experienced them frequently over the century; but its severity, as well as its qualitative difference from previous crises, stunned them. Of course, typical complaints arose concerning currency and bills of exchange: "I never knew the want of money so much as at present . . . I am so much in want of Cash I shall not have it in my power to accept your Bills if you should draw."[67] "Cash is so scarce," said David van Horne, "there is no selling anything for it." Newspapers reported that prices of wheat and flour at Barbados and Jamaica had plummeted and "all the Produce of the West Indies [was] extravagantly high," resulting in less trade and less specie for colonial needs. With the prospects of wartime currency being drawn out of circulation, merchants feared higher taxes would be imposed in order to retire paper money. As a consequence, they turned both against one another and against the farmers. Hoarding of available bills of credit added to the shortages, some charged, and since there was "no Corn at Market" because farmers withheld supplies, "scarcity of Cash" resulted when circulation of goods slowed. Even in mid 1765, a reduction of colonial grain prices did not substantially benefit the dry-goods importers, who needed specie and bills of exchange for London creditors; some merchants sought investment in land as a safe haven from "the vicissitudes of commerce," of which many were "heartily tired." "Trade in this part of the world is come to so wretched a pass," wrote a merchant in July, "that you would imagine the plague had been here, the grass growing in most trading streets; and the best traders so far from wanting the assistance of a clerk, rather want employment for themselves."[68]

The explanations New York merchants offered for the post-1760 depression were, however, more sophisticated than those they had given for earlier ones. In addition to the usual complaints about personal deceit or poor judgment, and about the sudden removal of military spending, city merchants hesitantly looked to deeper economic relationships to explain the widespread setbacks of the early 1760s. International banking and credit practices were one reason for the depression, they argued. Dutch firms had borrowed heavily from German bankers during the war, in part so as to offer colonists more credit, but the postwar slump in prices made it nearly impossible for the Dutch firms to pay back the bills of credit that they had given the Germans, which were drawn on the security of commodities shipped to the colonies and had declined in value. Unable to meet deadlines for repaying their German creditors, the De Neufvilles and others sold their securities to English firms at reduced prices in exchange for long-term credit to cover their debts. English securities buyers in turn sent large quantities of gold to Amsterdam, which further drained the British empire's reserves.[69]

British colonists in North America suffered as a result. As John Watts lamented, "the good folks at home [in England] are quite overshooting the mark about trade here [in New York]." Large quantities of goods sent to the colony would not find buyers, he was sure, and "little do they think [about how] the Mother Country will pay for it all at last, and when that happens commerce will be dispassionately considered [as its reputation sinks]."[70] Moreover, English merchants had begun to send auction agents to New York City again, "by which Methods great Quantity's of British Goods" passed into colonists' hands cheaply. And New York City's five or six auction firms, controlled by London factors, ignored Assembly legislation after the war to regulate and tax auction sales.[71]

By 1764, English manufactures piled up on city shelves, and lesser merchants could not sell grain in the West Indies. During the summer, John van Cortlandt and John Rhinelander closed their refineries, and the Waltons, Rays, and Bayards felt the closure of their distilleries to be imminent. Those who had borrowed sums of money from fellow traders or English commercial agents in the city and defaulted on those loans lost goods and real estate at auction sales held to recover debts. "Men of very considerable Interests (having become Surety for large Sums of Money, to be paid to Gentlemen in New York)" caused fellow merchants to suffer "unreasonably" when they called in the loans during the bitter winter months of late 1766. Wealthy traders "who were foresighted enough to procure Executions in Season; so that they might get their Money" forced defaulting debtors to auction as much as £400 or £500 "worth of Estate . . . for just such or such a Sum of Money as the most monied Man there present seems to be possessed of—and that Sum seldom exceeds a Tenth of the real Worth, and the Buyer commonly appears to be the Officer [of customs], or Vendue master . . . or Bum-Bailiff, and made up of the most Trickish of our Species."[72] Although the situation abated for some well-placed importers during 1766, a spiral of rising domestic food costs, and impossible webs of indebtedness to small retailers, exacerbated wholesale merchants' problems for years to come. In the fifteen years after 1760 until the Revolution, dry-goods importers supposedly knew "but six good years."[73]

Two Systems of Interest

The Seven Years' War and its aftermath wrought an intense phase of ambivalence about the proper balance between growth and restraint, self-interest and imperial obligations; the period had promoted much postwar optimism and then tempered it with economic trauma and policy disputes. The war had created great expectations of prosperity and called upon colonists to sacrifice much for its victories, but it left a disrupted economy in its wake, as well as heightened awareness by imperial authorities of the potential for colonial development. On the one hand, all imperial subjects seemed to be "Linked in a Chain of Mutual Dependence" and promising development; on the other hand, interests had been served differently by policies and economic circumstances in the first months after the war. In the atmosphere of Parliament's postwar "Narrow Scrutiny into the mysterys of Trade," which began in 1761, merchants had been "rendered . . . very cautious" and perceived "a melancholy stagnation on all business."[74] Recovery and internal development, said some, would have to await the return of commercial prosperity. When Prime Minister George Grenville's government began to design a "new system of interests" for the empire in 1763, city traders exhibited a heightened sensitivity to policy decisions— especially those that might break the "Chain of Mutual Dependence."[75]

Colonists were uncertain what kind of political economy would emerge in the "new system of interests" after 1763. The tremendous energies being released by England's industrial revolution, rural development, and demographic stability called attention to the home country's domestic economy more than ever. And the divisions between New York's wholesalers over the balance between international commerce and internal development, importation and exportation, and protection of privilege or encouragement of new wealth, arose again in the English discussion that emerged after the war.

Some writers urged imperial authorities not to neglect integrating the colonies into their scenarios. For example, the pamphleteer who styled himself "Impartiality" supported New York's "free foreign trade" and advised against a goal of national self-sufficiency in England, for the country's demand for sugar was rising faster than its possessions in the West Indies could satisfy it; French islands supplied more than twice as much sugar as Jamaica, St. Kitts, or the neutral ports. Moreover, New York had shipped more illegally acquired or captured French sugar to England than any other commodity during the Seven Years' War. "Impartiality" concluded that the foreign sugar trade was necessary, not only to New York merchants, but to English consumers and retailers as well; a less stringent policy toward that trade would serve the greatest number of interests simultaneously.[76]

"Impartiality" seconded the growing opinion that it was better to have no commercial regulations at all than to have unenforceable laws. Illegal commerce, agreed a Boston writer, "opens a door to corruption. This introduces a looseness in morals . . . This entirely destroys the distinction which ought invariably to be preserved in all trading communities between a merchant and a smuggler."[77] The same "looseness of morals" in commerce mocked imperial admiralty jurisdiction; most city traders knew how the provincial courts had dismissed cases in which officials had seized vessels for smuggling, declaring such suits to be outside civil jurisdiction and a matter for the admiralty courts to handle, and the best way to undercut smuggling's continuance lay in opening all imperial ports.[78] Many admitted colonial need for foreign West Indies markets at particular moments; and prescient observers knew that sharp fluctuations in the English capital and credit available for investment in trade with the northern colonies would alienate the affections of important dry-goods merchants. New manufactures in the home country had siphoned off many of those valuable funds, but once greater production of finished goods became evident, colonists would be essential buyers.[79]

Some English writers went so far as to announce the rise of compatible manufactures in the colonies. Already much earlier, a few influential writers had argued that colonial manufacturers might compete for certain markets where English products did not have customers, and thereby rise together with their counterparts in England. Following the reasoning of Dudley North, Charles Davenant, and William Paterson, John Oldmixon had defined the empire in 1708 as one large unit of enterprise whose components provided one another with necessities.[80] Later, Francis Hutchinson explained that "to form grand unwieldy empires, without regard to the obvious maxims of humanity, has been one great source of human misery." Why? Because policy makers in England paid excessive attention to controlling and restraining the activities of colonists, and gave insufficient credit for their natural drive to exchange material articles, by which means all peoples prosper toward higher "civilized states."[81] David Hume proposed in 1758 that all goods, regardless of their definition as necessities or luxuries, could find markets if someone wanted them. Expanded production everywhere in the empire would speed circulation and satisfy demand much better than artificial calculations by governments of what was best for inhabitants of the empire to enjoy. Matthew Decker in the 1750s and Israel Mauduit in the 1760s agreed that free circulation of colonial goods, even to foreign West Indian islands, would maintain the flow of specie into England; and even if some of these goods were not merely agricultural, but processed manufactures, interdependency would prevent colonial disaffection from the empire.[82]

But a tide of contrary sentiment was rising among high-level policy makers and eminent merchants in England, based on fears of insubordination, illegality, and excessive autonomy in the colonies. The end of war, which made the precariousness of English government finance manifest, heightened concerns about illicit trade and independent colonial development. Parliament must restructure the empire, argued some, because the mainland and West Indies colonies were developing along lines that, whether by internal expansion or by free exchange with other nations, challenged the very premise of subordination to England itself.

Some arguments for tightening imperial authority held that although they provided raw materials upon which England depended, British North Americans were no more than a "poor people." As the colonies became markets for finished products and expanding consumption, however, their standard of living would mature alongside the mother country's. Many colonists were anxious, after 1763, to give the impression that this had already happened, but debate at Westminster emphasized the need to sustain colonial subordination. Nevertheless, when the Rockingham ministry took over from Grenville in 1765, it reformulated commercial policy to take into consideration not only the West Indies lobby but a "North American interest" of manufacturers in England who hoped that more open imperial trade would give them the new colonial markets they sought.

Until the 1750s, the West Indies produced more wealth for England than all the northern colonies put together. Moreover, West Indian trade underwrote northern payments to England for colonial imports of finished goods. However, the Seven Years' War brought about a reassessment of circumstances that had previously been taken for granted: the small British Caribbean islands could absorb neither migrating populations nor large quantities of English finished goods, especially textiles. Furthermore, the grain-growing colonies, including New York, had provided an invaluable supply of food during England's years of dearth. As these relationships became clearer, the peace of 1763 took on special meaning for British woolen and clothing-manufacturing interests and the West Indies lobby, which feared competition from the French sugar-growing territories. When the choice arose of whether to return Canada and Florida or the French West Indies to France in settlement of the war, English manufacturers and West Indian planters joined together to support retention of the continental territories and return of the islands. They remained committed to uneven spheres of power in the empire, but emphasized that the northern colonists were consumers of manufactures and not just conveyors of naval stores and re-exporters of Caribbean goods.[83]

As Thomas Pownall, one of England's most important mercantile administrators, wrote, sugar had become a daily social necessity to hundreds of thousands of Europeans and a fundamental economic necessity to the mercantile system. Colonial maturation should not be accomplished at the expense of long-established mercantile tenets, and the persistent reality of cheap sugar in foreign ports should not increase the strain on the balance of trade. But by the

1760s, hard-liners, such as Pownall, also believed that "the several changes of territories, which at the last Peace took place in the Colonies of the European world, have given rise to *A NEW SYSTEM OF INTERESTS; have opened a new channel of business; and brought into operation a new concatenation of powers, both commercial and political.*"[84]

The Sugar Act reached New York in early April 1764 while colonists were discussing their postwar opportunities and setbacks. Although the act lowered duties from 6d. to 3d. per gallon of molasses or hundredweight of muscovado sugar, it carried provisions to enforce collection of the duties—a blow to smugglers—and it raised the duty for exported refined sugar and rum—which would, wrote John van Cortlandt, lead to the "total Destruction of Sugar Refiners." The act would stifle the commercial relations essential to colonial development, as laid out to Parliament by Captain Fayer Hall in 1733 and reiterated time and again in correspondence and the press. Lesser merchants were especially fearful about keeping their footholds in the West Indies trade.[85]

The Sugar Act also struck at the consumption of commodities central to new attitudes about private economic expectations. A writer styling himself "Z" noted in the *New-York Mercury* in January 1764 that colonists had hitherto been able to acquire foreign West Indies goods more cheaply than British ones, "which helped us considerably in our own Consumption, and had a Tendency to check the rising Value of several Articles, esp. Sugar in our own Islands." In return, cash, bills of exchange, and reexports had flowed toward England, so that "we have been enabled from Time to Time to support an incredible and luxurious Importation." Under the provisions of the Sugar Act, everyone would be forced into frugality: "Necessity will oblige [colonists] to turn their Eyes to different Objects, to consider what the Soil and Climate are capable of affording, to set on Foot home Manufactures, which . . . yet may sufficiently answer the Service of Decency and Warmth."[86]

Another writer argued that not only colonial property but the trade of "British Merchants and Manufacturers" would suffer "grievous Detriment." The "Artificers . . . [and] The Manufacturing Towns [of England] . . . The Rents of Lands, Iron Works, and Collieries, [would] fall; and Trade, in general, languish and decline." In New York, immigrants and small producers would not be able to find means of making a living; for example, the lumber and potash sent from the colony—a "natural product" of clearing the land—would be utterly wasted if colonists did not find markets for them in North America. "Can good reason," the writer asked, "be given why we should not change Ashes into Sugar?"[87] Decreasing colonial purchasing power would have serious consequences, railed John Watts: "the Intercourse between the Dutch &ca.: & the Colonys (I mean the dry Goods everywhere) ought to be entirely supress'd, but the rigirous Execution of the Sugar Act is very injurious," for if colonists suffered by it, Englishmen everywhere would fall "like Nine pins."[88]

Parliamentary acts to prevent colonial importation of foreign logwood, Madeira, and coffee threatened not only to cut off much importation for New York consumers but also to deprive reexporters of their cargoes. Moreover, in early 1764, Parliament halved the drawbacks on foreign goods reexported through London to New York and placed higher duties on many foreign goods New Yorkers were growing fond of, such as coffee, wine, raw silk, and citrus fruits. Finally, Parliament enumerated some of the goods colonists had begun to export extensively by 1764, including whale fins, potash, and pearl ash. Some colonists perceived Parliament's efforts to eradicate illegal trade, create commercial order, and raise revenues as efforts to channel and tax consumption so as to hold them in subjection at a low standard of living. A few believed that the intended effect of the Sugar Act and other new legislation was to bind colonists to London dry-goods firms with greater debts.[89]

John van Cortlandt noted that the duty of "5% sterling on all foreign sugars imported," was a measure "of great severity." Under the weight of the lingering recession and the new legislation, "getting the freedom of our commerce" became the "universal Cry" of New York merchants.[90] In a public statement of their intention to organize themselves, a large group of city merchants lamented that "our Debt in Europe increases, [but] our Power to pay it off decreases." In order to ascertain "the Causes, and point out a Remedy for this growing Evil," they assembled "at Mr. Burns' Long-Room where a very considerable Body of them met, and appointed a Committee to prepare a Memorial to the Legislature of this Province, representing the Decline of Trade, and the Distresses of the Merchants and Traders of this City." Eminent dry-goods importers were well represented, but the largest number present were West Indies merchants, some of them known to have smuggled from or traded with foreign ports in recent years. In a message to the Assembly in October 1764, they asked for "relief from the act commonly called the Sugar Act" and for recognition of the "right and necessity of a customs of less consequence to the libertye of our trade."[91]

That same year, the Currency Act announced restrictions on the authority of northern colonies to emit paper currency or mint copper coins. This new act, if enforced, would have made it impossible for colonists to circulate a satisfactory supply of bills of credit with legal-tender provisions. "The forbidding Paper Money to be legal tender would in my opinion take away what little energy it [the money] has," John Watts commented. "To suppose we can keep either silver or gold in the Colonies while our Mother Country will trust us for both necessaries and for luxuries is entirely ideal and destroying intercourse between Mother and her offspring may be very injurious to both." Gerard Beekman despaired that "unless a large sum of money is struck in this and the neighboring governments we shall never get in our debts," and William Lux stated flatly that "we cannot buy either wheat or flour for bills, for the millers want cash to pay the farmers and the farmers having no connection with London will not be concerned with bills."[92] Money of any type, they agreed, was a vehicle for exchange, a measure but not the embodiment of wealth and welfare; "reasonable sorts" of people knew that the balance of payments improved when there was greater consumption and greater production resulted when there was more investment capital. Merchants who dealt regularly with local colonists saw no reason to deny the effect of paper currency, minting coins, or overvaluing specie within their local sphere of trade.[93]

The New York Assembly had actually made important strides toward retiring outstanding wartime emissions of currency. Representatives had redeemed some of the currency with new taxes, as in the past, but when Parliament sent £195,330 in sterling as a reimbursement for colonial contributions to the war effort, the Assembly diverted large sums to merchants who had remained creditors of the government since their days as military suppliers.[94] Then, with news of the Currency Act, the Assembly resolved in November not to renew the Loan Office Act of 1737 in an attempt to cut off funds for crown officers' salaries and to evoke agreement from royal officials that they had already permitted colonists to circulate colonial paper money responsibly for many years.[95]

Not all merchants favored issuance of paper money, but large numbers of them agreed with the Assembly that it was up to the colony, not Parliament, to decide whether to print a local currency. Where they differed with the Assembly was over what kind of currency to circulate. A few well-placed city merchants asserted that regular bills of credit issued against future taxes had been of little good to them in international trade, and that these were the target of parliamentary attack in 1764; the same men tended to grow alarmed, however, at the prospects of curtailing all provincial currency, arguing that the Loan Office had served the colony well. Philip Livingston, for example, urged that the "landed interest" of the Assembly reconsider its animus against the crown and revive the Loan Office, with its notes based on the collateral of land and its significant interest payments into provincial coffers. Colonists, he pleaded, could no longer afford to deny themselves the beneficial effects of the Loan Office simply because they wished to assert the Assembly's power of the purse; deny-ing the self-interest of important commercial interests would court economic disaster.[96]

Others writers, including a few vocal merchants, did not distinguish between the Loan Office and regular provincial bills of credit, but simply noted that cur-rency shortages of any kind could lead to "the stagnation of our Trade." Paper money facilitated the "flow of arts and industry among the various parts of the world" and had become a "custom held as right" by colonists. As John Watts said, "We have no resources upon an Emergency but in Paper Money and if it be duly sunk we dont see the great Mischief of it to the Publick." He scorned those who "here abominate the abuse of paper money, because the conse-quences fall upon himself [the merchant], but there is just the same difference in the use and abuse of it as there is in food itself": too much of either produced "consumptive" people; but too little of either "starved" the body and trade.[97]

Lieutenant Governor Colden told the colonial agent Robert Charles that Parliament's insistence "that Paper Money may not be a legal tender are un-answerable." As city merchants argued, "the Debtor is obliged to make good to [the Creditor] the Value of a pound Sterling, whatever be the Exchange or de-nomination of our paper Currency." As a result, London creditors would be the losers as well. Dry-goods merchants watched their fortunes continue to sink as gluts and tightened English credit persisted into the fall of 1764; they blamed the Currency Act for "an unreasonable restriction on our own property" as well as "the general interests of the empire." When, by spring 1765, New Yorkers' transatlantic correspondents did not order large shipments of flour and flax-seed for the second consecutive season, they assumed a leadership role in pub-lic protests against the imperial legislation.[98]

Already, however, the recession of the early 1760s had evoked a discussion within the merchant community about whether, and how, to extend their op-position beyond formal petitioning procedures and informal evasion of the Acts of Trade. In December 1764 about a dozen city wholesalers—most of them men of middling means—embarked on a creative use of capital that appealed to broad layers of New Yorkers; they formed the Society of Arts, Agriculture, and Oeconomy to begin "useful manufactures" that would attract investment capital from "the discrete sort," employ the poor, and redirect some commerce toward domestic production. Proposing to be above "Party spirit, personal In-terest, political Views or private Motives," the Society attracted numbers of lesser merchants whose West Indies trade lay in distress and whose connections to myriad small producers had been extensive for years. Members vowed to "advance husbandry, promote manufactures and suppress luxury." They procured "several hundred pounds paid in" from twenty-shilling subscriptions and promised to pay premiums for outstanding workmanship on the fourteen looms engaged to produce linsey-woolsey for sale to city artisans, and to donate part of the proceeds of sales to the poor; soon they employed some three hundred residents, among them "Numbers of distressed Women, now in the Poor-House," as spinners. Obadiah Wells, who owned the factory building, also "put out" flax and took in yarn "every Tuesday, Thursday, and Saturday, in the Afternoon." Within a few months, the society's thirty-three members hired "the Itinerant Weavers who travel about the Country" to work up the thread spun in the factory.[99]

By the time the society began operations in the spring of 1765, New Yorkers had received word that yet another act had been passed by Parliament: the Stamp Act. City merchants bristled quickly with the judgment that the act was contrary to good reason and equity, as it raised revenues from the personal businesses of colonists directly. Scholars have explained admirably how this measure affected political thinking, as well as its pervasive impact on colonists. Not only did the act require that duties be paid in silver; it added the burden of stamping all insurance policies, admiralty records concerning privateering and vessel seizures, notarial documents, and clearance bonds, thereby falling heavily on the shoulders of dry-goods importers. The latter registered fears that colonists would "rescind our great demand for English Clothing" because the costs of imports would rise while the means to pay for them would shrink. Coming upon the heels of earlier legislation, the Stamp Act "would not have met with so violent an opposition, had not the Colonists in general, previous to that, been greatly chagrined at the rigorous execution of the laws of trade."[100]

Despite their universal wish for the act's repeal, city merchants divided more than ever about how to achieve it. Cautious petitioners wrote that despite the unreasonableness of the new law, "the Authority of the Parliament of Great Britain, to model the Trade of the whole Empire, so as to subserve the Interest of her own, we are ready to recognize in the most extensive and positive Terms."[101] Others agreed with this view in principle, but did not wish to ignore the Sons of Liberty, which was formed in August 1765 and assumed widespread public approbation for its open protests against the act. A few dry-goods importers accepted James De Lancey's proposal to take the leadership of the Sons of Liberty in order to steer a course toward moderation. De Lancey was known already as leader of a "court faction" that was reluctant to pass measures favorable to commercial farmers and West Indies exporters; he was also connected by marriage, blood, and commerce to a few English families in positions of significant power. He had little in common socially with either the Society of Arts or the rank and file of the Sons of Liberty; but his personal self-interest and the stability of his faction in the Council required that he give nominal support to popular public measures. His leadership in Sons of Liberty actions would, he reasoned, win the deference of a potentially "licentious mob" and keep that same crowd from aligning itself with the rival Livingston faction; he would also represent merchants who wished to make "reasoned objection" to "measures originating at home." John Cruger and John Stevens, merchant De Lanceyites, attended the Stamp Act Congress in October 1765 to argue about the "impracticable" nature of the act, and how it would "render them unable to purchase manufactures of Great Britain." In November, the port collector in charge of the stamp, James McEvers, resigned amid a flurry of merchants' efforts to clear vessels from the port without stamped papers or bonds. Another energetic mercantilist, Archibald Kennedy, "sour[ed] the inhabitants greatly" when he tried to stop the vessels.[102]

During the fall of 1765, both eminent and lesser merchants joined the infectious outrage spreading deeply through the city. Although their economic interests had not brought them into the public arena for the same reasons, lesser exporters and West Indies merchants of all ranks rallied behind transatlantic merchant leaders to promote a plan to reduce importation until Parliament repealed the act. On November 1, 1765, the day the Stamp Act was to go into effect, some two hundred merchants in the city signed a nonimportation agreement that would commence the following January 1. By declaring their intention to halt the flow of English goods into the colony, city merchants of this first nonimportation movement showed temporary unity of purpose. In January 1766, forty-eight Albany merchants joined the agreement.[103]

However, joining the same movement did not mean that they shared goals for the city's economy. Under the banner of temporary self-denial and frugality, which nonimportation required of consumers, lesser merchants were convinced that colonists would turn to expansive domestic production in future years, an example already set by the Society of Arts. By early 1766, their efforts overreached the control of eminent merchants when new manufacturing schemes for woolens, paper, checked linens, iron stocking looms, flax mills, gristmills, a bleaching apparatus for the main "manufactory," muslin, and potash took root and gave confidence to middling merchants, who could now "laugh at [England's] Blunder by shutting up the Port" to imports. Nonimportation and manufactures together would ensure that consumers would have necessities and that retailers would be able to stock their shelves with goods made throughout the interior.[104]

For their part, at least sixteen of New York City's eminent dry-goods importers refused to invest in the new manufactures, on the grounds that the non-importation movement had narrower goals. Most transatlantic wholesalers had agreed to join in what they believed was a "dangerous" provincewide protest and pursue the negative step of curtailing importation in order to reduce both the number of goods "dumped" on them by overzealous English creditors and their swollen inventories of unsold items. The connection they made between imperial taxation measures and nonimportation became abundantly clear in a *New-York Mercury* article in October 1765: "Most of the Gentlemen in Town, have entered into a Resolution not to buy any European Manufactures till their trade is more opened, the *Sugar Act* altered, and the *Stamp Act* is repealed." Still, when they countermanded all recent orders for goods, and refused to vend all goods sent on commission from England, they reassured each other that their actions were temporary and would not damage their commercial reputations with English firms. Even more tellingly, some of the city's scions of the West Indies trade insisted that sugar and rum from the islands be exempt from the nonimportation pledge.[105]

Although dry-goods importers who remanded orders from English firms probably had a more direct effect in bringing about repeal of the Stamp Act than did middling merchants connected to West Indies, internal trade, and manufacturing efforts, the latter's activities strengthened attachments with the "generalitye" of colonial consumers. Nonimportation appealed to the voluntary efforts of great numbers of people to become self-reliant, dress "in the new mode" with homespun and leather, in modest attire that served to symbolize both the extent to which the "new system of interests" might reduce colonists to poverty and the strength of their own determination to overcome the obstacles to their material rise. Certain colonists believed that these obstacles involved, not only pernicious parliamentary legislation, but also general business snags such as specie shortages, rising import prices, unemployment occasioned by periodic depressions, the presence of many foreign agents, the overabundance of unsolicited commodities, and obstacles to expanding manufactures in the colony.[106] The "quickening of the circulation [of goods] amongst us" created an aura of important activity despite new imperial laws. Woolens, all sorts of leather goods, woven hose, snuff, linseed oil, and potash manufactures required relatively little capital outlay and could be expanded or contracted easily according to levels of demand. No voices yet proposed colonial autonomy from imperial control; but many marveled at New Yorkers' newfound internal economic potential.[107]

Another intellectual dimension of nonimportation that appealed to wide layers of colonists involved the curtailment of spending on "unnecessaries" or luxuries. Even as material abundance became visible, an older language of community welfare or a general good was not totally moribund; indeed, it was useful in the 1760s to validate merchants' economic interests to the wider public. Merchants revitalized, if only temporarily, the appeal of generalized self-denial of luxuries and restraint against desiring to consume "a multiplicity of goods in each home" when fewer were adequate, for the sake of defeating the corruption of selfish parliamentary ministers. By presuming the virtue and endless abilities of New York's inhabitants, by blurring the distinction between self-interest and the general good, city traders helped foreclose doubts about whether nonimportation and manufactures would lead to the evils of luxury.[108]

In practice, domestic production plans softened the difficulties of achieving self-denial among New York's ambitious and striving population by promising colonists that, in time, they would not want for cheaper quality goods if they would only apply themselves with industry for the time being. As the Society for Arts continued its operations, merchants joined in praising the "Homespun Market." A number of them created a "Market for Home Manufactures" at the Exchange, and expressed pleasure that "every Thing was immediately bought up, as all Ranks of People take a laudable Pride in wearing what is made among ourselves." Support groups among Albany merchants and New York City merchants' wives and daughters widened appeal for the combination of nonimportation and manufacturing.[109]

Meetings of the Sons of Liberty overlapped with these efforts and led to a somewhat different kind of public action: in February 1766 a number of colonists destroyed the city's stamps and chastised two eminent southern European merchants for attempting to use stamped customs bonds. Predictably, eminent wholesalers pleaded with New Yorkers to avoid divisive violence, and pledged themselves to self-policing against further violations of nonimportation; indeed, with the exception of one cargo sent from Bristol to Theophylact Bache in May 1766, and one sent from London on the *Prince George* in April, nonimportation seemed to be working well.[110] Furthermore, transatlantic wholesalers threw their efforts into garnering support in London. For example, Barlow Trecothick, creditor of many city importers, organized a supportive petition to Parliament with twenty-seven names appended. Self-interest, agreed the petitioners, governed all commerce; "we find America in confusion, our property in danger, our Remittances uncertain, and the Trade in danger of annihilation." They dared to hope that Rockingham's ministers could be persuaded to declare free ports in the West Indies and the northern colonies. In London, "Wet goods" traders to the West Indies, in alliance with representatives of the logwood, rum, and sugar traders of the northern colonies, struggled for repeal, and Edmund Burke spoke out for New York and Philadelphia merchants.[111]

The same dry-goods importers who joined nonimportation with the modest goal of reducing their stocks of goods and achieving repeal of the Stamp Act, while affirming their loyalty to the crown's objectives in colonization, joined citywide celebrations upon hearing word of the act's repeal in the spring of 1766. But their accomplishments seemed minimal by July, when the Rockingham ministry fell, signaling the fall of their own hopes of commercial relief. They wrung their hands during a long wait for imports that did not arrive until November and December. When the flow of imports remained steady, city stores became glutted with goods and everyone experienced a "want of trade and Sufficient Amount of Circulating Currency." Parliament's short-sighted policies and London firms' willingness to extend too much credit, said importers, lay behind the city's "many Failures" during the winter of 1766–67. In anger, 240 petitioners—a representative group of men engaged in all kinds of city trade—again protested to Parliament about the limitations on their trade.[112]

Eventually, when bills went unpaid, goods stopped flowing into the colony, so that supplies then sank "below the level of Necessitye," and James de Peyster, for one, began to "Breake for a Large Sum" in late 1766; although he dunned debtors that entire year in order to secure small sums for personal use, they, too, were unable to circulate goods or money and repay debts. Having hoped to reduce an "overplus" of goods, a few prominent city importers now could not build up inventories. De Peyster "took many of his relatives along with his own fall" in early 1767.[113]

Interest-group tensions in the city also muted wholesalers' pleasure at repeal of the Stamp Act. Although hopes ran high that everyone would be "cemented together as Individuals" "in harmony and peace" following nonimportation, struggles over shaping the provincial economy resurfaced; interest groups kept "a Jealous Eye over Each other," believing that "private Interest and favors prevail . . . Among the Best of them," while less well endowed inhabitants could not measure the gains of their victory as easily. Dry-goods importers who joined in the nonimportation movement gained the tangible benefit of selling off goods that had been stagnating on their wharves, but now saw themselves as victims of transatlantic credit and debt. Lesser West Indies traders had already experienced long years of fluctuating prices for regional provisions, as well as Caribbean goods; they competed, sometimes fiercely, with a rising number of captains and vessels for unpredictable markets, which were now directly affected by the extant Sugar Act. Indeed, their calls for "enlarged freedoms" for commerce in the Caribbean did not abate with the end of nonimportation.[114]

Differences within the merchant community had consequences that reached beyond international trade. Although nonimportation ended for the time being, the Society of Arts continued to have a visible impact on city life. In 1767, Governor Moore assured the Board of Trade that its merchant operators sold pieces of cloth of decidedly inferior quality "for three times their value" and believed that the high cost of labor made it "easy to imagine with what difficulty it is supported, and how short the duration of it is like to be," but he also had to admit that the society inspired other manufacturing experiments. David Clarkson, a dry-goods importer active in the Dutch and English trades, was more positive about its success. He noted that the society provided a "fair, or Market, for all kinds of woolens . . . Many gentlemen are already Cloathed in This Produce." By mid 1766, wrote Clarkson, the society made "People throughout the Colony . . . determined to Incourage Every Manufactory the Country is Capable of," as well as to compete with New Jersey for sales of clothing. Moreover, the high prices of these domestic productions was not a deterrent, but rather an encouragement to more enterprise:

They have had so high a price . . . that it has Encouraged them to Exert themselves, to out do Each other, and to Get all they Possably Can, Before the [Sugar] Act is Repealed. The following manufactory's are already Established[:] an oar Furnace for Casting of Iron potts, kettles, Backs, etc. . . . Severall manufactory's of woman's Silks and Worsted[,] Shoes which have been judged Cheaper and Better . . . Hose, Woollen, Cloaths . . . Scant and Wide which is now Worn by Principall Gentlemen of the City . . . Linen . . . Pipes for Smoking, made very Cheap and Vests of all sizes, Paper, though not fitt to write upon, Paper Hangings, Cuttlery, very Neat, but Dear, Earthen Ware factory, glasses, dishes . . . Iron into Piggs . . . Ankirs . . . of different Weights, heavy Enough for any of our Vessell's, Snuff of Different Sorts, Distilleries for Rum, Brandy, Cordialls, etc., Sugar Baker's in Great Abundances, Weaver's of Stockings, Cap's, Breaches, etc., etc., etc.

Soon, said Clarkson, New Yorkers would have "Everything we want within our Selves." On Long Island, "a company of gentlemen" established a "woolen manufactory" modeled upon the society's work, where they produced knitted stockings and leather work clothes, and hoped to make shoes by 1767. "Americus" invited colonists to develop wool manufactures by giving bounties for prize sheep and quality wool in late 1765.[115]

    In addition, the society, while not a direct instrument of political consciousness in New York, spurred the "sincere expectation" that colonists could live outside the constraints of mercantilism and its associated wisdom about private economic endeavor. Observers in the colony recommended that sugar refiners, distillers, and iron manufacturers set their prices lower than what the market would bear, in order to promote additional budding enterprises, and then raise prices once a consumer market had been secured. This view departed from the wisdom of most eighteenth-century merchants, who preferred to buy low and sell dear, or who competed for the lowest price among agricultural producers but hoped their imported goods would sell high. To suggest that low selling prices and high wages were the most competitive, reversed received notions, and recognized that consumers and manufacturers constituted economic interest groups. But the society's promoters did more than recommend low consumer prices to stimulate new enterprise; they also associated new economic opportunities with freedom from imperial interests and negative restraints, and departed from the notion that commerce alone would increase the wealth of a people.[116]

The "new system" was a powerful recognition of divided economic commitments following the Seven Years' War. As policy makers pointed out in the postwar debates, customs duties from the colonies were not "sufficient to defray a fourth part of the expense necessary for collecting [them]," and English people were shouldering more of the enormous war debt than the colonists. Accordingly, both political authority and economic necessity required that new "Laws . . . confine the European Commerce of the Colonies to the Mother Country" and that colonists cease their "groundless" "Clamour." What made these affirmations of imperial relationships especially poignant to colonists was the simultaneous maturation of New York's economy. War had furthered the opportunities for paper money, privateering, smuggling, and internal expansion, all of which brought challenges to the requirements of colonial subordination. War had also tied the destinies of English manufacturers and colonial consumers together more inextricably: in 1700, as much as 80 percent of England's exports went to European countries, while only 10 percent went to the North American and West Indian colonies; by 1772, 40 percent went to Europe, while 42 percent went to the colonies. An unquestionable rise in England's ability to manufacture commodities for household and farm demand in the colonies underlay some of this shift in export patterns, a rise that was related to aggressive entrepreneurial strategies for industrializing England, as well as to colonists' better ability to afford new, and more, items.[117]

But colonists, too, produced far more than their own subsistence by the late colonial period; population grew faster in the colonies than in England, and England depended on colonists for many supporting commodities. Although New York's balance of trade with England had been unfavorable every year since officials had begun to keep records in 1697, glimpses of a developing interior and the mutual interests of colonists producing and exchanging in ever wider circles provided powerful incentives to ignore the formal relationships of empire, as well as its economic doctrines. And although imperial officials continued to promulgate trade laws over the eighteenth century, they grew no less apprehensive about enforcing them, for decades of profitable opportunities outside those laws, as well as evasion of extant ones, had kept alive the presumed advantages of freer trade.[118]

Some English observers realized the folly of continuing to believe that colonies should be backward outposts of the imperial metropolis. All human beings aspired to expand and acquire, said one writer. "It would be ridiculous to imagine that people bread in all the improvements of Europe should, by crossing the Atlantic, so unaccountably lose all remembrance of former skill and knowledge, as to betake themselves entirely to agriculture, and not once dream of improving those advantages, or applying those materials with which the country abounds, to the common use of human life." It was, he continued, utterly unrealistic to expect "that because there may as yet be no such manufactory as those at Abbeville or Sheffield, that every planter in America raise flocks of sheep only for the table, and flax only to supply Ireland with seed."[119] During the final colonial years, New Yorkers began to see the truth of these views.

Economic Freedom and Political Conviction

In the midst of a credit and currency crisis in 1766 and 1767, New York's Assembly issued forbidden paper money in large sums. In subsequent months, its representatives proposed to revive the Loan Office and emit legal tender bills, which the Currency Act expressly forbade. In early 1768, an anonymous merchant proposed a provincial bank based on colonial tax funds to help ease indebtedness.[120] And, as might be expected, lesser flour and grain exporters were among the prominent supporters of these measures; without a flexible medium of exchange, they could neither buy from farmers nor expand trade with neighboring colonists. As the merchant David Clarkson put it, "Crops in General, have been very Good," but farmers' prices were "Surprising high" over 1766 and 1767. The merchants extracting wheat from the interior suffered losses upon reselling the commodity to transatlantic traders, who in turn earned "large Commissions transporting it to Europe."[121]

Over this period reports of a precipitous rise in smuggling reached officials' desks, too. Rem Rapalje, Luke van Ranst, the Van Zants and Bogerts, Lawrence Kortright, John van Cortlandt, Isaac Roosevelt, Leonard Lispenard, Francis Lewis, Peter Keteltas, David van Horne, George Folliott, Philip Cuyler, and William Walton evaded customs collectors regularly; "neither would it have been prudent [for admiralty officials] to take any Notice of them." Or, as Colden put it to the earl of Shelburne, "no officer at this time, dare make a seizure in the Colonies where all restraints on Trade are unpopular; and where it may be in the power of a single Man, to set the Mob upon him." Informants assured Governor Moore "that a greater quantity of goods has been run without paying duties since the repeal of the stamp act than had been done in ten years before. Whole cargoes from Holland and shiploads of wines has been run, besides what is done in the usual way [by secreting portions of cargoes into the city]." Smuggling reached such proportions in the final colonial years that New Yorkers became "reconciled to it by example, habit, and custom," and "amuse themselves with some very superficial arguments in its favour, such as, that every man has a natural right to exchange his property with whom he pleases, and where he can make the most advantage of it." Furthermore, colonists had come to believe "that there is no injustice in the nature of the thing, being no otherwise unlawful than as the partial restrictions of power have made it."[122]

By 1767, military personnel passing through New York gawked at the variety of goods that entered the city undutied:

The principle Articles Smuggled into North America, are several sorts of Dutch East-India Goods, Particularly Teas in great Quantitys, Spices, Chintzes, &a Dutch Gun-Powder, German Linnens, Hemp, Yarn, &a from Holland, Hamburgh, Curosoa, Monte Christie, St. Eustatia. Likewise, from our own Islands, where it is brought in from the foreign Islands. Formerly Fruits, Pickles and Wines were smuggled from Ports South of Cape Finisterre . . . foreign Logwood, brought here from the Bay.

In a 1767 edition of *The Regulations Lately Made*, the author held that "they are no longer British colonies, but Colonies of the Countries with which they trade." By the final colonial decade, merchants imported great quantities of the city's tea illegally, and as much as a quarter of all provincial coffee, sugar, molasses, wine, tobacco, and other enumerated goods.[123]

While smugglers continued to thrive in their individual endeavors through the 1760s, fair traders to the West Indies and England blamed the new parliamentary legislation, including the Declaratory, Quartering, and Townshend Acts, for specie scarcity and high rates of exchange. Bankruptcies and near failures of partnerships reached a frightening level by early 1768, when dry-goods importers felt the pinch of another glut. Having experimented successfully with nonimportation in the last crisis, merchants renewed calls for a boycott of British imports and luxury commodities like tea. Colonists started up a number of potash manufactories, and some printed promotional tracts for hemp production. Ambitious merchants began two small linen manufactories, one with fourteen looms, but a hat manufactory, and a "glass house" failed that year, as did a hollow-ware furnace and a paper mill.[124]

The second nonimportation movement in New York nevertheless began. On April 14, 1768, merchants circulated a nonimportation agreement that announced their intentions to cease importing in October if Philadelphia and Boston merchants would join them.[125] By August 27, as some importers stockpiled in anticipation of stopping their orders for English goods, other colonists justified nonimportation in much broader terms. As one writer put it, "nearly all the Merchants and Traders in Town" agreed there was a shortage of circulating currency with which to conduct trade and that "the Colony in general is in a State of Poverty and Distress, chiefly arising from the Decline of Commerce, and a vast Consumption of British Manufactures, and foreign Commodities." Successful trade depended on larger issues of currency, more manufactures, and cessation of smuggling.[126]

A remonstrance against the Townshend duties signed by about 250 merchants and retailers denounced the duties on sugar, the new registration and warehousing restrictions, and the damage to regular West Indies trade, which would bring less specie to the colony and "severely clog and restrict" their shipping; together the laws "encreas'd the heavy burthen . . . [they] already laboured" under in the colony. "Free trade," the remonstrants declared, was not merely desirable but necessary; the French West Indies ports must be opened to American trade, free of customs duties. An additional document proposed a long list of items that colonists could eliminate from consumption.[127]

British observers dismissed merchants' confidence as "folly" in the "spirit of infatuation," but as nonimportation began, the volume of imports gradually fell, reducing both the remittances on sales and revenues from customs duties. In 1768, import values from England were still high, totaling about £482,000; in 1769, they fell to £74,000. But necessary emissions of currency, as well as removal of British troops and commissions agents, weighed heavily on merchants' minds by the end of the latter year. Prices had begun to rise dangerously high, too. Bickering rose among merchants about whether goods that had arrived on the eve of the boycott should be stored away in "public warehouses" or sold openly; and public meetings divulged rumors about certain merchants violating the nonimportation agreement by removing commodities from the warehouses. John Wetherhead, for example, believed that some of the Sons of Liberty, especially "Isaac Low, Isaac Sears, and Jo. Allicocke who are our present Tyrants," "had severall Times got their own Goods clandestinely out of the Store and were daily Selling them by little and little." Wetherhead, for his part, hired a man "to break open the Store in the Dead of the Night and take the Goods out he Wanted." But, he added to his correspondent, "perhaps the Next News you have will be that He and I have been carted about the Town" as examples of violating nonimportation.[128]

Along with some New York City importers, Albany's Indian goods suppliers began to lament scarcities by the fall of 1767; Robert Sanders, Jacob Cuyler, and Robert Lansing wrote of their hope that nonimportation would end soon. As tea smugglers, these men also found the language of "freedom of personal property" appealing and useful when they reassessed nonimportation and began to doubt its efficacy. About that time, West Indies and southern European merchants encountered gluts in wheat and flour markets abroad, and frankly expressed the desire to export those goods to England, where poor harvests raised demand for imported foodstuffs. "The Merchants are already tired of their Project and there is a Jealousy of each others Conduct," General Thomas Gage wrote to Lord Hillsborough. Cadwallader Colden, who became governor in September, was sure that extreme currency shortages provided the only incentive to continue nonimportation.[129]

The movement weakened early in 1769 for other reasons as well. De Lanceyites, who were in their majority dry-goods importers, had won inclusion of rum and sugar on the list of boycotted items, and they expected compliance from the smugglers of Dutch and foreign West Indies goods. Instead, nonimportation leaders confronted regular violations of the boycott. An enforcement committee comprised of importers discovered that Peter Clopper had instructed his agents in Philadelphia to receive all manner of West Indies commodities and ship them to New York by any means. When enforcers discovered one of his cargoes of British sugar entering through Sandy Hook by nightfall, they labeled Clopper "an Enemy to his Country, a Pest to Society." Watchdogs also found that Alexander Robertson, a southern European merchant who had been allowed to export grain in late 1768, returned with a clandestine shipment of forbidden goods in June 1769; a public meeting declared that "all Ranks and Degrees amongst us . . . shew their just Abhorrence and Detestation of such scandalous Practices, that they will avoid any Connections and all Intercourse with him, treat him . . . with the Contempt he deserves, regard him in the odious Light of an Enemy to his Country." Robertson found social and economic ostracism too much to endure and apologized for his errors.[130]

An Albany enforcement committee also pointed to fissures among merchants: "The Agreement operated no longer to any other Purpose, than tying the Hands of *Honest* Men, to let *Rogues, Smugglers,* and *Men of no Characters,* plunder their Country." Fair traders, who were in principle opposed to smuggling, blamed the "free trade interest" for the many "Distresses of the Country," distresses "really so grim that I cannot get [payments] either for Goods, Interest of Bonds or House Rent." Yet they were helpless to prevent violations of the agreement. As John Wetherhead put it, "I am convinced the True Meaning of not importing any [tea] from England is only a villanous Scheme to putt Money into the Pocketts of a pack of Smuglers in this City."[131]

While many leading merchants withdrew from nonimportation, expressing the hope that the "Rockingham Squadron of old Whigs will . . . make themselves gracious to the [merca]ntill, and Manufacturing Interest in England [and] to All the Colonies," an increasingly vocal layer of lesser merchants, artisans, and radicals in the Sons of Liberty insisted on another course. They could still agree that it was better to wear "a Cotton Smock" than "a Holland one" and to "see industry flourish" while importing stopped. But prolonged commercial distress, no currency, falling land values, and two successive bad harvests were unbearable, and when artisans and marginalized lesser merchants got wind that large importers contemplated placing orders with England, they attempted to mobilize New Yorkers to continue nonimportation. Public articles condemned the self-interest of "Mercantile Dons" who had abandoned the general will once they won their narrow economic ends. Peter Vandervoort and Isaac Sears, two lesser—but rising—merchants in the city, sent articles to Providence and Boston newspapers asking for the continued support of their neighbors in nonimportation.[132]

In December 1769, Alexander MacDougall issued his famous pamphlet *To the Betrayed Inhabitants of the City and Colony of New York*, and city radicals increased their efforts to force reluctant importers to continue nonimportation. "Informers have been punished in many Places, one was tarred, rolled in Feathers, and in that Condition carted through this Town at Noon Day," General Gage reported. "Some particulars who persisted in their Right to import, have been forced accordingly to Send back their Goods . . . and Some to read a Paper of Excuses to the People . . . or undergo the Discipline of the Populace." Retailers and middling merchants often led these public expressions of outrage, and formulated most movement demands to continue with nonimportation until Parliament repealed all Sugar and Townshend Act duties.[133]

But support for the movement was further undermined when Parliament gave permission in March 1770 to issue £120,000 in bills of credit, which counteracted the restive mood of New York's "lesser sort" and eased credit in the colony. Dry-goods importers felt relieved to pay some of their debts to English firms, and as "Friends of Liberty and Trade," to move colonists closer to the end of nonimportation.[134] As a writer in the *New-York Mercury* put it, "An Agreement not to import Articles, which were free from Duty, and which, it was notorious, the Colonies could not long do without, was as imprudent and absurd, as for a Man to make a Vow not to eat or drink . . . which he was very uncertain of effecting Time enough to prevent starving." Besides, the writer continued, new manufactures were still weak and inadequate to New York's demand; others noted that since merchants acquired most of their tea from Holland, colonists need not be concerned about continuing a perfunctory boycott on the British commodity.[135]

Although radicals of the Sons of Liberty, along with many lesser merchants of the West Indies trade, continued to uphold the agreement, repeal in March 1770 of all the Townshend duties—with the notorious exception of the tea tax—dampened importers' enthusiasm even more. House-to-house canvasses in June and July 1770 gave overwhelming support to "reopen the trade of the city," and importers insisted that the demand for "Liberty and no Importation" was now impossible to uphold: they were "starving on the slender Meals of Patriotism." Some dry-goods importers prepared to outfit vessels for the voyage to London; William Kelly and Abraham Lott notified fellow merchants that they would go into "a direct ready money Trade."[136]

Irreconcilable Divisions

Division among city merchants that made it difficult to sustain the second nonimportation movement portended deeper difficulties for the third. Although they did not yet contemplate separation from English mercantile authority altogether, a number of lesser merchants had grown confident about autonomous commercial and internal development. Only late in the gathering imperial crisis did many of these coastal and lesser West Indies traders, the city's commercial majority, begin to articulate that the consequences of significant colonial changes might include a distinct political economy. Eminent wholesalers, however, remained focused on commerce and its regulation. Since April 1768, before the second nonimportation movement formed, a Chamber of Commerce had been meeting, often with the specific objectives of setting commission rates for merchants' services, agreeing upon allowable rates of exchange among themselves, promoting "fair prices," adjusting trade disputes, and drawing up valuation tables for colonial currencies. But through its early years, members of the chamber could not agree on a few substantial matters. In some respects, they conceptualized their place in the empire differently. For example, President John Cruger affirmed in 1770 that the chamber would henceforth resort to nonimportation when expedient, but otherwise adhere to the general framework of mercantilism, which had proved "extensively useful and permanent, and more adequate to the purposes of so benevolent an Institution." Lesser merchant traders disagreed. When, in debates over three years, Isaac

Low—a rising trader—attempted to sponsor devaluation motions at monthly meetings, he was defeated by eminent merchants like John Cruger, Isaac Roosevelt, Leonard Lispenard, John Hoffman, Gerard Beekman, Isaac Gouverneur, and Richard Duyckinck, who upheld intrinsic value arguments until 1772.[137]

Also in 1772, for reasons which the minutes of the Chamber of Commerce do not divulge, lesser merchants sponsored a measure calling for provincial paper money and setting New Jersey currency above par with New York currency, which would have depreciated the latter as a circulating medium and thereby benefited internal trade. Successful importers protested, however, that this would harm international trade. Threatened by middling traders' outspoken insistence on the direction the chamber should take, eminent leaders expelled some of their lesser colleagues from the organization between June and December; so many lesser members resigned in sympathy that remaining members could not raise quorums. Over the next two years, the chamber refrained from making any overtly political decisions, for fear that the organization would expire.[138]

In a third nonimportation movement, from 1773 to 1774, New York wholesalers were separated from the beginning, precisely as momentous political decisions demanded their attention. The immediate cause of renewed nonimportation was news of the Tea Act in 1773, which by granting the East India Company a monopoly of transportation and sale of tea to the colonies undercut colonial importers. The provisions of the act also inadvertently promoted tea exporting from the home country because English merchants obtained drawbacks of duties they paid upon registering tea at British ports—duties that amounted to about 25 percent of the commodity's value—while inland duties, storage fees, and domestic transportation costs remained unaffected by the act. Together, these advantages made it cheaper to market the commodity in the colonies than to sell it at home.[139]

Commentators in New York could agree that the East India Company practiced a "relentless Barbarity" because it "monopolized the absolute Necessities of Life" in "sordid and cruel Avarice." Some believed the Company would "dump rotten tea" on them and take advantage of a captive market. The city's Dutch tea smugglers stood to lose the primary item of their trade or be undersold by the East India Company should they continue to import it; indeed, some city observers believed that "the East India Company's tea is violently opposed here by a set of men who shamefully live by . . . the smuggling way." When Chief Justice William Smith received a delegation of the act's opponents, he scoffed at how "the Sons of Liberty and the Dutch Smugglers set up the Cry of Liberty."[140]

In fact, the group of merchants that had acted with speed in October 1773 to block the port and turn away cargoes sent earlier that year, and that dumped £9,000 worth of East India Company tea in the river during New York's Tea Party, was much larger than Smith indicated.[141] A substantial number of middling West Indies and regional traders helped reactivate the Sons of Liberty in November 1773, and declared that the conservative "Friends of Lord North"—dry-goods importers and English agents in the city—"ruin our Trade with Impunity."[142] At about that time, many commercial newcomers and rising younger merchants called for reviving the Society for Agriculture, Arts and Oeconomy in order to prevent shortages of necessities and strengthen the self-sufficiency of the colony, as the previous society had taught. Radical mechanics and merchants together sought repeal of all imperial measures passed since 1763, and when news of the Coercive Acts reached the city in early May 1774, they moved to extend and enlarge their movement to include nonconsumption, a form of insurance against backsliding merchants who tried to sell smuggled or stockpiled English tea as foreign tea, and to instill the requisite moral fortitude in everyone.[143]

In fact, they had more to worry about than backsliding. Many dry-goods merchants refused to join the movement. Some had felt the bite of renewed economic hardships in 1769 and after 1771, especially because ever-larger numbers of merchants in New York and other colonial cities competed for the same uncertain markets. Others believed that nonimportation was an ineffective means to keep out prodigious amounts of "British and Asiatick manufactures."[144] Despite new vessel construction—in 1769 nineteen new vessels were registered by New York merchants; in 1770, eighteen; in 1771, thirty-seven—merchants were helpless to thwart the misery of a general crisis in 1772, precipitated by failures of Dutch firms to which some city wholesalers were affiliated, and a serious credit crisis in England. New York City groaned as it had in the 1720s and early 1760s. James Beekman had "lately offered sundry persons my whole Store, which is considerable, and well assorted as any in this City," but did not receive any offers. Robert and John Murray failed in mid 1772, sending shock waves through the city about "an universal wreck of credit throughout Europe," especially because the "airy speculation" of a few individuals drew many other merchants "innocently . . . into the vortex." John van Cortlandt wrote creditors that he would collapse without longer credit; Samuel Franklin, Henry Remsen, Philip Livingston, Jacob van Zandt, David van Horne, Broome & Co., and others all complained of imminent ruin. As in other dire crises, New Yorkers were also prone to bemoan the profits of Philadelphians in the transatlantic grain trade. Ironically, then, merchants who had the most to lose and fell farthest from the peaks of commercial success turned against nonimportation and made every effort to revive their trade.[145]

Those who opposed nonimportation for principled reasons articulated them more loudly than before. Jonathan Boucher's pamphlet *A Letter from a Virginian, To the Members of the Congress*, which colonial printers distributed widely in early 1774, excoriated the smugglers who "grow Rich by the Spoils of the fair Trader" who was linked in commerce and political loyalty to England. John Wetherhead insisted that not Parliament's regulations but the illicit rum trade into New York City was ruining his business. A few tried to ally themselves openly with the East India Company: William Kelley and Abraham Lott agreed to become its agents in October 1773, in defiance of nonimportation proposals, but were stymied by other colonists. Then Lott, Henry White, and James Booth stepped forward to be consignees of tea, but when the *Nancy* arrived full of the commodity in November, the Sons Of Liberty forced its return. John Watts, formerly an advocate of paper money and nonimportation, turned against them and defended the tea importers. New Yorkers, he wrote, drank as much Dutch tea as English tea, so efforts to cut off consumption of the commodity hurt more than trade to the home country. And because nonimportation proposals included rum, sugar, and dyewoods this time around, Watts feared that the movement jeopardized the very foundations of West Indies trade.[146]

Fair traders' disdain for smugglers was misplaced in part, for by late 1774, the latter were abandoning nonimportation. Isaac Low, Philip Livingston, and Jacob Walton withdrew from leadership of the movement and brazenly smuggled tea and other French and Dutch goods until the Revolution. A Captain Chambers imported tea from Holland on the *London* in April 1774 and the previously failed partners Robert and John Murray smuggled tea through Elizabethtown, New Jersey, in the *Beulah* on February 9, despite public censure and other merchants' ostracism. James Jauncey and John Cruger communicated their profound disgust with secret meetings and Sons of Liberty activities, but learned "to save Interest" by holding their silence and conducting their own clandestine trade. In December 1774, movement enforcers seized Walter Franklin's vessel for importing goods from the London firm of Haley & Co. By then, at least ten others in "the smuggling Interest," and "the Sugar Interest," balked at the radical moral suasion and manufacturing program of their middling peers.[147]

Although smugglers as a group had been among the most radical elements of New York's reform efforts before this, by the final colonial years, the elite among them articulated views that ran counter to the goals of nonimportation. When they countered the movement's calls for frugality with open appeals to colonists to continue buying the goods to which they had become accustomed, they lost allies among the coastal and lesser West Indies merchants, who called them "rapacious" importers in violation of the public interest. Some smugglers gravitated toward the group of dry-goods importers led by James De Lancey, whose supporters packed city meetings in mid-May 1774 and became the majority of a Committee of 51 formed to police—and limit—nonimportation. Eleven radicals, all of middling stature in the West Indies trade, resigned from the group on July 8 and joined a new Committee of 25 to press on with nonimportation.[148]

Just then, the first Continental Congress convened delegates from the colonies. For the time being, the De Lanceyites could claim to have acted successfully for the "generality of voices" in New York, for "Firmness without Violence," and for restraint in the cause of nonimportation.[149] But before De Lanceyites could effectively redefine the meaning that radicals had given to nonimportation, a series of events took everyone's breath away. In mid 1774, delegates from New York to Congress committed themselves to initiating a wider nonimportation agreement, having been infected with the enthusiasm rising in other colonies. Support for their plan grew when city residents heard of George III's November 30 speech rejecting conciliation over the Coercive Acts and the authority that lay behind them. In subsequent weeks, colonists threw their approval behind the congressional proposal to reject further compromise with Parliament and to plan for nonimportation, nonexportation, and nonconsumption under an intercontinental Association Agreement. During these heady weeks, a number of lesser merchants flocked to the New York Sons of Liberty and helped regain control of the Committee of 51, remodeling it as the Committee of 60. Almost half of the former membership dropped out of sight, while "Holland free traders" and "our rising merchants" oversaw committees of safety to enforce the Association Agreement. Yet as the great dry-goods importers retreated from the organization that assumed leadership of many revolutionary committees, they also stocked their inventories once again before trade was to stop on December first. "I hear," General Gage wrote to his superiors, "the Merchants are sending for double the Quantity of Goods they usually import," although they assented to pleas from radical voices in the city not to raise prices.[150]

General colonial enthusiasm for the Association Agreement ran high for many months. In February 1775, reports held that "several ships have arrived within this fortnight from England, and two or three from Scotland; all of them are obliged to depart without unloading a single article." More worrisome to the fragile revolutionary movement in 1775, however, was the quickly diminished enthusiasm of "Holland free traders," who had less commitment to affirming colonial rights against parliamentary measures than to their zeal for trade with foreigners. Provisions in the agreement to halt importation of English tea after December 1, 1774, brought their ready assent, but the appeal to colonists to cease drinking tea after March 1, 1775, caused consternation among traders with Dutch connections. Their appeals to the New York Provincial Congress in April to allow sale of Dutch tea at a fixed price, plus a tax of 1s. per pound for the new state's revenue purposes, came to little action.[151]

Subsequent proposals to import military supplies from Dutch sources, couched in terms depicting their "clandestine trade" as patriotic, raised opposition from many quarters. Reverend Samuel Seabury, a future loyalist, scoffed, for example, that New Yorkers did not have "virtue enough to prevent the tea from being bought and sold." And although John Jay admitted to delegates in the Continental Congress that among merchants, "Public Virtue is not so active as private Love of Gain," the delegates could not agree among themselves about whether to place patriotic trust in "the Dutch men" and were distracted by more pressing matters.[152]

But the smugglers did not await their reply. Cadwallader Colden had already written to Lord Dartmouth in late 1774 that "the smugglers expect large quantities of Dutch tea and insist that it shall be exempt from the effects of the Association." From November 1774 to February 1775, the Committee of 60 seized at least twenty-one vessels for violation of the agreement, including again Robert and John Murray's, and held their owners up to pubic ridicule. Other city merchants refused to abide by patriotic measures when some of their peers made conspicuous gains from infractions; some raised prices, some forestalled, some stockpiled and otherwise profited from the virtue of fellow colonists. In August 1775, flaxseed merchants expressed their intention to export to forbidden ports, and merchants routed so much of New York's nails, metal goods, wagons, and provisions to Boston that New York's Provincial Congress imposed an embargo in August. In December 1775, at the second Continental Congress, southern delegates helped defeat a proposal to attach the "smuggler interest" to the Patriot effort.[153]

The negotiation of economic interests was only one part of the imperial crisis, and it was subsumed into discussions about sovereignty, rights, and duly constituted power that pressed for more immediate resolution. But even toward the end of the colonial era, the rubrics of economic freedom and economic regulation were compelling to all kinds of imperial subjects. Edmund Burke, for example, posed as, in part, an advocate of "commercial freedoms." He was paternalistic enough to want an end to all smuggling, so that "commercial servitude" could be restored, and yet republican enough to support universal development even as he disdained the "fantasy, passion, and excess" of the financial revolution's great speculators. In his 1774 speech to the House of Commons on "Conciliation with America," Burke extolled a reciprocal relationship in which the balance of trade continued to favor England and staple commodities flowed from America toward England's industrial production. England, he insisted, might also have to accept modest manufactures from the colonies; expanding production of foodstuffs in the "bread colonies," for example, supplied England's swelling urban centers.[154]

The trouble was, Burke's reasoning originated in the very thinking that mercantilism had sought to displace since the mid seventeenth century. His focus was not on London merchants and manufacturers trading to the colonies; their power derived, he said, from the detestable conditions of war and speculation. Nor, as New York's colonial agent in Parliament from 1770 to 1776, was Burke a particularly helpful advocate of the colony when it requested relief from tight credit and new commercial restrictions. Indeed, he veered closer in his loyalties to the gentry and woolen merchants who faced the challenges of both mercantile policy makers in England and the impulses toward more production in America. For Burke, England's material prosperity had advanced far too quickly, and New York's commerce threatened to pull colonists irretrievably out of an organic order that he believed should be restored throughout the empire. Parliamentary legislation had wronged colonists, but the mutual interests of citizens throughout the empire, reasoned Burke, ought to be based on the social relations of the past and spread to the widest possible geographic scale. Other English writers— Matthew Decker, Thomas Pownall, John Mitchell, Josiah Tucker, and others— tried to conceptualize mutual interests throughout the empire rather than cling to an outmoded mercantile vision of unequal spheres; but they never went so far as a few colonists who glimpsed the compatibility of commerce, agriculture, and manufactures in their province as a distinct political economy.

The colonists who pressed most often, although never consistently, for commercial freedoms that made restoration of an organic community impossible were the rising, ambitious, middling layer of city traders. Many lesser merchants had become convinced of the benefits of linking nonimportation to textile, hemp, potash, pearl ash, and naval stores manufacture; at some point, greater variety and quantities of goods would also become attractive to new markets that might lie outside the sphere of imperial enumeration. They raised hopes for domestic self-sufficiency and colonial self-reliance, based on connecting commerce to internal production, thereby helping to shape widespread public responses to imperial measures in the final colonial years. As they moved conceptually from a model of circulation toward a model of expanding consumption and productivity, they also found ways to distinguish their claims for freedom from the claims of other merchants and their allies in New York and from English mercantile tenets.

We have seen that most middling merchants also sought regulations in the regional economy, and they learned much about the benefits of mercantilism in particular contexts. But a material and conceptual gulf separated them from the city's eminent wholesalers, who were often traders with attachments to English firms and families, and who would not, or could not, sustain enthusiasm for a movement that broadened its demands and deepened its commitment to economic activities that challenged membership in the empire. Ideological consistency and practical considerations required their loyalty to the bloodlines, political places, and London business liaisons that had made their careers possible in the first place. With the exception of their opposition to import duties, they agreed that regulations protected opportunity, that they could reallocate economic privileges periodically under the guiding hand of worthy rulers, and could settle periodic clashes of interests with countervailing pieces of legislation. They affirmed the "balance" of payments and spheres of power, and remained wary about the far-reaching meanings of "freedom."

When faced with supporting nonimportation movements that overrode their goals of depleting gluts of goods and attaining repeal of unwanted legislation, many dry-goods importers began to leave active committee work; although many of them became patriots by oath, many others clung to imperial arrangements. For example, Peter Hasenclever, writing from London in the wake of Parliament's repeal of most Townshend Duties and the reassertion of its sovereignty over the colonies, reiterated the adage that colonists should buy England's manufactures and provide its raw materials; they should, he insisted, wish for policies to "divert th[em from] their Manufactures, by which means a flourish[ing trade] will for Ever Subsist." For, "As the North American Manufactures are a Natural Prohibition of the Importation of English Manufactures, it must Certainly appear a Mistery to the world, that England makes Treatys of Commerce with forring Nations to allow The importation of her Manufactures under the Payement of a Havy duty & that She Neglects her Colonies where She has an exclusive trade without paying Duties." John Campbell put forth the extreme proposition that colonists should "wear not a rag of their own manufacturing; drive not a nail of their own forging; eat not out of a platter or cup of their own making; nay . . . produce not even bread to eat."[155]

Campbell only stated what he, and other hard-liners, wished to be so. Economic and political reality militated against so glib a portrait of imperial relations, for there was a spectrum of political views inside Parliament and out, and shifting material circumstances in England and the colonies defied most of the economic "laws" writers knew and evoked continual reconsideration of the various spheres of economic influence in the empire. No wonder, then, that we should find even the most economically secure cluster of New York City merchants divided in their political choices. Some of these men would soon be found in Congress and the new state government; many would retreat from the war altogether or reiterate their commitment to imperial authority.

Dissenters from mercantile tenets—among them "free traders" of all ranks and the rising men in New York who grasped at internal development and manufactures—were also divided in their political loyalties. What marked the patriots among them, however, were their difficulties in directing the wider political and constitutional aspects of the province's revolutionary movement. Lacking the habits of provincial leadership and unused to being deferred to in most cases, rising city merchants could not quickly translate many of their optimistic projections of expansion and development into effective leadership of the Revolution. Then, too, their conflicts with other city merchants, and between merchants and rural producers, worked against the creation of a single commercial voice responsive to turmoil in the empire. Still, although colonists' impulses toward economic freedom never prevailed prior to the Revolution, they offered a valuable alternative to dominant expectations and policies on occasion, inspiring some colonists to reshape the political economy they had inherited so that it might reflect and further their particular opportunities. Moreover, middling traders created direct vital ties between changing commercial conditions and the great numbers of internal producers, ties whose consequences could not yet be forecast. However, the revolutionary and postrevolutionary years would shortly revitalize their hopes for unleashing their talents in internal and commercial development.

Conclusion

THERE WAS NO quintessential eminent or lesser merchant in colonial New York City. A range of opportunities and experiences gave rise to a protean commercial community, one in which imminent ruin might threaten a successful trader or a relatively modest trader might rise to notable stature. Indeed, much united wholesalers in their pursuit of commerce: their mutual antipathy to import duties, their desire to extend the "revolution in desires" for "more of life's necessitous goods," and their efforts to minimize the difficulties of conducting long-distance trade by building good reputations and trustworthy liaisons abroad. Together, they protected and furthered their commercial interests, with no particular group of city traders more profit-conscious, more ambitious, or more innovative than another. As elsewhere in the early modern world, New York's merchants scorned Crusoe-style isolation from the world's traffic and applauded material plenty, fuller employment, and maturing settlements. Few merchants in the city leveled sustained criticism at the Navigation Acts until well into the eighteenth century; the stronger voices in merchants' correspondence by the 1680s expressed frustration with the lingering—albeit fading—appeal of customary notions about production and exchange in the hinterlands and city markets.

Still, colonists also identified consequential differences between the well-placed and the rising or middling merchants. On the one hand, while some of the most successful city merchants rose to the top because they diversified into West Indian trade, they typically focused their business choices, partnerships, and credit relations on transatlantic sources. None of them could avoid conditions of exportation from the province, but their credit and reputations tended to hinge on the importation of finished manufactures for their everyday use, as well as the luxuries that validated the higher stature of others. Issues that drew their ire included import duties, rising port fees, fixed rates of interest on loans to government and other colonists, English commission agents who "dumped" too many goods in the city, and auction agents who sold "excessively low." On the other hand, some lesser merchants undertook transatlantic trade, and some of them built their modest reputations on importation from England, but most of them got their start and kept their toeholds in commerce by trading with New England and the West Indies. Moreover, colonists consistently identified exportation of agricultural staples and "country manufactures" with the lesser merchants who had connections in the interior. Middling traders attained less success as a group, and they fell harder as individuals; they reveled in the many opportunities for commerce in the eighteenth century but could rarely achieve economies of scale and often resorted to larger partnerships and more dispersed ownership of vessels.

We can make no facile equation between transatlantic dry-goods importation and commercial success. Nor can we equate both of these characteristics with loyalty to the model of "fair trade," or mercantilism. Most city traders believed mercantilism was the best model, whether they assigned its benefits to imperial or regional trade; commercial difficulties, they usually explained, could be traced, not to the mercantile model itself, but to its poor execution. After all, English policy makers left much of New York's trade unregulated, especially its agricultural exports. And even the most ardent enthusiasts of open commerce believed in the efficacy of particular government restraints; quarrels over the bolting monopoly were but one instance in which city merchants depended on the guiding hand of government regulations to help them secure competitive exports or negotiate favorable market conditions. The precise character of that regulation depended on who asked for, who granted, and who defended it; but no voices in colonial New York believed they freely chose values and lifestyles, and if at times some of them shunned the greater civic consciousness that republicanism taught, they never forgot their place in networks of kin, community, and polity that undergirded all of their economic efforts.

Still, a significant minority of city merchants—more often lesser traders rather than successful wholesalers, usually involved in the West Indies and coastal trade, and never a solid coalition of interests—struggled to defeat or circumvent some mercantile tenets from the earliest years of settlement. At first they emulated the Dutch example of commercial freedoms, which remained influential in New York City long after 1664, but in time the attractiveness of a more open commerce led them to criticize policies enacted in the Common Council, New York Assembly, or Parliament. Up the Hudson River, across colonial boundaries in the region, along the coastline, and into the West Indies, middling merchants introduced challenges to imperial expectations of commerce. Regulating the prices and quality of exports, forging alliances with merchants outside their province who were equally unattached to great families, pursuing the fur and grain trades, and encouraging rural productivity and small country manufactures in the hinterlands—all of these attracted the city's ambitious newcomers and rising young traders, and all of these linked myriad families to wider spheres of commerce. Without offering consistent and unremitting dissent, they nevertheless pursued opportunity and thinking about autonomous economic activities and reasserted the benefits of open trade repeatedly as the character of the city changed.

Lesser merchants were more likely than transatlantic wholesalers to support paper money, open commercial boundaries between colonies, and elimination of embargoes; they tended to be bolder about trading with enemies in wartime, more emphatic defenders of peacetime illicit trade, and more enthusiastic promoters of consumption that was served by exchange with neighbors in New England. Of course, many city traders presumed that the primary benefit of freer trade was the security of their profits. But they also urged colonists who were inclined to take new risks to extend their productive efforts, whether in agriculture or manufacturing; especially during the nonimportation movements, they helped shape the message that colonists need not stifle their economic energy in order to gain political satisfaction, but could instead pursue a degree of economic autonomy on their own terms. By doing so, they helped hasten colonists toward thinking of themselves as a producing and consuming, as well as an importing and exporting, people. By the final colonial decades, many New Yorkers found aspects of language about economic freedom appealing, even compatible with resurgent notions about Protestant self-reliance and republican collective virtue. Private and public statements sometimes exaggerated the extent of their material accomplishments, or miscalculated imperial intentions about stifling colonial opportunities, but at the same time colonists were unquestionably more self-conscious about producing necessities for themselves, especially in light of both rising agricultural exports and the urban nonimportation movements.

In the last colonial years, New York merchants still understood their economy only imperfectly, had contradictory ideas about market behavior, and promoted a patchwork quilt of policies aimed at satisfying the interests of shifting commercial coalitions. Actual implementation of either regulations or freedoms was tempered by the varying degrees of success, choices of markets, and personal predispositions within the trading community. Most lesser merchants lacked political authority to influence legislation decisively. Just as important, small producers, millers, and commercial farmers developed their own habits of criticism and dissent independent of merchants' goals, so that wider alliances of economic interests proved ephemeral, especially as the revolutionary crisis approached. In addition, the distillers, brewers, sugar refiners, snuff manufacturers, and other entrepreneurs in New York City shared concerns about labor, wages, and prices that did not usually overlap with those of rural producers. Nor could lesser merchants claim the deference that eminent transatlantic traders enjoyed when they joined Whig leaders in intercolonial union.

For a long time, notions about economic freedom had helped colonists depart from customary or traditional codes of social organization. Leading up to the Revolution, regular appeals to greater collective development also expanded the imaginations of colonists about consumption. The Seven Years' War brought renewed commercial opportunities for colonists of all strata, and when it was over imperial officials faced, not only the need to repay steep debts, but also the desire of colonists to eat and wear a variety of new commodities. New York's major exports continued to be wheat, flour, and naval stores; but by the final years of the war, colonists had added to these significant quantities of ginseng, flaxseed, whalebone products, oysters, and preserved foods, and a wide spectrum of colonists consumed greater amounts of cocoa, coffee, and exotic fruits.

But, as delegates to the Continental Congress and New York's committees would learn, the same ideas encouraged smuggling and bold references to self-interest, neither of which squared with the goal of political liberty as revolutionary leaders defined it. During the final colonial years, smugglers, prosperous West Indies traders, and those who turned toward the promise of manufacturing and internal development all became more self-consciously opposed to the constraints of economic regulation and special-interest politics. When the Revolution began, those who spoke the language of self, rather than society, identified poorly with a "common interest" or the "will of the people." As a consequence, the legacy of economic freedom could motivate both patriotic developers of significant virtue and detractors from the revolutionary cause.

English mercantilists were not blind to the quickening pace of change in New York during its final colonial years. They grew concerned about the extent to which colonists frequented Spanish and French markets, and about the regional exchanges that defied imperial laws and ensnared colonists in webs of debt and credit that shifted primary economic loyalties away from London. Not only profit, but power, was at stake in rising colonial expectations, some imperial officials argued. Yet mercantilists could provide few new responses to individuals who clamored for access to unfettered markets, abolition of trade duties, and exemption from special legislation to channel, regulate, price, and otherwise control particular arenas of commerce. They could only try to contain the centrifugal tendencies of private interest with the language of national self-sufficiency and imperial authority, as they had all along. Such declarations, however, only reintroduced the conundrum of power in the imperial political economy: what was the proper balance between the requirements of political authority and the collective interests that created material prosperity? What mixture of regulation and freedom would best promote the expanding material capacity of people everywhere in the empire?

Neither economic freedom nor economic regulation was thrown into utter disarray by the prerevolutionary crisis, for it was not in the nature of economic ideas to be defeated or victorious in any definitive way. Those years were less an end point of dialogue and experience than the next step in refining the rift between economic regulation and economic freedom in the new state's thought and behavior. At first, New Yorkers spilled much ink during the Revolution explaining their fears of private economic interests tyrannizing over public virtue, yet few of them proposed giving more central authority to Congress. Indeed, the Revolutionary War offered lucrative prospects for a few city merchants who were virtually unknown in 1772. Moreover, some leading and many middling citizens kept alive the expectation that under future conditions of political liberty, they would achieve economic freedom in the "natural harmony" of peace, bounty, and benevolence. Into the early national era, economic freedom, broadly conceived, continued to inspire the many New Yorkers who wished to exclude a revitalized mercantilism and deny a place to the conservative businessmen who discouraged some of the risks that more ambitious traders sought. Sometimes advocates cherished the ideas of economic freedom as principles of human action, but more often unfettered enterprise seemed the best antidote to pampered special interests. The content of those ideas was familiar to revolutionaries, and their advocates stretched them to encompass activities on the vast frontier, through a burgeoning population, and in untold numbers of manufactures and internal developments. Proponents of economic freedom continued to argue that one did not have to beggar one's neighbor to get a piece of a fixed economic pie, and that the wealth of a nation included not only its "stock" of goods but also its laboring people and capacity to grow in the future.

On balance, however, New Yorkers did not separate from England in 1776 in order to sweep away mercantilism and turn to an enlightened mixture of international free trade and domestic manufacturing. They chose, not the visionary route of economic freedom, but the familiar one that recognized the rewards of material improvement under the aegis of a moderately regulated political economy. They would continue to prescribe a degree of restraint for themselves, not a daring consuming and producing machine, for regulatory stewardship seemed most compatible with the formidable tasks of working out constitutional principles, securing diplomatic and commercial relations, and organizing expansive territory in the new republic, even as private interests of many sorts would be its mortar. After all, middling commercial interests and ambitious small producers had long argued for particular regulations to temper extreme economic freedom. And even Adam Smith knew that "perfect liberty"—what some people later would call unharnessed free-market capitalism—was the vain appeal of ambitious ideologues.

Appendix A

Tables and Graphs

TABLE 1

New York's Trade with Great Britain by Decade, 1701–1780

	Exports to Great Britain		Imports from Great Britain	
Decade	From New York[a]	From America[a]	To New York[a]	To America[b]
1701–10	100,000	2,900,000	284,000	267,000
1711–20	200,000	3,800,000	446,000	366,000
1721–30	225,000	5,188,000	658,000	471,000
1731–40	162,000	6,670,000	929,000	660,000
1741–50	174,000	7,059,000	1,518,295	813,000
1751–60	279,000	8,091,000	3,070,585	1,577,000
1761–70	629,000	10,426,000	3,497,000	1,763,000
1771–80	571,000	7,436,000	2,656,000[c]	1,331,000

[a]Herman Stoker, *Wholesale Commodity Prices at New York City, 1720–1800*, Cornell University Experimental Station, *Memoir*, no. 142 (Ithaca, N.Y., 1932), pt. 2, 221.

[b]John Baker Holroyd, 1st earl of Sheffield, *Observations on the Commerce of the American States, with Europe and the West Indies* (1783), 6th ed. (London, 1784), app. 9, whose estimates are quite low and thus represent only the relative rise of all colonial imports as compared to New York.

[c]David MacPherson, *Annals of Commerce, Manufactures, Fisheries and Navigation* (London, 1805), 3: 518–673; excludes 1775.

TABLE 2

New York's Trade with Great Britain by Year, 1699 to 1774

(in £ sterling)

Year	N.Y. Exports	(a) N.Y. Imports	(b) N.Y. Imports (rounded to 000)
1699	16,818	42,792	43
1700	17,567	49,410	49
1701	18,547	31,910	32
1702	7,965	29,991	30
1703	7,471	17,562	17
1704	10,540	22,294	22
1705	7,393	27,902	26
1706	2,849	31,588	31
1707	14,283	29,855	27
1708	10,847	26,899	25
1709	12,259	34,577	35
1710	8,203	31,475	35
1711	12,193	28,856	34
1712	12,466	18,524	18
1713	14,428	46,470	44
1714	29,810	44,643	42
1715	21,316	54,629	50
1716	21,971	52,173	48
1717	24,534	44,140	40
1718	27,331	62,966	56
1719	19,596	56,355	52
1720	16,836	37,397	35
1721	15,681	50,754	47
1722	20,118	57,478	51
1723	27,992	53,013	45
1724	21,191	63,020	56
1725	24,976	70,650	63
1726	38,307	84,866	80
1727	31,617	67,452	63
1728	21,141	81,634	77
1729	15,833	64,760	63
1730	8,740	64,356	60
1731	20,756	66,116	59
1732	9,411	65,540	57
1733	11,626	65,417	54
1734	15,307	81,758	69
1735	14,155	80,405	67
1736	17,944	86,000	71
1737	16,833	125,833	106
1738	16,228	133,438	112
1739	18,459	106,070	86
1740	21,498	118,777	109
1741	21,142	140,430	140
1742	13,536	167,591	160
1743	15,067	135,487	122
1744	14,527	119,920	106
1745	14,083	54,957	44
1746	8,841	86,712	78
1747	14,992	137,984	118

Tables and Graphs   321

TABLE 2 (continued)

Year	N.Y. Exports	(a) N.Y. Imports	(b) N.Y. Imports (rounded to 000)
1748	12,358	143,311	128
1749	23,413	265,773	242
1750	35,634	267,130	238
1751	42,363	248,941	212
1752	40,648	194,030	164
1753	50,553	277,864	234
1754	26,663	127,497	110
1755	28,054	151,071	143
1756	24,073	250,425	225
1757	19,168	353,311	349
1758	14,260	356,555	359
1759	21,684	630,785	616
1760	21,125	480,108	467
1761	48,648	289,570	274
1762	58,882	288,046	274
1763	53,989	238,560	234
1764	53,697	515,416	509
1765	54,959	382,349	381
1766	67,020	330,829	332
1767	61,422	417,957	423
1768	87,115	482,930	484
1769	73,466	74,918	70
1770	69,882	475,991	449
1771	95,875	653,621	639
1772	82,707	343,970	359
1773	76,246	289,214	307
1774	80,008	437,937	456

SOURCES: The first two columns are drawn from Charles Whitworth, *State of the Trade of Great Britain in Its Imports and Exports Progressively from the Year 1697* (London, 1776); David MacPherson, *Annals of Commerce, Manufactures, Fisheries, and Navigation* (London, 1805), 3: 564, 585, 599; reports of the governors of New York to the Board of Trade, found in *Documents Relative to the Colonial History of the State of New York*, ed. and trans. E. B. O'Callaghan and Berthold Fernow (Albany, N.Y., 1865–87), for 1699–1704, 1717–23, 1724, 1727–37, 1739, and 1745–54; selected years of the *New-York Gazette* and the *New-York Mercury*; G. N. Clark, *Guide to English Commercial Statistics, 1696–1782* (London, 1938); and *An Account of Her Majesty's Revenue in the Province of New York, 1701–1709*, ed. Julius M. Bloch et al., facs. repr. (Ridgewood, N.J., 1966). These two columns represent the customs registrations computed in fixed commodities valuations in about 1698, which valuations were used as a standard by which to assess duties throughout the next century. They do not represent the true values of goods imported into New York or exported to Britain, but rather the relative volume of trade from one year to the next. Moreover, merchants tended to overvalue goods moving through English ports, especially when they might gain a drawback.

The third column is taken from John J. McCusker, "The Current Value of English Exports, 1697 to 1800," *William and Mary Quarterly*, 3d ser., 28 (Oct. 1971): 607–28. McCusker has converted the constant value of exports in the second column into a current value series by using a commodity price index to compute the value of exports to America. While his figures are rounded off, they provide a useful means of understanding the values of commodities exchanged, rather than having to speak of volume alone. Trends, however, are the same between column (a) and column (b).

TABLE 3
Entering and Clearing Vessels at New York City
(selected years)

Year	Number Entering[a]	Registered Tonnage	Number Clearing	Registered Tonnage
1701	67			
1702	54			
1703 (9 mos.)	41			
1704	69			
1705	71		131	
1707 (11 mos.)	51		117	
1708 (7 mos.)	51		112	
1709			116	
1710			160	
1711			145	
1712			166	
1713			142	
1714			169	
1715			197	
1716			218	
(1714–16) (36 mo.)	64			
(1715–18)			215/yr.	7,464/yr.
1725	23			
1726 (11 mos.)	196		211	7,855
1727	202		215	8,052
1728	195		193	
1729 (10 mos.)	206		184	
1730	216	6,230	225	
1731 (43 wks.)	111		163	
1733	215	7,672	214	8,052
1734	213	7,442	184	6,374
1735	196	6,759	205	7,145
1736	194		176	
1738	233		258	
1739	261	9,738	269	10,012
1740			ca. 300	10,012
1746			99	4,513
1748	180		206	
1749	286		331	6,731
1750	294		371	
1751	325		369	
1752	334		374	
1753	376		413	
1754	390	12,506	406	12,686
1755			296	
1756			ca. 400	
1760	178	9,901	247	14,222
1762			477	19,514
1763		14,900		16,800
1764	264	16,660	340	17,022
1765		18,100		19,800
1766		17,400		21,800
1767		22,900		20,000
1768	462	21,600	480	23,600

Tables and Graphs

TABLE 3 *(continued)*

Year	Number Entering[a]	Registered Tonnage	Number Clearing	Registered Tonnage
1769	625	26,600	787	27,800
1770	600	25,500	612	26,600
1771	557	25,000	524	25,300
1772	710	28,900	709	29,132
1773		24,300		24,300
1774	720	28,500		27,700

SOURCES: United Kingdom, Public Record Office, Customs Records, C.O. 16: 1; C.O. 5: 1224, 1225–26, 1228; *An Account of Her Majesty's Revenue in the Province of New York, 1701–1709*, ed. Julius M. Bloch et al., facs. repr. (Ridgewood, N.J., 1966); for 1721, Gov. Hunter to Board of Trade, in *Documents Relative to the Colonial History of the State of New York*, ed. and trans. E. B. O'Callaghan and Berthold Fernow (Albany, N.Y., 1865–87), 5: 601, 618; for 1725, ibid., 5: 744; for 1715–18, ibid., 5: 601, 613–16; for 1705–16, C.O. 5: 1051, Bb98; for 1726–44, *New-York Gazette*; for 1749, Governor Clinton to Board of Trade, in *Docs. Rel.*, ed. and trans. O'Callaghan and Fernow, 6: 511; for 1746, *The Documentary History of the State of New York*, ed. E. B. O'Callaghan (Albany, N.Y., 1850–51), 1: 493, 513; for 1749, Edmund Burke, *An Account of the European Settlements in America* (London, 1759), 2: 185; for 1738, 1740–41, *New York Journal*; for 1748–50, 1755–56, 1764, 1773–74, *New-York Gazette*; for 1763–64, 1767, *New-York Mercury*; for 1763-64, 1767, *New-York Gazette* (Weyman's); "New York Entrances and Clearances for 1760," MSS Div., Massachusetts Historical Society Library; Governor Tryon to the Lords of Trade, 1774, in *Doc. Hist.*, ed. O'Callaghan, 1: 739–72, 756; Henry Prince, "New York before the Revolutionary War," in *Views of Early New York* (New York, 1904), 119–20.

[a]Figures for vessels entering in the years 1701–8 represent ships carrying dutied goods only: imports of wine, rum, dry goods, and exports of furs. Most coastal voyages are thus excluded, as are ships carrying cargoes of nonenumerated items, especially wheat and flour, to any destination. See also Table 4.

TABLE 4
Customs Revenues Collected in New York
(selected years)

Year	Commodities Dutied	Amount (in £.s.d.)
1690–91 (2 yrs)	dry goods, wine, rum, furs, Hudson reexports	2,521. 1.12
1692	same as above	2,463. 3.11
1693	same as above	1,916. 8.1
1694	same as above	3,055.11.3
1695	same as above	2,313.17.10
1698–99[a]	dry goods	1,149.16.11
	wine	525.10
	rum	835.13
	furs	542. 1.3
	Hudson reexports	102. 6.8
1699–1700[a]	dry goods	1,280. 8.10
	wine	1,205.14
	rum	782. 3.8
	furs	571.10.11
	Hudson reexports	68. 8.10
1721–22[a]	dry goods	62. 2.5
	wine	496.10.6
	rum	1,165.14.9
	molasses	649.12.4
	salt	270. 9.0
	cocoa	192.19.6
1722–23[a]	dry goods	79.16.4
	wine	1,493. 2.0
	rum	1,324. 1.9
	molasses	711.18.8
	salt	175. 7.0
	cocoa	130.13.9
1723–24[a]	dry goods	115. 2.11
	wine	513. 0.0
	rum	1,782.11.6
	molasses	456.10.10
	salt	91. 5.6
	cocoa	163. 3.0
1726 (Mar.–Sept. only)	enumerated goods and excise taxes	3,825. 6.10
1740–41 (Sept.–Mar.)	do.	5,392. 9.3
1742–43 (Sept.–Mar.)	do.	6,025. 4.2
1738	enumerated goods only	2,913. 6.8
1740	do.	2,328. 4.1
1742	do.	2,197. 7.2
1743	do.	2,402. 8.10
1752	do.	2,704.15.11
1753	do.	1,788. 8.3
1754	do.	2,566. 2.0
1755	do.	2,447.19.10
1764	tonnage duty, 3d./ton	487. 6. 9

SOURCES: *Journal of the Votes and Proceedings of the General Assembly of the Colony of New York, 1691–1765* (New York, 1764–66); *Journal of the Votes and Proceedings of the General Assembly of the Colony of New York, 1766–1776* (Albany, N.Y., 1820); *The Documentary History of the State of New York*, ed. E. B. O'Callaghan (Albany, N.Y., 1850–51), 1: 701, 703.
    [a]For one year from 5 June to the following 4 June.

TABLE 5
New York's Paper Currency, 1709-1771

Year	Amount Issued	Amount Canceled
1709	£5,000	unknown
1709	4,000	unknown
1709	4,000	unknown
1711	10,000	unknown
1714	27,680	£27,406
1715	1,200	1,190
1717	16,607	16,351
1720	2,000	1,896
1723	2,140	2,122
1724	9,630	9,469
1726	3,000	2,858
1730	3,000	2,999
1734	12,000	11,576
1737	48,350	43,153
1739	10,000	9,115
1746	13,000	12,618
1746	40,000	38,772
1747	28,000	27,098
1755	45,000	36,325
1755	10,000	7,550
1755	8,000	6,489
1756	10,000	7,649
1756	52,000	41,999
1758	100,000	66,155
1759	150,000	98,842
1759	100,000	71,876
1760	60,000	41,970
1771	120,000	none

SOURCES: *Colonial Laws of New York from the Year 1664 to the Revolution*, ed. James Lyon (Albany, N.Y., 1894), 1: chs. 190, 204, 207, 231, 280, 292, 347; 2: chs. 396, 437, 447, 450, 492, 551, 625, 666; 3: chs. 676, 825, 832, 854, 970, 977, 988; 4: chs. 1008, 1009, 1059, 1082, 1087, 1112; *Journal of the Votes and Proceedings of the General Assembly of the Colony of New York, 1766–1776* (Albany, N.Y., 1820), 2: 281, 325, 350, 362, 422, 457, 489, 518, 554, 602, 606, 634, 644, 668, 672, 707, 728, 750, 785.

FIGURE A.1
Selected Prices of Flour Sold to Merchants from New York City

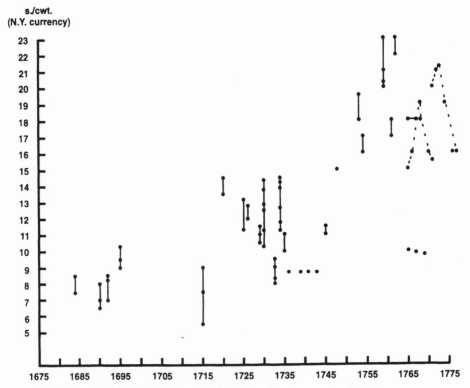

SOURCES: *The Annals of Albany*, ed. Joel Munsell (Albany, N.Y., 1850–59), 9: 21; Emory R. Johnson, *The History of Domestic and Foreign Commerce of the United States* (New York, 1915), 1: 120, 85; John J. McCusker, "The Current Value of English Exports, 1697 to 1800," *William and Mary Quarterly*, 3d ser., 28 (Oct. 1971), table 3; Marc Egnal, "The Economic Development of the Thirteen Continental Colonies, 1720–1775," *William and Mary Quarterly*, 3d ser., 32 (Apr. 1975): 191–222; Herman Stoker, *Wholesale Commodity Prices at New York City, 1720–1800*, Cornell University Experimental Station, *Memoir*, no. 142 (Ithaca, N.Y., 1932), 200–203, 215–16; *American Weekly Mercury*, 1720 to 1729 *New-York Gazette*, 1726 to 1738, 1739, 1754 to 1764, and 1766; *New-York Gazette, or Weekly Post-Boy*, 1765 to 1766; *New York Journal or General Advertiser*, 1767 to 1775; C.O. 323: 14, P 19 (for 1759); A. H. Cole, *Wholesale Commodity Prices in the United States: 1700–1861* (Cambridge, Mass., 1938), for 1748 to the Revolution; *Colonial Records of the New York Chamber of Commerce, 1768–1784*, ed. John Austin Stevens (New York, 1867); citation for July 14, 1740, in *The Papers of Sir William Johnson*, ed. James Sullivan et al. (Albany, N.Y., 1921–65), 1: 24; Henry Beekman to Gilbert Livingston Feb. 2, 1749, Beekman Papers; Van Schaick Papers; Glen-Sanders Papers; and John van Cortlandt Letter Book, all at the New-York Historical Society; Isaac N. Stokes, *The Iconography of Manhattan Island, 1498–1909* (New York, 1915–28), 4: 395, 453, 462, 468, 598; Cadwallader Colden to Lords of Trade, Mar. 9, 1764, in *Documents Relative to the Colonial History of the State of New York*, ed. and trans. E. B. O'Callaghan and Berthold Fernow (Albany, N.Y., 1865–87), 7: 612; Philip Cuyler to his father, Dec. 11, 1758, Dec. 17, 1759, Cuyler, Letter Book; *New-York Mercury*, May 1, Oct. 21, 1762; *The Aspinwall Papers*, Massachusetts Historical Society, *Collections*, 4th ser., vols. 9–10 (Boston, 1871–72), entries in vol. 10; John Watts, letters to various correspondents, in *Letter Book of John Watts of New York, 1762–1765*, New-York Historical Society, *Collections*, 2d ser., vol. 61 (New York, 1928), 5, 8–9, 33, 35, 45, 48, 65, 68, 80, 87, 94, 104, 109.

FIGURE A.2

Selected Prices of Wheat Sold to Merchants from New York City

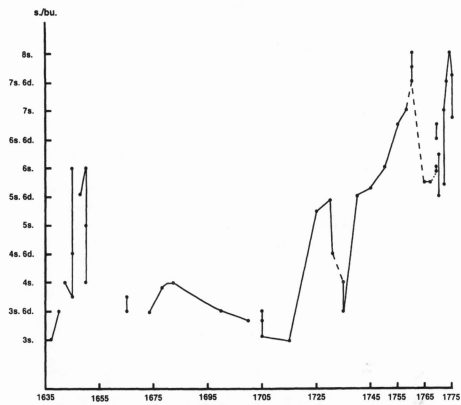

SOURCES: For 1634–44, see *The Van Rensselaer–Bowier Manuscripts*, ed. and trans. A. J. F. van Laer (Albany, N.Y., 1901), 252–53, 447, 478, 493, 511, 12, 563, 604–5, 650, 664–65. For conversion of gulden (florins) to shillings and pence, see John J. McCusker, *Money and Exchange in Europe and America, 1600–1775: A Handbook* (Chapel Hill, N.C., 1978), 44–45. For the years after the English conquest, see *The Annals of Albany*, ed. Joel Munsell (Albany, N.Y., 1850–59), 9: 21; Emory R. Johnson, *History of Domestic and Foreign Commerce of the United States* (New York, 1915), 1: 120, 85; John J. McCusker, "The Current Value of English Exports, 1697 to 1800," *William and Mary Quarterly*, 3d ser., 28 (Oct. 1971), table 3; Marc Egnal, "The Economic Development of the Thirteen Continental Colonies, 1720–1775," *William and Mary Quarterly*, 3d ser., 32 (Apr. 1975): 191–222; Herman Stoker, *Wholesale Commodity Prices at New York City, 1720–1800*, Cornell University Experimental Station, Memoir, no. 142 (Ithaca, N.Y., 1932), 200–203, 215–16; *American Weekly Mercury*, 1720–29; *New-York Gazette*, 1726–38, 1739, 1754–64, 1766; *New-York Gazette, or Weekly Post-Boy*, 1765–66; *New York Journal or General Advertiser*, 1767–75; C.O. 323: 14, P19, for 1759; A. H. Cole, *Wholesale Commodity Prices in the United States: 1700–1861* (Cambridge, Mass., 1938), for 1748 to the Revolution; Cadwallader Colden to Lords of Trade, Mar. 9, 1764, in *Documents Relative to the Colonial History of the State of New York*, ed. and trans. E. B. O'Callaghan and Berthold Fernow (Albany, N.Y., 1865–87), 7: 612.

Appendix B

Bills of Exchange

BILLS OF EXCHANGE facilitated merchants' transactions by providing an acceptable means of credit, a ready substitute for scarce specie, and a transferable instrument for transatlantic commerce. However, their usage depended ultimately on both the willing execution of their provisions and the availability of credit among correspondents who knew each other. When bad intentions, irresponsibility, and shortages of credit among familiar parties interferred with the smoothe circulation of bills of exchange, more than one merchant was affected adversely. Merchants' correspondence provide many examples of the frustrations that could arise. William Beekman's letters to correspondents, excerpted here from *The Beekman Mercantile Papers, 1746–1799*, ed. Philip L. White, 3 vols. (New York, 1956), 1: 517, 522, illustrate these frustrations.

To Alexander Ogilby, Newtown, Ireland, March 3, 1768

I Received your favour of the 28th September Relative to your Linens of which you have Inclosed [account of] Sales and you may be asshured you should have had Your money Er now if you had Ordered the proceeds in Dollars provided no bill Could be had Indeed it is Almost Next to Imposible to Obtain so Small a bill for Just your ballance. I have Applied to Every flaxseed Shipper but Could not Prevail on them to give me a bill. the sum Either Over run or fell short of the ballance they had to draw for.

To Evan and Francis Malbone, Rhode Island, March 10, 1769

Yours Inclosing Captain Dicksons bill Came duely to hand On Thompson and Alexander for 1339 1/16 Dollars which was Presented, but Mr. Alexander seemed much displeased that it was drawn on so short sight for so larg sum and said he Could not Accept it to be paid in dollars for it was Out of his power, Not knowing where to Collect them, however to make him Easey and prevent your disapointment, I told him he might take 8 or 10 days for Payment and I would take the Currency of the place. I Immediately Set About Collecting Specie which is very Scarce . . . I spoke to One hundred persons at least and was Obliged to take [coins valued at] 1, 2, 3 [pennyweight] . . . on 8 or 10 [pennyweight face value] at a place and those that had them would not part with the heavy [coins] unless I would take the Light Ones also.

Notes

Abbreviations

AAS — American Antiquarian Society

AJ — *Journal of the Votes and Proceedings of the General Assembly of the Colony of New York . . . 1691 . . . 1765,* vol. 1 (New York, 1764–66); and *Journal of the Votes and Proceedings of the General Assembly of the Colony of New York, 1766–1776,* vol. 2 (Albany, N.Y., 1820)

Bloch, *HMR* — *An Account of Her Majesty's Revenue in the Province of New York, 1701–1709,* ed. Julius Bloch et al. (Ridgewood, N.J., 1966)

Cal. Council Mins. — *Calendar of Council Minutes, 1668–1783,* ed. Berthold Fernow and A. J. F. van Laer, *New York State Library Bulletin* 58 (Apr. 1901–Mar. 1902)

C.O. 5: 1221–28 — United Kingdom, Colonial Office Papers, 5th ser., Records of the Customs Collectors, Records of Entrances and Clearances at the Port of New York, 1715 to 1764, Public Record Office, London

Colden — *The Letters and Papers of Cadwallader Colden,* New-York Historical Society, *Collections,* 2d ser., vols. 50–56, 67–68 (New York, 1917–23, 1934–35)

Col. Commissions — *Calendar of New York Colonial Commissions, 1680–1770,* ed. E. B. O'Callaghan (New York, 1929)

Colonial Laws — *Colonial Laws of New York from the Year 1664 to the Revolution,* ed. James Lyon, 5 vols. (Albany, N.Y., 1894)

Council Journal — *Journal of the Legislative Council of the Colony of New York, 1691–1775,* 2 vols. (Albany, N.Y., 1861)

Council Mins. — *Council Minutes, 1652–54,* trans. and ed. Charles T. Gehring (Interlaken, N.Y., 1983)

Doc. Hist. — *The Documentary History of the State of New York,* 4 vols., ed. E. B. O'Callaghan (Albany, N.Y., 1850–51)

Docs. Rel. — *Documents Relative to the Colonial History of the State of New York,* ed. and trans. E. B. O'Callaghan and Berthold Fernow, 15 vols. (Albany, N.Y., 1865–87)

Dutch MSS — *Calendar of Historical Manuscripts . . . Albany,* vol. 1: *Dutch Mss., 1630–1664,* ed. E. B. O'Callaghan (Albany, N.Y., 1866)

Fernow, *Records* — *The Records of the City of New Amsterdam from 1653 to 1674, Anno Domini,* ed. Berthold Fernow, 7 vols. (New York, 1897)

Laws and Ordinances — *Laws and Ordinances of New Netherland, 1638–1674,* ed. E. B. O'Callaghan (Albany, N.Y., 1868)

NYHS	New-York Historical Society
NYPL	New York Public Library
Osgood, *Mins.* Common Council	*Minutes of the Common Council of the City of New York, 1676–1776,* ed. Herbert Osgood, Austin Keep, and Charles Nelson, 8 vols. (New York, 1905)
Palsits, *Mins.*	*Minutes of the Executive Council of the Province of New York,* ed. Victor H. Palsits, 2 vols. (Albany, N.Y., 1910)
Postlethwayt, *Dict.*	Malachy Postlethwayt, *The Universal Dictionary of Trade and Commerce,* 2d ed., 2 vols. (London, 1774)
Smith, *History*	William Smith, *The History of the Late Province of New-York from Its Discovery to the Appointment of Governor Colden, in 1762,* New-York Historical Society, *Collections,* 2 vols. (New York, 1826, 1829)
State Papers,	*Calendar of State Papers, Colonial Series, America and West Indies, 1661–1738,* ed. W. Noel Sainsbury, J. W. Fortescue, and Cecil Headlam, 44 vols. (1860–1953; repr. London, 1964)
Stevens, *Records*	*Colonial Records of the New York Chamber of Commerce, 1768–1784,* ed. John Austin Stevens (New York, 1867)
Stoker, *Prices*	Herman Stoker, *Wholesale Commodity Prices at New York City, 1720–1800,* Cornell University Experimental Station, *Memoir,* no. 142 (Ithaca, N.Y., 1932)
Stokes, *Iconography*	Isaac N. Stokes, *The Iconography of Manhattan Island, 1498–1909,* 6 vols. (New York, 1915–28)
WLB	John Watts, *Letter Book of John Watts of New York, 1762–1765,* New-York Historical Society, *Collections,* 2d ser., vol. 61 (New York, 1928)
WIC	West-Indische Compagnie: the Dutch West India Company
Wills	*Abstracts of Wills on File in the Surrogate's Office, City of New York, 1665–1801,* ed. William S. Pelletreau, in New-York Historical Society, *Collections,* vols. 25–32 (New York, 1893–1909)

Introduction

1. For the relationships of empire, colonial settlement, and merchants' rise, see esp. Maurice H. Dobb, *Studies in the Development of Capitalism* (London, 1946), esp. chs. 1, 4, 6; C. B. Macpherson, *The Political Theory of Possessive Individualism: Hobbes to Locke* (Oxford, 1962); Robert Brenner, "Agrarian Class Structure and Economic Development in Pre-Industrial Europe," *Past and Present* 70 (1976), and the lively debate this article provoked in subsequent issues of the journal; id., *The Sinews of Power: War, Money and the English State, 1688–1783* (London, 1989); Jan de Vries, *The Economy of Europe in an Age of Crisis, 1600–1750* (Cambridge, 1974), chs. 4, 8; Charles Wilson, *England's Apprenticeship, 1603–1763* (London, 1965), 36–52; Barry Supple, *Commercial Crisis and Change in England, 1600–1642* (Cambridge, 1959), intro.; *Revisions in Mercantilism,* ed. D. C. Coleman (London, 1969), ch. 3; Violet Barbour, *Capitalism in Amsterdam during the Seventeenth Century* (Baltimore, 1950). These works treat merchant capitalism as a period of development predating wage-labor capitalism and industrialization, but not a market or

sophisticated financial and credit system, and this is the definition I have adopted. On English society, see Peter Earle, *The Making of the English Middle Class: Business, Society and Family Life in London, 1660–1730* (London, 1989), and on the English countryside, with a critique of literature on merchants' capitalism, David Ormrod, *English Grain Exports and the Structure of Agrarian Capitalism, 1700–1760* (Kingston upon Hull, 1985); Maxine Berg et al., *Manufacture in Town and Country before the Factory* (Cambridge, 1983); and Neal Wood, *John Locke and Agrarian Capitalism* (Berkeley, 1984). On intellectual and institutional changes, see Keith Horsefield, *British Monetary Experiments, 1650–1710* (London, 1960); William O. Letwin, *The Origins of Scientific Economics: English Economic Thought, 1660–1776* (London, 1963), ch. 3; J. A. W. Gunn, *Politics and the Public Interest in the Seventeenth Century* (London, 1969), esp. chs. 3, 5, 6; Albert O. Hirschman, *The Passions and the Interests: Political Arguments for Capitalism before Its Triumph* (Princeton, N.J., 1977), pt. 1; Wilson, *England's Apprenticeship*, 229–331; and P. G. M. Dickson, *The Financial Revolution in England: A Study in the Development of Public Credit, 1688–1756* (London, 1967), chs. 1, 2.

2. For comparisons to other northern ports, see Jacob Price, "Economic Function and the Growth of the American Port Towns," *Perspectives in American History* 8 (1974): 123–86, at 143–45; Gary Nash, *Urban Crucible: Political Consciousness and the Origins of the American Revolution* (Cambridge, Mass., 1979), 387–91. For studies that assume the eminent place of wholesalers, or are not concerned with distinguishing levels of economic and cultural accomplishment, see the otherwise outstanding studies of Joyce Goodfriend, *Before the Melting Pot: Society and Culture in Colonial New York City, 1664–1730* (Princeton, N.J., 1991), 19, 67–71, 79, 156–61, 173–74, 186; Oliver Rink, *Holland on the Hudson: An Economic and Social History of Dutch New York* (Ithaca, N.Y., 1986); and Nan Rothschild, *New York City Neighborhoods: The Eighteenth Century* (San Diego, 1990), and their bibliographies; for definitions of merchants, see Arthur M. Schlesinger Sr., *The Colonial Merchants and the American Revolution, 1763–1776* (New York, 1918), 15–29; and Jackson Turner Main, *The Social Structure of Revolutionary America* (Princeton, N.J., 1965), 86. Although many merchants had retail business in the city or country estates and public offices, this study focuses on the wholesaling activities of importers and exporters; it is further limited to wholesalers living in New York City, but cases of residents of the New York region whose primary commerce went through the port city are also noted. For contemporary definitions of international wholesalers, see Nathan Baily, *Dictionarium Britannicum* (London, 1730), s.v. "merchant"; Giles Jacob, *A New Law Dictionary* (In the Savoy, London, 1729), s.v. "merchant"; Richard Campbell, *The London Tradesman* (London, 1747), 284–85; and Thomas Sheridan, *A General Dictionary of the English Language*, 2 vols. (London, 1780).

3. The most important example is Virginia Harrington, *The New York Merchant on the Eve of the Revolution* (New York, 1935). Recent work returns to the equation of "merchants" with wealth or status. For example, in *The Emergence of the Middle Class: Social Experiences in the American City, 1760–1900* (New York, 1989), Stuart Blumin depicts "the most significant boundary" in late-eighteenth-century American cities as that which "separated the merchant and professional elite from everyone else" (p. 64). While that may be so, Blumin never addresses the middling success of lesser merchants, and the fine shading from artisan to financial elite—this, in a study about the emergence of the middle class. Furthermore, even the wealthiest city merchants did not equate their wealth,

status, or interests with the colony's landed elite, except in a few cases; see chapters 5–7 below. In contrast, see the very perceptive analysis of Thomas Doerflinger's *A Vigorous Spirit of Enterprise: Merchants and Economic Development in Revolutionary Philadelphia* (Chapel Hill, N.C., 1986), esp. pt. 1. For valuable studies that associate merchants with New York's politics and the cultural elite, see Patricia Bonomi, *A Factious People: Politics and Society in Colonial New York* (New York, 1971); Milton Klein, "Democracy and Politics in Colonial New York," *New York History* 40 (July 1959): 221–46; Beverly McAnear, "Politics in Provincial New York, 1689–1761" (Ph.D. diss., Stanford University, 1935); William Sachs, "The Business Outlook in the Northern Colonies, 1750–1775" (Ph.D. diss., Columbia University, 1957); Philip White, *The Beekmans of New York in Politics and Commerce, 1647–1877* (New York, 1956); and Lawrence Leder, *Robert R. Livingston and the Politics of Colonial New York* (New York, 1961). On the unrepresentative nature of New York's colonial politics, although without consideration of commerce, see Michael Kammen, "The American Revolution as a 'Crise de Conscience': The Case of New York," in *Society, Freedom, and Conscience: The American Revolution in Virginia, Massachusetts, and New York,* ed. Richard M. Jellison (New York, 1976), 125–89, at 129.

4. Harrington, *New York Merchant,* 77, estimates the merchant population to have been about 100, a low figure, which probably reflects her emphasis on the best-known members of the community; her estimate follows the earlier estimate of Henry B. Dawson, *New York during the American Revolution* (New York, 1861), 9–40. For sources used in this study, see the Essay on Sources. I have separated wholesalers from retailers and established the characteristics of great and lesser merchants by evaluating the number of voyages per year; ports of call and duration of voyages; relative sizes of cargoes; age at which data were available and years in trade; level of additional investments (loans, manufactures, real estate); level of debts over the years a merchant was known to be trading; and number of years in the city.

5. In the category "lesser merchant," I include those who outfitted one, two, or three voyages to the West Indies annually; who had shares with from two to five other merchants in West Indian or coastal trade; who had infrequent interests in transatlantic commerce; who did not own vessels; who held shares in vessels of under 80 tons burden; who exported small amounts of (usually) common staples; and who made few or no additional investments outside of commerce. Merchants with fewer than three years' residence in the port city have been excluded throughout. Merchants are also called middling with respect to their place in tax assessments and contemporary social and cultural evaluations. Accuracy is impossible, but it is possible to conjecture about the relative numbers of the wealthy and middling. Subsequent chapters examine the differences within this community over time and offer estimates of its numerical makeup. This study does not analyze agricultural production, rising rural consumption, or labor and prices in the countryside, and it looks at commercial farming only from the perspective of city commerce. Nor, for the New York City population, does it analyze labor conditions, wages, real-estate markets, or craft production.

6. On the terms *liberty* and *freedom,* see Cathy Matson and Peter Onuf, "Toward a Republican Empire: Interest and Ideology in Revolutionary America," *American Quarterly* 37 (1985): 496–531; and C. B. Macpherson, *Property: Mainstream and Critical Positions* (Toronto, 1978), 8.

7. For the term *mercantilism,* see Adam Smith, *An Inquiry into the Nature and Causes*

of the Wealth of Nations, ed. Edwin Cannan (1776; repr., Chicago, 1976), bk. 4, ch. 1, 412. For representative early rationales for mercantilism, see Sir William Petty, *Political Arithmetick,* in *The Economic Writings of Sir William Petty,* ed. Charles Hull (Cambridge, 1899), 259–61; Sir Walter Ralegh, *Observations Touching Trade and Commerce with the Hollander* (London, 1610), 6, 7, 8, 10; and "R.C.," "The Dutch Remonstrance, concerning the proceedings and practices of John de Witt, pensionary, and Ruwaert Van Putten, his brother" (1672), repr. in *Harleian Miscellany,* 12 vols. (London, 1808), 7: 504–21. For recent interpretations, see, e.g., Michael Duffy, *The Englishman and the Foreigner: The English Satiric Print, 1600–1832* (Cambridge, 1986), 27–31; Immanuel Wallerstein, *The Modern World-System II, Mercantilism and the Consolidation of the European World-Economy, 1600–1750* (New York, 1980), 35–71; and W. A. Speck, "The International and Imperial Context," in *Colonial British America: Essays in the New History of the Early Modern Era,* ed. Jack P. Greene and J. R. Pole (Baltimore, 1984), 384–407. On the controlling aspects of the Navigation Acts, see J. E. Farnell, "The Navigation Act of 1651, the First Dutch War, and the London Merchant Community," *Economic History Review,* 2d ser., 16 (1964): 439–54, and Charles Wilson, *Profit and Power: A Study of England and the Dutch Wars* (London, 1958), 12, 107. On the eighteenth-century shift from government protection and promotion to an emphasis on colonial subordination and imperial cultural domination, see James D. Tracy, introduction, *The Rise of Merchant Empires,* ed. id. (Cambridge, 1990).

8. For a summary of the debate about the benefits and drawbacks of mercantilism, see Gary M. Walton and James F. Shepherd, *The Economic Rise of Early America* (Cambridge, Mass., 1979), 173–77.

9. For favorable views of presumed Dutch freedoms, see Gerald Malynes, *The Maintenance of Free Trade* (London, 1622), and John Pollexfen, *A Discourse of Trade, Coyn, and Paper Credit* (London, 1697). For admiration of the Dutch carrying trades and economies of scale, see Lewes Roberts, *Treasure of Traffic,* in *A Select Collection of Early English Tracts on Commerce,* ed. J. R. McCulloch (London, 1856), 209, and Nicholas Barbon, *A Discourse of Trade* (London, 1690). On better Dutch ships, skills, and lower costs, see Tobias Gentleman, *England's Way to Win Wealth* (1614), repr. in *Harleian Miscellany,* 3: 398; John Keymor, *Observations touching Trade and Commerce with the Hollander* (London, 1620), 6–8, repr. in *A Select Collection of Scarce and Valuable Tracts on Commerce,* ed. J. R. McCulloch (London, 1859), 21–27; Carew Reynel, *The True English Benefit* (London, 1674), 14; Sir Thomas Culpepper, *A small Treatise Against Usury* (London, 1698); Sir Josiah Child, *Brief Observations* (1688), repr. in *Sir Josiah Child,* ed. William Letwin (Boston, 1949), app.; and John Cary, *Discourse of Trade* (London, 1695), 69, 124–25.

10. On the later English eighteenth century and approbation of economic freedom, see Alasdair MacIntyre, *After Virtue* (Notre Dame, Ind., 1981), 58; Louis Dumont, *From Mandeville to Marx: The Genesis and Triumph of Economic Ideology* (Chicago, 1977); Dorothy Ross, "Liberalism," in *Encyclopedia of American Political History,* ed. Jack Greene, 3 vols. (New York, 1984), 2: 750–63; and George Lichtheim, *Imperialism* (New York, 1971). For moral optimism and commerce's "sweetness," see Hirschman, *Passions and the Interests,* and Richard Teichgraeber III, *"Free Trade" and Moral Philosophy* (Durham, N.C., 1986), 1–13, 20–26. For overall views, see Joyce Appleby, *Economic Thought and Ideology in Seventeenth-Century England* (Princeton, N.J., 1979); James Tully, *A Dis-*

course on Property: John Locke and His Adversaries (Cambridge, 1980); C. B. Macpherson, *Possessive Individualism*; John Dunn, *Rethinking Modern Political Theory: Essays, 1979–1983* (Cambridge, 1985); and William Reddy, *Money and Liberty in Modern Europe: A Critique of Historical Understanding* (Cambridge, 1987), ch. 3. See also Alasdair MacIntyre, *Whose Justice? Which Rationality?* (Notre Dame, Ind., 1988), for a contrasting view.

11. On the overlapping influences of mercantile and free trade thought, see *Wealth and Virtue: The Shaping of Political Economy in the Scottish Enlightenment*, ed. Istvan Hont and Michael Ignatieff (Cambridge, Mass., 1977); Andrew S. Skinner, "Adam Smith: An Economic Interpretation of History," in *The Market and the State: Essays in Honour of Adam Smith*, ed. id. and Thomas Wilson (Oxford, 1976), 154–78; Duncan Forbes, "Skeptical Whiggism, Commerce, and Liberty," in ibid., 179–201; and Letwin, *Origins of Scientific Economics*, 216–20. For the appearance of both views in another important discourse, that of radical democracy, see E. P. Thompson, *Customs in Common* (New Press, 1992), and Peter Linebaugh, *The London Hanged: Crime and Civil Society in the Eighteenth Century* (Cambridge, 1992).

12. For examples in New York, see *Docs. Rel.*, 3: 233; and Cornelius Cuyler to Richard Janeway, Jan. 13, 1728, Cornelius Cuyler Letters, 1724–36, AAS. Ideas in this and the next two paragraphs were aided by Quentin Skinner, "Meaning and Understanding in the History of Ideas," *History and Theory* 8 (1969): 3–53, at 49; David Hollinger, *In the American Province: Studies in the History and Historiography of Ideas* (Bloomington, Ind., 1985), 130–51; John Toews, "Intellectual History after the Linguistic Turn," *American Historical Review* 92 (1987): 879–95; Lance Banning, "Jeffersonian Ideology Revisited: Liberal and Classical Ideas in the New American Republic," *William and Mary Quarterly* 43 (1986): 3–19; Joyce Appleby, "Republicanism in Old and New Contexts," ibid., 20–34; Michael Durey, "Thomas Paine's Apostles: Radical Emigrés and the Triumph of Jeffersonian Republicanism," ibid., 44 (Oct. 1987): 677–80; James T. Kloppenberg, "The Virtues of Liberalism: Christianity, Republicanism, and Ethics in Early American Political Discourse," *Journal of American History* 74 (1987): 9–33; Quentin Skinner, "Conventions and the Understanding of Speech Acts," *Philosophical Quarterly* 20 (1970), esp. 130, 133–37; and id., "Hermeneutics and the Role of History," *New Literary History* 7 (1975): 232.

13. Address of Cadwallader Colden, 1761, in *Journal of the Legislative Council of the Colony of New-York, December 8, 1743 . . . April 3, 1775*, 2 vols. (New York, 1764–66), 2: 1223.

ONE Establishing a Port, 1620–1664

1. On the founding of the Dutch West India Company and its colonial activities, see Jan de Vries, "On the Modernity of the Dutch Republic," *Journal of Economic History* 33 (Mar. 1973): 191–202; *Documents Relating to New Netherland, 1624–1626, in the Henry E. Huntington Library*, ed. A. J. F. van Laer (San Marino, Calif., 1924), intro.; and C. A. Weslager, *Dutch Explorers, Traders, and Settlers in the Delaware Valley* (Philadelphia, 1961). On the treaty, see *Docs. Rel.*, 3: 2, 16, 23.

2. On the founding of the colony, see Thomas J. Condon, *New York Beginnings: The Commercial Origins of New Netherland* (New York, 1968); Van Cleaf Bachman, *Peltries or Plantations: The Economic Policies of the Dutch West India Company in New Netherland,*

1623–1639 (Baltimore, 1969); and the stimulating work of Oliver Rink, *Holland on the Hudson: An Economic and Social History of Dutch New York* (Ithaca, N.Y., 1986), esp. 62–68, 102–16, 197–202.

3. "Freedoms and Exemptions for the Patroons and Masters," June 7, 1629, in *Laws and Ordinances*, 4–10; "Freedoms and Exemptions," 1629, in *Docs. Rel.*, 2: 551–57, and "Directors to Stuyvesant," 1646, in ibid., 13: 21. The basic duty was 5 percent ad valorem at Amsterdam; wine, brandy, and vinegar were taxed at 18 florins a cask. There were also provisions to initiate the slave trade officially in 1629.

4. *Laws and Ordinances*, 126, but see also 6, 17, 31, 40, 41, 70, 71, 84, 88, 175, 177, 233, 239, 249–50, 402, 441. And see Joseph Dorfman, *The Economic Mind in American Civilization*, 5 vols. (New York, 1946), vol. 1, ch. 5. For a representative free-trade statement, see *Docs. Rel.*, 3: 233. For early statements about the burdens of duties, see "Gaulter of Twiller . . . to the Governor of New England," Oct. 4, 1633, in *Docs. Rel.* 3: 18–19, and "The Privy Council to the Earl of Portland, Mar. 20, 1634," in ibid.

5. Laurence A. Johnson, *Over the Counter and on the Shelf: Country Storekeeping in America, 1620–1920* (Rutland, Vt., 1961), 22; "Capt. Mason to [?]," in *Docs. Rel.*, 3:17; and Adriaen van der Donck, *Description of the New Netherlands* (1656), ed. Thomas F. O'Donnell (Syracuse, N.Y., 1968), 97.

6. For this and the next paragraph, see "Proposed Articles for the Colonization and Trade of New Netherland," Aug. 1638, in *Docs. Rel.*, 1: 110–15; "Freedoms and Exemptions," 1629, in ibid., 2: 551–57; and "Directors to Stuyvesant," 1646, in ibid., 13: 21.

7. For estimates of entrances and clearances, see *Docs. Rel.*, vols. 1 and 2; see esp. 1: 432. For the many sizes and cargo capacities of vessels, see Charlotte Wilcoxen, "Ships and Work Boats of New Netherland, 1609–1674," in *A Beautiful and Fruitful Place: Selected Rensselaerswijck Seminar Papers*, ed. Nancy Anne McClure Zeller, intro. Charles T. Gehring (Albany, N.Y., 1991), 53–70. For population estimates, see E. B. O'Callaghan, *The History of New Netherland*, 2 vols. (New York, 1845–48), 1: 386. Details about merchants are from *New York Genealogical and Biographical Record* 6 (1875), 10–11; 94 (1963), 193–200; 14 (1883), 181–90; 15 (1883), 34–40, 72–77, and author's biographical compilation. Passenger lists of company-sponsored immigration leave out many middling craftsmen and merchants, so they have not been used.

8. For the number of ships, see *Docs. Rel.*, 1: 265; and for West Indies commodities, ibid., 1: 436–37.

9. *New York Historical Manuscripts: Dutch. Delaware Papers. English Period, 1664–1682*, ed. Charles T. Gehring (Baltimore, 1977). Augustus Heermans, for example, factored for Jean Gabry; Gouverneur Loockermans factored for Gilles Verbrugge at Curaçao and Aruba. Among city merchants in the coastal and Curaçao trade were Nicholas Varlet, Tieleman van Vleck, Nicholas de Sille, P. Tonneman, Johannes Ver Brugge, Cornelis van Ruyven, H. Jansen van der Vin, D. Hans Kiersteede, Gerrit van Tricht, Jacobus Backer, and—on behalf of the company—Pieter Stuyvesant. Most were not involved in trade to Amsterdam. A few city merchants, among them Augustus Heermans, had lived in the West Indies for a while before 1660. Company servants who traded between Curaçao and New Netherland during the 1640s were Sander Liendertsz and Hendrick Hendrickson, and, in the 1650s, were usually Jan Doncker and Johannes de Rasiere; see *The Curaçao Papers*, ed. Charles T. Gehring (Syracuse, N.Y., 1986) and sources cited in n. 8 above.

10. Some thirty merchants in the Virginia trade are listed at *Docs. Rel.*, 1: 437; a list of twenty-one merchants (principally exporters) whose names appeared on 1649 remonstrances against the Dutch Council is given in ibid., 14: 222. For connections mentioned in this paragraph, see "Journal or Log of Two Voyages from New Amsterdam to Holland and return, 1660–1663," Misc. MSS, Ships—Dutch, NYHS; "Certain Reasons" [1662], in *Docs. Rel.*, 3: 43–47; and ibid., 2: 127–63, 3: 42–43, 1: 436–39, 264, 2: 43–44, 230–34, 14: 431; Fernow, *Records*, 2: 169, 338–39, 4: 15, 39, 96, 189, 255, 298, 300, 309, 338; *State Papers, 1661–68*, p. 354; *Laws and Ordinances*, 126; Violet Barbour, *Capitalism in Amsterdam during the Seventeenth Century* (Baltimore, 1950), 93 n. 33.

11. Thomas C. Barrow, *Trade and Empire: The British Customs Service in Colonial America, 1660–1775* (Cambridge, Mass., 1967), 21, 47, and Rink, *Holland on the Hudson*, 257, 94–116.

12. *Docs. Rel.*, 1: 343–44, 425; 13: 6, 13, 35; 14: 484–85, 488; *Narratives of New Netherland, 1609–1664*, ed. J. Franklin Jameson (New York, 1909), 139; and O'Callaghan, *History of New Netherland*, 1: 181, 231, which notes a Mr. Lamberton trading from New Haven regularly. For the quotation, see *Docs. Rel.*, 14: 444.

13. *Docs. Rel.*, 1: 106, 110–15.

14. Ordinance, Apr. 15, 1638, and June 7, 1638, *Laws and Ordinances*, 11–12, 13; and "Eight Men to the Amsterdam Chamber of the West India Company," Oct. 28, 1644, in *Docs. Rel.*, 1: 201–3, 212–13.

15. See *Laws and Ordinances*, 29, 89, 251, and 364 on fairs and markets; and 16–17, 106–7, 112–15, 120, 125, 138–41, 146, 261–62, 307–9, 345, 348–50, and 358–61 on commodity prices; *Dutch MSS*, Apr. 15, 1638, 61, on the partial monopoly; and ibid., Apr. 3, 1642, 79, on duties. In 1645, the United Provinces also began to tax Baltic traders heavily, paralleling England's mercantile legislation in form; see *Docs. Rel.*, 2: 239.

16. "Petition for the Committee of the Commonalty of New Netherland," July 26, 1649; *Docs. Rel.*, 1: 260.

17. *Docs. Rel.*, 1: 259–61, 262–70, 307–18, 422, 425. The Eight Men were Joachim Pietersen, Jan Damen, Barent Dircksen, Abraham Pietersen, Isaac Allerton, Thomas Hall, Gerrit Wolfertson (Long Island), and Conelys Melyn.

18. *Laws and Ordinances*, July 4, 1647, 65–68; *Dutch MSS*, July 4, 23, 1647, 110, 111; Jan. 29, 1648, 115. Duties on peltry rose again in Sept. 1652 (*Council Mins.*, 32–33, 68) and in 1654 (ibid., 158–59, 160–63, and 174–79). As regards price-fixing, which would have limited markups and profits, see ibid., 78, and *Docs. Rel.*, 14: 225–26, on the rates set in 1653. There were no universal standards of value for Dutch coins in the seventeenth century. A guilder (gilder) was equivalent to twenty stuivers, and a piece of eight in New Netherland was equivalent to forty-eight stuivers, or eight reals.

19. On Vastrick's and Stuyvesant's trade to Fort Nassau, see *Delaware Papers*, ed. Gehring, 22–23, 24; and for Stuyvesant's measures, *Laws and Ordinances*, Mar. 10, 1648, and Sept. 18, 1648, 88–89, 101. For protests, see "Petition of the Commonalty," July 26, 1649, in *Docs. Rel.*, 1: 259–61, 262–70, quotation at 262; "Remonstrance . . . to the States General," July 28, 1649, in ibid., 1: 271–318, at 297–304, 307–18, 313–14, 318; "Memorial of Adriaen van der Donck, 1649," in ibid., 1: 438–40; and ibid., Nov. 29, 1650, 1: 422. The "Petition of the Commonalty" was signed by Adriaen van der Donck, Augustyn Heermans, Arnoldus van Hardenberg, Jacob van Couwenhoven, Oloff Stevens van Cortlandt, Michiel (Machyel) Jansen, Thomas Hall, Elbert Elbertsen, Gouvert Loockermans, Hen-

drick Hendricks Kip, and Jan Everts Bout; Van der Donck and Stevens van Cortlandt were not among the city's Nine Men, although the others were. Included among Stuyvesant's supporters from 1646 to 1650 were Jan Jansen van Dam; Jansen's sons-in-law Cornelis Tienhoven and Abraham Planck; Adrien Tienhoven, the brother of Cornelis; Jan Classen van Dam; and Charles van Brugge (*Delaware Papers*, ed. Gehring; *Docs. Rel.*, 1: 436–37; *Curaçao Papers*, ed. Gehring, passim). The new councillors were LeMontaigne, Newton, Tienhoven, Jochen Peitersz, Paulus Leendertsen, William Beekman, Hattern, and Isaac Forreest (*Council Mins.*, 33, 43).

20. *New York Historical Manuscripts: Dutch*, ed. A. J. F. van Laer et al., 4 vols. (Baltimore, 1974), 2: 289, 4: 140, 453–60; William Bradford, *Bradford's History of Plymouth Plantation, 1606–1646*, ed. William T. Davis (New York, 1908), 224–28; James W. Gerard, "The Administration of William Kieft, 1638–1647," in James G. Wilson, *The Memorial History of the City of New York*, 4 vols. (New York, 1893), 1: 228–30; *Narratives*, ed. Jameson, 422–24; and William Weeden, *Economic and Social History of New England, 1620–1789*, 2 vols. (New York, 1963), 1: 124, 279–80.

21. See, e.g., *Delaware Papers*, ed. Gehring, 26, 32, 132, 133; *Council Mins.*, 195; *Laws and Ordinances*, 63, 65, 72, 86, 89, 236–37, 314–15, 507–8; and *The Correspondence of Jeremias van Rensselaer, 1651, 1674*, trans. and ed. A. J. F. van Laer (Albany, N.Y., 1932), 46, 55–58, 77, 84, 91. For open ports in New England, see *Docs. Rel.*, 1: 267.

22. "Remonstrance of the Merchants of New Netherland against the Ordinance Fixing the Rates of Import Duties, Passed on the 19th of November, 1653, to the Director and Council of New Netherland, Nov. 22, 1653," in *Docs. Rel.*, 14: 221–22.

23. Fernow, *Records*, 3: 8–9, 13–15; 7: 225–26.

24. *Laws and Ordinances*, Sept. 4, 1652, Apr. 27, 1656, Aug. 11, 1656, and Apr. 23, 1658, 166, 172, 349–50. And see also ibid., 481, 484, on the reduction of duties to 2½ percent on Oct. 16, 1673. For narrative accounts, see Adriaen van der Donck, "A Dialogue Between A Patriot and a New Netherlander upon the Advantages which the Country Presents to Settlers, etc." (1655), repr. in id., *A Description of the New Netherlands*, ed. Thomas F. O'Donnell (Syracuse, N.Y., 1968), app., 120–33, at 122, 129, 130, 131; and "Representation of New Netherlands [to the Amsterdam directors], 1649," in *Docs. Rel.*, 1: 271–318, esp. 315.

25. *Laws and Ordinances*, Sept. 25, 1647, 75–78, and Jan. 30, 1657, 298–99; "Letter from the Nine Men to the States-General," July 26, 1649, in *Docs. Rel.*, 1: 259–61.

26. Fernow, *Records*, Sept. 23, 1658, 3: 17; "Petition of Certain Dutch Merchants to the States General" [1651], *Docs. Rel.*, 1: 436–37; "Remonstrance of the Merchants of New Netherland against the Ordinance Fixing the Rates of Import Duties, Passed on the 19th of November, 1653," Nov. 22, 1653, in ibid., 14: 221–22; and *Dutch MSS*, Jan. 28, 1653, 134, and Nov. 19, 1653, 310.

27. *Docs. Rel.*, 1: 422–23, 436–37.

28. "Directors to Stuyvesant," Feb. 13, 1659, in *Docs. Rel.*, 14: 431, 432.

29. *Docs. Rel.*, 1: 422, 429; 2: 58.

30. "The Dutch West Indies Company Directors to Stuyvesant," in *Docs. Rel.*, Feb. 13, 1659, Dec. 22, 1659, 14: 429, 431–32 (the quotation), 452; and Fernow, *Records*, 7: 225–26.

31. "Burghers of New Amsterdam to the Directors in Holland," Sept. 23, 1658, in Fernow, *Records*, 3: 17.

32. "Of the Reasons and Causes of the Great Decay of New Netherland," July 28, 1644, in *Docs. Rel.*, 1: 295; "Remonstrance of the Merchants of New Netherland against the

Ordinance Fixing the Rates of Import Duties, Passed on the 19th of November, 1653, To the Director and Council of New Netherland," Nov. 22, 1653, in ibid., 14: 221–22; see also ibid., 251, 431–32; "The Administration of Director Stuyvesant in Particular," 1659, in ibid., 307–13; and Fernow, *Records,* 3: 8–9, 13–15; 7: 225–26. On colonial duties, see *Dutch MSS,* June 12, Aug. 12 and 24, 1657, all at 311; *Laws and Ordinances,* Apr. 16 and 23, 1658, 348, 349–51. Lesser merchants who spoke out against the duties included Jacob Ryntgens, Jacob van Schermerhorn, Joost Theuniss Backer, and Pieter van der Linden.

33. On the individuals in this and the next paragraph, see *Docs. Rel.,* 1: 428, and *Curaçao Papers,* ed. Gehring, passim (for Reynsen); *Wills,* 25: 296 (for De Witt); *Council Mins.* (for Boon and Huck); *Wills,* 25: 42 (for Backer); 1653 petition and *Wills,* 25: 466 (for Nys).

34. *Correspondence of Jeremias van Rensselaer,* trans. and ed. Van Laer, 23; Harold Hancock, "Impressions of Delaware, 1675–1860" (MS), Hagley Museum and Library, Wilmington, Del. The Delaware area was still under Dutch control when Heermans and his family acquired their land. See also the 1653 petition.

35. For a population of about 8,000 in New Amsterdam in 1660, see *Docs. Rel.,* 2: 512; for a lower estimate, see David Valentine, *History of the City of New York* (New York, 1853), 213–14. The population of New Netherland as a whole had reached about 9,000; see Rink, *Holland on the Hudson,* 158, and Michael Kammen, *Colonial New York* (New York, 1975), 38, 44.

36. *Wills,* 25: 21, 30, 31, 59, 60, 191, 242, 356.

37. Ibid., 25: 21, 30, 60, 67, 121, 123.

38. This and the next two paragraphs draw on the author's biographical compilation; "Remonstrance . . . to the States General," July 28, 1649," in *Docs. Rel.,* 1: 313–14, 318; *The Van Rensselaer–Bowier Manuscripts,* trans. and ed. A. J. F. van Laer (Albany, N.Y., 1908), 40–85; "Remonstrance of the Merchants to the Director and Council of New Netherland," Nov. 1653, in *Docs. Rel.,* 14: 221–22; and "List of Inhabitants who Offered Loans [in 1653]," in David Valentine, *History of the City of New York* (New York, 1853), 313–14. By the 1650s, some merchants began to acquire city land, including the Kips, Webbers, Beekmans, Bayards, Van Cortlandts, and De Peysters; but most city merchants did not; see Stokes, *Iconography,* "Original Grants and Farms," 1: 70–76, 86, 88–93, 110–11, 164–65, 170, 4:158.

39. Some of the wealthiest residents of the 1650s were not Dutch but Sephardic Jews; see, e.g., Papers of Samuel Oppenheim (bound MSS), American Jewish Historical Society, New York City; and notations about the twenty-three Jews from Brazil in 1654 in Samuel Oppenheim, "Jews of New York," *Proceedings of the American Jewish Historical Society* 18 (1909): 2; surnames among the new arrivals included Barsimmon, Levy, Dandradi, De Lucena, Cohen, Dacosta, and Frera. For the 1695 assessment, see ch. 2.

40. Middling importers included Robert Vastrick, Reynier Rycke, Jan Withart, William Beekman, Cornelis van der Veer, Jacob de Weert, Jan Appel, Jacob Visch, Facog van Leeuwen, Abraham Nichel, Peter Schaffbanck, Jacob Jacobs, Dirck Claesen Boot, and Hendrick van der Vin. Middling fur (and less frequently, tobacco) exporters included Johannes Withardt, Paulus Leendertsz van der Grift, Hendrick Hendricks, Asser Levy, Asaac de Foreest, Paulus Schrijk, Abraham Delanoy, Barent van Marle, Jacob Steendam, Dirck Dircks, Allard Anthony, Nicholas de Meyer, Johannes van Brugge, Thomas and John Willett, Jan de Krupper, Abraham Staats, Claes Bordingh, Jan Harmens Wintdorp,

Gerrit Hendricks, Symon Janse Romeyn, Gilles van Brugge, Govert Loockermans, Andries de Haas, Johannes Provoost, Hendrick van de Water, Tielman van Vleeck. See sources cited in n. 38 above and "Assessment," Feb. 19, 1674, in *Docs. Rel.*, 1: 699–700.

41. *Delaware Papers*, ed. Gehring, esp. 22–23, 24, 26, 28, 109, 110, 254–56, 326; *Council Mins.*, 45; and Stokes, *Iconography*, 4: 129.

42. *Council Mins.*, 80–81, 114; Fernow, *Records*, Oct. 1655. The council also borrowed from city merchants in Sept. 1652, although it could not repay them and asked merchants to submit bonds for one-half of their loans, payable in one year (*Council Mins.*, 32–33). On the denial to the city of the right to collect taxes on registered vessels (a tonnage or *last* duty) or export duties, "because these duties concern the country in general and not a particular city or place," see *Council Mins.*, Feb. 1654, 213.

43. *Laws and Ordinances*, 298–303.

44. Author's biographical compilation; Fernow, *Records*, 4: 246, 247, 392, 7: 11, for the West Indies; and 5: 282, for whaling.

45. See, e.g., "Deduction Respecting the Differences about Boundaries," Nov. 5, 1660, in *Docs. Rel.*, 2: 155–56. There was little dispute in New Amsterdam over the issue of just price versus market price—certainly nothing like the clash between John Cotton and the defenders of Robert Keayne in early Massachusetts Bay; see Bernard Bailyn, "The *Apologia* of Robert Keayne," *William and Mary Quarterly*, 3d. ser., 7 (1950): 568–77. In New Amsterdam, usury, extortion, counterfeiting, and markups were the points of controversy.

46. See, e.g., *Laws and Ordinances*, Nov. 8, 1649, 111–13, and "Eight Men to the Amsterdam Chamber of the West India Company," Oct. 28, 1644, in *Docs. Rel.*, 1: 212.

47. *Laws and Ordinances*, July 4, 1647, Mar. 10, 1648, Aug. 18, 1653, Aug. 11, 1656, Jan. 3, Aug. 12, Nov. 29, 1657, 65, 72–73, 86–92, 148, 236–38, 292, 314–15, 317–19; *Dutch MSS*, July 4, 1647, 110; Jan. 28, 1653, 134; *Docs. Rel.*, Nov. 19, 1653, 14: 150–51. Amsterdam directors disallowed steep markups on Mar. 12, 1654 (*Docs. Rel.*, 14: 251–52). A list of prices in the 1640s is in O'Callaghan, *History of New Netherland*, 227; cf. prices in the 1650s in *Curaçao Papers*, ed. Gehring, passim. Complaints about high prices, due to both scarcities and high markups, were registered at New Amstel in the 1650s too; see, e.g., *Delaware Papers*, ed. Gehring, 77–78.

48. Van der Donck, *Description*, 40, 63; *Laws and Ordinances*, Nov. 29, 1657, 317–19; Kiliaen van Rensselaer's comments about markups are in *Van Rensselaer–Bowier MSS*, trans. and ed. Van Laer, 325–26.

49. *Laws and Ordinances*, Aug. 18, 1653, 148; *Docs. Rel.*, Nov. 19, 1653, 14: 150–51.

50. *Laws and Ordinances*, 1656, 357–60; *Dutch MSS*, Sept. 27, 1656, 311; Fernow, *Records*, 4: 153, 275, 288; Samuel Maverick, *Letters*, 1662–1665, in NYHS, *Collections*, vol. 3 (New York, 1869), 19–88.

51. *Van Rensselaer–Bowier MSS*, trans. and ed. Van Laer, 324;

52. "Governor Stuyvesant to the West Indies Company," 1660, in *Docs. Rel.*, 14: 470.

53. On devaluation, see John J. McCusker, *Money and Exchange in Europe and America, 1600–1775: A Handbook* (Chapel Hill, N.C., 1978), 157, 157n.; and for quotations, see *Docs. Rel.*, 1: 458–59.

54. The rates were as follows: in 1641, 5 beads per stiver for unpolished wampum, and 4 beads per stiver for polished (*Laws and Ordinances*, Apr. 18, 1641, 26); in 1650, 8 white or 4 black beads per stiver for "poor strung wampum," and 6 white or 3 black beads per

stiver for polished wampum (ibid., May 30, 1650, 115–16); in 1657, 1 white bead per half farthing, and 1 black bead per farthing (ibid., Jan. 3, 1657, 289–92), this latter ordinance being disallowed by company directors on Jan. 9, 1657. In November 1657, a general reduction of all wampum values to the 1650 rate for poor beads was instituted, with the effect of equalizing the value of all beads at poor rates and depressing good wampum (ibid., Nov. 29, 1657, 317–20). In 1662, wampum was further reduced in cases of wage payments to WIC employees, so that it took 16 to 24 white, and 12 black beads per stiver (ibid., Dec. 28, 1662, 433–34); see also ibid., Sept. 27, 1656, 255–57. Oliver Rink argues compellingly that a few Amsterdam merchants with a strong hold over New Netherland's commerce could keep up prices for necessities imported by colonists, which would have compounded their miseries respecting wampum and beaver (Rink, *Holland on the Hudson*, 210–11, 265).

55. "Governor Stuyvesant to the West Indies Company," 1660, in *Docs. Rel.*, 14: 470; and ibid, 1: 458–59.

56. The four millers serving New Amsterdammers over much of the 1640s to 1660s were Abraham Pietersen, Johannes de Witt, Adam Brower, and Hendrick Williams. John Robinson entered the city at the close of the Dutch period and stayed through the 1680s at least; he was the only miller/baker also to become an exporter before 1680; see Condon, *New York Beginnings*, 145–50, and Rink, *Holland on the Hudson*, 179, 183–84.

TWO   Where Returns Were the Richest

1. See Introduction, n. 1. Of course, discussions about international trade went hand in hand with those about labor, manufacturing, internal improvements, and relations between country and city; some "free traders" were manufacturers in their later careers. However, it is outside the scope of the present study to integrate these other issues, which are raised only cursorily in this chapter and to a greater extent in chapters 4 and 7. For the term *mercantilism*, see Adam Smith, *An Inquiry into the Nature and Causes of the Wealth of Nations*, ed. Edwin Cannan (1776; repr., Chicago, 1976), bk. 4, ch. 1, 412.

2. In general, see Charles Wilson, *England's Apprenticeship, 1603–1763* (London, 1965), 36–52; Barry Supple, *Commercial Crisis and Change in England, 1600–1642* (Cambridge, 1959), intro; *Revisions in Mercantilism*, ed. D. C. Coleman (London, 1969), ch. 3; E. Anthony Wrigley, "Urban Growth and Agricultural Change: England and the Continent in the Early Modern Period," *Journal of Interdisciplinary History* 15 (1984–85): 683–728; Keith Wrightson, *English Society, 1580–1680* (London, 1982); and Joanna Innes, "Jonathan Clark, Social History, and England's 'Ancien Régime,'" *Past and Present* 115 (May 1987): 165–200. On the West Indies, see, e.g., Gerard de Malynes, *Consuetudo, vel lex mercatoria*, 2d ed. (London, 1686), 144; Dalby Thomas, *An Historical Account of the Rise and Growth of the West India Colonies* (1690), repr., *Harleian Miscellany*, 12 vols. (London, 1808), 9: 414; John Cary, *An Essay on the State of England in Relation to its Trade* (Bristol, 1695), 124; "Answer of Charles Whe[e]ler, Governor of the Leeward Islands, to the inquiries of the Council for Foreign Plantations," Dec. 9, 1671, in *State Papers, 1669–74*, 7: 290; "Petition of the inhabitants of Antigua to Governor Lord Willoughby," in ibid., 1661–68, 5: 234; "Petition of the President, Council, and Assembly of Barbados," in ibid., 1661–68, 5: 29–30; "Petition of the President and Council of Barbados to the King, July 10," in ibid., 1661–68, 5: 46; "Lord Willoughby to the King," Jan. 11, Nov. 4, 1663, in ibid.,

1661–68, 5: 162, 167–68; "Propositions of Mr. Kendall, November 1664," in ibid., 1661–68, 5: 253; "An Account of His Majesty's Island of Barbados and the Government thereof, 1676," in ibid., 1675–76, 9: 348–49, and "Additional Instructions to Thomas Lord Windsor, Governor of Jamaica, April 8, 1662," in ibid., 1661–68, 5: 85. Lord Willoughby, the governor of Barbados, claimed in 1666 that "Free Trade is the life of all Colonies" and said that to regulate it as the Navigation Acts did was to invite disaster (quoted by H. E. Egerton, *A Short History of British Colonial Politics,* 5th ed. [London, 1918], 76). Following the second Anglo-Dutch war, many English writers promoted a "Free Trade" with the Dutch of Curaçao; see, e.g., Lewes Roberts, *The Merchant's Mappe of Commerce* (London, 1638), 120. Throughout the eighteenth century, some writers emphasized the desirability of freer trade in the Caribbean, with reference to Dutch successes there; see, e.g., the writings of Jonathan Swift, Daniel Defoe, Josiah Tucker, and Adam Smith. The original free-trade strain *in* the Caribbean had become a clamor for regulation by 1713, and mercantilism was dominant thereafter; see Klauss Knorr, *British Colonial Theories, 1570–1850* (Toronto, 1944), and Eric Williams, *Columbus to Castro* (New York, 1986), 529.

   3. See the works cited in Introduction, n. 9.

   4. Hugo Grotius, *The Freedom of the Seas, or the Right Which Belongs to the Dutch to Take Part in the East Indies Trade* (1608), trans. and ed. R. van Derman Magoffin (New York, 1916), 30, 36.

   5. Pieter de la Court, *The True Interest and Political Maxims of the Republic of Holland and West Friesland* (written 1662–68; publ. London, 1702), esp. 72–73, 86, 154, 239, 367, 487–88; and, on De Witt, Simon Schama, *The Embarrassment of Riches: An Interpretation of Dutch Culture in the Golden Age* (New York, 1987), 233–57. For discussion of Grotius and De la Court, see Charles Wilson, *The Dutch Republic* (New York, 1968), 51–69.

   6. See the works cited in Introduction, n. 9; and Sir Walter Ralegh, *Observations Touching Trade and Commerce with the Hollander* (London, 1610), 6, 7, 8, 10; Carew Reynel, *The True English Benefit* (London, 1674), 1: 14–15. On Dutch loans from the firms of Machado and Pereira, see *Calendar of State Papers, Foreign Series,* 1587, ed. S. C. Lomas (London, 1929), 427; ibid., July–Dec. 1588, ed. R. B. Wernham (London, 1936), 253, 390; ibid., 1586–87 (London, 1921), 184–85; *Calendar of State Papers, Domestic Series,* 1591–94, ed. M. A. and E. Green (London, 1867), 115, 574; ibid., 1595–97 (London, 1869), 414, 534; ibid., 1644, ed. W. D. Hamilton (London, 1888), 190–435; ibid., 1644–45 (London, 1890), 188; ibid., 1655–56, ed. M. A. and E. Green (London, 1882), 151; Sir William Temple, *Observations upon the United Provinces of the Netherlands* (1673; repr., Cambridge, 1932), 133. On Dutch insurance for enemy English vessels and sales of munitions to the English beginning in 1600, and coming largely from the De Geer, Girard, and Trip families in Amsterdam, see *Cal. State Papers, Domestic,* 1598–1602, and 1619–23, ed. M. A. and E. Green (London, 1858); ibid., 1638–39, ed. Bruce and W. D. Hamilton (London, 1871); ibid., 1639 (London, 1873), 98; ibid., 1644, ed. W. D. Hamilton (London, 1890), 366–67, 387, 466, 480; ibid., 1645–47 (London, 1891), 23, 66. On gunpowder trade to England, see William Carr, *A Description of Holland* (London, 1701), 17; [Anon.], *A Description of Holland; or, the Present State of the United Provinces* (London, 1743), 236. Merchants like the De Pintos, Medinas, Pereiras, Janssens, Da Costas, and others supported English provisioners in King William's War, and bailed out the Bank of England in 1695–97; see Charles Wilson, *Anglo-Dutch Commerce and Finance in the Eighteenth Century,* 2d ed. (London, 1966), 92–95. On Dutch skills, see Carl Bridenbaugh, *Vexed and Troubled Englishmen,*

1590–1642 (NewYork, 1968), 171; C. M. Andrews, *The Colonial Period of American History: England's Commercial and Colonial Policy,* 4 vols. (New Haven, Conn., 1938), 4: 25 n. 2, 24–31, 131, 133; Roberts, *Merchant's Mappe,* 256; Andrew Yarranton, *England's Improvement by Sea and Land* (London, 1677), 7, 141; *Defoe's Review,* 22 vols. (2d ed., Facs. Text Society, New York, 1938), 6: 23, 149; Roger Coke, *A Discourse of Trade* (London, 1670), 62–63; John Collins, *A Plea for the bringing in of Irish Cattle* (London, 1680), 21; Edward Misselden, *The Circle of Commerce* (London, 1623), 135; Reynel, *True English Interest,* 10–11; and [Anon.], *A Discourse . . . For the Enlargement and Freedom of Trade* (London, 1645), 22. On Dutch frugality, see Temple, *Observations,* 132; and Charles Davenant, *Discourses on Public Revenue,* in *The Political and Commercial Works of that Celebrated Writer Charles D'Avenant,* ed. Sir Charles Whitworth, 5 vols. (1697; repr., London, 1771), 2: 390–91. On liberal Dutch credit, see Roberts, *Merchants' Mappe,* 120. On Dutch prices, see *Docs. Rel.,* 8: 480; and Charles Wolley, *A Two Years' Journal in New York and Part of its Territories in America* (1701), ed. Edward G. Bourne (Cleveland, 1902), 29–30. For admiration of Dutch carrying trades and economies of scale, see Lewes Roberts, *Treasure of Traffic,* in *A Select Collection of Early English Tracts on Commerce,* ed. J. R. McCulloch (London, 1856), 209, 89; Nicholas Barbon, *A Discourse of Trade* (London, 1690), Reprints of Economic Tracts, ed. J. H. Hollander, 2d ser., no. 1 (Baltimore, 1905), 35, 38, 123; Temple, *Observations;* and Roger Coke, *England's Improvements* (London, 1675), 56, 82, 93, 97. Edmund Morgan, "The Puritan Ethic and the American Revolution," *William and Mary Quarterly* 24 (1967): 3–18, draws attention to the mixed beliefs of the English: admiration for aspects of Dutch culture and skill and scorn for their avarice, materialism, and unrestrained ambition. The apparent contradiction is resolved if we keep in mind that different writers started out with different goals for English commerce; optimists promoting new colonies and enterprise abroad found solace in Dutch success, while protectionist interests tried to build yet another wall to discourage the Dutch from influencing English national development.

   7. Wilson, *Anglo-Dutch Commerce,* 51–56; and David MacPherson, *Annals of Commerce, Manufactures, Fisheries, and Navigation,* 4 vols. (London, 1805), 3: 318, 302, 515. For the individuals named here, see Sir William Petty, *Political Arithmetick,* in *The Economic Writings of Sir William Petty,* ed. Charles Hull, 2 vols. (Cambridge, 1899), 2: 259–61; Gerard Malynes, *The Maintenance of Free Trade* (1622; repr. New York, 1971); [Matthew Decker], *An Essay on the Causes of the Decline of the Foreign Trade* (London, 1755), 14, 15, 26, 104, 106; and John Pollexfen, *A Discourse of Trade, Coyn, and Paper Credit* (London, 1697), 147–49. For another theory of freedom, one that most Englishmen rejected, see Stuart Hampshire, "Spinoza and the Idea of Freedom," in *Spinoza: A Collection of Critical Essays,* ed. Marjorie Greene (Garden City, N.Y., 1973), 297–317. For pamphlets favoring free trade as the Dutch were understood to practice it, see "S.E.," *The Touch-Stone of Money and Commerce* (London, n.d.), which argues for free out ports; [Anon.], *The Present Interest of England, Stated* (London, 1671), which calls for Anglo-Dutch trade reciprocity; Thomas Johnson, *A Plea for Free-mens Liberties* (London, 1648); [Anon.], *A Discourse, consisting of Motives for the Enlargement and Freedom of Trade* (London, 1645); Thomas, *Historical Account of the Rise and Growth of the West India Colonies,* 32, 48–49, which calls for free trade in sugar; and Coke, *Discourse of Trade,* 24–41, which says free trade is England's only weapon against the Dutch, mainly because it would bring down costs of ships, transportation, insurance, and even commodities; Coke allowed that the

colonies ought to have free trade in some fashion. "Trade is in its nature free, finds its own channel and best directeth its own course; and all laws to give it rules and directions, and to limit and circumscribe it, may serve the particular ends of private men, but are seldom advantageous to the public," Charles Davenant said (*An Essay on the East-India Trade* [London, 1697], in *Works*, ed. Whitworth, 1: 98; see also 95).

8. See Josiah Child, *A New Discourse of Trade* (London, 1693), and John Cary, *An Essay on the State of England in Relation to its Trade* (London, 1695), 123–24.

9. See, e.g., [Anon.], *A Discourse consisting of Motives for the Enlargement of Freedom of Trade* (London, 1645), and sources cited in n. 2 above.

10. In *The Century of Revolution, 1603–1714* (New York, 1966), 41, Christopher Hill notes a 6–7 percent rate in Holland and 10 percent in England for 1600–1620; in *Capitalism in Amsterdam during the Seventeenth Century* (Baltimore, 1950), 85, Violet Barbour cites 3 percent and 6 percent by the end of the 1660s. See also William Goffe, "How to Advance the Trade of the Nation, and to employ the poor" (n.d., n.p.), repr. in *Harleian Miscellany*, 12: 251; [Anon.], *Britannia Languens* (London, 1680), 48; Malynes, *Maintenance of Free Trade*; John Bland, "Memorial of 1660," *Virginia Magazine of History and Biography* 1 (1893–94): 141–55; and [Anon.], "An Essay towards carrying on the Present War Against France, and other Publick Occasions" (London, n.d. [1698?]), repr. in *Harleian Miscellany*, 10: 371–89. There was a fierce dialogue in England at midcentury centered on interest rates and wages and whether government should regulate either; only in the next century would some mercantilists support higher wages and free interest rates, although they retained a firm belief in controlling commercial markets; see chapter 5.

11. Sir Dudley North, *Discourses upon Trade* (1691; repr., Baltimore, 1907), ed. Jacob H. Hollander, 11–15; Barbon, *Discourse on Trade*; and Jacob Vanderlint, *Money Answers all Things; or, An Essay to Make Money Sufficiently Plentiful amongst All Ranks of People* (1734; repr., Baltimore, 1914), 543. See also Thomas Mun, *England's Treasure by Forraign Trade*, in *Select Collection of Early English Tracts*, ed. McCulloch, 115–209; Misselden, *Circle of Commerce*, 11, 12.

12. Thomas, *Historical Account*, repr. in *Harleian Miscellany*, 9: 438; and John Oldmixon, *The British Empire in America*, 2 vols. (London, 1708).

13. Charles Davenant, *Discourses on Public Revenue*, in *Works*, ed. Whitworth, 2: 390–91.

14. [Decker], *Essay on the Causes*, 14, 15, 26, 104, 106.

15. For this paragraph and the next one, see sources cited in Introduction, n. 4; and William de Britaine, "The Dutch Usurpation, or, A Brief View of the Behaviour of the States-General of the United Provinces, Towards the Kings of Great Britain" (1672), repr. in *Harleian Miscellany*, 7: 521–44; Bridenbaugh, *Vexed and Troubled Englishmen*, 18; Andrews, *Colonial Period*, 4: 48, 136; Wilson, *Dutch Republic*, 29–32; John Wheeler, *A Treatise of Commerce*, ed. G. B. Hotchkiss (1601; repr., New York, 1937), 37; and Ephraim Lipson, *The Economic History of England*, 3 vols. (London, 1929–31), 3: 74, 78, 90; "G.W.," "A Letter to a Country Gentleman, Setting Forth the Cause of the Decay and Ruin of Trade" (London, 1698), and [Anon.], "Elegy on the Death of Trade" (London, 1698), both repr. in *Harleian Miscellany*, 10: 361–71 and 351–59; Ralph Maddison, *Great Britain's Remembrancer* (London, 1665); [Anon.], *The Uses and Abuses of Money and the Improvements of It* (London, 1671); Henry Stubbe, *A Justification of the Present War against the United*

346   *Notes to Pages 44–45*

Netherlands (London, 1672); Sir Francis Brewster, *Essay on Trade* (London, 1695); and [Anon.], *The Naked Truth in an Essay on Trade* (London, 1696); Benjamin Worsley, *The Advocate* (London, 1651), 3–4; John Selden, *Of Dominion; or, Ownership of the Sea* (1652; repr., New York, 1972); and [Anon.], *A True and Exact Character of the Low Countreys* (London, 1652). Temple is quoted from *Observations*, 148–49, 208.

16. In addition to n. 2 above, see Temple, *Observations*, 148–49; Mun, *England's Treasure*, 81; Child, *New Discourse*, 22–23; Thomas, *Historical Account*; and Cary, *Essay on Trade*, 69.

17. See sources cited in Introduction, nn. 1 and 7. And on legislation before 1651, see Carole Shammas, "English Commercial Development and American Colonization, 1560–1620," in *The Westward Enterprise*, ed. K. R. Andrews et al. (Liverpool, 1978), 178, 186–87. Major Navigation Acts were passed in 1651, 1660, 1663, and 1673; see 12 Car. 2, c. 18, 1660; 15 Car. 2, c. 7, esp. sec. 6, 1663; Oliver Dickerson, *The Navigation Acts and the American Revolution* (New York, 1951), 7–10; and Andrews, *Colonial Period*, 4: 61–63, 77–82, 85–117, 119–22.

18. J. A. W. Gunn, *Politics and the Public Interest in the Seventeenth Century* (London, 1969), esp. chs. 3, 5, 6; Albert O. Hirschman, *The Passions and the Interests: Political Arguments for Capitalism before Its Triumph* (Princeton, N.J., 1977), pt. 1; William Letwin, *The Origin of Scientific Economics* (Garden City, N.Y., 1964), ch. 3; Wilson, *England's Apprenticeship*, chs. 6, 11; Charles Davenant, *An Essay upon the Probable Methods of Making a People Gainers in the Ballance of Trade* (London, 1699), 16–33; G. N. Clark, *Guide to English Commercial Statistics, 1696–1782* (London, 1938), intro. and 33–42; and Petty, *Political Arithmetick*.

19. In *Navigation Acts*, ch. 2, Oliver Dickerson concludes that mercantilism's benefits outweighed its costs to colonists, whereas Lawrence Harper emphasizes the costs to colonies and England's repressive intentions in *The English Navigation Laws: A Seventeenth-Century Experiment in Social Engineering* (New York, 1939). And see also Gary Walton, "The New Economic History and the Burdens of the Navigation Acts," *Economic History Review*, 2d ser., 24 (1971): 533–42; Robert Thomas, "A Quantitative Approach to the Study of the Effects of British Imperial Policy on Colonial Welfare," *Journal of Economic History* 25 (Dec. 1965): 625–38; Peter McClelland, "The Cost to America of British Imperial Policy," *American Economic Review* 59 (May 1969): 370–81; and Curtis Nettels, "British Mercantilism and the Economic Development of the Thirteen Colonies," *Journal of Economic History* 12 (Spring 1952): 105–14.

20. 10 Will. 3, c. 10, sec. 19. The Woolen Act did not stifle production and overland transport. Curiously, merchants on both sides of the Atlantic avoided discussion of the early Corn Laws as they affected New York's wheat and flour exports. The first time this legislation received serious treatment was in Smith's *Wealth of Nations*, bk. 2, ch. 5, where those laws are thoroughly criticized as injurious to the consumer and small producer.

21. P. G. M. Dickson, *The Financial Revolution in England, 1688–1756: A Study in the Development of Public Credit* (London, 1967), chs. 1–2, and pp. 294–96, 330–31; Keith Horsefield, *British Monetary Experiments, 1650–1710* (London, 1960); B. L. Anderson, "Provincial Aspects of the Financial Revolution of the Eighteenth Century," *Business History* 11 (1969): 12–20; Keith Tribe, *Land, Labor, and Economic Discourse* (London, 1978), 80–109; E. J. Gaines, "Merchant and Poet: A Study of Seventeenth-Century In-

fluences" (Ph.D. diss., Columbia University, 1953); and Daniel Defoe, *The Villany of Stock-Jobbers, Detected* (London, 1701).

22. Petty, *Political Arithmetick*, 239–40, 244. Albemarle is quoted by Andrews, *Colonial Period* 4: 61. See also Thomas Lydall, *Vulgar and Decimal Arithmetick, Demonstrated* (London, 1710); *Docs. Rel.*, 3: 43, 44–46; and *State Papers*, 1661–68, 5: 357.

23. See, e.g., "J.B.," *The Interest of Great Britain Considered ... proving ... that the Balance of Power ... is the Balance of Trade* (London, 1707); Davenant, *Essay on the Probable Methods*; Andrew Yaranton, *England's Improvement By Sea and Land* (London, 1677), 29; Richard Gouldsmith, *Some Considerations of Trade and Manufactures* (London, 1725); Richard Badcour, *Considerations Offered to all Corporations in England* (London, 1722); Pollexfen, *Discourse of Trade*; Cary, *Discourse of Trade*; Samuel Fortrey, *England's Interest* (London, 1663); and for extending credit and lowering export duties, [Anon.], *Essays on the National Constitution, Bank, Credit and Trade* (London, 1717).

24. See, e.g., Petty, *Political Arithmetick*, 259–60; Misselden, *Circle of Commerce*; and Mun, *England's Treasure*, 125. Davenant is quoted from *Essay on the Probable Methods*. Bacon is quoted from "Of Seditions and Troubles," in *Francis Bacon: A Selection of His Works*, ed. Sidney Warhaft (New York, 1965), 83. Also see William Loundes, *A Report Containing an Essay ... of the Silver Coins* (London, 1695), 42–45; and Roberts, *Treasure of Traffic*.

25. Temple, *Observations*, 185–90; Davenant, *Essay on the Probable Methods*, 45–46; Misselden, *Circle of Commerce*, 135; Gouldsmith, *Some Considerations*, 121; and John Houghton, *A Collection of Letters for the Improvement of Husbandry and Trade* (London, 1681). Joyce Appleby's discussion of this period in England has influenced my thinking; however, she proposes that after its heyday from the 1620s to 1690s, the balance-of-trade theory was weakened, and that as an ideological tool, it "had long been moribund" by the time of the American Revolution; this seems to exaggerate its demise, and I accord it an important place in chapters 5 and 8; see Appleby's thought-provoking explanation in *Economic Thought*, ch. 9. Another view is given in Wilson, *England's Apprenticeship*, 229–331, and his "Treasure and Trade Balances," *Economic History Review*, 2d ser., 2 (1949).

26. Ralegh, *Observations Touching Trade*, 6; John Dryden, "Annus Mirabilis: The Year of Wonders, 1666," in *The Poems and Fables of John Dryden*, ed. James Kingsley (Oxford, 1978), 169; Thomas Merchant, *Peace and Trade, War and Taxes or the Irreparable Damage of New Trade in Case of War* (London, 1729); Worsley, *Advocate*, 1–4; John Locke, *Second Treatise of Government*, in *Two Treatises of Government*, ed. Peter Laslett (1689; repr., Cambridge, Mass., 1966), secs. 36, 37, 46, 47.

27. The quotation is from [Anon.], *Some Considerations on the Late Mismanagement of the South Sea Stock* (London, 1721), 12. Pollexfen, *Discourse of Trade and Coyn*; Davenant, *Essay on the East India Trade*, 27–28; Child, *New Discourse*, 55–79; Petty, *Political Arithmetick*; Mun, *England's Treasure*, 190; Defoe, *Some Thoughts on the Subject of Commerce* (London, 1713); Charles Wilson, *Profit and Power: A Study of England and the Dutch Wars* (London, 1958), ch. 7; and Ralph Davis, *The Rise of the English Shipping Industry* (Trowbridge, Eng., 1962), 10, 20, 23, 49.

28. Statement of Martin Bladen to the Board of Trade, 1726, as quoted by Andrews, *Colonial Period*, 4: 106; [Anon.], *The Irregular and Disorderly State of the Plantation-Trade* (London, n.d.), repr. in *Annual Report of the American Historical Association for the Year 1892* (Washington, D.C., 1893), 37. In general, see Wilson, *England's Apprenticeship*,

chs. 4, 14; Peter Mathias, *The First Industrial Nation: An Economic History of Britain, 1700–1914* (New York, 1969), ch. 5. Thomas Barrow, *Trade and Empire: The British Customs Service in Colonial America, 1660–1775* (Cambridge, Mass., 1967), 59, finds that the act of 1696 systematically subordinated colonial commerce to England's need: "In no instance did the machinery of enforcement evolved depend on colonial participation . . . In all its varied aspects the Act of 1696 centered authority on London."

29. See Osgood, *Mins. Common Council,* 2: 1567–68, and 12 Car. 2, c. 19, sec. 18. And see also 9 Will. 3, c. 23, secs. 8, 9, for a drawback on sugar sent to England for refining.

30. For a description of the city, see Daniel Denton, *A Brief Description of New York* (1670; repr., Cleveland, 1902), 3–4. For a population estimate of the early Dutch years, see *Docs. Rel.,* 4: 420. For city population in 1660 and 1680, see David Valentine, *History of the City of New York* (New York, 1853), 213–14; for city population in 1698, see *Docs. Rel.,* 1: 467. For a provincial population estimate, see Michael Kammen, *Colonial New York* (New York, 1975), 38; and for a lower estimate of 8,000 in 1667, see the statement of Dutch merchants at *Docs. Rel.,* 2: 511. For Massachusetts in the 1660s, see Kammen, *Colonial New York,* 38.

31. "Answers of Governor Andros to Enquires about New Yorke," Apr. 1678, in *Docs. Rel.,* 3: 260–62; "Dongan to the Lords of Trade," Feb. 22, 1687, in *Docs. Rel.,* 3: 398; "Bellomont to the Lords of Trade," Apr., 1700, in *Docs. Rel.,* 4: 790, 791. There were fewer large ships in 1700 because of French privateering during King William's War. It is impossible to know how many vessels were built in New York and how many New Yorkers purchased from New Jersey and Boston.

32. *Docs. Rel.,* 3: 164–65; 2: 251–52, 283–97, 581–82, 602–16, 617–23. On the freezing of WIC assets, see "New York Colonial Records, General Entries, 1664–1665," *New York State Library Bulletin,* no. 2 (Albany, N.Y., 1899), 122–23, 133–43, 148–49, 183–85. Simultaneously, the crown sent Nicolls private instructions to secure "entyre submission and obedience" from Long Islanders, so "that the Dutch may noe longer ingrosse" trade, "which they have wrongfully possessed themselves of" ("Private Instructions to Coll. R. Nicolls," Apr. 23, 1664, in *Docs. Rel.,* 3: 70–74).

33. Fernow, *Records,* 5: 160–61, and *Docs. Rel.,* 3: 163–64, 164–65.

34. "Nicolls to Lord Arlington," Apr. 9, 1666, in *Docs. Rel.,* 3: 13–15; for the Dutch merchants' statement of 1667, see *Docs. Rel.,* 2: 511–14; and on New Jersey, "Gabriel Minvielle to Sir John Werden," Mar. 1685, in *Docs. Rel.,* 3: 361.

35. Osgood, *Mins. Common Council,* 1: 39, 40, 142; 2: 513, 398–99. Linen, hats, fine textiles, and bottled beer were New York's most usual "European goods."

36. *Docs. Rel.,* 3: 175–76, 177–78, 185, 2: 651; Palsits, *Mins.,* 1: 39–40, 56–57, 64, 113, 171, 194–95, and *Colonial Laws,* 1: 24–25, 111–16, 116–21, 121–23, 125–28, 137–41. Other New Yorkers who traded with the Dutch in the 1670s included Thomas Lovelace, Johannes de Peyster, Cornelis Steenwyck, Oloff Stevens van Cortlandt, Jacques Cousseau, Nicholas de Meyer, Frederick and Margareta Philipse, Cornelius van Ruyven, Thomas Delaval, and Johannes van Brugh. On "Boston invaders," see "Mr. Maverick to Col. Nicolls," July 5, 1669, in *Docs. Rel.,* 3: 182–83. On Dutch fears that English merchants would take over the tobacco trade with the southern colonies, see *Docs. Rel.,* 2: 230–34. On Dutch merchants from New York City who petitioned for a special voyage from Amsterdam, see *Docs. Rel.,* 3: 178–79. On continued requests for "free trade" from Amsterdam in cheap blankets

"worse than a sort called wadmoll," in about 1668, see Common Council petition in *Docs. Rel.*, 3: 187.

37. On the grant of three ships per year in 1667 and Stuyvesant's reasons, see *Docs. Rel.*, 3: 113–15, 163–64, 164–65, 165–66, 175–78, and Minutes of the Committee of Plantations, Oct. 17, 1667, in *State Papers, 1661–68*, 5: 511. *Docs. Rel.*, 3: 177–78, records that on Nov. 18, 1668, this privilege was revoked. On trade between Amsterdam and New York, see ibid., 2: 541–42; 3: 178–82; Osgood, *Mins. Common Council*, 1: 39, 40, 142; 2: 513, 398–99; and *Colonial Laws*, 1: 165–67, 170–71, 248, 287, 315–21, 322, 325, 403–4, 419.

38. Cathy Matson, "Commerce after the Conquest: Dutch Traders and Goods in New York City, 1664–1764," *De Halve Maen* 59 (Mar. 1987), pt. 1, 8–12; *Docs. Rel.*, 1: 263, 2: 155–56, 526, 539–42, 643, 734, 739–40, 3: 329; *State Papers*, 1697–98, 16: 456–59.

39. "Assessment of the best and most affluent inhabitants," Mar. 17, 1674, in *Docs. Rel.*, 2: 699–700; "New York Colonial Records, General Entries, 1664–1665," *New York State Library Bulletin*, no. 2 (Albany, N.Y., 1899), 122–23, 133–43, 148–49, 183–85; Lawrence Leder, *Robert R. Livingston, 1654–1728, and the Politics of Colonial New York* (Williamsburg, Va., 1961), 24, 37–38; *Ecclesiastical Records, State of New York*, ed. Hugh Hastings, 7 vols. (Albany, N.Y., 1901–16), 1: 641–43; Jasper Danckaerts, *Journal of a Voyage to New York and a Tour in Several of the American Colonies in 1679–1680*, ed. Henry C. Murphy (Brooklyn, N.Y., 1867), 353; *Wills*, 1: 203, 369–74; 2: 414; "Robert Livingston to William Blathwayt," in *Docs. Rel.*, 3: 846; also ibid., 4: 29, 33, 159, 172, 183; reports on the *Rebecca* and the *Blossom*, Dec. 1677 and Apr. 1683, in Records of the Exchequer (E), Public Record Office, London, E: 190: 644/2, 117/1, and, on unnamed New York vessels, 841/3. Many Jews who had arrived in the 1650s had died by the 1670s and 1680s leaving significant fortunes, although not usually the city's greatest ones; for example, Asser Levy died in 1682 worth some 57,000 guilders (*Wills Liber* [Albany, N.Y., 1913], 33–45). Some of the comfortable, rising traders of Dutch heritage in the 1680s included Johannes van Brugh, Johannes de Peyster, Nicholas Bayard, Eagidius Luyck, William Beekman, Jacob Kip, Antonio de Mill, Abraham and Samuel Staats, David Provoost, Nicholas Roosevelt, Benjamin Aske, Gabriel Minuit, and the merchants Thong, De Reimer, Sweeten, and Rombouts.

40. "Assessment of the best and most affluent inhabitants," in *Docs. Rel.*, 2: 699–700; Samuel Maverick, *Letters, 1662–1665*, in NYHS, *Collections*, vol. 3 (New York, 1869); *Docs. Rel.*, 2: 685, 697, 724–25; 3: 164–67, 175–79; Rink, *Holland on the Hudson*, 188–90, 202–6; and author's biographical compilation. As with all tax assessments, certain personal wealth was not counted at all, including smuggled items, outstanding debts and credits, and foreign-based assets—and many items would have been underrated. The nineteen top merchants were, in descending order of their assessments, Frederick Philipse, Cornelis Steenwyck, Nicholas de Meyer, Oloff Stevens van Cortlandt, Jacques Cousseau, Nicolas de Meyer, Margareta Philipse, Francis Hooghlandt, Michel Muyden, Jeronimus Ebbingh, Cornelis van Ruyven, Jacob Leisler, Johannes de Peyster, Johannis van Brugh, Matthew de Hart, Gabriel Minvielle, Nicholas Bayard, and Jan Lawrence. Below this layer there was a second one of about twenty city merchants who had begun what would prove to be prosperous careers over the next two decades, and another thirty-seven or so who would remain comfortable for five to ten years; the remaining forty-three in the assessment were probably of middling wealth at the peaks of their careers. Also compare these findings to the 1653 assessment discussed in chapter 1. Analyzing a 1677 assessment with regard to ethnic change, Thomas Archdeacon, *New York City, 1664–1710: Conquest*

and Change (Ithaca, N.Y., 1976), ch. 1, found roughly equal proportions of Dutch and English householders in all quartiles of wealth. But he did not set out to look at merchants as a class or occupational group represented within ethnic categories for that assessment, although he generalizes that most of the wealthiest families in the city were Dutch. Not surprisingly, he found that 79.3 percent of the households whose ethnicity he could identify were Dutch, 18.5 percent English, and 2.2 percent French and Jewish. For accounts of Dutch New Yorkers recovering some of their trade carrying tobacco from the Caribbean during the 1680s–90s, see Vertrees J. Wyckoff, *Tobacco Regulation in Colonial Maryland* (Baltimore, 1936), 45, 53–54, 76, 116; Thomas, *Historical Account*, 425; Eugene Sheridan, *Sugar and Slavery: An Economic History of the British West Indies* (Baltimore, 1974), 45–48; Barbour, *Capitalism in Amsterdam*, 93–94; Bloch, *HMR*; and Archdeacon, *Conquest and Change*, 48–50.

41. Author's biographical compilation; Curtis Nettels, "Economic Relations of Boston, Philadelphia, and New York, 1680–1715," *Journal of Economic and Business History* 3 (1931): 185–215; Bloch, *HMR*, intro.; "Sir John Werden to Gov. Andros," Sept. 15, 1675, in *Docs. Rel.*, 3: 232–33; Osgood, *Mins. Common Council*. On ethnicity, see Joyce D. Goodfriend, *Before the Melting Pot: Society and Culture in Colonial New York City, 1664–1730* (Princeton, N.J., 1992).

42. *The Correspondence of Jeremias van Rensselaer, 1651–1674*, trans. and ed. A. J. F. van Laer (Albany, N.Y., 1932), 376, 388, 390–91, 408, 412–13, 466–72; Bloch, *HMR*, intro.; C.O. 5: 1051, Bb98; author's biographical compilation; and Robert R. Livingston, "Freight List of the Brigantine *Robert*, Dec. 3, 1694," Livingston-Redmund MSS, NYHS. See also *Early Records of the City and Country of Albany and Colony of Rensselaerswyck: Deeds, 1678–1704*, trans. and ed. Jonathan Pearson and A. J. F. van Laer (Albany, N.Y., 1916), 324, for mention of "free trade" to Amsterdam in 1687 and the export "monopoly" of New York City's "great merchants," Cornelius Cuyler, Stephen De Lancey, and Frederick Philipse. Cargo tonnage amounts are difficult to ascertain with much accuracy for long periods of time, and vessel registrations were so falsified as to make discussion of ship capacity unfeasible; see Clark, *Guide to English Commercial Statistics*, intro; and John McCusker, "The Tonnage of Ships Engaged in British Colonial Trade during the Eighteenth Century," *Research in Economic History* 6 (1981): 73–105, esp. 90–91. "Tonnage" was a measure of a vessel's capacity, not its actual cargo sizes; it was determined by a formula (the length of the keel times the breadth of the ship, times one-half the breadth, divided by 94) and fixed at registration for the life of the vessel. Tonnage measurements became the basis for port fees and, on occasion, particular duties. However, the registered tonnage entered in port books was, according to McCusker's calculations, underestimated by about 50 percent below the actual tonnage capacity. The reason, of course, was to escape full payment of port duties. Also, fraudulent underestimation was even greater when the *cargo* loaded onto the vessel became the basis for tonnage duty payments; "cargo tonnage" was often estimated at about 100 percent less than the actual cargo until at least the 1780s, McCusker says. Merchants, that is, often loaded at least twice as much on vessels as they declared. For these reasons, we shall never know what ships really carried, and I have not frequently used tonnage figures. For a few colonial calculations, see *Docs. Rel.*, 5: 601, 608; 6: 511; 8: 446; and for vessel tonnage registered at the port, with missing quarters, see C.O. 5: 1222–28. Smuggling presents another set of problems, discussed later in this chapter. On London merchants in 1699, see *State Papers*, 1699–1700, 18: 59. On

merchants' moving to other ports and evading duties, see *Docs. Rel.*, 3: 846, 4: 29, 33, 159, 172, 183.

43. On the benefits to commerce of the English imperial system, see Gary Walton and James Shepherd, *The Economic Rise of Early America* (Cambridge, 1979), ch. 5; and *The British Empire before the American Revolution*, ed. Peter Marshall and Glyn Williams (London, 1980), intro.

44. On New York sentiments, see "Commissioners of the Customs to the Lords of the Treasury," Nov. 16, 1696, *State Papers, 1696–97*, 15: 213–15; "Anthony Brockholls to Andros," 17 Sept. 1681, in *Docs. Rel.*, 3: 281; and Robert Ritchie, *The Duke's Province: A Study of New York Politics and Society, 1664–1691* (Chapel Hill, N.C., 1977), 115–20.

45. *Colonial Laws*, 1: 116–21, 350; *Colonial Charters, Patents, and Grants to Communities Comprising the City of New York*, comp. Jerold Seyman (New York, 1939), 229; and Osgood, *Mins. Common Council*, 1: 213–14, 217–18. The charter also reserved significant powers to the freeholders of the city. Freemanship (like the burgher right before it) also remained a more inclusive category than that of freeholders; freemen included many craftsmen and petty retailers, while freeholders were white, male, property-holding, non-Jewish, non-Catholic New York City householders over twenty-one years of age—the category of urban residents most merchants fit.

46. See *Docs. Rel.*, 2: 526, 532, 539–42, 643, 734, 739–40; 3: 211–12, 233, 236, 279–82, 283–84, 302–8, 329. The crown also instructed Lewin to ferret out smugglers, counterfeiters, and dishonest port officials.

47. On lesser traders, see Sir John Werden to Gov. Andros, Sept. 15, 1675, in *Docs. Rel.*, 3: 233. On duties, see *Colonial Laws*, 1: 111–16, 116–21. The eight who refused the oath were Cornelis Steenwyck, Johannes van Brugh, Johannes de Peyster, Nicholas Bayard, Eagidius Luyck, William Beekman, Jacob Kip, and Antonio de Mill. See also *Docs. Rel.*, 1: 121–23, 125–28, 24–25, 116–21, 137–41; 2: 738–44, 3: 230, 236, 239; and Osgood, *Mins. Common Council*, 1: 25–26, 29–37, 50–62. Of the seven wealthiest merchants in 1676, only Leisler was not "assimilated" to English rule and rejected Andros's leadership; Gabriel Minvielle, William Beekman, Stephanus van Cortlandt, Johannes de Peyster, James Lawrence, and Nicholas Bayard accepted the new political arrangements under Andros. Matthias Nicholls, John Laurence, Henry Beekman, Frederick Philipse, Stephanus van Cortlandt, Samuel Wilson, John Young, Thomas Willett, Thomas Hicks, John Jackson, Samuel Moore, Richard Stillwell, William Darvall, and John Delavall, among others, refused, however, to pay duties in 1680–81 (*Colonial Laws*, 1: 111–16, and NYHS, *Collections*, vol. 45 [New York, 1912], 8–17, 24). On the roles of Frederick Philipse and Stephanus van Cortlandt, see Ritchie, *Duke's Province*, 98; and on Nicholas Bayard and Cornelis Steenwyck, see ibid., 267 n. 26; on Gabriel Minvielle, Johannes de Peyster, James Lawrence, Charles van Brugge, Charles Lodwick, and Evert Wendell, see Wendell Family Papers, NYHS. On Andros's reputation, see "Anthony Brockholls to Andros," 17 Sept. 1681, in *Docs. Rel.*, 3: 281; and "Account of the Revolution of New-York from 1690 to 1696," in ibid., 2: 173.

48. "Instructions to Gov. Dongan," May 29, 1686, in *Docs. Rel.*, 3: 374; *Colonial Laws*, 1: 24–25, 111–16, 116–21, 121–23, 125–28, 137–41; "Dongan to William Blathwayt," Sept. 11, 1686, in *Docs. Rel.*, 3: 363–64; "Dongan to the Board of Trade," in ibid., 3: 393–99; "Instructions to John Palmer," Sept. 8, 1687, in ibid., 3: 475–77; "The Mayor of New-York to John Werden," 1687, in ibid., 3: 361; "Address of the Mayor and Common Council to the

King," 1688, in ibid., 3: 424–25; "Duke of York to Governor Dongan," Aug. 26, 1684, in ibid., 3: 349–59. In 1683, export taxes rose to 9d. per beaver and 10 percent on dry-goods imports (*Colonial Laws*, 1: 165–67). In 1684, the 10 percent ad valorem tax was extended to all imports (ibid., 1: 170–71). The wine duty was 7½ oz. of silver per pipe; cocoa was 1 oz. of silver per cwt. Hudson River reexports were taxed at 3 percent ad valorem. On merchant opposition, see *Docs. Rel.*, 3: 268; 5: 897–89; 6: 127. Import revenues ranged from £1,560 to £3,055.11.3 over those years. In 1688, Bayard, Van Cortlandt, and Philipse changed sides and scorned tax revolters like Cornelius Cuyler, Gerard Beekman and Jacob Leisler; see Jerome Reich, *Leisler's Rebellion: A Study of Democracy in New York* (Chicago, 1953), 69–73.

49. For mention of John Hains, Thomas Willet, John Winder, John Robinson, Caleb Heathcote, Thomas Thatcher, Robert Sanford, Abraham Whearly, and the merchants Griffith, Lloyd, and Robson, see Osgood, *Mins. Common Council*, 1: 1–2, 9, 25–26, 29–37, 50–62.

50. See chapter 4.

51. Bloch, *HMR*, intro.

52. See, e.g., "Answers of Governor Andros to enquiries about New York," 16 Apr. 1678, in *Docs. Rel.*, 3: 260–62; Osgood, *Mins. Common Council*, 1: 18. On smuggling, see Osgood, *Mins. Common Council*, Sept. 19, 1677, which notes seizure of the *Elizabeth* and its cargo of Dutch goods, and the last section of this chapter.

53. Patricia Bonomi, *A Factious People: Politics and Society in Colonial New York* (New York, 1971), 60–68; *Docs. Rel.*, 2: 699–700, 4: 1133; John van Cortlandt Shipping Books, Aug. 12, 1699 to June 30, 1702, and 1702–5, NYHS; Bloch, *HMR*; Leder, *Robert R. Livingston*, 215, 217; Stanley Katz, *Newcastle's New York: Anglo-American Politics, 1732–1753* (Cambridge, Mass., 1968), 112–13, 208–9; *Correspondence of Jeremias van Rensselaer*, 26, 67, 150, 376, 388, 390–91, 408, 412–13, 431, 446, 448, 466–72; Palsits, *Mins.*, 1: 39–40, 56–57, 64, 81, 110, 113, 171, 194.

54. *Docs. Rel.*, 3: 183, 352, 393; Lt.-Col. Edward Thornburgh to the Assembly of Barbados, Apr. 1, 1673, in *State Papers*, 1669–74, 7: 475. On the West Indies connections, see "Governor Dongan to the Lords of Trade," Feb. 22, 1687, in *Docs. Rel.*, 3: 389–415. For Beekman, see *The Beekman Mercantile Papers, 1746–1799*, ed. Philip White, 3 vols. (New York, 1956), 1: 6–7, 8, 11, 12, 13, 15, 15–16, 16, 472, 473, 474, 476, 477, 478, 490, 491–92, 500–501, 502–3, and 506; and Gov. Hunter to the Board of Trade, in *State Papers*, 1716–17, 29: 256.

55. Bloch, *HMR*; Bonomi, *Factious People*, 60–68; C.O. 16: 1; Dickerson, *Navigation Acts*, 178–79.

56. Van Dam and Heathcote owned many plots of city real estate after 1700, and occupied political offices as well; see, e.g., "Jacobus van Cortlandt's Shipments from the Port of New York, 1695–1702," *New-York Historical Society Quarterly Bulletin* 20 (Oct. 1936): 118–20, and Van Cortlandt Shipping Books.

57. "An Account of a Voyage to Madagascar in the Ship *Prophet Daniel*" (MSS, 1698, NYPL); and Valentine, *History*, 221–22. See also evidence of John de Decker factoring in the slave trade for Dutch merchants; De Decker brought slaves to New Amsterdam and New York for merchants. And see *Wills*, 1: 82–83.

58. *Council Minutes, 1652–54*, ed. Charles T. Gehring (Interlaken, N.Y., 1983), 73, 115, 126–27, 129–30. Also on piracy, see *Laws and Ordinances*, 155–57, and *Wills*, 1: 84–88.

59. On seventeenth-century West Indies pirates, see *State Papers*, vols. 1–6; Violet Barbour, "Privateers and Pirates of the West Indies," *American Historical Review* 16 (Apr. 1911): 529–66, and her sources; and Marcus Rediker, *Between the Devil and the Deep Blue Sea: Merchant Seamen, Pirates, and the Anglo-American Maritime World, 1700–1750* (Cambridge, Mass., 1987), ch. 6, where he shows that despite the ultimate profits to merchants and captains, sailors seldom *chose* to become pirates; rather, they were usually seized and forced into piracy. For New York examples, see Records of the Exchequer, E: 190: 80/1, fols. 87–89; 117/1, 644/2, 841/3, and 834/9. Philipse, Barbarie, and Stephen De Lancey engaged in the African slave trade as well.

60. Willoughby to Council of Trade, Jan. 29, 1666, in *State Papers, 1661–68*, 5: 1124; Lynch to Council of Trade, Jan. 13, 1672, in ibid., *1669–74*, 7: 316. On piracy in the 1680s, see *Wills*, 1: 84–88.

61. On fortunes made by abetting piracy, see *State Papers, 1675–76*, 9: 812; ibid., *1697–98*, 16: 112–14; and ibid., *1699*, 17: 486–94; Philip van Cortlandt Letters; Howard Chapin, *Privateer Ships and Sailors: The First Century of American Colonial Privateering, 1625–1725* (London, 1926), 92, 115; James Lydon, "Barbary Pirates and Colonial New Yorkers," *New-York Historical Society Quarterly* 45 (July 1961): 281–90; and Bonomi, *Factious People*, 60–62. For the rise of Frederick Philipse, see *State Papers, 1697–98*, 16; 224, 794, and 904. For Gov. Fletcher's complicity, and his circle of merchant supporters, see ibid., *1697*, 15: 769; *1699*, 18: 495, 512, and 675; *1700*, 18: 400; "Earl of Bellomont to the Lords of Trade," May 8, 1698, in *Docs. Rel.*, 4: 302–6; "Report of Stephanus van Cortlandt," July 1, 1698, C.O. 5: 1048, no. 18; "Bellomont to the Lords of Trade," Dec. 14, 1698, in *Docs. Rel.* 4: 438. The quotations are from "Report of the Board of Trade on the Affairs of . . . New York," Oct. 19, 1698, in *Docs. Rel.* 4: 385–96, and *State Papers, 1697–98*, 16: 235. The same merchants almost to a man were involved in the illicit fur trade; see "Letter from Peter de la Noy," June 13, 1695, in *Docs. Rel.*, 4: 221–24; Gov. Bellomont's speech to the Legislature, *AJ*, 1: 111. Ritchie, *Duke's Province*, 39, 42, claims that "almost all the merchants in New York" were involved in piracy; this was true of the prominent wholesalers, but lesser merchants were often unable to enjoy its benefits. English merchants sought the protection of the East India Company in the Mediterranean during this period, but between 1694 and 1698, under the directorship of Sir Josiah Child, the company's privileges were rescinded. Not until 1698 did Parliament end this liberal phase and reinstate the company's monopoly. Thereafter, the monopoly established uniform standards among its imperial traders and gave company representatives greater leverage to negotiate with pirates. See "Bellomont to the Lords of Trade," June 27, 1698, in *Docs. Rel.*, 4: 327–28; William Letwin, *Sir Josiah Child* (Cambridge, Mass., 1959).

62. See *AJ*, 1: 3, and *Docs. Rel.*, 4: 326–28, 762; "New York Merchants to Governor Cornbury," 1705, in C.O. 5: 1048, no. 105; "Governor Nanfan to the Board of Trade," June 9, 1701, in C.O. 5: 1045, no. 20; "Thomas Quary to the Board of Trade," May 30, 1704, in C.O. 323: 5, no. 51; "Governor, Council and Assembly of New York to the Queen," Oct. 1708, in C.O. 5: 1049, no. 99; "New York Merchants to the Board of Trade," 1716, in C.O. 5: 1051, no. 67; and "Report of the British Board of Trade and Plantations," Nov. 1702, MSS Div., NYPL. For Admiralty Court cases, see Mayor's Court Records, Museum of the City of New York. For an overview of piracy after Queen Anne's War, see Marcus Rediker, "'Under the Banner of King Death': The Social World of Anglo-American Pirates, 1716–1726," *William and Mary Quarterly*, 3d ser., 38 (Apr. 1981): 203–27. On the decline of

piracy, see Gary M. Walton, "Sources of Productivity Change in American Colonial Shipping, 1675–1775," *Economic History Review*, 2d ser., 20 (1967): 77; and "Report on Piracy," May 19, 1721, *Cal. Council Mins.*, 280.

63. On a 1679 contract, see Leder, *Robert R. Livingston*, 24–25, 45. On the 1680s, see Lawrence Leder, "Military Victualling in Colonial New York," in *Business Enterprise in Early New York*, ed. Joseph R. Frese and Jacob Judd (Tarrytown, N.Y., 1979), 24–25. On the 1690s, see "Mr. Livingston to Mr. Ferguson," Mar. 27, 1690, in *Docs. Rel.*, 3: 698–99; and "Governor Bellomont to the Lords of Trade," Oct. 1700, in ibid., 4: 720, 723; "Governor Fletcher to Mr. Blathwayt," Sept. 10, 1692, in ibid., 3: 846; and *AJ*, 2: 680.

64. "Answers of Governor Andros to Enquires about New Yorke," Apr. 1678, in *Docs. Rel.* 3: 260–62; "City of New York Tax Lists, 1695–1699," in NYHS *Collections*, vol. 43 (New York, 1910), 1–36; Osgood, *Mins. Common Council*, 1: 154. The top 10 percent of all householders (76) made up fully 48 percent of the total of city valuations. Compare the analysis here with those for 1653, 1674, and 1677 above and the assessment of 1703 later in this chapter. The 1695 assessment does not identify occupations; these have been gleaned from other information. Also, the assessment does not state true values, only relative proportions of real and personal wealth. The top twenty-nine city traders were Miles Forster, Francis Huling, Paulus Richards, Jacob Kip, Johannes van Brugh, the widow Leisler, the widow De Peyster, Abraham de Peyster Jr., Joseph Bueno, Stephen De Lancey, Tunis de Kay, John de Bruyn, Francis Rombouts, Brandt Schuyler, Nicholas Stuyvesant, William Teller, Jacob van Cortlandt, William Beekman, Anthony Brockholls, Charles Lodwick, Rip van Dam, Caleb Heathcote, Cornelius Cuyler, Ounzeel van Sweeten, Philip French, Johannes Hoghlandt, Cornelius de Peyster, Robert Lurting, and Thomas Wenham. See also Johannes Kerfbyl to Abraham de Peyster, Oct. 3, 1690, Nov. 20, 1690, De Peyster Papers, 1690–1710, NYHS, 29–30; "Governor Fletcher to the Board of Trade," Dec. 24, 1698, in *Docs. Rel.*, 4: 443–51.

65. Richard Pares, *Yankees and Creoles: The Trade between North America and the West Indies before the American Revolution* (Cambridge, Mass., 1956), 63, and ch. 9; Chapin, *Privateer Ships and Sailors*, 116–19, 212–24.

66. John Ludlow, Invoice Book, Aug. 23, 1756, Feb. 2, Apr. 8, 1757, at the Hall of Records, New York City; Philip Livingston, account with Neate, Pigou and Booth, Ledger A, 1754, NYHS; Roberts, "Samuel Storke," 153–55; Philip White, *The Beekmans of New York in Politics and Commerce, 1647–1877* (New York, 1956), 365, 468; Rev. John Miller, *New York Considered and Improved, 1695*, ed. Victor H. Palsits (Cleveland, 1903), 45, 47; "Earl of Bellomont to the Lords of Trade," Apr. 17, 1699, in *Docs. Rel.*, 4: 506.

67. See the case of Lewin et al. against Andros and Fletcher's loans at good interest from English merchant newcomers in *JLC*, 1: 35, 49, 75, 85, 100, 114; *Cal. Council Mins.*, 70, 84, 100, 118, 125; *Docs. Rel.*, 3: 230.

68. See, e.g., *New-York Gazette*, Nov. 28, 1729. In general, see Joseph Ernst, *Money and Politics in America, 1755–1775: A Study in the Currency Act of 1764 and the Political Economy of Revolution* (Chapel Hill, N.C., 1973), 6–10, 16–17, 20–21; Jacob Price, "The Money Question," *Reviews in American History* 2 (Sept. 1974): 364–73; Robert C. West, "Money in the Colonial American Economy," *Economic Inquiry* 16 (1978): 1–15, at 5, 7–8, 10–14; William Baxter, *The House of Hancock: Business in Boston, 1724–1775* (Cambridge, Mass., 1945), 17–26; id., "Credit, Bills, and Bookkeeping in a Simple Economy," *Accounting Review* 21 (1946): 154–66; Margaret Martin, *Merchants and Trade of the Connecticut River*

Valley, 1750–1820, Smith College Studies in History, 25 (Northampton, Mass., 1938); and Byron Fairchild, *Messrs. William Pepperell* (Ithaca, N.Y., 1954), intro.

69. Compare the prohibitions of usury in Deuteronomy 14; Aristotle, *Politics,* ed. Ernest Barker (Oxford, 1981), bk. 1, ch. 10; the loopholes opened by Aquinas in *Summa Theologica,* question 78, art. 1, as explained by Raymond de Roover, *The Medici Bank* (New York, 1948), 57; and John Calvin's *Letter on Usury,* repr. in Richard H. Dana Jr., *Laws of Usury* (New York, 1881), 32–36. Calvin justified taking modest interest: "I confess what a child can see, that if you shut up money in a chest, it will bear no fruit." Luther, however, remained loyal to the extreme position against usury, saying, "since we break on the wheel, and behead, highwaymen, murderers, and housebreakers, how much more ought we to break on the wheel and kill . . . hunt down, curse, and behead all usurers" (*On Trade and Usury* [1527], repr. in *Luther's Works,* 54 vols. to date [Philadelphia, 1942–67], vol. 45, ed. Walter I. Brandt, 308). One of the greatest English critics of lending at interest was North (*Discourses upon Trade,* 6–7). For an influential statement about the value of taking interest, so long as rates were kept at a maximum, see Sir William Petty, *A Treatise of Taxes and Contributions* (1662), repr. in *Works of William Petty,* ed. Hull, 2: 20–51.

70. Ralph Davis, *The Rise of the Atlantic Economies* (Ithaca, N.Y., 1973), 240–41; Jan de Vries, *The Economy of Europe in an Age of Crisis, 1600–1750* (Cambridge, 1976), 192, 198, 208, 210, 214–35; Jacob Price, *Capital and Credit in the British Overseas Trade: The View from the Chesapeake, 1700–1776* (Cambridge, Mass., 1980), 22–31.

71. On New York, see Denton, *Brief Description;* Rev. John Miller, *A Description of the Province and City of New York* (1695; repr., New York, 1922).

72. See Leder, "Military Victualling in Colonial New York," 24–25; and on Livingston's attempts to speed up repayments of his loans, see "Mr. Livingston to Mr. Ferguson," Mar. 27, 1690, in *Docs. Rel.,* 3: 698–99; Leder, *Robert Livingston,* 45, 47–52, 79–80, 85–91. After about 1690, victualing contracts were separated from government loans; during warfare in the 1690s, some government loans brought 10 percent interest. For other evidence of the city borrowing from merchants at interest, see Osgood, *Mins. Common Council,* 3: 21–22, 47, 54–55, 97–98, 104; 4: 429; 5: 314, 342, 371, 471; 6: 90, 429. On Gov. Fletcher's loans, see n. 67 to this chapter. His land grants to merchants can be traced in *Docs. Rel.,* 4: 191, 1045, 1090; "Governor Fletcher to Mr. Blathwayt," Sept. 10, 1692, in *Docs. Rel.,* 3: 846; "Board of Trade's Report on the Northern Colonies," Sept. 3, 1696, in ibid., 4: 227–28; Fletcher to Blathwayt, Mar. 8, 1693, in *State Papers,* 1693, 14: 179; "Report from the New York Council Minutes," Apr. 14, 1693, in ibid., 1693, 14: 274; Osgood, *Mins. Common Council,* 1: 25–26, 29–37, 50–62; "Proceedings of the General Court of Assizes, 1680–1682," in NYHS, *Collections,* vol. 45 (New York, 1912), 8–17, 24. Assimilating Dutch merchants who benefited from these policies included Brandt Schuyler, Cornelius van Cortlandt, Evert Bancker, Frederick Philipse, Nicholas Bayard, Richard Delius, and E. ten Broeck. The merchants immigrating were John Young, Thomas Willett, Thomas Hicks, John Jackson, Richard Stillwell, John West, John Laurence, Samuel Moore, William Darvall, and John Delavall.

73. Bellomont to the Board of Trade, Oct. 17, 1700, in C.O. 5: 1045; "Petition of the Four Companies at New York to the Privy Council," in C.O. 5: 1046, no. 12; "An Account of Money Due to Robert Livingston," June 21, 1701, in C.O. 5: 1046, no. 22; New York Council to the Board of Trade, Mar. 6, 10, 30, May 5, 1701, in C.O. 5: 1046, nos. 5, 8, 12, 13; Treasury Order, July 15, 1701, in C.O. 5: 1047, no. 8; Council's List of Bills, in C.O. 5: 1048,

no. 82; Nanfan to the Board of Trade, Sept. 24, Dec. 29, 1701, Oct. 5, 1702, May 27, Oct. 11, 1703, and Feb. 15, 1705, in C.O. 5: 1047, nos. 1, 25; C.O. 5: 1119, 249–50; C.O. 5: 1048, nos. 57, 68, 103; List of Bills drawn by Nanfan, Mar. 29, 1701 to June 29, 1702, in C.O. 5: 1048, no. 63 (i). For later years, see [Gov. Robert] Hunter to Lords of Treasury, Treasury Office Papers (T), Public Record Office, London, Apr. 30, 1715, T: 1: 189, no. 64; Hunter to the Board of Trade, Oct. 3, 1710, in C.O. 5: 1050, no. 6.

74. *Docs. Rel.*, 4: 1045, 1090; T. S. Ashton, *An Economic History of England: The Eighteenth Century* (London, 1955), ch. 5; Dickson, *Financial Revolution*, chs. 1–2; De Vries, *Economy of Europe*, ch. 7; Price, *Capital and Credit*, 44–95; "Duke of York to Governor Andros," Apr. 6, 1675, in *Docs. Rel.*, 3: 230–31; "Sir John Werden to Governor Andros," 1675, in ibid., 236–37.

75. See petition of Robert R. Livingston, Peter Schuyler, and Stephen van Cortlandt to the Board of Trade, Aug. 1701, in C.O. 5: 1044, no. 46. Discounts were normally 5 to 7½ percent when customers paid in cash. Medieval bills of exchange were also used as loans from one party to another, with payments made by a third party to the first one, based upon credit that the second party had with the third.

76. De Vries, *Economy of Europe*, 226–28; Price, *Capital and Credit*, chs. 3, 4, 5; Postlethwayt, *Dict.*, 1: s.v. "bills"; Davis, *Atlantic Economies*, 242–44; Peter Burke, *Venice and Amsterdam: A Study of Seventeenth-Century Elites* (London, 1974), 56–59. Typically, "A"— the drawer of a bill who had credit with "B"—drew a bill on B, the drawee. If B accepted the bill, he would pay to "C"—in specie or another bill—a sum owed by A. For this and the next paragraph, see Edward Hatton, *The Merchants Magazine: or, Tradesman's Treasury*, 3d ed. (London, 1699), 205–12. For examples of bills in early years, see Fernow, *Records*, 5: 125; 6: 19, 165. For examples of assigning bills, see *The Register of Solomon La Chaire, Notary Public of New Amsterdam, 1661–1662*, ed. Kenneth Scott and Ken Stryker-Rodda (Baltimore, 1978). And see also Albert E. Feaveryear, *The Pound Sterling: A History of English Money* (Oxford, 1963), 150–52, 172; John McCusker, *Money and Exchange in Europe and America, 1600–1775: A Handbook* (Chapel Hill, N.C., 1978), 158–67; and Price, "Money Question," 369–70. On intrinsic value, see, e.g., John Locke, *Some Considerations of the Consequences of Lowering the Interest* (1692), repr. in J. R. McCulloch, *Principles of Political Economy* (London, 1870), 238–39; id., *Further Considerations Concerning Raising the Value of Money* (1694), repr. in *The Works of John Locke*, ed. Thomas Tegg, 10 vols. (London, 1823), 5: 131–206; John Law, *Of Money and Trade Considered*, 2d ed. (London, 1720), 19–22; and Curtis Nettels, *The Money Supply of the American Colonies before 1720*, University of Wisconsin Studies in the Social Sciences and History, no. 20 (Madison, Wis., 1934), 326. On rates of exchange in New York overall, see Ernst, *Money and Politics*, 284–5, 308–11; for rising rates—about 120 percent from 1664 to 1672, to 150 percent over 1684 to 1708, 155 percent in 1708, 170 percent in 1739, and 177.77 percent in 1740, when it was officially set to go no higher—see *Colonial Laws*, 1: 96–97; 4: 301, 305–6; Hunter to the Board of Trade, July 7, 1718, C.O. 5: 1051; Hunter to Lords of Treasury, Apr. 30, 1715, T: 1: 189, no. 64; Hunter to Board of Trade, Oct. 3, 1710, C.O. 5: 1050, no. 6; Leslie Brock, *The Currency of the American Colonies, 1700–1764: A Study in Colonial Finance and Imperial Relations* (New York, 1975), 73n; McCusker, *Money and Exchange*, 158. For early New York overvaluation, see Adriaen van der Donck, *Description of the New Netherlands*, ed. Thomas F. O'Donnell (1655; repr., Syracuse, N.Y., 1968), 62–63, 82; *Laws and Ordinances*, 1: 126; "An American," *An Essay Upon the Government of the English Plantations*, ed. Louis

B. Wright (1701; repr. San Marino, Calif., 1945), 42–43. For quotations, see "Duke of York to Governor Andros," Apr. 6, 1675, in *Docs. Rel.*, 3: 230–31; "Sir John Werden to Governor Andros," Jan. 28, 1676, in ibid., 3: 236–37; Osgood, *Mins. Common Council*, 6: 181–83. Also see Paul Hamlin, "Money Circulating in New York Prior to 1704," *New-York Historical Society Quarterly* 40 (Oct. 1956): 365.

THREE "Where There is the Least Hindrance"

1. "Governor Andros' Answer to Mr. Lewin's Report," Dec. 31, 1681, in *Docs. Rel.*, 3: 308–13.
2. Charles Lodwick to the Royal Society in London, May 20, 1692, in NYHS, *Collections*, 2d ser., vol. 2 (New York, 1849), 243–50; and John Miller, *Description of the Province and City of New York . . . in the Year 1695* (1843), repr. in *Historic Chronicles of New Amsterdam, Colonial New York and Early Long Island*, 1st ser., ed. Cornell Jaray (Port Washington, N.Y., 1969), 31.
3. Jasper Danckaerts, referring to Arnoldus de la Grange, *Journal of a Voyage to New York and a Tour in Several of the American Colonies in 1679–1680*, ed. Henry C. Murphy (Brooklyn, N.Y., 1867), 353.
4. For this and the next two paragraphs on the West Indies, see the sources cited in ch. 2, n. 2; "Governor Andros to the Lords of Trade," Dec. 1681, in *Docs. Rel.*, 3: 313; "John Lewin to the Board of Trade," May 24, 1680, in ibid., 3: 306; Stephen Saunders Webb, *1676: The End of American Independence* (New York, 1984), 331–42. Lord Windsor, the governor of Jamaica, urged planters to seek "free commerce with the plantations . . . of Spain and Holland" despite international rivalries and to try "to admit them to a free trade" (Apr. 8, 1662, *State Papers*, 1661–68, 5: 85).
5. *Voyages of the Slavers* St. John *and* Arms of Amsterdam, *1659, 1663*, ed. E. B. O'Callaghan (Albany, N.Y., 1867), intro., 106–225. In 1660, the city established its first slave auction, and merchants outfitted two ships that year to make a triangular voyage from New Amsterdam, to Amsterdam, to Africa, and back to the colony. That same year, twelve of the city's burghers petitioned the directors for permission to create a "free and unobstructed" trade between the colony and West Africa. Cornelis Steenwyck and Augustus Heermans engaged in this trade.
6. Thomas Barrow, *Trade and Empire: The British Customs Service in Colonial America, 1660–1775* (Cambridge, Mass., 1967), 21, 47; *Docs. Rel.*, 3: 46, 261 (where Gov. Andros welcomes slavery in New York in 1678 and notes that slaves cost £30 and £35 in "country pay," or New York currency); *State Papers*, 1677–80, 10: 41, 640; ibid., 1661–68, 5: 28, 539, 711; ibid., 1675–76, 9: 787, 840, 843; *Laws and Ordinances*, 81, 82, 127, 191, 455, 469; and "An American," *An Essay Upon the Government of the English Plantations* (London, 1701), ed. Louis B. Wright (San Marino, Calif., 1945), 60.
7. Bloch, *HMR*, passim.
8. *Docs. Rel.*, 2: 699–700; John van Cortlandt, Shipping Book, 1699–1702, 1702–5.
9. Bloch, *HMR*; Lawrence Leder, *Robert R. Livingston, 1654–1728, and the Politics of Colonial New York* (Chapel Hill, N.C., 1961), 215, 217; Stanley Katz, *Newcastle's New York: Anglo-American Politics, 1732–1753* (Cambridge, Mass., 1968), 112–13, 208–9; "Petition of the Merchants of the City of New York relating to Foreign Coin," Feb. 1705, in *Docs. Rel.*, 4: 1133.

10. Ralph Davis, *The Rise of the Atlantic Economies* (Ithaca, N.Y., 1973), ch. 1, and merchants' correspondence cited in notes to this chapter.

11. "City of New York Tax Lists, 1695–1699," in NYHS, *Collections*, vol. 43 (New York, 1910), 1–36; Stokes, *Iconography*, 4: 158; Abraham de Peyster Papers, NYHS; Jacobus van Cortlandt Letterbook, 1698–1700, NYHS; and author's biographical complilation. In *Before the Melting Pot: Society and Culture in Colonial New York City, 1664–1730* (Princeton, N.J., 1992), Joyce Goodfriend offers the most recent analysis of the 1695 assessment, but she is concerned with citywide ethnicity and race, rather than with divisions among merchants as a class or occupational group.

12. *Docs. Rel.*, 2: 699–700; John van Cortlandt, Shipping Book, 1699–1702, 1702–6; "Petition of the Merchants of the City of New York relating to Foreign Coin," Feb. 1705, in *Docs. Rel.*, 4: 1133.

13. On ethnic fears, see *Docs. Rel.*, 1: 263, 2: 155–56; "A Collection of Papers handed in by Mr. Weaver," Sept. 26, 1698, in *State Papers, 1697–98*, 16: 455–59; and Col. Nicholls to [the governor and Council of Massachusetts], July [?] 1664, in ibid., 1661–68, 16: 780, 222. On Manning, see Palsits, *Mins.*, 1: 127–29; and see also ibid., 1: 144–45, 2: 739, 740, 747–48. On Dutch privateers, see *Docs. Rel.*, 2: 572 n. 1, 662–63, 715–16, 725.

14. *The Register of Salomon La Chaire, Notary Public of New Amsterdam, 1661–1662*, ed. Kenneth Scott and Ken Stryker-Rodda (Baltimore, 1978), 124–25, 183–84; Fernow, *Records*, 4: 106–9, 75, 93; C. A. Weslager, *The Swedes and Dutch at New Castle* (New York, 1987), 223–30; *Docs. Rel.*, 2: 526–27.

15. *Docs. Rel.*, 2: 730–31; Fernow, *Records*, 7: 19, 18, 32, 53, 56, 59, 74; Records of the Exchequer (E), Public Record Office, London, E: 190/668–2, 669–4, 666–8.

16. See sources cited in ch. 2, nn. 64 and 67 on Andros and n. 72 on Fletcher; Van Schaick Papers, box 1, 1696, NYPL; Leder, *Robert R. Livingston*, 49, 77–95, where there is evidence that he traded directly with the London merchants Harwood and Blackall, and that Fletcher had shares in the 1692 Dutch voyages; and Charles Wolley, *A Two Years' Journal in New York and Part of its Territories in America* (1701), ed. Edward G. Bourne (Cleveland, 1902), 59.

17. "Governor Dongan to the Lords of Trade," Feb. 22, 1687, in *Docs. Rel.*, 3: 398; and ibid., 3: 288–89, 318–19, 321.

18. On country interests, see Cynthia Kierner, "Landlord and Tenant in Revolutionary New York: The Case of Livingston Manor," *New York History* 70 (Apr. 1989): 133–52; id., *Traders and Gentlefolk: The Livingstons of New York, 1675–1790* (Ithaca, N.Y., 1992), 25–26; Sun Bok Kim, *Landlord and Tenant in Colonial New York: Manorial Society, 1664–1775* (Chapel Hill, N.C., 1978); Robert Richie, *The Duke's Province: A Study of New York Politics and Society, 1664–1691* (Chapel Hill, N.C., 1977), ch. 9; Goodfriend, *Before the Melting Pot*. My view has benefited from the opinions of all of these scholars, although it differs.

19. Leisler's first marriage in 1663 linked him to a few major trading families, and by 1674, at thirty, he was trading regularly in Chesapeake tobacco, Dutch West Indies goods, coastal commodities, and Amsterdam dry goods. See Edwin Purple, *Genealogical Notes Relating to Lieutenant-Governor Jacob Leisler, and His Family Connections in New York* (New York, 1877), 5–7, 10–20; David M. Riker, "Govert Loockermans, Free Merchant of New Amsterdam," *De Halve Maen* 62 (1989): 4–10; *Docs. Rel.*, 2: 699–700; Osgood, *Mins. Common Council*, 1: 29–37 (1676). On economic distinctions mentioned in this and the

next paragraph, see *Docs. Rel.*, 3: 601, 610, 631, 599; 4: 223, 256, 274, 303–4, 324, 389, 327, 444–47, 456–61, 466–74, 306–8, 310, 385–88, 443–44, 479–83, 748–49.

20. On Leisler's legislation, see *Docs. Rel.*, 3: 629–33, 720–21, 737–48. On free bolting, see *Docs. Rel.*, 3: 300–301, 637, 717. When Cornbury became governor, he granted a renewal of the bolting monopoly from 1702 to 1704 but did not necessarily favor the Dutch trade; see Jerome Reich, *Leisler's Rebellion: A Study of Democracy in New York, 1664–1720* (Chicago, 1953), 164; and my ch. 4. Merchants of English origins who opposed the Leislerians included Chidley Brooke, Nicholas Bayard, William Emmott, John Laurence, Thomas and Richard Willett, Caleb Heathcote, Charles Lodwick, Thomas Wenham, William Smith, William Nicholls, Thomas Clark, and William Pinhorn; prominent Dutch resident opponents included Mathias Nicholls, Brandt Schuyler, Frederick Philipse, and Stephanus van Cortlandt. Van Cortlandt rose quickly through the ranks of city merchants, accommodating easily to English rule after 1664, and held the post of mayor, as an anti-Leislerian, during Leisler's tumultuous months in control. He continued to play a prominent role in restoring peace and royal rule after 1692 and served as port collector in 1698 under Bellomont. Rising merchants who turned against Leisler and figured prominently in commerce after the turn of the century included Jacobus van Cortlandt, Jonathan Morris, Jonathan Kip, Robert Lurting, Brant Schuyler, Matthew Ling, John Barberie, William Morris, Stephen De Lancey, Thomas Burrows, and Jonathan Cholwell. These details are drawn from the author's biographical information about individual merchants; David Valentine, *History of the City of New York* (New York, 1853), 79–80; and "A Letter from a Gentleman of the City of New-York, 1698," in *Narratives of the Insurrections, 1675–1690*, ed. C. M. Andrews (New York, 1915), 360–72, esp. 364. London firms with an animus against Leisler included those of Thomas Byfold, Micajah Perry, Thomas Starkey, Joseph King, William Shepperd, Nicholas Lofting, Samuel Waldenfield, Henry Adderly, Simon Lodwick, B. Hackshaw, William Cornelisen, Gerard van Heythuysen, and John Blackall; see "Some London Merchants Trading to New York," Feb. 9, 1698, in *State Papers*, 1699–1700, 18: 59.

21. The quotation is from "Colonel Nicholas Bayard to Sir Philip Meadows," Mar. 8, 1701, in *Docs. Rel.*, 4: 848. On Leisler's trial, see William Smith, *The History of the Late Province of New-York from Its Discovery to the Appointment of Governor Colden, in 1762*, NYHS, *Publications*, 2 vols. (New York, 1829–30), 1: 103.

22. Leder, *Robert R. Livingston*, 84–85.

23. On favoritism, see sources cited in ch. 2, n. 72. On King William's War, see Edmund Randolph to the Board of Trade, C.O. 323: 2, no. 6; Randolph to the Board of Trade, in *State Papers*, 1696, 15: 214; [?] to Board of Trade, in ibid., 1699, 17: 487, 553.

24. Van der Donck, *Description of the New Netherlands*, 62–63, 82; *Laws and Ordinances*, 1: 126; "An American," *Essay Upon the Government*, 42–43; Curtis Nettels, *The Money Supply of the American Colonies before 1720*, University of Wisconsin Studies in the Social Sciences and History, 20 (Madison, Wis., 1934), 226; Stokes, *Iconography*, 5: 175; and Paul Hamlin, "Money Circulating in New York Prior to 1704," *New-York Historical Society Quarterly* 40 (Oct. 1956): 361–68. This reasoning also appears in John Locke, *Some Considerations of the Consequences of Lowering the Interest* (1692), repr. in J. R. McCulloch, *Principles of Political Economy* (London, 1870), 238–39, and John Law, *Of Money and Trade Considered*, 2d ed. (London, 1720), 19–22.

25. On mints, see Nettels, *Money Supply*, 110–12, and Gov. Bellomont to [?], 1715, C.O.

5: 1051, no. 18. On inflation due to piracy, see "Report of the British Board of Trade and Plantations," Nov. 1702, MSS Div., NYPL; report of Stephen van Cortlandt, July 1, 1698, in C.O. 5: 1042, fol. 242; "Earl of Bellomont to the Lords of Trade," Dec. 14, 1698, in *Docs. Rel.*, 4: 438; James Lydon, "Barbary Pirates and Colonial New Yorkers," *New-York Historical Society Quarterly* 45 (July 1961), 281–90; and on Wood, [Anon.], "Coins and Currency of New York," in *Memorial History of the City of New York*, ed. J. G. Wilson, 4 vols. (New York, 1893), 4: 309–10. Clipping gold and silver coins was a nuisance in New York throughout the colonial period (see Stevens, *Records*, Aug. 1770, 104–5) and the chamber of commerce attempted to establish a weight of specie for all coins; "The Expediency of a Continental Paper Money," in *American Archives*, 4th ser., ed. Peter Force, 6 vols. (Washington, D.C., 1837–46), 2: 1262–64; *New-York Mercury*, Dec. 24, 31, 1753, Jan. 7, 21, 1754, Aug. 7, 1758; *New-York Post-Boy*, Jan. 14, Apr. 22, 1754; Joshua Delaplain Papers, NYHS; J. E. Pryor, Ledger, 1759–68, and Day Book, 1762–67, NYHS; *History of the State of New York*, ed. A. C. Flick, 10 vols. (New York, 1933–37), 2: 308–9; John McCusker, *Money and Exchange in Europe and America, 1600–1775: A Handbook* (Chapel Hill, N.C., 1978), 131–37, 159–61, 169–71, 181, 194–96, 216–20.

26. Daniel Defoe, *A Tour Through the Whole Island of Great Britain* (1724; repr. New York, 1978), 1: 139; Arthur Young, *A General View of the Agriculture of the County of Sussex, 1813* (London, 1813), 404–5; John Taylor, *The Ordinary of Newgate* (London, 1747), 23, cited by Cal. Winslow, "Sussex Smugglers," in *Albion's Fatal Tree: Crime and Society in Eighteenth-Century England*, ed. Douglas Hay et al. (New York, 1975), 119–66, esp. 148–49; H. and L. Mui, "Smuggling and the British Tea Trade," *American Historical Review* 74 (Oct. 1968): 50; Neville Williams, *Contraband Cargo: Seven Centuries of Smuggling* (London, 1959), 28; and Ralph Davis, *The Rise of the English Shipping Industry* (Trowbridge, Eng., 1962), 27.

27. See, e.g., "Answer of Sir Charles Whe[e]ller," in *State Papers*, 1669–74, 7: 290; Charles M. Andrews, *The Colonial Period of American History: England's Commercial and Colonial Policy*, 4 vols. (New Haven, Conn., 1938), 4: 114–15; *Correspondence of Jeremias van Rensselaer, 1651–1654*, trans. and ed. A. J. F. van Laer (Albany, N.Y., 1932), 26, 67, 150, 376, 388, 390–91, 408, 412–13, 431, 446, 448, 466–72; Palsits, *Mins.*, 1: 39–40, 56–57, 64, 113, 171, 194–95.

28. *Docs. Rel.*, 3: 288–89, 318–19, 321. See also Nuala Zahedieh, "The Merchants of Port Royal Jamaica and the Spanish Contraband Trade, 1655–1692," *William and Mary Quarterly* 43 (1986): 570–93. On the *Blossom* and *Rebecca*, see Records of the Exchequer (E), Public Record Office, London, E: 190: 664: 14; 663: 2, 5, 6; 664: 17; 665: 4, 11; 666: 8, 18. The *Hope* was seized and condemned in 1666 (*Wills*, 1: 71).

29. See, e.g., Osgood, *Mins. Common Council*, Sept. 19, 1677, which notes seizure of the *Elizabeth* and its Dutch goods; C.O. 5: 1038, no. 94, and C.O. 5: 1039, no. 10.

30. MSS Minutes of the Mayor's Court, City of New York, Nov. 13, 1674, to Sept. 21, 1675, Office of the New York County Clerk, 38, 61; Lawrence H. Leder and Vincent P. Carosso, "Robert Livingston (1654–1728): Businessman of Colonial New York," *Business History Review* 30 (Mar. 1956): 27; *Docs. Rel.*, 4: 304, 412, 446, 475; *Council Mins.*, 37; *The Curaçao Papers, 1640–1665*, trans. and ed. Charles T. Gehring (Interlaken, N.Y., 1987), 122–23, 145–25, 176–84, 187, 202; Abraham de Peyster Papers, 1695–1710, correspondence dated Jan. 22, Aug. 10, 17, 18, 24, Sept. 7, 14, Oct. 15, 18, Nov. 14, 28, 1702; Jan. 5, 11, 14, Feb.

23, Mar. 29, Apr. 5, 19, May 10, 24, June 5, 18, 1703; and for the quotation, De Peyster to Gov. Bellomont, Aug. 21, 1699.

31. "Lewin to the Board of Trade," Oct. 16, 1680, in *Docs. Rel.*, 3: 302–8. Andros denied the charge; see ibid., 309–11. On Dyer, see ibid., 3: 279–82, 283–84, 308–13, 314–16, 400–417; Order in Council, 1681, in ibid., 3: 362; "Report to the Committee of Trade on the Province of New York," Feb. 22, 1687, in ibid., 1: 160–61, 14: 567, 637; 2: 613–14; 3: 221–22, 318–19; and Osgood, *Mins. Common Council*, 1: 39, 40, 142; 2: 513, 398–99.

32. Santen's merchant helpmates were John Smith and John Harlow. Middling merchants' barbs were directed against Dongan, John van Cortlandt, and James Graham. On the episode, see *Docs. Rel.*, 3: 335, 389–417, 422–23, 493–501, 500–501; *Col. Commissions*, 2; and *State Papers*, 1686, 9: 258, 785–87, 826, 884, 889.

33. Under Collector Bayard, the merchants John Haynes, Paul Richards, and Thomas Wenham were appointed and quickly dismissed. *Docs. Rel.*, 3: 599–604, 608–9, 616–18, 636–48, 649–50, 661.

34. *Col. Commissions*, 45; *Docs. Rel.*, 3: 757, 818–24, 4: 25, 37, 302–6, 317–18, 320–21; *Colonial Laws*, 1: 248–53, 287–93, 325–26. Bellomont's choice, Thomas Weaver, was involved in a long controversy over back pay; see *Docs. Rel.*, 3: 354–58, 374–76, 417–18, 829. For the later quotations, see "Earl of Bellomont to the Lords of Trade," May 15, 1699, June 27, 1698, in *Docs. Rel.*, 4: 326–28, 518–26; and *State Papers*, 1700, 18: 718, 719.

35. "Mr. Nicholl's Pamphlet to Influence the Elections of the Assembly," Apr. 1699, C.O. 5: 1042, no. 23; William J. Hoffman, "A 'Tumult of Merchants' of New York in 1698," *New York Genealogical and Biographical Register* 74 (July 1943): 96–100; and "Earl of Bellomont to the Lords of Trade," June 6, 1698, in *Docs. Rel.*, 4: 323–24.

36. "Earl of Bellomont to the Lords of Trade," May 8, 18, 1698, in *Docs. Rel.*, 4: 302–6, 306–9; *Cal. Council Mins.*, 130–31; Bellomont's speech to the legislature, in *AJ*, 1: 111; Bellomont to the Commissioners of Customs, Oct. 27, 1699, in *State Papers*, 1699–1700, 18: 493; "Petition of Sundry Merchants of New York to the King," Mar. 1700, in *Docs. Rel.*, 4: 624. For the next years, see Report of the British Board of Trade and Plantations, Nov. 1702, MSS, NYPL; "Lord Cornbury to the Board of Trade," 1702, in *Docs. Rel.*, 4: 1003; and Edward Channing, *History of the United States*, 3 vols. (New York, 1912), 2: 258–59, 264–65, 267.

37. *Docs. Rel.*, 4: 544–55, 624; and "Some London Merchants Trading to New York to the Council of Trade and Plantations," Feb. 9, 1699, in *State Papers*, 1699–1700, 18: 90.

38. Charles Davenant, *Discourses on Public Revenues* (London, 1698), pt. 2, 15, 31; and id., *Essay upon the Probable Methods of Making a People Gainers in the Ballance of Trade* (London, 1699), 45–46; Edward Misselden, *Free Trade* (London, 1622), 7.

39. *Wills*, 1: 277–78, 352, 422.

40. Ibid., 388, 255, 290, 344, 350, 393, 97–98, 196, 257–58.

41. Ibid., 314, 355. A sampling of other merchants with small estates illustrates the point; e.g., ibid., 24 (Claes Melise), 25 (Thomas Badgord), 30 (Rogert Rugg), 112 (John Adams), 151 (Matthew Taylor), 179 (Thomas Phillips), 186 (Thomas Crundell), 196–97 (John Haines), 205, 211 (John Terry), 218 (Henry Mayle), 257–58 (Daniel Veenvos, Daniel Betts, Jacob Mayle, Thomas Coher), 363 (William Hodge), 366 (Samuel Burt), and 415 (John Vincent).

42. Nettels, *Money Supply*, 166; and for 1717, *Journal of the Commissioners for Trade and Plantations*, 14 vols. (London, 1920–38), 1718–22, 4: 63.

43. Willett's father was an English merchant who had been in New Amsterdam since 1643; his son Richard enhanced family commerce in the West Indies. Van Tright arrived by 1665 and was active until 1700 but never wealthy; Delanoy arrived in 1680 and was more active than many middling merchants but never wealthy either; Ludlow was the first of a family line of merchants that increased its fortunes over the early eighteenth century. These details derive from author's merchant biographies; J. H. Innes, *New Amsterdam and Its People* (New York, 1902), 192–95; and Purple, *Genealogical Notes*, 12. For the rise of Henry Van Vlecq and John Byvanck from shopkeepers to merchants before 1700, see Bruce Wilkenfeld, "The New York City Shipowning Community, 1715–1764," *American Neptune* 37 (1977): 65.

FOUR   Creating a Regional Economy, 1664–1700

1. I premise my discussion on the view that New York's economy developed through both staples exporting and internal development. Helpful starting points for examining this are John J. McCusker and Russell R. Menard, *The Economy of British America, 1607–1789* (Chapel Hill, N.C., 1985), intro.; D. A. Farnie, "The Commercial Empire of the Atlantic, 1607–1783," *Economic History Review*, 2d ser., 15 (Dec. 1962): 205–18; Jacob Price, "Economic Function and the Growth of American Port Towns in the Eighteenth Century," *Perspectives in American History* 8 (1974): 123–86; Curtis P. Nettels, "England's Trade with New England and New York, 1685–1720," *Proceedings of the Colonial Society of Massachusetts* 28 (1933): 322–50; id., "Economic Relations of Boston, Philadelphia, and New York, 1680–1715," *Journal of Economic and Business History* 3 (Feb. 1931): 185–215; Sun Bok Kim, *Landlord and Tenant in Colonial New York: Manorial Society, 1664–1775* (Chapel Hill, N.C., 1978); Ulysses Hedrick, *A History of Agriculture in the State of New York* (New York, 1933); Max Schumacher, *The Northern Colonial Farmer and His Markets* (New York, 1975); P. W. Bidwell and J. I. Falconer, *History of Agriculture in the Northern United States, 1620–1860* (Washington, D.C., 1925); Hans Medick, "The Proto-Industrial Family Economy: The Structural Function of Household and Family during the Transition from Peasant Society to Industrial Capitalism," *Social History* 3 (1976): 291–316; Allan Kulikoff, "The Economic Growth of the Eighteenth-Century Chesapeake Colonies," *Journal of Economic History* 39 (1979): 275–88; Jackson Turner Main, *The Social Structure of Revolutionary America* (Princeton, N.J., 1965), 180–83; Robert Zemsky, *Merchants, Farmers, and River Gods: An Essay on Eighteenth-Century American Politics* (Boston, 1971); James Henretta, "Families and Farms: 'Mentalité' in Pre-Industrial America," *William and Mary Quarterly* 35 (1978): 3–32; and Stoker, *Prices*, 213. Because this study focuses on port-city commerce, it does not address the many issues related to rural labor and productivity, rural household consumption, or the sources of internal change.

2. See, e.g., William Bayard mortgage of a long-term lease, May 1, 1742, Bayard-Campbell-Pearsall Papers, NYPL; Donna Merwick, *Possessing Albany, 1630–1710* (Cambridge, 1990), 115; "Tax List of the City of New York, December 1695," in NYHS, *Collections*, vol. 43 (New York, 1910), 1–35; and Nan Rothschild, *New York City Neighborhoods: The Eighteenth Century* (San Diego, 1990), esp. 185–204 (for 1703 assessment). It is possible to calculate roughly from these assessments which merchants turned partially to landlordism, since the owners of untenanted property were assessed and, if it was tenanted, the occupier was assessed. However, after the Dongan Charter was passed in 1686,

the city usually leased lots rather than sold them. The largest city properties sold to merchants included at least the following: the Bayards, Van Cortlandts, Beekmans, De Peysters, Kips, and Webbers by the 1670s; then Watts (Rose Hill); Thiebout (Rosborough), Norton (Hermitage), Youle (Spring Valley), Jones (Louve), Keteltas (Bellevue), the Bayard estate, and the Rutgers estate (Stokes, *Iconography*, 1: 169–70, 144–45, 125–26, 176–77, 108–9, 70–76, 134–36).

3. "William Nicolls to the Earl of Clarendon," Mar. 7, 1666, *Clarendon Papers*, in NYHS, *Collections*, vol. 3 (New York, 1869), 113–19; and see also Samuel Maverick, *Letters, 1662–1665*, in NYHS, *Collections*, vol. 3 (New York, 1869), 19–88, 126–28, 157–59.

4. Statement of Gov. Nicolls, July 7, 1668, in Fernow, *Records*, 6: 138–39.

5. See, e.g., *State Papers, 1677–80*, 10: 238, 254; *Colonial Laws*, 1: 116–21, 165–67. On the fur trade's connections to diplomacy and Indian affairs, see Arthur H. Buffington, "The Policy of Albany and English Westward Expansion," *Mississippi Valley Historical Review* 8 (1922): 327–66; Jean Murray, "The Fur Trade in New France and New Netherland, Prior to 1645," *Canadian Historical Review* 19 (1938): 365–67; Wilbur Jacobs, "Unsavory Sidelights on the Colonial Fur Trade," *New York History* 34 (1942): 135–48; W. J. Eccles, *The Canadian Frontier, 1534–1760* (New York, 1969); Lewis Saum, *The Indian and the Fur Trader* (Seattle, 1965); Allen Trelease, *Indian Affairs in Colonial New York: The Seventeenth Century* (Ithaca, N.Y., 1960). On the economics of the fur trade, see also esp. Thomas E. Norton, *The Fur Trade in Colonial New York, 1686–1776* (Madison, Wis., 1974); and cf. the staples-theory approach of Harold Innis, *The Fur Trade in Canada: An Introduction to Canadian Economic History* (New Haven, Conn., 1930). On Native American relations and diplomacy, see Daniel Richter, *The Ordeal of the Long House: The Peoples of the Iroquois League in the Era of European Colonization* (Chapel Hill, N.C., 1992), esp. ch. 4. The wealthiest city residents and top fur exporters in 1676 were Frederick Philipse, Nicholas de Meyer, and Oloff Stevense van Cortlandt (Bloch, *HMR*, intro.).

6. Palsits, *Mins.*, 1: 194–95, Nov. 18, 1668, and 1: 39–40, Oct. 18, 1669; *Colonial Laws*, 1: 111, 116, 484, 675. On the end of the century, see Thomas Weaver, New York Customs Report, Jan. 6, 1701 to Mar. 25, 1702, Hall of Records, New York City.

7. *Docs. Rel.*, 3: 216, 221–23, 260–63, 279–82, 287, 288–89, 302–6, 312–16; 5: 631, 708, 775, 778, 781–82. The merchant Peter Delanoy was implicated in Dyer's attempts to coerce export duties from merchants.

8. The London merchants are quoted from William Smith, *The History of the Late Province of New-York From Its Discovery to the Appointment of Governor Colden, in 1762*, NYHS, *Publications*, 2 vols. (New York, 1829–30), 1: 207, 221. See also Bloch, *HMR*, ix–xviii; and "Governor Dongan's Report on the State of the Province," Feb. 22, 1687, in *Docs. Rel.*, 3: 400.

9. Osgood, *Mins. Common Council*, 1: 1–2, 9, 25–26; "Instructions of Governor Dongan to Capt. Palmer," July 23, 1689, in *Docs. Rel.*, 3: 475–77; C.O. 5: 1222; *Docs. Rel.*, 3: 475–76, 651–53; Norton, *Fur Trade*, 43–59, 101; Bloch, *HMR*; *Early Records of the City and County of Albany and Colony of Rensselaerswyck: Deeds, 1678–1704*, trans. and ed. Jonathan Pearson and A. J. F. van Laer (Albany, N.Y., 1916), 324; Robert Ritchie, "London Merchants, the New York Market, and the Recall of Sir Edmund Andros," *New York History* 57 (1976): 5–31; and, in general, see Jack Sosin, *English America and the Restoration Monarchy of Charles II* (Lincoln, Nebr., 1981).

10. Johannes Kerfbyl to Abraham de Peyster, Oct. 3, 1690, Nov. 20, 1690, De Peyster

Papers, 1690–1710, NYHS, 29–30; "Governor Fletcher to the Board of Trade," Dec. 24, 1698, in *Docs. Rel.*, 4: 433–51; and Robert R. Livingston, "Freight List of the Brigantine *Robert*, Dec. 3, 1694," Livingston-Redmund MSS, NYHS.

11. See, e.g., the exports of Levy, Van Vleeck, Willet, Loockermans, De Meyer, and Van Brugge (Bridges) in merchants' accounts; and "The Corporation of New Orange to the States-General," in *Docs. Rel.*, 2: 526, 532, which was signed by nine Dutch merchants, eight of whom remained in the colony and included grain exporting among their other commercial activities.

12. See *Docs. Rel.*, 3: 46; Report [of the Lords of Trade and Plantations], Feb., 1677, in *State Papers*, 1677–80, 10: 15–16; Journal of Lords of Trade and Plantations, Mar. 28, 1678, in ibid., 1677–80, 10: 229–30; Commissioners of Customs to Sir Philip Warwick, Feb. 12, 1661, in ibid., 1661–1668, 5: 10; Circular Letter from the King to [the Governors of His Majesty's Plantations], Aug. 25, 1663, in ibid., 1661–68, 5: 155–56; Instructions for Col. Richard Nicolls, Sir Robert Carr, George Cartwright, and Samuel Maverick, Apr. 23, 1664, in ibid., 1661–68, 5: 200; Petition of divers of his Majesty's subjects trading to the ports of Europe, Jan. 19, 1676, in ibid., 1661–68, 5: 337; Order of the King in Council, Mar. 10, 1676, in ibid., 1661–68, 5: 358; Thomas Cole to the Commissioners of Customs, Mar. 16, 1676, in ibid., 1675–76, 9: 360. For general comments, see Curtis Nettels, *The Emergence of a National Economy* (New York, 1962), 435; Bloch, *HMR*, intro.; and Gary Walton and James Shepherd, *The Economic Rise of Early America* (Cambridge, 1979), ch. 2.

13. For population in 1664 and 1680, see David Valentine, *History of the City of New York* (Albany, N.Y., 1853), 213–14; for 1698, see *Docs. Rel.*, 1: 44, 467. For affirmation of the city's importance, see Stokes, *Iconography*, 4: 327, 961. On Indian relations, see Richter, *Ordeal of the Long House*, ch. 4. Merchants did not try to bring western Massachusetts trade to New York yet.

14. See Kim, *Landlord and Tenant*, esp. 142–60, and *Wills*, 2: 391, showing that the merchant Francis Richardson held 400 acres in Crittenham, Pa., by the 1690s. Important grants of land in the late seventeenth century are listed in Hedrick, *History*, 50.

15. On Pinhorne, see *Docs. Rel.*, 3: 716 n. 2. On Beekman, see Philip White, *The Beekmans of New York in Politics and Commerce, 1647–1877* (New York, 1956); on Van Cortlandt, see John van Cortlandt, Shipping Book, 1699–1702, NYHS; and on Levy, see *Wills*, 1: 123–24, 58. See also Jacob R. Marcus, *American Jewry, Documents: The Eighteenth Century* (Cincinnati, 1959), 235–36. This study does not address the concerns of those who were primarily landed and has not investigated the extent of landholdings among the commercial elite in systematic fashion. For hints at the latter, see Carl Becker, *The History of Political Parties in the Province of New York, 1760–1776* (1909; repr., New York, 1968); Patricia Bonomi, *A Factious People: Politics and Society in Colonial New York* (New York, 1971), esp. 83–97; and Virginia Harrington, *The New York Merchant on the Eve of the Revolution* (New York, 1935), ch. 1.

16. Donald R. Gerlach, *Philip Schuyler and the American Revolution, 1773–1777* (Lincoln, Nebr., 1964), 35, 37–38, 48.

17. Charles Wolley, *A Two Years' Journal in New York and Part of its Territories in America* (1701), ed. Edward G. Bourne (Cleveland, 1902), 69. On Livingston, see Lawrence Leder, *Robert R. Livingston, 1654–1728, and the Politics of Colonial New York* (Chapel Hill, N.C., 1961); on the two Philipses, see Charles Howell and Allan Keller, *The Mill at Philipsburg Manor Upper Mills and a Brief History of Milling* (Tarrytown, N.Y., 1977),

127–33, 135; Sleepy Hollow Restoration, Inc., *Philipsburg Manor* (Tarrytown, N.Y., 1969), 12–15; and *Wills*, 1: 369–74.

18. For Long Island sentiments, see Nov. 2, 1669, in *Docs. Rel.*, 14: 631–33.

19. Palsits, *Mins.*, 519–22. The middlemen John Schoute, Laurence Sluijsen, and William Darvall were granted exceptions to the embargo in order to grist corn at some distance from the city on Long Island and send it to New York.

20. See *Cal. Council Mins.*, Sept. 3, 1668, 10; and, for 1676, James H. Levitt, *For Want of Trade: Shipping and the New Jersey Ports, 1680–1783* (Newark, N.J., 1981), 10–11, 25–26.

21. *Docs. Rel.*, 3: 260–62, 281. On fisheries, see Price, "Economic Function," 158–59; and R. G. Lounsbury, *The British Fishery at Newfoundland* (New Haven, Conn., 1934), ch. 6. On the West Indies, see Palsits, *Mins.*, 1: 194–95, Nov. 18, 1668; ibid., 1: 39–40, Oct. 18, 1669. Cf. New York's level of grain exports with the vast quantities exported from, and consumed in, Amsterdam, cited in Jan de Vries, *The Economy of Europe in an Age of Crisis, 1600–1750* (Cambridge, 1976), 159–63.

22. "Petition of the Mayor and Common Council of New York," Nov. 9, 1683, in *Docs. Rel.*, 3: 337–38; "Petition of Mayor, Aldermen, and Principal Officers of New York," May 16, 1685, C.O. 1: 57, no. 119.

23. *Cal. Council Mins.*, Aug. 3, 1685, 42, and "Address of the Mayor and Common Council of New-York, to the King," 1687, in *Docs. Rel.*, 3: 424–25.

24. See "Governor Thomas Dongan to the Committee of Trade," Feb. 22, 1687, in *Doc. Hist.*, 1: 151; *Cal. Council Mins.*, 1: 621–23, 626–29; and Curtis Nettels, "Economic Relations of Boston, Philadelphia and New York, 1680–1715," *Journal of Economic and Business History* 3 (1931): 195–98. On Sloughter, see "Proposals Submitted by Colonel Sloughter to the Lords of Trade," Sept. 23, 1689, in *Docs. Rel.*, 3: 623–29; "The Commander-in-Chief and Council of New-York to Mr. Blathwayte," Aug. 6, 1691, in ibid., 3: 794–96; and "Address of the Governor and Council of New-York to the King," Aug. 6, 1691, in ibid., 3: 796–800.

25. Osgood, *Mins. Common Council*, 1: 18, 80, 94, 99, 130–35, 141–42, 149–50. For other comments on the 1680s, see Fernow, *Records*, 2: 115, 124–25; Jasper Danckaerts, *Journal of a Voyage to New York and a Tour in Several of the American Colonies in 1679–1680*, ed. Henry C. Murphy, Long Island Historical Society, *Memoirs* (Brooklyn, 1867), 253, 344; and Stanley G. Nissenson, *The Patroon's Domain* (New York, 1937), 75–79. Merchants making these arguments included a spectrum of former and continuing fur traders (e.g., Gerard Beekman, Robert Sanders, Cornelius Cuyler, Abraham Wendell); rising men just turning to commerce (e.g., David van der Heyden, Abraham ten Eyck); and sons of established and diversified merchants who started out in grain trading (e.g., Philip Livingston, John van Cortlandt).

26. Osgood, *Mins. Common Council*, 1: 80, and "Orders of the New York Governor in Council," Jan. 17, 20, 1680, C.O. 5: 1041, no. 4, for the first act. See also *Colonial Laws*, 1: 218; *Docs. Rel.*, 1: 263, 2: 155–56, 3: 232–43, 260–62, 308–13; and *State Papers*, 1697–98, 16: 456–59.

27. *Colonial Laws*, 1: 218, 326–28; Osgood, *Mins. Common Council*, 1: 152–53; "Petition of the Mayor and Common Council of New York," Nov. 9, 1683, in *Docs. Rel.*, 3: 337–39. The signers included prominent and rapidly rising city merchants: Cornelis Steenwyck, John van Brugge, John Laurence, Peter Marius, James Graham, Nicholas Bayard. On the city charter, see sources cited in ch. 2, n. 45.

28. Order of Governor Dongan in Council, May 22, 1684, in C.O. 5: 1041, no. 4; Reply to Mr. Weaver, 1684, in C.O. 5: 1042, no. 4; Petition of Mayor, Aldermen, and Council of New York, Apr. 6, 1684, in C.O. 5: 1041, no. 4.

29. *Wills*, 1: 244, 255, 152, 341, 244. Storey's estate was valued at over £8,000, including sloops and shares in the ship *Robert*.

30. "Sir John Werden to Governor Thomas Dongan," Mar. 10, Nov. 1, 1684, in *Docs. Rel.*, 3: 340–44, 351; *AJ*, 2: 294–95.

31. For this and the next two paragraphs, see Valentine, *History*, 180–81; "Thomas Dongan to the Privy Council," Feb. 22, 1687, in *Docs. Rel.*, 3: 391–93; Rothschild, *New York City Neighborhoods*; and merchants' correspondence cited in the notes to this chapter.

32. "John van Cortlandt to Edmund Andros," May 19, 1690, in *Docs. Rel.*, 3: 717.

33. See "Petition of Thirty-Six Merchants and Other Inhabitants to the King and Queen," May 19, 1690, in *Docs. Rel.*, 3: 748–49; Osgood, *Mins. Common Council*, 1: 230, 272, 280–81, 309, 311–13; Bloch, *HMR*, intro; and *Docs. Rel.*, 3: 279–82, 302–8; 5: 545–47; C.O. 5: 1042, no. 8; C.O. 1: 61, no. 75; and C.O. 5: 1264, no. 92. Merchants who at first were strong Leislerians included Gerard Beekman, Abraham de Peyster, Samuel Staats, Peter Delanoy, George Brewster, and Abraham Gouverneur. For anti-Leislerians, see ch. 3, n. 20 and sources cited in n. 21.

34. On prices, see *The Annals of Albany*, ed. Joel Munsell, 10 vols. (Albany, N.Y., 1850–59), 9: 21, for 1684; and Osgood, *Mins. Common Council*, 1: 150, 161, 202, 227, 248, 254, 256, 322, 339, 370, 375, 376, 405; 2: 1, 13, 25, 38–43, 94–95, 96, and 126, for years through 1700. On lesser merchants, see "Address of the Governor and Council of New-York to the King," Aug. 6, 1691, in *Docs. Rel.*, 3: 796–800; and John van Cortlandt, Shipping Book, 1699–1702, and Letter Book, 1698–1700, NYHS.

35. "Reply of Mr. Weaver to Colonel Fletcher's Answer," in *Docs. Rel.*, 4: 461, 462; *Cal. Council Mins.*, June 25, 1698, 132. "Address of the Governor and Council of New-York to the King," Aug. 6, 1691, in *Docs. Rel.*, 3: 796–800.

36. Osgood, *Mins. Common Council*, 1: 398–99, 513; 2: 7–9, 31–48; *Cal. Council Mins.*, June 25, 1698, 132; "Humble Address," Aug. 6, 1691, in Osgood, *Mins. Common Council*, 2: 44–58; and "The Case of New York, 1698," in C.O. 5: 1041, no. 4.

37. Stokes, *Iconography*, 1: 173, 4: 384, 395, 462, 468; Osgood, *Mins. Common Council*, June 10, 1696, July 2, 1696, Nov. 17, 1696, 1: 405–6, 418, 430–31; and *Cal. Council Mins.*, 115, 116, 117. Earlier embargoes in 1670–72 and 1673 can be followed in Palsits, *Mins.*, 1: 137, 2: 519, and *Colonial Laws*, 1: 96. See sources cited in ch. 2, nn. 67, 72, on Fletcher's role during these years respecting imposts, piracy, and land.

38. "Address of the Governor and Council of New-York to the King," Aug. 6, 1691, in *Docs. Rel.*, 3: 796–800; *State Papers*, 1697–98, 16: 846; and ibid., 1699, 18: 26, 769, 890, and 1209; *Cal. Council Mins.*, 621–23, 626–29; *Doc. Hist.*, 4: 127–30, 400–411; "A Letter from a Gentleman of the City of New York," 1698, in *Narratives of the Insurrections, 1675–1690*, ed. C. M. Andrews (New York, 1915), 360–72, esp. 364; and Robert Ritchie, *The Duke's Province: A Study of New York Politics and Society, 1664–1691* (Chapel Hill, N.C., 1977), ch. 9. See also "Abstracts of Colonel Nicholas Bayard's Journal," in *Docs. Rel.*, 3: 601, 631, 599; "Loyalty Vindicated from the Reflections of a Virulent Pamphlet," 1698, in *Narratives*, ed. Andrews, 375–401; and *A Modest and Impartiall Narrative* (1690), repr. in ibid., 402–10.

39. Statements of June 12, 1693, in *Docs. Rel.*, 4: 31–33. For a less choleric view of events, see Robert Livingston to Francis Nicholson, June 7, 1690, cited by Leder, *Robert*

Livingston, 72. On port duties in the 1690s, see *Docs. Rel.*, 3: 281, 260–62; Osgood, *Mins. Common Council*, 1: 50–62; and *Colonial Laws*, 1: 111–16.

40. *Council Journal*, 1: 423, 436, 428, 429, 430–31; *Docs. Rel.*, 3: 796–800, 4: 37; "Petitions of the Proprietors of East Jersey," Mar. 1, 1697, in C.O. 5: 980, no. A53; "Commissioners of Customs to Lords of Treasury," Aug. 31, 1697, in C.O. 5: 980, no. A53; Osgood, *Mins. Common Council*, 1: 398–99, 513; 2: 7–9, 31–48; *Cal. Council Mins.*, June 25, 1698, 132; "Humble Address," Aug. 6, 1691, in Osgood, *Mins. Common Council*, 2: 44–58; J. L. Bishop, *History of American Manufactures from 1608 to 1860*, 3 vols. (Philadelphia, 1863), 1: 134–35; "The Case of New York, 1698," in C.O. 5: 1041, no. 4.

41. "The Case of New York, 1698," in C.O. 5: 1041, no. 4; "Petition of Mayor, Alderman, and Recorder, and Assistants of New York," July 1, 1698, in C.O. 5: 1041, no. 4; Osgood, *Mins. Common Council*, 2: 6–8, 31, 32, 34, 36–54.

42. "James Graham to William Blathwayt," Sept. 19, 1698, in *Docs. Rel.*, 4: 461–62; "Proofs of the Heads of Complaint Against Col. Fletcher," Jan. 9, 1699, in ibid., 4: 375; *Council Journal*, 1: 45–46.

43. New York City ordinance, Sept. 24, 1700, in C.O. 5: 1045, no. 18; "Bellomont to the Lords of Trade," Nov. 28, 1700, in *Docs. Rel.*, 4: 790–91; Bellomont to Popple, Sept. 24, 1700, in C.O. 5: 1045, no. 18.

44. "Lord Cornbury to the Lords of Trade," July 1, 1708, in *Docs. Rel.*, 10: 57–58.

45. "Petitions of Proprietors of East Jersey," July 5, 1699, and "Memorial of Proprietors of East and West Jersey," Aug. 12, 1701, in C.O. 5: 1261, no. 16; Osgood, *Mins. Common Council*, 1: 84, 90, 111; "Lord Cornbury to the Lords of Trade," July 1, 1708, in *Docs. Rel.*, 10: 57–58; Ritchie, *Duke's Province*, 58–67, 191, 194.

46. See, e.g., Danckaerts, *Journal of a Voyage*, 153; Gov. Bellomont to Popple, July 7, 1698, in C.O. 5: 1040, no. 84; "Agent Nicolls' Payments Schedule, 1695," in C.O. 5: 1040, no. 18; Stuart Bruchey, review of *Money and Politics*, by Joseph Ernst, *William and Mary Quarterly*, 3d ser., 31 (October 1974): 673–75; and Curtis Nettels, *The Money Supply of the American Colonies before 1720*, University of Wisconsin Studies in the Social Sciences and History, 20 (Madison, Wis., 1934), 162–78.

47. Kiliaen van Rensselaer to Jacob Albertsz Planck, Oct. 3, 1636, in *The Van Rensselaer–Bowier Manuscripts*, ed. A. J. F. van Laer, New York State Library, *Annual Report* (Albany, N.Y., 1908), 74n., and a slight variation on pp. 325–26. See also John Hope, *Letters of Credit*, 2d ed. (London, 1784), 10–14, 16, 42, 61, 67.

48. Gerard de Malynes, *Consuetudo, vel lex mercatoria* (London, 1622), 8, 24; Sir William Petty, *A Treatise of Taxes and Contributions* (1662), repr. in *The Economic Writings of Sir William Petty*, ed. Charles Hull, 2 vols. (London, 1899), 2: 20–51; John Locke, *Consequences of Lowering the Interest and Raising the Value of Money* (1692), repr. in J. R. McCulloch, *Principles of Political Economy* (London, 1870), 220–360, esp. 226–27; Rice Vaughan, *A Discourse of Coin and Coinage* (1675), repr. in J. R. McCulloch, comp., *A Select Collection of Scarce and Valuable Tracts on Money* (London, 1933), pref., 37, 40; William Pollexfen, *Discourse of Trade, Coyne and Paper Credit* (London, 1697), cited by Joseph Dorfman, *The Economic Mind in American Civilization, 1606–1865*, 4 vols. (New York, 1946), 1: 168–77. Other arguments for low prices can be found in [Anon.], *Considerations on the Present High Price of Provisions and Necessaries of Life* (London, 1764); [Soame Jenyns], *Thoughts on the Causes and Consequences of the Present High Price of Provisions* (London, 1767); and Sir James Steuart, *An Inquiry into the Principles of Political Economy*,

ed. Andrew Skinner, 2 vols. (1767; repr., Edinburgh, 1966), 1: 175, 181, 485. For arguments favoring high prices in domestic trade, see Postlethwayt, *Dict.*, 1: s.v. "price"; and Arthur Young, *A Six Months Tour Through the North of England*, 2 vols. (London, 1768), 1: 187–94.

49. See also Barbon, *Discourse of Trade*, 15, 16; Petty, *Treatise of Taxes*, 35; Locke, *Consequences of Lowering the Interest*, 222–27; and Petty, *Political Arithmetick*, in *The Economic Writings of Sir William Petty*, 2: 89–90, 99.

50. "John van Cortlandt to Edmund Andros," May 19, 1690, in *Docs. Rel.*, 3: 717, and other merchants' correspondence cited in the notes to this chapter; Roger Sherman, *An Almanack for . . . 1750* (New York, 1750); and [Anon.], *The New York and Country Almanack for 1776* (New York, n.d.).

51. Stoker, *Prices*, 215–16; John H. Hickcox, *A History of the Bills of Credit or Paper Money Issued by New York from 1709 to 1789* (Albany, N.Y., 1866), 2–10.

52. Howell and Keller, *Mill at Philipsburg*, 127–33, 135; John van Cortlandt, Shipping Book, 1699–1702, and Letter Book, 1698–1700; Bonomi, *Factious People*, 60–68. On the association of the landed interest with unsympathetic governors, see *Council Journal*, 1: 35, 49, 85, 100, 114; and *Cal. Council Mins.*, 2: 70, 84, 100, 118, 125. On the alliance of wealthy importers with governors, and against lesser merchants associated with exporting, see Leder, *Robert R. Livingston*, 84–85, referring to the wealthy Robert R. Livingston, Stephanus van Cortlandt, Nicholas Bayard, Gabriel Minvielle, Frederick Philipse, Philip Schuyler, Charles Lodwick, James Graham and Lewis Morris; the rising J. Dudley, William Pinhorne, and Richard Townley; and the immigrant "wretches" John Lawrence and Thomas Johnson.

53. For example, Daniel Denton, *A Brief Description of New York* (1670; repr., Cleveland, 1902); Rev. John Miller *A Description of the Province and City of New York* (1695; repr., New York, 1862); and merchants' correspondence.

54. E.g., Osgood, *Mins. Common Council*, 6: 336; Maverick, *Letters*; *Docs. Rel.*, 14: 631–33; and *New-York Gazette*, Sept. 19, 1763.

55. Beekman to Henry Lloyd, Boston, May 28, 1767, cited in White, *Beekmans of New York*, 512–13.

56. On export prices rising faster than import prices, accounting for aspects of material improvement, see Appendix A, figs. A.1 and A.2; Francis Lewis, Letters, and Thomas Moffatt Letter Book, both NYHS; Marc Egnal, "The Economic Development of the Thirteen Colonies, 1720–1775," *William and Mary Quarterly*, 3d ser., 32 (Apr. 1975): 201–3, 217–21; and Carole Shammas, "How Self-Sufficient Was Early America?" *Journal of Interdisciplinary History* 13 (1982): 247–72.

F I V E   The Spur of Success

1. See Charles M. Andrews, *The Colonial Period of American History: England's Commercial and Colonial Policy*, 4 vols. (New Haven, Conn., 1938), 4: 31, 64, 294, 296; *The Dutch Republic in the Eighteenth Century: Decline, Enlightenment, and Revolution*, ed. Margaret Jacob and Wijnand W. Mijnhardt (Ithaca, N.Y., 1992), intro.; D. M. Joslin, "London Private Bankers, 1720–1785," *Economic History Review*, 2d ser., 7 (1954): 169; P. G. M. Dickson, *The Financial Revolution in England: A Study in the Development of Public Credit, 1688–1756* (New York, 1967), ch. 2; Jan de Vries, *The Economy of Europe in an Age of Crisis, 1600–1750* (Cambridge, 1976), ch. 8; Keith Horsefield, *British Monetary*

Experiments, 1650–1710 (London, 1960); William Letwin, *The Origins of Scientific Economics* (London, 1963), ch. 3; Ralph Davis, *The Rise of the Atlantic Economies* (Ithaca, N.Y., 1973), 239–40, 246–49.

2. William de Britaine, *The Interest of England in the Present War with Holland* (London, 1672); Carew Reynel, *The True English benefit; or, an Account of the Chief National Improvements* (London, 1674); James Whiston, *The Mismanagements in Trade Discover'd, and Adapt Methods to Preserve and Exceedingly Improve It* (London, 1704); and Daniel Defoe, *A Plan of the English Commerce* (London, 1728), 22. See also Joshua Gee, *The Trade and Navigation of Great Britain*, 2 vols. (1729; 3d ed., London, 1731); John Locke, MSS of 1674, cited by C. B. Macpherson, *The Political Theory of Possessive Individualism, Hobbes to Locke* (Oxford, 1962), 207; Charles King, *The British Merchant* (London, 1721); Jacob Vanderlint, *Money Answers All Things; Or, an Essay to Make Money Sufficiently Plentiful Amongst all Ranks of People* (1734; repr., Baltimore, 1914); Charles Davenant, *The True Picture of a Modern Whig* (London, 1701), 26; and Daniel Defoe, *A Review of the State of the British Nation* (London, 1711), where he says, "Money begets money, trade circulates and the tide of money flows with it; one hand washes the other and both hands wash the face."

3. *New-York Mercury,* Oct. 10, 1763; Daniel Defoe, *The Complete English Tradesman,* 2 vols. (London, 1727), 1: 241, 246, and id., *Defoe's Review,* no. 124 (1706). David Hume highly approved of merchants in 1752 in "Of Commerce," "Of Money," and "Of the Balance of Trade," in *David Hume: Writings on Economics,* ed. Eugene Rotwein (Madison, Wis., 1955), 3–18, 33–46, 60–77.

4. Richard Campbell, *The London Tradesman* (London, 1747), 284–86; Gary Nash, *The Urban Crucible: Social Change, Political Consciousness, and the Origins of the American Revolution* (Cambridge, Mass., 1979), 117–18; Carl Bridenbaugh, *Cities in Revolt: Urban Life in America, 1743–1776* (New York, 1955), 79.

5. On the Utrecht settlement, see Immanuel Wallerstein, *The Modern World-System, II, Mercantilism and the Consolidation of the European World-Economy, 1600–1750* (New York, 1980), 254–55, 270–71. Defoe is quoted from *Plan of the English Commerce,* 22. On mercantilist arguments against open trade with France, and the conception of France as a competitor, see the multi-authored work *The British Merchant; Or, Commerce Preserved* (London, 1713–14). On mercantile awareness about interior North American markets, see Richard W. Van Alstyne, *The Rising American Empire* (New York, 1960), 13–16, and H. T. Dickinson, *Liberty and Property: Political Ideology in Eighteenth-Century Britain* (London, 1977), 30–32, 41, 45–47, 81, 85, 91–96.

6. Joseph Harris, *An Essay upon Money and Coins,* in *A Selection of Scarce and Valuable Tracts on Money,* ed. J. R. McCulloch (1757; repr., London, 1856); Matthew Decker, *Essay on the Causes of the Decline of Foreign Trade* (London, 1734; repr., 1744); Davis, *Rise of the Atlantic Economies,* chs. 5–7, 12; Richard Kobener, *Empire* (New York, 1965), 79. There is growing material evidence that the ideological optimism of contemporaries about England's rapid development after 1713 involved more hope than reality; see N. F. C. Crafts, *British Economic Growth during the Industrial Revolution* (Oxford, 1985), 14–16. On the balance of trade, see my ch. 2. On Bacon, see source cited in ch. 2, n. 24.

7. Charles Davenant, *Discourse on the Public Revenue and on the Trade of England* (London, 1698), pt. 2, ch. 3, "On the Plantation Trade," at 204, 207. Davenant also forecast the loss of America if colonists challenged their subordination: "But otherwise they

are worse than members lopp'd from the body politic, being indeed like offensive arms wrested from a nation to be turned against it as occasion shall serve" (ibid., 204). Postlethwayt, *Dict.*, s.v. "colonies." And see John Cary, *An Essay on the Coyn and Credit of England* (London, 1696), 14, where he calls the colonies "our golden mines"; James Whiston, *The Mismanagements of Trade Discover'd* (London, 1704), 25, where he calls the colonies a "jewel in England's diadem"; John Houghton, *A Collection of Letters for the Improvement of Husbandry and Trade* (London, 1681); Dalby Thomas, *An Historical Account of the Rise and Growth of the West India Colonies* (1690), repr., *Harleian Miscellany*, 12 vols. (London, 1808), 9: 410–19; Sir William Petty, *Political Arithmetick*, in *The Economic Writings of Sir William Petty*, 2 vols., ed. Charles Hull (Cambridge, 1899), esp. 2: 290–96; John Pollexfen, *Discourse of Trade* (London, 1697), esp. 6, 87; William Wood, *A Survey of Trade* (London, 1718); Gee, *Trade and Navigation*, 1: 36–39, 173; Samuel Vetch to the Board of Trade, 1708, in *State Papers*, 1708–9, 2: 46–48; and [Anon.], *The Case of the Traders by Sea* (London, 1707).

8. "Lord Cornbury to the Board of Trade," July 1, 1708, in *Docs. Rel.*, 5: 57; C.O. 5: 1222–25; *New-York Gazette*, July 24, 31, Aug. 2, 9, 20, 1732; [Anon.], *The Present State of the British Sugar Islands Considered in a Letter from a Gentleman of Barbados* (London, 1731).

9. Gee, *Trade and Navigation*; and see also Richard Steele, *An Essay Upon Trade and Public Credit* (London, 1714); [Anon.], *The Present State of the British and French Trade to America* (London, 1745); Otis Little, *The State of the Trade in the Northern Colonies Considered* (London, 1748); [Anon.], *A Short History of the Progress of the French Trade and Navigation* (London, 1750); and François Crouzet, "England and France in the Eighteenth Century: A Comparative Analysis of Two Economic Growths," in *Causes of the Industrial Revolution in England*, ed. Peter Mathias (London, 1967), 146–48.

10. The most consequential acts for New Yorkers were the Wool Act, 10 Will. 3, c. 10, 1699; the Hat Act, 5 Geo. 2, c. 22, 1732; the Naval Stores Acts, 3 Anne, c. 10, sec. 8, 1705, and 2 Geo. 2, c. 35, sec. 16, 1729; the Iron Act, 23 Geo. 2, c. 29, 1750; the Molasses Act, 6 Geo. 2, c. 13, 1733; and acts dealing with copper ore, 8 Geo. 1, c. 18, par. 22, 1721, furs, 8 Geo. 1, c. 15, par. 24, 1722; and tobacco, cotton wool, and dyewoods (except logwood), 12 Car. 2, c. 19, par. 18, 1660. By 1706, English merchants paid £6 per ton for importing hemp, £5 per ton for masts, £4 per ton for pitch, £4 per ton for tar, and £3 per ton for rosin and turpentine. From 1723 to the Revolution, timber bore no duties; English ports granted drawbacks of all but 2 percent of the import duties on hemp and linen originating at imperial possessions. See also Irene D. Neu, "The Iron Plantations of Colonial New York," *New York History* 33 (Jan. 1952): 3–24; Charles S. Boyer, *Early Forges and Furnaces in New Jersey* (Philadelphia, 1931), 4–7. On the Molasses Act, see ch. 6; on colonial manufacturing, see ch. 7.

11. On benefits of English policies, see John J. McCusker and Russell R. Menard, *The Economy of British America* (Chapel Hill, N.C., 1985), 46–50, and Ralph Davis, *The Rise of the English Shipping Industry in the Seventeenth and Eighteenth Centuries* (Newton Abbot, Dev., Eng., 1962), chs. 1, 14. I make no attempt to assess the actual balance of payments between New York and England. On the difficulties of assessing tonnage, see ch. 2, n. 42. Turnaround times stayed about the same, as did voyage times and shipbuilding costs; see, e.g., William Walton, Insurance Book, Municipal Archives, New York. Some drawbacks, such as the one on sugar, provided benefits as well; see ch. 2. New Yorkers owned about 11 percent of the vessels clearing for Britain between 1715 and 1718, com-

pared with about 33 percent of their West Indies vessels. Curiously enough, merchants on both sides of the Atlantic avoided discussion of the early Corn Laws as they affected New York's wheat and flour exports. The first time this legislation received serious treatment was in Adam Smith's *Wealth of Nations*, bk. 2, ch. 5, where it is thoroughly criticized as injurious to the consumer and small producer.

12. Joshua Gee to Council of Trade and Plantations, Oct. 27, 1721, in *State Papers*, 1720–21, 32: 475, and id., *Trade and Navigation*, 5–9. See also Defoe's *Mercator*, May 26, 1713–July 20, 1714; Wood, *Survey of Trade*, 155, 136; and Decker, *Essay on the Causes*, 176.

13. See, e.g., Gov. Burnet to the Council of Trade and Plantations, Nov. 21, 1724, in *State Papers*, 1724–25, 35: 409; Charles Wilson, *England's Apprenticeship, 1603–1763* (London, 1965), esp. ch. 1, xi; Morton Horwitz, *The Transformation of American Law, 1780–1860* (Cambridge, Mass., 1977), intro.; Macpherson, *Political Theory of Possessive Individualism*, 58, ch. 5; and Nash, *Urban Crucible*, 303, 311. Economic freedom was also connected to changing notions of political liberty; the Glorious Revolution of 1688–89 had legitimated doubts about the unquestioned authority of the state, and gradual social and economic changes prompted revisions of the traditional prescription about liberty—a set of carefully delimited boundaries within which individuals could expend their energies under the eye of an outside authority, a "privilege held by grant or prescription by which men enjoy some benefit beyond the ordinary subject." The emerging meaning of liberty, as a more abstract set of rules to which one freely subscribed, and giving authority to accumulate unless restrained by the law, helped colonists move toward the belief that their property rights need not be subordinated to the public interest; rights and authority should be able to coexist. See Bernard Bailyn, *The Origins of American Politics* (New York, 1967), ch. 1; and Michael Kammen, *Spheres of Liberty: Changing Perceptions of Liberty in American Culture* (Madison, Wis., 1986).

14. Cornelius Cuyler to Richard Jeneway [*sic*], Jan. 13, 1728, Cornelius Cuyler, Letter Book, 1724–36, AAS.

15. On London and Amsterdam, see E. A. Wrigley, *Population and History* (New York, 1969), 148. On the 1703 census, see David Valentine, *History of the City of New York* (New York, 1853), 295, 345–65; and Thomas Archdeacon, *New York City, 1664–1710: Conquest and Change* (Ithaca, N.Y., 1976), 48–50. On 1731 numbers, see Robert Wells, "The New York Census of 1731," *New-York Historical Society Quarterly* 57 (1973): 256. On 1737, see *Docs. Rel.*, 5: 702, 929. On 1764, see Samuel McKee Jr., "The Economic Pattern of Colonial New York," in *History of the State of New York*, ed. A. C. Flick, 4 vols. (New York, 1933), 2: 263, 264.

16. Carl Bridenbaugh, *Cities in the Wilderness: The First Century of Urban Life in America, 1625–1742* (New York, 1938), 332; Beverly McAnear, "Politics in Provincial New York, 1689–1761" (Ph.D. diss., Stanford University, 1935), 359–60; Richard Lester, *Monetary Experiments: Early American and Recent Scandinavian* (Princeton, N.J., 1939), 117; McKee, "Economic Pattern," 2: 268–69; William I. Roberts III, "Samuel Stork: An Eighteenth-Century London Merchant Trading to the American Colonies," *Business History Review* 39 (1965): 147–70.

17. Bloch, *HMR*; "Earl of Bellomont to the Lords of Trade," Apr. 1700, in *Docs. Rel.*, 4: 790, 791.

18. On trade, for July 1715–July 1743, see quarterly reports (101 of a possible 112 quarters giving data on entrances and clearances) from the customs collector in Naval Office

Records, C.O. 5: 1222–28, and *New-York Gazette*, 1729–43; and for 1748–64, see C.O. 5: 1227–28; *New-York Evening Post*, 1749; *New-York Gazette, or Weekly Post-Boy*, 1752–67; *New-York Weekly Journal*, 1743–51; and *New-York Mercury*, 1752–67. For quotations, see Isaac Bobin to George Clarke, Sept. 12, 27, and Oct. 18, 1721, in *Letters of Isaac Bobin, Esq., 1718–1730*, ed. E. B. O'Callaghan (Albany, N.Y., 1872), 89, 95, 96; "Governor Cosby's reports to the Board of Trade," June 2, and Feb. 17, 1734, in *Docs. Rel.*, 6: 116, 112; "John Trusty," *New-York Weekly Journal*, Apr. 22, 1734. On the size of the fleet, see *Docs. Rel.*, 4: 790 (1700), 3: 398 (1749), 4: 511 (1749); *New-York Weekly Journal*, Apr. 8, 22, May 20, July 8, 1734; and *New-York Gazette*, Aug. 20, 1733. Many references suggest that New Jerseyans built small ketches and sloops to sell to New Yorkers in the 1720s–30s; Perth Amboy and Boston merchants sold vessels to New Yorkers over this period.

19. Jacob Price, "A Note on the Value of Colonial Exports of Shipping," *Journal of Economic History* 36 (1976): 704–24; Virginia Harrington, *The New York Merchant on the Eve of the Revolution* (New York, 1935), 176, 356, 358, 368; American Inspector General's Ledgers, Customs 16: 1, Public Record Office. Between 1750 and 1774, there were 362 clearances from New York to London; of these, 141 (40%) involved vessels owned by New Yorkers. See also sources cited in n. 41 below.

20. C.O. 5: 1225–28; Jacob Price, "Economic Function and the Growth of the American Port Towns," *Perspectives in American History* 8 (1974): 159, 185. Trends described here contrast sharply with those discussed in chs. 6 and 7.

21. See, e.g., Jacob Marcus, *American Jewry, Documents: The Eighteenth Century* (Cincinnati, 1959), 1; *New-York Gazette*, July 17, 1738. Osgood, *Mins. Common Council*, 6: 355; Gerard Beekman to Robert Crooke, July 19, 1753, to Henry Lloyd, Dec. 15, 1755, to Adam Schoales, Feb. 15, 1752, to Jacob Richardson, July 14, 1760, to James Searle, Mar. 25, 1760, to Thomas Reynolds, Dec. 24, 1753, to William Edmonds, Oct. 2, 1754, to Israel Boardman, Aug. 26, 1754, and to John Sayre, Dec. 15, 29, 1755, in *The Beekman Mercantile Papers, 1746–1799*, ed. Philip White, 3 vols. (New York, 1956); and for a comparison with England, see Defoe, *Complete English Tradesman*, 1: 354, on "forcing a vend."

22. *Colonial Laws*, 4: 925, 5: 67–71; Rita S. Gottesman, *The Arts and Crafts of New York*, NYHS, *Collections*, vol. 69 (New York, 1936), 263–67; J. R. Dolan, *The Yankee Peddlers of Early America* (New York, 1964), ch. 2, 256–58; H. A. Wooster, "A Forgotten Factor in American Industrial History," *American Economic Review* 16 (1926): 14–27; Campbell, *London Tradesman*; Defoe, *Complete English Tradesman*, 2: 2124; Fernand Braudel, *The Wheels of Commerce: Civilization and Capitalism, 15th–18th Century* (New York, 1982), 74–78, 79, 80.

23. Account books of Richard Sause, John Milligan, and Henry William Stiegel, NYPL; account books of Samuel Deall and John Wetherhead, NYHS.

24. See, e.g., *New-York Gazette*, Mar. 6, Oct. 16, 1727; June 3, 1728; Oct. 13, 1729; Oct. 8, 1733; Oct. 28, 1734; Apr. 7, Aug. 4, 1735; June 7, 1736; Oct. 10, 1737; July 31, 1738; Mar. 11, 1740; and *New York Journal*, Feb. 24, 1734; Feb. 3, 1735; Apr. 19, Nov. 29, 1736; Feb. 23, 1737; Mar. 10, 1740; Apr. 20, 1741; Jan. 11, 1742.

25. Marcus, *American Jewry*, 402.

26. Jaspar Danckaerts and Peter Sluyter, *Journal of a Voyage to New York, 1679–1680*, trans. and ed. Henry C. Murphy (Brooklyn, N.Y., 1867), 117, 133, 153; and Edward Hatton, *The Merchants Magazine; or, Tradesman's Treasury*, 3d ed. (London, 1699), 22.

27. "Governor Andros to the Board of Trade," Apr. 16, 1678, in *Docs. Rel.*, 3: 260–62,

at 261; and Charles Wolley, *A Two Years' Journal in New York and Part of its Territories in America* (1701), ed. Edward G. Bourne (Cleveland, 1902), 69, 36–37.

28. For Vetch, see G. M. Waller, *Samuel Vetch: Colonial Enterpriser* (Chapel Hill, N.C., 1960), 45; and *Wills,* 5: 244, 245. For Van Dam, and, in the next paragraph, Faneuil, see Bloch, *HMR,* and C.O. 5: 1222. Other examples include Nicholas Bayard, Philip French, Lawrence Reade, Stephen and Jacob van Cortlandt, and Frederick Philipse. Isaac Marquez, also a dry-goods importer and peltry exporter, acquired wealth without diversifying; his connections with Jewish firms in London assured him of clothing and textiles for city retailers and a position near the top of mercantile status and wealth in New York down to 1705, when Marquez's name disappears from port ledgers. David Provoost Sr. married a sister of Johannes de Peyster Sr. in 1666 and, after many years of business in New York City, left what was then a substantial fortune to his son David, who not only had the advantage of being born into an extended and wealthy family but also inherited important business connections and trading vessels from his uncle Johannes. By the turn of the eighteenth century, David Provoost Jr. had spent a few years as a bolter and retailer, and as a West Indies provisions trader, but he gave up the mills and stores after Queen Anne's War in order to devote himself to international trade. Provoost complained of a slow commercial start from 1713 to 1715 and of difficulties in providing for a household that included five indentured servants and three slaves, no doubt due to the postwar recession. John Cruger was assessed among the lowest third of city residents in 1703, but by 1708 he was one of the top forty merchants, and over the period 1713 to 1716, he imported European goods of greater value than most other importers did. Bloch, *HMR,* and C.O. 5: 1222–23.

29. *Proceedings of the American Jewish Historical Society* 21 (1913): 27, 31, 48; and *The Lee Max Friedman Collection of American Jewish Colonial Correspondence—Letters of the Franks Family, 1733–1748,* ed. Leo Hershkowitz and Isidore S. Meyer (Waltham, Mass., 1968), 24; *Wills,* 4: 202–3 (Van Cortlandt, 1748); 4: 230–32 (Philip Livingston, 1749); 5: 131–32 (Abraham van Horne, 1756); 6: 392–93 (Gerret van Horne, 1765). A 1728 assessment rated Moses Levy, Frederick Philipse, Augustus Jay, Daniel Jamison, Rodrigo Pacheco, and Stephen Richards the top personal and real property holders in the city; see Bruce Wilkenfeld, "The Social and Economic Structure of the City of New York, 1695–1796" (Ph.D. diss., Columbia University, 1973), 114–24; In 1730, the top 26 of 138 vessel owners constituted an elite with familiar family names (e.g., Walton, French, Van Horne).

30. On De Lancey, see *A History of Westchester County,* 2 vols., ed. J. Thomas Scharf (Philadelphia, 1886), and C.O. 5: 1222–25. Lesser merchants in the 1720s included John Theobold, John van Hose, John Halleck, Edward Burling, Robert Lurting, Gilbert Livingston, Humphrey Salisbury, William Hampton, Francis van Dyke, William Walton, Justice Bosche, Nathaniel Simpson, John VanderHuile, John Roosevelt, John van Brugh, Samuel Burdett, Vincent Bowdine, Robert Howard, Andrew Meade, John Bradock, John Conley, and others.

31. For the Van Hornes, see C.O. 5: 1222–25. Also active from the mid 1720s through the 1730s, and eminent among city merchants, were John and Philip van Cortlandt, John Barbarie, and Abraham de Lucena.

32. Bloch, *HMR,* passim; C.O. 5: 1224–25; and author's collective biographies.

33. For the 1701 assessment, see "Comptroller's Tax Book, 1699–1712," Paul Klapper Memorial Library, Queens College, New York, which shows 1,009 taxable persons. Wil-

kenfeld, "Social and Economic Structure," 28, 42, 53–54, 61–67, 71–73, 91–99, 103–21, uses this assessment to analyze the positions of 91 merchants, 36 of whom were among the wealthiest 10 percent, but he does not undertake an extensive analysis of the other two-thirds. For the 1703 assessment, see *Doc. Hist*, 1: 395–405; *The Burghers of New Amsterdam and the Freemen of New York*, NYHS, *Collections*, vol. 18 (New York, 1885); Osgood, *Mins. Common Council*, 4: 1–2; and Gottesman, *Arts and Crafts*, passim. For analysis of the Dutch merchants slipping from eminent to middling stature about this time, and an ethnic analysis of the merchant community, see Archdeacon, *New York City, 1664–1710*, 48–54, 60–64. In appendix I of her *New York City Neighborhoods: The Eighteenth Century* (San Diego, 1990), Nan Rothschild looks at these 110 merchants again and puts 47 of them in a category of merchants with unidentifiable property holdings. Using an eclectic array of materials, most of these 47 can in fact be identified with respect to commercial activities, entrance and clearance records, vessel shares and ownerships, household size, and other commercial characteristics, and most were of middling status. Rothschild's table 6.1, pp. 172–73, summarizes the positions of only 63 merchants in 1703, and thus leaves many uncounted; in any event, the fact that virtually half of the individuals she counts lie below the median assessment in this table qualifies her statement that merchants were found in "concentration . . . at one end [the top] of the wealth spectrum." In 1703, most taxed city residents were still colonial-born Dutch (42%); the next greatest number were English-born immigrants (30%), followed by African (18%), French (9%), and Jewish (1%) inhabitants. Alice Hanson Jones, *Wealth of a Nation to Be: The American Colonies on the Eve of the American Revolution* (New York, 1980), 126, finds that 1695, 1701, and 1730 assessments all show the top 10 percent owning about 45 percent of assessed city wealth; Archdeacon, *New York City, 1664–1710*, 148, confirms this. Merchants of eminent stature by the end of the decade also included Robert Watts, Andrew Fresneau, Patrick MacKnight, Abraham Wendell, Philip Schuyler, Rodrigo Pacheco, Lawrence Reade, and Barent Rynders, among others.

34. Author's biographical compilation; Bloch, *HMR*, passim; Valentine, *History*; *Doc. Hist.*, 1: 395–405, and C.O. 5: 1222–25. As in 1695, this assessment was based on land and does not include ship ownership, capital, or commercial inventories. Also, many residents are not included, and the merchant lists have been corrected according to the author's biographies.

35. See NYHS, *Collections*, vol. 43 (New York, 1910), 1–35, for the 1695 assessment; *Doc. Hist.*, 1: 395–405, for the 1703 assessment; and C.O. 5: 1222–25 for 1715 to 1728.

36. For 1708, see "Comptroller's Tax Book, 1701–1713," Klapper Memorial Library, Queens College, New York; for 1701, see n. 33 above; and for individuals, Bloch, *HMR*, and C.O. 5: 1222–25. Among those whose fortunes declined were Paul Droillett, Lewis Caree, Elias Noel, Cornelius Lodge, John Gurney, John Scott, John Carelse, Augustus Lucas, and William Anderson. Over the years 1701 to 1709 and 1713 to 1715, each of these was making one or two voyages per year with many others; all of them figured among the top forty merchants of 1703 but had fallen to places among the next forty by 1708. Jackson Turner Main, *The Social Structure of Revolutionary America* (Princeton, N.J., 1965), chs. 1, 3, and 4, estimates that the average annual income of laborers and seasonal craftsmen was £25–60; for artisans and small "manufacturers," £75–85; for a shopkeeper, £350.

37. *Wills*, 1: 314 (Marius); Wilkenfeld, "Social and Economic Structure"; Esther Sin-

gleton, *Social New York under the Georges*, 2 vols. (1902; repr., New York, 1969), 1: 53–65; Harrington, *New York Merchant*, 52–54; W. A. Duer, *The Life of William Alexander, Earl of Sterling*, New Jersey Historical Society, *Collections*, vol. 2 (1847), 6.

38. Bloch, *HMR*; *Docs. Rel.*, 5: 774; C.O. 5: 1223–25.

39. Thomas Pennington & Son, invoice, Sept. 10, 1755, in David Clarkson Invoices, 1751–55, NYHS; and "Sample Invoices of Shipment to James Beekman, 1753–1759," in *Beekman Mercantile Papers*, ed. White, 3: 1395–1411; *New-York Gazette*, advertisements of Samuel Bayard in 1730, and those of John Scott for snuff and perfume in 1732.

40. See, e.g., Charles Ludlow Misc. Business Papers, Columbia University; David Clarkson Correspondence, William Alexander Papers, Charles Nicoll Journal, and Ships File, all at NYHS; and *New-York Gazette*, advertisements for the 1730s–40s.

41. For June 1714–June 1717, see *Docs. Rel.*, 5: 618; for Dec. 1729–Dec. 1730, see *Boston Weekly Newsletter*, Mar. 4, 1731; for 1731, see *American Weekly Mercury*, Mar. 16, 1732; for the 1720s to 1760s generally, see C.O. 5: 1222–25; C.O. 16: 1; Howard Chapelle, *The History of American Sailing Ships* (New York, 1935), 33; Nash, *Urban Crucible*, 123–26; and Appendix A, table 3; *New-York Weekly Journal*, Mar. 28, 1737; "Governor George Clarke to the Board of Trade," June 2, 1738, in *Docs. Rel.*, 4: 116; McAnear, "Politics in Provincial New York," 361–65; Burnaby, *Travels in North America*, 167, 188; "Answer of the Collector of New York to Queries of the Board of Trade," 1738, 1747, in *Doc. Hist.*, 4: 182–83; 1: 725–26; "Governor Clinton to the Board of Trade," 1749, in *Docs. Rel.*, 4: 511; Price, "Note," 704–24; Harrington, *New York Merchant*, 176, 356, 358, 368.

42. Joseph Goldenberg, *Shipbuilding in Colonial America* (Charlottesville, Va., 1976), 20–21, 100–107.

43. *New-York Gazette*, advertisements of Joseph Reade for tea imports over the year 1736; C.O. 16: 1; Neil McKendrick, "Commercialization and the Economy," in id., John Brewer, and J. H. Plumb, *The Birth of a Consumer Society: The Commercialization of Eighteenth-Century England* (Bloomington, Ind., 1982), 28, 29, 81, 104–7; *New-York Post-Boy*, 1749–62; and Levi Coit to Abraham Wendell, Nov. 1759, Levi Coit Letter Book, NYHS.

44. C.O. 5: 1222–25. The three wine importers in 1708 were Thomas Bayeaux, Brandt Rhynderse, and Lewis Gomez; those in 1715 were Rip van Dam, Abraham de Peyster, and Abraham de Lucena. All of these men also shipped large amounts of grain and flour by then, and all were in the top 10 percent of the city tax assessments of 1708 or 1718. Gomez's daughters married De Lucena's sons.

45. William Bolton, *The Bolton Letters; or, The Letters of an English Merchant in Madeira, 1695–1714*, ed. André L. Simon, 2 vols. (London, 1928), entries for Dec. 15, 1695, Sept. 30, 1696, Oct. 18, 1697, July 17, Sept. 4, 1698, June 15, 1699, Feb. 24, 1700; Waller, *Samuel Vetch*, 59–62; Lawrence Leder, *Robert R. Livingston, 1654–1728, and the Politics of Colonial New York* (Williamsburg, Va., 1961), 17n; G. L. Beer, *The Old Colonial System*, 2 vols. (New York, 1912), 2: 345n; correspondence of the Cuylers, Ten Eycks, Van der Heydens, Wendells, Abraham de Peyster, and Charles Nicholl, NYHS; "Earl of Bellomont to the Lords of Trade," Nov. 28, 1700, in *Docs. Rel.*, 4: 790; Gov. Hunter to the Lords of Trade, Nov. 12, 1715, in *State Papers*, 1716, 29: 337, 340, 70, 32, 417; Caleb Heathcote to the Council of Trade and Plantations, Oct. 5, 1714, in ibid., 28: 388.

46. "Mr. Colden's Account of the Trade of New-York," 1723, in *Docs. Rel.*, 5: 686; C.O. 5: 1222–25; Gov. Hunter to the Board of Trade, in *State Papers*, 1716, 29: 256; Charles Whit-

worth, *The State of the Trade of Great Britain in Its Imports and Exports, 1697–1773* (London, 1776); *New-York Gazette,* 1735–36; Robert G. Albion, *The Rise of New York Port, 1815–1860* (New York, 1939), 6; John Huske, *The Present State of North America,* quoted in James G. Lydon, "Fish and Flour for Gold: Southern Europe and the Colonial American Balance of Payments," *Business History Review* 8 (1972): 172.

47. *New-York Gazette,* 1727–40, and correspondence of Cornelius Cuyler, Philip Cuyler, and Robert Livingston, NYHS. Duane and Richard are listed in the *New-York Gazette* advertisements, 1739. On salt imports and reexports, see Malcolm Kier, *The March of Commerce* (New Haven, Conn., 1727), ch. 1; and on trade to Newfoundland in the 1740s, see, e.g, *Cal. Council Mins.,* May 16, 1744, 344.

48. 3 Geo. 3, c. 12, sec. 1; "Report on the Trade in Lisbon," Aug. 3, 1765, in C.O. 388/95; Philip Cuyler to Scott, Pringle, Cheap & Co. of Madeira, Jan. 16, 1759, Cuyler, Letter Book; John Watts to George and John Riddell, Sept. 18, 1764, and to Scott, Pringle, Cheap & Co., Jan. 13, 1764, in *WLB,* 286, 214. Figures for the trade are in C.O. 16: 1. On English production of Port wine to compete with Madeira, and demand for more grain, see Thomas Pownall, *The Administration of the Colonies* (London, 1764), 1: 98–100, 256–57. The size and relative importance of New York's wine trade with southern Europe attracted the attention of England's mercantilists at the end of the Seven Years' War; it was taxed as of 1763 at steeper rates than the colonial ones of 1690 onward. The fee of £7 per tun (252 gallons usually) for importing wine direct from southern Europe, as compared to the £4 per tun if it was routed through English customs, evoked more than verbal protest. An article signed "P" in the *Providence Gazette,* Jan. 21, 1764, agreed that the illegal trade with the West Indies, Holland, and Hamburg ought to be suppressed because it was injurious to England's welfare. But the fruits, raisins, and wines of southern Europe did not compete with English exports and were "of little consequence" in profits. While it was probably savvy to argue that southern European commodities were scant competitive commercial threat to England's exports, the received wisdom that profits were from 25 percent to 40 percent in the southern European trade gives the lie to the claim that the trade was of little consequence.

49. C.O. 5: 1227–28; C.O. 16: 1; *Beekman Mercantile Papers,* ed. White, 1: 31–32, 39, 81, 83–84, 98, 135–39, 156–59, 162, 195; *Letters and Diary of John Rowe, Boston Merchant, 1759–1762, and 1764–1779,* ed. Anne Rowe Cunningham (Boston, 1903), 341, 390–91; Peter Kalm, *Travels in North America, 1748–1751,* ed. Adolph Benson, 2 vols. (New York, 1966), 1: 253–58, 237, 238–45; *Commerce of Rhode Island,* 9: 464–65, 476, 487, 508, 518; 10: 197, 221, 261, 308, 365.

50. Henry Cruger to Aaron Lopez, Feb. 1, 1772, in *Commerce of Rhode Island,* 9: 385–88. Philadelphia's exports of flaxseed grew even more rapidly than New York's.

51. Samuel Maverick to George Cartwright, *Clarendon Papers,* in NYHS, *Collections,* vol. 3 (New York, 1869), 126–29; Andrews, *Colonial Period,* 4: 24–28, 114; "Answer of Sir Charles Whe[e]ler, Governor of the Leeward Islands, to the inquiries of the Council for Foreign Plantations," in *State Papers,* 1669–74, 7: 290; "Report of the British Board of Trade and Plantations," Nov. 1702, MSS, NYPL; "Governor Cornbury to the Board of Trade," 1702, in *Docs. Rel.,* 4: 1003; Edmund Randolph to the Board of Trade, in C. O. 323: 2, no. 6; id. to the Board of Trade, in *State Papers,* 1696, 15: 214; [?] to Board of Trade, in ibid., 1669–74, 7: 487, 553; Jacob Judd, "Gleanings from a Captain's Letters," *New-York Historical Society Quarterly* 52 (1968): 270–74; Robert Ritchie, "London Merchants, the

New York Market, and the Recall of Sir Edmund Andros," *New York History* 57 (Jan. 1976): 5–30; and Barbour, *Capitalism in Amsterdam,* 21–23. These Dutch practices contrasted with those in England, where merchants remained relatively unspecialized and more capital went into government loans or manufactures. For the Morris quotation, see Charles M. Hough, *Reports of Cases in the Vice Admiralty of the Province of New York and in the Court of Admiralty of the State of New York, 1715–1788* (New Haven, Conn., 1925), 64–65.

52. Gov. Hunter to the Board of Trade, 1714, in *Docs. Rel.,* 5: 462; Andrews, *Colonial Period,* 4: 104–5; Leder, *Robert R. Livingston,* 68–70; *State Papers,* 1706–8, 23: 671; ibid., 1711–12, 26: 439; Joshua Gee to the Council of Trade and Plantations, Oct. 27, 1721, in ibid., 1721, 32: 474; Philip van Cortlandt Letter Book, NYHS; Ritchie, "London Merchants," 5–30; Cornelius Cuyler, Letter Books, AAS; Robert Sanders Letter Book, NYHS; C.O. 5: 1051, Bb98, which notes from two to four ships clearing for Amsterdam annually in the years 1705–16; and Richard Pares, *Yankees and Creoles: The Trade between North America and the West Indies before the American Revolution* (Cambridge, Mass., 1956), 19. And see C.O. 324: 10, pp. 386–87, for West Indian connections. For the years following Queen Anne's War, see also "Hunter to Mr. Popple," Apr. 9, 1715, in *State Papers,* 1714–15, 28: 144; Secretary Stanhope to the Council of Trade and Plantations, Jan. 15, 1715, in ibid., 69–70; and Council of Trade and Plantations to Gov. Hunter, June 22, 1715, in ibid., 108–10.

53. Joshua Gee to the Council of Trade and Plantations, Oct. 27, 1721, in *State Papers,* 1721, 32: 474; William Evert Wendell Correspondence, Philip van Cortlandt Letters, and Robert R. Livingston Correspondence, during the 1720s, all at the NYHS.

54. Thomas Norton, *The Northern Fur Trade in Colonial New York, 1686–1776* (Madison, Wis., 1974), 102, 109. For a dispute that developed between John Lewis and Cornelius Cuyler, and on the sizes of their shipments, see Osgood, *Mins. Common Council,* 1: 1–2, 9, 25–26.

55. Gabriel Ludlow to John de Neufville and Daniel Crommelin, Ludlow Letter Book, 1755–56; Philip Cuyler to John Hodshon, Aug. 9, 1755, Cuyler, Letter Book; William Alexander to John de Neufville, Jan. 14, 1755, Alexander Papers, NYHS, vol. 1; Christopher Bancker to Daniel Crommelin, Aug. 20, 1754, Bancker Waste Book; John Ludlow Account Book, 1756–61, vol. 2, NYHS.

56. Matthew Clarkson, *The Clarksons of New York,* 2 vols. (New York, 1875–76), vol. 1; Francis Goelet Journal, and Daniel Crommelin, Misc. MSS, box 8, no. 48, NYHS.

57. Cornelius Cuyler to Richard Jeneway [*sic*], Jan. 13, 1728; to Samuel Baker, Apr. 11, 1730; to John Cruger, Aug. 3, 24, Oct. 16, 1731, in Cuyler, Letter Book, AAS.

58. Osgood, *Mins. Common Council,* 1: 1–2, 9, 25–26; *Docs. Rel.,* 3: 475–77; Ritchie, "London Merchants," 5–31; Norton, *Northern Fur Trade,* 102, 109. David Armour, "The Merchants of Albany, New York, 1686–1760" (Ph.D. diss., Northwestern University, 1965), 175–76.

59. [Anon.], "Account Book of a New York City Merchant, 1706–1714," Library of Congress (in Dutch); Cadwallader Colden, *The Interest of the Country in Laying Duties* (New York, 1726); Hough, *Reports of Cases,* 64–65; *AJ,* 1: 544, 538–9; *Colonial Laws,* 2: 281–94, 350–371, 401, 485, 537, 553; Osgood, *Mins. Common Council,* 4: 1–2; and Singleton, *Social New York,* 1: 53–65, 84–88, 94; Bollan to the Board of Trade, Feb. 26, 1743, C.O. 5/883, Ee87; Barrow, *Trade and Empire,* 153. On vessel sales, see Joshua Gee to the Council of Trade and Plantations, Oct. 27, 1721, in *State Papers* 1721, 32: 474; David MacPherson,

Annals of Commerce, Manufactures, Fisheries, and Navigation, 4 vols. (London, 1805), 3: 164, 165–66. On credit and prices, see, e.g., Philip van Cortlandt to Richard Mico and Richard Lechmere, Sept. 9, Oct. 8, 1713, and to Thomas Richardson, July 11, 1715, in Philip van Cortlandt Letter Book, 1713–22, NYHS. Discounting ran from 5 percent to about 7½ percent for cash; see examples in William Alexander to Henry Walker & Co., Dec. 14, 1763, and to John Cocke, Dec. 14, 1763, Alexander Papers, NYHS, vol. 4; Alexander Ledger, 1770–72; Alexander Papers, 1773; John van Cortlandt to John Riddlehurst, June 20, 1764, Letter Book; Philip Cuyler to [?], Dec. 1, 1755, Cuyler, Letter Book; John Watts to James Napier, June 1, 1765, in *WLB*, 355; William Neilson Letters, 1747; John van Cortlandt's Sugar Accounts, 1762–69, where he notes selling sugar for 13s. 6d. per pound if by cash and 14s. per pound if on credit; and the Letter Books of Gerard Beekman, 1755, 1765, where he records selling rum for 2s. 1d. per barrel if by cash and 2s. 2d. if on credit.

60. Cornelius Cuyler to Storke & Gainsborough, Nov. 16, 30, 1734, Cornelius Cuyler, Letter Books, 1724–36, 1752–64, AAS. On drawbacks removed in 1737, see William Baxter, *House of Hancock: Business in Boston, 1724–1775* (Cambridge, Mass., 1945), 69–70. On the Rays, see Robert Sanders Voyage Book, 1748–56.

61. Bloch, *HMR*, passim, and C.O. 5: 1225, 1227, 1228. The most successful dry-goods importers in New York City over 1701 to 1709 owned many shares of ships, which they distributed widely through the fleet, although some merchants were sole owners; see the Account Books of Gregg, Cunningham & Co., Theophilus Bache, Elias Desbrosses, James Jauncy, Walter and Samuel Franklin, Henry van Vleck, Jacob and Moses Franks, Philip Cuyler, Walter Livingston, and Robert Livingston Jr., among others, NYHS.

62. C.O. 5: 1222–25, and author's biographical compilation.

63. C.O. 5: 1222–25. On the ability of interlopers to trade in New York, see Gary Nash, "Urban Wealth and Poverty in Pre-Revolutionary America," *Journal of Interdisciplinary History* 6 (1976): 547–74; Price, "Economic Function," 121–86; Davis, *Rise of the Atlantic Economies,* ch. 16.

64. On partnerships, see C.O. 5: 1222–28, and many merchants' correspondence. On competition, see *New-York Gazette,* Apr. and Nov. 29, 1731. A *New-York Weekly Journal* writer, "Paterculus," advised all would-be merchants of the rules by which to establish a reputation (July 15, 1734); governing the rules were the spirit of moderation, trust, neighborliness, and piety. For clerking in the West Indies later in the century, see the examples in Harrington, *New York Merchant,* 194–96.

65. Jacobus van Zandt, Jonathan Abeel, and William Alexander, *WLB*; Philip Livingston Papers, 1716–78; John van Cortlandt, Letter Book, 1762–92, entries for 1764–65; John Ludlow Papers, 1754–64; Thomas Doerflinger, "Commercial Specialization in Philadelphia's Merchant Community, 1750–1791," *Business History Review* 57 (Spring 1983): 42–45; Philip White, *The Beekmans of New York in Politics and Commerce, 1647–1754* (New York, 1956), 538, 543–48; Gary Walton, "New Evidence on Colonial Commerce," *Journal of Economic History* 28 (1968): 363–89; Stuart Bruchey, "Success and Failure Factors: American Merchants in Foreign Trade in the Eighteenth and Early Nineteenth Centuries," *Business History Review* 32 (Autumn 1958): 272–92.

66. Merchants' specialization also contrasts with the diversified relations of small producers and commercial farmers in the interior.

67. Dixon Ryan Fox, *Caleb Heathcote, Gentleman Colonist* (New York, 1926), ch. 1; Peter Jay Correspondence, 1720s, NYHS; Philip Livingston Family Letters, 1734–38, AAS.

For John van Cortlandt, Isaac Adolphus, and Nicholas Bayard, see Jacob van Cortlandt Letter Book, 1762–92; Day Book, 1757–62; Ledger B and C, 1757–70; Journal C, 1765–72, NYHS. Middling merchants diversified, too, but on a smaller scale and of necessity during difficult seasons or as a hedge against uncertain communications with new liaisons.

68. See, e.g., Cornelius Cuyler to David van Brugh, May 21, 1736, Cuyler Letter Book, AAS.

69. Examples abound; see esp., McKee, "Economic Pattern"; Gerard Beekman to Samuel Fowler, Feb. 23, 1753, to Adam Schoales, Feb. 15, 1752, Feb. 14, and Sept. 9, 1760, to M. Bowler, Sept. 7, 15, 1760, to Townshend White, July 29, Aug. 5, 1754, and to Francis Brown, Apr. 14, 1753, in *Beekman Mercantile Papers*, ed. White; John van Cortlandt to Ruscoe Sweeny, Oct. 9, 1762, to Robert van Rensselaer, Dec. 24, 1762, and to Richard Mackey, Nov. 26, 1764, Oct. 7, 1765, Feb. 10, 1766, and Feb. 15, 1767, Letter Book, 1672–92. John Watts to James Neilson, Feb. 1, 1762, and to Gedney Clarke, July 23, 1765, in *WLB*, 19, 360; Bayard, Lentz, & Van Cortlandt Papers, NYHS; Philip Livingston Papers, 1716–78, NYHS and AAS; *Calendar of the Stevens Family Papers*, New Jersey Historical Records Survey Project, 2 vols. (Newark, N.J., 1941), vol. 2, 1751–77; Philip Cuyler, Letter Book, 1755–60, NYPL; William Alexander, Papers, NYHS; and John Ludlow Account Book, 1754–74, AAS. Diversification might also include distilling, brewing, and manufacturing; see ch. 7.

70. See *Beekman Mercantile Papers*, ed. White, vol. 1, and William Smith, Letter Book, 1771–75, Historical Society of Pennsylvania.

71. Daniel Gomez Ledger, 1739–65, American Jewish Historical Society, New York City.

72. John Ludlow to Moses Franks, 1754, and to Elias Bland, 1754, Ludlow Miscellaneous Letters, NYHS; Philip Cuyler to his father, 1757–58, Cuyler, Letter Book, and to Evert Bancker, June 1771, Banker Journal, NYHS; and John van Cortlandt to Ruscoe Sweeny, Oct. 9, 1762, to Robert van Renselaer, Dec. 24, 1762, to Richard Mackey, Nov. 26, 1764, Oct. 7, 1765, Feb. 10, 1766, and Feb. 16, 1767, Letter Book. On West Indies captains, see Pares, *Yankees and Creoles*, ch. 3, 77–78, 84. On London agents, see, in general, Ralph Davis, "English and Foreign Trade, 1700–1774," *Economic History Review* 15 (1962): 300–321. Commissions varied from 2 to 5 percent; see John Watts to Gedney Clarke, July 31, 1762, and to James Napier, June 1, 1765, in *WLB*, 50, 354–355; John van Cortlandt to Robert van Rensselaer, Dec. 24, 1762, in Van Cortlandt Letter Book; William Alexander, Papers, box 11; John and Henry Cruger, Letter Book, 1766–67, NYHS.

73. They were Charles Lodwick, John Paice, T. Pitt, Richard Janeway, J. Lloyd, and Thomas Bayeaux. See petition of city merchants to the Lords of Trade, 1718, in *State Papers*, 1717–18, 30: 423; petition of London merchants, Aug. 28, 1718, in C.O. 5: 1051, no. 83; and "Petition of Mr. Lodwick, et al.," in *Journal of the Commissioners for Trade and Plantations*, 14 vols. (London, 1920–38), 4: 63 (1718–22).

74. Walter Livingston and Robert Livingston Jr., Waste Book, and Ledger; Philip Cuyler, Letter Book; John van Cortlandt, Nov. 1763 and Oct. 8, 1766, Letter Book; John Watts to Moses Franks, Oct. 11, 1764, and to Lord Rollo, Feb. 17, 1765, in *WLB*, 295–96, 331; William Roberts III, "Samuel Storke: An Eighteenth-Century London Merchant Trading to the American Colonies," *Business History Review* 39 (1965): 147–55. And on flaxseed, see Gerard Beekman to Robert Shaw and Snell, Nov. 1, 1748, to William Snell, Jan. 22, 1749, June 3, 1749, July 14, 1749, Jan. 31, 1750, and Mar. 15, 1751, and to Thomas Gilbert [of

Philadelphia], Sept. 31, 1750, in *Beekman Mercantile Papers*, ed. White, 1: 66, 74, 83, 87, 101, 104, 124–25. The London firms included John Blackburn; Neate, Pigou & Booth; Dirck van der Heyden; and David Barclay & Sons. On Ludlow, see letters to William Davy & Co.; Moses Franks; Kilby, Barnard & Parker; Pomeroy & Streatfield; Richard Durnford; Peach & Pierce; William Beekman & Clay; Midgeley & Co. (Liverpool); Touchet & Co. (Manchester), in his Letter Book, 1752–63, 2 vols. For commissions sales on behalf of other New Yorkers, see Ludlow Letter Book, 1752–63, various letters to Devonshire & Lloyd (Bristol), Thomas Pennington & Sons (Bristol), Henry Cruger Jr. (Bristol), and Hyde & Hamilton (Liverpool).

75. Bloch *HMR*, intro.; Nicholas Bayard Sr., Correspondence, 1743–44, NYHS; John van Cortlandt to Abraham Maer (of Virginia), Dec. 8, 1764, to Evan Jones, Apr. 7 and Dec. 19, 1766, and to Robert Tucker, Feb. 6, 1765, Van Cortlandt Letters; Philip Cuyler to John Cuyler, Mar. 19, 1757, Cuyler, Letter Book; John Watts to Joseph Maynard, Aug. 30, 1762, and to John Riddell, Mar. 24, 1764, in *WLB*, 81, 235; Gerard Beekman to Jacob Richardson, July 14, 1760, to Eleazer Fitch, May 4, 1761, to Adam Schoales, Feb. 14, 1752, and to Christopher Ellery (of Rhode Island), Oct. 3, 1765, in *Beekman Mercantile Papers*, ed. White; Robert and Walter Livingston, Ledgers, 1759–62; *New-York Mercury*, Dec. 11, 1769; and Stevens, *Records*, 50.

76. Gerard Beekman is quoted from a letter to Hugh Kirk, Jan. 20, 1769, in *Beekman Mercantile Papers*, ed. White 1: 519. See also Beekman to Samuel Fowler, Feb. 23, 1753, to Adam Schoales, Feb. 15, 1752, Feb. 14, and Sept. 9, 1760, to Townsend White, July 29 and Aug. 5, 1754, to Robert Crooke, July 19, 1753, to Henry Lloyd, Dec. 15, 1755, to Robert Rutherford, Mar. 16, 1752, to Daniel Dyson & Co., Nov. 22, 1752, and to Francis Brown, Apr. 14, 1753. And see John van Cortlandt to Ruscoe Sweeny, Oct. 9, 1762, to Robert van Rensselaer, Dec. 24, 1762, to Capt. Richard Mackey, Nov. 26, 1764, Oct. 7, 1765, Feb. 10, 1766, Feb. 16, 1767, and Jan. 28, 1768. Also on bills-of-exchange markets, see ch. 2, and on assigning bills of exchange, ch. 2, n. 76; Richard B. Morris, *Select Cases, Mayor's Court, 1674–1784* (Washington, D.C., 1935), 531 (1704), 535 (1707), and 539 (1708); Ludlow Letter Book, 1760–61; Cuyler, Letter Book; Van Cortlandt Letter Books, 1760 and 1766. English merchants discounted foreign bills of exchange at 4 percent over most of the eighteenth century; see D. M. Joslin, "London Private Bankers, 1720–1785," *Economic History Review* 7 (1954), 167–86. New York discounts for bills of exchange usually ran from 5 percent to 7½ percent, when paying cash; but for private and government paper, they varied from 8 percent to 30 percent, reaching 50 percent on occasion; see, e.g., Gov. Hunter's agreement to advance R. R. Livingston sterling bills of exchange at a 50 percent discount if the latter would receipt them for New York currency, in Leder, *Robert R. Livingston*, 220. For a 90-day allowance, see *Cal. Council Mins.*, May 5, 1747, 364.

77. On Barbarie, see *New-York Gazette*, Apr. 1731; on advance payments, see, e.g., Gerard Beekman to Stephen Hopkins, Oct. 25, 1746, to Channing, Nov. 17, 1747, and to Shaw and Snell, London, Nov. 25, 1747, in *Beekman Mercantile Papers*, ed. White, 1:10, 31, 32; and on Hamilton, letters to Jacob Walton and John H. Cruger, Nov. 27, 1771, to Nicholas Cruger, Nov. 4, 12, 1771, to Tileman Cruger, Nov. 16, 1771, to Walton & Co., Nov. 27, 1771, to Nicholas Cruger, Jan. 10, Feb. 24, 1772, to Henry Cruger, Feb. 24, 1772, in *The Papers of Alexander Hamilton*, ed. Harold C. Syrett and Jacob E. Cooke, 27 vols. (New York, 1961–87), 1: 8, 10, 11, 12–13, 17–18, 20–21, 25–26, 27–28.

78. On personal bonds, see Postlethwayt, *Dict.*, 1: s.v. "bond"; John McEvers, "List of

Bonds Due Him, 1752," NYHS; Cadwallader Colden to General Monckton, Sept. 20, 1762, in *The Aspinwall Papers*, Massachusetts Historical Society, *Collections*, 4th ser., vols. 9–10 (Boston, 1871–72), 1: 520–21; John van Cortlandt, Ledger, 1770–72; Hugh Wallace, Oliver De Lancey, George Folliot, John Watts, Isaac Low, Henry White, James McEvers, and John van Cortlandt, "American Loyalists: Transcripts of Various Papers Relating to the Losses, Services and Support of the American Loyalists . . . 1777–1783," 8 vols., NYPL; and the several advertisements in the *New-York Gazette* and *New-York Mercury* for "sums to let out," especially in 1763 and 1768. There is virtually no extant evidence that New Yorkers used bottomry bonds among themselves, by which merchant shipowners obtained the credit and goods necessary for a voyage by pledging the ship as collateral and paying interest on the loan if the ship completed the voyage, with all parties forfeiting property and profits if the vessel were lost. Bottomry bonds carried a steep rate of interest, normally 20 percent

79. Davis, *Rise of the Atlantic Economies*, 240–41; "Governor Clarke to the Board of Trade," June 2, 1738, in *Docs. Rel*, 6: 117; for commercial rates, see *Docs. Rel.*, 4: 13, 134, 136, 140; 5: 738; 6: 116; 8: 169; *New-York Gazette*, July 17, 1738.

80. On England and Europe, see De Vries, *Economy of Europe*, 192, 198, 208, 210, 214–15; Price, *Capital and Credit*, 22–31. On New York, see [Anon.], "Account Book of a New York City Merchant, 1706–1714," Library of Congress (in Dutch); *New-York Gazette*, Aug. 23, 31, Nov. 11, 1728.

81. Gerard Beekman to Thomas Freebody, Dec. 29, 1763, in *Beekman Mercantile Papers*, ed. White; John Watts to Thomas Astin, Jan. 1, 1762, in *WLB*, 1–3.

82. *WLB*, 8, 101, 142, 229, 342, 352. Wilson, *England's Apprenticeship*, 59–60, 332–33; Joseph Ernst, *Money and Politics in America, 1755–1775: A Study in the Currency Act of 1764 and the Political Economy of Revolution* (Chapel Hill, N.C., 1973), 14; John Law, *Of Money and Trade Considered*, 2d ed. (London, 1720), 19–22. In New York, see William Alexander account with David Barclay & Son, Letters, NYHS, vol. 1, 1760–69. Hume noted a received wisdom by the 1750s: falling exchange rates not only eased international payments, but also made the local economy stronger in relation to the pound sterling; see id., "Of Interest and Money" and "Of the Balance of Trade," in *David Hume: Writings on Economics*, ed. Rotwein, 48, 53. For the bills-of-exchange markets, see, e.g., "Memorial of Several Merchants . . . Proprietors of Bills of Exchange drawn by Col. Hunter," 1714, Treasury Office Papers (T), Public Record Office, London, T: 1: 186: 5. British and Dutch merchants preferred to loan money to the English government, which paid interest of from 8 to 10 percent after the Restoration, while the Dutch States General paid only from 3½ to 4 percent; Hunter to Lords of Treasury, Apr. 30, 1715, T: 1: 189: 64; Hunter to Board of Trade, Oct. 3, 1710, C.O. 5: 1050, no. 6; Pieter de la Court, *The True Interest and Political Maxims of the Republic of Holland and West-Friesland* (Amsterdam, 1662; trans., London, 1702), 33; Josiah Child, *A Short Addition to the Observations Concerning Trade and Interest of Money* (London, 1668), 10; Peter Burke, *Venice and Amsterdam: A Study of Seventeenth-Century Elites* (London, 1974), 56–59. For New York, see Philip Cuyler to his father, Dec. 11, 1758, Dec. 17, 1759, in Cuyler, Letter Book; Stokes, *Iconography*, 1: 303; comments of Isaac Low in 1770, in Stevens, *Records*, 10–18; Stoker, *Prices*, 203. The exchange rate fell from 85 in 1754 to 60 in 1759. See also *New-York Mercury*, May 1, Oct. 21, 1762; John Watts to Joseph Maynard, Jan. 2 and Apr. 3, 1762, to William Baker, Jan. 13 and May 12, 1762, to Maxwell & Udney, Apr. 7, 1762, to Gedney Clarke, May 9 and July 15, 1762, to John

Erving, July 1 and Dec. 6, 1762, and to Lasscelles Maxwell, Sept. 23, 1762, all in *WLB*, 5, 8–9, 33, 34–35, 45, 48, 65, 67–68, 87, 104. The exchange rate rose from 60 in 1759 to 85 in late 1760, to 95 in 1762; Sanders to Storke and Champion, Aug. 15, 1753, Letter Book; John van Cortlandt, Letter Book, 1762–69, entries for 1763–64; and, for the quotation, see White, *Beekmans*, 483.

83. See Jacob R. Marcus, *The Colonial American Jew, 1492–1776*, 2 vols. (Detroit, 1970), 2: 707–8, 713; Roberts, "Samuel Storke," 167, 169; and Lawrence Leder, "Military Victualling in Colonial New York," in *Business Enterprise in Early New York*, ed. Joseph R. Frese and Jacob Judd (Tarrytown, N.Y., 1979), 24–25. Robert R. Livingston's contract to supply the Albany forces in 1710 brought about suspicion of fraud, from which he was cleared; see James G. Wilson, *The Memorial History of the City of New York*, 4 vols. (New York, 1893), 2: 130–31. See also *Letters of the Franks Family*, ed. Hershkowitz and Meyer; Jonathan Swift, *The History of the Last Four Years of the Queen*, ed. H. Davis (Oxford, 1951), 68.

84. Frederick Lentz Papers and David Clarkson Correspondence, 1745–77, NYHS. *Cal. Council Ms.*, May 2, 1747, 2: 364; ibid., 2: 70, 84, 100, 118, 125; John Watts to Moses Franks, Feb. 14, 1764, in *WLB*, 228–29; and *Council Journal*, 1: 95–6, 35, 49, 75, 85, 100.

85. John Watts to Moses Franks, and to Thomas Astin, Feb. 14, 1764, Jan. 1, 1762, in *WLB*, 228–29, 1–3; John Carswell, *The South Sea Bubble* (London, 1960), 131, 133, 139, 161, 199; Frank Speck, *Stability and Strife: England, 1714–1760* (Cambridge, Mass., 1977), 157, 158–59; Larry Neal, *The Rise of Financial Capitalism: International Capital Markets in the Age of Reason* (Cambridge, 1990), 90–92, 94–99. The rapid expansion of South Sea Company stock triggered a bull market, which benefited myriad new companies seeking joint-stock company charters, some fraudulent, which undermined Parliament's ability to raise revenue by issuing corporate charters. Parliament tried to control the South Sea Company before the crash, but to little avail. Sir Robert Walpole, who was touted as a promoter of international commerce, nevertheless asked Parliament to reduce the land tax in 1731. Moreover, Walpole's commercial policies favored cautious trade and solid public credit, not a flamboyant rush to import fashionable goods for the wealthy, and most new trade laws from 1721 to 1740 promoted agricultural production and export, or infant manufactures. The excise tax Walpole proposed in 1733 would have raised revenues from neither land nor international commerce so much as from internal consumption, which would most have affected shopkeepers, retailers, and lesser merchants. And while it is true that Walpoleans supported a stronger Bank of England—a premier symbol of economic "fantasy" and speculation to its critics—they extended its privileges to many interests in commerce, manufactures, and finance, and to members of landed families. For distinct contemporary views of the events, see Defoe, *Complete English Tradesman*, 2: 226, 231–3, and Bernard Mandeville, *The Grumbling Hive; or, Knaves Turn'd Honest*, in *The Fable of the Bees* (1714), ed. F. B. Kaye, 2 vols. (London, 1924), 1: 17–37.

86. Newton quoted by Carswell, *South Sea Bubble*, 133; Daniel Defoe, *An Essay on the South Sea Trade* (London, 1712), 8, 22; id., *Plan of the English Commerce*, xii. See also Bishop George Berkeley, "Essay towards the Preventing the Ruin of Great Britain" (1720), in *Complete Works*, 4 vols. (Oxford, 1901), 4: 321–38, and id., *The Querist* (1736), repr. in *The Works of George Berkeley*, ed. A. C. Fraser, 3 vols. (London, 1871), 3: 474.

87. John Watts to Moses Franks, Feb. 14, 1764, in *WLB*, 228–29; William Alexander, "Account with David Barclay and Sons," 1760–69, in Alexander Letters, box 1, NYHS.

88. On London brokers, see Nicholas Magens, *Essay on Insurances* (London, 1755); Dickson, *Financial Revolution*, ch. 1; Wilson, *England's Apprenticeship*, 372. For New York, see Letter Books of John Ludlow, John Watts, Philip Cuyler and Gerard Beekman; *New-York Mercury*, Aug. 27, Nov. 5, 1759. By 1759, the merchants Abraham van Dam, Richard Nicholls, Abraham Keteltas, and Richard Sharpe offered insurance brokerage services to fellow merchants in New York, and since the 1740s, the Cuyler, Beekman, Van Horne, Lewis, and Franklin families had boasted of their ability to insure Newport, Perth Amboy, and some Philadelphia vessels. On the last colonial years, see William Walton, Insurance Book.

89. William Walton, Insurance Book. On Hugh Wallace, see Bridenbaugh, *Cities in Revolt*, 93, 73; Harrington, *New York Merchants*, 155–163; and White, *Beekmans*, 7, 13–15, 17, 480, and for the quotation, Corbyn Morris, *An Essay towards Illustrating the Science of Insurance* (London, 1747), 2. In peacetime, the rate for a trip from London to New York was from 2 to 3 percent of the cargo's value each way; the rate for a trip from the West Indies to New York was from 4 to 4½ percent each way; the rate for vessels that touched at additional ports rose to 6 percent, and merchants trading at French sugar islands often paid 9 percent for the return voyage to New York.

90. For the 1704 law, see Osgood, *Mins. Common Council*, 2: 261. For concern about auctions, see Philip Cuyler, Letter Book; Evert Bancker, Journal, comments at June 1771; John Ludlow, letters to Moses Franks and Elias Bland, 1754, in Ludlow Letter Book; *Beekman Mercantile Papers*, ed. White, 2: 860, 865, 888; *Journal of Madam [Sarah Kemble] Knight* (1704; orig. published in 1825), ed. Theodore Dwight (New York, 1920).

91. *New-York Gazette*, July 21, 1729, Sept. 10, 1733, and Mar. 20, 1739; Bridenbaugh, *Cities in Revolt*, 79; Philip Livingston to Storke & Gainsborough, Mar. 13, 1734, Philip Livingston Business Letters; *New-York Gazette*, Apr. 3, 1732. See also Marc Egnal and Joseph Ernst, "An Economic Interpretation of the American Revolution," *William and Mary Quarterly* 29 (1972): 15–18; and *Beekman Mercantile Papers*, ed. White, 1: 92, 134, 139–40, 287–88, 322, 345–46, 350, 379; 2: 839, 851, 867, 1023, 1055–56, 1065.

92. John Ludlow to Moses Franks, Jan. 8, 1754, to Sheldon & Wright, Dec. 30, 1757, and to Franks, Dec. 20, 1757, and Nov. 6, 1761, Ludlow Letter Book; *Calendar of the Stevens Family Papers*, 1760s; and Beekman to Henry Lloyd, Boston, May 28, 1767, quoted in White, *Beekmans*, 513.

93. William Sachs, "The Business Outlook in the Northern Colonies, 1750–1775" (Ph.D. diss., Columbia University, 1957), 253–54; *Beekman Mercantile Papers*, ed. White, 1: 21, 49–50, 54, 64, 254, 437; Bridenbaugh, *Cities in Revolt*, 277; *Colonial Laws*, 5: 74, 284–87; and "Governor Moore to Earl of Hillsborough," May 26, 1769, in *Docs. Rel.*, 8: 617.

94. Rodrigo Pacheco to James Alexander, May 12, 1732, Jan. 16, 1737, box 6, James Alexander Papers, NYHS; *New-York Gazette*, Mar. 14, 27, Apr. 3, 24, 1738.

95. Gerard Beekman to Shaw & Snell, London, Nov. 25, 1747, to Stephen Hopkins and others of Rhode Island, Oct. 25, 1746, and to Benjamin Burrows, Nov. 20, 1746, in *Beekman Mercantile Papers*, ed. White, 1:32, 10, 12.

96. Frederick Jay to John Jay, Jan. 23, 1770, in *John Jay: Unpublished Papers, 1745–1780*, ed. Richard B. Morris (New York, 1975), 99; Gerard Beekman to Fowler, Mar. 21, 1767, to the Rosses of Connecticut, Jan. 24, 1768, and to Henry Lloyd of Boston, July 22, 1767, in *Beekman Mercantile Papers*, ed. White, 1: 509, 516, 514; Christopher Bancker, Journal; Philip Cuyler, Letter Book; John van Cortlandt, Journal, 1760, and Letters, 1766; John

Watts to William Baker, Jan. 13, 1762, to Thomas Pennington & Son, May 24, 1762, to Lasselles Clark & Daling, May 13, 1763, and Apr. 1, 1765, to Telemen Cruger, Jan. 14, 1764, to Moses Franks, June 1, 8, 1765, and to Thomas Astin, Jan. 1, 30, and Apr. 10, 1762, in *WLB*, 8, 60, 142, 215, 342, 352, 357, 1–3, 13–16, 40–43; and David Clarkson Correspondence.

97. See, e.g., New York City Mayor's Court Minute Books, 1674–1821, Municipal Archives, New York City; *Colonial Laws*, 5: ch. 1568.

98. See, e.g., Gerard Beekman to Robert Crooke, July 19, 1753, to Henry Lloyd, Dec. 15, 1755, to Adam Schoales, Feb. 15, 1752, to Jacob Richardson, July 14, 1760, to James Searle, Mar. 25, 1760, to Thomas Reynolds, Dec. 24, 1753, to William Edmonds, Oct. 2, 1754, to Israel Boardman, Aug. 26, 1754, and to John Sayre, Dec. 15 and 29, 1755, in *Beekman Mercantile Papers*, ed. White. See also John van Cortlandt to John Riddelhurst, Nov. 10, 1763, to Edward Travis, Apr. 17, 1764, to John Batyer, Oct. 15, 1767, and to John Hilton, Dec. 2, 1762, Van Cortlandt Letter Book; Philip Cuyler to John Cuyler, Mar. 19, 1757, to William G. Beekman, Dec. 1, 1758, Cuyler, Letter Book, NYPL; John Watts to Joseph Maynard, Aug. 30, 1762, to John Riddell, Nov. 27, 1762, to Samuel Horner, Dec. 21, 1762, to Gen. Monckton, Mar. 11, 1764, to Christopher Kilby, Apr. 5, 1764, and to Scott, Pringle, Cheap & Co., Aug. 28, 1765, in WLB, 81, 97, 110, 234, 237, 381; John Ludlow to Nicholas Hallam, July 25, 1755, Ludlow Letter Book; Peter Livingston to Christopher Champlin, Nov. 11, 1771, in *Commerce of Rhode Island*, 382.

99. Defoe, *Complete English Tradesman*, 2: 118; Vanderlint, *Money Answers All Things*. See also Charles Davenant, *The True Picture of a Modern Whig* (London, 1701), 26; Defoe, *Essay upon Projects* (London, 1697); Charles Davenant, *An Essay on the Probable Methods of Making a People Gainers in the Balance of Trade* (London, 1699), 157–66; North, *Discourses upon Trade*, 14; Postlethwayt, *Dict.*, 1: s.v. "trade." A new definition of *treasure* emerged, too, one that held it was not specie, but the labor added to goods; see works by Davenant, William Wood, Richard Gouldsmith, and John Houghton, as well as John Locke, *Some Consequences of the Lowering of Interest and Raising the Value of Money*," in J. R. McCulloch, *Principles of Political Economy* (London, 1870), 326, 238–39.

100. Colden, *Interest of the Country*, 8; "Mr. Colden's Account of the Trade of New-York," 1723, in *Docs. Rel.*, 5: 685–90; and *New-York Gazette*, Jan. 21, 28, 1735. See also De Vries, *Economy of Europe*, 240–41; *New-York Mercury*, Oct. 17, 1768; *The Tradesman's Director; or, The London and Country Shopkeeper's Useful Companion* (New York, 1753); John Watts to William Baker, Jan. 13, 1762, to Gedney Clarke, July 5, 1762, to John Erving, May 30, 1762, and to Moses Franks, June 1, 1765, in *WLB*, 8, 60, 65–66, 352–54; Philip Cuyler to William G. Beekman, Oct. 27, 1758, Cuyler, Letter Book. For earlier complaints about cash scarcity, see *Laws and Ordinances*, 1: 126, 171, 248; *Colonial Laws*, 1: 248, 287, 322, 325, 419, 403; *Docs. Rel.*, 1: 634, 3: 217, 246, 289; 5: 519, 520, 581, 643, 706, 767. On long credits, see Wilson, *England's Apprenticeship*, ch. 10, and Nettels, *Money Supply*, 202–28.

101. Isaac Gervaise, *The System or Theory of the Trade of the World* (1720), ed. Jacob Viner (Baltimore, 1954), 8; David Clarkson, Correspondence, 1745–77, and Francis Goelet, Correspondence, 1746–78, NYHS; John Ludlow to Sheldon & Wright, June 9, 1753, Ludlow Correspondence; John Hope, *Letters of Credit*, 2d ed. (London, 1784), 10–14, 16, 42, 61, 67; Davis, *Economic Rise*, 240–41; De Vries, *Economy of Europe*, 192, 198, 208, 210, 214–35; Price, *Capital and Credit*, 22–31. As a writer in the *New-York Weekly Journal*, May 20, 1734, put it, "the Difference between ready Money and Trust will always be in proportion to the Height of the Interest." See also ibid., July 8, 1734.

102. Stevens, *Records*, 144; *New-York Gazette*, Aug. 23, 31, Nov. 11, 1728; Beekman to Samuel Fowler, Dec. 29, 1763, in *Beekman Mercantile Papers*, ed. White, 1:152; John Watts to Thomas Astin, Jan. 1, 1762, in *WLB*, 1–3. For examples of protested bills, see, e.g., John Ludlow to Moses Franks, Jan. 9, June 28, 1758, and to S. Touchet & Co. Dec. 14, 1754, in Ludlow Letter Books; Stephen van Cortlandt to Samuel Purviance, Dec. 19, 1763, and to Charles Cox, June 25, 1764, Van Cortlandt Letter Books; and Philip Cuyler to Elihu Lyman, Oct. 29, 1757, Cuyler, Letter Book. Chamber of Commerce rates were 5 percent for North American bills, 10 percent for West Indian bills, and 20 percent for European bills, plus recovery of the face value of the bill. On how the price of a bill of exchange was determined, see ch. 2 and notes there. On the Seven Years' War, see Julian Gwyn, "Private Credit in Colonial New York: The Warren Portfolio, 1731–1795," *New York History* 37 (1956): 269–93.

103. "Governor Cornbury to the Board of Trade," 1701, in *Docs. Rel.*, 4: 1059; "Robert Quary to the Board of Trade," June 1703, in ibid., 4: 1047; "Capt. Thomas Wenham to the Lords of Trade," Nov. 2, 1704, in ibid., 4: 1119; Nettels, *Money Supply*, 242–43.

104. "Lord Cornbury to the Lords of Trade," Feb. 5, 1704, in *Docs. Rel.*, 4: 1131–33; "Petition of Merchants of the City of New-York relating to Foreign Coin," June 25, 1705, in ibid., 4: 1133–35; Robert Quary to the Board of Trade, May 30, 1704, in C.O. 323: 5, no. 51; Governor, Council and Assembly of New York to the Queen, Oct. 1708, in C.O. 5: 1049, no. 99; New York Merchants to the Board of Trade, [1718], in C.O. 5: 1051, no. 67. For later complaints, see [Anon.], "Reflections on the Present State of the Province of Massachusetts Bay" (1720), repr. in *Tracts Relating to the Currency of Massachusetts Bay, 1682–1720*, ed. Andrew McFarland Davis (Boston, 1902), 329; and Colden, *Interest of the Country*, 8–11. The quotations are from Roger Sherman, *A Caveat against Injustice; or, An Enquiry into the Evil Consequences of a Fluctuating Medium of Exchange* (New York, 1752).

105. "Lord Cornbury to the Board of Trade," Feb. 19, 1705, in C.O. 5: 1048, no. 105; "Petition of Merchants [to the Council]," 1705, in C.O. 5: 1048, no. 105a; "Petition of Merchants of the City of New-York relating to Foreign Coin," June 25, 1705, in *Docs. Rel.*, 4: 1133–35; Board of Trade to Cornbury, Mar. 26, 1705, in C.O. 5: 1120, no. 280–81; Cornbury to the Board of Trade, Oct. 18, 1708, in ibid., no. 99; New York Council to the Board of Trade, Dec. 13, 1711, in C.O. 5: 1050, no. 45a; Ingoldsby to the Board of Trade, July 5, 1709, in C.O. 5: 1049, no. 107; Gov. Hunter to the Board of Trade, Nov. 28, 1710, Jan. 1, June 23, Nov. 1, Dec. 12, 1712, Mar. 14, May 11, July 13, 1713, and Aug. 27, 1714, in C.O. 5: 1050, no.'s 8, 45, 51, 60, 59, 63, 65, 67a, 68, 82; "Governor Hunter to the Lords of Trade," Nov. 12, 1715, in *Docs. Rel.*, 5: 414; MacPherson, *Annals*, 3: 574. On devaluation after the Seven Years' War, see Stevens, *Records*, 10–18, 52, 56; Gerard Beekman to Samuel Fowler, Dec. 29, 1763, in *Beekman Mercantile Papers*, ed. White; John Watts to R. Rogers, Jan. 1 and Nov. 15, 1762, in *WLB*, 130, 95; Gov. Moore to Hillsborough, May 29, 1769, in *Docs. Rel.*, 8: 169; Charles Bullock, *Essays on the Monetary History of the United States* (New York, 1900), 21–39; and Leslie Brock, *The Currency of the American Colonies, 1700–1764: A Study in Colonial Finance and Imperial Relations* (New York, 1975), 66–74, 336–53. For opposition to the colony's overvaluations see Postlethwayt, *Dict.*, 1: svv. "coin," and "balance of trade."

106. C.O. 5: 1050, Aa, 131; Lewis Morris, *Address to the Inhabitants of Westchester County, 1713* (New York, 1713); William Smith, *The History of the Late Province of New-York from Its Discovery to the Appointment of Governor Colden, in 1762*, NYHS, *Publications*, 2 vols. (New York, 1829–30), 1: 232–36.

386 Notes to Pages 165–167

107. *Colonial Laws*, 1: 248, 287, 322, 325, 403, 419, 2: 32; "Governor Hunter to the Board of Trade," Nov. 14, 1700, May 21 and 25, 1715, in *Docs. Rel.*, 5: 177–82, 402–5, 416–19; and letters with merchants' comments in ibid., 1: 634, 3: 317, 246, 289; 5: 519, 520, 581, 603, 643, 706, 707, 767; Bloch, *HMR*, ix–xviii; *Council Journal*, 1: 516, 479.

108. For the duties, see ch. 2, n. 48. For renewal of the laws in the eighteenth century, see *Colonial Laws*, 1: 315–21, 165, 403; 2: 8–12, 98–105, 197–98, 248–51, 263, 281–94, 372–403; 3: 951, 1000; 4: 215–35, 306–9. The liquor excise and brewing taxes seem to have been renewed through at least 1760; see George Edwards, *New York as an Eighteenth-Century Municipality* (New York, 1918), 69–79. On merchant opposition, see *Docs. Rel.*, 3: 268, 5: 897–99, 6: 127; George Schuyler, *Colonial New York*, 2 vols. (New York, 1885), 1: 99–120; Donald R. Gerlach, *Philip Schuyler and the American Revolution, 1773–1777* (Lincoln, Nebr., 1964), 2, 48–62, 316–18; *AJ*, 1: 548, 551–52 (1726); 1: 638, 641, 645 (1732); *New York Journal*, Mar. 18, 1734. For mercantilist statements on the wisdom of this legislation, see "Governor Hunter to the Lords of Trade," Dec. 22, 1719, in *Docs. Rel.*, 5: 534–37; "Governor Burnet to the Lords of Trade," Nov. 26, 1720, Sept. 24, 1720, Aug. 9 and Nov. 7, 1724, in ibid., 5: 576–81, 573, 707–13

109. "George Clarke to Robert Walpole," Nov. 24, 1725, in *Docs. Rel.*, 5: 768–71; Cadwallader Colden to William Burnet, Nov. 19, 1728, in *Colden*, 50: 273; James Alexander to Colden, June 28, 1729, in ibid., 50: 287–89; Leder, *Robert R. Livingston*, 265–67. For the English debate see, e.g., [Anon.], *Essays on the National Constitution, Bank, Credit, and Trade* (London, 1717), and Wood, *Survey of Trade*. Early arguments in New York are in, e.g., Rev. John Miller, *A Description of the Province and City of New York* (1695; repr., New York, 1862); Lewis Morris, *Dialogue Concerning Trade* (New York, 1713); id., "To All Whom These Presents May Concern, 1713," NYPL; "Governor Hunter to the Lords of Trade," Aug. 7, 1718, in *Docs. Rel.*, 5: 514; *AJ*, vol. 1, June 5, 1716, and Nov. 29, 1717.

110. Colden, *Interest of the Country*; [id.], *The Second Part of the Interest of the Country in Laying Duties* (1726), in *Colden*, 68: 267–79. Colden and others wanted to defeat sumptuary legislation and avoid the rise of charity or relief institutions in New York City too; see Richard B. Morris, *Government and Labor in Early America* (New York, 1946), 77, 84–86; Arthur Peterson, *New York as an Eighteenth-Century Municipality Prior to 1731* (New York, 1917), 183; and David M. Schneider, *History of Public Welfare in New York State* (Chicago, 1938), 39, 70.

111. [Colden?], *The Interest of the City and Country to Lay No Duties* (New York, 1727), 1–23; Cadwallader Colden to Dr. Robert Whytt, Sept. 3, 1763, in *Colden*, 55: 272; John Watts to Gedney Clarke, Feb. 18, 1764, in *WLB*, 233; *AJ*, 2: 775; Bridenbaugh, *Cities in the Wilderness*, 253, 413–14.

112. *AJ*, 1: 548, 551–52, 638, which also contains similar arguments by Stephen De Lancey, John Watts, John Erving, and Moses Franks, among others; Bonomi, *Factious People*, 58–59, 83–92; Archibald Kennedy, *Observations on the Importance of the Northern Colonies under Proper Regulations* (New York, 1750), 10–11, 14–18, 20–23, 27–28; *New York Journal*, Mar. 18, 1734, Sept. 5, 1757; *New-York Evening Post*, Jan. 25, 1748; *New-York Mercury*, Apr. 12, 1762;

113. *New-York Gazette, or Weekly Post-Boy*, Nov. 11, 1751; also Feb. 17, 1755.

114. [Cadwallader Colden], *The Two Interests Reconciled . . .* (New York, 1726), 11–12, as quoted by Beverly McAnear, "Mr. Robert R. Livingston's Reasons against a Land Tax," *Journal of Political Economy* 48 (1940): 72.

115. In addition to the sources cited in n. 112 above, see William Alexander to John Provoost, New York, Nov. 16, 1750, in William Alexander, Papers, vol. 1, no. 20, NYHS; *Colonial Laws*, 1: 484, 675, 789, 799, 810–11, 884–85, 898–901, 918–20, 1010–12; 2: 16, 32, 254, 426, 843, 867; 3: 31–34, 754, 963; 4: 370, 741, 766; 5: 280, 741, 860, 923, 956, 1039; "Lt. Gov. Clarke to the Lords of Trade," 1738, in *Docs. Rel.*, 6: 116; Smith, *History*, 2: 27–37; *Docs. Rel.*, 5: 551, 599, 607, 700, 736, 738, 769, 889–91; *AJ*, 2: 287, 333, 360, 403, 466, 507, 545, 573, 613, 643, 679, 712, 728, 754, 790; "Governor Hardy to the Board of Trade," Dec. 2, 1756, in *Docs. Rel.*, 5: 906–8; "Governor Moore to Shelburne," Feb. 21, 1767, in ibid., 7: 711. The Duty Act raised an average annual revenue of £2,226 between 1753 and 1755, amounts ranging between £3,174 and £10,346 during the Seven Years' War, and on average about £4,500 annually between 1764 and 1775; *Council Journal*, 1: 433, 520; 2: 1180; David Valentine, *Manual of the Corporation of the City of New York*, 27 vols. (1842–69), 17: 505–6, 509.

SIX   The Prospects for Satisfying Appetite

1. "Letter from Peter Delanoy, Relative to Governor Fletcher's Conduct," June 13, 1698, in *Doc. Hist.*, 4: 321–24; Peter Kalm, *Travels in North America, 1748–1751*, ed. Adolph Benson, 2 vols. (New York, 1966), 1: 125–35; Lord Adam Gordon, *Journal* (1774), cited in *Travels in the American Colonies*, ed. Newton D. Mereness (New York, 1916), 414. And see also Andrew Burnaby, *Travels through North America, 1748–1751, 1760* (New York, 1904), 63–64, 84–85; and Michael Kammen, *Colonial New York* (New York, 1975), 292.

2. For some English writings, see Sir William Petty, *Political Arithmetick*, in *The Economic Writings of Sir William Petty*, ed. Charles Hull (Cambridge, 1899), 196; Postlethwayt, *Dict.*, 2: s.v. "luxury"; Henry St. John, Viscount Bolingbroke, *The Craftsman*, 1742–43; Charles Davenant, *Discourse on the Public Revenue and on the Trade of England*, 2 parts (London, 1698), pt. 1; Andrew Fletcher, *Discourse of Government* (London, 1698); Anthony Ashley Cooper, 3d earl of Shaftesbury, *Characteristicks of Men, Manners, Opinions, Times*, 2 vols. (1711; facs. repr., Gloucester, Mass., 1963); Jonathan Swift, *Gulliver's Travels* (London, 1723), pt. 3; Peter Kalm, *Account of his Visit to England . . . 1748* (London, 1892). This line of thinking continued in, e.g., Richard Price and Joseph Priestley, discussed in Jack Fruchtman Jr., *The Apocalyptic Politics of Richard Price and Joseph Priestley: A Study in Late-Eighteenth-Century English Republican Millennialism*, American Philosophical Society, *Transactions*, 73 (Philadelphia, 1983). And its roots lay deep in the past; see, e.g., *The Politics of Aristotle*, ed. Ernest Barker (Oxford, 1958), 1.3.6–21; Thomas Hobbes, *Leviathan, or the Matter, Form, and Power of a Commonwealth, Ecclesiastical and Civil* (1651; repr., London, 1974), chs. 24, 30. For New York, see sources cited in notes to this chapter below.

3. Petty, *Political Arithmetick*, 196. See also Richard Steele, *An Essay upon Trade, and Public Credit* (London, 1714); and Matthew Decker, *Essay on the Causes of the Decline of Foreign Trade* (1734; repr., London, 1744); Neil McKendrick, John Brewer, and J. H. Plumb, *The Birth of a Consumer Society: The Commercialization of Eighteenth-Century England* (Bloomington, Ind., 1982); E. A. J. Johnson, *Predecessors of Adam Smith: The Growth of British Economic Thought* (New York, 1937); Isaac Kramnick, *Bolingbroke and His Circle: The Politics of Nostalgia in the Age of Walpole* (Cambridge, Mass., 1968); and William O. Letwin, *The Origins of Scientific Economics* (Garden City, N.Y., 1964).

4. For this and the next two paragraphs, see, in general, Sir William Temple, *Obser-*

vations upon the United Provinces of the Netherlands (1673; repr., Cambridge, 1932); Charles Davenant, *On the Plantation Trade,* in *The Political and Commercial Works of that Celebrated Writer Charles D'Avenant,* ed. Sir Charles Whitworth, 5 vols. (1697; repr., London 1771), 2: 75; [Anon.], *An Account of the French Usurpation upon the Trade of England* (London, 1679); "Scheme of Trade" (1699), signed by fourteen London merchants, repr. in *The Mercator,* no. 2; *The Tatler,* no. 148 (Mar. 21, 1710); George Coade, *A Letter to the Honourable the Lords Commissioners of Trade and Plantations* (London, 1747); [Anon.], *State of the Nation considered* (London, 1747); Henry Martin, articles in *The British Merchant,* 1713–14; John Withers, *The Dutch better Friends than the French* (London, 1713); J[ohn] E[gleton], *A Vindication of the House of Commons, in rejecting a Bill confirming . . . the treaty . . . between England and France* (London, 1741); and [Anon.], *Considerations on the Present State of the Nation* (London, 1720). Daniel Defoe opposed luxury trade with France but favored reciprocal trade relations in other commodities; at his most extreme, he said, "If there were no wines drunk in England at all, it would be no loss to the public stock. All our consumption of foreign production is a loss to the national wealth" (*The Mercator,* no. 142). See also Malachy Postlethwayt, *Great Britain's Commercial Interest Explained and Improved,* 2 vols. (London, 1759), 2: 366–91, 551, for later distinctions between wealth and luxury. For secondary treatments, see Charles M. Andrews, *The Colonial Period of American History: England's Commercial and Colonial Policy,* 4 vols. (New Haven, Conn., 1938), 4: 355–57, 358–61, 361 n. 2; Neil McKendrick, "Commercialization and the Economy," in id., Brewer, and Plumb, *Birth of a Consumer Society,* 9–194; and Alasdair MacIntyre, *After Virtue* (Notre Dame, Ind., 1981), intro.

5. Temple, *Observations,* 208; Postlethwayte, *Great Britain's Commercial Interests,* 2: 551; Nathaniel Forster, *An Enquiry into the Present High Price of Provisions* (London, 1767); Davenant, *On the Plantation Trade,* pt. 2, 75; Joseph Harris, *An Essay upon Money and Coins,* 2 parts (London, 1757), pt. 1, 28; Joseph Massie, *The Natural Rate of Interest,* in *Reprints of Economic Tracts,* ed. Jacob Hollander (Baltimore, n.d.), 20; Louis Dumont, *From Mandeville to Marx: The Genesis and Triumph of Economic Ideology* (Chicago, 1977), 75–76. For New York, see William Smith, *The History of the Late Province of New-York From its Discovery to the Appointment of Governor Colden in 1762,* NYHS, Collections, 2 vols. (New York, 1826, 1829), 1: 281.

6. William Pitt Sr. quoted from Bernard Bailyn, *The Ideological Origins of the American Revolution* (Cambridge, Mass., 1967), 134–35.

7. Compare language against luxury in Adam Smith, *An Inquiry into the Nature and Causes of the Wealth of Nations,* ed. Edwin Cannan (1776; repr. Chicago, 1976), 2: 388–92, quotation at 391, with statements apparently favoring expanded consumption beyond necessity in ibid., 328–32 and bk. 5, ch. 2. For interesting—albeit divergent—insights see Albert O. Hirschman, *Shifting Involvements, Private Interests, and Public Action* (Princeton, N.J., 1982); William Reddy, *Money and Liberty in Modern Europe: A Critique of Historical Understanding* (Cambridge, 1987); and Hiram Caton, *The Politics of Progress: The Origins and Development of the Commercial Republic, 1600–1835* (Gainesville, Fla., 1988), chs. 5–7.

8. Sir Dudley North, *Discourses upon Trade* (1691; repr. Baltimore, 1907), ed. Jacob H. Hollander, 14, 18, 21, 27, 7. Others gave qualified defense of expanded consumption too: see Daniel Defoe, *A Plan of the English Commerce* (London, 1728); Addison and Steele's *Spectator,* 1711–14, esp. nos. 55, 260, 294, 331, 478, 574; Joshua Gee, *The Trade and Naviga-*

tion of Great Britain, considered (1718; 3d ed., 1731; facs. repr., New York, 1883); David Hume, "Of Commerce," "Of the Balance of Trade," "Of Interest," and "Of Refinement in the Arts," all in *David Hume: Writings on Economics,* ed. Eugene Rotwein (Madison, Wis., 1955), 3–33, 47–59, 66–77; Adam Ferguson, *Essay on the History of Civil Society* (1767; repr., New Brunswick, N.J., 1980); Alexander Pope, *Essay on Man* (1733–74), ed. Maynard Mack, 2 vols. (London, 1970), 2: 41–42, 43–52, 53–59; Sir James Steuart, *An Inquiry into the Principles of Political Oeconomy,* ed. Andrew S. Skinner, 2 vols. (1767; repr. Edinburgh, 1966), 1: 43–6, 131–39, 265–69, 185–86, 255–56, 228–34, 279–82; Adam Smith, *Wealth of Nations,* bk. 5, ch. 2. Hume, who was no enemy to luxury or to the French trade, decided that "there are few Englishmen who would not think their country absolutely ruined were French wines sold in England so cheap and in such abundance as to supplant in some measure all ale and home brewed liquors"; yet "we transferred the commerce of wine to Spain and Portugal, where we buy worse liquor at a higher price" (*Writings on Economics,* ed. Rotwein, 66–67).

9. Barbon, *Discourse of Trade,* 32, 37–38; North, *Discourses,* 12. For later comments, see Bernard Mandeville, *The Grumbling Hive; or, Knaves Turn'd Honest,* in *The Fable of the Bees* (1714), ed. F. B. Kaye (London, 1924), 1: 193. John Trenchard and Thomas Gordon were calling for additional restraints on luxury consumption in *Cato's Letters,* 1: 25, 65, 266; 2: 43, 3: 84, 118, 136–48, 201; and see the ambivalence in Bolingbroke, *The Craftsman,* nos. 888 and 891. Mandeville wrote one of the most widely read condemnations of contemporary magistrates and bureaucrats who stifled the opportunities of middling inhabitants to enjoy a better standard of living. His dictum of 1714 that "Frugality is, like Honesty, a *mean, starving, virtue,*" was written at the height of the republican country opposition's popularity. On the notion of production for desire rather than need, see Mary Douglas, *The World of Goods: Towards an Anthropology of Consumption* (New York, 1979), ch. 1. Note also Bolingbroke's call in *The Mercator* (1713) for "as full and free a trade, and as open a market for manufactures in France as possible," and Charles Davenant's dictum that "trade is in its nature free, finds its own channel and best directeth its own course [with respect to France]," in *Works,* ed. Whitworth, 1: 98.

10. *New-York Gazette,* June 2, 9, 16, 1729 (ibid., Nov. 14, 1737, reprints and discusses Mandeville's *Grumbling Hive*); William Livingston et al., *The Independent Reflector,* ed. Milton M. Klein (Cambridge, Mass., 1963), Jan. 25, 1753, 111; *Docs. Rel.,* 5: 81. See also Philip Livingston to Samuel Storke, May 18, 1734, Philip Livingston Business Letters, AAS; *A Letter from a Merchant in London to His Nephew in North America* (London, 1765); Johnson, *Predecessors of Adam Smith,* 295–97.

11. "Mr. Thomas Cockerell to Mr. Popple," July 2, 1709," in *Docs. Rel.,* 5: 80–81; William Alexander to Peter van Brugh Livingston, Mar. 1, 1756, Rutherfurd Collection, vol. 3, no. 93, NYHS; Philip Livingston to Jacob Wendell, July 23, 1737, Livingston Papers, Museum of the City of New York, and to Samuel Storke, May 18, 1734, Philip Livingston Business Letters. These paragraphs are indebted to Drew McCoy, *The Elusive Republic: Political Economy in Jeffersonian America* (Williamsburg, Va., 1980), 96–104; and Joyce Appleby, "The Social Origins of American Revolutionary Ideology," *Journal of American History* 64 (1978): 935–58. However, McCoy sees luxury validated primarily in the crucible of the Revolution and after, not in the urban merchant settings of the colonial period; and Appleby sees a more thorough self-interest permeating American society

very early, but does not pinpoint the historical struggles of particular layers of colonial society.

12. Josiah Child, as quoted by John Smith, *Chronicon Rusticum-Commerciale,* 2 parts (London, 1747), pt. 1, iv.

13. Isaac Gervaise, *The System or Theory of the Trade of the World* (1720), ed. Jacob Viner (Baltimore, 1954), 15, 17–18, 23–24.

14. [Matthew Decker], *An Essay on the Causes of the Decline of the Foreign Trade* (London, 1750), 14, 15, 26, 31–32, 104, 106, 107, 109, 145.

15. See, e.g., Jacob Viner, "English Theories of Foreign Trade before Adam Smith," *Journal of Political Economy* 38 (1930): 269.

16. See, e.g., *Wealth and Virtue: The Shaping of Political Economy in the Scottish Enlightenment,* ed. Istvan Hont and Michael Ignatieff (Cambridge, Mass., 1977), intro.; P. G. M. Dickson, *The Financial Revolution in England: A Study in the Development of Public Credit, 1688–1756* (New York, 1967), 16; D. W. Jones, "London Merchants and the Crisis of the 1690s," in *Crisis and Order in English Towns, 1500–1700,* ed. P. Clark and P. Slack (London, 1972), 322–27.

17. Hume, Smith, and others qualified their hopes for a "natural balance" with the assumption that it was probably unobtainable, given individual passions; see Hume, "Of Commerce," in *Essays, Moral, Philosophical, Political, and Literary* (Oxford, 1963), 263; *The Spectator,* no. 287 (Jan. 29, 1712); Bishop George Berkeley, *The Querist* (1735), repr. in *The Works of George Berkeley,* ed. A. C. Fraser, 3 vols. (London, 1871), at 3: 374; Albert O. Hirschman, *The Passions and the Interests: Political Arguments for Capitalism before Its Triumph* (Princeton, N.J., 1977), pt. 1.

18. Daniel Defoe, *A Tour Through the Whole Island of Great Britain* (1724; repr. New York, 1978), 6, 15; Horace Walpole, *Memoirs of the Reign of King George the Third,* 3 vols. (1768; repr., New York, 1894), 3: 136.

19. Thomas Dalby, *Historical Account of the Rise and Growth of the West India Colonies and of the Great Advantage they are to England in respect of Trade* (London, 1690); John Oldmixon, *The British Empire in America,* 2 vols. (London, 1708); and Davenant, *On the Plantation Trade.*

20. [Anon.], *An Enquiry into the Causes of the Present High Price of Muscovado Sugars* (London, 1735), 6–9. John Campbell is quoted by Klaus Knorr, *British Colonial Theories, 1570–1850* (Toronto, 1944), 94.

21. E.g., *New-York Gazette, or Weekly Post-Boy,* Apr. 12, 1773. See also ibid., June 16, 1755, for hints about imitating "Japan-work."

22. "Mr. Colden's Account of the State of the Province of New-York," in *Docs. Rel.,* 7: 795.

23. "A Glance at New York in 1697: The Travel Diary of Dr. Benjamin Bullivant," ed. Wayne Andrews, *New-York Historical Society Quarterly* 40 (1956): 63–64.

24. "Archibald Kennedy to the Lords of Plantations," Jan. 5, 1747, in *Docs. Rel.,* 6: 393; Virginia Harrington, *The New York Merchant on the Eve of the Revolution* (New York, 1935), 201–2; *The Beekman Mercantile Papers, 1746–1799,* ed. Philip White, 3 vols. (New York, 1956), 1: 362, 368–70, 413. See also the *New-York Gazette, New York Journal,* and *New-York Gazette, or Weekly Post-Boy,* 1730s–60s.

25. On merchants' homes, see J. A. Stevens, "Old New York Coffee Houses," *Harper's New Monthly Magazine* 64 (Mar. 1882); William Loring Andrews, *Views of Early New York*

(New York, 1904), 89–110; James G. Wilson, *The Memorial History of the City of New York*, 4 vols. (New York, 1893), 2: 166–70, 472–73; and Henry Moscow, *The Street Book* (New York, 1979). For other details of merchant lifestyle, see, e.g., David Clarkson Papers; William Alexander, boxes of receipts; and Cornelius and Robert Ray Papers, all at the NYHS; Esther Singleton, *Social New York under the Georges, 1714–1776*, 2 vols. (New York, 1902), 1: 269, 174–75, 18–19, 42–43, 66–76; Dr. Alexander Hamilton, *Gentleman's Progress: The Itinerarium of Dr. Alexander Hamilton*, ed. Carl Bridenbaugh (1744; repr., Chapel Hill, N.C., 1948), 89; Burnaby, *Travels*; Stevens, *Records*, 61–62; and Harrington, *New York Merchant*, 14–15, 19, 22–25.

26. Adriaen van der Donck, *A Description of the New Netherlands*, ed. Thomas F. O'Donnell (1665; repr., Syracuse, N.Y., 1968), xix; James Rivington to Sir William Johnson, May 3, 1769, in *The Papers of Sir William Johnson*, ed. James Sullivan et al., 14 vols. (Albany, N.Y., 1921–65), 6: 733; Hugh Gaine to William Johnson, May 17, 1774, in ibid., 8: 1156; and for Samuel Judah's list, Jacob Marcus, *American Jewry, Documents: The Eighteenth Century* (Cincinnati, 1970), 10–11.

27. My generalizations are based on merchants' accounts and correspondence; Singleton, *Social New York*, 1: 337–39, 261; and Gary Nash, *The Urban Crucible: Political Consciousness and the Origins of the American Revolution* (Cambridge, Mass., 1979), 117–18. Thomas Doerflinger finds little evidence of this reading in *A Vigorous Spirit of Enterprise: Merchants and Economic Development in Revolutionary Philadelphia* (Chapel Hill, N.C., 1986).

28. Cathy Matson, "'Damned Scoundrels' and 'Libertisme of Trade': Freedom and Regulation in Colonial New York's Fur and Grain Trades," *William and Mary Quarterly*, 3d. ser., 51 (July 1994): 389–418. I am, again, emphasizing the role of commerce, both perceptually and materially, in New York City, although real-estate development, gentrification, and northern expansionism are also broached. Cf. Hedrick Hartog, *Public Property and Private Power: The Corporation of the City of New York in American Law, 1730–1870* (Chapel Hill, N.C., 1983), and Elizabeth Blackmar, *Manhattan for Rent, 1785–1850* (Ithaca, N.Y., 1989), ch. 1.

29. Singleton, *Social New York*, 2: 378–79, 380–81; see also 375; William Smith, *History*, 1: 277; "A Glance at New York in 1697," ed. Andrews; "Letter from Peter Delanoy," in *Doc. Hist.*, 4: 321–24; Kalm, *Travels*, 1: 125–35.

30. C.O. 5: 1222–28; *New-York Gazette, New York Journal,* and *New-York Gazette, or Weekly Post-Boy,* 1731–68; Kalm, *Travels,* 1: 134–36; Lawrence J. Bradley, "The London-Bristol Trade Rivalry: Conventional History and the C.O. 5 Records for the Port of New York" (Ph.D. diss., University of Washington, 1963), 201, 204.

31. C.O. 5: 1224–25, and merchants' correspondence cited in the notes to this chapter. "Cocoa nuts" refers to cocoa beans used to make chocolate.

32. Singleton, *Social New York,* 2: 364.

33. "Petition of the Merchants of the City of New-York relating to Foreign Coins," Feb. 1704, in *Docs. Rel.,* 4: 1133–35; Kalm, *Travels,* 1: 238–45, 49–50; David MacPherson, *Annals of Commerce, Manufactures, Fisheries, and Navigation,* 4 vols. (London, 1805), 3: 186–91; Robert G. Albion, *The Rise of New York Port* (New York, 1939), 1–3; Eric Williams, *From Columbus to Castro: The History of the Caribbean, 1492–1969* (New York, 1984), chs. 9–10. For New York City's sugar trade, start with C.O. 5: 1222–28; John van Cortlandt, Sugar House Accounts, Feb. 15, 1764; *New-York Gazette, or Weekly Post-Boy,* Aug. 18. 1766;

Kalm, *Travels*, 1: 238–45, 49–50; statement of Samuel Vetch, 1708, quoted in Andrews, *Colonial Period*, 4: 347; and Abraham de Peyster Papers, 1695–1710, NYHS.

34. C.O. 5: 1223–28; C.O. 3: 51–75; C.O. 390: 9, B6–B7; *Doc. Hist.*, 1: 493, 513; Edmund Burke, *An Account of the European Settlements in America*, 2 vols. (London, 1757), 2: 185; A. P. Newton, *The European Nations in the West Indies, 1493–1688* (London, 1933), concl.; Richard Pares, *Yankees and Creoles: The Trade between North America and the West Indies before the American Revolutin* (Cambridge, Mass., 1956), ch. 3; *New-York Gazette*, 1730–44; *New-York Mercury*, 1764; *New-York Post-Boy*, 1770–74; for 1715–18, see Albion, *Rise of New York Port*, 6. For comparison with Philadelphia, see Arthur Jensen, *The Maritime Trade of Colonial Philadelphia* (Madison, Wis., 1963). From 1715 to 1765, between 49 percent and 51 percent of the vessels moving through New York were employed in the West Indies trade; from 1715 to 1718, an average of 51 percent of New York's annual cargo tonnage cleared for the West Indies, about 112 vessels a year; in 1730, 51 percent of New York's entering vessels came from the West Indies and 56 percent of its vessels cleared for there, some 112 ships; by 1750, 43 percent of New York's cargo tonnage was intended for the West Indies; by 1764, 63 percent of entering vessels arrived from the West Indies, and 60 percent—166 vessels—cleared for West Indian ports. By 1770–74, the city averaged 273 clearances a year to the Caribbean ports. See C.O. 5: 1222–28; "An Essay on the Trade of the Northern Colonies," *Providence Gazette*, Jan. 14, 21, 1764; *The Commerce of Rhode Island, 1720–1800*, Massachusetts Historical Society, *Collections*, 7th ser., vols. 9–10 (Boston, 1914–15), vol. 9; and Herbert Bell, "The West Indies Trade before the Revolution," *American Historical Review* 22 (1916–17): 272–87. For voyage and layover times, see Noel Deerr, *The History of Sugar*, 2 vols. (London, 1949–50), 1: 193–201, 235–39; Charles Whitworth, *The State of the Trade of Great Britain in its Imports and Exports, 1697–1773* (London, 1776), 49, 57–58; Samuel Gilford Account Books, 1759–63, NYHS; Thomas Witter Papers, 1748–63, NYHS; John Taylor Log Book, 1743–47, NYHS; and William Walton Insurance Book, Municipal Archives, New York City, where we find that it took 30 to 40 days to arrive at Barbados or Jamaica over most of the eighteenth century, that times in port averaged 50 to 70 days at New York City, with large oceangoing ships taking longer to prepare for a voyage, and that ships lay in port at Barbados for about 25 to 35 days during the eighteenth century.

35. On West Indies smuggling via the Dutch since at least the 1580s, see D. W. Davies, *A Primer of Dutch Overseas Trade* (The Hague, 1961). On the rise of the Dutch in the Caribbean in general, see Cornelis C. Goslinga, *The Dutch in the Caribbean and on the Wild Coast, 1580–1680*, (Gainesville, Fla., 1971). For an example at New York, see Philip van Cortlandt Letterbook, 1713–22, NYHS.

36. [Anon.], "Account Book of a New York City Merchant, 1706–1714," Library of Congress (in Dutch). The city merchants included Moses Levy, Francis Gordon, Joseph Bueno, Octavo Cortlandt, Jacob Minvielle, Charles Crommeline, Robert Walton, Cornelius de Peyster, Nicholas Bayard, William Pratner, Dirck van Brugh, Benjamin Aske, Joseph Tiebout, Andrew Gravenraat, Thomas Clark, Josiah Ogden, Elias Low, Samuel Giebent, Henry Courteen, John van Brugh, Joseph Talmadge, Cornelis Langeveld, Adolphe Philipse, Ebenezer Wilson, Isaac Naftaly, Joseph Nimos, David Provoost Jr., Hendrick ten Eyck, Isaac Gouverneur, Adrian Hooglandt, Leonard Lewis, Garrit van Horne, William Walton, William Davis, Johannes Hartenburgh, Patrick Macknight, Jacob Ruitzen, and Nicholas Roosevelt.

37. "Mr. Colden's Account of the Trade of New-York," in *Docs. Rel.*, 5: 685–700, at 686; Cornelius Cuyler to Richard Jeneway [*sic*], Jan. 13, 1728, to Samuel Baker, Apr. 11, 1730, and to John Cruger, Aug. 3, 24, and Oct. 16, 1731, Cuyler, Letter Book, AAS. Other merchants in the Dutch Caribbean trade by 1715 included Philip Livingston, Philip van Cortlandt, Abraham de Peyster, Cornelius ten Broeck, Johannes de Peyster, Hans Hansen, Rutger Bleecker, Evert Wendell, and Ryer Gerritse; *AJ*, 1: 538–39, 544; *Colonial Laws*, 2: 281–94, 350–71, 401, 485, 537, 553; David Armour, "The Merchants of Albany, New York, 1686–1760" (Ph.D. diss., Northwestern University, 1965), 175–76; Ships File, NYHS; Jacob Wendell, Letterbook, NYHS; Peter and Robert Livingston Jr., Letterbook, Museum of the City of New York. Livingston's business with Samuel Storke alternated between legal and illicit voyages. Other networks, including the Schuyler, Van Cortlandt, and De Vries family connections with Surinam, St. Eustatius, and Curaçao, and by 1710, Jamaica and Barbados, can be discerned in *Docs. Rel.*, 2: 699–700, 4: 1133, and John van Cortlandt, Shipping Book, Aug. 12, 1699–June 30, 1702, and 1702–5.

38. John Campbell, *A Concise History of the Spanish Americas* (London, 1741); George Lyttleton, *Considerations upon the Present State of our Affairs at Home and Abroad* (London, 1739), 12–14; and Philip Livingston to Storke & Gainsborough, Nov. 13, 1735, Philip Livingston Letters; Gov. Bellomont to the Lords of Trade, Nov. 28, 1700, in *State Papers*, 1700, 18: 676; id. to the Lords of Trade, May 25, 1698, in *Docs. Rel.*, 4: 317; Gov. Hunter to the Lords of Trade, Nov. 12, 1715, in *State Papers*, 1714–15, 28: 337, 338, 340; Michael Kammen, *Colonial New York* (New York, 1975), 151–52; Nash, *Urban Crucible*, 66.

39. "Representation to Her Majesty on the State of the Plantations in America," Sept. 8, 1721, in *Docs. Rel.*, 5: 591–630; MacPherson, *Annals*, 3: 174; *New-York Gazette*, July 19, 26, Aug. 2, 9, 1731, July 24, 31, Aug. 2, 9, 20, 1732; [Anon.], *The Present State of the British Sugar Islands Considered in a Letter from a Gentleman of Barbados* (London, 1731); Dalby Thomas, *An Historical Account of the Rise and Growth of the West India Colonies* (1690), repr., *Harleian Miscellany*, 12 vols. (London, 1808), 9: 410–19; *AJ*, 1: 633. On the duty, see Frank W. Pitman, *The Development of the British West Indies, 1700–1763* (New Haven, Conn., 1917), 48.

40. Gov. Tryon to the Board of Trade, 1774, in *Doc. Hist.*, 1: 758–59.

41. C.O. 5: 1227, 1228; John Watts to Joseph Maynard, 10 Jan. 1763, to Gedney Clarke, Jan. 30, 1762, and to Francis Clarke, Jan. 30, 1762, in *WLB*, 113, 18, 17, 130; Pitman, *Development of the British West Indies*, 281–82. Agents purchased dyewoods for cash or bills of exchange, having already disposed of goods from New York in other parts of the West Indies on the way to Honduras and Curaçao lumber "factories"; see e.g., C.O. 390: 9, B6–B7.

42. John van Cortlandt, Account Book, 1754–59; C.O. 16: 1; John Baker Holroyd, 1st earl of Sheffield, *Observations on the Commerce of the American States, with Europe and the West Indies* (1783), 6th ed. (London, 1784), app. 12; Henry Cruger to Aaron Lopez, Feb. 1, 1772, in *Commerce of Rhode Island*, 1: 385–88; and ibid., Mar. 11, July 14, 1772, 1: 391–92, 405. Rice accounted for about £3,000 a year of New York's reexports after 1760, and southern naval stores for about £1,000 to £3,000 a year; by contrast, merchants exported about 130,000 bushels of flaxseed a year by then.

43. Bloch, *HMR*. Levy is one example of many, and the sources in the following notes would reveal many patterns like his.

44. C.O. 5: 1222–24. Other owners of shares in the *Abigail* were Jacob Franks and, until 1721, Samuel Levy; and thereafter, Adolphe Philipse and John van Cortlandt.

45. C.O. 5: 1224–28. The relatives were Isaac (1706–77), Michael (1709–ca.1760), Hayman (1721–89), Eleazer (d. 1811), and Joseph (unknown dates).

46. Author's biographical compilation; Bloch, *HMR*; David Valentine, *History of the City of New York* (New York, 1853), 345–65; for the 1701 and 1703 tax assessments, a source of important information for my generalizations, see ch. 5, n. 33; for the 1708 assessment, ch. 5, n. 36.

47. C.O. 5: 1222–24; Bloch, *HMR*; Archdeacon, *Conquest and Change*, 64, 72–75. Minvielle died in 1702, so there is no continuous record of his trade.

48. Philip Cuyler to John Ludlow, June 13, 1758, Cuyler, Letter Book; Christopher Bancker, Waste Book, Feb. 20, 1750; John van Cortlandt, Letter Book, Nov. 11, 1763; John and Henry Cruger, Letter Book, 1766–67; Alexander Hamilton to Jacob Walton and John H. Cruger, Nov. 27, 1771, to Nicholas Cruger, Nov. 4, 12, 1771, to Tileman [*sic*] Cruger, Nov. 16, 1771, to Walton and Co., Nov. 27, 1771, to Nicholas Cruger, Jan. 10, Feb. 24, 1772, and to Henry Cruger, Feb. 24, 1772, in *The Papers of Alexander Hamilton*, ed. Harold C. Syrett and Jacob E. Cooke, 27 vols. (New York, 1961–87), 1: 8, 10, 11, 12–13, 17–18, 20–21, 25–26, 27–28; and William Lux to John Bradford, July 15, 1768, Lux Letter Book, NYHS.

49. Appendix A, table 2; Anne Grant, *Memoirs of an American Lady . . . Previous to the Revolution*, 2 vols. (1808; repr., New York, 1970), 2: 241–43.

50. For this paragraph and the next, see C.O. 5: 1227–28; *Boston News-Letter*, July 27, 1749, quoting *New-York Gazette* for July 17, 1749; Isaac Gouverneur, Walter Livingston, Henry Cruger, John van Cortlandt, William and John Walton letter books, all at NYHS; letter book at the AAS of Philip Livingston, who traded at Jamaica, Honduras, St. Kitts, Antigua, the Virgin Islands, St. Croix, and Surinam. The Crugers traded at Jamaica, Mosquito, St. Eustatius, Curaçao, Antigua, St. Kitts, and Montserrat. Pitman, *British West Indies*, 279–80, writes that Jamaica received one-third to one-half of New York's Caribbean trade, an average of 3,400 tons a year after 1730; this is based on assessing legal traffic and overstates New York's preference for that island. John J. McCusker, "The Current Value of English Exports, 1697–1800," *William and Mary Quarterly* 28 (1971): 607–28, table 3, shows the rise in Chesapeake wheat production that met some island demand; by 1770, Virginians exported one-fourth of the wheat New Yorkers and Philadelphians did.

51. John Cary, *Essay on Trade* (London, 1695), 115–16, 122, 125–28; Oldmixon, *British Empire in America*, 2: 152; [Anon.], *High Price of Muscovado Sugars*; [Anon.], *A Short Answer to an Elaborate Pamphlet* (London, 1731), 21; and [Anon.], *Remarks upon a Book, Entitled, The Present State of the Sugar Colonies Consider'd* (London, 1731), 7, 9; Pitman, *British West Indies*, 416–17; and Richard B. Sheridan, *Sugar and Slavery: An Economic History of the British West Indies, 1623–1775* (Baltimore, 1963), 136–71.

52. Micajah Perry to Cadwallader Colden, Dec. 27, 1731, in *Colden*, 51: 46–47. Earlier, Charles Davenant had proposed that Parliament allow the colonies to have the provisions trade with the West Indies in order to distract them from undermining England's interest in the Newfoundland fisheries—a greater plum until the early eighteenth century; see *Works*, ed. Whitworth, 12: 9, 21, 22. Also see Charles Whitworth, *State of the Trade* (London, 1776), pt. 2, 85–86; and William Wood, *Survey of Trade* (London, 1718), 136–41, for understatements of French influence in the Caribbean.

53. Captain Fayer Hall, "Capt. Fayer Hall's Evidence before a Committee of the Whole House," *New-York Gazette,* July 24, 31, and Aug. 2, 9, 20, 1732.

54. Examples of New York's responses to the proposed Molasses Act may be traced in C.O. 324 in general; Gov. Hunter to the Board of Trade, Aug. 11, 1720, in C.O. 5: 1052, Cc38; "Representation to Her Majesty on the State of the Plantations in America," Sept. 8, 1721, in C.O. 324: 10; "An Account of the Trade of New York by Cadwallader Colden," June 25, 1723, in C.O. 5: 1053, Cc117; Rip van Dam to the Board of Trade, Oct. 29, 1731, in ibid; and "The Humble Representation of the President[,] Council and General Assembly of the Colony of New York," Oct. 29, 1731, in C.O. 5: 1055, Dd161. The quotation is from [Anon.], "Letter from St. Croix," reprinted from the *New-York Gazette* in the *Providence Gazette,* Aug. 26, 1769; but also see MacPherson, *Annals,* 3: 186–91; Sheridan, *Sugar and Slavery;* John J. McCusker Jr., "The Rum Trade and the Balance of Payments of the Thirteen Continental Colonies, 1660–1775" (Ph.D. diss., University of Pittsburgh, 1970), 313, 398, 400. For the view that French merchants undersold British ones, see William Perrin, *The Present State of the British and French Sugar Colonies, and our own Northern Colonies considered* (London, 1740).

55. [Anon.], *The Importance of the British Plantations in America to this Kingdom* (London, 1731), 66–67; [Anon.], *A Comparison between the British Sugar Colonies and New England as they relate to the Interest of Great Britain* (London, 1732); [Anon.], *A True State of the Case between the British Northern Colonies and the Sugar Islands* (London, 1732); John Ashley, *Sugar Trade with the Incumbrances thereon, laid open* (London, 1734). On declining prices, see Pitman, *British West Indies,* 418–20.

56. The Molasses Act is at 6 Geo. 2, ch. 13. See also Smith, *History,* 1: 279–82; *Docs. Rel.,* 7: 759; MacPherson, *Annals,* 3: 397; correspondence cited in notes to this section; and, on distilling, ch. 7.

57. William Beekman, Daybook C, 1752–56; Lawrence Kortright, Letters, NYHS; *Colden,* 50: 27, 51, 195.

58. Albion, *Rise of New York Port,* 6; C.O. 16: 1; C.O. 324: 10, pp. 386–87; William Sachs, "The Business Outlook in the Northern Colonies, 1750–1775" (Ph.D. diss., Columbia University, 1957), 175–88; *New-York Gazette,* for the 1750s; Walton Insurance Book, 1774. From 1715 to 1718, an average of 68 (33%) of the 215 vessels clearing New York annually listed coastal destinations, most of them Boston, Perth Amboy, Providence, Charles Town, and Philadelphia. In 1754, a combined 10,840 cargo tons entered from, and cleared to, coastal ports; in 1764, 30 percent of New York City's tonnage cleared for coastal ports; by 1772, 592 (42%) of 1,410 vessel clearances were for coastal destinations, and carried 22,000 cargo tons (26.5% of the total) that year. Coastal voyages usually did not involve the "triangles" of most interpretations (e.g., those of Harrington and Albion) but rather a series of direct voyages, as the examples of Isaac Sears and Jacobus van Zandt show; see Robert Jay Christen, "King Sears: Politician and Patriot in a Decade of Revolution" (Ph.D. diss., Columbia University, 1968). Over the century, coastal trade occupied about 35 percent of all vessels moving through the port of New York, William Davisson and Lawrence Bradley estimate in "New York Maritime Trade: Ship Voyage Patterns, 1715–1765," *New-York Historical Society Quarterly* 55 (Oct. 1971): 309–17.

59. E.g., C.O. 5: 1222–27; "Governor Dongan to the Board of Trade," 1687, in *Docs. Rel.,* 3: 393; John Watts to George and John Riddell, Jan. 14, 1764, in *WLB,* 322; John van

Cortlandt to John Riddlehurst, Nov. 17, 1762, Van Cortlandt Letter Book; "Mr. Colden's Account of the Trade of New-York," in *Docs. Rel.*, 5: 686.

60. Sachs, "Business Outlook," 175–88; Curtis Nettels, *The Money Supply of the American Colonies before 1720* (Madison, Wis., 1934), 110; *Docs. Rel.*, 6: 511; William Weeden, *Economic and Social History of New England, 1620–1789*, 2 vols. (Boston, 1890), 2: 615.

61. James Levitt, *For Want of Trade: Shipping and the New Jersey Ports, 1680–1783* (Newark, N.J., 1981), 56–58, 113–17, 119–20, 123; records of the *Burnet, Mary and Catharine, Eagle of Amboy, Molly,* and *Two Friends,* in C.O. 5: 1222–25; *Calendar of the Stevens Family Papers,* New Jersey Historical Records Survey Project, 2 vols. (Newark, N.J., 1941), vol. 2, 1751–77; *Beekman Mercantile Papers,* ed. White, vol. 1; Philip Livingston to Storke & Gainsborough, Sept. 31, Nov. 28, 1734, Philip Livingston Letters, AAS; and the Matthew Clarkson letters, NYHS.

62. *Docs. Rel.*, 5: 686; *Archives of the State of New Jersey, 1631–1800,* ed. W. A. Whitehead et al., 3d ser. (Trenton, N.J., 1880–1928), 9: 402–4, 442–44, 26: 122, 553; 27: 439; E. R. Johnson, *History of Domestic and Foreign Commerce of the United States,* 2 vols. (New York, 1915), 1: 163–69; "Petition of New York Merchants to the House of Commons," (Weyman's) *New-York Gazette,* May 4, 1767; Kalm, *Travels,* 1: 31, 49–50, 179, 199, 200, 201, 253–58; C.O. 16: 1; Gov. Tryon, "Report to the Board of Trade," 1774, in *Doc. Hist.*, 3: 434–57. The *New-York Mercury,* June 14, 1762, carried a notice from a Perth Amboy merchant, Andrew Johnson & Co., that the company had just been delivered a large supply of "India goods" from London via New York City.

63. *New-York Gazette, or Weekly Post-Boy,* June 10, 1754; 12 Car. 2, c. 18, par. 18; *New-York Gazette,* 1732; and J. L. Bishop, *A History of American Manufactures, from 1608 to 1860,* 3 vols. (Philadelphia, 1868), 2: 22.

64. *Docs. Rel.*, 6: 510–11; (Holt's) *New York Journal,* 1774–75; Bishop, *American Manufactures,* 1: 461; John van Cortlandt, Sugar House Accounts, Feb. 7, 15, 1764, NYHS; *New-York Gazette, or Weekly Post-Boy,* Aug. 18, 1766; Sachs, "Business Outlook," 175–88.

65. John van Cortlandt, Sugar House Accounts, 1757–67; id., Letter Books, 1762–69.

66. William Alexander to Capt. Dunbiben, Dec. 20, 1749, Alexander Letters, vol. 1, fols. 1744–50, NYHS; Gerard Beekman to James E. Powell, Nov. 2, 1755, in *Beekman Mercantile Papers,* ed. White, 1: 261; John Watts to George and John Riddell, Jan. 14, 1764, in *WLB,* 322; John van Cortlandt to John Riddlehurst, Nov. 17, 1762, Van Cortlandt Letter Book.

67. *New-York Gazette,* Dec. 18, 1732; Nettels, *Money Supply,* 118–19. New York vessels carried rice but not South Carolina's naval stores, salted meat, and hides; some Carolina exports had been engrossed by the Scottish factors, too; see, e.g., Gerard Beekman to James E. Powell, Nov. 2, 1755, in *Beekman Mercantile Papers,* ed. White, 1: 261; Philip Cuyler to William Proctor, Cuyler, Letter Book, July 5, 1755; John van Cortlandt to Roscoe Sweeny, to Robert Tucker, and to Abraham Maer, Van Cortlandt Letter Book, 1757–59.

68. "Mr. Colden's Account of the Trade of New-York," in *Docs. Rel.*, 5: 685–700, at 686; *Independent Reflector,* ed. Klein, May 10, 1753, 221–27. The Connecticut trader is quoted from the *New London Gazette,* Aug. 17, 1770; see also *Connecticut Journal,* Jan. 19, 1770; *Docs. Rel.*, 5: 686.

69. John van Cortlandt to John W. Hoffman, Van Cortlandt Letter Book, 1756; John Watts in *WLB,* 214–15; Philip Cuyler to David Franks, Oct. 4, 1756, Mar. 21, Dec. 19, 1757, and Aug. 14, 1758, Cuyler, Letter Book; Thomas Wharton to Gerard Beekman, Apr. 15,

1756, and to John Waddell, Mar. 13, Apr. 17 and 26, and June 23, 1758, in *Beekman Mercantile Papers*, ed. White. In general, see the correspondence of Robert C. Livingston, John Harris Cruger, Isaac Adolphus, James Kennedy, John Watts, David Franks, David van Horne, Philip Cuyler, Hugh and Alexander Wallace, Jacobus van Zandt, Lawrence Kortright, Gerard Duyckinck, Garret Rapalje, Henry Cuyler, Henry White, Abraham Lott, John Alsop, and John Remsen.

70. C.O. 5: 1222–25.

71. C.O. 5: 1222–23; Hugh Hall Jr. to his father, Sept. 25, 1717, Hugh Hall Journal, 1716–20, and Hugh Hall Letter Book, 1716–20, NYPL.

72. C.O. 5: 1222–25; correspondence of Walton, Philip Livingston, the Van Hornes, and Rip van Dam, all at NYHS; James Lydon, "New York and the Slave Trade, 1700–1774," *William and Mary Quarterly*, 3d ser., 35 (1978): 374–94.

73. C.O. 5: 1222–27; *Historical Statistics of the United States* (Washington, D.C., 1970), ser. Z, p. 1193.

74. *State Papers*, 1700, 18, no. 953; ibid., 1701, no. 378; C.O. 5: 1222, pp. 74, 123, 138, 172, 186, 256, 272; "Archibald Kennedy to the Board of Trade," Dec. 16, 1726, *Docs. Rel.*, 5: 814, for numbers of slaves imported, 1701–26; Lydon, "New York and the Slave Trade," 375–94, esp. 381–83; John Walter, Arnot Schuyler, David Griffiths, Stephanus van Cortlandt, Nathaniel Marston, Philip Livingston, William Walton, Rip van Dam, Brandt Schuyler, and Garrett van Horne, Account Books, all at NYHS, and C.O. 5: 1222–27.

75. C.O. 5: 1227, 1228; Smith, *History*, 1: 280; Pitman, *British West Indies*, 133–36, 242–46; J. F. Jamison, "St. Eustatius in the American Revolution," *American Historical Review* 8 (July 1903): 683, 708; E. B. Schumpeter, *English Overseas Trade Statistics, 1697–1808* (Oxford, 1960), 60–62; Marc Egnal, "The Economic Development of the Thirteen Colonies, 1720–1775," *William and Mary Quarterly*, 3d ser., 32 (Apr. 1975): 191–222, esp. 208; and Waldemar Westergaard, *The Danish West Indies under Colonial Rule, 1671–1754* (New York, 1917), 194–235, 250–51, 308.

76. Cornelius Cuyler to Richard Janeway, Jan. 13, 1728, and to Storke & Gainsborough, Nov. 16, 30, 1734, Cornelius Cuyler, Letter Books, AAS.

77. For New York reflections along these lines, see "Mr. Nicholl's Pamphlet to Influence the Elections of the Assembly," Apr. 1699, in C.O. 5: 1042, no. 23; "The Interest of the City and Country," *New York Journal*, Sept. 5, 1757; *Assembly Journal*, 1: 548, 551–52, 638, 641, 645; *New York Journal*, Mar. 18, 1734; *Papers of Sir William Johnson*, ed. Sullivan, 6: 762–64; 7: 11, 153–54, 301, 569; *New-York Mercury*, Apr. 12, 1762; and *New-York Evening Post*, Jan. 25, 1748.

78. See nn. 53, 58 above; *Docs. Rel.*, 5: 686; and Decker, *Essay on the Causes*, 48–49, 106, which promotes the engrossing and hoarding of goods in English ports until merchants could obtain the highest prices. For the rise of these ideas in other quarters, see David Hume, "Of Interest" and "Of Money," in *Writings on Economics*, ed. Rotwein, 48, 53; Adam Smith, *Wealth of Nations*, 1: 376, 98, 375; 2: 16–19; Janet Ann Riesman, "The Origins of American Political Economy, 1690–1781" (Ph.D. diss., Brown University, 1983), 55–87; Dickson, *Financial Revolution*, ch. 2; De Vries, *Economy of Europe*, ch. 8; Davis, *Atlantic Economies*, 239–40, 246–49.

79. "Lord Cornbury to the Lords of Trade," 1702, July 1, 1708, and Feb. 1, 1706, in *Docs. Rel.*, 4: 1003, 5: 55–60, 1049; Smith, *History*, 1: 280; *Docs. Rel.*, 6: 511.

80. The English law is at 7 & 8 Will. 3, c. 22, 1696, cited in Sir Thomas Parker, *The Laws*

of Shipping and Insurance, with a Digest of Adjudged Cases (London, 1775). The merchants in this illicit trade network included Robert R. and John L. Livingston, Samuel Vetch, Thomas Fowles, Levinus van Schaick, Micajah Perry, Margaret Schuyler, Jacobus van Cortlandt, Caleb Heathcote, Philip French, Thomas Wenham, Dirk Wessels, David Jamison, Peter Fauconnier, and others. The vessels were named *Catherine, Industry, Mary and Margaret,* and *Dove*; see "Lt.-Gov. Clarke to the Lords of Trade," in *Docs. Rel.,* 6: 154–556; Lawrence Leder, *Robert Livingston, 1654–1728, and the Politics of Colonial New York* (Chapel Hill, N.C., 1961), 174–75, 181; and Bloch, *HMR.* For logwood trading with Spanish factors, see [Anon.], *The Irregular and Disorderly State of the Plantation-Trade* (1696), repr. in *Annual Report of the American Historical Association for the Year 1892* (Washington, D.C., 1893), 36; and Edmund Randolph, "Report to the Board of Trade," Prince Society, *Publications,* vols. 24–28, 30–31 (Boston, 1898–1909), 25: 250, 28: 118. For punishments, see, e.g., *New-York Weekly Journal,* May 27, 1734, reporting on a hanging at an unspecified location on May 3, 1734. Cornbury is cited in n. 79.

81. Ch. 3 discusses sources of early smuggling and attitudes about it; ch. 8 returns to the Seven Years' War.

82. *Colden,* 55: 161–62, 210–12, 149–51, 178, 138–39; Peter R. Livingston and Lawrence Kortright jointly owned the *Industry* and the *Phoenix*; separately, Kortright also owned the *Sally*; and for John Tabor Kempe on the extent of the Newport trade, see *The Aspinwall Papers,* Massachusetts Historical Society, *Collections,* 4th ser., 2 vols. (Boston, 1871–72), 1: 449–50, 470–71. On sales of "flags of truce," see Philip Cuyler to William Tweedy, Mar. 11, 1760, Cuyler, Letter Book; Pitman, *British West Indies,* 317, 328; Harrington, *New York Merchant,* 266, citing Thomas Riche of Philadelphia to Jacobus van Zandt, Mar. 24, and Apr. 2, 1759, Letter Book of Thomas Riche, Historical Society of Pennsylvania. "Flag of truce" was the colonial name for a merchant ship commissioned by the governor to carry prisoners to an enemy country to be exchanged. They were expressly forbidden to trade goods for profit at any point of entry.

83. "Earl of Bellomont to the Lords of Trade, 1700," in *Docs. Rel.,* 4: 792.

84. Two to four registered vessels went to Amsterdam a year between 1706 and 1716, and an uncertain number of illicit ones, which matches New York's level of trade with Amsterdam before 1689; from 1724 to 1731, two to six ships cleared and up to three ships entered New York from Amsterdam a year; from 1740 to 1764, only one to three vessels cleared and up to two entered New York City legally. Albany merchants also traded to Amsterdam through New York City merchants, who were instructed to avoid paying duties: in the 1720s, Hendrick ten Eyck, Robert Sanders, David van der Heyden, Jelles Fonda, and Jacob Glen; in the 1730s to 1740s, Hendrick ten Eyck and Cornelius Cuyler. *New-York Gazette,* 1724–31, 1737–64; C.O. 5: 1222–23, 1225–26; Charles Lodwick Papers, NYHS; William Roberts III, "Samuel Storke: An Eighteenth-Century London Merchant Trading to the American Colonies," *Business History Review* 39 (1965): 147–70; Cornelius Cuyler to Henry Bonnin (Antigua), July 27, 1753, to William Darlington, Mar. 16, 1754, to Philip Cuyler, n.d., 1754, to a Mr. Hansen, Oct. 31, 1754, to Daniel Crommelin, Dec. 23, 1755, and to Philip Cuyler, Mar. 20, July 13, Aug. 16, and Sept. 7 and 24, 1756, Cuyler, Letter Book.

85. On the 1720s, see Thomas Norton, *The Fur Trade in Colonial New York, 1686–1776* (Madison, Wis., 1974), 84–85; C.O. 5: 1224; Barrow, *Trade and Empire,* 151; William van

Nuys to Evert Wendell, July 4, 1716, Wendell Ledger, 1711–38; William van Nuys Papers, and Charles Lodwick Papers, both at the NYHS.

86. Gov. Cornbury to Lords of Trade, July 1, 1708, Feb. 1, 1706, in *Docs. Rel.,* 5: 55–60, 1049.

87. Archibald Kennedy to the Board of Trade, Jan. 10, 1738, in *Doc. Hist.,* 3: 101–12; William S. McClellan, *Smuggling in the American Colonies* (New York, 1912), 2–7; *New-York Mercury,* June 6, 1748; Burnaby, *Travels,* 118, 128, 129n; Collector to Board of Trade, 1739, in *Docs. Rel.,* 6: 154–55; Cadwallader Colden's comments in ibid., 7: 476, 479, 483–84, 797. The court may have tolerated smuggling because its members held office on good behavior and thus depended for reappointment upon an Assembly where some smugglers periodically sat, although the evidence for this is conjectural; *Docs. Rel.,* 7: 467, 468, 470, 705; 6: 792; William Beekman to Samuel Fowler, Apr. 2, 1754, to Thomas White, Dec. 1, 1754, in *Beekman Mercantile Papers,* ed. White; John Watts to Gedney Clarke, Mar. 30, 1762, in *WLB,* 31–32; Philip Cuyler to Joseph Wanton Jr., Oct. 16, 1755, Cuyler, Letter Book.

88. Report of the British Board of Trade and Plantations, Nov. 1702, MSS Div., NYPL, 271–78; Thomas Query, *Report on the Advances of the Navigation Acts* (1708), repr., Massachusetts Historical Society, *Proceedings,* 2d ser., vol. 4 (Boston, 1887–89), 148, 149, 152; "Robert Query to the Board of Trade," in *Docs. Rel.,* 4: 542; "Earl of Bellomont to the Lords of Trade," 1700, in ibid., 4: 793; and Philip Cuyler to John Hodshon, Oct. 4, 1757, and June 26, 1759, to Richard and Coddington, Sept. 25, 1758, Apr. 18, May 8, Sept. 27, and Nov. 7, 1759, and July 23, 1760, Cuyler, Letter Book.

89. See Gov. Clinton's report, May 23, 1749," in *Docs. Rel.,* 6: 511; John van Cortlandt, Sugar House Accounts, 1757–67; id., Letter Books, 1762–69.

90. "Earl of Bellomont to the Lords of Trade," Nov. 28, 1700, in *Docs. Rel.,* 4: 792–93; on Jeffries, see *Doc. Hist.,* 3: 183, 352, 393; Harmanus Veening (of Amsterdam) to Rutger Bleecker, May 5, 1707, June 16, 1708, Apr. 19, 1709, and June 15, 1710, all in Bleecker-Collins-Abeel Papers, NYPL; on the anonymous venture, *Docs. Rel.,* 2: 33; on the northern fisheries, see *New-York Gazette,* entries of vessels clearing the city, 1730–37; on the Antigua incident, see Andrews, *Colonial Period,* 4: 94. For other evidence of early-century smuggling, see "Earl of Bellomont to the Lords of Trade," May 13, 1699, in *Docs. Rel.,* 4: 516–17; ibid., 4: 792, 323, 542, 307, 762; Miller Papers, Abraham de Peyster Papers, and Abraham Wendell Papers, all at the NYHS. For the complicity of tide waiters and other port officials, see *Docs. Rel.,* 4: 302, 324, 354, 516. Logwood, a commodity of high value and demand from Campeche and the Bay of Honduras, was not enumerated; however, merchants paid duties for its reexport from New York City; England taxed the importation of logwood, but Amsterdam entered it duty-free; see C.O. 3: 51–75; C.O. 390: 9, B6–B7; Abraham Keteltas Account Book, 1744–61, John Keteltas Correspondence, 1761–69, Samuel Gilford Correspondence, and Peter du Bois Accounts, all at the NYHS; Geoffrey L. Rossano, "Down to the Bay: New York Shippers and the Central American Logwood Trade, 1748–1761," *New York History* 70 (July 1989): 233–34; "Report of Robert Query to the Board of Trade," Apr. 6, 1708, Massachusetts Historical Society, *Proceedings,* 2d ser., vol. 4 (Boston, 1887–89), 152; *New-York Gazette,* 1724–31, 1737–64; Cornelius Cuyler, Letter Books, and Philip Livingston Business Letters, 1734–39, AAS; John Ludlow, Account Book, vols. 1–2; John Alsop Letters; William Alexander to John de Neufville, Jan. 14, 1755, and Mar. 19, 1758, Alexander Papers, vol. 2; Christopher Bancker, Waste Book, 1754; and Philip Cuyler, Letter Book, all at the NYHS. Danish ports were duty-free after 1735, a pol-

icy meant to attract New York and New England business in provisions and lumber; the Dutch ports were duty-free over the entire century; see Pitman, *British West Indies*, 271–79, 331–33; Andrews, *Colonial Period*, 4: 98–100, 114. On Surinam, Curaçao, and St. Eustatius in the 1730s, see Archibald Kennedy to the Board of Trade, Jan. 10, 1738, in C.O. 5: 1059; "Archibald Kennedy, Esq. vs. Sloop *Mary and Margaret*, Thomas Foweles, Reclaimant," 1739, in C.O. 5: 1059, fols. 132–33; and Joseph Goldenberg, *Shipbuilding in Colonial America* (Charlottesville, Va., 1976), 20–21, 100–105.

91. John van Cortlandt Shipping Book, Aug. 12, 1699–June 30, 1702; Abraham de Peyster Papers, 1695–1710; William van Nuys (of Amsterdam) to Evert Wendell, July 4, 1716, Evert Wendell Ledger, 1711–38, all at NYHS; Davies, *Dutch Overseas Trade*, ch. 12; Leder, *Robert R. Livingston*, 37–38, 90 n. 35; Sheridan, *Sugar and Slavery*, 45–48; and Pares, *Yankees and Creoles*, 19.

92. Cornelius Cuyler, Letter Books, AAS; Philip Livingston to Robert Livingston, Mar. 25, Apr. 21, and June 10, 1724, and Philip Livingston to and from Isaac Gomez (of Curaçao), 1725, Philip Livingston Letters, Museum of the City of New York; Gerard Bleecker to and from David Minville (of Barbados), and to Hendricke ten Eyck, Jan. 1729, box 1, Bleecker Papers, NYPL; C.O. 5: 1224; *New-York Gazette*, Oct. 1, 1739; Philip Livingston to Storke & Gainsborough, Apr. 10, 1735, to Samuel Storke, Nov. 13, 1735, June 7, 1736, and June 7, Apr. 25, Oct. 17, 1737; Robert Sanders, Letter Book, 1750–58, and Invoice Book, "Exports," all at NYHS; Cornelius Cuyler to David van Brugh, May 31, 1736, to John Livingston, 1735, and to and from John Cuyler, 1749–50, Cuyler, Letter Book; and Barrow, *Trade and Empire*, 146, 151, 166.

93. Ludlow to Capt. Richard Jeffrey, Apr. 6, 1755, to Daniel Crommeline, Apr. 3 and Oct. 13, 1755, Jan. 5 and 8, 1756, and July 12 and 16, 1757, all in John Ludlow Letters, 1752–62. For the 1750s, see C.O. 5: 1228; Sheffield, *Observations*, 234; McClellan, *Smuggling in the American Colonies*, 30; *Messages from the Governors, 1683–1776*, ed. Charles A. Lincoln (Albany, N.Y., 1909), 1: 83, for Oyster Bay; Philip van Cortlandt Letters; Samuel Gilford Papers, 1760; and *Calendar of the Stevens Family Papers, 1754–77*. William Walton, Insurance Book, 1774, shows interest charges as high as 25 percent for voyages to the West Indies, which normally cost 3 percent to 4½ percent, because he was aware that Antigua, St. Eustatius, and other foreign ports exported contraband in New York vessels.

94. See, e.g., Philip Livingston to Storke & Gainsborough, Dec. 29, 1734, and Feb. 24, June 2, 1735.

95. Cornelius Cuyler to Henry Bonnin (Antigua), July 27, 1753, to William Darlington, Mar. 16, 1754, to Philip Cuyler, n.d., 1754, to a Mr. Hansen, Oct. 31, 1754, to Daniel Crommelin, Dec. 23, 1755, and to Philip Cuyler, Mar. 20, July 13, Aug. 16, and Sept. 7 and 24, 1756, Cuyler, Letter Book.

96. Robert Sanders, Voyage Book, 1748–56; Richard and Robert Ray, Correspondence; Francis Lewis Correspondence, 1751–86; Abraham Keteltas Account Book, 1744–61, all at the NYHS.

97. C.O. 5: 1222, and *Journal of the Voyage of the Sloop Mary . . . 1701*, ed. E. B. O'Callaghan (Albany, N.Y., 1866), 1–5. De Lucena also shared voyages of the *Hester* with Stephen De Lancey in 1714 and 1715, but many were legitimate ones to South Carolina for rice.

98. James B. Hedges, *The Browns of Providence Plantations: Colonial Years* (Cambridge, Mass., 1952), ch. 1; Richard Pares, *War and Trade in the West Indies, 1739–1763* (Ox-

ford, 1936), 449–60. "Greasing palms" was not new; Frederick Philipse and Stephanus van Cortlandt were reported to bribe collectors in the 1680s; see *Docs. Rel.*, 2: 279–82, 3: 335.

99. *Colden*, 55: 63, and *Cal. Council Mins.*, 369.

100. E.g., Gee, *Trade and Navigation; State Papers*, 1661–68, 5: 28, 539, 771; 1675–76, 9: 787, 840, 843; 1677–80, 10: 41, 640; 1708–9, 24: 268; *Doc. Hist.*, 3: 46. For Dutch West Indies smuggling during Queen Anne's War, see "Lord Cornbury to the Board of Trade," July 1, 1708, in *Docs. Rel.*, 5: 57; "Richard Ingoldesby to Lord Nottingham," June 14, 1704, in ibid., 4: 1090; [Anon.], *The Trade of the Port of New York (Colony)* (New York, 1711), 10.

101. Christopher Bancker, Waste Book, May 11, 23, and Aug. 24, 1752; Cornelius Cuyler, Letter Books; Philip Cuyler to his father, 1756–57, Cuyler, Letter Book; and John Ludlow, Account Book, 1752–95.

102. *New-York Gazette*, 1727–44, 1746, 1767; George Clark to the Board of Trade, *New-York Gazette*, July 5, 1736; Osgood, *Mins. Common Council*, Aug. 15, 1721, where there is a report about the seizure of many casks of French brandy entering New York City from New Jersey; ibid, Apr. 3, 1722; "Earl of Bellomont to the Lords of Trade," 1700, in *Docs. Rel.*, 4: 793; Philip Livingston to Storke & Gainsborough, Apr. 10, 1735; Philip Cuyler to his father, n.d., 1756, Cuyler, Letter Book.

103. Anonymous entry, 1705, in C.O. 5: 1211; *Docs. Rel.*, 4: 1150, 5: 57; "Richard Ingoldesby to Lord Nottingham," June 14, 1704, in ibid., 4: 1090; "Lord Cornbury to the Board of Trade," July 1, 1708, in ibid., 5: 57; C.O. 5: 913, 464–71, and C.O. 390: 5, no. 46.

104. George Clark to the Board of Trade, *New-York Gazette*, July 5, 1736; Hugh Home, *A Study of the Rise and Progress of Our Disputes with Spain* (London, 1739); C.O. 388: 1: 95 (13), 95 (22); and Rossano, "Down to the Bay," 237.

105. Malachy Postlethwayt, *British Commercial Organization Explained* (London, 1747), 344; id., *Great Britain's Commercial Interest*, 1: 485–98; "Governor Clinton's Report on the Province of New-York, May 23, 1749," in *Docs. Rel.*, 6: 511; Gov. Hardy to the Board of Trade, July 10, 1757, in ibid., 7: 271; Colden to Board of Trade, Dec. 7, 1763, in *Colden Letter Books*, NYHS, *Collections*, vols. 9–10 (New York, 1876–77), 9: 259; *Military Affairs in North America, 1748–1765*, ed. Stanley Pargellis (New York, 1936), 376.

106. Williams, *Columbus to Castro*, 127–30, 174–75; Gov. Hardy to the Board of Trade, July 10, 1757, in *Docs. Rel.*, 7: 271; C.O. 5: 1227–28. New Yorkers' arguments for open commerce also gained poignancy because of increased provincial regulation of trade before and during the war; see ch. 5.

SEVEN   The Promise of the Domestic Economy

1. In addition to the sources cited in ch. 4, n. 1, see C.O. 5: 1222–28 for evidence of eighteenth-century changes.

2. See Nan Rothschild, *New York City Neighborhoods: The Eighteenth Century* (San Diego, 1990), 57–58.

3. *American Jewry, Documents: The Eighteenth Century*, ed. Jacob R. Marcus (Cincinnati, 1959), 325, 328, 329; on chapmen, see the *New-York Gazette* advertisements over the 1730s.

4. *New-York Gazette*, advertisements, 1730s; Thomas F. DeVoe, *The Market Assistant*

(New York, 1867), 141–44, 145–46; and Virginia Harrington, *The New York Merchant on the Eve of the Revolution* (New York, 1935), 62–65.

5. See, e.g., *Colonial Laws*, 1: 755, 955; 2: 242, 417; 4: 926; Hedrick Hartog, *Public Property and Private Power: The Corporation of the City of New York in American Law, 1730–1870* (Chapel Hill, N.C., 1983), 15–18, 38–40; George W. Edwards, *New York as an Eighteenth-Century Municipality, 1731–1776* (New York, 1917), 197–205; Osgood, *Mins. Common Council*, 7: 77–79.

6. Osgood, *Mins. Common Council*, 2: 305–6; *Cal. Council Mins.*, 241.

7. *Council Journal*, 1: 435; *Docs. Rel.*, 3: 798; 4: 37. Because they anticipated that the legislation would result in higher prices when shortages occurred, the Assembly also allowed the colony's first emission of paper money at this time; see discussion later in this chapter.

8. Osgood, *Mins. Common Council*, 2: 305–6; *Cal. Council Mins.*, 241; and Marcus, *American Jewry*, 311–12.

9. *Cal. Council Mins.*, 336, 337, 355; *New-York Post-Boy*, June 9, 1746; *Docs. Rel.*, 6: 162; and *Colonial Laws*, 3: 569–70, 370–71. See also *Docs. Rel.*, 5: 684–92; and Stokes, *Iconography*, 4: 571–73, 613, 737.

10. Osgood, *Mins. Common Council*, 5: 242–44; and Beverly McAnear, "Politics in Provincial New York, 1689–1761" (Ph.D. diss., Stanford University, 1935), 2 vols., 1: 75–78, 130, 150, 179.

11. *Colonial Laws*, 3: 403, 548, 578, 660; *AJ*, 2: 337, 339, 341, 524–25 (May 30, June 5, 14, 1753; Feb. 18, 1757); *New-York Post-Boy*, Jan. 18, 1748; "Public Virtue to be distinguished by Public Honours," Jan. 25, 1753, in *The Independent Reflector*, ed. Milton Klein (Cambridge, Mass., 1963), 111–17. On the embargo, see Osgood, *Mins. Common Council*, 5: 242–44, and Stokes, *Iconography*, 4: 737.

12. C.O. 5: 1222; Osgood, *Mins. Common Council*, 1720s; Gov. Cornbury to the Board of Trade, 1706, C.O. 5: 1049, no. 18; id., July 1, 1708, C.O. 5: 1049, no. 96; Gov. Nanfan to the Board of Trade, 1701, and Oct. 5, 1702, C.O. 5: 1047, nos. 1, 250.

13. "Governor Hunter to the Lords of Trade," Oct. 3, 1710, Jan. 1, 1712, Aug. 27, 1714, Nov. 25, 1715; to St. John, Sept. 12, 1711, in *Docs. Rel.*, 5: 170, 252, 379–80, 390, 254–65; Gov. Hunter to the Board of Trade, Feb. 3, 1717, in *State Papers*, 1717–18, 30: 255; "Representation of the Grand Jury . . . to Hunter," Nov. 29, 1717, in ibid., 244; "Merchants Trading to New York to the Board of Trade," May 2, 1718, in ibid., 243; *Colonial Laws*, 1: 165–67, 170–71, 248, 287, 322, 325, 403–4, 419, 439; 2: 423, 843, 852, 3: 240; *Docs. Rel.*, 3: 241–42; 5: 296; and *Council Journal*, 1: 435–36.

14. William Smith, *The History of the Late Province of New-York from its Discovery, to the Apointment of Governor Colden, in 1762*, NYHS, *Collections*, 2 vols. (New York, 1829–30), 1: 166; *AJ*, 1: 223–24.

15. *Docs. Rel.*, 3: 241–42, 796–800, 4: 37; *Colonial Laws*, 1: 675, 912, 918–20, 801, 812, 847, 898, 1010; 2: 18, 254 843–44, 861; 3: 754; 4: 370, 741, 766; 5: 280; *Council Journal*, 1: 423, 436, 428, 429, 430–31. Prominent advocates of discrimination included Frederick Phillipse, Stephen van Cortlandt, Nicholas Bayard, Gabriel Minvielle, Chidley Brooke, and William Nichols. On tonnage, see ch. 2, n. 43.

16. See *Council Journal*, 1: 433–36, and activities of merchants Leo Lewis, Jacobus Kip, John Stillwell, Thomas and William Willett, Johannes Ferbos, Garrett van Horne, Carrill Hansen, Abraham Lakerman, Isaac Hicks, Robert Livingston, Cornelius Sebring, Jacob

Ruston, David Provoost, Jacob Cuyler, Hendrick Harring, and John Jansen, in C.O. 5: 1224–27.

17. *Council Journal,* 1: 433, 520; 2: 1180; *Docs. Rel.,* 5: 551, 599, 607, 700, 736, 738, 769, 889–91, 7: 908; *Colonial Laws,* 1: 18, 843, 844, 675, 799, 801, 847, 898, 912, 913, 918–20, 1010; 2: 16, 18, 843, 867; 3: 754; 4: 370, 741, 766; 5: 280, 741, 860, 923, 956.

18. "Mr. Colden's Account of the Trade of New-York," 1723, in *Docs. Rel.,* 5: 685–700, at 687; Bloch, *HMR;* C.O. 5: 1222; and U.S. Census Bureau, *Historical Statistics of the United States* (Washington, D.C., 1961), ser. Z, secs. 108–21, p. 762.

19. Bloch, *HMR; Docs. Rel.,* 4: 789; Bleeker-Collins-Abeel Papers, NYPL; and Evert Wendell Account Book, 1695–1726, NYHS. Peltry exporters in the first decade of the century included Mary Teller, Benjamin Faneuil, Frederick Philipse, Onzeel van Sweeten, Caleb Cooper, Thomas Wenham, Abraham Schuyler, John Scott, Hendrick van Bal, Abraham Wendell, Lawrence Richards, Benjamin Aske, Mary Coler, and Hannah Noel.

20. "Petition of the Merchants of the City of New-York Relating to Foreign Coin," Feb. 1704, *Docs. Rel.,* 4: 1133–35; Curtis Nettels, "Economic Relations of Boston, Philadelphia, and New York, 1680–1715," *Journal of Economic and Business History* 3 (Feb. 1931): 185–215; Robert Ritchie, *The Duke's Province: A Study of New York Politics and Society, 1664–1691* (Chapel Hill, N.C., 1977), ch. 2, 58–67, 115, 119; Philip Cuyler, Letter Book, AAS; Jacob Price, "Economic Function," 158–59; R. T. Lounsbury, *The British Fishery at Newfoundland* (New Haven, Conn., 1934), ch. 6; Philip Livingston to Jacob Wendell, Sept. 4, 1744, Jan. 14, 1746, Livingston Letters, Museum of the City of New York; Cadwallader Colden to Archibald Kennedy, Nov. 17, 1756, in *Colden,,* 68: 165–67; [Philip Livingston?], "About the Act prohibiting Indian goods going to Canada," Nov. 1729, Livingston-Redmond MSS, NYPL; Colden to William Johnson, Jan. 11, 1769, in *Colden Letter Books,* NYHS, *Collections,* vols. 9–10 (New York, 1876–77), 9: 183–85; *The Papers of Sir William Johnson,* ed. James Sullivan et al., 14 vols. (Albany, N.Y., 1921–65), 6: 762–64, 7: 11, 153, 301, 569; *New-York Mercury,* Apr. 12, 1762. Others who continued in the fur trade were Jonas Phillips (*New-York Mercury,* Jan. 4, 1762), Heyman Levy (*Papers of Sir William Johnson,* 1: 336), Richard and Robert Ray (Robert Sanders, Letter Books; Cornelius Cuyler, Letter Books, AAS), Philip Cuyler (Philip Cuyler, Letter Book), Henry Holland (ibid.), Christopher Bancker (Bancker, Waste Book), David van der Heyden (Cornelius Cuyler, Letter Books), and Oliver and Stephen De Lancey (ibid.).

21. Thomas Norton, *The Fur Trade in Colonial New York, 1686–1776* (Madison, Wis., 1974), 43–59; Osgood, *Mins. Common Council,* 1: 1–2, 9, 25–26; Bloch, *HMR,* 3: 475–77; Robert Ritchie, "London Merchants, the New York Market, and the Recall of Sir Edmund Andros," *New York History* 57 (1976): 5–31.

22. Bloch, *HMR;* Cornelius Cuyler, Letter Books.

23. C.O. 5: 1222–25; Cornelius Cuyler, Letter Books; *Papers of Sir William Johnson,* vols. 8–9; Stephen De Lancey Papers, 1716–24; William van Nuys Papers; and Charles Lodwick Papers, all at the NYHS.

24. "An American," *An Essay upon the Government of the English Plantations* (1701), ed. Louis B. Wright (San Marino, Calif., 1945), 4–8; "Mr. Thomas Cockerill to Mr. Popple," July 2, 1709, in *Docs. Rel.,* 5: 81.

25. Gov. Burnet to the Council of Trade and Plantations, Nov. 21, 1724, *State Papers,* 1724–25, 34: 114; and Smith, *History,* 1: 207, 221. On merchant opposition, see David Armour, "The Merchants of Albany, New York, 1686–1760" (Ph.D. diss., Northwestern

University, 1965), 117–18; Lawrence Leder, *Robert R. Livingston, 1654–1728, and the Politics of Colonial New York* (Williamsburg, Va., 1961), 251–60, 277–90. In 1725, colonists exported 70 cases, 305 hogsheads, and 87 packs of beaver and deer skins (*Docs. Rel.*, 5: 774).

26. Philip Livingston to Storke & Gainsborough, June 5, July 16, 24, Dec. 29, 1734, Feb. 24, 1735, Philip Livingston Letters, AAS; Cornelius Cuyler to Samuel Baker, July, Aug. 18, 1732; to Mico, Nov. 5, 1733; to Christopher Bancker, Oct. 19, 1734; to David Clarkson, Sept. 2, Oct. 11, 1735, and to Philip Livingston, Nov. 7, 1735, Cornelius Cuyler, Letter Books.

27. Gov. Burnet is quoted from Smith, *History*, 1: 229–30, in connection with a petition signed by R. Walter, Rip van Dam, John Barbarie, Francis Harrison, Cadwallader Colden, James Alexander, and Abraham van Horne. See also Burnet, address, June 14, 1722, in *AJ*, 1: 473; "Mr. Colden's Account of the Trade of New-York," 1723, in *Docs. Rel.*, 5: 687; "Mr. Colden's Memoir on the Fur Trade," Nov. 10, 1724, in ibid., 5: 733; and "Governor Hardy to the Lords of Trade," Jan. 16, 1756, in ibid., 7: 6. On the city "monopolists," see "Mr. Robert Livingston to Col. Schuyler," Aug. 23, 1720, in ibid., 5: 559–61; "Lords of Trade on the New York Acts Regulating the Indian Trade," in ibid., 5: 745–56; Philip Livingston to Robert R. Livingston, Dec. 4, 1720, Duane Papers, NYHS; statement of merchants grievances against fur regulations, 1708, in *AJ*, 1: 238–39. On smuggling to Amsterdam in the 1720s, see, e.g., Cornelius Cuyler, Isaac Low, Philip Livingston, and Hendrick ten Eyck, Letter Books.

28. "Representation of the Lords of Trade to the King," 1724, in *Docs. Rel.*, 5: 707–8; Smith, *History*, 1: 211, 216–30; Cornelius Cuyler, Letter Books; Philip Livingston Letters, 1722; Van Nuys Letters, 1716; Philip van Cortlandt Letters.

29. Board of Trade report on the Colonies, Sept. 8, 1721, in *State Papers*, 1721, 32: 408–49. Also see Cornelius Cuyler to Richard Janeway, Jan. 13, 1728; and Cuyler to Samuel Baker, Apr. 11, 1730, June 10, 1731 and May 20, 1732, Cuyler, Letter Books; Jacob Wendell Correspondence, 1729; Norton, *Fur Trade in Colonial New York*, 101–2; Robert Sanders, Letter Book; Smith, *History*, 1: 223–24. Isaac Bobin also noted on July 2, 1723, that "Coll. John Schuyler has been discovered to Trade with Canada"; see Bobin to George Clarke, *Letters of Isaac Bobin, Esq., 1718–1730*, ed. E. B. O'Callaghan (Albany, N.Y., 1872), 101–2.

30. Smith, *History*, 1: 207, 221.

31. James G. Wilson, *A Memorial History of the City of New York*, 2 vols. (New York, 1892), 2: 182; Council and Assembly of New York to the Board of Trade, Dec. 21, 1730, *State Papers*, 1730–31, 37: 403–4; *Colonial Laws*, 2: 8–12, 98–105, 197–98, 248–50, 281–94, 350–65, 366–71, 372–403, 484–97, 535–71.

32. Archibald Kennedy, *Serious Considerations on the Present State of the Northern Colonies* (New York, 1754). See also id., *Observations on the Importance of the Northern Colonies under Proper Regulations* (New York, 1750), esp. 6–9, 10–11, 14–18, 20–23, 27–28; id., *On the Importance of Gaining and Preserving the Friendship of the Indians to the British Interest* (New York, 1751); and "Cadwallader Colden to Governor Clinton," Oct. 1, 1751, in *Docs. Rel.*, 6: 738–47.

33. Cornelius Cuyler, Letter Books. Robert R. Livingston, James Alexander, Lewis Morris, Cadwallader Colden, and "Governor Clinton's faction" in the Assembly welcomed Cuyler's trade.

34. William Johnson to the Earl of Loudoun, Apr. 28, June, 1757, in *Papers of Sir William Johnson*, 6: 184–87, 280, 314, 336, 9: 699, 723.

35. "Petition of the Merchants of the City of New-York Relating to Foreign Coin," Feb. 1704, in *Docs. Rel.*, 4: 1133–35.

36. Osgood, *Mins. Common Council*, 1: 74, 84, 90, 111; and Gov. Fletcher to the Board of Trade, Dec. 24, 1698, *Docs. Rel.*, 4: 443–51. See also "Petition of the Merchants of the City of New-York relating to Foreign Coin," Feb. 1704, in ibid., 4: 1133; "Earl of Bellomont to the Lords of Trade," July 22, 1699, in ibid., 4: 532; Bloch, *HMR*.

37. "Mr. Colden's Account of the Trade of New-York," 1723, in *Docs. Rel.*, 5: 685–700, at 686.

38. Cornelius Cuyler to David Clarkson, Sept. 2, 1735, Oct. 11, 1738, Cuyler, Letter Books; Smith, *History*, 1: 279

39. Writers noted that 80 to 120 acres of field, arable, timber, and house lot was necessary for a family of 4 or 5 in the eighteenth century; see, e.g., Peter Warren to William Johnson, Nov. 20, 1738, *Papers of Sir William Johnson*, 13: 2; and *New York Mercury*, Mar. 11, 1765. In "Slave Life, Slave Society, and Tobacco Production in the Tidewater Chesapeake, 1620–1820," in *Cultivation and Culture: Labor and the Shaping of Slave Life in the Americas*, ed. Ira Berlin and Philip D. Morgan (Charlottesville, Va., 1993), 181, Lorena Walsh finds that Chesapeake maize production reached 10 barrels per hand in the 1730s, and "about half of the crop was marketable surplus." See also James Lemon, *The Best Poor Man's Country: A Geographical Study of Early Southeastern Pennsylvania* (Baltimore, 1972). For wheat and flour prices, see Appendix A, figs. A.1 and A.2.

40. Based on letters and account books of merchants cited in this chapter; collection of storekeepers' accounts at the NYHS and the NYPL; "Lord Cornbury to the Board of Trade," July 1, 1708, in *Docs. Rel.*, 5: 59; Caleb Heathcote to the Board of Trade, Aug. 3, 1708, *Doc. Hist.*, 1: 712–13; Archibald Kennedy to the Board of Trade, 1738, ibid., 4: 725–27; "George Clinton to the Board of Trade," May 23, 1749, in *Docs. Rel.*, 6: 511; Andrew Burnaby, *Travels through North America, 1748–1751, 1760* (New York, 1900), 114–15; Gov. Moore to Board of Trade, 1767, *Doc. Hist.*, 1: 734; David MacPherson, *Annals of Commerce, Manufactures, Fisheries, and Navigation*, 4 vols. (London, 1805), 3: 163; J. L. Bishop, *A History of American Manufactures, from 1608 to 1860*, 3 vols. (Philadelphia, 1868), 1: 315. For studies on other colonies, see Bettye Hobbes Pruitt, "Agriculture and Society in the Towns of Massachusetts, 1771: A Statistical Analysis" (Ph.D. diss., Boston University, 1981); and Aubrey Land, "Economic Behavior in a Planting Society: The Eighteenth-Century Chesapeake," *Journal of Southern History* 33 (1967): 469–85. On European factors that influenced American migration and agricultural settlement, see Hans Medick, "The Proto-Industrial Family Economy: The Structural Function of Household and Family during the Transition from Peasant Society to Industrial Capitalism," *Social History* 3 (1976): 291–316; Joan Thirsk, "Industries in the Countryside," in *Essays in the Economic and Social History of Tudor and Stuart England*, ed. F. J. Fisher (Cambridge, 1961), 70–88. Contrast to James Henretta, "Families and Farms: 'Mentalité' in Pre-Industrial America," *William and Mary Quarterly*, 35 (1978), 3–32; and Michael Merrill, "Cash Is Good to Eat: Self-Sufficiency and Exchange in the Rural Economy of the United States," *Radical History Review* 9 (Winter 1977): 42–71.

41. E.g., Beekman to Ross, Oct. 18, Nov. 30, 1764, in *The Beekman Mercantile Papers, 1746–1799*, ed. Philip White, 3 vols. (New York, 1956), 1: 475, 477–78.

42. "A Memorial of Several Aggrievances and Oppressions of His Majesty's Subjects in the Colony of New-York in America," repr. in *Annual Report of the American Histori-*

cal Association for the year 1892 (Washington, D.C., 1893), 45–53; "Capt. Mulford's Representation against the Government of New York," in *Docs. Rel.*, 3: 363–71, 372–83; statement of 1714, in C.O. 5: 1051, Bb.64; and *Docs. Rel.*, 4: 516–17, 591, 1058, 1155; 5: 58.

43. See, e.g., address of the Assembly to Gov. Cornbury, May 27, 1703, *AJ*, 1: 166–67, and James H. Levitt, *For Want of Trade: Shipping and the New Jersey Ports, 1680–1783* (Newark, N.J., 1981), 59–61, who calculates that about one-third of Perth Amboy's vessels were built and registered at New York City. For New Jersey's later Philadelphia connections, see Harrington, *New York Merchant*, 223–29.

44. Cornbury to the Board of Trade, 1706, in C.O. 5: 1049, no. 18; id., July 1, 1708, in C.O. 5: 1049, no. 96; C.O. 5: 1222; Nanfan to the Board of Trade, 1701, and Oct. 5, 1702, in C.O. 5: 1047, nos. 1, 250; Gov. Hunter to the Board of Trade, Aug. 27, 1714, in C.O. 5: 1050, no. 82; and id., July 25, 1715, in C.O. 5: 1051, no. 3; Levitt, *For Want of Trade*, 113–17; C.O. 5: 1035–6; *Calendar of the Stevens Family Papers*, New Jersey Historical Records Survey Project, 2 vols. (Newark, N.J., 1941); Low Family Papers, NYHS; and Peter Kalm, *Travels in North America, 1748–1751*, ed. Adolph Benson, 2 vols. (New York, 1966), 1: 122.

45. On prices, see *New-York Gazette*, May 11, 1730; Charles Wolly, *A Two Years' Journal in New York, and Part of its Territories in America* (1701; repr., Cleveland, 1902), 70; Gerard Beekman to David and William Ross, in Newry, Ireland, Feb. 3, 1768, Dec. 15, 1766, in *Beekman Mercantile Papers*, ed. White, 1: 504–5, 516; John Wetherhead to Sir William Johnson, Jan. 7, 1771, in *Papers of Sir William Johnson*, 7: 1071; and Appendix A, figs. A.1 and A.2. Helpful comments appear in Douglas Vickers, *Studies in the Theory of Money, 1690–1776* (Philadelphia, 1959), 239–90; David Hume, "Of Refinement in the Arts" and "Of the Balance of Trade," in *David Hume: Writings on Economics*, ed. Eugene Rotwein (Madison, Wis., 1955), 36, 60–77; Sir James Steuart, *An Inquiry into the Principles of Political Economy*, ed. Andrew Skinner, 2 vols. (1767; repr., Edinburgh, 1966), 1: 160–73, 475–520; Adam Smith, *An Inquiry into the Nature and Causes of the Wealth of Nations*, ed. Edwin Cannan, 2 vols. in 1 (1776; repr., Chicago, 1976), 1: 289, 340, 453–54; Ronald Meek, "The Scottish Contribution to Marxist Sociology," in *Economics and Ideology and Other Essays* (London, 1967), 34–50.

46. See Philip Livingston to Storke & Gainsborough, 5 June, 16, 24 July, 29 Dec. 1734, 24 Feb. 1735, Livingston Letters; Beekman to David and William Ross, Newry, Ireland, Feb. 3, 1768, Dec. 15, 1766, in *Beekman Mercantile Papers*, ed. White, 1: 504–5; and John Wetherhead to William Johnson, Jan. 7, 1771, in *Papers of Sir William Johnson*, 7: 1071.

47. Philip Cuyler, Letter Book, 1755–60, NYPL; Gerard Beekman to Eleazer Trevet, Feb. 4, 1765, to Samuel Fowler, Nov. 5, 1764, Oct. 24, 1765, Mar. 21, 1767, to Joseph Chew, Aug. 26, 1765, to Henry Lloyd, July 22, 1767, in *Beekman Mercantile Papers*, ed. White, 1: 476, 480–81, 486, 485, 509–10, 513–14.

48. Beekman to David and William Ross, Newry, Ireland, Oct. 18, Nov. 30, 1764, in *Beekman Mercantile Papers*, ed. White, 1: 475; John van Cortlandt, Account Book, 1754–59; Colden to William Alexander, 1763, *Colden Letter Books*, 1: 312–13; *Docs. Rel.*, 5: 591, 617; Henry Cruger to Aaron Lopez, Feb. 1, 1772, *Commerce of Rhode Island, 1720–1780*, Massachusetts Historical Society, *Collections*, 7th ser., 2 vols. (Boston, 1914–15), 1: 385–88; and ibid., Mar. 11, July 14, 1772, 1: 391–92, 405.

49. Philip Cuyler, Letter Book, 1755–60; Beekman to Eleazer Trevet, Feb. 4, 1765, to Samuel Fowler, Nov. 5, 1764, Oct. 24, 1765, Mar. 21, 1767, to Joseph Chew, Aug. 26, 1765, to Henry Lloyd, July 22, 1767, in *Beekman Mercantile Papers*, ed. and White, 1: 476, 480–81,

486, 485, 509–10, 513–14. Similar evidence appears in the Cristopher Bancker Journal, 1718–39, William Alexander Papers, vol. 4, Walter Livingston Pig Iron Accounts, 1767–74, and John van Cortlandt Journal, 1760, all at NYHS.

50. Osgood, *Mins. Common Council*, 6: 336; *New-York Gazette*, Sept. 19, 1763.

51. E.g., John Clarkson moved to Philadelphia in 1747, from where he kept liaisons with his family and the Beekmans (William Beekman to Samuel Greenleaf, Boston, Mar. 17, 1747, in *Beekman Mercantile Papers*, ed. White, 1: 16–17).

52. Philip Livingston to Storke & Gainsborough, 5 June, 16, 24 July, 29 Dec. 1734, 24 Feb. 1735, Livingston Letters.

53. "Mr. Colden's Account of the Trade of New-York," 1723, in *Docs. Rel.*, 5: 688.

54. *New-York Gazette*, May 11, 1730; William Roberts III, "Samuel Storke: An Eighteenth-Century London Merchant Trading to the American Colonies," *Business History Review* 39 (1965): 153–55; *Beekman Mercantile Papers*, ed. White, 1: 365, 468; Philip Cuyler to his father, Dec. 2, 1755, Cuyler, Letter Book; John Ludlow, Letter Book and Invoice Book, 1752–63, Hall of Records, New York City; Gov. Tryon to the Lords of Trade, in *Doc. Hist.*, 1: 758.

55. Marc Egnal, "The Economic Development of the Thirteen Colonies, 1720–1775," *William and Mary Quarterly*, 3d ser., 32 (Apr. 1975): 214–17. European goods included linens, silks, distilled beverages, and many dry goods that originated outside of Britain.

56. These are generalizations drawn from many merchant accounts and letters cited in this chapter; see, e.g., John Ludlow, Invoice Book, Aug. 23, 1756, Feb. 2, Apr. 8, 1757; Philip Livingston, Account with Neate, Pigou & Both, Ledger A, 1754, 9; C.O. 5: 1224–27; Appendix A, figs. A.1 and A.2.

57. "Cadwallader Colden to the Lords of Trade," Mar. 9, 1764, in *Docs. Rel.*, 7: 612; John Watts to James Neilson, Feb. 1, 1762, to Gedney Clarke, July 23, 1765, in *WLB*, 19, 360; Bayard, Lentz, and Van Cortlandt Papers; Philip Livingston Papers, 1716–78; Philip Cuyler, Letter Book; William Alexander, Account Books, 1756–70; John Ludlow Papers, 1754–64.

58. See, e.g., account books of Samuel Deall, John Wetherhead, Richard Sause, and John Milligan, at the NYPL; *New-York Mercury*, Feb. 27, 1764, and June 1, 1768; *The Arts and Crafts of New York*, comp. Rita S. Gottesman, NYHS, *Collections*, 69 (New York, 1936); and Merrill, "Cash Is Good to Eat." For England, see Daniel Defoe, *The Complete English Tradesman*, 2 vols. (London, 1727), 1: 89–90, 356, 2: 121, 209, 211, 332, 335, 300; and John Moore, *Daniel Defoe: Citizen of the Modern World* (Chicago, 1959), 85–92, 306–24. On chapmen and commission merchants, see the *New-York Gazette* over the 1730s.

59. See, e.g., *New-York Post-Boy*, Mar. 19, 1745; ibid., May 20, 1745; *New-York Gazette*, Aug. 29, 1748; Charles Howell and Allen Keller, *The Mill at Philipsburg Manor Upper Mills and a Brief History of Milling* (Tarrytown, N.Y., 1977), 100, 102. Country mills gristed three to four bushels per hour with one set of stones, which created demand for many millers in areas of high production.

60. "Humble Address," Aug. 6, 1691, in Osgood, *Mins. Common Council*, 2: 44–58; Bishop, *History of American Manufactures*, 1: 134–35. Merchant mills were not more technologically advanced, but simply larger, and their owners enjoyed beneficial business connections.

61. *New-York Post-Boy*, May 20, 1745; C.O. 5: 1223–26; and Howell and Keller, *Mill at Philipsburg*, 134–37, 161.

62. Osgood, *Mins. Common Council*, 1: 80, 94, 99, 130–35, 141–42, 149–50, 152, 311–13; 2: 7–9, 31–98; and *State Papers*, 1697–98, 16: no. 846; ibid., 1669–1700, 18: nos. 26, 769, 890, 1209. The same arguments were raised later by Philip Livingston, Abraham Wendell, Gerard Beekman, Abraham ten Eyck, David van der Heyden, and Robert Sanders.

63. C.O. 5: 1092, sec. 122–23; and *State Papers*, 1699–1700, 18: no. 953; *Docs. Rel.*, 4: 811–12.

64. "Lord Cornbury to the Lords of Trade," July 1, 1708, *Docs. Rel.*, 5: 58; ibid., 3: 798, 4: 37, 1180; *Council Journal*, 1: 435.

65. *AJ*, 1: 223–24 (1708); *Council Journal*, 2: 1223; 3: 289.

66. Stoker, *Prices*; C.O. 5: 1050, Aa, 131; *State Papers*, 1714–15, no. 35.

67. Minute Books of the Mayor's Court, Dec. 19, 1715, Hall of Records, New York City; C.O. 5: 1042, no. 8.

68. Osgood, *Mins. Common Council*, 4: 169–70, 251–52; *AJ*, 1: 563, 654. For examples of this discussion in 1727, 1728, 1734, 1736, 1741, and 1750, see the failed bolting proposals in *AJ*, 2: 292–95, 563, 577, 605, 654, 659, 662–63, 689, 736, 738, 807, 809; and *Colonial Laws*, 3: 788–93, 4: 1096–98, 5: 198–202.

69. "Governor Cosby's Speech," Apr. 1734, in *Messages from the Governors, 1683–1776*, ed. Charles A. Lincoln (Albany, N.Y., 1909), 245–48; *AJ*, 1: 689, 736, 738, 807, 809.

70. *New York Journal*, Mar. 1, 1736; *New-York Weekly Journal*, Mar. 18, May 20, and July 8, 1734, and Feb. 17, 24, 1735; *New-York Gazette*, Sept. 19, Oct. 17, 1737; [Anon.], *An Unanswerable Answer to the Cavils and Objections* . . . (New York, 1739), in NYPL; and for 1743, Smith, *History*, 2: 71, 78–85, 100–104.

71. Smith, *History*, 2: 272–73; Patricia Bonomi, *A Factious People: Politics and Society in Colonial New York* (New York, 1971), 75–97, 140–72; Ten Eyck and Seaman, item, *New-York Gazette and Weekly Mercury*, Oct. 17, 1768; letters of Gerard Beekman, John van Cortlandt, Philip Cuyler, and William Alexander. On trucking, see Beekman to D. and W. Ross, Newry, Ireland, Mar. 7, 1765, in *Beekman Mercantile Papers*, ed. White, 1: 484. On book credit, see *Laws and Ordinances*, 255, 289; William Baxter, *The House of Hancock: Business in Boston, 1724–1775* (Cambridge, Mass., 1945), 17–21; and Curtis Nettels, *The Money Supply of the American Colonies before 1720* (Madison, Wis., 1934), 162–78.

72. On export prices in this period, see Stokes, *Iconography*, 4: 395, 453, 462, 468, 598; Emory R. Johnson, *History of Domestic and Foreign Commerce of the United States* (New York, 1915), 1: 120, 85; Stoker, *Prices*, 200–202; for quotations covering Jan. to Sept. 1720, and occasional weeks of 1721, see *American Weekly Mercury* (Philadelphia); for 1725 through 1732, *New-York Gazette;* for 1733 to 1750, *New-York Weekly Journal;* for the entire period, see Appendix A, figs. A.1 and A.2. Prices in the West Indies followed a similar trajectory: flour that the wholesaler sold for 18s. per barrel in the early 1730s sold at Jamaica for 25s. to 30s. near the end of the decade, and at Barbados for 32s. to 34s. per barrel by about 1740 (Stoker, "Prices," 201–3, 215–16).

73. On European conditions, see B. H. Slicher van Bath, *The Agrarian History of Western Europe, 800–1850* (London, 1963), 221–28, where he says that wheat prices rose 100 percent between 1721–45 and 1791–1820, much of the rise falling in the earlier years of the eighteenth century. On West Indies conditions, see ch. 6 above.

74. In addition to the sources cited in n. 73 above, see *Independent Reflector*, ed. Klein, 79–80, 106, 108–10, 433–35; and *New-York Post-Boy*, Oct. 22, 1750.

75. William Alexander to John Provoost in London, Nov. 16, 1750, Alexander Papers,

vol. 1, fol. 20; "Petition of Merchants to the New York Assembly," Oct. 26, 1750, in *AJ*, 2: 294–95; ibid., Oct. 28, 1750, 2: 295–96; McAnear, "Politics in Provincial New York, 1689–1761," 1: 75–78, 130, 150, 179.

76. *Colonial Laws*, 3: 788–94, 1096–98, 4: 1096, 5: 197, 580; Smith, *History*, 2: 228; *AJ*, 2: 294–95; Stevens, *Records*, 310–11; "Governor Hardy's Speech," 1757, in *Messages from the Governors*, ed. Lincoln, 617; and William Livingston, "Reasons for the farther regulating of Beef and Pork; together with the Necessity of an Act for the Inspection of Butter," *Independent Reflector*, ed. Klein, May 10, 1753, 221–27.

77. Muscovado sugar sold wholesale at New York for 40s. per cwt. in 1739, 55s. in 1748, and rose slowly thereafter until 1763; see C.O. 5: 1225–28; for comparative prices of other commodities, see Stoker, *Prices*, 201–3, 215–16; and A. H. Cole, *Wholesale Commodity Prices in the United States, 1700–1861* (Cambridge, Mass., 1938), for a continuous series of New York price quotations starting with 1748; Philip Cuyler to his father, Dec. 11, 1758, Dec. 17, 1759, Cuyler, Letter Book; *New-York Mercury*, May 1, Oct. 21, 1762; *WLB*, 5, 8–9, 33, 35, 45, 48, 65, 68, 80, 87, 94, 104, 109. For wheat and flour prices, see Appendix A, figs. A.1 and A.2.

78. DeVoe, *Market Assistant*, 141–4, 145–6; and for the quotation, see John Watts to John Riddle, Mar. 24, 1764, in *WLB*, 235–36.

79. Stevens, *Records*, 3, 21, 30, 59; *AJ*, May 5, 1769, 52; *Colonial Laws*, 4: 1021, 1096; 5: 833. The same petition called for regulation of potash and iron production. On flour inspection in 1769 and city storage facilities, see DeVoe, *Market Assistant*, 250, referring to the merchants Francis Maerschalk and Henry Bryant.

80. Bishop, *History of Manufactures*, 1: 134–35; *Colonial Laws*, 5: 198–202; Stevens, *Records*, 110–13. The quotation is from *The American Correspondence of a Bristol Merchant, 1766–1776: Letters of Richard Champion*, ed. G. H. Guttridge (London, 1974), 27; see also ibid., 52, 56. Wheat, flour and bread made up almost 19 percent of the total exports from North America by 1770, a value of over £636,000 sterling in official prices. More than £500,000 of this value originated in the regions dominated by New York and Philadelphia exporters; New Yorkers exported about £222,600 sterling by the 1740s, although Philadelphia's proportion of the total rose faster than New York's; see "Impartiality," *Impartial Observations to be Considered on by the King, his Ministers, to the People of Great Britain*, Mar. 25, 1763, cited in MacPherson, *Annals*, 3: 495; C.O. 16: 1; *New-York Mercury*, Apr. 13, 1761, Mar. 15, 1762, Apr. 9, 1764, and Dec. 8, 1766; Stevens, *Records*, 152–53; and correspondence and accounts of Walter and Robert Livingston Jr., Henry Cruger, Philip Cuyler, Evert Bancker, John Ludlow, William Neilson, Perry & Hayes, Perry, Hayes & Sherbrook, Waddell & Cunningham, and Evert Wendell. In 1763, England imported more grain and flour from New York than any other commodity; and in 1767 and 1772, agricultural harvests were poor, and grain imports rose high again. The value of England's wheat and flour imports from New York in 1767 was £12,171; in the following year it stayed high, at £12,433, falling only slightly in the next years. Beginning with the late-1772 crisis, imports rose to £19,538 by 1774, and a record high of £119,970 in 1775.

81. William Lowndes, *A Report Containing an Essay . . . of the Silver Coins* (London, 1695); John Pollexfen, *Discourse of Trade, Coyn, and Paper Credit* (London, 1697), 2–8; Vickers, *Studies in the Theory of Money*; Arthur E. Monroe, *Monetary Theory before Adam Smith* (Cambridge, Mass., 1923), 157–288; Joseph Dorfman, *The Economic Mind in American Civilization, 1606–1865*, 4 vols. (New York, 1946), 1: 151–55; Albert Feaveryear, *The*

410 Notes to Pages 241–244

Pound Sterling: A History of English Money (Oxford, 1963), 150–58; Paul Hamlin, "Money Circulating in New York Prior to 1704," *New-York Historical Society Quarterly* 40 (Oct. 1956): 361–68.

82. E.g., "A General State of the Public Funds," 1767, in *Docs. Rel.*, 1: 103–5.

83. *Colonial Laws*, 1: 654–58; *Journal of the Commissioners of Trade and Plantations*, 14 vols. (London, 1920–38), vol. 3, Oct. 31, Dec. 22, 1709, Jan. 12, 1710, at 82, 108, 113; entries for Nov. 29, Dec. 15, 1709, *State Papers*, 1708–9, 24: 537, 552; Leder, *Robert R. Livingston*, ch. 5; Nettels, *Money Supply*, 274–75, 259n, 260n. Opponents of paper money continued to use the intrinsic-value notion and specie-fund argument until the Revolution; see, e.g., Stevens, *Records*, 10, 18, 50, 84–85, 308. Compare this paragraph and those that follow in this section with Jan de Vries, *The Economy of Europe in an Age of Crisis, 1600–1750* (Cambridge, 1976), ch. 7, esp. 229–31.

84. *State Papers*, 1714–15, 28: 170–72, 203–4, 222–25, 273; *Colonial Laws*, 1: 846–57, 858–63; *AJ*, June 5, 1716, 1: 32; Leder, *Robert R. Livingston*, 236–41.

85. William Potter, *The Key of Wealth* (London, 1650), 1–4; *Council Journal*, 1: 435; and *Docs. Rel.*, 3: 798, 4: 37.

86. On sinking funds in England, see Richard Price, *An Appeal to the Public on the Subject of the National Debt* (1774), repr. in *A Select Collection of Early English Tracts on Commerce*, ed. J. R. McCulloch (London, 1856), 301–58; Vickers, *Studies in the Theory of Money*, ch. 2. For New York, see *Council Journal*, 2: 1585, 1600; *Docs. Rel.*, 7: 844; and Bruce Smith, "American Colonial Monetary Regimes: The Failure of the Quantity Theory and Some Evidence in Favor of an Alternative View," *Canadian Journal of Economics* 18 (Aug. 1985): 531–64. For the predominant view that paper currency and rates of silver were connected, see, e.g., *Journal of the Commissioners*, vol. 4 (1718–22), Apr. 28, 1718, 74. Merchant supporters in New York included Cornelius van Horne, Stephen Bayard, Simon Johnson, Peter Schuyler, Peter Jay, John Moore, William Broome, David Clarkson, Anthony Rutgers, and Philip van Cortlant. Earlier, emissions had been supported by Robert R. Livingston, James Alexander, Cadwallader Colden, Stephen De Lancey, Frederick Philipse, and other notable traders.

87. Smith, *History*, 1: 280. Also see *Docs. Rel.*, 5: 514, 522, 525, 700, 736, 738; *AJ*, 1: 410–12.

88. "The Expediency of a Continental Paper Money," in *American Archives: Fourth Series*, ed. Peter Force, 6 vols. (Washington, D.C., 1837–46), 2: 1262–64; notation of a petition submitted, in *Journal of the Commissioners*, vol. 4, Apr. 23, 1718, 63; "Humble Representation of the Grand Jury for the City and County of New York," Nov. 29, 1717; and "Some Considerations to be Humbly Offered to the Lords of Trade," Dec. 1717, in Jay Papers, reel 1, NYHS; "Robert Hunter to Secretary Popple," Dec. 3, 1717, in *Docs. Rel.*, 5: 494–95; "Governor Hunter to the Board of Trade," Jan. 27, 1718, in ibid., 5: 499–500; John H. Hickcox, *A History of the Bills of Credit or Paper Money Issued by New York from 1709 to 1789* (Albany, N.Y., 1866), 53–66; and for a little later, *New-York Gazette*, May 11, 1730.

89. "Memorial of Eight Merchants trading to New York," 1718, in C.O. 5: 1051, no. 67; "Petition of Merchants Trading to New York," Aug. 28, 1718, in C.O. 5: 1051, no. 77.

90. "Robert Hunter to Edward Popple," Dec. 3, 1717, *Docs. Rel.*, 5: 494–495; Leder, *Robert R. Livingston*, ch. 5; Nettels, *Money Supply*, 271; *Colonial Laws*, 1: 815–26, 846–57, 858–63, 898–901, 938–91; *AJ*, June 5, 1716, Nov. 29, 1717, Oct. 9, 1718, 1: 32, 312, 389; "Governor Hunter to the Board of Trade," May 21, July 25, 1715; July 7, Aug. 7, Nov. 3, 1718, in

Docs. Rel., 5: 402–5, 416–19, 512, 514, 518–20; "Lords of Trade to Governor Hunter," Feb. 25, 1718, ibid., 5: 501; Gov. Burnet to the Council of Trade and Plantations, Nov. 21, 1724, *State Papers*, 1724–25, 34: 409–11. For early emissions, see Cadwallader Colden, *Colden Letter Books*, 9: 350–2; *Colonial Laws*, 1: 190–91, 204, 206–7, 222, 227, 231, 2: 292, 347, 396, 437, 447, 450, 492, 551, 631, 676; 3: 688–92; 4: 57, 60, 215, 317, 350, 398.

91. Eugene Sheridan, *Lewis Morris, 1671–1746: A Study in Early American Politics* (Syracuse, N.Y., 1981), 123–34; Hickcox, *History of the Bills of Credit*, 53–79; William Sachs, "Interurban Correspondents and the Development of a National Economy," *New York History* 36 (1955): 320–35; *AJ*, 1: 392 (1717), 416 (1718); *New York Journal*, May 20, July 8, 1734; John J. McCusker, *Money and Exchange in Europe and America, 1600–1775: A Handbook* (Chapel Hill, N.C., 1980), 131–37, 159–61, 169–71, 181, 194–96, 216–20; "The Expediency of a Continental Paper Money," in *American Archives*, ed. Force, 2: 1262–64; *New-York Gazette*, June 2, 9, 16, 1729, May 11, 1730.

92. For Maryland, see Gov. Leonard to Charles Calvert, Oct. 28, 1729, Maryland Historical Society, *Publications*, 34: 68–81, cited by Victor Clark, *The History of Manufactures in the United States, 1607–1860*, 3 vols. (Washington, D.C., 1929), 1: 128. For Boston, [John Wise], *A Word of Comfort to a Melancholy Country . . .* (1721), repr. in *Colonial Currency Reprints*, ed. Andrew McFarland Davis, 4 vols. (New York, 1901), 2: 204; *The Weekly Rehearsal*, Mar. 25, 1734, repr. in ibid., 3: 106; [William Douglass], *An Essay Concerning Silver and Paper Currencies*, repr. in ibid., 3: 222; [Anon.], *An Inquiry into the Nature and Uses of Money, etc.* (1740), repr. in ibid., 3: 440; Boston *Gazette*, Jan. 7, 1751.

93. Hickcox, *History of the Bills of Credit*, 53–79; Sachs, "Interurban Correspondents," 320–25; Abraham Lott to Gov. Moore, Nov. 14, 1766, *The Aspinwall Papers*, Massachusetts Historical Society, *Collections*, 4th ser., vols. 9–10 (Boston, 1871–72), 10: 520–21.

94. The first argument for the Loan Office, with bills at 4 percent interest, was in the *New-York Gazette*, June 2, 9, 16, 1729. On the 1737 Loan Office, see *Colonial Laws*, 2: 666, 1015–40; *New York Journal*, May 23, 1737; John Hickcox, *History of the Bills of Credit*, 25–28. Compare the Loan Office rate of 4 percent and 5 percent to the legal rate of interest, which was lowered from 8 percent to 7 percent in 1738, and government loans at 6 percent in the period 1720–50: "Lt. Gov. Clarke to the Duke of Newcastle," Dec. 17, 1737, in *Docs. Rel.*, 6: 110–11. New York entertained no proposals for a land bank until 1784 when Robert R. Livingston stepped forward; however, Massachusetts began an experiment in 1740, which promised to be successful until disallowed by Parliament. Even in 1765, when Charles Townshend proposed land banks for America, and Benjamin Franklin developed an elaborate plan for them in response to the imperial crisis, New Yorkers turned a cold shoulder to them. See my M.A. thesis, "The New England Paper Money Tradition and the Massachusetts Land Bank of 1740" (Columbia University, 1979).

95. *Colonial Laws*, 2: 1015–47; 3: 294–95, 381–82, 745, 784–87; 4: 156–59, 199–202, 301–4, 385–87, 491–94, 554–56, 649–52, 708–10. Merchants sharing this view about real estate included James Alexander, John Le Count, Julian Verplanck, Johannes Lott, John Chambers, John Wallace, Adolph Philipse, and Peter Schuyler.

96. *New-York Gazette*, Dec. 1737; *New York Journal*, May 23, 1737. The West Indies commentators included Isaac Hicks, Colonel Philipse, David Matthews, Peter and Philip Livingston, Gerard Beekman, and Abraham Lott. In practice, Loan Office interest payments amounted to about £2,000 a year from 1737 to 1764, and they were—as lesser traders predicted—largely paid out to military supply agents, most of whom were

prominent dry-goods importers. Except for revenues raised by the Duty Act after 1753, the Loan Office was New York's greatest source of government revenue; see ch. 5, n. 115; "Governor Hardy to the Lords of Trade," Dec. 2, 1756, in *Docs. Rel.,* 7: 202–5; "Governor Moore to the Earl of Shelburne," Feb. 21, 1767, ibid., 7: 906–9; John Watts to Robert Monckton, June 30, 1764, in *WLB*, 269–70.

97. Joseph Ernst, *Money and Politics in America, 1755–1775: A Study in the Currency Act of 1764 and the Political Economy of Revolution* (Chapel Hill, N.C., 1973), 39–42.

98. "James DeLancey to the Lords of Trade," May 21, 1754, in *Docs. Rel.,* 6: 840; "Lords of Trade to Lt.-Governor De Lancey," July 5, 1754, in ibid., 848; *AJ*, 2: 409–10, 411, 420–21; Leslie Brock, *The Currency of the American Colonies, 1700–1764: A Study in Colonial Finance and Imperial Relations* (Ph.D. diss., University of Michigan, 1941; New York, 1975), 339, 347; *Colonial Laws*, 3: 1038–50, 1078–93, 4: 350–55; McCusker, *Money and Exchange,* table 3.5, 162–65; Ernst, *Money and Politics,* 43–51; Hickcox, *History of the Bills of Credit,* 88–94.

99. On depreciation, see Hickcox, *History of the Bills of Credit,* 39–41; Brock, *Currency of the American Colonies,* 336–37; *AJ*, 2: 696; *Colonial Laws*, 3: 861; and Appendix A, table 5. On becoming supporters, see John Watts to William Baker, May 13, 1763; to Moses Franks, June 1, 1765, in *WLB*, 142, 352; Gerard Beekman to David Beekman, July 17, 1766, in *Beekman Mercantile Letters,* ed. White; and Theodore Thayer, "The Army Contractors for the Niagara Campaign, 1755–1756," *William and Mary Quarterly,* 3d ser., 14 (1957): 32–46.

100. William Douglass, "A Discourse Concerning the Currency of the British Plantations in America" (1745), repr. in American Economic Association, *Economic Studies,* vol. 5 (Boston, 1897), 265–375, see esp. 329, 366; Hickcox, *History of the Bills of Credit,* 22–23; *AJ*, 2: 281, 325, 336, 350, 362, 422–3, 424, 457, 518–19, 554, 570, 602, 606, 634, 644, 668, 672, 707, 728, 750, 785; 3: June 28, Dec. 13, 1766; June 6, 1767; Nov. 23, Dec. 29, 1768, Dec. 12, 1769, Jan. 11, 1771, Jan. 14, 1772, Jan. 12, 1773, Jan. 22, 1774, Jan. 25, 1775; [Anon.], *An Inquiry into the Nature and Uses of Money,* repr. in *Colonial Currency Reprints,* ed. Davis, 3: 419–20; [Cadwallader Colden], *New-York Weekly Journal,* Mar. 28, 1737; "Mr. Colden to the Earl of Hillsborough," Oct. 4, 1769, in *Docs. Rel.,* 8: 189. Supporters in transatlantic trade included Cornelius van Horne, Paul Richard, Henry Cruger, Robert Livingston Jr., Isaac de Peyster, Abraham Lynsen, David Jones, John van Cortlandt, William Alexander, Philip Schuyler, James De Lancey, and John Watts.

101. On exchange rates, devaluation, and bills of exchange, see ch. 2, nn. 75, 76, and ch. 5, nn. 76, 81, 82, 102. Historians today still disagree about whether prices and specie supply are linked to the rates of exchange. Ernst, *Money and Politics,* intro., argues against the validity of a quantity theory and looks for sociopolitical explanations of the economy; Jacob Price, "The Money Question," *Reviews in American History* 2 (1974): 364–69, defends the neoclassical argument affirming a primary role for the supply of specie and its relation to prices; and E. James Ferguson, "Currency Finance: An Interpretation of Colonial Monetary Practices," *William and Mary Quarterly,* 3d ser., 10 (Apr. 1953) 153–80, esp. 155–57, gives an older—yet perhaps more satisfactory—solution that relates the quantity of specie and bills of exchange to interest-group politics in his appreciation of colonial behavior. See also E. James Ferguson, "Political Economy, Public Liberty, and the Formation of the Constitution," ibid., 3d ser., 40 (July 1983): 389–412. David Hume reversed some aspects of this debate; he believed that exchange rates declined to

desirable levels, not by reason of devaluation, but rather by careful emission and with-drawal of modest amounts of paper currency, combined with sound banking; see Hume, "Of Interest and Money" and "Of the Balance of Trade," in *Writings on Economics*, ed. Rotwein, 48, 53.

102. See, e.g., *AJ*, 1: 223–24.

103. Daniel Denton, *A Brief Description of New York* (1670; repr., Cleveland, 1902), 18; "Lord Cornbury to Mr. Secretary Hodges," July 15, 1705, in *Docs. Rel.*, 4: 1151; and Peter Hasenclever to Sir William Johnson, Jan. 6, 1768, in *Papers of Sir William Johnson*, 10: 69. In 1751, Benjamin Franklin wrote, "It is the multitude without land in a country . . . that enables undertakers to carry on a manufacturing" (*The Writings of Benjamin Franklin*, ed. Albert H. Smyth [New York, 1905–7], 3: 65, 66, 4: 49). John Adams voiced the notion that "America will not make manufactures enough for her own consumption these thousand years" (Adams to Franklin, Aug. 17, 1780, in *Works of John Adams*, ed. Charles Francis Adams, 10 vols. [Boston, 1853], 7: 247). See also Cathy Matson, "Liberty, Jealousy, and Union: The New York Economy in the 1780s," in *New York in the Age of the Constitution*, ed. William Pencak and Paul Gilje (New York, 1992), 112–50.

104. "Governor Cosby to the Duke of Newcastle," Dec. 18, 1732, in *Docs. Rel.*, 5: 941; "Mr. Colden's Account of the Trade of New-York," 1723, in ibid., 5: 688–90. See also "Caleb Heathcote to the Board of Trade," 1708, in ibid., 5: 63, 64; "Governor Hunter to the Lords of Trade," 1715, in ibid., 5: 457; *New-York Gazette*, Jan. 21, 1735, Oct. 18, 1736; Clark, *History of Manufactures*, 1: 164–66; and Bishop, *History of Manufactures*, 2: 24, 32, 46, 56–57.

105. Kalm, *Travels*, as cited by Stokes, *Iconography*, 5: 612; Bishop, *History of Manufactures*, 2: 24, 32, 46, 56–57; Smith, *History*, 1: 280. See also *New York Journal*, Jan. 5, 1769; *AJ*, 2: 746; *Colonial Laws*, 4: 737–39; Cornbury to Secretary Hodges, 1702, in *Doc. Hist.*, 1: 711–14; Caleb Heathcote to the Lords of Trade, Nov. 12, 1715, in ibid., 1: 713–14; George Clarke, "Reasons in Support of Triennial Elections," Dec. 1737, in ibid., 4: 245–53; "Lt.-Governor Clark to the Lords of Trade," June 2, 1738, in *Docs. Rel.*, 6: 116; and *Independent Reflector*, ed. Klein, 79–80, 106, 108–10.

106. On the division between natural and artificial, see Gov. Nicholson to the Board of Trade, 1697, in *State Papers*, 1697–98, 16: 391; and sources cited in nn. 107–10 below. Benjamin Franklin argued more strongly than many for a strict bifurcation between "natural" and "artificial" production; see Drew McCoy, *The Elusive Republic: Political Economy in Jeffersonian America* (Chapel Hill, N.C., 1980), ch. 1. But even Adam Smith felt that expansion could not be infinite, and that there were "natural" limits to both agriculture and commerce; he also advocated manufactures on a small scale of division of labor and capital investment—which was roughly where they stood at that time, and the kind of manufactures New Yorkers would have understood (*Wealth of Nations*, 1: 454–56, 117, 346n, 348–49; 2: 419).

107. [Anon.], *Interest of the Merchants and Manufacturers of Great Britain in the Present Contest with the Colonies, Stated and Considered* (London, 1734), 20. For New York merchants who hesitated to begin manufactures, see, e.g., the letters of William Gilliland, Abraham Lynsen, David Jones, Paul Richard, and David Clarkson.

108. E.g., *The British Merchant; or Commerce Preserv'd* (1713–14, repr., London, 1721). This periodical of 181 issues featured essays by Charles King, Charles Cooke, Theodore Jansen, James Milner, Nathaniel Torians, Joshua Gee, Christopher Haynes, David Mar-

tin, and Henry Martin; its writers opposed the open or free trade. For the conscious distinction between merchant and manufacturer in New York City, see *Arts and Crafts*, comp. Gottesman, 267. A valuable discussion of agriculture, rural manufactures, and their effects on commerce is Maxine Berg, *Manufactures in Town and Country before the Factory* (Cambridge, 1983), ch. 1.

109. "Freedoms and Exemptions" (decreed 1629, published 1630), in *Docs. Rel.*, 2: 551–57; *Laws and Ordinances*, 1–10; Charles Wilson, *England's Apprenticeship, 1603–1763* (London, 1965), chs. 4, 14; Peter Mathias, *The First Industrial Nation: An Economic History of Britain, 1700–1914* (New York, 1969), ch. 5.

110. "An American," *An Essay upon the Government*, ed. Wright.

111. [Anon.], *The Irregular and Disorderly State of the Plantation-Trade* (1731), repr. in *Annual Report of the American Historical Association for the Year 1892* (Washington, D.C., 1893), 36–44, at 37. See also works of Cary, Whiston, Thomas, Petty, Pollexfen, and Gee cited in ch. 2.

112. Statement of Martin Bladen to the Board of Trade, 1726, quoted by C. M. Andrews, *The Colonial Period of American History: England's Commercial and Colonial Policy*, 4 vols. (New Haven, Conn., 1938), 4: 106; 4 Geo. III, c. 15, sec. 26; *New York Gazette*, Oct. 8, 1764; and for the Acts of Trade prohibiting or protecting New York manufactures, see Introduction, nn. 1, 7; ch. 2, n. 17; and ch. 5, n. 10.

113. William Wood, *A Survey of Trade, together with Considerations on our Money and Bullion* (London, 1718), 147; and citations in nn. 104, 107, and 108.

114. See, e.g., citations in nn. 104, 107, and 108. For other colonies, see Thomas Doerflinger, "Farmers and Dry Goods in the Philadelphia Market Area, 1750–1800," in *The Economy of Early America: The Revolutionary Period, 1763–1790*, ed. Ronald Hoffman et al. (Charlottesville, Va., 1988), 166–95; Margaret Martin, *Merchants and Trade of the Connecticut River Valley, 1750–1820* (Northampton, Mass., 1938); Jackson Turner Main and Gloria Main, "Standards and Styles of Living in Southern New England, 1640–1774," *Journal of Economic History* 48 (1988): 27–46; Lois Carr and Lorena Walsh, "Changing Life Styles and Consumer Behavior in the Colonial Chesapeake," in *Of Consuming Interests: The Style of Life in the Eighteenth Century*, ed. Cary Carson et al. (Charlottesville, Va., 1992), 59–166; and Wilbur C. Plummer, "Consumer Credit in Colonial Philadelphia," *Pennsylvania Magazine of History and Biography* 56 (1942): 385–409.

115. Gov. Hunter to the Board of Trade, Nov. 12, 1715, in *Doc. Hist.*, 1: 713–14; George Clarke, "Reasons in Support of Triennial Elections," Dec. 1737, in ibid., 4: 245–53; Cadwallader Colden on the trade of New York, 1723, in ibid., 1: 714–21; *New-York Gazette*, Jan. 21, 28, Feb. 4, 1735. Clarke actively promoted New York manufactures in the 1730s; *Messages from the Governors*, ed. Lincoln, 256 (1736); 260 (1737); 280 (1739).

116. *New-York Gazette*, Aug. 29, 1748, on the Livingston mills; ibid., May 9, 1763, on the Van Cortlandt mill; Clark, *History of Manufactures*, 1: 176; Letter Books of Philip Livingston, William and Jacob Walton, Samuel Bayard, and William Gilliland; Bishop, *History of Manufactures*, 1: 105–8.

117. *New-York Gazette*, Aug. 18, 1755; Clark, *History of Manufactures*, 1: 32–38, 42–43, 52–57, 167, 176; Anne Grant, *Memoirs of an American Lady . . . Previous to the Revolution*, 2 vols. (1808; repr., New York, 1970), ch. 26; *Colonial Laws*, 1: 171, 248, 339 752, 755, 991, 995; 2: 242; *Docs. Rel.*, 5: 706; Egnal, "Economic Development," 191–222; Robert Sanders to Stork & Champion, Aug. 15, 1753, Sanders Letter Book; John van Cortlandt, Letter Book,

1762–69, entries for 1763–64; John Watts to William Baker, Jan. 13, 1762, to Charles Hardy, Dec. 1, 1762, to Lasscelles, Clarke & Daling, May 13, 1763, Apr. 1, 1765, to William Allen, Feb. 14, 1764, to Moses Franks, June 1, 1765, in *WLB*, 8, 101, 142, 229, 342, 352; William Alexander, "Account with David Barclay and Son," 1760–69, Alexander Letters, box 1, NYHS.

118. Caleb Heathcote to the Lords of Trade, Nov. 9, 1705, in C.O. 5: 1949; *Docs. Rel.*, 5: 501, 617; "Mr. Colden's Account of the Trade of New-York," 1723, in ibid., 5: 688–90; Archibald Kennedy to Board of Trade, 1738, in *Doc. Hist.*, 4: 725–26.

119. See, e.g., *Docs. Rel.*, 3: 263, 4: 668–70; 5: 59, 591ff., 610, 617; 6: 19, 207, 511; MacPherson, *Annals*, 3: 49, 159, 162; *Council Journal*, 1: 661, 713; 2: 1540, 1541. Flaxseed was separated from the fibers; the former was exported, while farmers cleaned the fibers with a "break," beat them with a wooden paddle called a "swingling," and then combed and carded the dried results. Linsey-woolsey was half flax.

120. "Mr. Colden's Account of the Trade of New-York," 1723, in *Docs. Rel.*, 5: 688–89; Gov. Clarke to the Assembly, 1736, in *AJ*, 1: 689; Colden to William Alexander, 1763, in *Colden Letter Books*, 1: 312–13; *Docs. Rel.*, 5: 591, 617. On the urge to cease paying the Scandinavians and encourage colonial hemp production, see Andrews, *Colonial Period*, 4: 78 n. 9 and 103.

121. *Council Journal*, 1: 661, 713; 2: 1540, 1541. The most influential writers on bounties in England were James Whiston, *The Mismanagements of Trade* (London, 1704), see esp. 25; and Postlethwayt, *Dict.*, 1: 107–8. On New York's bounties, see Philip White, *The Beekmans of New York in Politics and Commerce, 1647–1877* (New York, 1956), 348, 384, 443. Indigo, for which England paid 6d. per pound after 1748, was probably the most successful bounty in all the colonies, but New Yorkers transported only a portion of South Carolina and Georgia indigo. See also Gov. Cornbury to Hedges, July 15, 1705, in C.O. 5: 1084, no. 28; Heathcote to the Board of Trade, Aug. 3, 1708, in C.O. 5: 1049, no. 98; Gov. Hunter to the Board of Trade, Nov. 12, 1715, in C.O. 5: 1051, no. 19, and Oct. 31, 1712, in C.O. 5: 1050, no. 58; and Report of Board of Trade, Mar. 28, 1717, in C.O. 390: 12, 35–36.

122. William Alexander to the earl of Shelburne, Aug. 6, 1763, cited by W. A. Duer, *The Life of William Alexander, Earl of Stirling* (New York, 1847), 74–77. For other merchants' support, see William Beekman to David & Ross, Ltd., Newry, Ireland, Oct. 18, 1764, Nov. 30, 1764, in *Beekman Mercantile Papers*, ed. White, 1: 475, 477–78; *Docs. Rel.*, 5: 501, 617.

123. Potash is potassium carbonate, which was made in colonial New York by leaching wood ashes, usually from deciduous trees, and then evaporating the solution in large iron pots. The value of these exports in 1771 was £29,611, fully one-third of New York's legal exports. In 1773, the value increased to £32,247, or 40 percent of New York's legal exports. See MacPherson, *Annals*, 3: 49, 159, 162; *Colonial Laws*, 4: 926–27, 1090; and Gerret van Zant Correspondence, Albany Institute of History and Art; *Docs. Rel.*, 3: 798, 5: 610; *Council Journal*, 1: 435: 1205, a.57.

124. Denton, *Brief Description*, 17–18.

125. Cornbury to Secretary Hodges, 1702, in *Doc. Hist.*, 1: 711–14; "Lord Cornbury to Secretary Hodges," 1705, in *Docs. Rel.*, 4: 1151.

126. "Caleb Heathcote to the Lords of Trade," Aug. 3, 1708, in *Docs. Rel.*, 5: 63.

127. "Governor Hunter to the Lords of Trade," 1715, in *Docs. Rel.*, 5: 460; and *London Daily Post*, Mar. 28, 1737, repr. in *New-York Gazette*, June 20, 27, 1737. See also "Governor Cornbury to the Lords of Trade," July 1, 1708, in *Docs. Rel.*, 5: 59; Colden on the trade of New York, 1723, in *Doc. Hist.*, 4: 714–21; Gov. Hunter to the Board of Trade, Nov. 12, 1715,

in ibid., 4: 713–14; Archibald Kennedy to the Board of Trade, 1738, ibid., 4: 725–27; "George Clinton to the Lords of Trade," May 23, 1749, in *Docs. Rel.*, 6: 511; Burnaby, *Travels*, 114–15; "Governor Moore to the Board of Trade," Jan. 12, 1767, in *Docs. Rel.*, 1: 734.

128. Kennedy, *Observations*, 6–9, 16; and *Docs. Rel.*, 5: 897–99.

129. Kennedy, *Observations*, 10–11, 14–18, 20–23, 27–28.

130. Clark, *History of Manufactures*, 1: 92–94, 120; and George Chalmers, *Political Annals of the Present United Colonies, From their Settlement to the Peace of 1763*, 2 vols. (1783; repr., New York, 1968), 2: 39, 40, 41, 116, 319; and *Docs. Rel.*, 5: 617.

131. For a sense of the extent to which this is true, see C.O. 5: 1222–28; Philip Livingston, Letter Books; Cornelius Cuyler, Letter Books and Ledgers; MacPherson, *Annals*, 3: 163; Bishop, *History of Manufactures*, 1: 315; and Clark, *History of Manufactures*, 1: 116–17.

132. "Governor Moore to the Board of Trade," Jan. 12, 1767, in *Docs. Rel.*, 7: 888.

133. "George Clinton to the Lords of Trade," May 23, 1749, in *Docs. Rel.*, 6: 511.

134. "Governor Bellomont to the Board of Trade," June 22, 1700, in C.O. 5: 931, no. 3; Nov. 28, 1700, in C.O. 5: 1045, no. 18; statement of the New York Council, Mar. 5, 1701, in C.O. 5: 1046, no. 5; and "Mr. Colden's Account of the Trade of New-York," 1723, in *Docs. Rel.*, 5: 688–90. For bounties, see 3 Anne, c. 10; 8 Anne, c. 13; 12 Anne, c. 9; 5 Geo. 1, c. 11; 8 Geo. 1, c. 12; 2 Geo. 2, c. 35; 24 Geo. 2, c. 52; 25 Geo. 2, c. 35; 4 Geo. 3, c. 11.

135. "Instructions for Governor Andros," in *Docs. Rel.*, 3: 216–19; *Colonial Laws*, 1: 1022; 2: 423, 852; 3: 240. The merchant protests are in *Docs. Rel.*, 3: 798, 4: 37; *Council Journal*, 1: 435.

136. *Colonial Laws*, 3: 77–79, 346, 788–93; 4: 1021–22; 5: 71–73, 65–66, 198–202, 266–68; Osgood, *Mins. Common Council*, 4: 95, 306; 6: 239–41, 161; *AJ*, 1: 563, 820, 822–23, 2: 291–96; Stevens, *Records*, 3, 59, 63, 70–71, 176, 178, 190–95; *New-York Post-Boy*, Oct. 22, 1750, June 4, 1753, and *Beekman Mercantile Papers*, ed. White, 1: 465–66, 472.

137. *Docs. Rel.*, 4: 668; 5: 72, 610, 688; Caleb Heathcote to Lord Bolingbroke, Oct. 15, 1714, in *State Papers*, 1714–15, 28: 338.

138. In 1724, the shipwrights of London lost their appeal for restrictions on colonial shipbuilding (*Journal of the Commissioners*, 3: 138). Vessels were built more cheaply in the colonies—some for as little as £4 per ton—than those built on the Thames, despite the high cost of labor. About half of New York's annual average of twelve to twenty-two new vessels built from the 1720s to 1750s were registered outside of the colony, and it is likely that English merchants purchased many of them. See *New-York Gazette*, 1727–44; "Samuel Maverick to Richard Nicolls," July 5, 1669, "Answers of Inquiries of New York received from Sir Edmund Andros," Apr. 16, 1678, and "Earl of Bellomont to the Lords of Trade," Nov. 28, 1700, in *Docs. Rel.*, 3: 183–85, 261, 4: 790; Gov. Hunter to the Board to Trade, Nov. 12, 1715, in *State Papers*, 1714–15, 28: 70, 337; Caleb Heathcote to Lord Bolingbroke, Oct. 15, 1714, in ibid., 1714–15, 28: 338. On the general characteristics of shipbuilding in colonial New York, see Nash, *Urban Crucible*, 93, 123–26.

139. "Governor Hunter to the Lords of Trade," 1715, in *Docs. Rel.*, 5: 460; Lawrence Leder, "Military Victualling in Colonial New York," in *Business Enterprise in Early New York*, ed. Joseph R. Frese, S.J., and Jacob Judd (Tarrytown, N.Y., 1979), 16–54.

140. *Docs. Rel.*, 5: 610.

141. Marcus, *American Jewry*, 325, 328, 329; Samuel Mulford's speech to the Assembly at New York, Apr. 2, 1714, MSS Div., NYPL, 6; Hugh Wallace to William Johnson, Dec. 10,

1762, in *Papers of Sir William Johnson*, 3: 968; Peter Hasenclever to William Johnson, in ibid., 4: 540–41, 811; 5: 11–14, 475–78; Gov. Tryon to the Board of Trade, 1774, in *Doc. Hist.*, 1: 758–59; *Beekman Mercantile Papers*, ed. White, 1: 229–31, 265; [Gov. Robert Hunter], *Androboros* (1714), repr. in NYPL *Bulletin*, ed., Lawrence H. Leder, 68 (1964): 153–90. For a 1726 request for a monopoly of porpoise fishing, see Mordecai Gomez Papers, American Jewish Historical Society, New York City. On the premiums the Assembly offered to the United Whale Fishery Company in 1774, see *Archives of the State of New Jersey, 1631–1800*, 1st ser., ed. W. A. Whitehead et al. (Trenton, N.J., 1880–1928), 5: 205, 208. On other merchants' support, see William Alexander to earl of Shelburne, Aug. 6, 1763, cited by Duer, *Life of William Alexander*, 74–77; Beekman to David & Ross, Ltd., Newry, Ireland, Nov. 30, 1764; Oct. 18, 1764; May 2, 1766; Beekman to Ross, Newry, Feb. 27, 1768, all in *Beekman Mercantile Papers*, ed. White, 1: 478, 475, 517–18; *Docs. Rel.*, 5: 501, 617, 688.

142. Burnaby, *Travels*, 115; David Valentine, *History of the City of New York* (New York, 1853), 542.

143. *Reasons Humbly Offered for the Encouragement of Making Iron in his Majesty's Plantations of America*, repr. in *Annual Report of the American Historical Association for the Year 1892*, 56–65; Bishop, *History of Manufactures*, 1: 524–26; Arthur C. Bining, *Pennsylvania Iron Manufactures in the Eighteenth Century* (Harsby, Pa., 1938), 143–47; Francis Eastman, *A History of the State of New York* (New York, 1831), 26; *New-York Mercury*, Oct. 20, 1755; Archibald Kennedy to the the Board of Trade, 1738, *Doc. Hist.*, 1: 725–26; Irene Neu, "The Iron Plantations of Colonial New York," *New York History*, 33 (Jan. 1952), 3–24.

144. Kennedy, *Observations*, 95–96; Marcus, *American Jewry*, 380–81; "An Account of Iron Made at Ancram," *Doc. Hist.*, 1: 730; Peter Hasenclever to Sir William Johnson, Jan. 6, Mar. 4, 22, 1764, in *Papers of Sir William Johnson*, 11: 3–4, 621–23, and 648–49; "The Case of Peter Hasenclever," cited by Clark, *History of Manufactures*, 1: 147; Samuel McKee Jr., "The Economic Pattern of Colonial New York," in *History of the State of New York*, ed. A. C. Flick, 4 vols. (New York, 1933), 2: 276–77; *New-York Mercury*, Aug. 24, 1767; F. J. Tuttle, "The Hibernia Furnace and the Surrounding Country in the Revolutionary War," New Jersey Historical Society, *Proceedings*, 2d ser., 6 (1880); and Gov. Tryon to Board of Trade, 1774, in *Doc. Hist.*, 4: 711–12. For other examples, see, e.g., *New-York Mercury*, Nov. 17, 1760, Aug. 24, 1767, and Oct. 17, 1768; *New-York Gazette*, Oct. 8, 1764.

145. Burnaby, *Travels*, 84–85; *New-York Gazette*, Aug. 21, 28, 1732, Aug. 27, Sept. 3, 1733; John Baker Holroyd, 1st earl of Sheffield, *Observations on the Commerce of the American States, with Europe and the West Indies* (1783), 6th ed. (London, 1784), app.; and Appendix A, table 1.

146. "Hunter to the Lords of Trade," 1714, in *Docs. Rel.*, 5: 462; *State Papers, 1706–8*, 23: 671; ibid., 1711–12, 26: 439; 8 Geo. 1, c. 18, sec. 22; Andrews, *Colonial Period*, 4: 104–5.

147. On distilling, see *New-York Gazette*, Sept. 21, 1730; "George Clinton to the Lords of Trade," May 23, 1749, in *Docs. Rel.*, 6: 511; Colden to the Board of Trade, 1738, in *Doc. Hist.*, 4: 727, 729; MacPherson, *Annals*, 3: 176; Bishop, *History of Manufactures*, 1: 161, 162. Wine never became a viable colonial production; by the 1720s, merchants imported large quantities; see C.O. 5: 1223–24. On other manufactures, see Osgood, *Mins. Common Council*, 5: 118–20, 357; 7: 25–26, 181, 210, 287–88; and Clark, *History of Manufactures*, 1: 164–80. Peter Warren owned New York City's only glassworks (Wilson, *Memorial History*, 2: 130).

148. Bellomont to the Lords of Trade, Nov. 2, 1700, in *Docs. Rel.*, 4: 439–40; *New-York Gazette*, Dec. 13, 1731, May 8, 1732, Sept. 19, 1763; Wilson, *Memorial History*, 2: 92. For brewing in the Dutch period, see ch. 1, n. 38.

149. Refined sugar was made by boiling raw sugar, adding milk of lime (a very diluted calcium carbonate) and egg albumen, and skimming off the impurities as the mixture continued to cook. The resulting syrup was poured into molds (usually cones) and crystallized. Merchants sold the syrup that dripped from the tip of the cone as treacle; they wrapped the cones in paper and dried the sugar at 130–40 degrees for three to five days. Granulated sugar appeared in northern shops only in the 1870s. The earliest English discouragement of colonial sugar refining that I find was in 1697, which is about the time English refining and distilling began to grow. See [Anon.], *The Case of the Refiners of Sugar in England stated* (London, 1697). On New York refining, *Council Journal*, 1: 461, 536, 557, 558, 562; Gov. Clinton to the Lords of Trade, in *Docs. Rel.*, 6: 511; *New-York Gazette*, Aug. 17, Sept. 21, 1730; John van Cortlandt to Christopher Jacobson, Nov. 21, 1763; to John Badger, Feb. 22, 1766, Van Cortlandt Letter Book; Wilson, *Memorial History*, 2: 452–54; William Barret, *The Merchants of Old New York*, 5 vols. (New York, 1886), 5: 26, 1: 270. On chocolate, see James Baker Correspondence, 1761–1823, AAS; Evert Wendell Day Book and Ledger, 1711–38; Andries Teller Correspondence, 1726–30; and on importation of cocoa beans, C.O. 5: 1222–28.

150. Marcus, *American Jewry*, 315. 152; Bishop, *History of Manufactures*, 2: 22; John van Cortlandt Letter Book. See also *New-York Gazette*, advertisements over 1732;

151. Marcus, *American Jewry*, 288, 393–95; *Arts and Crafts*, comp. Gottesman, 293.

152. *New-York Gazette, or Weekly Post-Boy*, Aug. 19, 1751, May 19, 1763, Jan. 8, 1767, Feb. 5, 1770; *New York Journal*, Dec. 24, 1767; Comptroller Weare, "Observations on the British Colonies on the Continent of America," Massachusetts Historical Society, *Collections*, 1st ser., vol. 1 (Boston, 1794), 74, 75, 79; "George Clarke to the Lords of Trade," June 2, 1738, in *Docs. Rel.*, 6: 116; "Mr. Colden's Account of the Trade of New-York," 1723, in ibid., 5: 688–90; "Governor Moore to the Lords of Trade," Jan. 12, 1767, in ibid., 7: 888; and "Colden to the Lords of Trade," Mar. 9, 1764, in ibid., 7: 612. On the stages of history, see also, e.g., Benjamin Franklin, "The Interests of Great Britain in America," in *Works*, 4: 61–62.

EIGHT　　The Vagaries of War and Depression, 1754–1770

1. "Governor Clarke to the Board of Trade," Dec. 15, 1741, in *Docs. Rel.*, 6: 207–9; Gov. Clinton to duke of Newcastle, Nov. 18, 1745, in ibid., 6: 284–85; *The State of the Trade of Great Britain in Its Imports and Exports, 1697–1773*, ed. Sir Charles Whitworth (London, 1776); various letters of William Alexander to Henry and William Livingston in Antigua, Alexander Papers, 1744–50; John Ludlow to Chauncey, Brown & Chauncey, Nov. 30, 1753, John Ludlow Letter Book, AAS; John Baker Holroyd, 1st earl of Sheffield, *Observations on the Commerce of the American States, with Europe and the West Indies* (1783), 6th ed. (London, 1784), 234; Thomas Pownall, *The Administration of the American Colonies* (1764), 4th ed. (London, 1768), 5–12; *New-York Mercury*, Nov. 13, 1752; Charles H. Wilson, *Anglo-Dutch Commerce and Finance in the Eighteenth Century* (Cambridge, 1941), chs. 6–7.

2. Gerard Beekman to William Beekman, June 6, 1752, in *The Beekman Mercantile*

Papers, 1746–1799, ed. Philip White, 3 vols. (New York, 1956), 1: 143–44; and letters of Gabriel Ludlow, Waddell Cunningham, and Robert and Richard Ray.

3. On French trade, see, e.g., Philip Cuyler to his father, 1756, Cuyler, Letter Book. On logwood at Honduras, see Cornelius Ludlow to John de Neufville, Jan. 5, 1756, Ludlow Letter Book. On Amsterdam trade, see Edmund and Josiah Quincy to Thomas and Adrian Hope, 1745, in C.O. 323, fol. 13; Christopher Bancker, Waste Book, May 11, 23, Aug. 24, 1752; and Wilson, *Anglo-Dutch Commerce*, chs. 6–7.

4. Philip Cuyler to his father, 1756, Cuyler, Letter Book; *Docs. Rel.*, 5: 686, 6: 154–55, 7: 162, 215, 271, 612, 8: 255.

5. C.O. 5: 5, fol. 246; Gov. George Clinton to the Board of Trade, May 23, 1749, in C.O. 5: 1062, Hh 48; Gary Walton and James Shepherd, *The Economic Rise of Early America* (Cambridge, 1979), ch. 4; Marc Egnal, "The Economic Development of the Thirteen Continental Colonies, 1720–1775," *William and Mary Quarterly*, 3d ser., 32 (1975): 191–222; Jacob Price, "The Transatlantic Economy," in *Colonial British America*, ed. Jack Greene and J. R. Pole (Baltimore, 1984), 18–42; Richard Sheridan, "The British Credit Crisis of 1772 and the American Colonies," *Journal of Economic History* 20 (1960): 166–86, esp. 166–67; and Appendix A, table 2. Sheridan notes that in 1776, British creditors set New York's sterling debts to them at £88,000, but that chronic exaggeration of American debts suggested they were lower. An annual average of only 11.27 percent of New York's ships, representing 24.5 percent of its vessel tonnage, plied between New York and England from 1749 to 1754.

6. David MacPherson, *Annals of Commerce, Manufactures, Fisheries, and Navigation*, 4 vols. (London, 1805), 1: 6; Gerard Beekman to Samuel Fowler, Apr. 2, 1754, to William Beekman, June 6, 1752, and to Henry Lloyd, June 21, 1756, in *Beekman Mercantile Papers*, ed. White, 210–11, 143–44, 282–83; William Alexander to Henry and William Livingston (in Antigua), 1750, Alexander Papers, fol. 1; Gabriel Ludlow to Chauncey, Brown & Chauncey, Nov. 30, 1753, and three letters to Moses Franks, Elias Bland, and Sheldon and Wright, Jan 8, 1754, Ludlow Letter Book.

7. Gerard Beekman to William Edmonds, June 29, 1755, and to Samuel Fowler, July 10, 1755, in *Beekman Mercantile Papers*, ed. White.

8. Gov. Hardy to William Pitt, Mar. 11, 1757, in *State Papers, 1757*, 64: 71; Thomas Barrow, *Trade and Empire: The British Customs Service in Colonial America, 1660–1775* (Cambridge, Mass., 1967), 160–73; Gary B. Nash, *The Urban Crucible: Political Consciousness and the Origins of the American Revolution* (Cambridge, Mass., 1979), 238; Virginia Harrington, *The New York Merchant on the Eve of the Revolution* (New York, 1935), 308–9. For comments hopeful of war profits, see Gerard Beekman to William Edmonds, June 29, 1755, and to Samuel Fowler, July 10, 1755, in *Beekman Mercantile Papers*, ed. White, 1: 256–57, 258; John Ludlow to Sheldon and Wright, July 1, 1755, to Moses Franks, Nov. 7, 1755, and to John de Neufville, Jan. 5, 1756, Ludlow Letter Book; Philip Cuyler to Dirk van der Heyden, July 17, 1756, Cuyler, Letter Book. The merchant councillors were Charles Apthorpe, William Axtell, Henry and John H. Cruger, James Jauncey Jr., Joseph Reade, Hugh Wallace, William Walton, John Watts, Henry White, and the two "merchant-landowners," William Alexander and Oliver De Lancey.

9. Insurance rates rose from 5 percent to 15 percent for the trip from New York to London in 1757, from 15 percent to 18 percent for the trip to Amsterdam in 1757–58, and from 4½ percent to 10 percent and higher for the trip to the West Indies; see London bro-

kers discussed in Nicholas Magens, *Essay on Insurances* (London, 1755); P.G. M. Dickson, *The Financial Revolution in England: A Study in the Development of Public Credit, 1688–1756* (New York, 1967), ch. 1; Charles Wilson, *England's Apprenticeship, 1603–1763* (London, 1965), 372; and Postlethwayt, *Dict.*, 1: 136. For New York, see John Ludlow, Philip Cuyler, and Gerard Beekman, Letter Books, and *WLB*; brokerage service announcements in the *New-York Mercury,* Aug. 27, Nov. 5, 1759; and Jacob and William Walton, Insurance Book, 1774, Museum of the City of New York.

10. For military supply movements, see *The Papers of Sir William Johnson*, ed. James Sullivan et al., 14 vols. (Albany, N.Y., 1921–65); William Alexander Papers, and Gabriel Ludlow Account Books, NYHS; and Theodore Thayer, "The Army Contractors for the Niagara Campaign, 1755–1756," *William and Mary Quarterly*, 3d ser., 14 (1957), 31–46; mention of the merchants Watts, Cruger, Walton, Richards, Thomas, Philipse, De Lancey, Beekman, Filiken, Verplanck, LeCount, and Walton in *AJ*, esp. Sept. 11, 1755; Jeffrey Amherst to Cadwallader Colden, Apr. 18, 1762, in *Colden*, 55: 143–44.

11. *WLB*, 1750–64; *New-York Mercury,* Dec. 31, 1759; *New-York Gazette,* Aug. 29, Sept. 12, 19, 1763.

12. Harrington, *New York Merchant,* 297–303; *Sir William Johnson Papers,* 2: 367–68, 463, 466–67, 504–5, 782–83.

13. See, e.g., Receipt Book of Judah Hays, 1759–62, American Jewish Historical Society, New York City.

14. Osgood, *Mins. Common Council,* 6: 22, 90, 91–92, 429; 7: 253; *WLB*, 142, 76, 352, 118, 342; *Docs. Rel.*, 4: 13, 134, 136, 140; 5: 738; 6: 116; 8: 169; Julian Gwyn, "Private Credit in Colonial New York: The Warren Portfolio, 1731–1795," *New York History* 37 (1956): 269–93; *Cal. Council Mins.*, May 2, 1747, 364. The quotation is from Corbyn Morris, *An Essay towards illustrating the Science of Insurance* (London, 1747), 2. Watts also invested in the 3 percent consolidated Bank of England debt and the 4½ percent annuities offered by the English government during the war, rates more in line with peacetime levels. Samuel Baker to William Johnson, Aug. 14, 1772, *Sir William Johnson Papers,* 8: 574–75, indicates Johnson's investment of £4,000 in 3 percent consolidation stocks offered by the English government, and see John Ludlow Account Book, 1756–60, for evidence of annuities purchased by successful dry-goods importers.

15. On Queen Anne's War, see Board of Trade and Plantations, report, Nov. 1702, MSS, NYPL; Anne Grant, *Memoirs of an American Lady . . . Previous to the Revolution,* 2 vols. (1808; repr., New York, 1970), 2: 243; "New York City Merchants to the Lords of Trade," Feb. 20, 1712, in *Docs. Rel.,* 5: 331–32; Richard Pares, *Yankees and Creoles: The Trade between North America and the West Indies before the American Revolution* (Cambridge, Mass., 1956), 63; and Howard Chapin, *Privateer Ships and Sailors: The First Century of American Colonial Privateering, 1625–1725* (London, 1926), 116–19, 212–24. On King George's War, see "Governor Clinton to the Lords of Trade," 1744, in *Docs. Rel.,* 6: 260; *AJ*, 1744; C.O. 5: 1061; *New-York Post-Boy,* Feb. 25, 1745; *New-York Gazette,* May 19, 1740, Oct. 1, 1746; *New-York Evening Post,* Mar. 4, Apr. 11, 1745; James Lydon, *Pirates, Privateering, and Profits* (Upper Saddle River, N.J., 1970), 154–59.

16. Philip Cuyler to Henry Cuyler, July 15, 1756, to Capt. Stoddard, Mar. 31, 1757, Cuyler, Letter Book; Waddell Cunningham to Isaac and Zachariah Hope of Amsterdam, July 16, 1756, Waddell Cunningham Letterbook, NYHS; Charles Nicholl, Sept. 28, 1756, Nicholl Account Book, 1753–59; *Lloyd Family Papers,* NYHS, *Collections*, vols. 59–60

(1926–27), 60: 562; Thomas Witter, Apr. 26, 1759, Account Book, 1755–61, NYHS; C.O. 5: 1227–28; Lydon, *Pirates, Privateering, and Profits,* 154–59. I have eliminated captains from consideration in this paragraph. The logwood traders included Philip Cuyler, Philip Livingston, Alexander McDougal, Isaac Sears, Jacob and William Walton, John Watts, Hayman Levy, and Sampson Simpson. Lesser merchants included Ephraim Cooke, David van der Heyden, Samuel Stilwell, Thomas Witter, and Charles Nicholl. Among the dry-goods men were David Provoost, George Folliott, John Lawrence, John Jauncey, John Waddell, Joseph Hayes, John Ludlow, Evert Bancker, and Lawrence Kortright. The large rum traders included Isaac Gouveneur, Philip Livingston, the Crugers, the Van Cortlandts, the Waltons, the Franklins, and the Wallaces. During the first thirty months of the Seven Years' War, New York privateers returned with at least 248 French prizes, more than they had taken in the entire nine years of King George's War; see *New-York Mercury,* June 27, 1757; *New-York Post-Boy,* Aug. 1, 1757; *Docs. Rel.,* 7: 343; Waddell Cunningham Letterbook, 1756–57; Lydon, *Pirates, Privateering, and Profits,* 211, 214–15, 223, 278; *New-York Gazette,* June 27, 1757; Philip Cuyler to Tweedy, Dec. 15, 1758, to Henry Cuyler, Sept. 13, Oct. 19, 1756 and May 16, 1757, and Oct. 3, 1758, to John Stevenson, Apr. 27, 1757, Cuyler, Letter Book.

17. In addition to the sources in n. 16, see C.O. 5: 1226–27; author's collective biography; *New-York Gazette,* Mar. 12, Apr. 9, 30, 1759, Jan. 6, 1763, Sept. 18, 25, 1769; Moses Gomez Letter Book, American Jewish Historical Society, New York City; Philip Cuyler, Letter Book.

18. Statement of Stephen Hopkins, C.O. 5: 1276, 704.

19. Gov. George Clinton to the Board of Trade, Oct. 4, 1752, in C.O. 5: 1064, fol. 144; "Hardy to the Lords of Trade," July 10, 1757, in *Docs. Rel.,* 7: 271; De Lancey to the Board of Trade, July 30, 1757, in C.O. 5: 1068, Mm 14; Gerard Beekman to Thomas Gilbert, Sept. 31, 1750, to Samuel Fowler, July 28, 1752, Sept. 6, Sept. 25, 1753, Apr. 1, 2, 1754, to Gamaliel Wallice, Oct. 1, 1753, to Samuel Fowler, June 17, 1755, Dec. 5, 1763, to Samuel Fowler and Jacob Richardson, July 14, 1760, to James Green, July 14, 1760, and to Christopher Champlin, July 3, 1762, in *Beekman Mercantile Papers,* ed. White, 124, 146, 165, 185, 188, 210, 211, 255, 362, 413, 452, 503; John Ludlow to Moses Franks, Dec. 24, 1756, Ludlow Letter Book; Robert Sanders to Samuel Osborne, May 23, 1756, Sanders Letters; Philip Cuyler to his father, Jan. 14, May 13, 1760, Cuyler, Letter Book. The smuggling trade with French islands is described in "Colden to the Lords of Trade, 1763," in *Docs. Rel.,* 7: 499; John Ludlow to Daniel Crommelin, and to Moses Franks, July 12, 18, 1757, Ludlow Letter Book; John Rowe to Philip Cuyler, Sept. 24, 1759, in *Letters and Diary of John Rowe: Boston Merchant, 1759–1762, and 1764 to 1779,* ed. Anne Rowe Cunningham (Boston, 1903), 337–38.

20. John Ludlow to John de Neufville, Amsterdam, Jan. 5, 1756, Ludlow Letter Book. The merchants included John Ludlow, William Ludlow, John Waddell, Elias Desbrosses, and Capt. Richard Jeffrey. For the Rule of 1756, see James Marriott, *The Case of the Dutch Ships Considered,* 3d. ed. (London, 1759), ch. 3.

21. *Docs. Rel.,* 7: 162; Alexander Colden to Cadwallader Colden, May 8, 1756, in *Colden,* 54: 71–74; Philip Cuyler to Cornelius Cuyler, Oct. 31, 1754, Jan. 4, 1755, Mar. 20, May 19, Aug. 16, Sept. 7, 24, Oct. 28, 1756, to Isaac Clockener & Zoon, June 4, 1756, and to John Hodshon, June 9, 15, and 30, 1756, Cuyler, Letter Book. On the seizures and repurchase of goods, see Philip Cuyler to his father, July 7, Sept. 13, 1756, to John Lloyd, July 12, 1756, and to Daniel Crommelin in Amsterdam, July 16, 1756, in ibid.; and William Smith,

The History of the Late Province of New-York from its Discovery, to the Apointment of Governor Colden, in 1762, NYHS, *Collections,* 2 vols. (New York, 1829–30), 2: 350.

22. "Hardy to the Lords of Trade," July 10, 1757, in *Docs. Rel.,* 7: 271; "An Essay on the Trade of the Northern Colonies," *Providence Gazette,* Jan. 14, 21, 1764; Philip Cuyler to John Lloyd, July 12, 1756, to William Tweedy, Feb. 18, 1760, to Samuel Townshend, Jan. 23, 1760, to Richards and Coddington, Nov. 7, 1759, Cuyler, Letter Book; Cornelius Ludlow to John Lloyd, Sept. 24, 1755, to Capt. Richard Jeffrey, Apr. 6, 1755, Ludlow Letter Book; Thomas Wharton to John Waddell, 1756, Waddell Letter Book; Charles M. Andrews, "Colonial Commerce," *American Historical Review* 20 (1915): 61–62; Lt. Gov. Colden, report to the Board of Trade, Dec. 7, 1763, in *Colden Letter Books,* NYHS, *Collections,* 2d ser., vols. 9–10 (New York, 1876–77), 9: 257–59, 375–76; John Watts to the New York Council, 1763, and John Freebody to Christopher Champlin, Dec. 12, 1771, in *Commerce of Rhode Island, 1720–1790,* Massachusetts Historical Society, *Collections,* 4th ser., vol. 9 (1914), 383, and vol. 10 (1915), 507.

23. Harrington, *New York Merchant,* 250–52; and Philip White, *The Beekmans of New York in Politics and Commerce, 1647–1877* (New York, 1956), 271n, 297–98, 384–85, 281, 298, 401–2.

24. John van Cortlandt to David Purviance (of Martinique), Dec. 15, 1752, Van Cortlandt Letter Book, NYPL; Wilson, *Anglo-Dutch Commerce,* ch. 1; Waddell Cunningham to Thomas Greg, Dec. 11, 1756; Greg and Cunningham to William Snell and Co. (of London), June 4, 1756, Waddell Cunningham Letter Book; Barrow, *Trade and Empire,* 151–52; Joshua Gee to Council of Trade and Plantations, Oct. 27, 1721, in *State Papers,* 1721, 32: 470–75, esp. 474; MacPherson, *Annals,* 3: 164–66; Francis Lewis Correspondence, 1751–86; Hugh Wallace, Letters; John Alsop Correspondence, 1733–94; Charles Nicoll, Account Books; Walter and Samuel Franklin Correspondence; all at the NYHS.

25. John Ludlow to Moses Franks, Dec. 24, 1756, Ludlow Letter Book; Philip Cuyler to John Hodshon, Jan. 17, 1758, to his father, Dec. 3, 1759, Cuyler, Letter Book; Lt. Gov. De Lancey to the Board of Trade, Jan. 5, 1758, C.O. 5: 1068, fols. 160–62. The return voyages from Amsterdam usually involved one of five Dutch firms: those of Thomas and Adrian Hope, who would fund American patriots in the future; John Hodshon, whose ties to London banking and government loans were well known by the 1740s; Daniel Crommelin, long a familiar liaison to New Yorkers; William van der Grift; and William van Nuys. Logwood was not all that went to Amsterdam; the Robert Sanders Voyage Book, 1748–56, shows voyages to John and William van der Grift, with Robert and Richard Ray of New York, with sugar. The *Mary and Margaret,* outfitted by about sixteen New Yorkers, entered the city with Dutch gunpowder and rounded St. Eustatius to pick up sugar, which was taken direct to Amsterdam; in 1760, the *Venus* landed at Sandy Hook without stopping for inspection by tide waiters, carrying tea and "Dutch ducks and checks" (Barrow, *Trade and Empire,* 149–50). Also on tea, see John Sherburne (of Portsmouth) to John Reynell, Mar. 15, 1760, Coates-Reynell Papers, box 11, Historical Society of Pennsylvania; Pares, *Yankees and Creoles,* 148–49; Gerard G. Beekman to Adam Schoales, Sept. 9, 1760, in *Beekman Mercantile Papers,* ed. White, 1: 366; Cornelius Cuyler, Letter Book, 1752–64, AAS; Abraham Yates, Papers, box 1, 1760, NYPL; Lt. Gov. De Lancey to the Board of Trade, Jan. 5, 1758, in C.O. 5: 1068, fols. 160–62; Edmund and Josiah Quincy (of Boston) to Capt. Sinclair, Apr. 10, 1745, in C. O. 323: 13, fols. 179–80.

26. Gov. George Clinton to the Board of Trade, Oct. 4, 1752, in C.O. 5: 1064, fols.

144–47; Cadwallader Colden to his son, 1759, in *The Colden Letters on Smith's History, 1759–1760*, NYHS, *Collections*, vol. 1 (New York, 1868), 183–84; "Colden to the Lords of Trade," 1763, in *Docs. Rel.*, 7: 499; John Ludlow to Daniel Crommelin, and to Moses Franks, July 12, 18, 1757, Ludlow Letter Book; *Public Advertiser* (London), Jan. 26, 1775; *Address of the People of Great Britain to the Inhabitants of America* (London, 1775), 5; and John Alsop Correspondence, 1733–74, NYHS.

27. Loudoun is cited in *Military Affairs in North America, 1748–1765*, ed. Stanley Pargellis (New York, 1936), 376; Gov. Hardy to the Board of Trade, July 15, 1757, in C.O. 5: 1068, Mm 13; testimony of William Kelly, Feb. 11, 1766, British Museum, Additional MS 33030; De Lancey to the Board of Trade, Jan. 5, 1758, in C.O. 1068, fols. 160–62; Pownall, *Administration of the American Colonies*, 192, 195. For embargoes, see *Docs. Rel.*, 7: 162, 215, 346, 356; 8: 255; *Cal. Council Mins.*, Dec. 29, 1756, 431; July 9, 1757, 434; May 17, 1758, 439; and *New-York Mercury*, June 27, 1757. The Flour Act is at 30 Geo. 2, c. 9.

28. Smith, *History*, 2: 261–76, 287, 292–93, 303–5; statement of Lt. Gov. De Lancey, Jan. 5, 1758, in C.O. 5: 1068, Mm 42; also, id., C.O. 5: 1068, Mm 11, 15; Philip Livingston to Philip Cuyler and Walter Livingston, Livingston Business Letters; Records of the *Charming Polly, Gregg, Sharp, Penguin, Fair Lady*, and *Catharine*, summarized in *Reports of Cases Determined by the High Court of Admiralty and Upon Appeal Therefrom*, ed. Reginald G. Marsden (London, 1885), 223–25; Cadwallader Colden's report to Pitt, Oct. 27, 1760, in C.O. 5: 19; and *Council Journal*, Dec. 20, 1760. Smuggling into England diminished during the war, probably because of the heightened dangers at sea and universally higher prices in Europe, although House of Commons committees insisted, as they had in the 1740s, that the decline was due to reduced duties in English ports; see W. A. Cole, "Trends in Eighteenth-Century Smuggling," *Economic History Review* 10 (1958): 402–8, and MacPherson, *Annals*, 3: 583. French sugar imported into New York was estimated to be worth about £9,000 in 1755 and rose to about £40,000 in 1760, constituting fully two-thirds of New York's reexports to the mother country.

29. *New-York Gazette*, 1756–58; John J. McCusker, "The Current Value of English Exports, 1697–1800," *William and Mary Quarterly*, 3d ser., 28 (1971): 607–28, table 3; Egnal, "Economic Development," 191–222; A. H. Cole, *Wholesale Commodity Prices in the United States* (Cambridge, Mass., 1938), 117; MacPherson, *Annals*, 3: 373, 524n.; John Watts to Gedney Clarke, Aug. 23, 1762, in *WLB*, 78–79; John van Cortlandt to [?], Mar. 19, May 5, 1764, Van Cortlandt Letterbook.

30. Trade of Garret van Horne, Robert Crommelin, and Richard and Cornelius Ray, in C.O. 5: 1227–28; *Calendar of Historical Manuscripts in the Office of the Secretary of State, Albany*, ed. E. B. O'Callaghan, 2 vols. (Albany, N.Y., 1866), 2: 679, 692, 735; C.O. 3: 51–63; and Stokes, *Iconography* 4: 395, 453, 462, 468, 598.

31. Gerard Beekman to William Beekman, June 14, 1760, to Solomon Townshend, July 14, 1760, in *Beekman Mercantile Papers*, ed. White, 1: 285–86; *Calendar of Historical Manuscripts*, ed. O'Callaghan, 2: 679, 692, 735; Waddell Cunningham to Leggs, Hyde, & Co., Dec. 31, 1757, Gregg and Cunningham Letter Book, NYHS; John van Cortlandt to Robert Tucker, Oct. 3, 1762, July 11, 1765, Mar. 20, 1766, to Christopher Jacobson, Nov. 21, 1763, Van Cortlandt Letter Book; Cole, *Wholesale Prices*, 14–16, 31–70; Evert Wendell, Account Book, entries for the 1760s; Philip Cuyler, Letter Book, letters for 1755–59.

32. Smith, *History*, 2: 287; Richard Sanders to Moses Franks, Nov. 7, 1755, to John

Wendell, Nov. 11, 1755, Sanders Letter Book; and letters of Aaron Lopez of Rhode Island, in *Commerce of Rhode Island*, vol. 9

33. Gerard Beekman to William Beekman, June 14, 1760, in *Beekman Mercantile Papers*, ed. White, 1: 285–86; John van Cortlandt to Robert Tucker, Oct. 3, 1762, July 11, 1765, Mar. 20, 1766, Van Cortlandt Letter Book; Evert Wendell, Account Book, 1760s.

34. John Ludlow to Moses Franks, July 1, 1755, Dec. 24, 1756, Ludlow Letter Book, 1752–63; Philip Cuyler to Richards and Coddington, Jan. 14, May 13, 1760, Cuyler, Letter Book. For logwood trade later, see Stevens, *Records*, Oct. 3, 1769, 57–58; and Elmus Wicker, "Colonial Monetary Standards Contrasted: Evidence from the Seven Years' War," *Journal of Economic History* 45 (Dec. 1985): 869–84.

35. Carl Bridenbaugh, *Cities in Revolt: Urban Life in America, 1743–1776* (New York, 1955), 5, 39, 216; Evarts B. Greene and Virginia D. Harrington, *American Population before the Federal Census of 1790* (1932; repr., Gloucester, Mass., 1966), 95–103; James G. Wilson, *Memorial History of the City of New York*, 4 vols. (New York, 1893), 2: 466–68, 472–73; Stokes, *Iconography*, 4: 688–93, 703.

36. *New-York Mercury*, Aug. 7, 1758; Dec. 24, 31, 1753; *New-York Post-Boy*, Sept. 18, 1766, Jan. 18, 1768; Joshua Delaplain Papers, NYHS; John Pryor Ledger, 1759–68; and Pryor Day Book, 1762–67, NYHS; *Docs. Rel.*, 7: 825–26, 845–46, 849–50; Peter R. Livingston to Philip Schuyler, New York, Feb. 27, 1769, in Schuyler Papers, NYPL; Robert Livingston Jr. to William Alexander, Mar. 26, 1753, William Alexander Papers, vol. 1. For the comparison to Byzantium, see F. J. Hinkhouse, *Preliminaries of the American Revolution as Seen in the English Press, 1763–1775* (New York, 1926), 107.

37. Nash, *Urban Crucible*, 9, 257. In addition to these four, Paul Richards, William Walton, Oliver De Lancey, John Wetherhead, William Axtell, and William Alexander may have accumulated large fortunes, although their incomes cannot be ascertained; see their private account books and letters.

38. Harrington, *New York Merchant*, 16–17, 313. Henry White, who had married into the Van Cortlandt family by the late 1740s, was a diversified merchant who exported bread and flour to South Carolina and the West Indies, imported an array of English goods, and owned at least three large vessels; in 1773 he served as one of the British tea consignees. Hugh Wallace married into the Low family and was a linen factor for Irish merchants and a vendue master from the 1750s to 1776. Similar rises were enjoyed by the four Buchanans in commerce and by Peter Curtenius and two Goelet brothers, who privateered and imported hardware and ironware.

39. Smith, *History*, 1: 284, and *Military Affairs in North America, 1748–1765*, ed. Stanley Pargellis (New York, 1936), 376.

40. Gabriel Ludlow Account Books; *The Lloyd Family Papers*, NYHS, *Collections*, vol. 60; C.O 5: 1226–28; Marsden, *Admiralty Cases*, 30–46; Philip Cuyler to John Hodshon, 17 Jan. 1758, and to his father, 3 Dec. 1759, Cuyler, Letter Book; Barrow, *Trade and Empire*, 149–50; John Sherburne (of Portsmouth) to John Reynell, 15 Mar. 1760, Coates-Reynell Papers, box 11; Pares, *Yankees and Creoles*, 148–49; Gerard G. Beekman to Adam Schoales, 9 Sept. 1760, *Beekman Mercantile Papers*, ed. White, 1: 366; Yates Papers, box 1, 1760; and David van der Heyden Papers, Invoice Book, NYHS. Hints of similar activities can be found in correspondence of Samuel Townsend, John Tiebout, John Watts, and David Provoost. Interesting remarks about risks are to be found in Geoffrey L. Rossano, "Down to the Bay: New York Shippers and the Central American Logwood Trade, 1748–1761,"

New York History 70 (July 1989): 243–46;; correspondence of Samuel and Walter Franklin, Thomas Buchanan, and John and Henry Cruger; and *New-York Gazette*, Oct. 21, 1765.

41. For general observations, see Cadwallader Colden to Jeffrey Amherst, May 22, 1762, in *Colden Letters on Smith's History*, 209. On Lynch, see John Tabor Kempe to Gen. Monckton, Nov. 3, 1762, in *The Aspinwall Papers*, Massachusetts Historical Society, *Collections*, 4th ser., vols. 9–10 (Boston, 1871–72), 9: 470–73; Cadwallader Colden to William Pitt, Oct. 27, 1760; and to Jeffrey Amherst, Apr. 23, 1762, in *Colden*, 50: 195–96, 312–13. On Watts, see John Watts to Lt. Col. Isaac Barre, Feb. 28, 1762, in *WLB*, 24–27.

42. On methods of secreting goods, see Philip Cuyler to Nicholas Lechmere, Aug. 19, 1760; to Richards & Coddington, Dec. 3, 1760, Cuyler, Letter Book. Other prominent merchants who engaged in West Indies smuggling included William Bayard, Philip Cuyler, Gerard and William Beekman, Isaac Gouverneur, Nicholas Roosevelt, John Ludlow, and Robert Sanders. Slave traders included Jasper Farmer, Nathaniel Marston, Paul and Thomas Miller, Thomas Greenall, and David Griffiths. Neutral Dutch St. Eustatius received large amounts of flour and bread from New York via Antigua or the Leeward Islands. The Danish Virgin Islands charged an import duty of 25 percent until 1773, but New Yorkers nonetheless traded there occasionally, buying brandy and gin.

43. Wilson, *Memorial History*, 2: 467; correspondence of Abraham de Peyster, William Walton, Walter Franklin, Gabriel Ludlow, Walter Livingston, Cornelius van Horne, Nathaniel Marston, Isaac Roosevelt, John Cruger, David Clarkson, William Wallace, and William White; Stokes, *Iconography*, 4: 683, 863; and Osgood, *Mins. Common Council*, 5: 188–19, 357; 7: 25–26, 287–88.

44. John Watts to Gedney Clark, Feb. 18, 1764, in *WLB*, 233; L. H. Gipson, "A View of the Thirteen Colonies at the Close of the Great War for Empire, 1763," *New York History* 40 (1959): 327–57. Records of these activities are scattered in the papers of late-colonial writers; they are in direct conflict with the arguments made by imperial writers who chose to keep the West Indian sugar islands and to give up the frontier west following the Seven Years' War.

45. "Governor Moore to the Lords of Trade," Jan. 12, 1767, in *Docs. Rel.*, 7: 888–89.

46. See, e.g., Stevens, *Records*, 21, 30; Harrington, *New York Merchant*, 165–171; *Colonial Laws*, 4: 1021, 1096; 5: 833. For Hume, see "Of the Jealousy of Trade," 1758, in *David Hume: Writings on Economics*, ed. Eugene Rotwein (Madison, Wis., 1955), 78–82.

47. "Report of Governor Tryon on the Province of New York," June 1, 1774, in *Docs. Rel.*, 8: 466–49; C.O. 5: 1227–28; Cathy Matson, "'Damn'd Scoundrels' and 'Libertism of Trade': Freedom and Regulation in Colonial New York's Fur and Grain Trades," *William and Mary Quarterly*, 3d ser., 51 (July 1994): 389–418. On home manufactures, see also ch. 7 above.

48. Cadwallader Colden to William Pitt, Dec. 27, 1760, in *Colden*, 51: 52; and "P," *Providence Gazette*, Jan. 14, 21, 1761.

49. Colden to Pitt, Dec. 27, 1760, in *Colden*, 51: 52; Pitt's Aug. 23, 1760, speech to the House of Commons is reprinted in *Quincy's Massachusetts Bay Reports*, ed. Harrison Gray (Boston, 1865), 407–10. See also Barrow, *Trade and Empire*, 163; Cadwallader Colden to Sir Jeffrey Amherst, Apr. 23, 1762, in *Colden*, 55: 195–96; and C.O. 5: 848–51.

50. Smith, *History*, 2: 287.

51. *An Account of the Value of Exports . . . to the North American Colonies from Xmas*

1739 to Xmas 1761, orig. in Earl of Shelburne Papers, 3: 22, Clements Library, photocopy in NYPL.

52. Gen. Jeffrey Amherst to Cadwallader Colden, Aug. 2, 9, 16, 1761, in *Colden*, 55: 62, 64, 66.

53. Gov. Thomas Fitch to Cadwallader Colden, Aug. 14, 1761, in ibid., 66: 166–68.

54. Gen. Jeffrey Amherst to Cadwallader Colden, Apr. 16, 1762, in ibid., 66: 137–40.

55. Amherst to Colden, May 6, 1762, in ibid., 66: 161–63; C.O. 5: 1226–28; "Lt.-Gov. Colden to the Lords of Trade," Dec. 7, 1763, in *Docs. Rel.*, 7: 584; Gerard Beekman letters, in *Beekman Mercantile Papers*, ed. White, 1: 465–66, 472. Five or six vessels made their way to Amsterdam and Rotterdam by the end of 1764; whether two or three of these paid duties or smuggled through English ports, or the vessels were sold, is unclear because there is no further record of them; three returned from Amsterdam to Rhode Island with dutiable goods. Forty-one more vessels cleared for the West Indies that year than entered from that area; although some smuggled molasses and sugar through New England and Long Island and a few re-routed legally via southern Europe, at least three, and perhaps six, of them went direct to Amsterdam.

56. Stokes, *Iconography*, 5: 725, citing the pledge of May 26, 1762.

57. Jeffery Amherst to Peter Randolph, Apr. 24, 1762; Amherst to Cadwallader Colden, Apr. 16, May 6, 1762, in *Colden*, 55: 151–52, 137–40, 161–63; Colden to Lord Egremont, May 1763, and Colden to Lord Dartmouth, Nov. 2, 1774, in *Colden Letter Books*, 9: 230; 10: 371; [Anon.], *An Essay on the Trade of the Northern Colonies* (London, 1764), 10, 22, 24–25; "A Few Thoughts on the Method of Improving and Securing the Advantages which accrue to Great Britain from the Northern Colonies," *New-York Mercury*, Aug. 27, 1764.

58. John Watts to Gov. Clarke, Jan. 2, 1762, in *WLB*, 6.

59. John Watts to Thomas Pennington & Son, May 24, 1762; to Scott, Pringle & Cheap, June 20, 1762, in *WLB*, 60, 62–63.

60. Appendix A, table 1, shows the rise in imports by values recorded per year; *New-York Gazette*, Feb. 2, 1764; Philip Cuyler to his father, Dec. 11, 1758, Dec. 17, 1759, Cuyler, Letter Book; *New-York Mercury*, May 1, Oct. 21, 1762; *WLB*, 5, 8–9, 33, 45, 48, 65, 68, 80, 87, 94, 104, 109. London's exports of dry goods to New York City remained high through the 1760s except for the years of nonimportation, and northern colonists as a whole took as much as two-fifths of England's textile exports; see James F. Shepherd and Gary Walton, *Shipping, Maritime Trade, and the Economic Development of Colonial America* (Cambridge, 1972), 167. On falling West Indies prices, see John Watts to various correspondents, 88–89, 91–92, 157, 180, 229, 231, *WLB*; and the *Newport Mercury*, Oct. 19, 1762, Feb. 4, 1763.

61. On rising English prices, see, e.g., John Ludlow, Account Book and Letters, 1752–63. On agricultural prices, see the correspondence of Cornelius Ray, Philip Livingston, and William Alexander.

62. On exportation, see Gerard Beekman to William Davis, Jan. 30, June 14, 1760, to Alexander White, Aug. 20, 1760, in *Beekman Mercantile Papers*, ed. White, 285–86; and testimony of William Kelly, Feb. 11, 1766, British Museum, Additional MS 33030. On logwood, see John Watts to Isaac Barre, Feb. 28, 1762, in *WLB*, 24–27; and C.O. 3: 51–63.

63. Quoted in Marc Egnal and Joseph Ernst, "An Economic Interpretation of the

American Revolution," *William and Mary Quarterly,* 3d ser., 29 (1972): 17; and Harrington, *New York Merchant,* 316–24.

64. John Watts to Scott, Pringle, Cheap & Co., Feb. 5, 1764, to Gedney Clark, July 17, 1765, to Thomas Astin, Apr. 10, 1762, to Colborn Barrell, May 10, 1762, in *WLB,* 228, 359, 40, 46; William Douglass to William Bayard, Apr. 3, 1765, Bayard-Campbell-Pearsall Collection, NYPL. For bankruptcies, see Philip Cuyler to Henry Cuyler, Dec. 3, 1759, to his father, Oct. 5, 1760, Cuyler, Letter Book; William Alexander, Papers, vol. 3, fol. 26; *New-York Mercury,* May 1, Oct. 21, 1762, Feb. 27, 1764; John van Cortlandt to Roscoe Sweeney, Oct. 9, 1762, Van Cortlandt Letter Book; Harrington, *New York Merchant,* 333–41.

65. John van Cortlandt to [?], Dec. 1763, Van Cortlandt Letter Book; letter to a London merchant firm, Nov. 1764, Charles Thomson, Letters, NYHS.

66. Grant, *Memoirs of an American Lady,* 2: 244.

67. John van Cortlandt to Abraham Maer, Mar. 19, 23, 1764, to William Smith, Feb. 16, 1764, and to John Riddlehurst, Feb. 15, 1764, Van Cortlandt Letter Book; John Watts to Moses Franks, July 23, 1763, to Gen. Monckton, July 23, 1763, to Scott, Pringle, Cheap & Co., Jan. 13, 1764, and to William Allen, Feb. 14, 1764, in *WLB,* 157, 158, 214–15, 229–31; James Watts to Gen. Robert Monckton, Feb. 23, 1767, and Oct. 30, 1763, in *Aspinwall Papers,* 10: 597, 449–50. See also Benjamin Franklin, "The Interest of Great Britain Considered" (1760), in *The Papers of Benjamin Franklin,* ed. Leonard W. Labaree et al., 25 vols. to date (New Haven, Conn., 1959–), 9: 47–49, esp. 58; Dr. John Mitchell, *The Present State of Great Britain and North America* (London, 1767), 280; and [Arthur Young], *American Husbandry,* 2 vols. (London, 1775), 2: 124–26.

68. David van Horne to Nicholas Brown & Co., Aug. 18, 1765, Brown Papers, as cited by William Sachs, "The Business Outlook in the Northern Colonies, 1750–1775" (Ph.D. diss., Columbia University, 1957), 137; *New-York Mercury,* Apr. 9, 1764; John Macomb to Sir William Johnson, Apr. 14, 1765, William Darlington to Sir William Johnson, Apr. 15, 1765, in *Sir William Johnson Papers,* 11: 690–91, 695–96. The last quotation is anonymous, July 30, 1765, Upcott Collection, 2 vols., NYHS, 2: 289. For later reflections, see Thomas Gage to Lord Hillsborough, Dec. 10, 1770, Jan. 1771, in *Correspondence of General Thomas Gage, 1763–1775,* ed. Clarence E. Carter, 2 vols. (New Haven, Conn., 1931–33), 1: 287, 289.

69. T. S. Ashton, *An Economic History of England: The Eighteenth Century* (London, 1955), 176–77.

70. Watts to Gen. Monckton, in *Aspinwall Papers,* 10: 506; James Shepherd and Gary Walton, "The Coastal Trade of the British North American Colonies, 1768–1772," *Journal of Economic History* 32 (1972): 783–810, esp. 800–804; and Walton, "New Evidence on Colonial Commerce," *Journal of Economic History* 28 (1968): 363–89.

71. Thomas Gage to William Barrington, Oct. 7, 1769, in *Correspondence of General Thomas Gage,* ed. Carter, 2: 527; *AJ,* 2: 741; *Docs. Rel.,* 7: 548, 710; Charles M. Andrews, *The Colonial Period of American History,* 4 vols. (New Haven, Conn., 1938), 4: 419–28. The five vendue masters in the 1760s were More & Lynsen Co., Patrick McDavitt, Daniel McCormick, a Mr. Hoffman, a Mr. Ludlow, and David Clarkson. For evidence of French agents, see Harrington, *New York Merchant,* 292–303.

72. *New-York Gazette,* Aug. 27, Oct. 1, Dec. 3, 10, 24, 1764, Jan. 3, 1765; John van Cortlandt to John Hoffman, May 16, Sept. 2, 1764, and to Robert Tucker, July 11, 1765, Van Cortlandt Letters; *New-York Mercury,* Jan. 13, 1766; *Connecticut Courant,* Feb. 17, 1766. See

also *New-York Gazette, or Weekly Post-Boy*, Nov. 22, 1764, Apr. 4, 11, May 2, 30, July 25, Aug. 1, Sept. 5, 12, Oct. 3, Dec. 27, 1765; and *AJ*, Apr. 20, 1764, 2: 740–44, Oct. 18, 1764, 2: 769–79.

73. *Colden Letter Books*, 9: 27, 51, 195; Stoker, *Prices*, 201–3, 215–16; and letters of John Ludlow, Evert Bancker, and Walter Livingston, NYHS.

74. Optimism is at *New-York Mercury*, Jan. 23, 1764; dismay is at John Watts to Thomas Pennington & Son, May 24, 1762; to Scott Pringle & Cheap, June 20, 1762, in *WLB*, 60, 62–63.

75. Grenville is quoted by Carl Becker, *The History of Political Parties in the Province of New York, 1760–1776* (1909; repr., New York, 1968), 23.

76. "Impartiality," *Impartial Observations to be Considered on by the King, his Ministers, and the People of Great Britain*, Mar. 25, 1763, cited in MacPherson, *Annals*, 3: 495. The author also makes the following calculations of imports into England: £1,763,200 from all northern colonies; £2,385,700 from British West Indies; £200,500 from French Canadian conquests; £4,485,633 from French colonies in the Caribbean.

77. *Boston Evening Post*, Nov. 21, 1763, cited by Arthur Schlesinger, *The Colonial Merchants and the American Revolution, 1763–1776* (New York, 1918), 45.

78. *New-York Gazette*, May 19, 1760; George Spenser to Jeffrey Amherst, Nov. 29, Dec. 17, 1760, in *State Papers*, 1760, 73: 95; Cadwallader Colden to the earl of Egremont, Sept. 14, 1763, in *Colden*, 56: 231.

79. MacPherson, *Annals*, 3: 533–34; Sheridan, "Credit Crisis of 1772," 161–63.

80. John Oldmixon, *The British Empire in America*, 2 vols. (London, 1708). See also Bishop George Berkeley, "Empire for Liberty," in *Complete Works*, 4 vols. (Oxford, 1901), 4: 321–38.

81. Hutchinson is cited in Caroline Robbins, *The Eighteenth Century Commonwealthmen: Studies in the Transmission, Development and Circumstances of English Liberal Thought from the Restoration of Charles II Until the War with the Thirteen Colonies* (Cambridge, Mass., 1959), 185–95.

82. Hume, "Of the Jealousy of Trade" (1758), in *Writings on Economics*, ed. Rotwein, 78–82; Duncan Forbes, "Skeptical Whiggism, Commerce, and Liberty," in *Essays on Adam Smith*, ed. Andrew S. Skinner and T. Wilson (New York, 1976), 194–201; Matthew Decker, *Essay on the Decline of Trade* (London, 1751), 176; and Israel Mauduit, *Some Thoughts on the Methods of Improving and Securing the Advantages which Accrue to Great-Britain* (London, 1765), 18.

83. Lucy Sutherland, *Politics and Finance in the Eighteenth Century* (London, 1984), 312–14. See also Benjamin Franklin, *The Interest of Great Britain Considered* (London, 1760); and citations of Lord Shelburne's speech on consumption in Dec. 1762, in J. H. Parry, *Trade and Dominion: The European Overseas Empires in the Eighteenth Century* (New York, 1971), 128.

84. Pownall, *Administration of the American Colonies*, 1; see also 5, 285. The language is virtually identical to that of Malachy Postlethwayt's *Great Britain's Commercial Interest Explained and Improved* (London, 1759), 482–83, and it was present much earlier, as in, e.g., *State Papers*, 1719–20, 31: 73; *Docs. Rel.*, 5: 593–630; Joshua Gee, *The Trade and Navigation of Great Britain, considered*, 3d ed., 2 vols. (London, 1731), 1: 5–9, 44–45, 164–66; William Wood, *A Survey of Trade* (London, 1718), 155; and [Anon.], *The Irregular and Disorderly State of the Plantation-Trade* (1731), repr. in *Annual Report of the American Historical Association for the Year 1892* (Washington, D.C., 1893), 36–44. By 1764, some

English writers were also concerned about the home country's reliance on grain imports; see Phyllis Deane and W. A. Cole, *British Economic Growth, 1688–1959: Trends and Structure* (Cambridge, 1962), ch. 1; and Jacob Price, "Economic Function and the Growth of American Port Towns in the Eighteenth Century," *Perspectives in American History* 8 (1974): 151–80; and William Lux, Feb. 20, 1766, Lux Letter Book. The total number of vessels, cargo tonnage, and value of goods cleared for England did not rise significantly in the final colonial years, but the value of grain and flour rose to about two-thirds of New York's exports to the mother country. Also of concern to English policy makers was whether the proper balance of agricultural output, wages of labor, and urbanization was being met by England's own domestic economy; see Deane and Cole, *British Economic Growth*, 78–95, 106–22; Brinley Thomas, "The Rhythm of Growth in the Atlantic Economy of the Eighteenth Century," *Research in Economic History*, ed. Paul Uselding, 3 (1978): 29–30, 84–86; Larry Neal, "Interpreting Power and Profit in Economic History: The Causes of the Seven Years' War," *Journal of Economic History* 37 (Mar. 1977): 20–35; and A. H. John, "War and the English Economy, 1700–1763," *Economic History Review*, 2d ser., 7 (Apr. 1965): 329–44.

85. 4 Geo. 3, c. 15; John van Cortlandt to John Riddlehurst, May 5, 1764, Van Cortlandt Letter Book. See also nn. 86–88.

86. *New-York Mercury*, Jan. 23, 1764.

87. See petition of merchants to the Assembly, Apr. 20, 1764, in *AJ*, 2: 740–44; memorial of New York City merchants to Lords of Trade, Mar. 8, 1764, in *Cal. Council Mins.*, 464, and *New-York Mercury*, Jan. 2, 1764.

88. John Watts to Gen. Robert Monckton, Dec. 29, 1763, in *Aspinwall Papers*, 10: 506. Ideological divisions based on economic behavior are not necessarily incompatible with the findings of scholars who write about political factionalism; see Edward Countryman, *A People in Revolution: The American Revolution and Political Society in New York, 1760–1790* (Baltimore, 1981); and Patricia Bonomi, *A Factious People: Politics and Society in Colonial New York* (New York, 1971).

89. MacPherson, *Annals*, 3: 395–99, 401, 567–68; 4 Geo. 3, c. 15. By this act, shipmasters were also required to post bond for all goods, whether or not they were enumerated.

90. John van Cortlandt to Abraham Maer, Nov. 10, 1763, to John Riddlehurst, Feb. 16, 1764, and to Isaac Youngblood, Nov. 10, 1763, Van Cortlandt Letter Book; *Colden Letter Books*, 10: 68.

91. "Lt.-Gov Colden to the Lords of Trade," Mar. 9, 1764, Dec. 6, 1765, *Docs. Rel.*, 7: 612, 799; testimony of William Kelly, Feb. 11, 1766, British Museum, Additional MS 33030; *Colden Letter Books*, 10: 77–88; *New-York Gazette*, Jan. 5, 30, Feb. 2, June 28, Aug. 27, Oct. 1, Dec. 3, 10, 24, 1764, Jan. 3, 1765; *New-York Mercury*, Jan. 2, 23, Mar. 5, Apr. 23, 1764; *AJ*, Apr. 20, 1764, 2: 740–44; Oct 18, 1764, 2: 769–79; John van Cortlandt to John Hoffman, May 16, Sept. 2, 1764, and to Robert Tucker, July 11, 1765, Van Cortlandt Letter Book.

92. 4 Geo. 3, c. 34; John Watts to Gen. Robert Monckton, Apr. 14, 1764, in *Aspinwall Papers*, 10: 520; Gerard Beekman to David Beekman, June 17, 1766, May 9, 1767, in *Beekman Mercantile Papers*, ed. White; William Lux to Molleson, Nov. 9, 1766, Lux Letter Book. See also *Docs. Rel.*, 7: 612, 820–21, 827–28, 843–45, 878, 884; Philip Livingston, Business Letters, 1758–69; *New-York Mercury*, Apr. 28, 1766; *AJ*, 2: 741–44; and MacPherson, *Annals*, 3: 398.

93. John van Cortlandt to Thomas Shipboy, June 18, 1767, to Evan Jones, Jan. 30, May

17, 1767, to John Hoffman, June 6, 1767, Feb. 24, 1768, and to Evan and Jones, Feb. 10, 1768, Van Cortlandt Letter Book; *New-York Mercury,* Apr. 25, 1768; *New York Journal,* Feb. 4, 1768. On London merchant opposition to the Currency Act, see Lucy Sutherland, "Edmund Burke and the First Rockingham Ministry," *English Historical Review* 47 (1932): 46–70.

94. *Colonial Laws,* 4: 801–4; John Watts to William Baker, Apr. 22, 1763, in *WLB,* 138; Lawrence H. Gipson, *The Triumphant Empire: Thunder Clouds Gather in the West, 1763–1766* (New York, 1961), 76–81.

95. Stevens, *Records,* 10, 18, 50, 84–85, 308; *AJ,* 2: 733–39; John Watts to Robert Monckton, Nov. 10, 1764, in *WLB,* 309–10; Wilson, *Memorial History,* 4: 321–22; "Governor Moore to the Board of Trade," Mar. 28, 1766, in *Docs. Rel.,* 7: 820–21; "Representation of the Lords of Trade on the Circulation of Bills of Credit," May 16, 1766, in ibid., 7: 827–28; "Lords of Trade to Governor Moore, July 11, 1766, in ibid., 7: 843–45.

96. *AJ,* 2: 739, 769–80. See also MacPherson, *Annals,* 3: 398; Cadwallader Colden to Robert Charles, June 8, 1764, in *Colden Letter Books,* 9: 301–02.

97. See John Watts to Moses Franks, June 9, 1764, to Gen. Monckton, Apr. 14, 16, June 30, 1764, in *WLB,* 263–64, 243, 245, 269–70.

98. Cadwallader Colden to Robert Charles, in *Colden Letter Books,* 9: 330–31; Philip Cuyler to John Mico, June 14, 1760, Cuyler, Letter Book; John Watts to Gen. Monckton, Sept. 23, 1765, in *WLB,* 385. For popular opposition to the Currency Act, see *New-York Gazette, or Weekly Post-Boy,* May 30, 1765; and "The News Boys's Verses," Jan. 1, 1767, *New York Journal, or General Advertiser,* supplement.

99. Statement of the Society of Arts, Agriculture, and Oeconomy, *New-York Gazette,* Dec. 3, 1764; also ibid., Dec. 10, 17, 1764, and issues of the paper through May 30, 1767; *New-York Mercury,* Dec. 3, 10, 17, 24, 1764; *New-York Gazette, or Weekly Post-Boy,* Dec. 27, 1764; *AJ,* 2: 744; *New York Journal,* Dec. 24, 31, 1767, Jan. 14, 21, June 14, 1768.

100. *New-York Gazette, or Weekly Post-Boy,* May 30, 1765.

101. "The New York Petition to the House of Commons," Oct. 18, 1764, repr. in *Prologue to Revolution: Sources and Documents on the Stamp Act Crisis, 1764–1766,* ed. Edmund S. Morgan (Chapel Hill, N.C., 1959), 8–14.

102. On factions, see Becker, *History of Political Parties,* ch. 2; Bonomi, *Factious People;* Dorothy R. Dillon, *The New York Triumvirate* (New York, 1949), 91–99. On the Stamp Act protests, see Edmund S. Morgan and Helen M. Morgan, *The Stamp Act Crisis* (New York, 1952); Becker, *History of Political Parties,* ch. 2; and Cadwallader Colden to Secretary Conway, 1765, in *Docs. Rel.,* 7: 759. For quotations, see John Watts to Robert Monckton, Nov. 7, 1765, in *WLB,* 404, and John van Cortlandt to John Hilton, Dec. 9, 1765, Van Cortlandt Letter Book. On the Stamp Act Congress, see Morgan and Morgan, *Stamp Act Crisis,* 142–43; *Docs. Rel.,* 5: 685, 738, 6: 116, 179; and *New-York Gazette,* Nov. 7, 1765.

103. *New-York Mercury,* Oct. 28, 1765, Jan 27, 1766; *New-York Gazette, or Weekly Post-Boy,* Oct. 31, Nov. 7, 1765, Feb. 13, Mar. 27, Apr. 10, 1766; *New-York Gazette,* Sept. 30, 1765, Jan. 2, 27, Feb. 3, Mar. 10, 17, 1766. In *Wealth of Nations,* bk. 4, ch. 7, Adam Smith makes interesting comments about the coincidence of politics and economics, with reference to the Stamp Act Congress and nonimportation. For merchant comments, see David Clarkson to Levinus Clarkson, Nov. 13, 1765, and to John Bennett of London, Dec. 28, 1766, in Clarkson Letters, NYHS.

104. *New York Journal,* Dec. 17, 24, 31, 1767, Jan. 14, 21, June 14, 1768; *Docs. Rel.,* 7: 548,

710; William Alexander, Papers, box 1, 1760–69; John van Cortlandt, Letters, 1762–69; [Anon.], *The Commercial Conduct of the Province of New York Consider'd and The True Interest of that Colony attempted to be Shewn In a Letter to The Society of Arts, Agriculture, and Economy* (New York, 1767), 6, 16; *Docs. Rel.,* 4: 346–47. Radicals wanted to continue city business illegally without stamps, a measure middling merchants countenanced more frequently than eminent ones. See Bernard Friedman, "The New York Assembly Elections of 1768 and 1769: The Disruption of Family Politics," *New York History* 46 (1965): 3–24; Sachs, "Business Outlook," 142–64, 170–72, 216–23; James Shepherd and Gary Walton, "Estimate of 'Invisible' Earnings in the Balance of Payments of the British North American Colonies, 1768–1772," *Journal of Economic History* 29 (1969): 230–63.

105. *New-York Gazette, or Weekly Post-Boy,* Nov. 7, 28, 1765; *New-York Mercury,* Oct. 28, 1765, Jan. 27, 1766; Frances Armytage, *The Free Port System in the British West Indies* (London, 1953), 35–42. The dry-goods merchants favoring limited nonimportation goals included Henry Cruger, William Hicks, Nicholas Roosevelt, John Watts, James De Lancey, Francis Filkin, George Brencoton, Dirk Brinkerhoff, John Bogert Jr., Cornelius Roosevelt, John Vanderspeigel, David van Horne, James Jauncey, Walter Rutherfurd, John Alsop, and William Livingston; see *New-York Gazette, or Weekly Post-Boy,* Nov. 28, 1765, and Becker, *History of Political Parties,* 32–38, 51. John Tyler, *Smugglers and Patriots: Boston Merchants and the Advent of the American Revolution* (Boston, 1986), concludes that nonimportation in Boston was almost exclusively the work of dry-goods merchants who had a stake in reducing stockpiles, while new entrants to trade and younger merchants in West Indies business had little reason to support the movement. Thomas Doerflinger, *A Vigorous Spirit of Enterprise: Merchants and Economic Development in Revolutionary Philadelphia* (Chapel Hill, N.C., 1986), finds that Philadelphia's wealthiest traders, most of them dry-goods importers, were not central to the nonimportation movement or other political opposition developing in 1769 and 1770, a finding closer to the case of New York.

106. *New-York Gazette, or Weekly Post-Boy,* Jan. 2, 9, 23, Feb. 27, Mar. 27, 1766; *New York Journal,* Dec. 17, 24, 31, 1767.

107. See *New-York Mercury,* Oct. 28, 1765, Jan. 27, 1766, Mar. 30, 1767; *New-York Gazette, or Weekly Post-Boy,* Oct. 31, Nov. 7, 1765, Feb. 13, Mar. 27, Apr. 10, 1766.

108. *New-York Gazette, or Weekly Post-Boy,* Feb. 2, 1764; Stokes, *Iconography,* 4: 690. The first nonimportation movement occasionally went further than merchants had intended, as when on May 10, 1766, rioters attacked the theater as a symbol of luxury and noncompliance with the movement (*New-York Gazette,* May 12, 1766).

109. *New-York Mercury,* Oct. 28, 1765; *New-York Gazette, or Weekly Post-Boy,* Nov. 7, 1765, Feb. 13, Mar. 27, Apr. 10, 1766; *New-York Gazette,* Mar. 10, 17, 1766.

110. John Watts to Gen. Robert Monckton, Dec. 30, 1765, in *Aspinwall Papers,* 10: 587; *New-York Gazette, or Weekly Post-Boy,* Jan. 2, 9, 23, Feb. 27, Mar. 27, 1766; *New-York Gazette,* Feb. 15, 1766; *New-York Mercury,* Apr. 28, 1766; Wilson, *Memorial History,* 2: 379.

111. British Museum Additional MSS 38339, fol. 166; 35430, fol. 31; and 33030, fols. 101, 243, 245, 247; "The Letters of Dennys de Berdt," in Colonial Society of Massachusetts, *Publications,* vol. 13 (Boston, 1910–11), 314, 315, 431.

112. Sutherland, "Edmund Burke and the First Rockingham Ministry," 46–70; Stokes, *Iconography,* 5: 980; "Governor Moore to the Lords of Trade," Mar. 28, Nov. 15, 1766, in *Docs. Rel.,* 7: 821, 878; *AJ,* June 17, 1766; John van Cortlandt to Robert Tucker, Mar. 20,

1766, and to William Hoffman, July 25, 1766, Van Cortlandt Letter Book, 1762–69. Frank Speck, among other historians, believes that William Pitt was an aggressive imperialist allied with London interests against the landed, rather than a free trader; by early 1766, Edmund Burke and the Rockingham Whigs favored repeal of Grenville's Stamp Act, and many colonists accepted this as a sign of Rockingham's moderation. See Speck, *Stability and Strife, England, 1714–1760* (Cambridge, Mass., 1977), ch. 12; Armytage, *Free Port System*, 24–25; and Isaac Kramnick, *The Rage of Edmund Burke: Portrait of An Ambivalent Conservative* (New York, 1977), 2–5, 10, 73, 99, 106–15.

113. David Clarkson to "My Dear Friend," Nov. 11, 1766; and to Thomas Streatfield, Feb. 6, 1768, Clarkson Letters; Gerard Beekman to David and William Ross, Newry, Ireland, May 2, 1766, in *Beekman Mercantile Papers*, ed. White, 1: 497

114. *New York Journal*, Dec. 24, 31, 1767, Jan. 14, 21, June 14, 1768; *Docs. Rel.*, 7: 548, 710; William Alexander, Papers, box 1, 1760–69; Van Cortlandt Letter Book, 1762–69.

115. "Governor Moore to the Lords of Trade," Jan. 12, May 7, 1767, and to Lord Hillsborough, May 7, 1767, in *Docs. Rel.*, 7: 888–89, 8: 66; David Clarkson to "My Dear Friend," Jan. 6, Mar. 15, 1766, Clarkson Letters; *New York Journal*, Dec. 24, 31, 1767, Jan. 14, 21, 1768; "Americus," *New-York Gazette, or Weekly Post-Boy,* June 28, 1764, May 30, Aug. 1, Sept. 12, 1765; also [Anon.], *Commercial Conduct*; New York Council to the Board of Trade, Nov. 7, 1766, in *Doc. Hist.*, 1: 732–33; and for Long Island, *London Chronicle*, 1764, pp. 413, 518.

116. E.g., Peter Hasenclever to Johnson, Jan. 6, 1768, in *Sir William Johnson Papers*, 10: 69; New York Council to the Board of Trade, Nov. 7, 1766, in *Doc. Hist.*, 1: 732–33. In "'Baubles of Britain': The American and Consumer Revolutions of the Eighteenth Century," *Past and Present* 119 (May 1988): 73–104, Timothy Breen argues that such nonimportation and nonconsumption discourse provided a shared basis for "the needs of a national consciousness." My analysis finds that the desire for new and more goods led to greater awareness of domestic productive capacity and recognition of economic interests; but New Yorkers rarely expressed their views on how these would translate into an intercolonial political community during the 1760s.

117. Andrews, *Colonial Period*, 4: 121; Pownall, *Administration of the American Colonies*, 192, 195; W. Sclote, *British Overseas Trade from 1700 to the 1930s*, trans. W. O. Henderson and W. H. Chaloner (Oxford, 1952); Ralph Davis, "English Foreign Trade, 1700–1774," *Economic History Review*, 2d ser., 15 (1962): 285–303.

118. See Appendix A, tables 1 and 2; Pownall, *Administration of the American Colonies*, 1, 5; Wood, *Survey of Trade*, 155; [Anon.], *Irregular and Disorderly State of the Plantation Trade*, 36–44.

119. Comptroller Weare, "Observations on the British Colonies on the Continent of America," Massachusetts Historical Society, *Collections*, 1st ser., vol. 1 (Boston, 1794), 74, 75, 79. Similar sentiments are at, e.g., "George Clarke to the Lords of Trade," June 2, 1738, in *Docs. Rel.*, 6: 116; "Governor Moore to the Lords of Trade," Jan. 12, 1767, in ibid., 7: 888; and "Cadwallader Colden to the Lords of Trade," Mar. 9, 1764, in ibid., 7: 612.

120. "Governor Moore to the Lords of Trade," Nov. 15, Dec. 19, 1766, in *Docs. Rel.*, 7: 878, 884; *AJ*, Nov. 13, 1766, Nov. 21, 1769, Jan. 27, 1770; *New York Journal*, Nov. 27, 1766, Feb. 20, 1768, Mar. 16, 1769; *New-York Mercury*, Feb. 22, 1768; David Clarkson to "My Dear Friend," Feb. 17, 1767, and to Pomery & Hodgkins, Feb. 24, 1768, Clarkson Letters. On the emissions, see Cadwallader Colden to Lord Hillsborough, Oct. 4, 1769, and Hillsborough to Colden, Nov. 4, Dec. 9, 1769, in *Docs. Rel.*, 8: 189, 190; Gov. Moore to Lord Shelburne,

in ibid., 7: 920–21; Nicholas Varga, "The New York Restraining Act: Its Passage and Some Effects, 1766–1768," *New York History* 37 (1956): 233–58; *New York Journal*, Aug. 16, Nov. 8, 1770; and Gov. Tryon to Board of Trade, in *Hist. Docs.*, 4: 767. The Assembly emitted £120,000 at 5 percent interest in 1768–69, and £120,000 in 1771, in both cases for fifteen years.

121. Clarkson to "My Dear Friend," Nov. 11, 1766, Clarkson Letters; *Docs. Rel.*, 7: 157, 167–68, 169–70, 8: 168–70, 193–96; *New York Journal*, Feb. 15, 1770; *Colonial Laws*, 2: 24–26; Stokes, *Iconography*, 4: 800–805.

122. *New-York Gazette*, Jan. 19, May 4, 1767; Cadwallader Colden to the earl of Shelburne, Nov. 1767, in *Colden Letter Books*, 10: 133–34; "Governor Moore to the Lords of Trade," Jan. 14, 1767, in *Docs. Rel.*, 7: 891; "A Tradesman of Philadelphia," *Pennsylvania Journal*, Aug. 17, 1774, cited by Schlesinger, *Colonial Merchants*, 44; Sheffield, *Observations*, 248; Morgan and Morgan, *Stamp Act Crisis*, 208–9, 215, 216. For the names, see letters of John van Cortlandt, John Watts, Francis Lewis, and Philip Cuyler of New York, and John Rowe of Boston.

123. Thomas Gage to Lord Shelburne, Apr. 28, 1767, in *Correspondence of General Thomas Gage*, ed. Carter, 1: 135–36; [Anon.], *The Regulations Lately Made Concerning the Colonies and the Taxes Imposed on Them Considered* (1765; repr., London, 1767), 92; C.O. 5: 1228; and Carole Shammas, "Consumer Behavior in Colonial America," *Social Science History* 6 (1982): 67–86.

124. "Governor Moore to the Earl of Shelburne," 1768, in *Docs. Rel.*, 8: 1; see also 13, 72, 96; *New York Journal*, Dec. 17, Nov. 19, 1767, Feb. 4, Aug. 4, May 19, June 31, 1768; *New-York Mercury*, Dec. 21, 1767, Jan. 18, 25, Feb. 1, 8, 1768; "The Committee appoint'd . . . to consider of the Expediency of entering into Measures to Promote Industry and Frugality," *New-York Mercury*, Jan. 18, 1768; and Victor Clark, *The History of Manufactures in the United States, 1607–1860*, 3 vols. (Washington, D.C., 1929), 1: 208.

125. *New York Journal*, Apr. 14; also Apr. 21, Nov. 12, 19, 26, Dec. 3, 10, 1768; John van Cortlandt to John Hoffman, Sept. 30, 1768, Van Cortlandt Letters. The initial committee consisted of Isaac Low, James Desbrosses, John Alsop, John Broome, William Neilson, Theodorus van Wyck, Walter Franklin, John Murray, Jacob Walton, Theophylact Bache, Thomas Franklin Jr., Samuel Verplanck, Isaac Sears, Peter Vandervoort, Thomas William Moore, Henry Remsen Jr., John Harris Cruger, John Thurman Jr., Thomas Walton, Peter T. Curtenius, Herbert Van Wagenen, Joseph Bull, Edward Laight, and Charles McEvers. All but three of these merchants were in the Chamber of Commerce (see below). Only Remsen, Sears, Curtenius, and Broome were patriots. Murray and Franklin were Quakers, and thus neutral, at the opening of the Revolution.

126. *New York Journal*, Sept. 8, 15, 1768.

127. "The Committee appointed by the Inhabitants of the City of New-York . . . to Encourage Frugality and Employ the Poor," Dec. 29, 1768; *The Committee Appointed by the Inhabitants . . . on Wednesday the 29th of December Last*, (New York, 1769); *New York Journal*, Sept. 15, 1768; *American Archives*, 4th ser., ed. Peter Force, *Containing a Documentary History of the English Colonies in North America*, 6 vols. (Washington, D.C., 1837–46), 3: 736, 1294, 1424–26, 4: 437, 1071–72, 1104; *New York Post-Boy*, Sept. 12, 1768; David Clarkson to Pomery & Hodgkins, June 2, 1768, and to John Bennet, Nov. 17, 1768, Clarkson Letters; [John Almon], *A Collection of Interesting, Authentic Papers, Relative to the Dispute between Great Britain and America: Shewing the Causes and Progress of the*

Misunderstanding, from 1764 to 1775 (London, 1777), 163–67; Edmund Burke, "A Short Account of a Late Short Administration," *Gentleman's Magazine* 36 (1766): 396.

128. Thomas Gage to Lord Shelburne, Jan. 23, to Lord Hillsborough, Sept. 26, and to Lord Barrington, May 13, Sept. 10, 1768, Feb. 4, 1769, in *Correspondence of General Thomas Gage*, ed. Carter, 2: 467–68, 487, 499, 1: 159–62, 196–97; MacPherson, *Annals*, 3: 339, 351, 365, 385, 410, 435, 456, 475, 486, 495; Wetherhead to Sir William Johnson, Sept. 15, 1769, in *Sir William Johnson Papers*, 7: 172–73.

129. On smugglers, see *New York Journal*, Nov. 9, 30, 1769, and *New-York Gazette, or Weekly Post-Boy*, Aug. 28, 1769. On the West Indies, see *Advertisement of Great Importance to the Public* (New York, 1769); *An Advertisement of Greater Importance to the Public . . . New York, July 20, 1769* (New York, 1769). For the quotations, see Thomas Gage to Lord Barrington, Dec. 2, 1769, and to Lord Hillsborough, Dec. 4, 1769, in *Correspondence of General Thomas Gage*, ed. Carter, 2: 530, 1: 241–42; Colden to Hillsborough, Oct. 4, 1769, in *Docs. Rel.*, 8: 189.

130. For the committee of enforcement, see *New York Journal*, Mar. 9, 16, 1769; July 5, 1770. See also the case of David Hill, a peddler who was denied the right to bring forbidden goods overland into New York City, took his case of "illegal restraint of trade" to court, and lost on the grounds of violating the public will as it was outlined in the nonimportation agreement (William Fowler Jr., "A Yankee Peddlar, Nonimportation, and the New York Merchants," NYHS *Quarterly* 56 [Apr. 1972], 147–54).

131. *New-York Gazette, or Weekly Post-Boy*, July 31, 1769; John Wetherhead to Sir William Johnson, June 26, 1769, and (after nonimportation) to id., Mar. 28, 1771, in *Sir William Johnson Papers*, 7: 44–45, 8: 48. See also *New-York Mercury*, July 2, 16, Aug. 20, Sept. 3, 1770; *New-York Gazette*, June 5, July 30, 1770. David Clarkson to John Bennett, June 4, 1770, Clarkson Letters, where he notes that the tea duty was still "a bone of contention" with tea importers; and "A Merchant," "The Times," Jan. 27, 1770, repr. in Evans Early American Imprints, no. 11881, which relates the concerns of the poor and war veterans to nonimportation.

132. See *Colden Letter Books*, 10: 153, 193; James Rivington to William Johnson, July 11, 1769, in *Sir William Johnson Papers*, 7: 57; "At This Alarming Crisis" (July 7, 1769), repr. in Evans Early American Imprints, no. 11379, on attempts to remobilize the city; "Brutus" (1770), repr. in James Bancker, *New York Broadsides, 1762–1779*, NYPL, *Bulletin* 1 (1897): 28, on "Mercantile Dons"; *New-York Gazette, or Weekly Post-Boy*, Apr. 10, 1769, and Becker, *History of Political Parties*, 80–86, on riots associated with sustaining the boycott; and *Providence Gazette*, June 23, 1770, on Vandervoort and Sears.

133. Alexander McDougall, *To the Betrayed Inhabitants of the City and Colony of New York* (1769), repr. in *Hist. Docs.*, 3: 317–21; Gage to Lord Barrington, Aug. 6, 1770, to Hillsborough, Dec. 4, 1769, and to Barrington, May 14, 1769, in *Correspondence of General Thomas Gage*, ed. Carter, 2: 550, 1: 241–42, 2: 510. "The Sons of what ever you chuse to call them" proposed to prevent English soldiers from working in "the flax Seed and flour Stores" in New York City, resulting in a riot, Norman MacLeod wrote Sir William Johnson on Jan. 27, 1770 (*Sir William Johnson Papers*, 12: 772–74).

134. *New York Journal*, Apr. 12, May 17, 1770.

135. *New-York Mercury*, Aug. 27, 1770.

136. *New-York Gazette and Weekly Mercury*, July 2, 23, Sept. 3, 1770; *New York Journal*, July 12, 19, 26, Aug. 2, 1770; William Kelly to Sir William Johnson, and Abraham Mortier

to Johnson, June 12, Dec, 11, 1770, in *Sir William Johnson Papers*, 7: 733–37, 971; Gage to Hillsborough, July 10, 1770, to Barrington, July 6, Aug. 6, 1770, in *Correspondence of General Thomas Gage*, ed. Carter, 1: 264, 546–47, 550; and *Docs. Rel.*, 8: 218–20. Samuel Wharton, "Observations on the Consumption of Tea in North America, 1773," *Pennsylvania Magazine of History and Biography* 25 (1901): 139–41, notes continued smuggling.

137. The Chamber of Commerce lowered the price of flour casks in August 1768. When millers and retailers balked, New York City merchants coordinated a pool of resources through Lewis Pintard and Anthony van Dam to buy from Philadelphia- and Boston-area farmers and millers, until the Hudson Valley millers gave in to the chamber's decree (Stevens, *Records*, 20–28). The chamber also passed resolutions on branding and quality control of potash, casks, flour, flaxseed, and the like (ibid., 8–46). The initial members were John Cruger, Elias Desbrosses, James Jauncey, Jacob Walton, Robert Murray, Hugh Wallace, George Folliott, William Walton, Samuel Verplanck, Theophylact Bache, Thomas White, Miles Sherbrooke, Walter Franklin, Robert R. Waddle, Acheson Thompson, Lawrence Kortright, Thomas Randall, William McAdam, Isaac Low, Anthony van Dam, John Alsop, Henry White, Philip Livingston, and James McEvers. Thirty more merchants joined in 1768, and twenty in 1769; see Stevens, *Records*, 3–8, 15–16, 54; and Charles King, *A History of the New York Chamber of Commerce* (New York, 1856), 49, 57–58. Support for fixed rates of currency exchange came from Robert C. Livingston, Charles McEvers, Isaac Low, and others. Support for the "intrinsick value" notion came from John Cruger, Isaac Sears, Isaac Roosevelt, John Hoffman, Gerard Beekman, Isaac Gouverneur, Leonard Lispenard, and others (Stevens, *Records*, 105–6). The intrinsic-value argument finally lost in 1772, but opposition to paper currency remained strong into the 1780s (King, *History*, 76–79). Only seven members of the chamber supported nonimportation in 1769–70, namely, Desbrosses, Alsop, Low, Kortright, McAdam, Franklin, and Cruger, all of whom exported flaxseed and grain to southern Europe and Ireland and imported English dry goods. Four of the five first Continental Congress representatives were in the chamber, although the majority opposed sending them (Stevens, *Records*, 105–8; *AJ*, 2: 759–86).

138. Stevens, *Records*, 77, 105–6, 108, 143, 152–53, 170–72, 161, 168, 187, 299–303, 393–95. John Thurman Jr., Thomas McAdam, Nicholas Hoffman, Daniel Phoenix, John Amiel, William Imlay, and Joseph Bull were among the lesser merchants. The resignations came from Jacob Watson, Isaac Roosevelt, James Beekman, Nicholas Hoffman, Daniel Phoenix, Gerard Beekman, Henry Remsen, Gerard Duyckinck, John Amiel, Herman Gouverneur, William Neilson, James Thurman, William Imlay, John Schuyler, Leonard Lispenard, Edward Laight, Hamilton Young, and John Cruger.

139. 13 Geo. 3, c. 44; Max Farrand, "The Taxation of Tea, 1767–1773," *American Historical Review* 3 (1898): 266–69; Joseph Reid, "Economic Burden: Spark to the American Revolution?" *Journal of Economic History* 38 (Mar. 1978): 81–100.

140. *The Alarm* (New York, 1773); "Governor Tryon to Lord Dartmouth," Nov. 3, 1773, Jan. 3, 1774, in *Docs. Rel.*, 8: 400, 407–8; and William Smith, *Historical Memoirs . . . of William Smith*, ed. Lorenzo Sabine (New York, 1958), 157–60.

141. C.O. 5: 133; *Rivington's New-York Gazetteer*, Apr. 28, 1774; Stokes, *Iconography*, 4: 841; *Docs. Rel.*, 8: 400–401; Becker, *History of Political Parties*, 104–5; and [Anon.], *To The Public* (June 20, 1774), repr. in Evans Early American Imprints, no. 13670.

142. [Anon.], *The Association of the Sons of Liberty of New-York* (New York, 1773).

143. *American Archives*, 4th ser., ed. Force, 3: 1263–64, 1424–26; merchants advocating nonconsumption included Alexander McDougall, Isaac Sears, Leonard Lispenard, John Alsop, Abraham Brasher, Theophilus Anthony, Francis van Dyck, Jeremiah Platt, and Christopher Duyckinck. See also Roger Champagne, "New York and the Intolerable Acts, 1774," NYHS *Quarterly* 45 (Apr. 1961): 195–207.

144. For city merchants' reactions to hardships, see letters of Henry White, Abraham van Horne, John and Isaac Roosevelt, and Anthony Bleecker; on economic conditions, see Egnal and Ernst, "Economic Interpretation," 17; MacPherson, *Annals*, 3: 572–73.

145. [Anon.], *Political Essays Concerning the Present State of the British Empire* (London, 1771); [Almon], *Collection of Interesting, Authentic Papers*, 54; *Commissioners of the Customs*, Massachusetts Historical Society, *Collections*, 7th ser. (1910); MacPherson, *Annals*, 3: 524, 533–34; John van Cortlandt to John Hoffman, Oct. 17, 1772, Van Cortlandt Letters; and the correspondence of the merchants Jacob van Zandt, Philip Livingston, Broom & Co., David van Horne, Samuel Franklin, and Henry Remsen, NYHS. The Murrays descended from Quakers who owned flour mills in Lancaster, Pennsylvania, during the 1730s and 1740s, then moved to North Carolina during the early 1750s, and finally to New York City, where they acquired ships and excelled in the West Indies trade; their insurance company was the largest in New York. For 1772, see Shepherd and Walton, "Coastal Trade," 783–810, esp. 800–804; Walton, "New Evidence"; Sheridan, "Credit Crisis of 1772," 161–81; Sheffield, *Observations*, 74, 96; and Richard Champion, *Considerations on the Present Situation of Great Britain and the United States of America* (London, 1784). Harrington, *New York Merchant*, 289–319, ignores the economic downturns after 1766. For observations about Philadelphia, see, e.g., Stoker, *Prices*, 201–3. Flaxseed provided a substitute commodity for only a few merchants, and never for the middling; see Isaac Sears' letters in *The Jacksons and the Lees*, ed. Kenneth Porter (Cambridge, Mass., 1937), 183–84, and Gerard Beekman to Bristol correspondents, 1764–67, in *Beekman Mercantile Papers*, ed. White, 469, 475, 477, 535–40, 562, 603–28. For New York's sterling debt to England in 1774, see Earl of Chatham, "List of Debts Due by Citizens of the United States of America to Merchants and Traders of Great Britain . . . to the Year 1776 with Interest to Jan. 1, 1790," cited by Edward Channing, *History of the United States*, 3 vols. (New York, 1912), 3: 247; and Alice Hanson Jones, "Wealth and Growth of the Thirteen Colonies: Some Implications," *Journal of Economic History* 44 (June 1984): 239–54. New York's share was probably about £175,095, less than 3 percent of the total American colonial debt, which helps explain why colonial merchants focused on their structural hardships rather than the mercantile relationship.

146. [Jonathan Boucher], *A Letter from a Virginian, To the Members of the Congress* (New York, 1774), repr. in Evans Early American Imprints, no. 13167; Smith, *Historical Memoirs*, ed. Sabine, 152–55, 156; Becker, *History of Political Parties*, 103–5; Rivington's *New-York Gazetteer*, Nov. 18, 1773.

147. *American Archives*, 4th ser., ed. Force, 2: 48, 144–48, 284; Smith, *Historical Memoirs*, ed. Sabine, 162. The De Lancey faction was by then a coherent grouping set apart from radical Whig merchants and the Sons of Liberty (Bonomi, *Factious People*, 275–80). Low, Livingston, and Walton also refused to serve on nonimportation enforcement committees and on the Committee of Correspondence formed in 1773.

148. Stevens, *Records*, supplement; *New York Journal*, Oct. 13, 1774. For the merchants on the Committee of 51, see Becker, *History of Political Parties*, 116. Of this list, Isaac Low,

James Jauncey, William and Abraham Walton, James De Lancey, John Alsop, William Alexander, William Wallace, Francis Lewis, John Aspinwall, and twenty-five others made up the majority of thirty-six that went to the De Lanceyites. For the Committee of 25, see *Docs. Rel.*, 8: 433; *American Archives*, 4th ser., ed. Force, 1: 258, 294–31, 342; Smith, *Historical Memoirs*, ed. Sabine, 186–89; and Becker, *History of Political Parties*, 113 n. 4, 127. The radicals who resigned from the Committee of 51 were Peter van Brugh Livingston, Francis Lewis, Joseph Hallet, Thomas Randall, Abraham Lott, John Broome, and Jacobus van Zandt, in addition to Sears, McDougall, Lispenard, and Brasher.

149. *Docs. Rel.*, 8: 433; *American Archives*, 4th ser., ed. Force, 1: 248; *A Serious Address to . . . New-York . . . [on] the Boston Port Act, Calculated to excite Our Inhabitants To Conspire, with the other Colonists on This Continent* (New York, 1774); *London Packet*, Apr. 14, 1775; Stokes, *Iconography*, 4: 874. The first Continental Congress delegates were Robert R. Livingston, John Cruger, Philip Livingston, William Bayard, and Leonard Lispenard, four of whom were merchants; the second Continental Congress delegates were John Alsop, Philip Livingston, Isaac Low, James Duane, and John Jay, three of whom were merchants; Low became a loyalist, and Alsop resigned in July 1776, leaving Philip Livingston as the sole merchant delegate from New York to the Congress.

150. The Association Agreement banned all purchase and sale of British, Irish, and foreign tea, molasses, coffee, wines, indigo, and slaves; none of the colonies' exports were to go to Britain, Ireland, or the British West Indies (Schlesinger, *Colonial Merchants*, app.). On the Committee of 60, see "Letter of the Committee of Sixty to the New Haven Committee," in *John Jay: Unpublished Papers, 1745–1780*, ed. Richard B. Morris, vol. 1 (New York, 1975), 1: 143; Becker, *History of Political Parties*, 168 nn. 34–36; *New-York Mercury*, Nov. 28, 1774. On the dry-goods merchants, see Thomas Gage to Dartmouth, July 20, Aug. 27, 1774, in *Correspondence of General Thomas Gage*, ed. Carter, 1: 361–62; Stokes, *Iconography*, 5: 871; *Public Advertiser* (London), Jan. 26, 1775; *Address of the People of Great Britain to the Inhabitants of America* (London, 1775), 5; and John Alsop Correspondence, 1733–94, NYHS.

151. On tea smugglers, see Lt. Gov. Colden to the earl of Dartmouth, May 4, 1774, in *American Archives*, 4th ser., ed. Force, 1: 249; Colden to Gov. Tryon, Dec. 7, 1774, in *Colden Letter Books*, 2: 375; and William Barrett, *The Merchants of Old New York*, 5 vols. (New York, 1886), 4: 279–80. The first Provincial Congress included, among others, the merchants Philip Livingston, Isaac Low, Francis Lewis, and Isaac Roosevelt; see *Journals of the Provincial Congress, Provincial Convention, Committee of Safety and Council of Safety of the State of New York*, 2 vols. (Albany, N.Y., 1842), 1: 92, 123, 136, 166.

152. Rev. Samuel Seabury, *The Congress Canvassed* (New York, 1774), 22; for the Jay quotation, see Gordon Wood, *The Creation of the American Republic, 1776–1787* (1969; repr., New York, 1972), 96; for Jay's involvement, see *John Jay . . . Papers*, ed. Morris 1: 162–64; "New York Provincial Congress to New York Delegates, Sept. 1, 1775," in ibid., 1: 165; and Jay to Alexander McDougall, Dec. 4, 1775, in ibid., 1: 188.

153. "Colden to the Earl of Dartmouth," Dec. 7, 1774, in *Docs. Rel.*, 8: 512. For violations, see *Rivington's New-York Gazetteer*, Jan. 19, 26, Apr. 6, 1775; *New York Journal*, Nov. 10, Dec. 15, 1774, Feb. 2, 9, 23, Mar. 9, 23, 30, Apr. 6, 13, 27, 1775; on flaxseed merchants, see *American Archives*, 4th ser., ed. Force, 3: 96, 529, 661–62; and for continued English trade, see ibid., 2: 242, 282–83, 636–37, 3: 445–47, 536–37, 558–59; and *Rivington's New-York Gazetteer*, Apr. 17, 24, 1775. On events in Congress, see Bernard Mason, "Robert R. Liv-

ingston and the Non Exportation Policy: Notes for a Speech in the Continental Congress, October 27, 1775," NYHS *Quarterly* 44 (1960): 296–307. Wheat (and tobacco) were exempt from the Association Agreement, but an English act forbade colonial exporters to send them to English possessions as of Mar. 1, 1776 (*The American Correspondence of a Bristol Merchant, 1766–1776: Letters of Richard Champion*, ed. G. H. Guttridge [New York, 1974], 25, 26, 27).

154. "Speech on Moving Resolutions for Conciliation with the Colonies, March 22, 1775," in *The Works of Edmund Burke*, 9 vols. (Boston, 1839), 6: 27, 50–51; and *Edmund Burke, New York Agent, with his Letters to the New York Assembly and Intimate Correspondence with Charles O'Hara, 1761–1776*, ed. Ross Hoffman (Philadelphia, 1956), esp. 99, 191.

155. On limiting the protest movement, see, e.g, Cadwallader Colden to the Assembly, *AJ*, 2: 673; John Ludlow to Daniel Crommelin, 1762–64, Ludlow Letter Book; Philip Cuyler to Richards and Coddington, 1764, Cuyler, Letter Book; Barrow, *Trade and Empire*, 143–44. On colonial subordination, see Peter Hasenclever to Johnson, Jan 6, 1768, in *Sir William Johnson Papers*, 10: 69; James Rivington to Johnson, July 11, 1769, in ibid., 7: 57; John Campbell, *Political Essays Concerning the Present State of the British Empire* (London, 1772), 327. Gov. Tryon to the Lords of Trade, 1774, in *Doc. Hist.*, 1: 759–61, emphasized the poor balance of trade between New York and the mother country, and underscored what so many merchants knew: that Bristol and Liverpool merchants were shifting their provisions and grain orders to Philadelphia. Nevertheless, 40 percent of what New Yorkers shipped to England after 1760 involved foodstuffs, and the value of wheat and flour exports grew from under 9,000 tons per year in the 1750s to 15,000 tons in 1772; moreover, New York's sterling debt to England was much lower than that of some other colonies (see n. 145 above).

Essay on Sources

O VER THE YEARS, I have unearthed myriad sources of information about colonial New York City wholesalers, including customs data, newspapers, legislative and insurance records, pamphlet literature, public legislative and enforcement records, and above all, the correspondence and account books of merchants. These latter often stretched over decades, but some show only a glimpse of city commerce for a month or a year. Moreover, no great or lesser merchant left a record of his own commerce or reflections on the empire over an entire lifetime; only a few link the details of business, family, and more general cultural life together for sustained periods of time. Still, even though a full portrait of any one merchant is impossible to limn, wholesalers as a group shared certain attributes, and using an array of sources provides a more satisfying view of commercial life in the city than the record of any single merchant's life could yield. At the same time, compiling all these sources into an extensive computerized bibliographical index permits the separation of wholesalers from retailers and of eminent from lesser merchants in the city, as the Introduction has defined this.

Merchants' correspondence and account books at eighteen historical societies and libraries in England and America are at the core of this study. At times, more than one account or letter book has survived a merchant; for many city wholesalers, however, only official sources or the references of other merchants provide evidence. In all, I read 252 account and letter books, most of which yielded valuable information that has found its way into notes to this study. Only the most important ones are listed here: at the American Antiquarian Society, the James Baker Records (1761–1823), Cornelius Cuyler, Letter Books (1724–36, 1752–64), Philip Livingston Family Business Letters (1734–38), George Ludlow Ledger (1772–74), and John Ludlow Account Book (1752–74); at Columbia University, the John Crooke Estate Records (1764–94), Joseph Laurence Accounts (1765–68), and records of Robert and Peter Livingston and Co. (1733–40), Charles Ludlow (1733–1815), and George Ludlow (1772–74); at the Hall of Records, New York City, the John Ludlow Letter Book and Invoice Book (1752–63) and Templeton and Stewart Records (1769–74); at the Long Island Historical Society, Elias Pelletreau's accounts; at the Library of Congress, [Anon.],

"Account Book of a New York City Merchant, 1706–1714" (in Dutch), Amory Family Papers, Thomas Amory Letters (1697–1823, 1723–25), Nicholas Cruger Business Letters (1766–75), Neil Jamieson Papers, Nicholas Low Papers, and Alexander Woodrup Account Books (1719–34); at the Museum of the City of New York, William Walton's Insurance Book (1774), Thomas Weaver, New York Customs Report (1701–2); the Garret Rapalje Record Book (1758–64), Accounts of Ship *Ambitious* (1712), Samuel Vetch Letter Book, and Jacob Wendell Correspondence; at the New Jersey Historical Society, Newark, the John Waddell Papers (1714–62) and John Cruger Account Book (1713–21); at the New-York Historical Society, the William Alexander Papers, Account Books, and Correspondence (many boxes and volumes, 1710–1800), John Alsop Correspondence (1733–94), Christopher Bancker Journal, Ledgers, Waste Book (various volumes, covering 1718–63), Evert Bancker Account Books and Ledgers (1760–1801, 1772–76, 1760–76), Nicholas Bayard Sr. and Jr. Correspondence, Sugar House Accounts, etc. (1743–90, 1743–55, 1763, 1762–72, 1765–74), Bayard, Lentz, and Van Cortlandt, Snuff Mill Accounts (1763–68), David Clarkson Correspondence and Letter Book (1745–77), John and Henry Cruger Letter Books (1766–67, 1767–1802), papers of Abraham, Henry, and Cornelius Cuyler, papers of James, Oliver, and Stephen De Lancey, papers of many De Peyster family members, piracy papers, ships file, various Samuel Gilford Account Books covering 1759–75, Francis Lewis letters (1713–1802), papers and accounts of Livingston family members, covering 1716 to 1778, marine insurance files, vendue sales files, John, Philip, and Stephanus van Cortlandt Letter Books, Shipping Books, Sugar House Accounts, and Family Papers, covering 1695 to 1786, and Abraham and Evert Wendell Day Books, Ledgers, Dockets, and Account Books covering 1695 to 1746. At the New York Public Library, valuable collections include Philip Cuyler, Letter Book (1755–60), Thomas Moffatt Letter Book (1715–16), Elias Pelletreau Account Books; and many files of storekeepers' records. New Jersey, Connecticut, and Pennsylvania repositories have also been used for their letters and accounts of many New York City merchants, and the notes to this study cite printed editions of some New York City merchants' correspondence.

Public records, some of them printed, have also been central to this study. Most heavily used are the Colonial Office Papers, series 5 and series 390, at the Public Record Office, Kew, London, which record names of ships, captains, vessel owners, quantities and types of goods, destinations and points of origins, for many quarters of the eighteenth century; *An Account of Her Majesty's Revenue in the Province of New York, 1701–1709*, ed. Julius Bloch et al. (Ridgewood, N.J., 1966); *Documents Relative to the Colonial History of the State of New York*, ed. and trans. E. B. O'Callaghan and Berthold Fernow, 15 vols. (Albany, N.Y., 1865–

87); *Minutes of the Common Council of the City of New York, 1675–1776*, ed. Herbert Osgood et al., 8 vols. (New York, 1905); *Abstracts of Wills on File in the Surrogate's Office, City of New York, 1665–1801*, ed. William S. Pelletreau, New-York Historical Society, *Collections*, vols. 25–32 (New York, 1893–1909); *Calendar of State Papers, Colonial Series, America and West Indies, 1661–1738*, ed. W. Noel Sainsbury, J. W. Fortescue, and Cecil Headlam, 44 vols. (London, 1860–1953); Isaac N. Stokes, *Iconography of Manhattan Island, 1498–1909*, 6 vols. (New York, 1915–28). In addition, compilations of laws, tax lists, property assessment records, and court and legislative records, for both the Dutch and English periods, have been indispensable, as have the many newspapers printed in New York beginning in 1725.

Views about economic conditions—as they were and as they should be, according to contemporaries—are present in the 273 pamphlets and treatises I read for this study and cite in the notes. Some of them are lengthy discourses by Englishmen about England's place in a world of commerce, including those by well-known theorists or publicists such as Sir William Petty, Joshua Gee, Josiah Tucker, and many others. Some pamphlets, written by travelers or newly arrived residents, reflect on the culture and material progress of New York City, and include important perspectives on the merchant community. Other, shorter works issued in New York City promote specific remedies for languishing trade or specific means to propel the city's commerce forward, and along the way they usually offer important evaluations of the causes of commercial failures and successes. Together, this pamphlet literature comprises a body of transatlantic economic thought that gives historians a glimpse of how merchants might have responded to particular opportunities and difficulties—indeed, of what they regarded as opportunitites and difficulties in the first place. Many pamphlets can be found in the *Goldsmiths'-Kress Library of Economic Literature: Resources in the Economic, Social, Business and Political History of Modern Industrial Society, Pre-1800–1850* (Woodbridge, Conn., 1975–present). This collection merges the holdings of the Kress Library at Harvard and the Goldsmiths' Library at the University of London.

Lastly, as citation of secondary sources throughout the notes reveals, my study of New York City's colonial commerce is deeply indebted to many distinguished scholars who have examined aspects of the colony's politics, religion, racial and gendered textures, labor development, and ethnicity.

Index

Barbados *(cont'd)*
importance to New Amsterdam, 28; prices
fall at, 106
Barbarie, John, 63, 84, 140, 154, 209, 222–23,
353n.59, 359n.20, 373n.30
Barbon, Nicholas, 42, 114, 173, 242
Barcelona, grain to, 210
Baxter, Thomas, 62
Bay of Campeche, 186
Bay of Honduras, 134, 210
Bayard: family, 27, 61, 283; Nicholas, 63, 65,
76, 82, 85, 95, 101, 141, 153, 261, 268–69, 276,
349n.39, 350n.41, 351n.47, 355n.72, 359n.20,
365n.27, 368n.52, 373n.28, 392n.36, 402n.15;
Samuel, 27, 86, 269; Stephen, 163, 179,
410n.87; William, 64, 68, 163, 261, 267–68,
437n.149
Bayeaux, Thomas, 224, 374n.36
Bedloe, Isaac, 53, 55
Beekman: David, 191; Gerard, 60, 115–16, 145–
46, 151, 153–55, 158–61, 163, 197, 201, 222,
229, 246, 267–68, 275, 289, 304, 352n.48,
365n.25, 366n.33, 425n.42, 435nn.137, 138;
Henry, 95, 151, 153, 222, 246, 351n.47; James,
142, 152, 271, 276, 305, 435n.138; William, 28,
95, 98, 108, 135, 168, 179, 230, 234, 261,
339n.19, 340n.40, 350n.41, 351n.47, 354n.64,
425n.42
Bellomont, Governor. See Coote, Richard
Berkeley, Bishop, 242
Bermuda, 77, 128, 189, 202
bills of exchange, 59, 69, 90, 153–54, 162–63,
204, 328–29; in Amsterdam, 147; in Bristol,
146; and farmers, 112; in Ireland, 145–46;
and military spending, 68–69; and paper
money, 241, 244, 413n.102; shortages of,
267, 282; sold in Philadelphia, 201; from
South Carolina, 200; from southern
Europe, 60, 143; from the West Indies, 90,
125, 184–85, 189, 191, 202
Blanck, Jurien, 29
Blathwayte, William, 54, 82
Bleeker (Bleecker): Anthony, 153; Johannes,
146, 209; Rutger, 148, 208, 393n.37
Blundel, Jane, 132
Board of Eight Men (1643–44), 20–22
Board of Nine Men (1647–48), 20–21
Board of Trade, 13, 45
Board of Twelve Men (1641), 20, 29
Bobin, Isaac, 130

Bogert: Henry, 272, 298; John, 156, 268,
431n.105
bolting (flour): and Leisler's Rebellion, 81;
and lesser merchants, 89; in New Jersey,
217–18; New York City monopoly of, 99,
102–6, 108–9, 116–17, 190, 228, 234, 314. See
also farmers; flour; mills and millers; regulations, economic
Bolton, William, 144
Boon, Francis, 26
Boot: Dirck Claesen, 340n.40; Jan Everts
(Evertsen), 28, 338n.19
Booth, James, 306
Bosch, Justus, 220
Boston, 53, 60, 83, 102, 107, 128, 134–35, 143,
146, 151, 153, 160, 190, 197, 201, 209, 221, 231;
devaluation of coin, 163; grain trade to,
100, 102, 109; New Amsterdam trade to, 29;
vs. New York, 22, 89, 129–30; vs. New York
City, 3
Boucher, Jonathan, 306
bounties, 47, 252, 255–56, 296
Bourdet, Samuel, 132
Bradford, William, 132
brandy, 187, 196, 207
Brasher, Abraham, 269, 436n.143
Brencoton, George, 431n.105
brewing, 21, 28, 166, 184, 261
Brewster, George, 85, 366n.33
Brinkerhoff, Dirk, 431n.105
Bristol, 135, 145–46, 152, 191; copper to, 260;
flaxseed to, 188
Brockholls (Brockholst), Anthony, 73, 79, 141,
354n.64
Brooke, Chidley, 85, 359n.20, 402n.15
Broome: John, 305, 437n.147; William,
410n.87
Brower, Adam, 342n.56
Buchanan, Thomas, 276
Bueno, Joseph, 77, 354n.64, 392n.36
Bull, Joseph, 435n.138
Burke, Edmund, 294, 308
Burling, Edward, 197
Burnaby, Andrew, 208, 249, 259
Burnet, Gov. William, 165, 223–24, 245
Burrows, Thomas, 359n.20
Byvanck: Evart, 267; John, 362n.43

Campbell: John, 177, 199, 310; Richard, 123,
225

Library of Congress Cataloging-in-Publication Data

Matson, Cathy D., 1951–
    Merchants and empire : trading in colonial New York / Cathy
Matson.
        p.   cm. — (Early America)
    Includes bibliographical references and index.
    ISBN 0-8018-5602-7 (alk. paper)
    1. Merchants—New York (State)—New York—History—17th century.
    2. Merchants—New York (State)—New York—History—18th century.
    3. Wholesale trade—New York (State)—New York—History—17th
century.   4. Wholesale trade—New York (State)—New York—
History—18th century.   5. New York (N.Y.)—Commerce—History—17th
century.   6. New York (N.Y.)—Commerce—History—18th century.
    7. Great Britain—Colonies—America—Commerce—History.   I. Title.
II. Series.
HF3163.N7M38   1998
381'.09747'109032—dc21   97-2768
                                                                                                    CIP

Printed in the United States
135769LV00003B/17/A

9 780801 872471

Made in the USA
Lexington, KY
22 October 2012